RA 1147.5 .D57 1998
40837948
Disorders of executive
 functions

S0-BXY-399

DATE DUE

MAY - 5 2009	
AUG 2 7 2009	
DEC 1 4 2009	

DEMCO, INC. 38-2931

Disorders

of

Executive Functions

Civil and Criminal Law Applications

Disorders
of
Executive Functions

Civil and Criminal Law Applications

Edited by

Harold V. Hall, Ph.D., A.B.P.P., A.B.F.P.
Forest Institute of Professional Psychology
Kaneohe, Hawaii

Robert J. Sbordone, Ph.D., A.B.C.N., A.B.P.N.
Private Practice, Irvine, California
and
Departments of Neurosurgery, Physical Medicine, and Rehabilitation
University of California at Irvine College of Medicine
Irvine, California

THE RICHARD STOCKTON COLLEGE
OF NEW JERSEY LIBRARY
POMONA. NEW JERSEY 08240

S^t_L

St. Lucie Press
Boca Raton, Florida

Contents of the following articles were first published in the *American Journal of Forensic Psychology*, a publication of the American College of Forensic Psychology, 26701 Quail Creek, Number 295, Laguna Hills, California 92656:

    a. Hall, H. V. (1984). Predicting dangerousness for the courts.

    b. Hall, H. V., Catlin, E., Boissevain, A., and Westgate, J. (1984). Dangerous myths about predicting dangerousness.

    c. Hall, H. V. (1985). Cognitive and volitional capacity assessment: A proposed dicision tree.

    d. Hall, H. V. (1986). The forensic distortion analysis: A proposed decision tree and report format.

Permission to reproduce sections of the following have been received:

    a. Chaffee, E. E. and Lytle, I. M. (1982). *Basic Physiology and Anatomy (4th edition)*. Philadelphia, PA: J. B. Lippincott Company.

    b. Hall, H. V. and McNinch, D. (1988). Linking crime-specific behavior to neuropsychological impairment. *International Journal of Clinical Neuropsychology*, 10, 113-122.

    c. Rosenzweig, M. R. and Leiman, A. L. (1982). *Physiological Psychology*. Lexington, MA: D. C. Heath and Company.

    d. Stuss, D. and Benson, D. F. (1986). *The Frontal Lobes*. New York: Raven Press.

Library of Congress Cataloging-in-Publication Data

Catalog record is available from the Library of Congress.

This book contains information obtained from authentic and highly regarded sources. Reprinted material is quoted with permission, and sources are indicated. A wide variety of references are listed. Reasonable efforts have been made to publish reliable data and information, but the author and the publisher cannot assume responsibility for the validity of all materials or for the consequences of their use.

Neither this book nor any part may be reproduced or transmitted in any form or by any means, electronic or mechanical, including photocopying, microfilming, and recording, or by any information storage or retrieval system, without prior permission in writing from the publisher.

All rights reserved. Authorization to photocopy items for internal or personal use, or the personal or internal use of specific clients, may be granted by CRC Press LLC, provided that $.50 per page photocopied is paid directly to Copyright Clearance Center, 27 Congress Street, Salem, MA 01970 USA. The fee code for users of the Transactional Reporting Service is ISBN 1-878205-16-1/93/$0.00+$.50. The fee is subject to change without notice. For organizations that have been granted a photocopy license by the CCC, a separate system of payment has been arranged.

The consent of CRC Press LLC does not extend to copying for general distribution, for promotion, for creating new works, or for resale. Specific permission must be obtained in writing from CRC Press LLC for such copying.

Direct all inquiries to CRC Press LLC, 2000 Corporate Blvd., N.W., Boca Raton, Florida 33431.

Trademark Notice: Product or corporate names may be trademarks or registered trademarks, and are used only for identification and explanation, without intent to infringe.

© 1993 by PMD Publishers Group, Inc.
© 1998 by CRC Press LLC
St. Lucie Press is an imprint of CRC Press LLC

No claim to original U.S. Government works
International Standard Book Number 1-878205-16-1
Printed in the United States of America   2 3 4 5 6 7 8 9 0
Printed on acid-free paper

Dedications

This work is dedicated to Vali Hall McKeown, H.V.H.'s beloved daughter, Frank R. Ervin, M.D. (R.J.S.'s mentor), and Phyllis Vella, R.J.S.'s beloved mother.

Contents

Chapter 6

Chapter 7

Foreword

Neuropsychologists are experts in the relationship between brain and behavior. It is not surprising that the neuropsychologist has found a home in the legal arena where implications of neurological impairment to various civil and criminal matters are relevent. A large percentage of civil matters involve neurologic injury affecting the frontal lobe system. Many criminal matters of relevance to the neuropsychologist pertain to the defendant's ability to regulate and monitor behavior. Any exploration of the frontal lobes and regulation and monitoring of behavior brings into focus potential disorders in executive functions.

Entering into the forensic arena can be a daunting prospect for even the most competent psychologist and neuropsychologist. The demands and expectations are different then a clinical practice and the challenges to and scrutiny of one's basic credentials, training, expertise, and conclusions can be intimidating. The contributors to this book display obvious knowledge of these demands and challenges. They communicate valuable insights and practical "nuts and bolts" guidance in conducting a thorough evaluation and providing optimal testimony in civil and criminal matters where executive functioning is at issue.

Appropriately, the repetitive theme is that of ecological validity that emphasizes that the role of the forensic neuropsychologist is to offer informed opinions about executive functioning in the real world. The contributors instruct how to integrate multiple sources of information—well beyond utilizing only test data—in formulating defensible conclusions that the trier-of-fact will find credible. Psychologists and neuropsychologists interested in enhancing their own executive capabilities when entering the forensic arena will benefit from this book.

Arnold D. Purisch, Ph.D
June, 1992

Dr. Purisch is nationally recognized for his expertise in neuropsychological assessment of brain-injured and psychiatric disorders Dr. Purisch holds a Diplomates in Clinical Neuropsychology from the American Board of Clinical Neuropsychology and the American Board of Professional Neuropsychology. He has been elected a Fellow and is past Vice President of the National Academy of Neuropsychologists. He is co-author of the Luria-Nebraska Neuropsychologocal Battery, one of the most widely used assessment instruments in the field of Clinical Neuropsychology. His breadth of interest is reflected in his 30 articles and publications, which cover a wide range of topics from neuropsychological assessment methodology, psychiatric disorders, recovery of function after brain injury, rehabilitation, and medi-legal applications of neuropsychological evaluation. Dr. Purisch serves on the editorial boards of the *International Journal of Clinical Neuropsychology* and the *Archives of Clinical Neuropsychology*. He is currently in private practice in Irvine, CA.

Preface

Disorders of Executive Functions: Civil and Criminal Law Applications was designed to provide an understanding of deficits of executive functioning in legal settings and forensic situations. In instances where executive-impairment is suspected, this book will assist the forensic evaluator to demonstrate the relationship between frontal lobe impairment and criminal/civil behavior. (An earlier conceptualization of decision analysis and executive deficits was published inthe Summer 1988 issue of *International Journal of Clinical Neurospychology.*)

This sourcebook is intended for psychologists, psychiatrists, attorneys, and other professionals in the mental health and law system where disorders of executive functions in criminal defendants, victims, or litigants are common.

For civil cases, the focus is on personal injury actions. The material is pertinent to a variety of executive functions-related deficit conditions. The same decision analysis can be applied toward workers' compensation and disability determination examinations.

For neuropsychology in the criminal arena, the emphasis is on disorders of executive functions that may have contributed to instant offense behavior. The focus is on serious violence. This means the reader should become aware of the empirical and clinical lore on human aggression. Relevant topics include criminal responsibility (mental capacity), competency to legally proceed (fitness), dangerousness prediction, and assessment of victim credibility.

This work draws upon the neuropsychological and forensic psychological literature in varied interdisciplinary settings and situations. A comprehensive glossary of forensic and neuropsychological terms follows the main text. To assist the reader, a core reading list in the two specialties, as compiled by the American Board of Professional Psychology (ABPP), follows the glossary.

Harold V. Hall
Honolulu, Hawaii
and
Robert J. Sbordone
Laguna Beach, California
June, 1993

Contributors

Paul J. Bach, Ph.D., The Western Montana Clinic, Missoula, Montana

Raquel E. Gur, M.D., Ph.D., Brain Behavior Laboratory and the Neurospsychiatry Program, University of Pennsylvania, Philadelphia, Pennsylvania

Ruben C. Gur, Ph.D., Brain Behavior Laboratory and the Neurospychiatry Program, University of Pennsylvania, Philadelphia, Pennsylvania

Harold V. Hall, Ph.D., A.B.P.P., A.B.F.P., Forest Institute of Professional Psychology, Kaneohe, Hawaii

B.L.J. Kaczmarek, Ph.D., Developmental and Defective Psychology Department, Uniwersytet Marie Curie-Sklodowskiej Wydzial, Pedagogiki i Psychologii Instytut Psychologii, Lublin, Poland

Rolland S. Parker, Ph.D., A.B.P.P., A.B.C.N., Department of Psychiatry, New York Medical College, New York, New York

Robert J. Sbordone, Ph.D., A.B.C.N., A.B.P.N., Private Practice, Irvine, California; Departments of Neurosurgery, Physical Medicine and Rehabilitation, University of California at Irvine College of Medicine, Irvine, California

Chapter 1

Forensic Neuropsychology and Claims of Personal Injury

Rolland S. Parker

This chapter describes the application of neuropsychological concepts and procedures to claims of personal injury stemming from alleged potential traumatic brain injury (TBI). It addresses legal issues, relationships with clients and their respective attorneys of each side, misassessment of TBI victims, the concepts of baseline functioning, neuropsychological impairment, and their relationship to the diagnosis of TBI, various neuropsychological dysfunctions, the ability of the patient to accurately describe own impairments, report writing, depositions, and court appearances.

THE NEUROPSYCHOLOGIST IN THE FORENSIC PROCESS

DESCRIPTION OF THE SPECIALTY

Forensic neuropsychology is a specialty that addresses particular issues, and utilizes a specialized body of facts, concepts, and procedures. Psychologists are recognized by law as the recognized expert in the area of psychological assessment and behavior. Evaluation by a psychologist may be requested by a neurologist or other medical professionals, an attorney for the plaintiff or defendant (they have the right to examine the plaintiff), the court, or an administrative agency (e.g., social security disability, family).

SOME LEGAL ISSUES

Litigation for personal injury (establishing liability for damages and estimating their dollar value) represents an adversarial process (e.g., someone wins, someone loses). A personal injury claim involves establishing "liability" (e.g., responsibility) for an accident, an injury, and estimating the consequent "damages" for which some form of financial compensation is sought. Many cases involve "torts" (a civil wrong not arising from a contract). Injured parties are entitled to compensation for harms intentionally inflicted by a defendant, negligently inflected through lack of reasonable care, or inflicted without intention or negligence (Dennis, 1989). The trier-of-fact (jury or judge) determines the weight given to the neuropsychologist's testimony, based on his or her experience and training. Errors by neuropsychologists can be committed in both directions (i.e., large awards to plaintiffs who sustain minimal injuries or are malingering, or even worse a defense victory against the severely injured plaintiff). Satz (1988) has reviewed court decisions examining the credibility of the psychologist, which may be determined by a lower court. He concluded that the mere possession of the Ph.D. in clinical psychology may not be sufficient grounds for rendering expert testimony. Even when the psychologist has some relevant expertise, overextending the psychologist's conclusions can lead to reversal of a verdict on appeal. The reader can find a more comprehensive description of legal issues in Barton (1985), Palagi and Springer (1984), and Kurke and Meyer (1986).

THE QUESTIONS ADDRESSED BY THE FORENSIC NEUROPSYCHOLOGIST

Cases involving a personal injury require an understanding of the following concepts: *attribution* (e.g., can any detected impairment be reasonably attributed to a particular trauma or event?), *impairment* (identification of deficits) and/or in what way is the patient's functioning reduced (e.g., pathologic or maladaptive), *prognosis* (are the observed impairments expected to be permanent or improve?), and *treatment* (what kinds of treatments are necessary to return the patient to his or her original state) or prevent deterioration of functioning (this will help to estimate costs of rehabilitation or care), *damages* (estimated from factors such as lost earnings and reduced quality of life), and *opinions* (e.g., location of brain dysfunction, proximar causes, etc.)

Qualifications

A forensic neuropsychologist should be board certified. Neuropsychology has been recognized as a specialty area in Psychology by The American Board of Professional Psychology (in collaboration with the American Board of Clinical Neuropsychology) for nearly 10 years. Clinical neuropsychologists typically are primarily engaged in the evaluation of brain-behavior relationships in individuals with known or suspected involvement of the central nervous system.

The Division of Clinical Neuropsychology (1989) of the American Psychological Association offers the following definition of a Clinical Neuropsychologist: It is a doctoral level professional psychologist, who applies principles of assessment and intervention based upon the scientific study of human behavior as it relates to normal and abnormal functioning of the central nervous system. A clinical neuropsychologist should have received training in neuropsychology and the neurosciences at a university or medical school setting; 2 or more years of appropriate supervised training in a clinical setting, licensure (as a psychologist), and board certification in this speciality by one's peers, as well as additional training and/ or experience for the particular patient population served (e.g., traumatic brain injury, dementia).

Matarazzo (1987) has pointed out that the courts require a higher level validity on the procedures utilized by neuropsychologists in forensic issues than in a hospital or clinic. Since large amounts of money are at stake, the neuropsychologist in an adversarial situation must be prepared from the moment a client is first seen to carefully explain and properly document any conclusions or inferences drawn. Therefore, the neuropsychologist should not mutilate or lose any notes or materials. The neuropsychologist should also assume that any notes or test results will be carefully scrutinized by the opposing side, including another (perhaps even more competent and experienced) neuropsychologist or knowledgable attorneys.

Special Contributions

The neuropsychologist and related vocational/educational professionals have far greater experience and expertise in assessing academic and vocational potential and occupational achievements of a brain-injured client than medical professionals. The neuropsychologist should possess considerable expertise in general psychological issues and skills, including the ability to interview and utilize a wide variety of psychological and neuropsychological tests and procedures. The forensic neuropsychologist's tasks may include the assessment and diagnosis of brain insults, documentation of the level and nature of impairment, determination of pre-existing conditions, estimation of probable baseline functioning, and prognosis, as well as provide recommendations for further examinations and/or treatment. Law suits for damages can arise from the following sources: accidents, negligence (e.g., poorly maintained buildings and roadways), and medical malpractice. Examples of such sources would include: vehicular and airplane accidents; falls; falling objects; assaults; exposure to neurotoxins (e.g., cleansing agents, pesticides; lead; mercury); hypoxic insults, electrical injuries; toxic shock; and improper diagnoses/treatment resulting in brain damage.

The neuropsychologist can enter at any phase of litigation:

- Assessment can begin shortly after an accident to evaluate the patient's deficits, treatment needs, and establish a baseline to determine the rate of recovery and prognosis. Such data would be utilized in negotiation with the adversary (defendant).

- Offering advice to an attorney on the significance and presentation of neuropsychological and related evidence.

- Reviewing records and integrating technical information, without actually examining the patient. For example, performing a "psychological postmortem" on a deceased patient, or establishing the presence of visual neglect after an accident.

- Initial or re-examination of client before trial.

- Appearance as an expert witness at a trial.

CLAIMS MAY INVOLVE LARGE SUMS OF MONEY

Attorneys and insurance companies commonly try to estimate "how much a case is worth." The relative shrewdness and preparation of each attorney, the attitudes of judge and jury, and the personal qualities of the claimant and defendant, frequently make the outcome of a particular case unpredictable, particularly in terms of the size of the award. However, personal injury law has been criticized as an inefficient system of victim compensation (Sugarman, 1990). Therefore, neuropsychological reports, made in writing or testimony in court, are subjected to a kind of skepticism and requirement for verification beyond the demands of usual clinical situations. A psychologist used to relying upon his or her intuition to arrive at the conclusion of brain damage will often painfully discover in court that the ultimate criterion is "objective evidence."

EDUCATING LEGAL PARTICIPANTS

It is important to educate the attorney who has retained the services of a neuropsychological expert about brain damage, particularly its neurobehavioral manifestations. For example, with respect to the issue of lead poisoning: The seriousness of lead poisoning, the length of time that is required before patients begin manifesting symptoms of brain damage, and an understanding of such symptoms. This might also include information about organic vs. inorganic lead exposure, and how lead is absorbed into the body.

The neuropsychologist can utilize models of brain, skull, and diagrams that illustrate the effects of lead upon brain tissue, particularly on midbrain and subcortical brain centers during trial if the court permits such testimony over the objections of opposing counsel.

SCIENTIFIC BASIS FOR FORENSIC TESTIMONY

Weiner (1985) has stressed that a psychologist is more than someone who just gives tests. The psychologist instead is a knowledgable mental health professional who possesses a broad range of knowledge and skills. A psychologist's testimony in court, however, will be limited in value if it is solely restricted on a report of test findings. In other words, technical awareness is needed to address the issues involved in litigation of personal injury (e.g., whether the trauma could have caused the alleged impairments) and the prognosis for this injury. As a consequence, the neuropsychologist should be knowledgable in the scientific and medical literature that supports his or her opinions. This should include a good understanding of the pathophysiology resulting from physical accidents (e.g., impact, acceleration, deceleration) and the separate consequences of immediate damage (e.g., contusions, lacerations, shearing, hemorrhage) vs. secondary damage (e.g., edema, metabolic problems, see Parker, 1990), the effects of neurotoxins such as lead; side effects of various medications; the complex anatomy and relationships between the central, autonomic, and peripheral nervous systems; the symptoms and manifestations of various types of brain damage (e.g., hypoxic, traumatic); the physiologic and neurologic development of children; and the effects of brain damage on behavior and physiological systems.

Many cases may require factual knowledge beyond the neuropsychologist's wealth of information since a thorough neuropsychological assessment frequently requires specific knowledge in the areas of medicine, chemistry, physics, neurology, clinical psychology, career counseling, child development and educational psychology, general science, technology, vocational counseling, education, social psychology, and social sciences. For example, the medical records of a child referred to the writer after lead poisoning cited various blood studies. To avoid vulnerability in court, the writer had to become familiar with classifications of lead level toxicity (Berkow & Fletcher, 1987; Ellenhorn & Barcelous, 1988), and the effects of lead upon blood cell formation (Ellenhorn & Barcelous, 1988).

Database searches can provide access to the most recent literature on specific topics (e.g., brain functioning and pathology, toxins). The reader should be familiar with Biosis Connection, Medline, and Medical Abstracts. Some reprints are also available from UMI, Inc. For example, an attorney asked the author if recollection of specific information following a traumatic brain injury could return if a patient were brought to the scene of the accident that occurred 3 years earlier. A search of the literature on memory functioning did not offer evidence to support a loss of retrograde amnesia. In another case, a woman stated that she had particular sexual difficulties after a steel cable hit her head. A database search did not reveal any medical evidence to support her claim, although it should be pointed out that this does not mean that she was exaggerating or histronic, rather that her particular complaint would be difficult to prove.

STRESS-RELATED INJURIES MAY INCLUDE A HISTORY OF TBI

The neuropsychologist should be familiar with modern concepts of stress (e.g., Kolb, 1987), since the examination of a patient to assess emotional distress may elicit evidence of a TBI. The following cases illustrate this:

- A woman was a passenger in a small plane that crashed into the ocean. She struck her head against the cockpit and was briefly rendered unconscious. After she came to she feared death from sharks or drowning.

- A female professional was in a taxicab collision, carrying her young child. While her child's injury resulted in a claim of emotional distress, she admitted that she had banged her head against the hard partition and had felt bewildered for several minutes.

- A child's parents sued a Board of Education for negligence, after she was repeatedly harassed and once knocked to the ground by a young male bully. The fall resulted in brain damage when her head struck the ground.

HEAD INJURY VICTIMS ARE OFTEN POORLY EVALUATED

Due to inadequate examinations, and the widespread lack of information concerning the causes and effects of brain damage, many TBI patients are often characterized as malingerers, compensation neurotics, or hysterics, particularly if their neurological examinations are negative. Consequently, they often fail to receive any compensation for their injuries.

NO EXAMINATION

TBI victims may be asked by the police if they want to go to a hospital. Because they are usually in a state of confusion they often refuse, because they want to go home or go about their business. As a consequence, some TBI victims may never be examined by a physician following an accident or injury.

Incorrect Statements or Inferences Concerning
Loss of Consciousness (LOC)

Errors concerning LOC frequently occur. The first error is the statement contained in the medical records that there has been "no LOC." This may be made by emergency personnel at the scene of accident, or by a staff member in the hospital who fails to observe the brief LOC (e.g., the patient had "come to" by the time the paramedics arrived or recognized the patient's confused state). For example, a bricklayer was struck on the head by a piece of lumber estimated to have fallen 18–20 stories. The emergency room record stated "No loss of consciousness," although he woke up at the scene of the accident with his head bleeding, recalling somebody saying 'Take him to the shack.'" The neuropsychologist should be aware that a cerebral concussion and cerebral contusion can occur without a LOC (Gennarelli, 1987).

CLINICAL EXAMPLE

A computer programmer was in an automobile that was struck from the rear. He struck his head against the windshield, causing sufficient damage to his nose to require extensive surgery. There was no loss of consciousness, although he appeared confused when the paramedics arrived. Since his injury 9 months ago he cannot organize his daily schedule. However, he acknowledged that he does much better in structured situations (i.e., when others set up a plan for him). He is unable to generate any plans for himself. If somebody tells him what to do he can perform the task. In comparing his problem to computers he stated, "If you slip a computer disk in me, and press *enter*, I will know what to do. I am missing the program that tells me what to do. I have the hardware, but not the program."

Momentary loss of consciousness may not be recognized by observers or medical personnel. However, TBI patients who experience brief LOC will typically report symptoms such as feeling dizzy or dazed, bewilderment, seeing stars, or confusion.

IMPROPER OR INCOMPLETE EXAMINATION

Emergency room physicians frequently assume that a patient did not sustain a TBI when the skull x-rays, neurologic exam, or computed tomography (CT) scan is normal. However, these tests are often ineffective in detecting focal or diffuse axonal brain injury (DAI).

Claims of significant adaptive dysfunction (i.e., inability to study, work, maintain domestic responsibilities, enjoy leisure time) is often a sign that a TBI has occurred. Complaints of headaches can indicate considerable damage to soft tissues and bone (temporomandibular joint [TMJ] syndrome) and suggest that considerable trauma to the head or brain may have occurred (Adams & Victor, 1985; Gelb & Siegal, 1980; Herskowitz & Rosman, 1982; Parker, 1990; Rimel, Giordani, Barth, & Jane, 1982; Speed 1982; Spindler & Reischer, 1982; Zohn, 1982).

THE RELATIVE INSENSITIVITY OF THE NEUROLOGIC EXAMINATION TO EVALUATE TBI

According to Livingston (1985), the sensory and motor functions of the human brain probably involve about 20 percent of the cortex. The remaining 80 percent of the cortex represents the "decision-making capacity" of the brain. Unfortunately, the neurologic mental status examination (which is frequently 5–15 minutes) is inappropriate to assess complex functions, such as language, memory, perception, problem solving, abstract thinking, adaptive skills, and other cognitive skills that influence the ability to work and study (Tupper, 1987). As a consequence, a normal neurologic exam can lead to the spurious erroneous conclusion that the patient is neurologically intact.

It should also be pointed out that the neurologic examination is entirely subjective, nonstandardized, varies considerably from one clinician to another, and generally lacks any firm objective norms.

INSENSITIVITY OF NEUROIMAGING TECHNIQUES TO TBI

X-rays, CT scan, and magnetic resonance imaging (MRI) are typically negative in the presence of neurobehavioral symptoms such as cognitive difficulties, anxiety, depression, distractibility, and impulsivity. These tests unfortunately are too insensitive to detect such phenomena as petechial hemorrhages, or axonal damage.

EMOTIONAL PROBLEMS FOLLOWING TBI

Many examiners do not explore the patient's emotional problems after a TBI. As a consequence, emotional reactions due to brain damage, post-traumatic emotional reactions (which are more variable than PTSD alone), and the patient's reactions to being cognitively impaired or disabled are often overlooked.

THE NATURE OF TRAUMATIC BRAIN INJURY

The following concepts concerning brain damage are useful in explaining neuropsychological findings to attorneys and courts:

1. *Significant cognitive and behavioral functions require complex brain processing.* Complex functions are not mediated at a particular brain location. Instead complex functions typically involve a dynamic interaction between peripheral, central, and subcortical systems (Aysto & Hanninen, 1988; Parker, 1990). The brain is highly interconnected (see, for example diagrams in Pansky, Allen, & Budd, 1988, pp. 98–99; Duus, 1989, pp. 258–259), which makes it vulnerable to shearing, stretching, tearing, long distance effects (diaschisis), and generalized brain injury. The integrity of long nerve pathways are effected by impact and acceleration/deceleration injuries, particularly commissural (between hemispheres); association (within hemispheres); and projection (different levels) pathways. A symptom may result from damage at different points along a neural pathway (remote or distant effects).
2. *Local brain damage can create brain dysfunctioning elsewhere (diaschisis).* Brain dysfunctioning can occur due to localized damage interfering with the input or output of different brain areas.
3. *The brain is highly vulnerable to damage from a variety of sources.* The impact, and acceleration and deceleration forces of high speed injuries, assaults, and falls can produce tearing, stretching, shearing, tension, contusions, and lacerations of brain matter as well as skull deformation and cavitation (Becker & Povlishock, 1985; Cooper, 1987; Parker, 1990).
4. *Trauma typically causes generalized brain damage.* While focal functions such as language may be intact, generalized brain damage can impair abstract thinking, our ability to process information, judgment, memory, and planning skills.
5. *Secondary brain pathology can produce cognitive and behavior deficits and can also be fatal.* The following secondary pathologic processes can occur following a direct impact injury to the brain: hemorrhage; edema; anoxia; seizures; pressure against the skull and dura, and extrusion through the foramen magnum, due to swelling and edema; infection into the cerebral spinal fluid through skull fractures near the nose and ear; osteomyelitis after depressed skull fractures; metabolic derangements within the brain; systemic effects such as changes in heart rate and blood pressure; shock; hyperthermia; and dehydration. Each of the pathologic conditions will produce alterations of cortical functioning. Any condi-

tion that compromises the functioning of the lower brain stem is likely to produce death.

6. *So-called "minor" head injury can have grossly impairing effects.* Recent studies have demonstrated that "minor" head injuries can result in a variety of disabling cognitive, behavioral, and emotional problems even without evidence of head impact during whiplash injuries or LOC (Dacey & Dikmen, 1987; Haas & Ross, 1986; Rimel et al., 1982; Uzell, Langfitt, & Dolinkas, 1987).

7. *The relationship between the duration of coma and disability can be misleading.* While it is generally accepted that the severity of brain damage is roughly proportional to the duration of coma, a surprising number of patients become disabled after so "minor" head trauma. The writer has known several patients who suffered whiplash injuries without LOC who were so impaired they could not practice at their profession. Severe impairment can follow a blow to the head causing only momentary dizziness (e.g., cerebral contusion). It is well known that penetrating brain injury can occur without LOC. Conversely, some patients who have been in a coma for a month have made surprisingly good recoveries when they receive rehabilitation and sympathetic family support.

8. *Some cognitive effects are inconspicuous.* Aphasia can exist immediately after an accident then seem to disappear. However, the patient may have subclinical communication problems that may not be recognized or are concealed by the patient until the patient undergoes formal neuropsychological testing.

9. *There are multiple effects upon the symptom pattern and level.* These include: locus and extent of neurologic damage; interval since injury; the age at injury; interaction of cognitive reserves and the particular demands of the patient's environment; prior brain damage; and different rates and extent of improvement for different cognitive functions (Boll, 1982; Bond, 1986).

10. *Even without detectable deficits, cognitive reserves can be depleted.* After trauma, cognitive reserves against further injury, or ability to cope with more difficult or changed circumstances are reduced. The patient's judgment and ability to avoid further accidents is lessened. Such individuals typically show a greater pronensity to injure themselves or sustain further trauma.

11. *Cognitive deficits generally persist over time.* Individuals who sustain significant brain damage will frequently exhibit cognitive deficits in a variety of areas that can often be detected on careful neuropsychological testing several years later (Parker, 1990).

TAXONOMY OF NEUROPSYCHOLOGICAL

SYSTEMS AND DYSFUNCTIONS

A taxonomy is proposed in order to categorize symptoms resulting from brain damage. A systematic study of behavior after TBI has the following advantages:

*   It fosters a comprehensive examination of the TBI victim.

*   It encourages the completeness of available patient data.

*   It identifies the need for referrals to other experts.

- It assists in rehabilitation planning.

- It provides for comprehensive assessment of damages for forensic purposes.

- It conveys valuable information to victims, family, schools, psychotherapists, courts, and significant others.

- It overcomes gaps in collecting information due to the patient's poor awareness of his or her problems.

Definition of a System

A system refers to a set of behaviors that have an adaptive function that is mediated by a specific neural subset. A variety of systems that regulate our sensory, perceptual, physiologic, cognitive, and emotional functioning are described below along with their symptoms when these systems become dysfunctional.

I. CONSCIOUSNESS, ORIENTATION, ATTENTION, AND AROUSAL

This would include the following adaptive functions: self-awareness; alertness to the environment; selection of new or ongoing events for continued appraisal; alertness to possible danger; determining the relevance of ongoing activities for prior plans, curiosity, and bodily needs.

Symptoms of dysfunction: Seizures, confusion, strange experiences, depersonalization, derealization, problems with attention, sleeping difficulties, problems staying awake, disorientation to one's surroundings; becoming easily distracted by external or internal stimuli; and oversensitivity to noise and light .

II. INTEGRATED SENSORIMOTOR FUNCTIONS AND BODILY IMAGE

This system performs the following adaptive functions: analyzes sensory information and encodes this information for current use and later retrieval; regulates muscular activity, orients sensory receptors to receive meaningful information; integrates newly acquired information with motor functions; modifies ongoing physical activities based on sensory feedback originating from various sites in a person's body; organizes purposeful movements based on sensory feedback, and provides the basis for an individual's "body image."

Symptoms of dysfunction: Loss of strength, decreased psychomotor speed, poor coordination, ataxia, sensory deficits, dizziness, and vertigo.

III. NEUROPHYSIOLOGIC, HUMORAL, AND VISCERAL FUNCTIONING

This system integrates neural and visceral organ systems under conditions of relaxation and survival as well as during acute or chronic stress. It controls our energy levels and metabolism. It modulates our sensitivity to sensory information and controls our moods and emotional responses to the environment. This system relies on the pineal gland and other endocrinologic sites to transform environmental information (e.g., light, cold, heat) into signals that modulate our neuroendocrine mechanisms that generate neurohormones, neuromodulators, and neuroimmune responses, which effect our endocrine system and alter the functioning of the central nervous system.

Symptoms of dysfunctions: Loss of energy, reduced sexual libido, autonomic nervous system hyperarousal or hypoarousal, headaches, pain; impaired physical development, chronic anxiety, hypersexuality, changes in weight, changes in appetite, hyperactivity, depression, sleep difficulties, and hypertension.

IV. INTELLECTUAL FUNCTIONING

General intelligence can be described as the ability to form concepts and abstractions as well as the capacity for creative approaches to novel tasks. Intellectual efficiency depends upon a variety of complex functions such as perception, motivation, mental control, attention and concentration, memory, positive health, physical stamina, psychomotor skills, a constructive sense of one's identity, and freedom from disruptive emotional factors (e.g., loss of hope, rejection, failure, depression).

Intellectual functioning can be evaluated according to specific environmental demands (e.g., structured vs. unstructured), the nature of the information to be processed (e.g., verbal vs. nonverbal), skills (e.g., mechanical, spatial, numerical, clerical), and temporal factors (e.g., sequential and holistic or simultaneous). Each of these factors may be evaluated separately or simultaneously.

Symptoms of dysfunction: General (dementia) or specific deficits (e.g., spatial), reduced speed of informational processing, changes in problem solving effectiveness, diminished insight, and/or concrete thinking.

V. MENTAL EFFICIENCY: PROBLEM SOLVING STYLE, CONCENTRATION, CONTROL, AND PLANNING

Mental efficiency refers to the style and effectiveness with which meaningful tasks are approached. It facilitates intellectual functioning through task selection, concentration, and efficient problem solving skills. It plays a prominent role in the monitoring of ongoing mental activities by comparing our performance with our expectations or intentions. It also involves processing problems at an effective pace; planning and foresight to anticipate the consequences of our actions; our ability to recognize, avoid, and reject errors (e.g., judgment); flexibility to adapt to novel events or unexpected circumstances; planning future actions; and appropriately initiating and terminating our actions. These behaviors, which are related to the integrity of our frontal lobes, have been termed our "executive functions" by Lezak (1983).

Symptoms of dysfunction: Poor planning; inability to recognize or correct one's mistakes; loss of initiative, perseveratory behavior, inability to maintain conversations, ongoing events, follow through on intended tasks, maintain goal-directed behavior, and anticipate possible negative consequences.

VI. COMMUNICATION

Communication allows us to express our thoughts and feelings in response to the needs and thoughts of others. It can be broken down into the following components: the reception and analysis of verbal and nonverbal information, expression of thoughts and feelings, use of grammatical rules and proper syntax, and acquisition and mastery of learned skills such as reading, writing, and spelling.

Symptoms of dysfunction: Inability to express one's ideas or feelings, word finding difficulties, empty or meaningless language, paraphasic errors, difficulties repeating sentences, loss of prosody, dyslexia, and aphasia.

VII. MEMORY

Memory cansimply be defined as the process of storing and retrieving previous information, experiences, or events. Memory gives meaning to our current sensory experiences and enhances our survival through recalling prior rules, warnings, signals, and conditions of safety and danger. Our short-term memory contributes to efficient problem solving (rejection of previous unsatisfactory solutions, while saving effective solutions or techniques).

Symptoms of dysfunction: Difficulty recalling recent conversations, events and learning; inability to recall information from long-term memory (e.g., specific skills and facts learned in school or work); confabulation, disorientation, loss of continuity, difficulty following through on planned tasks, and confusion.

VIII. EMOTIONAL RESPONSIVITY

The brain is responsible for our emotions, moods, motivation and drive for action, sense of one's self, and adaptive functions such as self-protection, anger, sex, and love.

Symptoms of dysfunction: Organic personality and affective syndromes characterized by reduced motivation, apathy, flat affect; emotional dyscontrol, irritability; rapid mood swings; mutism; emotional lability; euphoria; poor frustation tolerance; changes in sexuality; and drive, paranoia, rage, violence; and changes in aggressive behavior.

IX. ADAPTABILITY, INDEPENDENCE, AND DAILY FUNCTIONING

Adaptive functioning refers to solving problems of daily living and dealing with difficult or changing circumstances in our environment. Effective adaptive functioning depends on our relative independence, mobility, judgment, freedom from dysphoric feelings such as anxiety, lack of pain and suffering, adequate sensory abilities, strength, range of motion, and relative absence of significant emotional problems. Effective adaptability frequently leads to productivity, pleasant moods, and positive self-esteem.

Symptoms of dysfunction: Loss of independence; inability to travel due to anxiety or loss of physical mobility; social introversion; inability to maintain past friendships or make friends; problems with study, work, shopping, use of public facilities, or driving; marital difficulties; agoraphobia; rigidity; denial; and anxiety reactions.

X. ANXIETY, STRESS, AND PSYCHODYNAMIC REACTIONS

The unimpaired person conducts his or her life relatively calmly, with good emotional control. There is a sense of self-esteem, capacity to enjoy life, and ability to make plans for the future. Problems are faced directly with the belief that they can be resolved.

Symptoms of dysfunction: Nightmares and other sleep disturbances; flashbacks; unrealistic fears; paranoia; avoidance behaviors; generalized anxiety reactions; inability to enjoy life; fatigue; depression; psychosomatic illness; somatoform disorders; suicidal ideation or behavior; pessimissism about future; poor self-esteem; social withdrawal; and self-defeating behavior.

XI. SPECIAL PROBLEMS OF CHILDREN

TBI in children is sufficiently complex to warrant special consideration. Differences between TBI in children and adults include: a smaller repertoire of available information and adaptive skills; impairment of physical and cognitive development; lack of synchronization of cognitive skills that normally function together; failure to develop skills on which later skills are dependant; and failure to develop the capacity to perform several cognitive functions simultaneously.

TBI in children is often accompanied by slow physiologic development due to damage to the hypothalamico-pituitary-adrenal axis, which often results in slow or incomplete achievement of puberty.

Symptoms of dysfunction: Loss of ability to maintain rank or grades in school; behavioral problems at school or at home; difficulty making friends; rejection by peers; social withdrawal; failure to reach cognitive, physiologic, and emotional milestones; poor self-esteem; coordination difficulties; social immaturity; impaired judgment; poor self-image; irritability; and poor frustration tolerance.

EXPRESSIVE DEFICITS HAMPERING SELF-DESCRIPTION

"Expressive deficits" is a term proposed by the writer to describe the inability or reluctance of brain damage victims to describe their accident, or its adaptive and emotional consequences (Parker, 1987, 1988, 1990). Consequently, obtaining a complete and objective account of their accident or post-traumatic personal difficulties can be extremely difficult. To obtain an accurate self report from the TBI patient requires the awareness that a change has taken place. Lack of awareness of an illness itself is called *anosognosia* (Bisiach, Vallek, Perani, Pagagno, & Berti, 1986), the ability to experience distress, the ability to recall one's problems as deficits (Levin, 1987), sufficient intelligence and judgment to evaluate the consequences of one's actions, and sufficient motivation to communicate one's distress.

Westermeyer and Wahmenholm (1989) point out the difficulties of assessing victimized patients directly, due to their dysphoria, and the additional problem relating their symptoms to a given injury. Self-awareness shortly after injury may be relatively low or the patient may be motivated by denial (Lam, McMahon, Priddy, & Gehred-Schultz, 1988). Poor orientation or amnesia frequently result in unreliable self-reports on questionnaires (Priddy, Mattes, & Lam, 1988). As a consequence it is essential that the significant others or family members be interviewed to gather an appreciation of the patient's impairments, which are often highly salient in unstructured settings.

Expressive deficits can increase the difficulty of establishing damages in a given TBI case. The following examples illustrate this:

Case Example 1

A young woman, 10 years earlier, had been rendered unconscious after being knocked down by a truck while riding a bicycle. When the case was settled, the writer asked the attorney about the contribution of the neuropsychological report. The writer was informed that "they did not pursue brain damage as she would not have made a credible witness. Instead the case went to court to pursue loss of hearing!"

Case Example 2

A woman at age 16 hit a pothole while riding a bicycle, resulting in a TBI and coma. She did not admit to a single symptom on a four-page symptom checklist. This information (available through subpoenaed records) was used by the defense attorney as evidence of lack of damages produced by the accident. At her deposition she admitted that she didn't remember seeing the pothole, the accident, falling off her bike, hitting her head, or being on the ground. Her case went to trial and eventually lost since it was not possible to establish the community's liability for the pothole.

TAXONOMY OF EXPRESSIVE DEFICITS

1. *Pre-existing conditions*
   (a) *Alexythymia.* A condition not necessarily caused by brain damage, in which the person does not identify or label feelings, fantasies, or physiologic reactions (Acklin & Bernat, 1987; Taylor, 1984), or misinterprets them (Papciak, Feuerstein, & Spiegel, 1985).
   (b) *Intellectual deficits.* The unintelligent or illiterate subject (Lecours, Mehler et al., 1987) may be unable to offer a personal statement.
2. *Concealing legitimate symptoms*
   (a) *Fear of loss of employment.* Job inefficiency is concealed and covered up by the employee and co-workers/supervisors (Parker, 1987).
   (b) *Reduced social acceptability.* Fear of losing friends should their limitations be known (e.g., bragging with friends about sex with their wives).
   (c) *Embarrassment caused by impaired verbal expression.* The patient avoids conversation or people, or uses nonverbal expressions or generalities to conceal deficits.
   (d) *Embarrassment about particular symptoms.* One woman's seizures were concealed since she was reluctant to tell her neurologist that she lost bladder control. A child may not tell his parents about a serious fall resulting in unconsciousness, or a woman may be fearful revealing a beating by her TBI husband (Hales & Yudofsky, 1987, p. 180).
   (e) *A "Spartan mentality"* (i.e., the belief that it is improper to complain). Pride in being able to overcome affliction can also lead people not to state the extent of impairment. Many people have been trained not to ask for what is coming to them, assert their rights, etc. Some people are trained not to express emotional pain to appear strong (Parker, 1981). They may not complain for religious reasons (i.e.,God had willed this affliction upon the individual). One religious woman engaged in litigation only at her husband's insistence.
3. *Reducing anxiety*
   (a) *Reluctance to relive the trauma.* Since memories may be repetitive or "intrusive," and impairment, pain, and loss of quality of life pervasive, victims may avoid discussion of the experience. One woman who was knocked down by a car "pretended that there was no accident."
   (b) *The defense of denial.* It is difficult to accept that brain damage is highly impairing and generally permanent, leading to self-concealment. This is to be distinguished from "agnosias" (i.e., lack of awareness of a deficit).
   (c) *Compensation for deficits.* Tricks are used to overcome problems (e.g., using lists to compensate for a bad memory, but not revealing this).
4. *Lack of awareness*
   (a) *Impaired consciousness.* Ongoing confusion, poor alertness, dizziness, lack of self aware-

ness, etc., all impair memory, ability to evaluate one's current condition, ability to process complex situations, and even the ability to respond to questions.

(b) *The victim may not associate injury with the symptoms for years.* As one automobile accident victim, a physician, stated: "I didn't see the change in myself. I didn't know that was wrong." His psychotherapist pointed out that he was once better able to concentrate.

(c) *Sensory neglect or agnosias.* A lack of general awareness (anosognosia) or the ability to recognize specific information (agnosia), or neglect of incoming sensory information originating from one side of the body (Livingston, 1985; Mesulam, 1985).

5. *Problems of concentration.* Inability to focus or sustain attention may create problems of self-awareness and communication.

6. *Communication deficits.* The patient may be unable to understand others, find appropriate self-descriptive words, or express the understood problem (see *embarrassment*, above).

7. *Impaired intelligence or comprehension.* This refers to the patient's inability to understand or express their deficits, or to adequately understand verbal questions of the examiner.

8. *Poor memory.* A deficit cannot be reported if it is not remembered. Anterograde and retrograde amnesia, seizures, and post-traumatic confusion hamper a description of the circumstances of the accident and consequent problems. For example, a TBI patient was taken by his attorney to see a physician for a medical exam. The patient denied having any problems and stated that he was not aware of sustaining any problems during his motor vehicle accident. After the examination was completed the patient was taken home. Shortly after he arrived home his wife asked him what happened at his doctor's appointment. The patient responded, "What appointment?"

9. *Misleading organic affective dysfunctions.* One of the primary signs of brain damage is dysfunction of emotional expression, with positive and negative signs (Heilman, Bowers, & Valenstein, 1985; Heilman, Watson, & Bowers, 1983; Parker, 1990; Ross, 1985). These dysfunctions are presented below:

    Emotional dullness. Flat affect and lack of facial expression are common among TBI victims. The patient seemingly lacks concern, even when describing distressing impairment or despair. Social credibility may be weakened by prosodic difficulties (i.e., nonverbal and emotional components that convey feeling tone).

    Quasi-emotional disorders. Bizarre thinking, temporal-limbic seizure disorders can give rise to visual hallucinations, illusions, rapid mood swings, laughter, feelings of impending doom or death, irritability, obsessive thoughts, automatic or ritualistic behaviors, self-mutilation, and abnormal motor and sensory phenomena.

    Apparent immaturity. Problems such as poor judgment, inability to regulate one's behavior, euphoric behavior, self-destructive behavior, or the apparent inability to learn from experience, which are frequently seen in TBI patients, often give the impression of indifference and immaturity ("frontal lobe syndrome").

10. *Psychodynamically Based Hyporeactivity*

    Reluctance to describe the accident or its consequences. The individual may be reluctant to discuss the trauma, injury, or its consequences to avoid re-experiencing the emotional trauma produced by the accident.

    Depression or constricted style of emotional expression. This may be erroneously misconstrued as indifference.

    Denial. It is difficult to accept that brain damage is highly impairing and generally permanent. The loss of ability to enjoy life and valued assets are often painful, as a consequence self-concealment (denial) is common. For example, a woman who was knocked down by a car later said that she "pretended that there was no accident." This should be distinguished from "agnosias" and inability to express emotional pain (Parker, 1972, 1981).

Avoidance. Most individuals avoid situations in which failure is certain or that produce intense anxiety. Many TBI patients may take a less challenging job or stay away from situations where their impairments will be quickly recognized. Through such avoidance the cognitive, behavioral, or emotional problems of the TBI patient may go unrecognized.

11. *Effects of chronic pain.* Chronic pain is likely to result in a severe depression that may produce an inability to express intense anger and/or fear directly as well as mask the intensity of one's feelings (Hendler, Long, & Wise, 1981).

MISLEADING PROFESSIONAL REPORTS

The competency of TBI assessment is frequently inadequate as a result of one or more of the following reasons: the conclusions are based entirely upon limited test data; failure to understand the natural history of brain damage (i.e., how it effects the brain and its varied consequences); failure to interview collateral sources (e.g., family members, significant others); failure to obtain behavioral observations of patient in "real world" settings; and the failure to integrate test data with the patient's medical records (Sbordone, 1991).

Overview of Behavioral Effects of TBI

Behavioral manifestations of brain damage commonly observed by the neuropsychologist typically are those behaviors that are relatively conspicuous (though by no means universal), and supplementary (problems that produce subtle impairments or are the consequences of conspicuous characteristics).

Examples of Conspicuous Characteristics

- Dementia. Characterized by a marked loss of intellectual or cognitive functioning resulting in gross incompetence.
- Unilateral hemiparesis
- Expressive aphasia

Examples of Supplementary Characteristics

- Cognitive inflexibility (e.g., difficulty switching attention or going from one task to another)
- Visual-perceptual impairments
- Impaired executive functions (e.g., difficulty initiating tasks, recognizing errors)

The neuropsychological examination frequently includes reviewing medical, neurologic, or psychological reports that are based upon a poor understanding of brain damage. For example:

- "There is no neurological evidence of any brain damage or impairment" following a neurologic examinations often lasting 5–15 minutes (!)
- Orthopedic and other medical examinations that make no mention of the behavioral manifestations of TBI.

• Psychological examinations that are based entirely on the results of IQ test scores or personality testing.
• Psychiatric examinations that are based entirely on verbal behavior of patient.
• Superficial examinations by physicians in busy and crowded emergency rooms.

Case Example

Several examples of this were found in the records of a 28-year-old woman referred for neuropsychological assessment. She had been referred for psychotherapy after her TBI and recalled that "I took a course requiring a lot of concentration and couldn't keep up with the course. I asked my therapist whether I was having trouble with the course because of the accident, and she said "probably not" since her neurologic examination was normal. Subsequently, she remained in treatment for 1 1/2 years although her therapist failed to relate her problems with anger, sex, depression, and anxiety to her TBI, but instead felt it was due to masturbating at the age of 5.

SOME MAJOR ADAPTIVE PROBLEMS ACCOMPANYING TBI

Reduced Mental Efficiency and Control

Manifestations of this problem in the TBI patient are concentration-attention difficulties, impaired short-term memory, diminished speed of cognitive processing, rapid fatigue, diminished frustration tolerance, and frequent errors.

While such impairments are often attributed to frontal lobe pathology, this problem is not confined to any particular area of the brain since these impairments can be produced by damage to widely scattered areas of the brain, and can range from subtle to profoundly disabling.

Impairment

In adults, an impairment may be defined as a reduction in the individual's capacity to function in such areas as employment, social and family life, or to become independent, or enjoy life.

For children, an impairment may be defined as an inability to perform school and domestic responsibilities and/or problems in getting along with peers, family, teachers, etc. It may be expressed immediately as cognitive or personality problems, or as delayed development or unattained maturity.

"Disabled" means "Not Able" (i.e., unable to work or function). This extreme condition can be brought about by general impairment (e.g., gross cognitive dysfunctioning), or by deficits of relatively narrow functions, health problems, or emotional problems (e.g., embarrassment due to scarring, anxiety, loss motivation, irritability and temper).

An impairment can exist without deficits of measured general intellectual function (e.g., normal IQ scores).

Emotional Reactions

The issue of preinjury emotional problems frequently arises in TBI cases. It is the author's opinion that after TBI the primary emotional distress is generally due to the injury. However, the issue of pre-existing factors must be addressed by the neuropsychological expert regardless of whether the expert is retained by the plaintiff or defendant. Attempting to determine a preinjury condition, and/or attributing any deficits to an injury and/or emotional stress is difficult, particulary if there have been multiple accidents, and/or pre-existing psychiatric disorders that may have been exacerbated by the injury, or subsequent stress and cognitive impairments.

EXAMPLES OF EMOTIONAL DISTURBANCE AFTER TBI

Specific emotional effects of brain damage. The examiner should be alert for endogenous depression, anger and/or aggressive outbursts, affective flattening (apathy and reduced ability to express feelings), depersonalization, mood swings, or euphoria.

Clinical example. A 44-year-old man reported tenderness in his left temporal area after his car was struck laterally by another vehicle moving at high speed. After his TBI, his wife stated that "He doesn't want to do anything. He wants everybody to be unhappy because he is unhappy." Prior to his TBI he enjoyed repairing household appliances and furniture. Now he sits on a broken chair and has made no attempt to repair it. He fails to finish what he starts. He never asks his children about their activities, and no longer participates in parent-teachers' meetings. He shows little interest in previously enjoyed activities.

Neuropsychological implications. His wife describes a personality change that is frequently observed after brain injury (i.e., the frontal lobe syndrome). After the accident he was observed at the hospital to have left temporal tenderness. A blow in this region can move the brain, causing the frontal and temporal lobes to move over sharp edges in the floor of the cranial cavity, and against the frontal crest and crista galli separating the frontal lobes. The observed changes in his behavior are consistent with an injury to this region of the brain yet may be so subtle that it is missed completely by neurologists or psychologists who base their opionions entirely on their test data (Berg, 1986; Sbordone, 1991).

Stress-reaction. Head injury and/or multiple trauma are associated with marked increases in catecholamine activity, ECG changes, depression of thyroid function and hypoxia (Marshall & Marshall, 1985). This may account for long-lasting effects in cognitive, physiologic, and emotional functioning. The examiner should be alert to the following symptoms: intrusive anxiety (somatic expression, nightmares, flashbacks, preoccupation with the accident); identity as a victim, pessimism about the future; disturbed Weltanschauung (view of the world); dysphoric mood; guilt; depression, anger at life and the individual who caused the injury; psychic and enhanced somatic pain; poor control over anger and irritability; somatic reactions; hyporeactivity and/or hyperarousal (reduced affective expression); somatic forms of anxiety; and sleep disturbances.

Psychodynamic defenses and regressive reactions. The following symptoms suggest the presence of psychodynamic defenses and regressive reactions: reduced self-esteem due to loss of status, feelings of unattractiveness, poor morale, feeling unable to cope, feelings of incompetence, pessimism about the future, inablity to pursue personal goals, wish-fulfilling fantasies,or constructive activities; regression to former levels of adaptation (i.e., use of immature modes of adaption), denial, social distress, withdrawal, and feeling of isolation and shame.

Catastrophic reaction. The brain-damaged individual may react to problem solving difficulties by crying, giving up prematurely, self-criticism, angry outbursts, and depression. While catastrophic reactions are traditionally associated with left cerebral hemisphere damage (Broca's and

Wernicke's areas), it has also been observed with right hemisphere damage and has been attributed to release of limbic centers (Bruno, 1984). It is unknown whether the right hemisphere processes "negative" emotions, or merely expresses feelings in a nonpropositional or nonverbal manner.

SOCIAL REACTIONS

Reduced social interactions are frequently observed after brain damage. TBI patients often report that they are lonely and disinterested in being with family and friends. They cannot participate in social activities or sports due to injuries. Since they are unable to work they are unable to pursue activities that resulted in social acceptance and positive self-esteem. Physical mobility may be reduced due to the physical injury, pain, fear, seizures, and dizziness. Facial and bodily scarring secondary to trauma or surgery may create a loss of self-esteem, social uneasiness, and social isolation.

EMPLOYMENT CONSIDERATIONS

Returning to work appears to depend upon the extent of the neurologic injury; the patient's motivation (including the type of work to which the patient will return); the passage of time since injury; level of premorbid intelligence; preinjury personality characteristics; social and family support; residual communications skills; professional support and correct handling (e.g., job coaching); and the nature of somatic injuries.It should also be kept in mind that some attorneys may advise their client not to return to work regardless of whether the patient is motivated or capable of returning to work in order to build up "damages." The patient is also informed that returning to work would "jeopardize your case." However, continued unemployment may be seriously questioned and challenged, even to the point of surreptitious videotapes of the patient's activities by investigators hired by the defendent's attorneys.

THE FORENSIC NEUROPSYCHOLOGICAL EXAMINATION

General Principles of Neuropsychological Assessment

ESTABLISHING A BASELINE

Deficits from a baseline are the most significant and common diagnostic features for TBI. The baseline is defined as the estimated or documented level, quality, and style of performance before an injury. Information to determine a baseline can be elicited from: vocational records (samples, commendations, salary, personnel decisions); interviews with collaterals and colleagues; known association between IQ, education, and particular occupations; personal documents (drawings, photographs); academic performance (percentiles, grades, teachers' evaluations); and leisure time activities (e.g., art and crafts).

Intellectual functioning. The courts frequently accept an estimate of the patient's preinjury IQ based on WAIS-R scale scores (Matarazzo & Herman, 1984).

Demographic considerations. Performance effectiveness is a function of age, education, health, constitution (stature, health), personal and employment experience, lifestyle, and IQ scores. The examiner must also assess the patient's job duties, training, personality and quality of job performance to determine the patient's postinjury status (e.g., how long the patient was unemployed, relative skill level, problems in performing the job). These findings can then be compared to the estimated baseline (see Parker, 1990).

Direct observation. An estimate of current performance can also be elicited by direct clinical observation (e.g., patient's demeanor, vocabulary, detection and avoidance of errors, persistence, quality of standards applied to performance).

VARIED PATTERNS REVEAL BRAIN INJURY

Deficits compared to a preinjury baseline:
1. Generalized (dementia).
2. Factorial (e.g., verbal, perceptual-spatial, freedom from distractibility).
3. Narrow functions.
   a. Cognitive (e.g., agnosias, acalculia, anomia, visual memory).
   b. Sensorimotor. For example, dizziness, a common complaint after impact, often accompanies problems of balance, and is experienced when a finger is rotated in front of both eyes (vestibulo-ocular reflex). The anatomic basis for sensory deficits can be contingent upon whether trauma caused damage to nerve pathways above or below the point of decussation from the opposite hemisphere. Some sensory or motor deficits are due to damage to the sense organs directly (e.g., the eye), while others may be due to brain damage. Somatic damage and pain can mimic damage to the CNS. Damage to the anterior portion of the skull can cause olfactory loss. Vestibulo-ocular deficits are commonly observed following TBI.
4. Psychometric. The use of the concept of "organicity" should not be used since it connotes a lack of expertise in the field of neuropsychology. Instead, the neuropsychologist should utilize more specific terms (e.g., cerebral concussion, dementia), if they are supported by a review of the records.

   Many psychologists rely on cut-off scores to determine the likelihood of brain damage, or site of inferred lesion . However, such cut-off scores may not be realistic in light of the patient's pre-injury education, IQ, background, or age. In many cases the examiner must estimate the patient's pre-injury baseline and determine whether the patient's scores have significantly deviated from the estimated baseline.

   Pathognomonic signs:

   Specific patterns of responses are likely to occur following brain damage, and usually absent in nonbrain-damaged individuals (e.g., seizures; perceptual rotations; perseveration; catastrophic reactions).

   Test patterns:
1. Combinations suggesting a localized lesion. For example, combination of verbal dysfunctioning and right visual field defect can be used to indicate a left cerebral hemisphere injury.
2. Patterns of reduced and maintained functions. For example, a gross difference between verbal and performance IQ scores (Matarazzo & Herman, 1985; Matarazzo, Bornstein, McDermott, & Noonon, 1986).

MALINGERING AND LYING IN CASES OF PERSONAL INJURY

Malingering may be defined as making a claim of injury, that is false or exaggerated, for some personal gain. This would include concealing the extent of recovery. While opinions vary concerning the frequency of malingering (Grant & Alves, 1987), there is no evidence that patients become less symptomatic when their case has settled. The examiner should be particulary alert to personality styles such as an Antisocial Personality Disorder (Binder, 1990). Lishman (1987, pp. 150–151, 170) asserts that "impending litigation can strongly motivate the aggravation and prolongation disability. . .The injured person is invited to complain. . .repeatedly. . .to a number of specialists." However, Lishman does not differentiate between the patient with a valid claim and the exaggerator.

Malingering should be differentiated from the Somatoform Reaction "for which there are no demonstrable organic findings or known physiologic mechanisms. . .(since). . .symptom production. . .is not intentional" (American Psychiatric Association, 1987, p. 255); the motivation and pattern of an insanity defendant, which is likely to differ from the personal injury claimant (Lees-Haley, 1989); and physical conversion symptoms (the hysteric), which are motivated to avoid personal responsibility characterized by bland indifference (Solomon & Masdeu, 1989; Binder, 1990). The latter disorder should be differentiated from an organic emotional disorder.

Livingston (1985, p. 1153) has observed that when a physician interprets a patient's difficulties in terms of what is reasonable in light of current physiologic knowledge, the frequency of individuals who are diagnosed as malingerers tends to be quite high. Physical signs attributed to a "functional overlay" in noninjury cases (i.e., apparently competent limbs and nerves that misbehave according to the examiner's beliefs) are likely to be attributed to malingering (Cartlidge & Shaw, 1981). For example, Binder (1990) has assumed that bizarre results on double simultaneous stimulation of face and hand is evidence of malingering. He also offers examples of the patient's statements of personal history that are not supported or contradicted by the record. Malingering is likely to occur at the various points during an examination.

The "Personal Statement" (Questionnaire and Interview)

The examiner, under pressure to obtain information with limited time available, assumes that the patient is honest (Lees-Haley, 1990). Attempts at malingering or deception can include: concealing pre-existing conditions (e.g., drug addiction; psychiatric hospitalization); and lies about the patient's age that make test scores imprecise. Lees-Haley (1990) demonstrated that a questionnaire could be faked using a situation related to forensic neuropsychological claims (e.g., assumed toxin exposure and the Impact Events Scale).

Test Procedures

Faust, Hart, and Guilmette (1988) review malingering detection on commonly used neuropsychological procedures. In general, there may be a slight proportion over chance of the detection of malingering, but no test or general procedure has evolved that significantly improves the clinician's ability to combat being fooled. Binder (1990) recommends that forced choice procedures be utilized where the probability of unusual responses can be used to estimate faking. However, without objective evidence concerning the presence or absence of brain damage (a finding that would render the diagnosis of malingering inaccurate, and often not available today) the external criterion establishing the effectiveness of this technique does not exist.

RORSCHACH

Preston and Lieben (1990) assert that the Rorschach's popularity in part "has come about because the Rorschach will often reveal hidden aspects of one's personality and is therefore instrumental in evaluating individuals who either hide their innermost feelings and ideas, or, who are malingering." Yet, there has been a controversy whether the Rorschach can be faked, whether scored clinically or through an Exner computer program (Cohen, 1990; Kahn, Fox, & Rhode, 1990). Faust et al. (1988, citing Albert, Fox, & Kahn, 1980) have indicated that experienced clinicians may confuse the Rorschachs of psychotic individuals with those of normals who were feigning psychosis. The unfamiliar nature of the Rorschach task may also lead to a higher level of functioning than a deliberately depressed IQ score. There seems to have been no Rorschach study of faked brain damage, but faking of other conditions (Schretlen, 1988). Perry and Kinder (1990) concluded that prior Rorschach studies of malingering were questionable because of statistical problems, although some uninstructed individuals may fake serious emotional disturbance.

IQ TESTS

Schretlen (1988) lists three characteristics found in the protocols of malingerers: absurd or grossly illogical answers, approximate answers (correct answer is inwardly calculated and then slightly changed), and inconsistent performance between tests (level of difficulty passed or failed). However, this may also be due to fatigue or cognitive difficulty.

SENSORIMOTOR PROCEDURES

Some patients who sustain traumatic brain damage will complain of a loss of olfaction. The claim of lost olfactory sensation can be studied using ammonia since it creates tearing.

IF YOU ARE RETAINED BY THE DEFENDANT

When a client is referred by the defendant, the defendent has the right, through the adversary system, to have the plaintiff examined by their own neuropsychological expert. Eventually the neuropsychologist's report will be sent to the plaintiff's attorney during the "discovery process" (exchange of information between opposing attorneys).

The Plantiff's Attorney May Be Present

Often the patient will be accompanied by his attorney to your office. In the writer's experience, probably without exception, their presence (which is permitted) is ultimately harmful to their own cause. They may intrude to try to prevent the examiner from obtaining legitimate information that they wish to exclude from exposure to a jury (e.g., details of employment, severe parental conflict that may affect a child's personality or performance). If this occurs, proceed as far as possible with your intended examination, but make notes of any problems, call the attorney who retained you if feasible, and avoid a confrontation.

Do Not Mistreat the Plaintiff

The writer has heard numerous stories about the mistreatment of plantiffs who undergo a required examination by psychologists or physicians. Sometimes the presumption is made that the patient is faking, and this can be detected with a forthright confrontation. One brain-injured patient told the psychologist that he was feeling badly, that he needed to rest. The psychologist refused to grant the patient a rest break, which resulted in the patient having generalized seizures (which did not appear in his report). One psychologist precipitated an asthmatic attack after being told that the patient was allergic to two cats in the office (one jumping on his lap). Regardless of the source of referral, all persons referred for a forensic psychological examination should be treated with respect and dignity.

PRINCIPLES FOR SELECTING A BATTERY

One selects a particular forensic neuropsychological battery on the basis of the questions that are asked, and the manner in which evidence should be presented. The overall guiding principle for neuropsychological assessment was offered by Zygmunt A. Piotrowski over 50 years ago (Piotrowski, 1937): "The victim of brain damage displays both cognitive deficit and emotional distress. Be aware of the limitations of neuropsychological procedures in localizing lesions."

The writer recommends an eclectic battery: Relatively frequently administered procedures administered to individuals of a particular age group; supplemented according to the demographic and other characteristics of the plaintiff: education, vocation, type of symptoms, cultural background, etc. This permits substitution with various kinds of patients, as well as replacement as more effective or better normed (type of patient and recency of sampling) tests become available. The examiner recommends the procedures listed below:

Sample a Wide Range of Functions

A taxonomy of neuropsychological dysfunctions can guide the development of a comprehensive examination and organizing a report. Attempting only to document symptoms reported by the patient or others, or routine use of a pre-established battery of procedures, will often ignore many of the patient's dysfunctions.

Evaluation of cognitive functions, rather than the location of injury, has a higher priority in forensic neuropsychology. Localization helps to document damage and make the cognitive findings credible. Due to the long neural tracts, multiple input, and decussation to the opposite side of the nervous system, psychological procedures require multiple and overlapping evidence for localizing functioning, even for such simple tasks as sensation and motor efficiency.

Use Procedures Permitting Comparison to a Baseline

Deficits from an estimated or "real" baseline is a key issue in both the diagnosis and assessment of damages.

Alter Procedures According to the Background and Personal Statement of Patient

For example, the use of the Wechsler Adult Intelligence Scale—Revised (WAIS-R) may be inappropriate and misleading when evaluating the intellectual functioning of an individual who was raised in a difficult culture, has a limited command of English, or is aphasic. In such cases the examinoer should attempt to use relatively culture-free measures which place little emphasis on the patient's verbal or motor skills such as the Raven Progressive Matrices Test (Sbordone, 1991).

Avoid a Practice Effect

It may be necessary to substitute a different test for one previously administered (regardless of need for a baseline), or to administer the same test and an alternative. If a case is going to court, regardless of the practice effect, it may be useful to readminister it for comparison.

Select Procedures that Have a High Ceiling and Low Floor

Tasks with a low ceiling, often administered in a medical mental status examination (e.g., simple arithmetic), give the illusion of success, when the presence of more difficult items in the context of age-determined norms, often reveal deficits from baseline.

Tasks without a floor (i.e., that give no minimal standard credit for inability to perform administered items) implicitly ignore low ability. Instead they artificially raise the estimate of cognitive ability by substituting tests on which the patient can succeed. The forensic neuropsychologist who indicates that he or she did not report functioning in which there was so grievous a deficit would have his or her objectivity questioned.

Test Complex Functions

Complex functions often become more impaired than simple cognitive functions following TBI. Thus, a complex motor task is more useful than simple tapping speed, and reading comprehension more useful than reading recognition.The psychologist should select procedures emphasizing complexity or having a high ceiling as being most likely to detect impairment.

Use Tests That are Sensitive to Both Brain Damage and Adaptive Functioning

Some tests measure general functions, such as intelligence, success of adaptation, or a specific ability, and are not sensitive to focal brain damage (e.g., the Wisconsin Card Sorting Test, Heinrichs, 1990). Do not assume that particular procedures test localized damage (Parker, 1990).

Use the Latest Edition of the Test

Up-to-date norms are needed for accurate measurement. For example, the difference between scores obtained from the WAIS and WAIS-R have been described by Smith (1983). In contrast, Reitan and Wolfson (1990) have argued that the WAIS-R (with subjects tested between 1976 and 1980) has not been shown to be sensitive to brain damage, and thus, should not be substituted for WAIS (published in 1955). The use of out-of-date norms leads to significant errors in obtaining quantifiable findings (Flynn, 1984; Lippold & Claiborn, 1983; Parker, 1990; Wechsler, 1981). Yet, an attorney stated, "I am superconservative, but I would prefer that you use accepted tests, not new ones even if better." The examiner may find it necessary to use both familiar and new tests.

Select Procedures that Have Suitable Norms

Well-standardized tests with reasonably relevant norms are useful. An example would be level of achievement for academic functions, using high school seniors as the norm. The examiner must take into account the educational and vocational achievement, age, cultural and linguistic background of the patient (Sbordone, 1991).

Unstandardized Procedures Integrate with Standardized Ones

This permits a frame of reference for evaluation of unstandardized tests.

Realize the Sensorimotor Examination is Relevant to Forensic Questions

Many accident victims are unaware that vague sensory and motor dysfunctions are effects of a TBI. This is particularly true if there has not been a careful neurologic examination. TBI patients are likely to state that they bump into things, without realizing that this symptom arose after their head trauma. Examination of peripheral visual fields often reveals that the field of vision is generally restricted, or restricted in one area, which can create serious problems if the patient returns to driving.

Recognize the Limitations of any Given Procedure

No test is perfect in terms of its psychometric considerations: standardization of procedures, validity, reliability, and norms. Moreover, the range of even a so-called simple function is too great to be completely sampled by any test, particularly if practical considerations of examination time are considered (Sbordone, 1991).

THE COMPREHENSIVE NEUROPSYCHOLOGICAL REPORT

The report is an important factor in pretrial negotiation by both sides. In most cases, attorneys prefer to avoid the expense and unpredictability of a trial. Therefore it should be well-organized, thorough, unbiased, and include sufficient documentation for another neuropsychologist to determine whether its conclusions are reasonable. It should be forthright within ethical limitations (see Ethical Considerations, below). If one cannot come to a firm conclusion, this should be stated. The examiner should also specify which functions have not been examined. The examiner may state that (in the case of children) dysfunctions could appear later, or that poor emotional control limited the conclusions that could be drawn.

The report should include:

- A heading consisting of name of patient, referral source, date of examination, age at examination, age at accident, interval since accident, nature of the TBI (e.g., closed head injury).
- A summary of available records (educational, medical, employment, personal) and statements made by collaterals, with their neuropsychological implications. The summary is a complete, chronologic narrative report that is often read into the record of a trial.

- A history of prior injury or emotional distress, with an attempt to determine the sequence of impairment following various accidents or illnesses.
- Considerable numerical data (e.g., WAIS-R IQ Scales, Factor Averages, percentiles, and age-scaled scores).
- Verbatim report of the interview. The neuropsychologist should take great pain to take as detailed of a history as possible. Such information, however, may be discrepant with statements elsewhere in the patient's medical records.
- A comprehensive formation of the patient's impairments, particularly their relationship to the accident or injury and required treatments.

The outline used by the writer is: review of medical records; review of educational records; statements made by collaterals; personal statement; clinical observations; sensorimotor examination; cognitive functioning in structured situations (mental level and achievement); cognitive functioning in unstructured situations; supplementary cognitive functioning (efficiency and neuropsychological screening procedures); personality; and formulation.

Formulation

1. Background: What information is relevant to the victim's present situation (e.g., education, pre-existing medical or psychological conditions, job history).
2. Baseline: A summary of findings, as suggested in "Baseline" above. Where there is a pre-existing condition, an attempt should be made to evaluate the patient's impairments from the pre-existing baseline.
3. Injury: Whether there was LOC, amnesia, what parts of the body were injured, documentation of brain damage, hospitalization, treatment, etc.
4. Impairment Evaluation: This is a summary of findings listed in consecutive order by all 10 Taxonomic areas, with special reference to children where appropriate.
5. Diagnosis: Separate statements are made concerning brain damage and any personality or psychotic disturbances. Concerning the use of the DSM-III-R (American Psychiatric Association, 1987), contrary to a widespread impression among lawyers and psychologists that it must be used, there is no ethical or legal obligation to use it. If it is used, the diagnostic categories should be carefully applied, or the examiner is vulnerable to the accusation of incompetence on cross-examination. Other classifications can be utilized (e.g., ICD-9-CM [Cunningham Support Services]).
6. Attribution: "Can the deficits or dysfunctions be attributed with reasonable neuropsychological certainty to a particular injury?"
7. Prognosis for Adaptability, Employment, Development: Are the various dysfunctionings likely to be temporary or permanent?
8. Implications for Quality of Life: What are the effects of pain, anxiety, various other losses upon adaption and daily living?
9. Recommendation: Further evaluation (e.g., equivocal results may invite further neurologic, medical, or neuropsychologic study). The writer often recommends examination by medical specialists (e.g., endocrinologist, ophthamologist). Recommendations for treatment (e.g., cognitive rehabilitation, family counseling, personal psychotherapy, vocational retraining, residential treatment, etc.).

When treatment is recommended (e.g., psychotherapy) the patient may be asked in court whether he or she followed this suggestion. If the patient has not followed through, and one is asked in court why not, the reply is that many brain damaged patients do not follow through with recommendations, as a result of their brain injury (e.g., denial, loss of initiative, poor resent memory, etc.).

Enlivening Documentation

Some test results can be used to exemplify one's findings:

Photographs of such responses as WAIS-R Object Assembly (OA) and Block Design (BD) are helpful. The photos are matched against a photocopied model of the designs OA, and include in the photograph for BD the model and the response.

Photocopies of Drawings and Bender-Gestalt (B-G) Performance & Recall (and a copy of the B-G model), when their deficits are apparent to the untrained observer, can be used to exemplify the findings.

ETHICAL CONSIDERATIONS

Accuracy

Although the neuropsychologist is retained as part of an adversary process, there is an ethical responsibility to be truthful and objective (Blau, 1984). Statements should be forthright, yet findings and opinions should be reported as objectively as possible. The writer believes that careful documentation is helpful in keeping one's conclusions reasonable.

Competence

The neuropsychological examination should not be undertaken by an untrained psychologist. Experience in performing psychological assessment does not qualify an examiner for the high proficiency needed for neuropsychological assessment in forensic cases. The unqualified psychological examiner should either avoid an assignment, or perform it only with consultation with an experienced and competent neuropsychologist and considerable study of the relevant literature.

Thoroughness

A comprehensive neuropsychological examination, combined with good documentation to support the opinions contained within the report is likely to result in a document that will withstand the criticisms and attacks of the neuropsychological expert retained by opposing counsel. It also represents a barrier to altering findings under pressure by the retaining client. Yet, one must be aware that our procedures are often imprecise, and can lead to overzealous statements that often cannot be supported.

Avoiding Misinterpretation

While it is tempting to attribute the patient's dysfunctioning to prior conditions or events, the neuropsychologist must not attempt to ignore the problems created by the injury, or vice-versa

The writer, at the request of the plaintiff's lawyer, recently reviewed a neuropsychological report written on behalf of the defendant. The patient, a woman who had completed 3 years of college, had suffered a minor blow to the head in a car accident.

All of the patient's cognitive test scores (about two dozen) were below the 50th percentile. The psychologist persistently described percentile ranks of 30 as average and 22 percentile as low normal range. These deficits were attributed to her foreign origin, although surprisingly, she subsequently graduated college.

She was being treated for seizures. Her low scores on measurements of concentration (both in the author's prior examination, and the psychologist's later one) were attributed to the medication, without considering whether the seizures themselves were a symptom of brain damage.

When the patient arrived for the examination she was asked whether she was bothered by the cats in the office. She said, "Yes, I am allergic." The examiner proceeded with one cat sitting 2 feet away, the other leaping into his lap. Subsequently she sneezed for an extended period, and had an allergic attack that required self-administered medication. None of this appeared in the psychologist's report, which stated that the patient was a malingerer because of variability in her performance. A high memory score on one test was used to prove that other memory scores represented willful deception!

Confidentiality

The patient should be made aware of the limits of confidentiality. The client should be told that his or her only task is to give the examiner an accurate statement (i.e., leaving nothing out, but not exaggerating or inventing any problems) and to reveal any pre-existing conditions or improvement. He or she is told about "discovery" (i.e., the exchange of information), the likelihood of being examined by professionals retained by the defendant, and the adversary's examination before trial (EBT).

The writer obtains authorization to send a copy of the report to the attorney and even to a referring or treating physician. The patient is told that no telephone requests to forward a report will be honored.

There are two ways in which the psychologist yields confidential records, and the details found here may vary according to the jurisdiction within which the reader practices. *(The writer keeps authorizations and subpoenas indefinitely as a part of the patient's file).*

An "Authorization"

An authorization is permission by a patient to forward particular materials to a third party. The writer uses this procedure:

There should be a signature by the patient or legal guardian that is less than 6 months old. This prevents difficulties if there has been a change of attorneys, and the professional is not privy to any disagreements. There should also be a release to a particular party (not "to bearer").

A typical authorization may read:

> To Dr. Rolland S. Parker, Re. Mr. T.B. Injury. You are hereby requested and authorized to disclose to attorney A. Lincoln, whose address is 41 Covered Wagon Lane, NY, NY, or authorized representative all information, records, X-rays, etc., approximate date of admission to hospital, first examination, treatment or consultation.

This is an excessive request. One would not send copies of correspondence from the attorney or other doctors' reports (see below). Even the term "records" is ambiguous. Some attorneys interpret this to mean simply dates of "treatment," not technical data.

The writer received an authorization from an attorney representing an "infant" client, whose case had been transferred from the initial attorney. The guardian grandmother was illiterate. The writer requested an authorization, and received one by return mail, with an illegible scrawl purporting to be the child's mother. The writer returned this document stating that the handwriting was illegible and he needed a connection between the child, the attorney, and the authorizer. Since there was no reply the writer assumed the authorization to be fraudulent. An attorney called stating that he had sent the writer an authorization, and asked only for page 6 of the report, since he had the remainder. The writer discovered that there was no authorization in my files. The writer then told him that he received the report from someone else, but that the writer would not provide a copy without an authorization.

In another case, a psychologist refused to deliver authorized records to an attorney except to another psychologist stating that "this would be a violation of copyright laws." Since the scribbling of a Man or definition of Breakfast is not copyrightable, the psychologist was ignorant of her duties under the law.

Subpoenas

When a case cannot be settled through negotiation (litigation), it is assigned to the "calendar" (i.e., it will be scheduled when court facilities are available). In New York State a subpoena is issued in the name of the court, and may indeed may come unsigned by either a judge or an attorney. The records are to be sent to the record room of the court. You may or may not be entitled to payment for the cost of duplicating your records.

It is probably legitimate if there is a calendar number, but if there is no attorney's signature the writer does not comply but calls and asks for a properly signed document. Then, a particular person is taking responsibility for requesting my records. This is some protection against a forged or inappropriate request. An attorney indicated that the subpoena should even be signed by the judge, although it is customary to receive them without this. There are ambiguities and one should determine requirements for compliance.

A typical subpoena is signed by a particular attorney, with legal file numbers, a judge's name, and a request to send to the clerk of a particular court, "any and all medical records, charts, x-rays, bills, insurance claim forms, correspondence and reports having reference to your treatment and/or examination, including but not limited to, any other physicians' reports, therapists' reports, psychiatrists' reports, or other medical reports, CT scan plates, contained in your files, regarding the plaintiff's injury."

This is a fishing expedition for confidential material useful to the defense, but not authorized to be released by the patient to this attorney. It is not the psychologist's job to do the attorney's "discovery."

The man who delivered the above subpoena said, "Would you please send a copy to Mr. John Smith." If they could not obtain my records at the court house, the writer would have delivered them improperly without any authorization directly to the lawyer. *Subpoenaed records are sent only to court.*

Leins

Some attorneys representing plaintiffs expect the psychologist to accept a contingency fee payable for the entire examination from the proceeds of a settlement (which could be 10 years later). A dishonest attorney will avoid paying you by closing their files without examination to determine whether anybody has a lien against the settlement. Thus, care is advised before you agree to do work on a lein basis. In addition, accepting a particular case on a lein basis means if the attorney doen not win the case you probably will not get paid.

IF YOU ARE CALLED TO TRIAL

In forensic cases, from the moment the patient walks in the door, you should assume that anything said or written may be scrutinized in court. The writer knows of no clinical presentation that may undergo so relentless, hostile, and often intelligent, well-informed criticism. Matarazzo (1987) observes that in the courtroom, an adversary relationship may exist between the psychologist (if representing a defendant) and patient that does not occur in ordinary clinical practice. Other psychologists may be called in to examine the (subpoenaed) records to offer leads to how to discredit the conclusionsof the opposing neuropsychological expert.

Preparing for Trial

1. Review the materials (this may require several hours). Make a summary in terms understandable to laymen (i.e., the judge and jury). Make an outline of the key points, and present a copy to the attorney that retained you. If more than 1 year has elapsed, the question will be asked whether any change has taken place. It may be claimed that any dysfunction is due to a subsequent event, or that the examiner does not know whether the plaintiff has improved.
2. The writer recommends re-examination if more than 1 year has elapsed since the last examination. While a high proportion of individuals show permanent impairment, you will be asked in court, "Doctor, you have not seen this person for (1–10) years. You really don't know how they are getting along, do you?" The answer, of course, is that you don't unless you have examined the person shortly before the trial. In one trial, the writer was confronted by a sharp attorney, who pointed out that an assault victim, whom the writer had assessed some time previously as having diffuse brain injury with impaired cognitive functioning, was currently earning a very large sum of money.
3. Meet with the attorney in advance. Gain some impression of the opposing attorney and the judge that will try the case. Explain the key points of your evaluation. Go over the procedures to "qualify you as an expert." Make available a resume, with points emphasized that make you an expert in the issues at stake. Since neuropsychological evidence is relatively unfamiliar, and frequently opposes (inaccurate) general opinion concerning brain damage, be ready to help the attorney and court understand the nature of brain damage, and how you arrived at your conclusions. Diagrams of the brain, and a model of skull and brain, can be used to illustrate particular points of anatomy and trauma.
4. Expressive deficits should be made clear to retaining attorney, judge, and jury (i.e., how they may prevent an impaired person from giving a completely accurate presentation). As Kolpan (1986) points out, for the victim to obtain his legal rights the jury must understand that the witness can be significantly impaired, but may appear cognitively intact, since the courtroom is relatively orderly.
5. Find out what new information has been revealed in recent reports or testimony in court. At this point, your knowledge of general psychology will be useful in integrating these

findings into your own conclusions. If you are first presented with this information while on the stand, quick thinking and general technical knowledge will be quite helpful.

6.   Alert the plaintiff's attorney of the great anxiety that people experience as they are required to review the accident and their impairment. The defense counsel is often aggressive to the patient, and to opposing witnesses, in order to discredit them. They (properly) anticipate intimate and damaging details of their life to be revealed in an unfriendly way.

Who is an Expert

Whether one may testify will be decided by the judge who determines "whether the expert's background demonstrates sufficient knowledge and competence in a particular field that the court recognizes as valid" (Kolpan, 1989). Expertise is established through review of qualifications (e.g.,training, meetings, writings, boards, teaching and practice affiliations, relevant experience), the legal definition of psychological practice, and the relevance of procedures to the questions before the court. The writer strongly recommends that the psychologist refuse to accept a case in areas in which there is specialized information and procedures beyond his or her current abilities and knowledge.

An expert (Blau, 1985) is "one who is so qualified by study or experience that he can form a definite opinion of his own respecting a division of science, branch of art, or department of trade concerning which persons having no particular training or special study are incapable of forming accurate opinions or of deducing correct conclusions." Schwartz (1987, citing Maloney, 1985) states that a psychologist as an expert is based in part on education and training, relevant experience, research and publications, knowledge and application of scientific principles, and use of specific tests and measures. Thus, personal experience or thorough literature review is highly relevant.

The definition of an expert may be interpreted differently by different judges. For example, one judge may not let a psychologist introduce his or her opinion concerning the diagnosis of brain damage, when it had not previously been introduced by a medical doctor. Another judge may say that while the psychologist was not a physician, the weight of his or her evidence should be determined by the jury. A third judge may listen carefully to an explanation of the effect of impact upon the brain, and ask intelligent questions for clarification.

Differences Between Witnesses

There is a difference between an expert witness, who is retained to present testimony concerning opinions, and a fact witness, who testifies as to facts (e.g., that one actually wrote a particular report or performed treatment). If you are subpoenaed by one party not as an expert, but because you have examined or treated a patient, you are then a fact witness, you need not give your opinion. Lawyers sometimes subpoena a professional as a fact witness as a way of getting around paying them a fee.

It should be brought out during qualification or presentation of findings that the psychological examination is usually considerably longer than that of the physician, and that the procedures used to study behavioral variables are more valid, reliable, are more frequently standardized, and have suitable norms. With a wide-range neuropsychological examination, dysfunctions can be detected that have been ignored, or are greater than previously estimated.

The neuropsychological witness should actually be an expert in a given area, which is relevant to the particular issues of the case. Schwartz (1987) states that presentation to a court of evidence involving brain trauma should be preceded by evidence of the expert's expertise (e.g., attendance at neuropathologic conferences, review of textbooks, and/or course work in neuroanatomy). He refers specifically to "pretenders" (i.e. inexperienced clinical psychologists). The writer has often seen erroneous conclusions reached in assessing TBI cases because of lack of knowledge or a narrow range of examination(e.g., WAIS-R, Bender-Gestalt and MMPI).

Example of psychologist using inappropriate generalizations. A 3 $\frac{1}{2}$-year-old boy fell 12 feet onto an asphalt surface, suffering a closed head injury with a loss of consciousness. He had seizures shortly after the accident. Examined about 5 years later, a clinical psychologist, retained by the defendant (who had access to my earlier report), with experience in examining children with attentional deficit disorder, took a diagnosis of ADD within the school as evidence that his condition was a developmental disorder with presumably unknown etiology (illustrating how many professionals do not inquire into prior accidents, so the true basis for neurologic disorders is unknown). He also used as evidence for a pre-existing condition a totally undocumented preinjury allegation of sexual molestation.

Taking the Witness Stand

Be aware of the ground rules of the jurisdiction you are testifying within. For example, in New York State Supreme Court, a witness may not be present when another witness presents evidence during personal injury cases. Curiosity to hear what goes on before your presentation can disqualify you. Unless asked to remain, leave when finished since a witness can be called back after testifying if a point is raised involving your testimony. However, in Federal court, however, witnesses can hear other testimony.

Bring in all test protocols (originals). Don't bring in tests themselves, unless you have a duplicate, since they may be "entered as evidence" and left behind in the court for weeks.

The retaining attorney will lead you through your training, qualification, previous and current experiences, boards, licensure, etc., or may ask you to describe your background.

Present the relevant points in a psychologically significant manner (i.e., not test by test). Organize it according to a taxonomy, which is more concise and meaningful.

Be prepared to be abused during cross-examination. With a skillful attorney on the attack, it is no collegial case conference!

Attacks can come from three directions: (1) errors—mistakes of judgment, or clerical errors will haunt you; honesty—your objectivity will be questioned. "You were paid for your testimony, weren't you, Doctor?" The proper reply is, "No. I am being paid for my time in court and my professional skill!" "You are in the business of personal injury, aren't you?" I informed the attorney, "No, I am in a licensed profession." "You're a hired gun, aren't you?" The only response, is "No", and (3) competence—justification of your findings will be demanded by the adversary. Be prepared for an attack on any weak points, particularly if your files have been subpoenaed in advance. You may have to demonstrate the utility or validity of particular procedures. If asked, "Did you rely upon such and such a test?" the answer is, "Not completely." "Do you recognize such a text as 'authoritative'." If you state that it is, you can be called upon to read aloud or to acknowledge anything in that text, whether or not you are familiar with it or disagree with it. The correct reply may be, "Only in part." I have stated that I do not know a certain book, pointed out that it was the 3rd not the 5th edition, stated that I disagreed with the conclusions of the authors of a neurology textbook being intimately familiar with what they had stated about TBI, and indicated that the *PDR* (*Physicians' Desk Reference*) was not a reliable source for neuropsychological drug effects. If you haven't read a book, don't acknowledge it, regardless of its renown.

You will be asked whether prior emotional disturbances (e.g., early family experiences, divorces), medications, or medical conditions are responsible for your or another examiner's findings. You may be asked whether any findings new to you are significant enough for you to modify your findings. If you cannot offer an opinion, don't do so.

If you have a considered opinion, state it in a clear and professional way. If you don't know, say so. The attorney may comment about your ability to your face, or behind your back to the jury. There may be objections to explaining in detail what you meant, for which judge's tolerance varies. You may be interrupted as being verbose. State that the problem is too complex to offer a *yes* or *no* response. If there can be alternatives or weak points in your presentation, acknowledge them or you will appear prejudiced. Since a wide-range report will offer details that are advantageous to the adversary, you will be asked whether you wrote them. A good attorney will observe points that you would like to make, but were interrupted, and in "re-cross"-examination will ask you to explain them. Alert the attorney in advance to watch for this.

If you have given a response, and the attorney repeats the question, simply say, "I have answered that question."

Stay within your areas of expertise. For example, you are not expected to know the neuropsychological side effects of medications. Conversely, when an attorney asked me, using the *Physicians' Desk Reference* as an authoritative text, whether a physician should have used certain laboratory tests, I stated that my opinion had no value to the court.

The plaintiff is usually present during your testimony. Attorneys like to have them there so the jury will empathize with them. You would ordinarily never discuss a patient's dysfunctions so plainly. On one occasion, to my regret, the writer presented his findings in the case of an adolescent girl, who was upset, started to cry, and left the court, leading to a mistrial.

If your attorney loses the case, follow through. Review the judge's decision, get a report from the attorney how the jury came to its decision. Try to find out how well you were received in court by the judge and the jury when you presented your testimony. Based on this feedback you can determine how future cases with psychological implications can be better or differently presented.

SUMMARY

The forensic neuropsychological examination is primarily concerned with detecting cognitive, behavioral and emotional impairments and their relationship to a specific event or injury, their implications (e.g., effect on the patient's ability to work, enjoy life, attend school, handle responsibilities, etc.), and prognosis (e.g., anticipated changes in the patient's future condition, needs for services, length of treatment/care, additional problems, etc.). The neuropsychological examiner should be the primary source of information and the integrator of the patient's medical, academic, employment, and psychiatric/psychological records. The forensic neuropsychological examination requires considerable knowledge in the fields of clinical psychology, neuropsychology, behavioral neurology, psychopharmacology, neurosciences, and a variety of related health disciplines. A taxonomy of neuropsychological functions frequently impaired after personal injury and stress has been presented, and recognition is given to the special problems of the brain-damaged child. A taxonomy of expressive deficits was also presented (i.e., why the TBI victim cannot offer a complete statement concerning dysfunctioning). Suggestions for selecting a wide-range eclectic battery were explained, with examples. The chapter also contains a discussion of TBI and stress, qualifications of the examiner, scientific basis for the examination, report writing, ethical and confidentiality considerations, fees, and preparation for and appearance at court.

ACKNOWLEDGMENT

The author would like to thank Andrew B. Rosenblum, Ph.D. Project Director, Narcotic and Drug Research, Inc., NYC, for statistical assistance.

REFERENCES

Acklin, M. W., & Bernat, E. (1987). Depression, alexithymia, and pain proneness disorder. Rorschach study. *Journal of Personality Assessment, 51,* 462–479.

Adams, R. D., & Victor, M. (1985). *Principles of neurology (3rd ed.)* New York: McGraw Hill.

Albert, S., Fox, H. M., & Kahn, M. W. (1980). Faking psychosis on the Rorschach: Can expert judges detect malingering? *Journal of Personality Assessment, 44,* 115–119.

American Psychiatric Association. (1987). *Diagnostic and statistical manual of mental disorders (3rd ed. rev.).* Washington, DC: Author.

Aysto, S., & Hanninen, R. (1988). Simultaneous and successive cognitive processes in brain damaged adults: Hemispheric and anterior-posterior effects. *Archives of Clinical Neuropsychology, 3,* 9–3.

Barton, W. A. (1985). *Recovering for psychological injuries.* Washington, DC: The Association of Trial Lawyers of America.

Becker, D. P., & Povlishock, J. T. (Eds.). (1985). *Central nervous system trauma status report-1985.* National Institute of Neurological and Communicative Disorders and Stroke, National Institutes of Health.

Berg, R. (1986). Neuropsychological effects of closed-head injury in children. In J. E. Obrzut & G. W. Hynd (Eds.), *Child neuropsychology (Vol. 2)* (pp. 113–135). New York: Academic Press.

Berkow, R., & Fletcher, A. J. (1987). *The Merck manual, (15th ed.).* Rahway, NJ: Merck Sharpe & Dohme Research Laboratories.

Binder, L. M. (1990). Malingering following minor head trauma. *The Clinical Neuropsychologist, 4,* 25–36.

Bisiach, E., Vallek, J., Perani, D., Pagagno, C., & Berti, A. (1986). Unawareness of disease following lesions of the right hemisphere: Anosognosia for hemiplegia and anosognosia for hemianopia. *Neuropsychologia, 24,* 471.

Blau, T. (1984). *The psychologist as expert witness.* New York: Wiley.

Blau, T. (1985). The psychologist as expert in the courts. *The Clinical Psychologist, 38,* 76–78.

Boll, T. J. (1982). Behavioral sequelae of head injury. In P. Cooper (Ed.), *Head injury.* (pp. 363–375). Baltimore: Williams & Wilkins.

Bond, M. R. (1986). Neurobehavioral sequelae of closed head injury. In I. Grant & K. M. Adams (Eds.), *Neuropsychological assessment of neuropsychiatric disorders.* (pp. 347–373). New York: Oxford University Press.

Bruno, R. S. (1984). The catastrophic reaction: Release of cortical inhibition following cortical lesion. *Newsletter: The New York Neuropsychology Group, 3,* 1–6.

Cartlidge, N. E. F., & Shaw, D. A. (1981). *Head injury.* Philadelphia: W.B. Saunders.

Cohen, J. B. (1990). Misuse of computer software to detect faking on the Rorschach: A reply to Kahn, Fox, and Rhode. *Journal of Personality Assessment, 54,* 58–62.

Cooper, P. R. (Ed). (1987). *Head injury (2nd ed.).* Baltimore: Williams & Wilkins.

Cunningham Support Services. The Extract of Mental Health ICD-9-CM Codes. POB 1347, Arlington VA.

Dacey, G. R., & Dikmen, S. S. (1987). Mild head injury. In P. R. Cooper (Ed.), *Head injury (2nd ed.)* (pp. 125–140). Baltimore: Williams & Wilkins.

Dennis, M. (1989). Assessing the neuropsychological abilities of children and adolescents for personal injury litigation. *The Clinical Neuropsychologist, 3,* 203–229.

Division of Clinical Neuropsychology. (1989). Definition of a clinical neuropsychologist. *The Clinical Neuropsychologist, 3,* 22.

Duus, P. (1989). *Topical diagnosis in neurology.* New York: Thieme.

Ellenhorn, M. J., & Barcelous, D. G. (1988). *Medical toxicology.* New York: Elsevier.

Faust, D., Hart, K., & Guilmette, T. J. (1988). Pediatric malingering: The capacity of children to fake believable deficits on neuropsychological testing. *Journal of Consulting and Clinical Psychology, 56,* 578–582.

Flynn, J. R. (1984). The mean IQ gains of Americans: Massive gains 1932–1978. *Psychological Bulletin, 95,* 29–51.

Gelb, H., & Siegel, P.N. (1980). *Killing pain without prescription.* New York: Harper & Row.

Gennarelli, T. M. (1987). Cerebral concussion and diffuse brain injuries. In P. R. Cooper (Ed.), *Head injuries (2nd ed.)* (pp. 108–124). Baltimore: Williams & Wilkins.

Grant, I., & Alves, W. (1987). Psychiatric and psychosocial disturbances in head injury. In H. L. Levin, J. Grafman, & H.M.Eisenberg (Eds.). *Neurobehavioral recovery from head injury)* (pp. 233–261). New York: Oxford University Press.

Haas, D. C., & Ross, G. S. (1986). Transient global amnesia triggered by mild head trauma. *Brain, 109,* 251–257.

Hales, R. E., & Yudofsky, S. C. (1987). *Textbook of neuropsychiatry.* Washington: American Psychiatric Press.

Heilman, K. M., Bowers, D., & Valenstein, E. (1985). Emotional disorders associated with neurological diseases. In K. M. Heilman, & E. Valenstein (Eds.), *Clinical neuropsychology (2nd ed.)* (pp. 377–402). New York: Oxford University Press.

Heilman, K. M., Watson, R. T., & Bowers, D. (1983). Affective disorders associated with hemispheric disease. In K. M. Heilman & P. Satz (Eds.), *Neuropsychology of human emotions* (pp. 45-64). New York: Guilford Press.

Heinrichs, R. S. (1990). Variables associated with Wisconsin Card Sorting Test performance in neuropsychiatric patients referred for assessment. *Neuropsychiatry, Neuropsychology, and Behavioral Neurology, 3,* 107–112.

Hendler, N. H., Long, D. M., & Wise, T. N. (Eds). (1981). *Diagnosis and treatment of chronic pain* (pp. 53–62). Boston: John Wright.

Herskowitz, J., & Rosman, N. P. (1982). *Pediatrics, neurology, and psychiatry-common ground.* New York: MacMillan.

Kahn, M. W., Fox, H., & Rhode, R. (1990). Detecting faking on the Rorschach: Computer versus expert clinical judgment: A reply to Cohen. *Journal of Personality Assessment, 54,* 63–66.

Kolb, L. C. (1987). A neuropsychological hypothesis explaining post-traumatic stress disorders. *American Journal of Psychiatry, 144,* 989–995.

Kolpan, K. I. (1986). Medicolegal issues: Amnesia and the law. *Journal of Head Trauma Rehabilitation, 1,* 81–82.

Kolpan, K. I. (1989). Expert courtroom testimony. *Journal of Head Trauma Rehabilitation, 4,* 95–96.

Kurke, M. I., & Meyer, R. G. (Eds.) (1986). *Psychology in product liability and personal injury litigation.* Washington, DC: Hemisphere.

Lam, C. S., McMahon, B. T. Priddy, D. A., & Gehred-Schultz, A. (1988). Deficit awareness and treatment performance among traumatic head injury adults. *Brain Injury, 2,* 235–242.

Lecours, A. R. Mehler, J., & others. (1987). Illiteracy and brain damage: I. Aphasia testing in culturally contrasted populations (control subjects). *Neuropsychologia, 25,* 231–245.

Lees-Haley, P. R. (1989). MMPI-F and F-K Scales: Questionable indices of malingering. *American Journal of Forensic Psychology, 7,* 81–83.

Lees-Haley, P. R. (1990). Malingering mental disorder on the impact of event scale (IES): Toxic exposure and cancer phobia. *Journal of Traumatic Stress, 3*, 315–321.

Levin, H. S. (1987). Neurobehavioral sequelae of head injury. In P. R. Cooper (Ed.), *Head injury (2nd ed.)* (pp. 442–463). Baltimore: Williams & Wilkins.

Lezak, M. (1983). *Principles of neuropsychological assessment (2nd ed.)*. New York: Oxford University Press.

Lippold, S., & Claiborn, J. M. (1983). Comparison of the Wechsler Adult Intelligence Scale and the Wechsler Adult Intelligence Scale-Revised. *Journal of Consulting and Clinical Psychology, 51*, 315.

Lishman, W. A. (1987). *Organic Psychiatry*. Boston: Blackwell Scientific Publications.

Livingston, R. B. (1985). Section IX. Neurophysiology. In J. B. West (Ed.), *Best & Taylor's physiological basis of medical practice (11th ed.)* (pp. 970–1295). Baltimore: Williams & Wilkins.

Maloney, M. P. (1985). *A clinician's guide to forensic psychological assessment*. New York: The Free Press.

Marshall, L. F., & Marshall, S. B. (1985). Current clinical head injury research in the United States. In D. B. Becker & J. T. Povlishock (Eds.), *Central nervous system trauma status report—1985* (pp. 45–51). National Institute of Neurological and Communicative Disorders and Stroke, National Institutes of Health (No location cited).

Matarazzo, J. D. (1987). Validity of psychological assessment: From the clinic to the courtroom. *The Clinical Neuropsychologist, 4*, 307–314.

Matarazzo, J. D., Bornstein, R. A., McDermott, P. A., & Noonon, J. V. (1986). Verbal IQ versus performance IQ differences scores in males and females from the WAIS-R standardization sample. *Journal of Clinical Psychology, 42*, 965–974, as corrected by JCP, 1987, 43, 293–297.

Matarazzo, J. D, & Herman, D. O. (1984) Relationship of education and IQ in the WAIS-R standardization sample. *Journal of Consulting and Clinical Psychology, 52*, 631–634.

Matarazzo, J. D. & Herman, D. O. (1985). Clinical uses of the WAIS-R: Base rates of differences between VIQ and PIQ in the WAIS-R standardization sample. In B. B. Wolman (Ed.), *Handbook of intelligence: Theories, Measurements and applications* (pp. 899–932).

Mesulam, M-Marsel. (1985). Attention, confusional states, and neglect. In M. Mesulam (Ed.), *Principles of behavioral neurology* (pp. 125–168). Philadelphia: F.A. Davis.

Palagi, R. J., & Springer, J. R. (1984). Personal injury law. In R. H. Woody (Ed.), *The law and the practice of human services*. San Francisco: Jossey-Bass.

Pansky, B., Allen, D. J., & Budd, G. C. (1988). *Review of neuroscience (2nd ed.)*. New York: Macmillan.

Papciak, A. S., Feuerstein, M., & Spiegel, J. A. (1985). Stress reactivity in alexithymia: Decoupling of physiological and cognitive responses. *The Journal of Human Stress*. 135–142.

Parker, R. S. (1972). The patient who cannot express pain. In R. S. Parker (Ed.), *The emotional stress of war, violence and peace* (pp. 71–85). Pittsburgh: Stanwix House.

Parker, R. S. (1981). *Emotional common sense*. New York: Harper & Row.

Parker, R. S. (1987). Recognizing employees who have suffered brain damage. *EAP Digest*, (Employees Assistance Program), 7, March/April, pp 55-60.

Parker, R. S. (1988). Brain damage victims: They may not be the best witnesses for themselves. *Trial, 24*, 68–73.

Parker, R. S. (1990). *Traumatic brain injury and neuropsychological impairment*. New York: Springer-Verlag.

Perry, G. G., & Kinder, B. N. (1990). The susceptibility of the Rorschach to Malingering: A critical review. *Journal of Personality Assessment, 54*, 47–57.

Piotrowski, Z. (1937). The Rorschach inkblot method in organic disturbances of the central nervous system. *Journal of Nervous and Mental Disorders. 86*, 525–537.

Preston, J., & Lieben, D. S. (1990). Defending the Rorschach in forensic cases. *American Journal of Forensic Psychology, 3*, 59–67.

Priddy, D. A., Mattes, D., & Lam, C. S. (1988). Reliability of self-report among non-oriented head-injured adults. *Brain Injury, 2*, 249–253.

Reitan, R., & Wolfson, D. (1990). A consideration of the comparability of the WAIS and WAIS-R. *The Clinical Neuropsychologist, 4,* 80–85.

Rimel, R. W., Giordani, B., Barth, J. T., & Jane, M. A. (1982). Moderate head injury: Completing the clinical spectrum of brain trauma. *Neurosurgery, 11,* 344–351.

Ross, E. G., (1985). Modulation of affect and nonverbal communication by the right hemisphere. In M. Mesulam (Ed.), *Principles of behavioral neurology.* Philadelphia: F. A. Davis.

Satz, P. (1988). Neuropsychological testimony: Some emerging concerns. *The Clinical Neuropsychologist, 2,* 89–100.

Sbordone, R. J. (1991). *Neuropsychology for the attorney.* Orlando: Paul M. Deutsch Press, Inc.

Schretlen, D. J. (1988). The use of psychological tests to identify malingered symptoms of mental disorders. *Clinical Psychology Review, 8,* 451–476.

Schwartz, M. L. (1987). Limitations on neuropsychological testimony by the Florida Appellate decisions: Action, reaction, and counteraction. *The Clinical Neuropsychologist, 1,* 51–60.

Smith, R. S. (1983). A comparison study of the Wechsler Adult Intelligence Scale and the Wechsler Adult Intelligence Scale-Revised in a college population. *Journal of Consulting and Clinical Psychology, 51,* 414–419.

Solomon, S., & Masdeu, J. C. (1989). Neuropsychiatry and behavioral neurology. In H. I. Kaplan & B. J. Sadock (Eds.), *Comprehensive textbook of psychiatry (5th ed.) Vol. I.* (pp. 217–240). Baltimore: Williams & Wilkins.

Speed, W. G. (1982). Headaches. In N. H. Hendler, D. M. Long, & T. Wise (Eds.), *Diagnosis and treatment of chronic pain* (pp. 141–152). Boston: John Wright.

Spindler, H. A., & Reischer, M. A. (1982). Electrodiagnostic studies in the evaluation of pain. In N. H. Hendler, D. M. Long, & T. N. Wise (Eds.), *Diagnosis and treatment of chronic pain* (pp. 53–62). Boston: John Wright.

Sugarman, S. D. (1990). The need to reform personal injury law leaving scientific disputes to scientists. *Science, 248,* 823–827.

Taylor, G. J. (1984). Alexithymia: Concept, measurement, and implications for treatment. *The American Journal of Psychiatry, 141,* 725–732.

Tupper, D. E. (1987). The issues with 'soft' signs. In D. E. Tupper (Ed.), *Soft neurological signs.* (pp. 1–16). Orlando: Grune & Stratton.

Uzell, B. P., Langfitt, T. W., & Dolinkas, C. A (1987). Influence of injury severity on quality of survival after head injury. *Surgical Neurology, 27,* 419–429.

Wechsler, D. (1981). *Wechsler Adult Intelligence Scale-Revised.* The Psychological Corporation.

Weiner, I. B. (1985). Preparing forensic reports and testimony. *The Clinical Psychologist, 38,* 78–80.

Westmeyer, J., & Westenholm, K. (1989). Assessing the victimized psychiatric patient. *Hospital and Comminity Psychology, 40,* 245-249.

Zohn, D. A. (1982). Mechanical (structural) headache. In N. H. Hendler, D. M. Long, & T. N. Wise (Eds.). *Diagnosis and treatment of chronic pain.* (pp. 117-139). Boston: John Wright.

Chapter 2

Criminal-Forensic Neuropsychology of Disorders of Executive Functions

Harold V. Hall

Psycholegal issues within the criminal justice system frequently become the focus of attention when the defendant's executive skills, judgment, or other ultimately interpersonally related functions are compromised. An examination of this nation's state and federal penal codes (Hall, 1983) revealed the use of words and terms with possible relevance both to executive skills (e.g., planning, resisting, self-control, deception, intention, anticipation) and dysfunctions (e.g., disorganization, incompetence, acts under extreme emotion, mental retardation, reckless behavior, heedless to consequences). Not surprisingly, a number of neuropsychologists, particularly those who discuss the executive functions of the brain, utilize similar terminology (e.g., see reviews in Filskov & Boll, 1986; Fuster, 1989; Lezak, 1983; Parker, 1990; Perecman, 1987; Strub & Black, 1981; Stuss & Benson, 1986). This raises the possibility that the criminal court and the neuropsychologist may be addressing the same behavioral phenomena. Although neuropsychological terminology is clearly not identical with these legal terms, the neuropsychologist who provides forensic input is obliged to clarify how similar terms overlap in their respective meanings and functions.

The connection between executive impairments, as seen by neuropsychologists, and criminal behavior, as seen by the courts, has not been precisely established (Kandel & Freed, 1989). Research studies examining specific executive-related dysfunctions, as demonstrated by neuropsychological tests and antisocial behavior, are virtually nonexistent or limited to only a few case studies, which will be discussed later. Yet, the forensic evaluator still frequently assesses for (1) current neuropsychological status (which has relevance to competency to stand trial); (2) criminal responsibility (examination for which extends evaluation data back over time to the instant offense); and (3) rehabilitation and risk analysis during the sentencing phase of the judicial proceedings (Blau, 1986; McMahon & Satz, 1981).

The forensic neuropsychologist attempts to communicate helpful information to the trier of fact or other referring party—a point admitted to even by those opposed to the admission of psychological data in court (Ziskin, 1981). To maximize the potential impact, two tasks may be necessary: (1) isolate those neuropsychological abilities and deficits that may operate for a defendant and (2) communicate to the referring party the decision path utilized by the evaluator in reaching his or her opinions. Hall has previously described the use of decision analysis for violence prediction (Hall, 1982, 1984a, 1987; Hall, Catlin, Boissevain, & Westgate, 1984), for mental capacity (Hall, 1983, 1985), for forensic distortion and deception (Hall, 1982, 1986), for post-traumatic stress disorder (Hall & Hall, 1987), and extreme emotion as mitigation to murder (Hall, 1990). Decision analysis will be discussed in this chapter only insofar as it relates to executive dysfunction.

EXECUTIVE FUNCTIONS: A DEFINITION

A broad definition of executive functions or systems is presented below. This definition will be used throughout the remainder of this book:

> Executive functions comprise a neuropsychological system that translates awareness into action and consists of those abilities that allow the person to engage in purposeful, autonomous, self-serving, and prosocial activities. Included are temporally oriented programming functions designed to accomplish tasks successfully such as task anticipation, goal selection, planning, implementation, monitoring, and use of feedback. Executive functions can be differentiated from cognition, sensation, perception, and other neuropsychological functions since the former is qualitatively unique (i.e., execution versus awareness) in that deficits in that executive dysfunction affect a broad set of behaviors. Disorders of executive functions, when they arise, typically produce deficits in either drive (e.g., inertia, apathy, labile behavior) or sequencing functions (e.g., perseveration, disorganization, impaired problem-solving ability). The primary neural systems that regulate executive functions consist of both the neocortex and the subcortex with a special contribution by the frontal and anterior temporal lobes due to their rich and intimate connections with the rest of the cerebrum. The ability of the executive system to integrate, select, modify, and eventually produce novel behaviors represents the highest form of human intellectual activity.

LEGAL ISSUES AND DECISION ANALYSIS

The central substantive question in both civil and criminal law becomes, "Is the defendant responsible for any wrongdoing and, if so, how responsible is he or she?" (Bartol, 1983; Blau, 1986; Monahan, 1981). This question is based upon the premise that adults have the ability to monitor and control their own behavior unless otherwise demonstrated to the contrary (Horowitz & Willging, 1984; Schwitzgebel & Schwitzgebel, 1980). When a person physically harms another person or property, the legal search is initiated for the agent or condition that allegedly created the illegal behavior (Rogers, 1986; Schuman, 1986; Ziskin, 1981). Once a case is prepared, a judicial battle waged in the courts determines the legal outcome.

Thus, one can see the issues raised by the forensic mental health professional have considerable bearing on civil and criminal matters since both deal with a self-control issue within an adversarial process. It makes little difference to the neuropsychologist whether the issue is an alleged social wrong resulting in possible criminal responsibility (i.e., a crime) or a civil wrong with ensuing personal or product liability (i.e., a tort). In both cases a neuropsychologist must determine the presence and extent of any disorder of executive function in an individual and assess its impact upon that individual's ability to control and regulate his or her behavior.

When presenting neuropsychological findings, the neuropsychological expert may offer a physical or mental condition (e.g., brain injury) as an explanation for the neuropsychological disorder. It is humbling, yet important, to realize that the expert's final opinion (e.g., brain injury) may never parallel the ultimate conclusion of the judge or jury (e.g., guilt or liability) since the court's decision typically rests upon different assumptive bases, a different language, and represents a higher level of abstraction. In this regard and for criminal cases, McMahon and Satz (1981) stated:

> In our years of experience we have never found an instance where the neuropsychological examination per se could answer any of these questions or where cortical dysfunction was, in and of itself, sufficient for a defense. There have been occasions when cortical dysfunction *was* a contributing factor, most particularly with regard to competency and intent. (p. 687)

The differences between civil and criminal forensic neuropsychology are instructive. In the civil arena, the three primary points of focus of neuropsychological assessment are personal injury, disability determination, and workers' compensation. The burden of proof is often lower than in criminal cases and calls for a "preponderance of evidence," which some forensic professionals equate with a 50–75 percent level of certainty (Frederick, 1978; Hall, 1987; Stone, 1975). A "clear and convincing" burden of proof, associated with a 76–89 percent level of certainty, is found both in the civil and criminal arenas. In contrast, criminal cases require that culpability be shown "beyond a reasonable doubt," which is associated with a 90–100 percent degree of certainty. Finally, in civil cases, a prognosis is usually required, whereas in criminal matters, a diagnosis of a mental or physical condition answers most referral questions.

Civil and criminal law converge when the evaluator considers retrospectively the decision path used in arriving at the proffered conclusions. This process, entitled "Forensic Executive Decision Tree," (Fig. 1) will be referred to throughout this text. Simply, it is a seven-step retrospective analysis of data that is designed to link disorders of executive function to relevant criminal or civil behavior. The seven steps represent fundamental activities the evaluator should perform in order to connect evaluation and incident-related data to answer specific referral questions. The evaluator must recognize first that collected data are relevant to different points in time. Behavior during an evaluation is rarely of interest in and of itself (i.e, right side of decision tree) but may be helpful in terms of possibly shedding light on alleged liability or culpability (i.e, left side of decision tree).

In sum, this post-hoc decision process involves obtaining an interdisciplinary data base from multiple sources or data points, accounting for nondeliberate distortion and deliberate deception in order to ensure that the data reflect what they purport to measure, and an analysis of the individual's history. For civil cases, there should be a competency assessment of relevant skills and a determination as to whether or not the person's premorbid adjustment was equal to or superior to behaviors that occurred subsequent to the incident in question. In criminal cases, there should be an examination of basal violence in terms of its frequency, severity, and recency.

Next, a disorder of executive function should be established by demonstrating the existence of a well-recognized and accepted neuropsychological syndrome for the time of the alleged condition, injury, or crime.

Self-control should be considered next. For civil cases, the question is to what degree did the injured party contribute to the net harm represented by the cerebral insult. In criminal cases, the evaluator must determine the level of volitional control exhibited by the accused in order to answer the referral question.

The primary issue is the linkage question. In civil cases, impairments that are uncovered must be linked to the alleged cerebral insult. In criminal cases, the linkage issue involves highlighting the similarities and behavioral limitations of the accused in terms of a disorder of executive functions

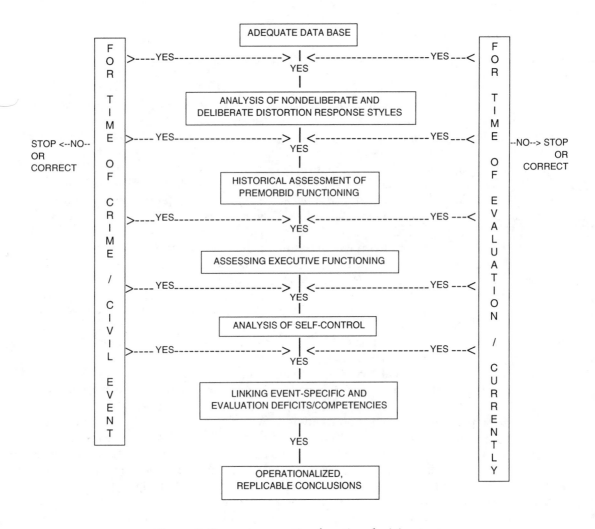

Figure 1. Forensic executive function decision tree.

for the time of the crime as opposed to the response sets shown during neuropsycho-logical testing.

Last, the evaluator can offer the court conclusions that have been arrived at by an independent neuropsychological examination.

The following sections discuss executive dysfunction, which may result in criminally violent response patterns. The focus is on the frontal lobes, not because disorders of executive functions cannot be caused by damage to other parts of the brain, but because the frontal lobes play a primary role in the planning, initiation, integration, and implementation of complex behavioral acts and, therefore, are relevant to an understanding of violent behavior.

Since virtually all violent acts involve complex motor acts and behavior. A clear understanding of the role of the frontal lobes and their relationships to executive functions is required. The evaluator should be able to articulate the decision path used in arriving at forensic conclusions.

EXECUTIVE FUNCTIONING AND VIOLENT RESPONSE PATTERNS

Establishing or refuting a functional relationship between neuropsychological deficits and instant offense behavior, such as in a mental capacity assessment, may be the crucial and exculpating determinant in criminal proceedings. Yet, this relationship has never systematically been addressed in the forensic research literature.

Violent criminal behaviors secondary to a disorder of the central nervous system have direct relevance to an accused's mental capacity at the time of an alleged offense, since the defendant is often seen as being incapable of suppressing or modulating such behaviors. The actions include, but are not limited to, aggressive and assaultive behaviors precipitated by the following: (1) acute confusional states; (2) degenerative conditions such as Huntington's disease, Alzheimer's disease, and alcoholic dementia; (3) repeated head (brain) trauma; (4) toxic conditions resulting in aberrant thinking or psychotic behavior caused by prescribed or illegal drugs, alcohol, and some heavy metals; (5) neoplastic disease processes of the central nervous system (e.g., tumors within brain); (6) seizure disorders such as psychomotor, complex-partial, and temporal lobe epilepsy; and (7) "borderland" organic mental disorders (c.f. Strub & Black, 1981) such as the episodic dyscontrol syndrome.

Anatomically, brain lesions that have been found to be possible etiologic factors in precipitating violent behavior are typically located in the ascending inhibitory component of the reticular activating system, limbic system (including such structures as the amygdala, hippocampus, and septum), the dorsomedial and anterior thalamic nuclei, the ventromedial hypothalamus, and the baso-orbital and posteromedial frontal lobe. Virtually all functional systems and sites, as discussed in detail later, may affect self-regulatory abilities in complex person–environment interactions, including violent two-person situations.

Disorders of executive functions due to frontal lobe problems should be of considerable relevance in the criminal responsibility examination, particularly criminal intent factors. This brain structure serves to mediate between the intellect and the emotions by analyzing and synthesizing both types of input. In addition, the frontal lobes' ability to modulate and control aggressive urges originating from the limbic system is adversely affected when the orbital regions of the frontal lobes are damaged.

The vulnerability of the frontal lobes to trauma has been known for the past 2,400 years. For example, Hippocrates is credited to have observed that more patients die from anterior than posterior brain trauma of equal severity, and in less time (Adams, 1952). Bilateral damage to the prefrontal areas of the cerebral cortex (Brodman areas 9, 10, and 11) produces a syndrome characterized by varying degrees of apathy, irritability, poor adherence to moral standards, shallow affect, and cognitive changes, such as marked perseveration with a decreased ability to shift cognitive strategies and response sets. Verbal fluency and sustained attention are also often affected adversely with this type of lesion (Stuss & Benson, 1986). The effects of frontal lobe damage has also been shown in animal studies. For example, Bianchi (1895) noted restlessness, indifference, decreased affect and other drive-related behavior with hypersensitivity towards noxious or threatening stimuli, defective reflection, judgment, memory, and adaptability, and stereotypic and automatic motor activities following damage to the frontal lobes.

Hecaen and Albert (1975) stressed that "the frontal lobes regulate the 'active state' of the organism, control the essential elements of the subject's intentions, program complex forms of activity, and constantly monitor all aspects of activity" (p. 137). Similarly, Lezak (1983) stated, "Thus, the frontal lobes are where already correlated incoming information from all sources—external and internal, conscious and unconscious, memory storage and visceral arousal centers—is integrated and enters ongoing activity" (p. 79). Stuss and Benson (1986), in their extensive review of the frontal lobes, added that "The human prefrontal cortex attends, integrates, formulates, executes, monitors, modifies, and judges all nervous system activities" (p. 248). In an earlier paper (Stuss & Benson, 1984) they concluded that deficits secondary to prefrontal damage included those of ordering sequential behavior, establishing or changing set, maintaining set (particularly in the presence of interference), monitoring personal behavior, attaining congruity between knowledge and direction of response, and consistency of attitudes. Finally, Strub and Black (1981) warned, "The frontal lobe patient who displays gross antisocial behavior and disinhibition can superficially resemble someone with psychopathic behaviors unless a careful history and examination are carried out" (p. 244).

It is important to isolate a disorder of executive functions from nonorganic causes when evaluating criminal behavior since judicial outcomes are typically determined according to attribution of blame and perceived rehabilitation potential. For example, violence-related psychopathology due to character defects is likely to be seen as being voluntary and, therefore, more indicative of culpability. Pseudopsychopathology due to frontal lobe damage may be seen as being voluntary, especially when the defendant contributed to the outcome by a reckless lifestyle. Lastly, individuals with brain damage are often seen as poorer risks for forensic intervention than nonimpaired persons, reflecting the poor success rates of rehabilitation efforts.

In summary, the functions mediated by the executive functions of the frontal lobes are susceptible to damage stemming from a variety of etiologies. The results of this damage are likely to have considerable bearing upon the forensic issue of the defendant's mental capacity.

FRONTAL LOBE THEORIES AND MODELS

Brown: Microgenesis

Brown's (1983, 1985a, 1985b, 1986, 1987) model of frontal lobe organization focuses on the "microstructure of action." His basic premise is that frontal "microaction" recapitulates the evolutionary development of the frontal lobes. Essentially, he sees evolutionary development as proceeding from the rostral brain stem and the basal ganglia, through the mesial frontal limbic cortex, to integration centers on the convexity to frontal motor areas.

Brown's model is important in that he attempts to take the cytoarchitechonic divisons of the frontal lobes and relate them to normal and deficit neural processing. His work goes far beyond the classic (and more easily studied) frontal mechanisms, namely those concerned with movement and speech. Brown has also explored movement and speech and has found forensic implications. For example, one of his classic findings is that the supplementary motor region (SMR) is the locus of planning and initiation of voluntary movement. In the microgenetic view, "Volition is not a faculty that can be independently impaired [in that] . . . the sense of volition is a product of action development; it is realized with the action and is not something that gives rise to it" (Brown, 1987, p. 255).

Legal theory seems to hold to the classic view, placing volition as a cause or effect rather than as occurring simultaneously with action sequences in an unfolding cognitive process. One consequence of such a view is that damaged frontal sites may be equated with loss of willpower or self-control. This interpretation neglects the impact of possible damage to subsequent levels and sites of executive functioning. A final limitation of Brown's theory is that he would seem to imply preplanned crimes would not occur, in violation to known cases where premeditation has been established.

Pribram: Oscillation Theory

Pribram's (1960, 1967) theory of frontal functioning partially assimilates and extends Brown's work by postulating various types and effects of frontal damage. According to Pribram's theory, intentional behavior is dictated by the anterior system and such behavior is too complex to be explained by the classic reflex arc. He proposed an oscillation theory based on the assumption that there is always a state of incongruity between the responding organism and an environmental stimulus, resulting in a feedback operation until the incongruity is no longer apparent.

One implication of Pribram's work to neuropsychological assessment is that the search for a "frontal lobe battery" may be in vain until complex integrative and monitoring functions are taken into account. Pribram (1960, 1967) found that medial and posterior orbital lesions are implicated in perseveration and distraction, with a decrease in aggression and an increase in mouthing objects as associated behavioral features. Thus, a decrease in flexibility can be seen in delayed alternation and go/no go tasks. Orbitoventral lesions resulted in a decrease in alertness causing delayed habituation and perseveration of "central sets" during conditioning experiments. Lateral frontal lesions in delayed response tasks resulted in an increase in distraction and visual stimulus confusion. Orbitoventral lesions resulted in impairments on tasks involving matching problems and nonspatial discrimination. Anterior ventrolateral lesions appeared to cause visual discrimination problems on place reversal tasks, whereas dorsal periarculate lesions resulted in auditory discrimination deficits during a functionally similar task.

On the basis of all of his findings, Pribram (1960, 1967) postulated three functions and neuroanatomic systems for the frontal lobes:

1. Response activation. Deficits create "stop" and "go" problems. "Stop" problems yield response bias, motor neglect, and similar difficulties, and are associated with the uncinate fasciulus frontolimbic connection. In contrast, nigrostriatal-frontal connections create "go" problems and are associated with a lack of initiative.
2. Response maintenance. Dysfunctions in this secondary subsystem contribute to derailment of action, distractibility, and confabulation. Distractibility is caused by dorsolateral lesions, whereas ventrolateral and periarculate lesions are implicated in confabulation.
3. Integration of output. Deficits in the integration of motor output were associated with damage to the superordinate frontal system (e.g., articulation and dyspraxia) while damage to the premotor and precentral cortex interfered with frontal integrative functions.

Since most of Pribram's work is based on lower primates, a generalizing of his findings to human frontal lobes is somewhat difficult. However, his work clearly illustrates that the role of the frontal lobes is extremely important in understanding executive functions, particularly disorders of execution.

NAUTA: NEUROANATOMIC CONNECTIONS

Nauta (1971, 1973) can be credited with the observation that the frontal lobes, with their telencephalic-limbic system relationships, represent the major (if only) neocortical representation of limbic structures. The relevance of Nauta's findings in regard to violence in which drive and affect are issues should be apparent to forensic neuropsychologists. For example, the organism's "flight or fight" response to substantial stress or threat, in an attempt at self-preservation, has been traditionally assumed by some to be isolated in the amygdala and other specific limbic sites. Nauta's theory highlights the possibility of this basic reaction occurring in the absence of amygdaloid damage following an injury to the frontal lobes.

HALSTEAD/REITAN: CENTRAL PROCESSING FACTORS

Halstead (1947a, b) presented a model of central processing functions consisting of three factors: a Central Integrative Field factor, consisting of stored historical information; an Abstraction factor, involving reasoning and logical analysis (e.g., taking apart complex situations into their component parts after identification of the significance of sensory input is a reflection of this ability), with which the anterior portion of the brain has been associated; and the third factor, involving an energy source, called a Power factor.

Reitan refined and amplified the above model but dropped the Power factor due to measurement problems (Reitan & Wolfson, 1985, 1986, 1988). Their model proposes that sensory input constitutes the first level of central processing. Functions such as alertness, attention, sensory registration, concentration, and comparing incoming data to prior experiences occur at this level.

The second level of cerebral processing involves receptive and expressive language and communication skills, associated with the left cerebral hemisphere, and spatial, temporal, and manipulatory skills, associated with right hemispheric skills. A dynamic integration of both sets of abilities is proposed throughout the entire model.

The third level of central processing is associated with abstraction, reasoning, and logical analysis. Of relevance to forensics, persons who have difficulty profiting from experience do poorly at this level, even though they may be otherwise intact on the first two functions. Yet, it should be recognized that the inability to profit from experience is often cited as a hallmark of the psychopath, who, because of repeated antisocial behavior, is often specifically *excluded* in many penal codes from alleging mental incapacity at the time of the instant offense. Reitan (1987) suggests that personality changes consisting of erratic behavior, deterioration of personal hygiene, and a lack of empathy for others may represent adverse changes in the highest level of central processing.

LURIA: CLINICAL/ANATOMICAL THEORY

The hierarchical clinical/anatomical/neuropsychological theory of Luria (1969, 1973a, 1973b) may have relevance for frontal dysfunctioning in criminal behavior. Luria viewed the frontal lobes as being the directing and controlling force of the brain. Planning and self-regulation take place primarily through language-mediated behavior. According to Luria, in the analysis of frontal lobes in any situation, one should consider each of the following factors individually: (1) the ability to analyze information, (2) the establishment of plans, (3) implementation efforts, and (4) comparison of results to the initial goal.

For many criminal offenses, it is legally important to determine whether or not the defendant went beyond his or her original intentions as this may bear on legal culpability for those offenses. Finally, Luria's assessment of frontal lobe functioning appears to be individually geared toward particular patients and functional deficits (an idiosyncratic approach) and relies on a qualitative analysis of the patient's behavior based on a conceptual model of brain-behavior relationships.

Golden and co-workers (1980, 1984; Golden, Ariel, McKay, Wilkening, Wolf, & MacInnes, 1982; Golden, Ariel, Moses, Wilkening, McKay, & MacInnes, 1982; Golden, Hammeke & Purisch 1980; Golden & Strider, 1986) have attempted to quantify Luria's conceptual model of brain-behavior relationships (i.e., the Luria-Nebraska Neuropsychological Battery). The courts, however, have shied away from using descriptions of defendants in actuarial/statistical terms as critical determinants in legal outcomes (Hall, 1982, 1984a, b, 1987). Moreover, the same objection could be made toward any normative approach to the measurement of executive functions. In general, the courts tend to be more receptive to idiosyncratic data on defendants (e.g., unique history, stress-related data). A note of caution is that no test battery (including the Luria-Nebraska Battery) is any better than the competence of the neuropsychologist utilizing a particular test battery. In this respect, Purisch and Sbordone (1986) have reported that many of the psychologists utilizing the Luria-Nebraska Battery lack an adequate background in behavioral neurology and neuro-anatomy.

DAMASIO: NEUROANATOMICAL THEORY

Damasio has proposed an anatomical-functional model of the frontal lobes (Damasio, 1979; Damasio & Van Hoesen, 1980, 1983). His observation that frontal lobe functioning reflects the ability to adjust to complex environmental stimuli "...within the context of the individual's own history" highlights the importance of evaluating a defendant's developmental history, especially the individual's violence history when this is an issue, as in sentencing or state-of-mind defenses.

History gathering is often an onerous task for forensic evaluators. Yet, it may be of fundamental importance in placing relevant behaviors into the proper historical context. In fact, many penal codes *require* that a defendant's viewpoint of the crime be taken into account. This includes both historical and momentary (i.e., offense-related) influences on the cognitions and perceptions of the accused. The extreme emotional/mental disturbance mitigation of murder to manslaughter, in most jurisdictions, would be an example.

TEUBER: COROLLARY DISCHARGE

Against tradition, Teuber's (1964, 1966, 1972) theory and empirical work on corollary discharge points out that anterior anticipation processing acts upon posterior systems, rather than primarily the reverse. Every behavior is seen to cause neural impulses to be sent to the effectors and a simultaneous discharge to the central receptor sites. Thus, Teuber expanded the concept of the frontal lobes beyond the role of an effector of motor action.

Interestingly, Teuber illustrates the lack of frontal lobe sensitivity on most commonly used psychological tests (e.g., tests measuring sorting skills, general intelligence, memory, attention). He found evidence of frontal lobe deficits on tests of perception of reversals and ambiguous perspectives, rod and frame (Aubert) tasks, personal orientation measurement, and visual search. According to Teuber, incorporation of these test procedures should be considered when assessing possible frontal lobe deficits.

GOLDBERG: PERSEVERATION ANALYSIS

Notwithstanding the finding that perseveration can be due to posterior/basal deficits (Critchley, 1964; Stuss & Benson, 1984, 1986), frontal perseveration may be possible in as many different forms as there are levels and types of discrete perceptual and cognitive abilities. Goldberg and his co-workers (1979, 1985, 1987) have attempted to extend Luria's work on the frontal lobes and their functions. His observations reflect the lore that frontal lobe dysfunction is essentially the study of the perseveratory behavior. Discussed in detail later, perseveration analysis has implication for alleged criminal violence. Often, serious violence, such as aggravated assault or murder, involves response perseveration on the part of the perpetrator in regard to striking the victim. Were the repeated strikes willful (as in instrumental behavior) or did they represent involuntary responses? It is essential to isolate the type of perseveration (e.g., nondominant arm-motor perseveration without weapon) and then compare it to other defendant abilities and deficits. Extending Goldberg's analysis to violent-related perseveration, a key question is whether the repeated responses are functionally and qualitatively similar to one another.

KACZMAREK: NEUROLINGUISTICS

A neurolinguistic perspective of frontal lobe functioning has been presented by Kaczmarek (1984, 1986, 1987), who stressed patients with prefrontal lobe damage have impaired verbal message processing. He reported that left dorsolateral damage is associated with difficulties in carrying out behavioral acts. On the other hand, verbal instructions (e.g., a command to do something other than an inappropriate behavior) have little effect. Therefore, impaired planning is the overriding deficit following left dorsolateral damage. Left orbitofrontal lesions lead to distractible behavior and impaired monitoring of ongoing events.

Right frontal lobe damage leads to difficulties in evaluating one's present condition or task performance. Denial and projection of blame for mistakes are associated features. Disorientation for time and place is also frequently noted. In general, an impaired holistic configuration of information is frequently observed following right frontal lobe damage.

These patients also exhibit greater displacement of propositions, and incorrect interpretations of standard stimuli (e.g., pictures, forms), but fewer sentence fragments than patients with left frontal lobe damage. With this in mind, the evaluator should examine the writing of the defendant (e.g., confessions, diaries, written statements about the instant offense). The reader should review the chapter by Kaczmarek on neurolinguistics in this book.

FUSTER: TEMPORAL DEFICITS

Most offenses require examiners and the courts to temporally restructure events, especially those that occurred prior to, during, and subsequent to the alleged violence. Fuster's (1981, 1989) emphasis on prefrontal temporal integration addresses this issue. He argues that the frontal lobe provides a temporal framework for any purposeful behavior or goal, especially in novel and complex situations. The degree to which offense behavior represented a novel situation to the perpetrator, as opposed to being routine, may be relevant to state-of-mind issues in legal contexts. For example, penal code definitions of mental disturbance defenses appear to be based on the assumption that the stress or threat experienced by the defendant was so overwhelming that it prevented the normal integration of time-related crime events.

SHALLICE: INFORMATION-PROCESSING

Shallice (1978, 1982) presents an information-processing model of cerebral functioning consisting of four components: cognitive units; schemas, consisting of higher-order behavioral activities that are usually routine (e.g., driving home, preparing a meal); contention scheduling or selection of schemas for routine behaviors; and a supervisory attentional system (SAS) for nonroutine goal-oriented behavior, which is mediated by the frontal lobes and kicks into operation when contention scheduling fails or whenever there is no readily apparent solution to a problem. Rather than monitoring contention scheduling, the SAS may not recognize errors (e.g., not checking for the defensive capability of the victim when engaged in routine thievery). The influence of substances, particularly alcohol and some drugs, should not be overlooked when determining possible causes for the SAS functioning in a given manner. Shallice's findings suggest that, following frontal damage, contention scheduling remains effective while the SAS is impaired. Perseveration and distraction would therefore be expected—the former because of shifting difficulties and the latter due to new input capturing contention scheduling procedures.

STUSS AND BENSON: EXECUTIVE DEFICITS

A model of executive functions of the frontal lobes developed by Stuss and Benson (1986) is promising in regard to linking violent behavior with neuropsychological deficits. The contributions of posterior and basal sites and systems has also been suggested (see Fig. 2).

They argue that the executive functions are called into play in novel situations and provide a sense of direction and control, resulting in the integrated processing of input. Frontal lobe systems are divided into drive and sequencing operations, representing continuous input from all modality/subfunction systems (e.g., attention, memory, cognition, language, and motor activity).

In regard to forensic contexts, their model suggests that superordinate executive functions of converging drive and sequencing operations are capable of linkage to task-oriented responses. This would include: anticipation, goal selection, preplanning, and monitoring of ongoing behavior. Expanded in the last chapter on linkage, the argument of this book is that each of these superordinate functions are inoperable to some extent in most cases involving criminal violence. Hence the task of the forensic neuropsychologist is to establish the link and demonstrate its probable effect during the instant offense.

DECISION ANALYSIS

It is not enough to demonstrate impairment of frontal lobe functions in order to show a cause and effect relationship between neuropsychological deficits and criminal behavior. The author has observed a number of court cases in which the expert failed to demonstrate the linkage between frontal lobe impairment and the alleged offense. Unfortunately, judges and juries, when confused or uninformed, often discount exculpable or mitigating data and base their decisions

EXECUTIVE FUNCTION

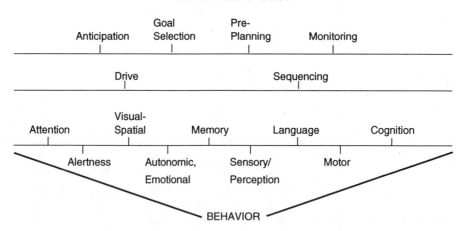

Note: Executive control functions, called into action in nonroutine or novel situations, provide conscious direction to the functional systems for efficient processing of information.

Source: Stuss, D., & Benson, D. (1986). *The frontal lobes*. New York: Raven Press.

POSTERIOR/BASAL FUNCTIONAL SYSTEMS

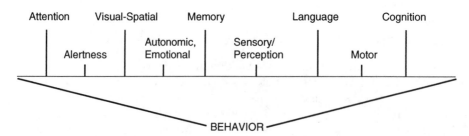

Note: Various organized integrated fixed functional systems hypothesized to be based, in relation to the frontal lobes, in more posterior/basal brain regions.

Source: Stuss, D., & Benson, D. (1986). *The frontal lobes*. New York: Raven Press.

Figure 2. Organized integrated functional systems.

upon their own idiosyncratic notions of whether or not the accused was impaired at the time of the offense. Such negative outcomes can be avoided by paying careful attention to processing as well as content aspects of the data base when formulating forensic neuropsychological findings.

Integrating information from the previous sections of this chapter, the seven-step retrospective decision path can be utilized for the individual forensic evaluation in the following manner.

Obtaining an Adequate Forensic Data Base

The evaluation of an executive function disorder as a possible causative factor in criminal cases rests upon a multisourced and interdisciplinary analysis of the defendant. This strategy recognizes that no single test or procedure is adequate to assess brain damage and that no one professional discipline can answer all the biological, neuropsychological, and social-historical questions that bear upon mental capacity. This does not necessarily imply a team approach. The forensic mental health professional need not uncover firsthand all the data necessary in this type of evaluation, but the data need to be obtained as an initial step in the forensic assessment process. This means that a mental capacity report attempting to link neurologic impairments with crime-specific behavior will, by necessity, include information from other disciplines.

Eventually, input from the actor (e.g., defendant), acted upon (e.g., victim), and crime context needs to be included in the data base. This is because all violence represents a three-way interaction of these factors. What actually occurred in this interaction is considered "ground truth" in forensic situations.

The selection and administration of relevant neuropsychological tests or other measures should be considered and retrospectively evaluated. This breaks down into considering which test measures tap different temporal aspects of executive functions associated with the frontal lobes, such as goal formulation and planning, behavioral implementation of these plans, effective performance, and response generalization. Asterisks (*) are assigned to measures that have some empiric support in detecting cognitive deficits secondary to cerebral dysfunction (Filskov & Boll, 1986; Lezak, 1983; Stuss & Benson, 1986).

GOAL FORMATION

      "Problems of Fact" items from Stanford Binet
      "Cookie Theft" picture from Boston Diagnostic Aphasia Examination
      Thematic Apperception Test
*   Wechsler Scales of Intelligence
*   Category Test
*   Raven's Progressive Matrices
      Rorschach Test
*   Structured clinical interview
      Self-description (e.g., written by assessee in the third person)
      Vineland Social Maturity Scale—Revised (administered by collaterals)
      Interviews of significant/knowledgable others regarding assessee
      Behavior analysis in naturalistic settings

PLANNING
All above, plus:

*   Bender-Gestalt Visual Motor Test (layout)
*   Porteus Maze Test
*   Complex Figure Drawing Task
*   Maze subtest from WISC-R
*   Draw-a-Clock

CARRYING OUT ACTIVITIES

All above, plus:

* * Thurstone Word Fluency Test
* * Babcock Sentence Test
* * Wisconsin Card Sorting Test
* Trail Making Test, Part A
* * Trail Making Test, Part B
* Trail Making Test, ABC
* Tinkertoy Test
* Uses of Objects Test
* Design Fluency Test
* Line Tracing Test
* * MacQuarrie Test for Mechanical Ability
* * Stroop Color and Word Test
* * Test of motor impersistence
* * Necker Cube Tasks
* * Contrasting motor programs procedure
* * Mirror Drawing

EFFECTIVE PERFORMANCE

All above, plus:

Austin Maze (electrically activated version)

* * Stylus Maze
* * Purdue Pegboard Test
* * Grooved Pegboard Test
* * Tactual Performance Test
* * Reading Adaptive Flexibility

RESPONSE GENERALIZATION

Wechsler Memory Scale—Revised (Associative Learning)
Parallel forms (where increased learning is expected)
Similar measures, established by regression equations
Free operant environment testing

Goal formulation measures tap the individual's ability to systematically analyze and integrate his or her awareness of self and the environment as well as the capability of productively elaborating on a goal from a relatively small number of cues. Planning depends upon goal formulation and includes the ability to show clear and logical cognitive preparation for subsequent behaviors. Carrying out activities depends upon the above and includes the ability to show concordance between intentions, plans, and actions. Effective performance includes a person's ability to monitor and correct the rate, intensity, and duration of their responses. Response generalization methods tap whether or not learning is confined to situation-specific contexts.

A composite neuropsychological battery should be administered (or results should be available). There are three reasons for this. First, patterning and configuration of the test results may suggest dysfunction in sites other than the frontal lobes. Second, some tests in neuropsychological batteries that poorly assess frontal lobe impairment may become useful when these test results are combined with other tests (e.g., greater impairment in finger oscillation than TPT scores suggesting frontal involvement). Third, a composite battery will yield more data about whether the lesion is progressive or static, the most likely pathologic process, and the individual's cognitive/behavioral strengths and weaknesses as they relate to forensic treatment and rehabilitation.

Other tests for executive impairment, which are available and relevant to a client's specific deficit or to the referral question, can be given in addition to a composite battery. In the author's experience, a comprehensive evaluation of executive-related functioning can be performed in 4–6 hours of direct contact with the evaluee. This can be shortened considerably if recent testing by a competent neuropsychologist has been performed.

In summary, a strategy is suggested, which involves the administration of a composite battery of neuropsychological tests, followed by tailoring further tests to assess possible disorders of executive functioning, especially if it is suspected during the instant offense.

Accounting for Distortion and Deception

Legal professionals often react with incredulity when confronted with certain executive dysfunctions. Malingering may be suspected at the very least. For example, consider the alien hand phenomenon associated with lesions in the isolated lateral premotor system of the damaged contralateral hemisphere. Afflicted persons may have to "talk" to their hand to induce compliance. The affected hand may have to be "peeled off" objects or persons once it has taken grasp.

The reduplication phenomenon (Capgras' syndrome), which occasionally follows frontal injuries originating from closed-head trauma, appears highly suspect to the neurologically uninformed. For example, the accused may believe that his victim-wife has been replaced by another person (e.g., see Alexander, Stuss, & Benson, 1979). The accused recognizes the impossibility of this occurring, and, just as unbelievably, may state that he would find his own story implausible if told to him by another.

In a final illustration, legal actors and jurors may have a hard time understanding that the frontally impaired can be aware of what is wrong (equated with "cognitive" capacity) and yet be unable to utilize this knowledge (equated with "volitional" capacity). In such cases, by affirming that his or her actions were wrong, the defendant is not necessarily implying that self-control was present during the offense.

The vested interest of the accused is substantial (e.g., he may end up in prison for a substantial time). Distortion, therefore, should always be investigated when the accused asserts loss of self-control during criminally violent behaviors.

The next section includes tests that assess deliberate distortion and deception by the forensic assessee. These should also be administered by the forensic neuropsychologist to counter the frequent argument by the opposing attorney that the test results were deliberately faked to exaggerate pathology. Hence, some of these tests should be included in the neuropsychological expert's evaluation, even if one is reasonably certain that valid test results were obtained. Poor performance on various "fake bad" (i.e., for malingering) subtests and measures, including those that follow, however, may suggest neuropsychological deficits of an organic etiology. These measures, therefore, should be used in combination with other "fake bad" methods, and then should be compared to cross-validating data.

- Parallel forms (where no increased learning is expected)
- Similar tests, as established by regression equations
- Illusory difficult tasks
    California Memory Test
    Dot counting (ungrouped dots)
    Cutaneous two-point threshold tasks
- Easy versus difficult versions of same test
    Dot counting (massed versus spaced dots)
    Word recognition tasks (recall versus recognition)
- Intrasubtest scatter on graduated scales
- Learning curves
- Validity scale analysis (e.g., F-K on MMPI)
- Test pattern analysis (e.g., subtle versus obvious items on MMPI)
- Perceptual and memory complaint tests
- Symptom Validity Testing (e.g., Wahler Physical Symptom Inventory; forced choice measures)
- Goodness of fit (e.g., test profile versus naturalistic behavior)

An analysis of specific types of faking bad needs is presented in Table 1.

Table 1. Faking bad.

Type	Behavioral Strategy	Example
1. Verbal fabrication	Saying there is a nonexistent problem	"I hear voices."
2. Verbal exaggeration	Amplifying real problem	"I'm more irritated."
3. Verbal denial	Disclaiming an ability	"I can't smell anything."
4. Verbal minimizing	Downplaying an ability	"I can walk only one block."
5. Behavioral fractionalizing	Shows crudely estimated fraction of ability	Finger tapping and hand grip scores only 50% of ability.
6. Behavioral approximating	Gets a close but not exact answer	"6 + 6 = 13" ; "7 x 3 = 22"
7. Behavioral infrequency	Sprinkles errors throughout performance on graduated scale	WAIS-R info and comp errors even with simple questions
8. Behavioral disengagement	Shows confusion, frustration, and slows down; deliberate forgetting	Claims total inability during blindfolded portion of TPT
9. Impulsive engagement	Quickly answering, false confidence, expansive, first thing on mind	Arithemetic items, digit span responses Show long latency of response
10. Perseveration	Irregardless of feedback, sticks with one response mode	Alternates errors on BCT or card sort
11. Randomizing	No consistent pattern of errors	Speech Perception Test errors due to deliberate inattention
12. Misattribution	Deliberately stating deficit due to one cause that was actually created by another event	Congenital back problems "caused" by accident

An analysis of deception for the time of the crime must also be performed. Hall (1986) discusses some deception factors including (1) amplifying past pathologic conditions (e.g., blood alcohol readings versus reported alcohol consumption), (2) presentation of paradoxical motives for the crime (e.g., presentation of altruistic motives versus chronic behavior patterns based upon sexual gratification), and (3) comparing present "faking bad" test profiles to that observed prior and subsequent to the crime.

"Forced choice" is a form of symptom validity testing that has been shown to be promising and accurate (Pankratz, 1979, 1983; Pankratz, Binder, & Wilcox, 1987; Pankratz, Fausti, & Peed, 1975; Theodor & Mandelcorn, 1973). Symptom validity testing can be directed towards suspected malingered sensory and memory recall deficits. The procedure always involves exposure to a task with a subsequent statistical analysis of test results. Possible malingered areas to be assessed include visual, auditory, tactile, and other sensory deficits, in addition to assessment for alleged short- and long-term memory problems. This technique requires test stimuli of the same modality as the claimed deficit. For example, when sensory problems are suspected to be feigned, the sensory stimulus (e.g., touch, light, sound) is presented at random over a total of 100 trials. During the task the subject is instructed to say whether or not the stimulus was perceived. If the subject does not say "yes" or "no," then the subject is instructed to guess. The subject's answers are then recorded on the form followed by immediate feedback as to the correctness of each response. With faked memory deficits, an interference procedure is used, consisting of a task lasting from 10–12 seconds after the initial stimulus is presented.

An intact subject who is not attempting to deceive the examiner is expected to answer virtually all trials correctly. If the subject is blind or has legitimate memory problems, the subject will typically obtain a score of 50, since there is a 50/50 chance of guessing the correct item. Scores less than 40 or greater than 60 deviate approximately two standard deviations from the mean and, therefore, should be suspect. Scores less than 40 suggest that the subject perceives the stimulus but denies seeing it. Scores greater than 60 suggest that the subject has perceived the stimulus far greater than chance (perhaps due to an unsuccessful cognitive strategy).

The forced-choice method can be adapted to previous criminal behavior. The technique is to select items from the crime scene that only the perpetrator would know. These items are then randomly spaced over 100 trials while the subject is instructed to guess whether or not that item occurred or existed at the time he or she was exposed to that stimulus. Episodic memory, which forms a basis for these items, is much more resistant to decay and interference than other forms of memory. An innovative forced-choice methodology termed *Explicit Alternative Testing* (Hall & Shooter, 1989; Shooter & Hall, 1990) was examined in two studies to detect feigned visual memory deficits.

The first study involved 52 simulators who served as their own control (Hall & Shooter, 1989). The procedure involved the presentation of one of two colored stimuli followed by an interference procedure. The results of this study indicated a hit rate of 84.6 percent in terms of accurately identifying simulators.

Shooter and Hall (1990) tested for faked visual memory deficits using an abbreviated format of 50 trials with 19 simulators serving as their own control. A hit rate of 94.7 percent was obtained in terms of accurately identifying fakers when the data from an additional 52 simulators who had obtained a hit rate of 84.6 percent in an earlier EAT investigation was utilized for comparisons. When the hit rate of the 19 simulators administered 50 trials was favorable when compared to the 52 simulators administered 100 trials, a loss of 4 percent in accuracy to 80.8 percent was found over the first 50 trials in the original 52 subjects. A hit rate of 84.5 percent was obtained when the first 50 trials for the original 52 simulators was combined with the performance of the 19 simulators in this study. These investigators found that shortening the EAT by 50 percent resulted in lower but relatively high hit rates.

Examination of Historic Violence

A key question is whether basal violence, especially when it is similar to the instant offense, was the result of a habitual set of violent acts or an isolated event. For example, violent behavior during the offense in question may be triggered by stress or involuntary factors that may be superimposed upon a presumed disorder of executive functions. Historic instances of violence should be examined in terms of variables such as frequency, severity, recency, acceleration, triggering stimuli, opportunity factors, and inhibitions to aggression. Factors that have traditionally indicated willfulness to commit violence include: (1) lengthy time delays between triggers to violence and the instant crime; (2) performance of complex chains of behaviors in order to execute the violent behavior; (3) flexibility of response (e.g., when the perpetrator has multiple weapons with which to inflict harm); and (4) predatory versus reactive violence.

Key forensic questions can be formulated as follows: Should the defendant have known the likely outcome of the chain of behavioral events culminating in violence? What does this imply for forensic intervention?

Consider the following two courtroom scenarios:

Prosecutor: Doctor, you testified that the accused suffered a substantial impairment in his (her) mental capacity at the time of the alleged offense. You cited a list of neuropsychological deficits in terms of his (her) lack of ability to self-control and monitor his (her) violent behavior as reasons for the substantial incapacity. You did not examine his (her) previous violence, focusing instead on his (her) behavior during your evaluation and at the time of the alleged crime.

Would your conclusions change if you knew the accused engaged in several dozen other very similar acts of previous violence, with rewarding consequences, high-stated self-control, some evidence of planning and rehearsal, and no observable loss of verbal or physical abilities during those violent acts? Why or why not? Cannot one's past violence influence affect appreciation of wrongdoing and self-control in later violence? Now please read the accused's rap sheet to the court...

Let's turn this around for the defense, assuming expert testimony to the effect that there was no substantial impairment:

Defense Attorney: Doctor, would you change your mind if you knew that (a) the defendant had no previous violence at all prior to the instant case and, in fact, was a model citizen; (b) his (her) cumulative stress level for the year before the violence was extreme, as measured by several standardized tests and independently by DSM III-R Axis IV criteria; and (c) he (she) believed that he (she) had to perpetrate the violence because his (her) life had been placed into danger by the victim? The other examiners considered these facts, why didn't you?

There is no escape from considering historic influences to crime behavior. This is because mental capacity to a greater or lesser degree is always influenced by previous experiences. Many studies, for example, have suggested that historic violence accounts for the major portion of the statistical variance in accounting for exhibited violence (Hall, Catlin, Boissevain, & Westgate, 1984). A history of violence or, conversely, a benign past, appears to act as a prepotent force of its own, determining to a large extent whether violence will or will not occur. In addition to history, triggers to violence and opportunity factors account for a higher incidence of exhibited violence (Hall et al., 1984b).

Repetitive violence, by an individual with an antisocial personality disorder, does not by itself imply willful self-control, since some acts of repetitive violence are largely neurophysiologically determined, as previously discussed, and in many forensic cases there appears to be a combination of external and internal contributors to violence. Likewise, isolated violence, represented by the instant offense, does not necessarily mean loss of self-control since isolated or unique violence can occur as the result of planning or special circumstances prior to instant violence.

VIOLENCE TYPOLOGIES

Many forensic professionals have attempted to categorize violence in order to analyze it for individual cases. As a consequence, a plethora of classification schemes has been developed over the last century for violence and other forms of criminality. Briefly, the two main types—heuristic (deductive) and empirical (inductive)—would include categorizations based upon: (1) cultural differences, (2) social class, (3) constitutional and physical characteristics, (4) conceptual level or developmental stage, (5) interpersonal maturity level, (6) psychological test responses, (7) psychoanalytic theory, (8) degree of deviance, (9) instant offense characteristics (i.e., felony type), and (10) repetitive crime patterns. While most of these schemes are fatally flawed, they often become resistant to extinction once they enter into forensic theory or broad-based programming. Some are untestable (e.g., psychoanalytic, constitutional) and lack homogenous subgroups (e.g., instant offense, degree of deviance), while some are unable to classify even a majority of offenders into one or more pattern types (e.g., repetitive crime patterns). Almost all of the schemes have substantial reliability and validity problems.

Various classification criteria have been proposed. The list varies according to perceived need and availability of data (e.g., see Gibbons, 1975; Hall, 1987; Megargee & Bohn, 1979). Ideally, the classification scheme needs to be reliable, valid, based on adequate normative data, and dynamic, with changes in the defendant's behavior over time reflected in reclassification. The violence-related categories should be parsimonious and mutually exclusive. The scheme should be comprehensive and consider all possible types of violence directed toward others. In particular, it should take into account relationship, recency, and severity factors. It should be applicable to all levels of the criminal justice system and minimize reliance on professionals. It should permit facilitation of rapid classification of individual violent acts and trends to assist the neuropsychological assessment process.

As a starting point, the scale suggested in Figure 3 classifies previous violence to others.

A principal consideration in the taxonomy is whether or not weapons were used to perpetrate the violence and the net harm to the victim. The forensic professional must determine whether weapons were involved in each previous act of violence, as this bears directly upon intent and

THREE DIMENSIONAL MODEL OF BASAL VIOLENCE

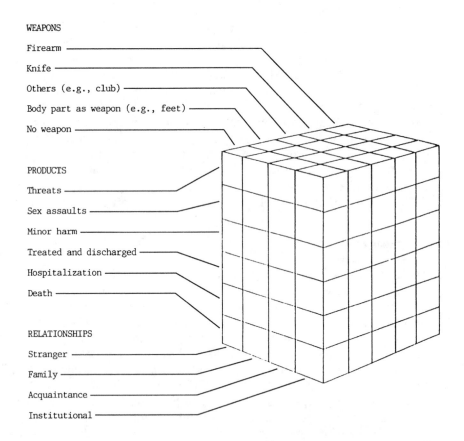

Figure 3. Three-dimensional model of basal violence.

self-control factors. Victim harm must be calculated, since this determines to a large extent the crime for which the perpetrator is charged.

Threatened violence and attempted acts are likewise scrutinized in the search for the true basal violence, as many of these are chargeable offenses. Attempted murder in many jurisdictions carries the same legal penalty as consummated murder. Victims are frequently severely emotionally traumatized, and their lifestyles are often severely disrupted from threatened/ attempted physical harm whether or not physical violence was actually consummated. For example, during robbery there is intimidation combined with theft without any physical harm to the victim. In another example there is vaginal, anal, and/or oral penetration in rape/sodomy cases without any bruises or lacerations.

A standardized system of calculating violence severity stems from the U.S. Department of Justice's National Survey of Crime Severity (NIJ-96017), (Wolfgang, Figlio, Tracy, & Singer1985). This classification system is based upon the responses of over 60,000 Americans. Scaling methods used in this system yield weighted values, which can then be used to assess violence trends for individuals over the period of their basal violence. Table 2 presents the weighted values for distinct crime categories.

Table 2. Seriousness scoring system.

Score sheet

Identification number(s): _____

Effects of event: I   T   D   (circle all that apply)

Component scored	Number of victims	x	Scale weight	=	Total
I. Injury					
(a) Minor harm	_____		1.47		_____
(b) Treated and discharged	_____		8.53		_____
(c) Hospitalized	_____		11.98		_____
(d) Killed	_____		35.67		_____
II. Forcible sex acts	_____		25.92		_____
III. Intimidation					
(a) Verbal or physical	_____		4.90		_____
(b) Weapon	_____		5.60		_____
IV. Premises forcibly entered	_____		1.50		_____
V. Motor vehicle stolen					
(a) Recovered	_____		4.46		_____
(b) Not recovered	_____		8.07		_____
VI. Property theft/damage	_____				_____
			Total score		_____

$.\log 10Y = .26776656 \log 10X$
where   Y = crime severity weight
       X = total dollar value of theft or damage

NIJ definitions follow for the violence-related events in this system.

1. *Number of persons injured.* Each victim receiving some bodily injury during an event must be accounted for. Physical injuries typically occur as a direct result of assaultive events, but they can be caused by other events as well. The four levels of bodily injury are:
   a. Minor harm—An injury that requires or receives no professional medical attention. The victim may, for instance, be pushed, shoved, kicked, knocked down, and receive a minor wound (e.g., cut, bruise).
   b. Treated and discharged—The victim receives professional medical treatment but is not detained for further medical care.
   c. Hospitalized—The victim requires inpatient care in a medical facility, regardless of its duration, or outpatient care for three or more clinical visits.

    d. Killed—The victim dies as a result of the injuries, regardless of the circumstances in which they are inflicted.

2. *Sexual intercourse by force.* This event occurs when a person is intimidated and forced against his/her will to engage in a sexual act (e.g., rape, incest, sodomy). Such an event may have more than one victim, and the score depends on the number of such victims. However, a continuous relationship with the victim may occur in forcible incest and is likely to be counted as one event.

      A forcible sex act is always accomplished by intimidation. Thus, the event must also be scored for the type of intimidation involved (see below). Intimidation is scored for all victims in a forcible sexual act (Author's note: such is not the case for other events, see below). The victim of one or more forcible sexual acts is always assumed to have suffered at least minor harm during the event. Even when medical examination may not reveal any injuries, the event must be scored for minor harm. This level of injury should also be scored (rather than treated and discharged) when the victim is examined by a physician only to ascertain if venereal infection or disease (e.g., AIDS) has been transmitted or to collect evidence that the sexual act was completed.

3. *Intimidation.* This is an element in which one or more victims are threatened with bodily harm (or some other serious consequences) for the purpose of forcing the victim(s) to obey the request of the offender(s) to give up something of value or to assist in a criminal event that leads to someone's bodily injury and/or to property theft or damage. In addition to rape, robbery is a classic example. Ordinary assault and battery, aggravated assault and battery, or homicide are not to be scored for intimidation merely because someone was assaulted or injured. The event must also have included the threat of force for intimidation to have been present. With the exception of forcible sexual acts, criminal events involving intimidation are scored only once regardless of the number of victims who are intimidated. The types of intimidation are:

    a. Physical or verbal—Physical intimidation means the use of strong-arm tactics (e.g., threats with fists, menacing gestures). Verbal intimidation means spoken threats only, not supported by the overt display of a weapon.

    b. Intimidation by weapon—Display of a weapon (e.g., firearm, cutting or stabbing instrument, or blunt instrument capable of inflicting serious bodily injury).

(Author's note: these definitions are not flawless. Problems of lack of specificity and some overlap emerges frequently when one also counts sexual assaults as physical harm. There has been, however, an attempt to operationalize violence and provide weighted values for discrete violence-related behavior and attempts. This has not been successfully accomplished in previous classification schemes on such a large normative base. Keep in mind, moreover, that for the next several decades, the major criminal justice system agencies in this country may use this system. The preceding system—the Standard Classification of Offenses [SCO]—persisted for over one-half century despite a demonstrated lack of accurate description and predictiveness.)

For the severity variable, the forensic expert notes and summates all acts of previous violence that fit the above definitions. Often, knowledge of previous violence is unavailable, as when juvenile records are sealed. For this reason, the author has focused on adult violence (since age 18) although the system could theoretically be applied to the lifetime of the descriptee.

The relevance of a total severity score (net harm) for global sentencing considerations should not be overlooked. Total net harm represented by the instant offense can be linked to victim restitution criteria, thus adding a quantitative dimension to a notoriously subjective task.

RELATIONSHIP FACTORS

The relationship of the perpetrator to the victim is important to consider because (1) all violence to others, as opposed to self or property, is an interactional phenomenon; (2) some types of relationship violence are highly recidivistic (e.g., family violence). If the family violence was isolated, contrary to the usual pattern in these cases, the examiner would look more to stress and situational factors to account for the violence; (3) some types of violence are not considered highly recidivistic except for certain offender groups. Compare the above to the low frequency of stranger violence for the average citizen; (4) Some types of recidivistic violence are irrelevant. Institutional violence is recidivistic, for example, when continual commands to aggress are given over time, along with victim opportunity and means to aggress; and (5) victim patterning effects have direct bearing on intent factors. This would include picking victims of a smaller size or weaker physical status, or selecting women as targets. Victim patterning effects are found within relationships (e.g., spouse abuse, rape).

The definitions of relationships are as follows, stemming from NIJ research (Wolfgang et al.,1985): The perpetrator is a stranger if the victim identifies the individual as a stranger, including perpetrators "known by sight." Family relationships include those perpetrators and victims related by blood or marriage. All others are acquaintances.

The key task for the evaluator in considering the relationship variable is to create three mutually exclusive categories. To assist the classification, the perpetrator may be assigned to the stranger category if the victim is killed. In this case, knowledge that a stranger relationship existed comes from other data base sources. For family relationships, add common-law and "live-in" arrangements between perpetrator and victim. Much violence occurs within the context of an impaired central love relationship, whether or not a formal marriage has been effected. The examiner should be consistent in assignment to one of the three types of relationships, since this has implications for violence trends (see below).

RECENCY

How long ago specific acts of violence occurred adds a dynamic quality to the taxonomy. As a final step in analyzing basal violence, the last act of substantial violence is time dated. This means that descriptees/predictees are not "frozen" into a prepotent level of basal violence. Recent as opposed to remote violence is more dangerous; in fact, most recidivism from prison occurs within the first 2 years of release. In general, base rates for recency are available for (1) up to 3 months past the prediction, (2) up to 1 year, (3) from 1–4 years following release, and (4) greater than 4 years.

The above suggested time blocks are tied to base rates. A history of violence accounts for most of the statistical variance within the 3-month period (Hall et al., 1984b) when compared to other factors, such as triggers to aggress and victim availability. The period close to the instant offenses may contain acts of violence relevant to the instant offense. The 90-day period is also useful for predictions of imminent violence. The 1-year period is useful for conditional release, usually after 1 year of hospitalization. The 4-year period is tied to the FBI recidivism base rates (Hall, 1987). Periods greater than 4 years should be considered to demonstrate that violence was within the behavioral pattern of the descriptee/predictee.

Violence trends for individuals can be studied by summating point values within specified temporal blocks. The time segments are geared toward your referral question. Short-term periods (up to 1 year) may be used for mental capacity examinations, for example, if the evaluator wishes to portray acceleration or deceleration before offense-related violence. This would mean that the examiner would count violence the year before the instant offense, not from the time of the evaluation. Long-term periods (e.g., 3-year blocks) may be considered for more protracted periods of time, say for sentencing or programming purposes.

Prepotent basal violence is a term used for a past history of violence that is recent (within 3 months), multiple (more than one previous act of violence), and severe, the last depending on the severity value obtained from the previous presented system. The suggested typology of basal violence may be helpful in determining true basal violence for individual perpetrators. It is partially normative-based with built-in reliability and validity values for some of its dimensions (e.g., severity). It is dynamic in terms of changes in classification over time. The classification scheme does not require highly skilled training and could be used in most settings where violence is an issue. Trends in violence for individuals can be crudely estimated in the search for extraneous factors that bear upon any increase or decrease of violence. Lastly, the scheme may have relevance to treatment.

The forensic expert must consider the basal violence of the examinee to help explain the instant offense. Basal violence is compared with behavior at the time of the instant offense in the same manner evaluation findings are retrospectively linked to the alleged offense. This places the examiner in the position of utilizing both current and historical data to understand the alleged offense. Violence prediction is a mandatory part of the sanity evaluation in many jurisdictions when an exculpatory conclusion is rendered. Basal violence is the key determinant of future violence. An examination of basal violence leads directly to the following. How much of the violence in a specific case could be self-controlled, and how can this be demonstrated to the satisfaction of the criminal court?

Assessing Executive Functioning

If warranted by the aforementioned data base, the evaluator should diagnose a disorder of executive functioning for both the times of the evaluation and the instant offense. By doing this, the court and all parties concerned would know that two distinct sets of observations were taken into account and that the executive impairment did not originate or worsen after the alleged crime. Further, all existing tests of insanity require a diagnosed condition at the time of the alleged offense in order to address the relationship between the accused's mental condition and the crime.

Specific reasons for an organic mental disorder in general and a disorder of executive functions in particular can be corroborated. First, composite neuropsychological test battery data associated with various characteristics of brain damage can be provided. Second, anterior dysfunctions can be elaborated. For example, involvement of the mesial aspect of the frontal lobe is associated with changes in sphincter control (bowel and bladder), as well as with blunt affect. Partial complex seizures, as well as *déjà vu* and *jamais vu* experiences can originate in the anterior temporal lobe. Impairment of the sexual libido sometimes stems from bilateral or right frontal damage. Disinhibition of sexual impulses can implicate baso-orbital lesions. Impaired olfactory discrimination can stem from tumors in the orbital region where Cranial Nerve I originates. Impaired orienting responses can involve the dorsolateral area of the frontal lobe, in addition to cingulate gyrus damage. Mutism or paucity of speech with no maintenance of speech flow is seen with berry aneurysms of the anterior cerebral artery territories. Frontal seizures may create eye/ head turning in the direction away from the seizure site. Other violence-related behaviors associated with anterior impairments have been mentioned. They include the baso-orbital and posterior medial regions, with their rich and intimate connections to the limbic system.

Lezak (1983) has indicated that the five most common behavioral symptoms of frontal lobe dysfunction are: (1) problems starting tasks, characterized by diminished spontaneity and initiative, reduced productivity, and diminished verbal output (generally associated with damage in the medial frontal areas); (2) problems in making behavioral/cognitive shifts, characterized by perseveration, mental rigidity, and stereotyped behaviors, all of which are supramodal in nature (generally associated in damage to the dorsolateral convexities); (3) problems stopping ongoing tasks, characterized by impulsivity and over-reactivity (generally associated with the baso-orbital area); (4) deficits in self-awareness, characterized by inability to see one's mistakes and their impact on others, and to properly evaluate social situations. Defective self-criticism and unconcern about social conventions are associated problems; and (5) a concrete attitude, where events are taken for their face value with an inability to separate one's self from one's surroundings. The abstract ability may or may not be intact, although this ability is likely to be impaired if the patient has damage in the dorsolateral frontal lobes.

Lezak (1983) also suggests that the florid, spontaneous confabulation occasionally seen in frontal lobe disorders is frequently associated with subcortical lesions in the medial basal white matter. Motor skill deficits are frequently attributed to lesions in the premotor association areas. An impaired sense of time is associated with bilateral frontal lesions. Cognitive integration deficits are more associated with damage to the dorsolateral convexities, whereas emotional control deficits are apt to reflect subcortical lesions or damage to the pathways from the neo-cortex to the diencephalon.

The value of such specificity is that it allows for other investigators from allied health disciplines to focus on expected behavioral deficits and anomalies. A positive computer tomography (CT) scan showing frontal lobe lesions or atrophy, combined with neuropsychological test findings suggesting the same results, may help in convincing the court that the accused was volitionally impaired. (Hit rates of medical tests for brain damage and laterality are generally inferior to neuropsychological testing results, see Boll, 1985.)

A second value of specificity concerns the notion of delay in impulse control and need gratification. For example, prosecuting attorneys make an issue of time delays between initial observation of the victim by the accused and subsequent criminal violence, as if the victim sighting—time delay—violent behavior sequence represents a unitary behavioral phenomenon (and therefore greater defendant culpability). Lezak's (1983) observations would suggest that such time delays would reflect slower initial goal formulation, slower shifting to an action plan, and slower stopping of the criminal behavior once it is initiated. Whether goal formulation and action planning occurred immediately after the victim was sighted or just prior to an assault certainly would suggest a new interpretation of any revealed time delay, at least for individuals with a disorder of executive functions.

The evaluator should look for behaviors associated with frontal lobe damage, in addition to anomalies from other sites and systems. The list of symptoms associated with frontal lobe dysfunction (Table 3) has been obtained from a wide variety of sources. The reader should be aware that the overlapping symptoms may reflect damage to other areas of the brain, or even functional impairments and that frontal lobe damage varies in symptomatology, depending on the site, severity, and recency of damage, and the intertwining of neuropathologic processes.

Self-Regulation and Self-Control

For criminal cases, the evaluator examines the alleged offenses according to the account presented by the accused versus that presented by the victim and other cross-validating sources.

Table 3. Symptoms Associated With Frontal Lobe Dysfunction

Motor/Physical (Abnormal grasping, groping, snout and sucking reflexes [i.e., frontal "release" signs])
  Kleist's gegenhalten (counterpull)
  Abnormal gait/posture
  Unexpected ratios in bilateral efficiency
  Frontal apraxia
  Impaired olfactory discrimination
  Urinary/fecal urgency or incontinence
  Sexual dysfunction: altered libido, erectile dysfunction in men
  Disturbances in eating habits
  Disturbances in sleep patterns
  (Overall general health may not be impaired)

Cognition
  Impaired temporal discrimination for recency and time span
  Defects in goal formulation
  Impaired ability to sustain attention
  Impaired ability to shift conceptual sets
  Difficulty in reversal of perspective
  Defects in planning behavior
  Spontaneous, florid confabulations with psychotic qualities
  Marked dissociation between verbalized intentions and actions
  Low creativity but may be maladaptively or primitively original
  (Overall intelligence as measured by IQ tests may not be impaired)

Affect
  Flat, blunt, or labile affect
  Violence occurring within background of flat affect
  Short-lived pleasure or pain
  Low frustration tolerance
  Shallow or inappropriate jocularity
  Inability to see the point in humorous pictures, anecdotes, cartoons, etc.

Individual Behaviors
  Marked perseveration
  Impaired self-control
  Incompetent or ineffectual behavioral productions
  Impaired ability to modulate or fine-tune complex behavior

Social-Interpersonal Behaviors
  Marital or familial conflict centering around impairments
  Inability to obtain/maintain employment
  Low conformance to societal values/norms with no maliciousness intended
  Little spontaneous speech
  No maintenance of word flow, or difficulty turning off verbage
  Inability to make appropriate shifts of "principle of action" (e.g., switching from attack to escape behaviors)
      during crime
  Boastful, loud verbal productions
  Insensitivity towards others
  Sexual disinhibition
  Impaired ability to modulate emotional response during sustained social interaction

The perpetrator should present a full crime account unless he or she was amnesic for some or all of the crime, or if malingering is an issue. If amnesia did occur, the evaluator should specify a condition that would account for that lack of information encoding or recall. Possible explanations include the following, either alone or operating in combination with one another: (1) extreme emotional states and stress characterized by pain, anger, fear, or loss; (2) dissociative states; (3) florid psychosis that may also create a psychotic recall; (4) epilepsy; (5) gross substance intoxication and blackouts; (6) poor comprehension; (7) aphasic difficulties; and (8) specific brain syndromes (e.g., an acute confusional state). The possibility of malingering should also be evaluated according to the previously suggested methods. Clinically, the "feeling of knowing" (e.g., when true amnesics state that they could recall if cued properly; malingerers state that their recall would not improve) has been isolated as being helpful in differentiating true amnesia from that that is being faked.

The evaluator should be on the alert for defendants with genuine amnesia-producing conditions, who, nevertheless, deceptively exaggerate the length of the amnesic episode or critical events of the instant offense. In such cases, the same procedures as previously suggested should be followed—the evaluator should first obtain a basal level of responding from data base measures, then test for deliberate distortion. When giving parallel IQ tests, (e.g., double administration of the Slosson Intelligence Test or Peabody Picture Vocabulary Test) or redundant testing (e.g., digit span tests on the Wechsler Scales or Wechsler Memory Scale) the evaluator should use the higher score to elicit the optimal level of neuropsychological performance on tests. The higher score implies the capability to perform at that level on the employed measure. Such a method may be used, for example, when "faking bad" is suggested. It is important to recognize that some serious attention deficits can produce inconsistent performances on some tasks in which attention is necessary (i.e., digit span, Wisconsin Card Sorting Test).

The evaluator should analyze the instant offense for the defendant's abilities and deficits in areas relevant to behavioral self-regulation. Parameters to be considered during the commission of the crime include: (1) coherence and other characteristics of speech suggesting intact verbal expressions; (2) intensity and appropriateness of affect (e.g., especially during portions of the crime sequence that would normally produce strong emotion); (3) the focus of the crime, ranging from nebulous to markedly specific; (4) substance intoxication; (5) current, long-range mental conditions such as retardation or focal brain damage; (6) behaviors requiring immediate, short-term, and historical memory skills of discrete sensory modalities or a combination of modalities; (7) gross-motor, fine-motor, perceptual-motor, and motor-sequencing skills; (8) level of substance intoxication (in most jurisdictions, all but pathologic intoxication is considered inculpatory); (9) presence of bizarre behavior; (10) level of anxiety; (11) presence of delusions and/or hallucinations; (12) presence of depressed or expansive mood; (13) planning and preparation; (14) awareness of criminality; (15) level of activity; and (16) self-reported control.

The defendant's activities during the week before the instant offense (see Rogers Criminal Responsibility Assessment Scales—R-CRAS below) should be checked for behavioral deterioration, especially in self-care, work productivity, and in the central love relationship. The evaluator must also consider whether or not the alleged crime represented the accused's first significant act of violence. For many of these parameters, quantitative measures on an empirically validated, likert-scale format can be obtained from the R-CRAS (Rogers, 1984) and the Schedule of Affective Disorders and Schizophrenia (Spitzer & Endicott, 1978).

Other considerations include the use of a weapon designed for attack (gun, knife, numchuka), which would indicate a chain of responses more subject to control (i.e., selecting, obtaining, concealing, carrying, reaching for, and attacking with the weapon). Chains of responses usually call for shifts in behavior programs and lessen the likelihood of impulsivity. The next level of complexity involves use of a weapon designed for attack that the perpetrator found at the scene of the crime. A defendant's use of his or her body to club, strangle, or kick a victim suggests a primitive response. An attack with certain parts of the body (e.g., biting, banging one's head against the victim) suggests an even more primitive level of aggression. Continuing to attack nonvictim entities suggests further loss of behavioral self-control.

The accused's flexibility of response and method of attack should also be considered. The use of multiple weapons or shifting back and forth from one method of attack to another suggests that different executive functions were utilized. This suggests the presence of self-control, even in frontal lobe-impaired persons.

Linkage of Deficits and Crime Behavior

The evaluator must now compare crime-specific behaviors reflecting a disorder of executive functions with those elicited during the neuropsychological assessment. This statement is based on two assumptions. The first is that the defendant's behaviors at the times of the evaluation and of the crime represent task responses, even if the production may be viewed as maladaptive.

The second assumption is that, given a valid and comprehensive data base, task behaviors shown by the defendant during the neuropsychological evaluation (with the built-in structure and encouragement for best performance) are the optimal responses that the defendant can produce. The defendant's behaviors exhibited during the instant offense should not exceed the evaluation performance. Instant offense behavior should be more maladaptive, considering the stress and contextual features of most violent crimes. For example, perseveration shown on motor-sequencing tasks should also be present in some form during the crime if the opportunity existed. The key here is to look for evaluation and crime behaviors that are functionally similar. The behavioral sequence involved in intercepting a victim, for example, should contain the same or a greater degree of behavioral disorganization as in tasks administered during the evaluation to tap this skill. If behaviors shown during the crime appear to be the functional equivalent of the type as well as the level of evaluation performance, this is an indication that stress or other events that act to disrupt the execution process were not operating. This suggests a higher level of self-control and means that, during the crime, the accused was acting at a near optimum level. The evaluator must also specify crime-specific factors that operate to disinhibit the accused or to deteriorate his or her coping abilities. Otherwise, one is left in the position of explaining why the defendant does not aggress continually, despite the presence of a presumably chronic organic condition.

If impairment of self-regulatory behaviors is elicited during the assessment, this information cannot be used in a forensic context to support loss of self-control unless the hypothesized frontal lobe dysfunction or other proffered mental condition caused those responses. This is because in all jurisdictions, impairments must always be the result of the accused's diagnosed condition. Further, the cause must be direct, and not secondary. Incapacitating, self-induced alcohol intoxication at the time of the crime that may have contributed to or was triggered by frontal lobe-related behavioral impulsiveness is considered an invalid argument for escaping criminal responsibility. This further decreases the range of behaviors that can be used as the basis for exculpation. The symptom pool is restricted even more by the exclusion of all disorders of executive functions that were operating at the time of the crime but had little to do with mental capacity interference (e.g., mild motor deficits in a "successful" assault).

Illustrations of possible instant offense-evaluation links are presented in the following section. These are presented only as hypotheses to consider and not as proofs of their existence. The evaluator may note their possible operation during the instant offense in order to select neuropsychological tests to assess those functions and deficits.

ATTENTION AND ALERTNESS

In analyzing violent-related responses, the evaluator may consider the degree to which the defendant attended to the victim and contextual stimuli. Proper attention and alertness are considered necessary to effectively plan, select, shift, and monitor task-oriented responses. Key issues in this regard include the following.

Look for confusion. Frontal inattention, sometimes involving conjugate deviation of the eyes and forced circling (toward the side of the lesion) should be ruled out. Insensitivity to other sources of stimuli should be analyzed (e.g., noise, lights, presence of bystanders). Did the accused miss important details, such as whether the victim was carrying a weapon? The normal response is a "weapon focus" in attending to others who use, threaten with, or otherwise handle potentially lethal weapons, particularly guns and knives.

Given adequate attention, orientation to time, place, person, and circumstances should not be impaired. The "wrong" victim, due to misidentification, is occasionally chosen in what appears to be random stranger violence. On occasion, the "wrong" person may be aggressed upon because of the defendant's distractibility and difficulty in focusing towards the intended victim.

The evaluator should be on the alert for attention and alertness deficits in verbal interaction between the perpetrator and the victim. In almost all cases, physical aggression is preceded by verbiage from and/or to the victim or others. Is the perpetrator speechless, akinetically mute, or is there normal quantitative output and articulation? Does the victim have to repeat questions? If so, the implications are twofold: First, the perpetrator may not be attending properly to verbal stimuli; second, the victim's frustration may have increased, thus creating a synergistic phenomenon in regards to the initiation of violence. Look for dissociation between the perpetrator's words and actions (e.g., expressing willingness to discuss a problem while preparing to attack the victim).

The presence of substance intoxication may interact with frontal lobe deficits to create violence. Although some experts view intoxication due to substances as a disorder of executive function that is associated with disinhibition of aggressive impulses from the limbic system, the law sees voluntary substance ingestion as inculpatory. In a lesser sense, the voluntary cessation of stabilizing medication may be seen by the law as a sign of culpability.

Substance intoxication, superimposed on supposed frontal lobe deficits that culminate in violence, may make it impossible to isolate specific executive function deficits that created an alleged mental incapacity. When substance intoxication is involved, "all bets are off" in terms of accurate forensic description and isolation of neuropathologic processes. In such cases, the evaluator must rely on identification of crime behavior that is congruent with the loss of presence of self-control, irrespective of possible brain damage.

Did the accused confabulate due to inattention? Often, confabulation represents an attempt to fill in the gaps due to inattention or to frontal lobe recall deficits (see the following section). The impact of confabulation on the victim prior to the instant violence should be considered.

SENSORY-PERCEPTUAL

All sensory systems may be involved in executive functions. Frontal damage can create hemi-inattention which affects the ability to respond appropriately to environmental stimuli contra-lateral to the lesion site. The evaluator should attempt to determine whether the defendant's inattention was consistently right- or left-sided, as this may have affected his or her ability to respond appropriately in interpersonal situations.

Problems in detecting fast-moving objects and other related deficits (e.g., head and eye deviation, placing response deficits, forced circling of eyes) by the perpetrator may create a tendency for the victim or witnesses to perceive the accused as "weird" or intoxicated, and predispose them to act defensively. For example, the perpetrator may fixate on one physical spot (e.g., the victim's eyes, a barroom television) even after that stimulus has been removed (e.g., head moved, TV turned off). If two objects are presented, such as a victim's upright arms to indicate surrender, the perpetrator may perceive only one of the objects, in this case, only one of the victim's raised arms, and interpret the action as possible aggression. The perpetrator may interpret a single detail in the visual search and scanning process and thereby commit errors as described above. The perpetrator's actions would also predispose the victim and witnesses to believe that the perpetrator is paranoid or is magnifying the events out of proportion. The victim may be more likely to react defensively rather than in a task-oriented manner. This may lower the threshold for victim responses that may lead to maladaptive interactions between the perpetrator and victim.

A response bias deficit has been suggested as the cause for misperception in pitch quality in right frontal areas extending, by convergence and control mechanisms, the temporal lobe's processing of this ability. The pitch quality of the victim's voice, as perceived by the accused, should be noted because verbal content may be identical in two messages despite completely different motivations.

Defendants with frontal lobe damage often deny their sensory-perceptual problems. Right frontal damage is particularly associated with deficit denial.

VISUAL-SPATIAL

Defendants with frontal visual-spatial deficits may perform well on simple tasks as long as the examiner is providing structure, guidance, and monitoring. However, difficulties in visual-spatial shifting are found in (1) reversal of perspective, (2) judgment of visual and postural vertical positioning, (3) constructional deficits, and (4) focus on details. Frontally impaired individuals are notoriously hazardous on the road for all of the above reasons and may contribute more than their proportionate share of negligent homicides (Undeutsch, 1982, 1984).

Personal orientation tasks are usually considered mediated by the parietal lobes. Yet, the shifting, sequencing, and reversal requirements may cause deficient performance in individuals with frontal lobe impairments, particularly in the right hemisphere. In these tasks, the subject is shown a profile of a human body and is required to touch the part of his or her body that corresponds to that indicated on the profile. Deficits in tasks of finding and naming body parts, right-left orientation, and change in action tasks should be worse for the time of the crime than for the time of the evaluation.

Evaluators should also consider the victim's responses to visual-spatial deficits. For example, stimulus boundedness may cause the victim to believe that he or she is being stared at. As suggested by animal research and clinical literature with humans, physical and sexual aggression are seen by the average person as the usual motivations for prolonged staring. The steady gaze of the frontal lobe-damaged person may be upsetting, or at least disconcerting, to the victim and others. It may be perceived as a challenge and, thereby, contribute to a possible violent encounter.

AUTONOMIC/EMOTIONAL

Premorbid personality patterns may largely dictate frontal lobe affective disturbances although the evidence is weak, particularly for distinctive qualities of behavior as opposed to generalized release (Parker, 1990). Thus, although a lesion may not create new behaviors, it may accentuate old response patterns. To investigate deficits in drive-related behaviors for the instant offense, the neuropsychological expert needs to determine the degree of change as determined from baseline (i.e., premorbid) functioning. Whether the presence or absence of emotion was appropriate to the situation should be considered, as measured by weighing crime context factors. The task is to (1) evaluate for deficits or excesses in emotional expression, (2) look for functionally similar behaviors during the offense, (3) determine the difference, and (4) see if it was beyond the accused's ability to exercise self-control over the expression, compared to the accused's premorbid history.

Decreased motivation or affect-blunted behavior may contribute to violence. Pseudodepressive affect often seen in individuals with medial frontal lobe damage may lead to suicidal behavior or contribute to depression in others by contagious depression. "Despontaneity," which involves a sharp drop in initiative, may contribute towards allowing another person to commit suicide, or towards refusing to assist in another's injuries. Both of these acts of omission are crimes in many jurisdictions.

The frontal lobe-damaged individual may have difficulty verbalizing feelings to the point when violence is seen as the only viable option. A decreased concern for social propriety may contribute towards others perceiving the person as being insensitive, although this perception may be inaccurate. For example, the frontal lobe-impaired defendant may act without considering the feelings of others, rather than consciously rejecting or humiliating them. Increased affect-related behaviors may lead to violence. The "pseudopsychopathic" triad of facetiousness, sexual/personal hedonism, and an impulsive lack of concern for others could, under the right circumstances, be misperceived as a sexual intrusion.

Inappropriate or prolonged laughter or crying, which represents a reciprocal innervation (MacLean, 1986), may occur due to deficits in the thalamocingulate division of the limbic system (e.g., The laughter and crying are not in keeping with the patient's feelings.) Huntington's disease, Central Nervous System (CNS) syphilis affecting the frontal cortex, Pick's disease, and some other conditions may involve the above affective deficits. They may be exculpatory since substantial incapacitation is usually apparent.

In general, three affective styles are suggested: (1) those creating decreased behavior or affect, (2) those increasing behavior or affect, and (3) most commonly, a mixed style, with prolonged reduced activity coupled with occasional labile behavior, especially when demands are made of the accused.

MOTOR

Frontal lobe motor deficits are typically characterized by slowed initiation, excessive responses (i.e., perseveration), motor impersistence once started, and difficulty in changing one's own behavior. Motor impairments are often accompanied by emotional excess (seen as disinhibition) or a lack of emotion, as when perpetrators commit acts of violence with no apparent emotional reaction. The law appears to equate motor execution with "volition" and intent or anticipation with "cognition." The volitional arm of the federal tests of insanity under the American Law Institute (ALI) has been recently dropped in an increasing effort to delimit the mental incapacity concept. The net effect is that motor behaviors are viewed as secondary to intent.

Motor deficits are now seen legally as that which is relevant to the *actus reus* (deed of crime) rather than *mens rea* (evil intent). *Mens rea* is seen as a cognitive capacity and is the standard by which mental capacity is judged. The law seems to say, "The significance of motor deficits beyond describing the guilty act is minimal, since (evil) thoughts are behind all serious illegal violent acts." A connection between evil intent and an unlawful behavior is seen as necessary in order to demonstrate the occurrence of a crime. Such a view ignores the motivational components of motor behaviors.

Motor impairments do have relevance to *mens rea*. The grasp reflex, for example, which is a frontal release sign whereby objects or people may be grabbed and held for a few moments, may easily be interpreted as a threat involving physical contact. Frontal signs may be absent except for a lack of drive. Therefore, the victim and onlookers may not suspect brain damage, especially since the grasp reflex is known to be set off by stress and depression. In magnetic apraxia, the accused may spontaneously explore the environment in pursuit of a stimulus to grasp (utilization behavior). This is hardly the picture of an individual who is out of control, especially since successful utilization behavior requires some skill integration. Yet, utilization behavior is rarely, if ever, seen without frontal lobe dysfunction. If some frontal lobe-impaired persons are touched by an object, there may be active pursuit, with headturning. A "gluing" effect (e.g., of a frontal lobe-impaired person to a victim) occurs if the perpetrator tries to move, with leg stiffening and Kleist's *gegenhalten* (counterpull). The degree to which these behaviors occurred in criminal contexts should be explored fully.

Motor perseveration occurs in many crimes. With some frontally impaired persons, the initiation of the violence may have been well-planned or impulsive, but in either case, it quickly shifts to disorganized behavior. Continuing to strike someone past the point of resistance is an example. Other normal inhibitors fall off. Injury to the victim, blood and gore, urgings to stop, threats to his own safety if he continues, may all have little or no impact.

MEMORY

Loss of short-term recall for what one was supposed to remember differentiates frontal lobe memory from more posterior recall deficits, although classic amnesia signs in individuals with frontal lobe damage are usually absent. "Frontal amnesia" or provisional memory deficits may be due to difficulty in switching from one memory trace to another, especially when interference factors are present. The frontal "memory" system has intimate connections with the limbic-diencephalic system. Therefore, motivational and emotional problems may also be present. The dissociation between verbalized intentions (or agreement) and actions can often be observed, even with adequate attention and mental alertness, and is often seen as a blatant disregard of instructions or commitments. In sexual assault cases, anything short of a clear "no" before the aggression often results in persistent sexually aggressive behaviors. This is very different from nonorganic sadistic rapists (as in serial rape murderers) who may thrive on the pain cues of the victim.

After arrest, Miranda warnings regarding the rights against self-incrimination may be violated if frontal lobe recall problems are not taken into consideration. In forensic settings, individuals with frontal lobe damage may understand that they are "frying" themselves, but nevertheless persist in offering confessions. Even worse, they may not recall what they have previously confessed to, and often contradict themselves.

COGNITION

Overall intelligence may not be affected in individuals with frontal lobe pathology. For the accused, a social situation involving violence may represent a novel event. Simultaneous stimulation from a variety of context sources may cause the accused to show disorganization in convergence and integration abilities. Simultaneous sources of material may confuse perpetrators beyond their abilities to deal with them. Thus, they may respond to a fragment of the situation. For example, a victim's manner of dress may represent seductiveness or an invitation to engage in a sexual act. The perpetrator may see a person carrying a weapon as having an intent to harm, despite an actual intention to protect if other victim characteristics were taken into consideration.

Abstraction abilities may be impaired in violent defendants. An inability to conceptually remove themselves from their surroundings certainly adds to the potential of violence. However, a switch in principle ("change of action") may not have occurred until that time (e.g., from emotional venting to assault). The switch may require an extraneous stimulation (e.g., a loud noise, sudden movement by the victim). Potential victims may want to wait until the accused shows tiredness, when they can physically leave the scene of the possible assault. The chances of such aggression reoccurring increase if the victim insists on remaining at the scene.

LANGUAGE

Virtually all significant crimes of violence involve some prior verbal statements, even if only brief, by the perpetrator or victim, or both. Characteristics of the perpetrator's language that may create emotional responses from the victim include (1) flaccid paretic dysarthria (hypernasality, breathy phonation, stridor); (2) explosive speech (e.g., due to cerebellar atrophy); (3) flat tonal quality, combined with an apathy often seen in left frontal lobe damage. This last trait may then lead witnesses to conclude falsely that they should increase their efforts to properly communicate with the perpetrator. Hyperphonia may result in the victim missing the perpetrator's words or asking that the words be repeated or spoken louder (these requests are likely to be ignored or perceived negatively by the perpetrator); and (4) pressured speech. Pressured speech, noted in posterior aphasics, may represent a release of frontal speech control mechanisms.

Almost all speech problems secondary to frontal lobe damage are characterized by white matter and subcortical involvement. Therefore, motor and emotional overtones to speech deficits can be expected.

Aphemia is a good indication of frontal lobe pathology. Acute mutism or poor articulation may occur and worsens when the perpetrator is under stress. The occasional tendency of aphemics to speak with an apparent foreign accent may result in strangers believing that the perpetrator was a foreigner or had attempted to disguise his or her voice. Aphemia is usually associated with Broca's area lesions or a subcortical undercutting of Brodman's area 44.

Impaired supplementary motor area (SMA) functions may cause involuntary motor activities of the perpetrator's dominant arm during the alleged offense. These actions may be seen as threatening to witnesses, especially since they are usually accompanied by a reduced verbal output. Yet, the perpetrator's expressed sentences may still be grammatically correct.

Consider Broca's aphasics who may exhibit frontal alexia in relationship to postarrest behavior. They may read the title correctly, but may not understand the details on the actual constitutional rights form. In terms of forensic treatment, offenders may state a desire to return to work, but fail to mobilize the resources to do so. The perpetrator may be seen as lying in order to obtain a reduced sentence.

In sum, language deficits may affect victim behaviors, contexts involving confession, and rehabilitation. Further, if the regulatory powers of speech are lost, inner speech becomes impaired, along with the ability to properly implement or monitor one's verbal and motor behavior during interactional behavior.

Circumscribed Conclusions

It is important that the evaluator offers only the conclusions that are relevant to the forensic referral question. The conclusions should be presented in a sequential fashion and in a language comprehensible to those outside the neuropsychological field.

Sample conclusions for a hypothetical examinee assessed for mental capacity are offered as follows:

1. The forensic data base was sufficient to draw some relevant conclusions beyond a reasonable degree of psychological probability. All conclusions were rendered independently of other forensic examiners in this case.
2. An analysis of possible distortion of data base material suggests that the evaluation is an accurate representation of the accused at the time of the evaluation and the alleged crime.
3. The mental condition of the accused for the time of the evaluation was *Organic Mood Disorder* (DSM III-R Code 293.83). This is consistent with a frontal lobe dysfunction and is represented by a discrete set of neuropsychological deficits and behaviors, including disturbance in mood (i.e., flattened/blunted affect) and marked behavioral perseveration. A *Specific Developmental Disorder* NOS (Code 315.90) is suggested as a DSM-III-R Axis II disorder. Other relevant physical problems for the time of the evaluation include polyuria and polydipsia as DSM III-R Axis III conditions.
4. The mental condition of the accused for the time of the alleged offenses includes *Organic Mood Disorder* and *Adjustment Reaction with Mixed Disturbance of Emotion and Conduct* (Code 309.40) in addition to the *Specific Developmental Disorder* and above-noted Axis III physical problems. Severity of psychosocial stressors (Axis IV) for the year before the instant offenses is seen as being between "severe" and "extreme" using DSM III-R criteria and as exceeding the 90th percentile of cumulative stress as measured by several standardized stress scales. The highest level of adaptive functioning (Axis V) is "poor" for the six months prior to the instant offenses

using DSM III-R criteria and was reflected by a marked deterioration in self-care, work functions, and/or marital/sexual relationship.

5. The accused is competent to proceed legally. He or she has a basic understanding of the nature and quality of the legal proceedings, of some but not all of the possible consequences to himself or herself, and can cooperate with his or her attorney in his or her own defense within his or her capabilities and limitations. Competency to proceed is not likely to improve substantially, given the expected chronicity of his or her organic brain condition. On two standardized measures of legal competency, he or she scored as fit to proceed, with previously noted deficiencies.

6. In the examiner's opinion, the extent to which the above-diagnosed mental conditions impaired the defendant's cognitive ability to appreciate the wrongfulness of his or her acts was mild to moderate on a scale of negligible, minimal, mild, moderate, considerable, and substantial. The defendant stated at the time of the alleged crime that he or she knew he or she was doing wrong and had full recall for instant offense events.

7. In the examiner's opinion, the extent to which the above-diagnosed conditions impaired the defendant's volitional capacity to conform his or her conduct to the requirements of the law was substantial. This is based upon the interactive effects of (1) impaired self-control and other executive-related deficits resulting from the suggested mental disorder, (2) substantial and cumulative psychosocial stress, (3) significant behavioral deterioration both for several months and just prior to the instant offenses, and (4) [specify other factors].

8. An assessment of the defendant's risk of danger and proposed intervention are required in this jurisdiction if a potentially exculpating mental condition is proffered as in the present case. Violence potential for this individual is seen as substantial due to predisposing variables such as his or her mental condition, present triggering stimuli, opportunity factors, and recent and severe violence. Forensic hospitalization is recommended.

SUMMARY

The foregoing discussion must, by necessity, rest upon the limited assumptions and state-of-the-art neurodiagnostic technology in the area of brain-behavior relationships in general and a disorder of executive functions secondary to frontal lobe damage in particular. Nevertheless, it may have applicability to the analysis of crime-specific behavior. The focus of this chapter is on ways for the forensic evaluator to demonstrate the crucial link between the neuropsychological evaluation and alleged offense behaviors. Failing to do this is often the bane of defense strategies where, in fact, brain damage may have been established.

A decision path is recommended for criminal cases using the following process and content factors:

1. *Obtaining a multisourced and interdisciplinary forensic data base.* This data base targets in on known correlates to disorders of executive functions, utilizing a wide range of neuro-psychological tests and measures, all within a composite battery that yields information on other impaired brain functions, lateralization, progression, etiologic and prognostic factors, and potential intervention.

2. *Accounting for retrospective and current distortion,* particularly malingering, in order to obtain a deliberately poor performance.

3. *Examining basal violence* in terms of relevant parameters in order to determine the degree to

which past dangerousness was proactive and voluntary versus reactive due to stress or factors interacting with the disorders of executive functions.

4. *Diagnosing a disorder of executive functions,* if warranted, for both the time of the evaluation and for the alleged offense.

5. *Analyzing self-regulation and self-control during the instant offense* for factors that ordinarily rule out mental capacity (e.g., complex partial seizures, gross perseveration, psychotic symptoms) and for factors that suggest ruling in mental capacity (e.g., crime rehearsal and preparation, acts resulting in financial or other gain, use of weapons).

6. *Linking a disorder of executive functions with instant offense behavior.* This linking occurs by searching for symptoms that are functionally similar to neuropsychological evaluation behavior, and that represent a deterioration from baseline evaluation performance and hence point to other operative factors that explain the alleged crime behavior. The other factors may be mental conditions or events in addition to brain damage (cumulative stress resulting in an adjustment disorder, deteriorative patterns, concurrent acute schizophrenic disorder).

7. *Presenting circumscribed conclusions.* Presenting these in terms of accurate representativeness of the data base, diagnosed mental conditions, fitness to proceed, mental capacity, and imminent dangerousness, the last only if an exculpatory mental condition is proffered.

At the very least, the above seven-step procedure will, in the author's experience, communicate to the court that the forensic evaluator was comprehensive and willing to share his or her decision process. This approach emphasizes the all-important connection between a diagnosed mental condition, causing a disorder in executive functions and alleged offense responses. Finally, this approach is open-ended, in contrast to the usual advice to render short, terse reports that present only conclusions and exclude the basis of the evaluator's reasoning process and content.

A final observation about disorders of executive functions is that the current *Zeitgeist* in this country appears to be one of limiting volitional impairments (i.e., motor output) in favor of assumed cognitive deficits (e.g., thought disorders, suicide ideation). Federal jurisdictions have dropped the volitional arm of the American Law Institute (ALI) guidelines. Others that use the M'Naghten type of insanity defenses focus on all-or-none cognitive impairment.

Attempts to limit the insanity defense may be unreasonable for two intertwining reasons. First, to exclude volitional impairments violates contemporary conceptualizations about brain-behavior relationships. From a neuropsychological perspective, this is tantamount to saying that some brain lesions are morally superior to others, such that temporal lobe, or brain stem damage, for instance, is possibly exculpatory, while damage in the regions of the brain that deal primarily with executive functions are not.

Second, the forensic evaluator should remember that even primarily cognitive impairments must always be expressed through overt behavior because it is the only manner by which those impairments can be observed or deduced. Cognitive impairments are second-order inferences derived from possible behavioral aberrations. All cognitive impairments, therefore, presuppose volitional impairments in the sense that problems in thinking must be reflected through behavioral responses.

American and English appellate cases reflect a rudimentary judicial decision-path in regards to mental incapacity. It is based on the belief that cognitive impairments, as mental elements in thinking and intent, always imply behavioral impairment, but not the reverse. Thus, florid psychosis, gross encephalopathy, dissociative states, mental retardation, and other mental conditions wipe out cognition as well as volition. Yet, it is possible to have impaired volition (e.g., due to frontal lobe dysfunction or other organic states) and still have intact cognition. Theoretically, it would be more parsimonious and scientifically pure to remove the cognitive arm of the ALI test and leave volition as the focus of inquiry.

Mens rea, or evil intent, surely presupposes the ability to carry out those intended actions. How else can criminal responsibility be assigned or even implied? Until judicial wisdom catches up to the current thinking in the science of brain-behavior relationships, it may be necessary for the forensic evaluator to expand the meaning of "appreciation" in truncated versions of ALI tests of insanity to include behavior, affect, and ability to modulate behavior, as well as cognitive activity. For does it not affect appreciation of wrongdoing if one is unable to exercise self-control over one's behavior, modulate extremes of emotion, or engage in reasonable or productive behavior? Compelling questions such as this are expected to reoccur in the literature as neuropsychological information is increasingly applied to forensic settings and situations.

REFERENCES

Adams, F. (1952). Hippocrates writings. In R. M. Hutchins & M. J. Adler (Eds.), *Great books of the western world: Hippocrates, Galen.* (Vol. 10, pp. 1–160). Chicago: William Benton, Publisher.

Alexander, M. P., Stuss, D. T., & Benson, D. F. (1979). Capgras' syndrome: A reduplicative phenomenon. *Neurology, 29,* 334–339.

Bartol, C. R. (1983). *Psychology and American law.* Belmont, CA: Wadsworth Publishing Company.

Bianchi, L. (1895). The function of the frontal lobes. *Brain, 18,* 497–522.

Blau, T. (1986). *The psychologist as expert witness.* New York: John Wiley & Sons.

Boll, T. (1985). Developing issues in neuropsychology. *Journal of Clinical and Experimental Neuropsychology, 7,* 473–484.

Brown, J. W. (1983). The microstructure of perception: Physiology and patterns of breakdown. *Cognition and Brain Theory, 6,* 145–184.

Brown, J. W. (1985a). Frontal lobe syndromes. In *Handbook of clinical neurology, Vol. 45. Clinical neuropsychology* (pp. 23–41). Amsterdam: Elsevier.

Brown, J. W. (1985b). Imagery and the microstructure of perception. *Journal of Neurolinguistics, 1,* 89–141.

Brown, J. W. (1986). Cognitive microgenesis: Review and current status. *Progress in Clinical Neurosciences, 2.*

Brown, J. W. (1987). The microstructure of action. In E. Perecman (Ed.), *Frontal lobes revisited.* New York: IRBN Press.

Critchley, M. M. (1964). The problem of visual agnosia. *Journal of Neurological Science, 8,* 274–290.

Damasio, A. R. (1979). The frontal lobes. In K. M. Heilman & E. Valenstein (Eds.), *Clinical neuropsychology* (pp. 360–412). New York: Oxford University Press.

Damasio, A. R., & Van Hoesen, G. W. (1980). Structure and function of the supplementary motor area. *Neurology, 30,* 359.

Damasio, A. R., & Van Hoesen, G. W. (1983). Emotional disturbances associated with focal lesions of the limbic frontal lobe. In K. M. Heilman & P. Satz (Eds.), *Neuropsychology of human emotion* (pp. 85–110). New York: Guilford Press.

Filskov, S. B., & Boll, T. J. (Eds.). (1986). *Handbook of clinical neuropsychology,* Vol. 2. New York: John Wiley & Sons.

Frederick, C. (1978). An overview of dangerousness: Its complexities and consequences. In *Dangerous behavior: A problem in law and mental health* (NIMH, DHEW Publication No. ADM 78-563). Washington,

DC: U.S. Government Printing Office.

Fuster, J. (1981). Prefrontal cortex in motor control. In V. B. Brooks (Ed.), *Handbook of physiology—The nervous system, Vol. II. Motor control* (pp. 1149–1178). Bethseda: American Physiological Society.

Fuster, J. M. (1989). *The prefrontal cortex: Anatomy, physiology, and neuropsychology of the frontal lobe* (2nd ed.). New York: Raven Press.

Gibbons, D. C. (1975). Offender typologies—two decades later. *British Journal of Criminology, 15,* 141–156.

Goldberg, E., & Bilder, R. (1987). The frontal lobes and hierarchical organization of cognitive control. In E. Perecman (Ed.), *The frontal lobes revisited.* (pp. 159-187).New York: IRBN Press.

Goldberg, E., & Costa, L. (1985). Qualitative indices in neuropsychological assessment: Executive deficit following prefrontal lesions. In K. Adams & I. Grant (Eds.), *Neuropsychological assessment of neuropsychiatric disorders* (pp. 48–64). London & New York: Oxford University Press.

Goldberg, E., & Tucker, D. (1979). Motor perseveration and long-term memory for visual forms. *Journal of Clinical Neuropsychology, 1,* 273–288.

Golden, C. J. (1980). In reply to Adam's in search of Luria's battery: A false start. *Journal of Consulting and Clinical Psychology, 48,* 517–521.

Golden, C. J. (1984). The Luria-Nebraska Neuropsychological Battery in forensic assessment of head injury. *Psychiatric Annals, 14,* 532–538.

Golden, C. J., Ariel, R. N., McKay, S. E., Wilkening, G. N., Wolf, B. A., & MacInnes, W. D. (1982). The Luria-Nebraska Neuropsychological Battery: Theoretical orientation and comment. *Journal of Consulting and Clinical Psychology, 50,* 291–300.

Golden, C. J., Ariel, R. N., Moses, J. A., Wilkening, G. N., McKay, S. E., & MacInnes, W. D. (1982). Analytical techniques in the interpretation of the Luria-Nebraska Neuropsychological Battery. *Journal of Consulting and Clinical Psychology, 50,* 40–48.

Golden, C. J., Hammeke, T. A., & Purisch, A. D. (1980). *The Luria-Nebraska Battery manual.* Palo Alto, CA: Western Psychological Services.

Golden, C. J., & Strider, M. (Eds.). (1986). *Forensic neuropsychology.* New York: Plenum Press.

Hall, H. V. (1982). Dangerousness prediction and the maligned forensic professional: Suggestions for estimating true basal violence. *Criminal Justice and Behavior, 9,* 3–12.

Hall, H. V. (1983). Guilty but mentally ill: Feedback from state attorneys general. *Bulletin of the American Academy of Forensic Psychology, 4,* 2–8.

Hall, H. V. (1984a). Dangerous myths about predicting dangerousness. *American Journal of Forensic Psychology, 2,* 173–193.

Hall, H. V. (1984b). Predicting dangerousness for the courts. *American Journal of Forensic Psychology, 2,*   5–25.

Hall, H. V. (1985). Cognitive and volitional capacity assessment: A proposed decision tree. *American Journal of Forensic Psychology, 3,* 3–17.

Hall, H. V. (1986). The forensic distortion analysis: A proposed decision tree and report format. *American Journal of Forensic Psychology, 4,* 31–59.

Hall, H. V. (1987). *Violence prediction: Guidelines for the forensic practitioner.* Springfield, IL: Charles C. Thomas.

Hall, H. V. (1988). Book review. Understanding and treating the psychopath by D. Doran. *Clinical Psychology Review, 8,* 253.

Hall, H. V. (1990). *Extreme emotion.* University of Hawaii Law Review, University of Hawaii, Honolulu, Hawaii, 12, 39-82.

Hall, H. V., Catlin, E., Boissevain, A., & Westgate, J. (1984). Dangerous myths about predicting dangerousness (1). *American Journal of Forensic Psychology, 2,* 173–193.

Hall, H. V., & Hall, F. L. (1987). Post-traumatic stress disorder as a legal defense in criminal trials. *American Journal of Forensic Psychology, V,* 45–53.

Hall, H. V., & Shooter, E. (1989). Explicit alternative testing for feigned memory deficits. *Forensic Reports, 2,* 277–286.

Halstead, W. C. (1947a). *Brain and intelligence: A quantitative study of the frontal lobes.* Chicago: University of Chicago Press.

Halstead, W. C. (1947b). Specialization of behavioral functions and the frontal lobes. *Research Publication of the Association of Nervous and Mental Diseases, 27,* 59–66.

Hecaen, H., & Albert, M. (1975). Disorders of mental functioning related to frontal lobe pathology. In D. F. Benson & D. Blumer (Eds.), *Psychiatric aspects of neurological disease.* (pp. 175-218).New York: Grune & Stratton.

Horowitz, I. A., & Willging, T. E. (1984). *The psychology of law: Integrations and applications.* Boston: Little, Brown and Company.

Kaczmarek, B. L. J. (1984). Neurolinguistic analysis of verbal utterances in patients with focal lesions of frontal lobes. *Brain and Language, 21,* 52–58.

Kaczmarek, B. L. J. (1986). *Frontal lobes, language, and human behavior* (in Polish). Wroclaw: Ossolineum.

Kaczmarek, B. L. J. (1987). Regulatory function of the frontal lobes: A neurolinguistic perspective. In E. Perecman (Ed.), *The frontal lobes revisited* (pp. 225–240). New York: The IRBN Press.

Kandel, E., & Freed, D. (1989). Frontal-lobe dysfunction and antisocial behavior: A review. *Journal of Clinical Psychology, 45,* 404–413.

Lezak, M. (1983). *Neuropsychological assessment* (2nd ed.). New York: Oxford Press.

Luria, A. R. (1969). Frontal lobe syndromes. In P. J. Vinken & G. W. Bruyn (Eds.), *Handbook of clinical neurology* (pp. 725–757). North Holland, Amsterdam.

Luria, A. R. (1973a). The frontal lobes and the regulation of behavior. In K. H. Pribram & A. R. Luria (Eds.), *Psychophysiology of the frontal lobes* (pp. 3–26). New York: Academic Press.

Luria, A. R. (1973b). *The working brain: An introduction to neuropsychology,* translated by B. Haigh. New York: Basic Books.

MacLean, P. D. (1986). Culminating developments in the evolution of the limbic system: The thalamocingulate division. In B. K. Doane & K. E. Livingston (Eds.), *The limbic system: Functional organization and clinical disorders* (pp. 1–28). New York: Raven Press.

McMahon, E., & Satz, P. (1981). Clinical neuropsychology: Some forensic applications. In S. Filskov & T. Boll (Eds.), *Handbook of clinical neuropsychology.* New York: John Wiley & Sons.

Megargee, E. I., & Bohn, Jr., M. J. (1979). *Classifying criminal offenders: A new system based on the MMPI.* Beverly Hills: Sage Publications.

Monahan, J. (1981). *The clinical prediction of violent behavior* (DHHS Publication No. ADM 81–921). Rockville, MD: National Institute of Mental Health.

Nauta, W. J. H. (1971). The problem of the frontal lobe: A reinterpretation. *J.ournal of Psychiatric Research 8,* 167–187.

Nauta, W. J. H. (1973). Connections of the frontal lobe with the limbic system. In L. V. Laitinen & K. E. Livingston (Eds.), *Surgical approaches in psychiatry* (pp. 303–314). Baltimore: University Park Press.

Pankratz, L. (1979). Symptom validity testing and symptom retraining procedures for the assessment and treatment of functional sensory deficits. *Journal of Consulting and Clinical Psychology, 47,* 409–410.

Pankratz, L. (1983). A new technique for the assessment and modification of feigned memory deficit. *Perceptual and Motor Skills, 57,* 367–372.

Pankratz, L., Binder, L., & Wilcox, L. (1987). Assessment of an exaggerated somatosensory deficit with Symptom Validity Assessment. *Archives of Neurology, 44,* 798.

Pankratz, L., Fausti, S. A., & Peed, S. (1975). A forced choice technique to evaluate deafness in a hysterical or malingering patient. *Journal of Consulting and Clinical Psychology, 43,* 421–422.

Parker, R. (1990). *Traumatic brain injury and neuropsychological impairment: Cognitive, emotional and adaptive problems of children and adults.* New York: Springer-Verlag.

Perecman, E. (1987). *The frontal lobes revisited.* New York: IRBN Press.

Pribram, K. H. (1960). The intrinsic systems of the forebrain. In J. Field, H. W. Magoun, & H. V. Hall, *Handbook of physiology, Vol. II.* Neurophysiology (pp. 1323–1344). Washington, DC: American Physiological Society.

Pribram, K. H. (1967). The new neurology and the biology of emotion: A structural approach. *American Psychologist, 23,* 830–838.

Purisch, A.D., & Sbordone, R.J. (1986). The Luria-Nebraska Neuropsychological Battery. In G. Goldstein & R. A. Tarter (Eds.), *Advances in clinical Neuropsychology* (Vol. 3) (p. 291-316). New Jersey: Plenum.

Reitan, R. M., & Wolfson, D. (1985). *Neuroanatomy and neuropathology: A clinical guide for neuropsychologists.* Tucson, AZ: Neuropsychology Press.

Reitan, R. M., & Wolfson, D. (1986). *Traumatic brain injury: Vol. I. Pathophysiology and neuropsychological evaluation.* Tucson, AZ: Neuropsychology Press.

Reitan, R. M., & Wolfson, D. (1988). *Traumatic brain injury: Vol. II. Recovery and rehabilitation.* Tucson, AZ: Neuropsychology Press.

Rogers, R. (1984). *R-CRAS: Rogers Criminal Responsibility Assessment Scales.* Odessa, FL: Psychological Assessment Resources.

Rogers, R. (1986). *Conducting insanity evaluations.* New York: Van Nostrand Reinhold.

Schuman, D. W. (1986). *Psychiatric and psychological evidence.* New York: McGraw-Hill.

Schwitzgebel, R. L., & Schwitzgebel, R. K. (1980). *Law and psychological practice.* New York: John Wiley & Sons.

Seyle, H. (Ed.). (1980, 1983, 1983). *Selye's guide to stress research* (Vols. 1-3). New York: Van Nostrand Reinhold.

Shallice, T. (1978). The dominant action system: An information-processing approach to consciousness. In K. S. Ope & J. L. Singer (Eds.), *The stream of consciousness* (pp. 117–157). New York: Plenum Press.

Shallice, T. (1982). Specific impairments of planning. In D. E. Broadbent & L. Weiskrantz (Eds.), *The neuropsychology of cognitive function* (pp. 199–209). London: The Royal Society.

Shooter, E., & Hall, H. V. (1989). Distortion analysis on the MMPI and MMPI-2. *Bulletin of the American Academy of Forensic Psychology, 10,* 9.

Shooter, E., & Hall, H. V. (1990). Explicit alternative testing for deliberate distortion: Towards an abbreviated format. *Forensic Reports., 4,* 45-49.

Spitzer, R. L., & Endicott, J. (1978). *Schedule of affective disorders and schizophrenia.* New York: Biometric Research.

Stone, A. (1975). *Mental health and the law: A system in transition* (DHEW Pub. No. ADM 76–176). Washington, DC: U.S. Government Printing Office.

Strub, R., & Black, F. (1981). *Organic brain syndromes.* Philadelphia, PA: F. A. Davis Company.

Stuss, D. T., & Benson, D. F. (1984). Neuropsychological studies of the frontal lobes. *Psychological Bulletin, 95,* 3–28.

Stuss, D. T., & Benson, D. F. (1986). *The frontal lobes.* New York: Raven Press.

Teuber, H. L. (1964). The riddle of frontal lobe function in man. In J. M. Warren & K. Akert (Eds.), *The frontal granular cortex and behavior* (pp. 410–444). New York: McGraw-Hill.

Teuber, H. L. (1966). The frontal lobes and their function: Further observations on rodents, carnivores, subhuman primates and man. *International Journal of Neurology, 5,* 282–300.

Teuber, H. L. (1972). Unity and diversity of frontal lobe functions. *Acta Neurobiologiae Experimentalis (Warsz.), 32,* 615–656.

Theodor, L. H., & Mandelcorn, M. S. (1973). Hysterical blindness: A case report and study using a modern psychophysical technique. *Journal of Abnormal Psychology, 82(3),* 552–553.

Undeutsch, U. (1982). Statement reality analysis. In A. Trankell (Ed.), *Reconstructing the past.* Deventer, the Netherlands: Kluver, Law and Taxation Publishers.

Undeutsch, U. (1984). *Methods in detecting assessee misrepresentation.* European Military Psychologists Conference, Nuremberg, Federal Republic of Germany.

Wolfgang, M. E., Figlio, R. M., Tracy, P. E., & Singer, S. I. (1985, June). *The national survey of crime severity.* (U.S. Department of Justice Publication No. NCJ–96017). Washington, DC: U.S. Government Printing Office.

Ziskin, J. (1981). *Coping with psychiatric and psychological testimony.* Beverly Hills, CA: Law & Psychology Press.

Chapter 3

Neurolinguistic Aspects of Crime-Related Frontal Lobe Deficits

B. L. J. Kaczmarek

THE FRONTAL LOBES AND CONTROL OF VERBAL BEHAVIOR

It is commonly accepted that the frontal lobes are important for the regulation of complex behavior. Of particular importance, however, is the role of frontal lobes in self-control and avoiding criminal behavior. The function of the prefrontal area is believed to be involved with planning activities and maintaining a course of action, particularly modifying one's actions to conform to changing environmental demands, since these functions are severely disturbed after frontal lesions. This is corroborated by the increasing ability of children to plan, organize, and perform complex tasks as the prefrontal cortex matures. Similarly, patients with frontal lobe injuries who manifest difficulty in behavioral regulation show a considerable impoverishment of their language output (Goldstein, 1948; Luria, 1966, 1973, 1982; Novoa & Ardila, 1987; Stuss & Benson, 1987).

The writer's own studies (Kaczmarek, 1984, 1986, 1987) have revealed a notable simplification of the grammatical structure of narrative language in patients following frontal lobe injury. An analysis of the syntactic complexity of verbal narratives has revealed several different variants of the frontal lobe syndrome. For example, differences between the structure of narratives elicited from patients with dorsolateral and orbitofrontal lesions of the left frontal lobe as well as of the right frontal lobe have been observed.

The diagnostic value of the linguistic structure of verbal utterances has been demonstrated in a series of interesting studies (Morice, 1986; Morice & Ingram, 1982; Morice & McNicol, 1986) that revealed detectable language changes in schizophrenic patients. These authors, however, stressed a probable frontal lobe deficit in their patients' behavioral control deficits.

Similarly, Pontius and Yudowitz (1980) examined 30 young, healthy criminals and found that the form of their offensive actions reflected an inability to switch the principle of action (POA), and that this problem was manifested in the form of the verbal narratives they produced. Pontius has argued that such an inability follows an injury to the frontal lobes. A consequence of this inability is that social interactions deteriorate due to impaired frontal lobe mediation. (Author's note: This type of deviant behavior should be contrasted with the impulsive seizure-like aggression that is considered to be mediated by the limbic system where the violent action is evoked by a strong emotional component.) This problem creates a disorder of executive functions that causes a person to continue a criminal action despite the appearance of intervening circumstances. Pontius stressed that when this occurs, the "action deteriorates into destructiveness or violence without the presence of a corresponding emotional component directed at the person or property to be violated by the criminal action" (Pontius & Yudowitz, 1980, p. 114).

A typical example of such behavior is provided by Pontius and Yudowitz (1980): "I was shoplifting, a cop came and asked me questions, and I threw the cop to the ground. It was stupid, I got charged with A and B [assault and battery] of a cop." (p. 115)

Such a discrepancy between "knowing and doing" has been reported by a number of authors as a typical feature of a frontal lobe deficit (Ackerly, 1964; Luria, 1973; Milner, 1964; Stuss & Benson, 1987, 1990; Teuber, 1972). It is presumed that the above disturbances reflect impairment of the regulatory function of language that are closely connected with the executive functions of the frontal lobe (i.e., the ability to control an integrated goal-directed human behavior that is linked with self-awareness and self-analysis).

Development of Language and Self-Control

Most psychologists stress the significance of language in programming and performing willful actions. The development of language for the mediation of verbal behavior has been proposed by Luria (1961, 1982). The main idea behind Luria's research is that a child is at first instructed to do various tasks by an adult, and then learns to give himself linguistic commands. These self-instructions are at first uttered aloud and then gradually take the form of internal covert instructions. Luria's theory has received some criticism, particularly his ideas of the dominance of the verbal system over the motor behavior, and its developmental aspects (Bloor, 1977). The question of whether the human capacities of the brain are an outcome of acquiring language, or that language acquisition is due to the specific organization of the brain, is not the central issue there, instead, the main point is that relationships between linguistic skills and the ability to perform complex behavioral acts can commonly be observed. These relations can frequently be observed in children since their ability to control their motor behavior develops both as a consequence of the maturation of the brain, particularly the frontal lobes, and the acquisition and mastery of language. It is also a well-known clinical observation that language-deficient children exhibit various behavioral problems, among which conduct disorders are most common (Baker & Cantwell, 1982, 1987; Giannopoulou, 1990).

Pontius and her co-workers (Pontius, 1974, Pontius & Ruttinger, 1976, Pontius & Yudowitz, 1980) have identified four stages in the development of the child's ability to tell stories, taking into account the form of action described. Stage I is characterized by disjointedness of activities. Stage II is characterized by an inability to switch the principle of action of an ongoing activity. Planning competence appears in Stage III. In Stage IV the child is able to switch the principle of action appropriately. Pontius has stressed that these stages correspond to the maturation of the frontal lobes. For example, she has observed a distinct increase of the ability to regulate behavior along with the decrease of the inability to switch the principle of action when children reach age four, the period in which the frontal area is reported to undergo its greatest maturational spurt. Furthermore, Pontius has found a positive correlation between the developmental stages of actual behavior and "the maturational phases of the form of action as expressed in narratives" (Pontius & Ruttinger, 1976, p. 510).

Neurolinguistic Analysis of the Frontal Lobe Syndrome

One of the basic aims of the field of neurolinguistics is to establish relationships between the brain, language, and behavior. However, this is not an easy task since each of these phenomena are of a complex and multilevel nature. Recent developments in both linguistics and brain research have made this a more feasible endeavor. Linguistic analysis, in particular, can provide a precise tool to investigate language. Yet, when carrying out the linguistic analysis of verbal narratives produced by brain-damaged subjects, it is important to consider neuropsychological factors that influence their verbal output. Thus, one must utilize neurolinguistics, which integrates the fields of neurology, psychology, and linguistics, since its main focus is the neural mechanisms of language and speech.

A neurolinguistic approach becomes particularly useful when examining patients with frontal lobe injuries because of the complexity of the frontal lobes and their interactions with cortical and subcortical brain structures. The frontal lobes not only play an inhibitory role in behavior, but also color our emotional experiences. No wonder that all complex functions tend to be disturbed after frontal lesions. However, the observed symptoms depend, to a large degree, upon the task the patient is asked to perform, since frontal lobe dysfunctions reveal themselves only during novel or complex tasks while tasks that are based on prior experiences or rote learning are only minimally affected by frontal lobe injuries. For example, IQ scores are only minimally affected by frontal lobe pathology (Sbordone, 1991).

Since the symptoms of frontal lobe pathology are complex, the symptoms observed are of a diverse nature. One possible solution is to analyze the verbal behavior of such individuals at a common linguistic level. The results of these investigations (Kaczmarek, 1984, 1986, 1987) have proved promising since they allow us to delineate the symptoms characteristic of frontal lobe pathology. Thus, language analysis may be of considerable importance to the forensic evaluator.

Yet, as pointed out by Morice (1986), the diagnostic efficacy of such a procedure is seriously limited by its complexity, which makes it a time-consuming task; besides it requires some linguistic training. However, our investigations have allowed us to construct a diagnostic methodology that permits an evaluator with only limited grammatical training to analyze language samples. This methodology is described below.

METHOD

Subjects. Two experimental groups were selected; one with a history of serious offensive behavior but without evidence of brain damage and the other with clear-cut frontal lobe damage.

The first group consisted of eight subjects who had been given a diagnosis of schizophrenia after having committed serious crimes. Five subjects were tried for homicide, two for arson, and one for serial robberies. All were kept in custody on a psychiatric hospital unit after their trial (Group A).

The second group consisted of eight patients who had sustained an injury to their frontal lobes. Five subjects had the lesions in the right frontal lobe, while three subjects suffered from left frontal damage. The offenses of this group were limited to mild forms of aggression (e.g., scuffles, brawls) (Group B).

Both experimental groups displayed a tendency to react with aggression to complex situational stimuli that seemed to surpass their coping skills. Consequently, their conduct in a highly structured clinical setting was sedate with a marked tendency toward social isolation. Both groups, however, could exhibit outbursts of anger if pressed too hard to complete the examination task. Four control groups without any history of violence were included in the study. These groups were composed on the following subjects: eight schizophrenic subjects (Group C); patients with lesions of the right and left frontal lobes that were matched with Group B for the localization of injury (Group D); eight posterior brain-damaged patients with no evidence of aphasia, half of which (four) suffered from left hemisphere injuries; the remaining half (four) had right hemisphere lesions (Group E); and a group of eight nonbrain-damaged subjects who stayed in the same hospital as the frontal lobe-damaged patients. Each subject in this group had been treated for radiculalgia, a disorder of a peripheral spinal nerve including the nerve roots of teeth (Group F).

All the subjects utilized in this study were males with a mean age of 42.9. All subjects had IQs between 85 and 120; however, the IQ of the frontal and schizophrenic (aggressive) patients were somewhat lower than the control groups. This appeared to be due to their distractibility as well as partial cooperation. As a consequence, the level of prior education was utilized to determine their intellectual ability. The precise location of the lesions of the brain-damaged patients were determined during surgery. Each subject was evaluated by Luria's original neuropsychological battery.

Procedure. A variety of tasks were utilized to facilitate language production. These tasks consisted of: (1) repeating a story (a) that was told by an examiner or (b) that the subject read himself; (2) describing a situation presented in (a) a single representational picture or (b) a sequence of pictures; and (3) talking about a given topic (a) relating to the subject's personal experience (e.g., hometown, work) or (b) of a more general interest (e.g., the mountains, sea).

Subtests (a) and (b) permitted us to gain a better understanding of the linguistic behavior exhibited by our subjects since it stimulated them to produce long narratives suitable for language analysis. The particular subtests represented various degrees of difficulty for individual patients based on our previous research since frontal lobe subjects typically performed better when they were asked to reproduce a story they had listened to rather than if they were required to read it themselves. As a rule, they said much more about a picture story than about a single picture. In comparison, subjects with posterior lesions found it easier to describe a picture rather than a picture story. Accordingly, patients with frontal lobe damage were likely to talk more about personal matters that aroused their feelings. In summary, our previous research had demonstrated that constructing a story on a given topic when neither the content nor grammatical structure is given is a most difficult task for the subjects with frontal lobe damage (see Kaczmarek, 1984, 1986).

The complexity of linguistic tasks given to the subjects in this study permitted us to carefully analyze both the semantic and syntactic structure of their mental narratives. Each narrative was tape-recorded and then transcribed verbatim.

Content deformations. The most striking language disturbances observed in subjects with frontal lobe injuries are content deformations. For example, their utterances are often incoherent and generally characterized by numerous repetitions, digressions, and confabulations. However, the content of their language varies considerably according to the type of task the subject is asked to perform. As a consequence, the scores of individual tasks will be presented separately.

Reproducing a story. In each story both semantic and syntactic structures are already organized, which permits us to observe the subject's ability to reproduce the structured information. For the purpose of semantic analysis, elementary propositions (carrying the essential information) were

Table 1. Percentage of semantic errors in reproducing a story.

Error type	Subject group*					
	A	B	C	D	E	F
Perseveration of propositions	27.0	30.6	12.0	37.1	0	0
Perseveration of words	28.4	22.1	52.0	12.1	21.0	0
Digression	17.6	9.7	12.0	9.7	10.5	0
Displacement of propositions	14.9	24.2	10.0	35.2	21.0	0
Confusion of events and characters	12.1	13.4	8.0	5.9	0	0
Peculiar phrases	0	0	6.0	0	0	0
No errors	0	0	0	0	0	100.0

*A - aggressive schizophrenics; B - aggressive frontals; C - nonaggressive schizophrenics; D - nonaggressive frontals; E - posterior lesions; F - controls.

identified in each story by at least 21 healthy, normal subjects (see Appendix A). In this way both the number and the sequence of propositions were determined in each story.

A distribution of semantic errors in the examined groups while reproducing stories is presented in Table 1. It should be noted that perseveration of propositions as well as confusion of events and characters are typical of both frontal (Groups B and D) and schizophrenic patients (Groups A and C). There were also qualitative similarities, especially between Groups A and B, since the subjects in these groups were unable to initiate the story without prompting by an examiner. Furthermore, digressions in these patients often lead to confabulations, while the subjects with posterior brain lesions did not produce the confabulations.

At the same time, some differences between the groups were observed. For example, the two "criminal" Groups (A and B) exhibited a greater tendency to confuse events and characters than Groups C and D. Their scores were also found to be more similar to those of nonagressive frontal lobe subjects (Group D) than to the nonagressive schizophrenics.

Another characteristic feature of subjects with frontal lobe injuries is their inability to give the moral of the story. This was also observed in schizophrenic subjects, but was more pronounced in the agressive group.

We noted that perseveration of words, digression, and displacement of propositions occurred in all groups except Group E. Therefore, these errors can be considered general indicators of the brain dysfunction.

Describing pictures. Complex situational pictures or picture stories also provide an opportunity for detailed semantic analysis. Table 2 presents the results of the second task in terms of percentage or erroneous productions. Striking similarities between the scores obtained by schizophrenics with a criminal history (Group A) and frontal lobe subjects (Groups B and D) can be noted. These particular groups exhibited considerable difficulty describing the situation presented in the pictures. As a consequence they can only name single objects within the picture. Also when describing a sequence of pictures, they treat each picture as a separate unit, and are not able to relate the story the pictures present. Another

Table 2. Percentage of semantic errors in describing pictures.

Error type	Subject group*					
	A	B	C	D	E	F
Perseveration of propositions	22.8	24.2	20.0	26.6	0	0
Perseveration of words	19.0	17.5	30.0	9.8	10.5	0
Naming single objects	30.4	30.7	18.8	30.4	0	0
Misnaming	11.4	10.6	2.5	13.3	23.8	0
False interpretation	8.8	10.1	15.0	12.2	10.3	6.6
Digression	7.6	6.9	1.2	7.7	0	0
Peculiar phrases	0	0	12.5	0	0	0
No errors	0	0	0	0	55.4	94.5

*A - aggressive schizophrenics; B - aggressive frontals; C - nonaggressive schizophrenics;
D - nonaggressive frontals; E - posterior lesions; F - controls.

characteristic is their perseveration of propositions as a consequence of their inability to formulate a narrative.

As in the previous task, the perseveration of words is a common error for all brain-damaged groups in contrast to the controls (Group F). However, describing pictures is certainly an easier task for the patients with posterior brain lesions than for the schizophrenics and frontal lobe subjects since the former (Group E) performed it correctly in over 50 percent of the time. Table 2 also shows that misnaming is the most pronounced error in the posterior brain-damaged group, which may be attributable to deficits in visual perception. Hence, they are much better at describing complex pictures than picture stories. A possible explanation is that the situational picture gives more information than one picture of a story, which helps overcome the shortage of visual information. It should be noted that posterior lobe subjects frequently give the name of an object that is most probable to occur in a picture presented to them. In contrast, patients with frontal lobe injuries give names that, even though they resemble the presented object, are highly improbable to appear in a given setting. For example, they may call a "lamp" an umbrella; a "heater" a carpet, and a "snowman" a bear. This difficulty often produces an inaccurate interpretation of the entire picture. These patients appear to lack the ability to select the correct names to correspond to the situation presented in the picture. The performance of agressive schizophrenics (Group A) is analogous to this. For example, when describing The Bad Helper story one subject called the little dog "a cat standing at the woman's head." It appears, therefore, that the misnaming errors of both the frontal lobe and the schizophrenic subjects are due to their use of inaccurate verbal terms that prevent them from making sense out of the picture.

As seen in the first task the features of brain dysfunction are more evident in Groups A and B than in the nonagressive frontal subjects. The frequency of verbal perseverations was found to be greatest in the nonagressive schizophrenic Group (C). However, patients in Group C produced the lowest number of misnamings and digressions. Their use of peculiar phrases, such as "the thing is on the girl's back" to designate a dress clearly differed from Groups A, B, and D.

Spontaneous narratives. Kaczmarek (1984, 1986, 1987) has reported that the spontaneous delivery of ideas is much disturbed in patients with prefrontal injuries. This was also true for frontal (B and D) as well as schizophrenic (A and C) groups in the current study, in that these patients tended to perseverate individual propositions or stick to stereotyped phrases when talking about topics of a more abstract nature. This tendency was more commonly observed in the aggressive subjects (Table 3, Groups A and B). Thus, when the subjects are asked to tell a story about the mountains or the sea, they either state they cannot describe it as they have never been there or they give an account of their personal experiences. As a consequence, whether they talk much or say very little, they are not able to pass much information on the matter in question (e.g., concrete thinking).

In contrast to the frontal (B and D) and schizophrenic (A and C) groups, the posterior group (E) performed much better on the third task than the four previous tasks.

Concluding remarks. Regarding scores across the examined groups, we see that despite the differences in the pattern of errors (which depends on the type of a task) obvious similarities between Groups A, B, C, and D can be observed. A close resemblance can be seen between the two groups with a criminal history (A and B), in that they both exhibit distinct frontal features (the major distinction being the perseveration of propositions) while their scores have characteristics of the generalized brain dysfunction. It is of interest to note that nonaggressive schizophrenics (Group C) constitute a distinct group characterized by features of marked global cerebral dysfunction. This finding is consistent with the observations of Goldberg and Bilder (1987) that "... any diffuse brain dysfunction, affecting much of the brain ... will disrupt executive functions before it will disrupt other functions" (p. 183).

Similar formulations have been offered by Jackson (1958) and Mazurkiewicz (1980) in connection with the notion of hierarchical organization of the central nervous system and the theory of dissolution. They believe that so-called positive or hyperpositive symptoms complicate a clinical picture of a given disease since they reflect the activity of lower levels released from the inhibitory control of the upper cortical level. This leads to the conclusion that only the negative symptoms are a direct result of the dysfunction of a particular brain area.

Table 3. Percentage of semantic errors in spontaneous narratives.

Error type	Subject group*					
	A	B	C	D	E	F
Perseveration of propositions	28.9	27.4	17.6	29.5	0	0
Perseveration of words	27.8	21.2	29.4	8.6	25.0	0
Stereotyped phrases	32.2	37.2	23.5	25.1	0	0
Digression	7.8	11.0	1.5	23.3	0	0
Misnaming	3.3	3.2	20.6	13.5	0	0
Peculiar phrases	0	0	7.4	0	0	0
No errors	0	0	0	0	75.0	100.0

*A - aggressive schizophrenics; B - aggressive frontals; C - nonaggressive schizophrenics; D - nonaggressive frontals; E - posterior lesions; F - controls.

The previous considerations make us realize why it is so difficult to delineate the frontal syndrome on purely behavioral grounds.

Syntactic Deformations

As pointed out in the previous section the semantic structure of narratives produced by subjects with frontal lobe deficits is unstable, and is not easy to analyze. Besides, the qualitative features of the narratives are typically more important to identify frontal lobe pathalogy than the quantitative ones. The qualitative analysis frequently turns out to be the main clinical indication of frontal lobe deficits, which, however, requires considerable clinical experience on the part of the evaluator. Syntactic deformations tend to be stable since the overall proportions of utterance types remain the same across each task. Therefore, the scores of the groups will be presented together.

The total number of particular sentence types and their percentages found in the narratives of each subject group are given in Table 4. A chi square statistical analysis of the distribution of all sentence types within each group was computed. This analysis revealed that the distribution of particular sentence types in the groups was different, in that the difference reached statistical significance (Chi $^2 = 305.600$; df = 25; $p < 0.001$). The difference in the distribution of simple and complex sentences was also found to be statistically significant (Chi$^2 = 165.682$; df = 5; $p < 0.0001$), and the same was found to be true of the differences in the distribution of the remaining sentences (Chi $^2 = 76.265$; df = 15; $p < 0.0001$).

Table 4. Distribution of utterance types in narratives of examined subject groups.

		Subject group*						
Utterance type		A	B	C	D	E	F	Total
1. Simple sentence	N	152	121	151	74	56	56	608
	%	44.05	44.81	39.43	33.79	23.73	22.50	
2. Complex sentence	N	46	37	99	35	124	129	470
	%	13.33	13.70	25.85	15.98	52.54	53.75	
3. Sentence fragment	N	25	11	20	14	7	5	82
	%	7.25	4.07	5.22	6.39	2.97	2.08	
4. Interfected phrase	N	37	3	15	9	7	10	81
	%	10.72	1.11	3.92	4.11	2.97	4.17	
5. Nonfinite clause	N	67	97	78	71	40	42	395
	%	19.42	35.93	20.37	32.42	16.95	17.50	
6. Phatic phrase	N	18	1	20	16	2	0	57
	%	5.22	0.37	5.22	7.31	0.85	0.00	
7. Total	N	345	270	383	219	236	240	1693
	%	100.00	100.00	100.00	100.00	100.00	100.00	

*A - aggressive schizophrenics; B - aggressive frontals; C - nonaggressive schizophrenics; D - nonaggressive frontals; E - posterior lesions; F - controls.

A careful analysis of the ratio of simple to complex structures of the following groups, that do not statistically differ, allows us to pair the following groups:

A and B (Chi ^{2} = 0.001; df = 1; ns)
C and D (Chi ^{2} = 1.823; df = 1; ns)
E and F (Chi ^{2} = 0.110; df = 1; ns)

Taking into account the distribution of other sentences (numbers 3 to 6) also allows us to group the scores into three pairs. However, the distribution of these structures in groups A and B is significantly different (Chi ^{2} = 51.267; df = 3; p <0.001), while in the remaining two pairs the differences were not found to be significant (Chi ^{2} = 1.163; df = 3; p >.05 for Groups C and D, and Chi ^{2} = 1.362; df = 3; p >.05 for Groups E and F).

These findings suggest that the ratio of simple to complex sentences can serve as an indicator of syntactic complexity, and, consequently, of the frontal lobe dysfunction. This is consistent with other findings (Morice, 1986; Morice & Ingram, 1982; Morice & McNicol, 1986). Moreover, this ratio proves to be the same in both "criminal" groups (A and B) in which simple sentences outnumber complex ones by a factor of three (3.3 to 1). It is a little lower in the frontal nonaggressive group (D = 2.1 to 1), while in the nonaggressive schizophrenic (Group C) it drops down to 1.5 to 1. Yet, in all the above groups the proportions of simple structures are higher than those of complex ones, while in the posterior brain-damaged group (E) and in controls (F) the ratio discussed is reversed (E = 0.5 to 1 and F = 0.4 to 1). These data suggest that the score pattern typical of frontal lobe deficits is expressed to a higher degree in the aggressive groups and reveals that they may have a greater frontal lobe deficit.

In order to evaluate the validity of the above findings, the ratio of simple to complex sentences was tested with the use of the Spearman correlation rank coefficient. The correlation coefficient, means, standard deviations as well as the ratio discussed above is shown in Table 5.

Table 5. Means, standard deviations (SD), Spearman rank correlation coefficient, and ratio of simple to complex sentences in narratives of examined subject groups.

	Group	Simple Sentences	Complex Sentences	Correlation Coefficient	Ratio
A	Mean	19.00	5.75	0.627	3.3:1
	SD	8.88	3.17		
B	Mean	15.13	4.63	0.550	3.3:1
	SD	5.25	1.51		
C	Mean	18.88	12.38	0.310	1.5:1
	SD	5.62	5.73		
D	Mean	9.25	4.38	0.213	2.1:1
	SD	1.16	2.33		
E	Mean	7.00	15.50	0.849*	0.5:1
	SD	2.93	4.72		
F	Mean	6.75	16.13	0.826†	0.4:1
	SD	2.49	4.12		

* p < .01; † p < .05

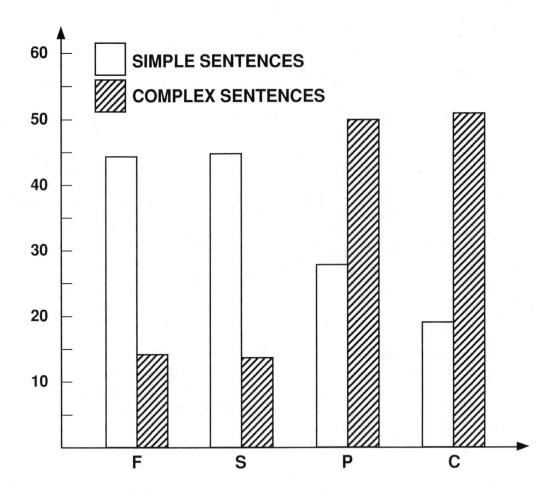

Figure 1.   Mean percentage of simple and complex sentences in all narratives. F = frontals. S = schizophrenics, P = posteriors, C = controls.

The data contained in Table 5 can be seen in Figure 1, which illustrates the mean numbers of the sentences in each group. The data included in Figure 1 and Table 5 indicate that the groups differ if a simultaneous comparison is made of both parameters with the exception of Groups E and F (t = 0.184; df = 14; ns for simple sentences, and t = 0.284; df = 14; ns for complex sentences). An analysis of the Spearman coefficient of simple to complex structures reveals that significant correlations occur only in Groups F and E, and in Groups A and B, while in groups C and D the correlations are modest.

   Since the means, correlation coefficients, and the ratios of evaluated sentence types are of diverse nature (with the exception of Groups E and F) a graphic comparison of simple and complex constructions was performed among the scores of all groups. As Figure 2 indicates, the scores of subjects in Groups E and F differ from the remaining four groups.

For example, the scores of Group A (schizophrenics with a criminal history) cover an area of a broad division of simple sentences (from low to very high numbers) and of complex sentences (from low to average numbers). Scores of Group B (aggressive subjects with frontal lesions) occupy a fraction of the area covered by Group A, centering in its bottom-middle part.

In comparison, Group D subjects (frontal patients without signs of violence) uttered a low number of both simple and complex structures. Consequently, they take up a very small region common with the lower parts of the areas formed by Groups A and B. This illustrates that these three groups exhibit features characteristic of a frontal lobe syndrome, but some additional features can also be observed in the utterances of aggressive subjects.

At the same time, the number of simple and complex sentences occurring in Group C (nonaggressive schizophrenics) is only partially common with Groups A and B. A great deal of the Group C region extends outside the A and B areas, moving towards Groups E and F. Yet it is separated from the latter groups by a considerable distance. Moreover, Groups C and D constitute two distinct sets. This suggests that Group C (nonaggressive schizophrenics) is not homogeneous, and might be further divided into an additional subgroup separate from all other groups so that it would occupy a zone lying between the norm and organic brain pathology. The possible subgroup is marked with a broken line in Figure 2.

The results obtained confirm the hypothesis that the disturbances observed in Groups A and B reflect prefrontal dysfunction despite some additional features that might be attributed to aggressiveness. Furthermore, only some schizophrenics with no history of violent behavior (Group C) seem to suffer from frontal lobe deficits, as the problems encountered by them appear to be due to other factors.

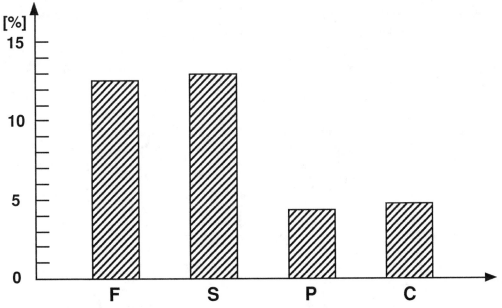

Figure 2. Mean percentage of repeat and part words in all narratives. F = frontals, S = schizophrenics, P = poeteriors, c = controls.

Another important linguistic variable suggestive of frontal lobe dysfunction is the proportion of repeated and part words to all the words (tokens) occurring in a given narrative. This variable has been delineated by Morice (1986), who used a microcomputer to identify measures of high diagnostic reliability. In our material the distribution of the words discussed is similar in the following pairs of the groups:

A and B (Chi^2 = 2.070; df = 1; p >.05)
C and D (Chi^2 = 2.449; df = 1; p >.05)
E and F (Chi^2 = 0.411; df = 1; p >.05)

The scores of other groups differ to a significant degree from each other (Chi^2 = 178.084, df = 5; p <0.001). The resemblance between each of the above pairs confirms the findings of the analysis of the syntactic structure of narratives.

The ratio of repeated words to tokens in Groups A, B, C, and D (with specified or presumed frontal deficit) was generally similar. For example, the percentages of repeated words ranged from 9.82 percent to 12.28 percent in the above groups, while the ratio in Groups E and F (without the frontal lobe dysfunction) was considerably lower—3.24 percent and 3.62 percent respectively (see Table 6).

These observations were further evaluated by testing the intercorrelations between the numbers of all words (tokens) and of repeated words with the Spearman rank coefficient. The values for the individual groups as well as the means and standard deviations (SD) of the scores in question are presented in Table 7.

Practical Implications

An analysis of deviations observed in the narratives of patients with specific brain injuries, both in the previous and the present studies, has made it possible to delineate a number of features characteristic of the frontal lobe deficit. It has also permitted us to distinguish between features of frontal lobe generalized brain dysfunction (i.e., brain damage irrespective of its

Table 6. Number of tokens and repeated words as well as percentage of repeated words in utterances of examined subject groups.

Group	Number of Tokens	Number of Repeated Words	Percent of Repeated Words
A	1621	199	12.28
B	1412	147	10.41
C	2566	252	9.82
D	1958	224	11.44
E	2036	66	3.24
F	2129	77	3.62
Total	11722	965	8.23

Table 7. Means and standard deviations (SD) of tokens and repeated words as well as Spearman rank correlation coefficient between these variables in examined groups.

Group		Tokens	Repeated Words	Correlation Coefficient
A	Mean	202.6	24.9	0.952[†]
	SD	96.4	22.2	
B	Mean	176.5	18.4	0.819[*]
	SD	56.5	7.5	
C	Mean	320.8	31.5	0.262
	SD	81.6	13.1	
D	Mean	244.8	28.0	0.925[†]
	SD	65.0	9.8	
E	Mean	254.5	8.3	0.731[*]
	SD	72.1	2.5	
F	Mean	266.1	9.6	0.238
	SD	68.9	3.7	

[*] $\alpha = 0.05$
[†] $\alpha = 0.01$

localization). These characteristic features of both the content and the syntactic structure of the narratives produced by these groups are described below:

SEMANTIC STRUCTURE

Features of Frontal Lobe Dysfunction
A. Reproducing a Story
   1. Inability to initiate a story
   2. Perseveration of propositions
   3. Confusion of characters and events
   4. Digression (confabulation)
   5. Inability to state the moral of a story
B. Describing Pictures
   1. Treating each element (picture) as a separate unit
   2. Perseveration of propositions
   3. Misnaming (pseudoagnosia)
   4. Digression (confabulation)
   5. Improbable/false interpretation
C. Spontaneous Narratives
   1. Inability to initiate a story
   2. Perseveration of propositions
   3. Sticking to stereotyped phrases
   4. Misnaming
   5. Digression (personal outpourings)

Features of Generalized Brain Dysfunction
  A. Reproducing a Story
      1. Perseveration of words
      2. Digression
      3. Displacement of propositions
  B. Describing Pictures
      1. Perseveration of words
      2. Misnaming (agnosia)
      3. False interpretation
  C. Spontaneous Narratives
      1. Perseveration of words
      2. Misnaming (in aphasia)

The above features are presented separately for each type of narrative to reflect the diversity of symptoms observed in subjects with frontal lobe dysfunction performing individual tasks. A common disorder is an inability to develop a narrative in accordance with its inner plan; hence, perseveration of propositions as well as difficulty in initiating a story are the most commonly observed in these subjects. Another feature is created by improperly connecting elements into an ordered sequence. This is typically manifested by a confusion of the characters and events in the reproduced stories, misnaming in describing pictures, and highly personalized descriptions when discussing a given topic. It is also extremely difficult for the individuals with frontal pathology to draw conclusions based on the set of events they are provided. As a consequence, they cannot provide the moral of the story they are asked to reproduce nor are they able to properly describe the situation presented in a picture or a series of pictures.

It should be noted that delinquent subjects do exhibit features of a frontal lobe disorder. Their symptoms include the loss of ability to organize incoming information and to control their own actions. In addition, they show symptoms of generalized brain dysfunction, most pronounced of which is perseveration of separate words since it occurs twice as frequently as nonaggressive individuals with frontal deficits. Interestingly enough, the perseveration of words is highest in schizophrenic subjects with no records of violence. However, they also exhibit some positive symptoms, such as the use of neologisms or peculiar phrases, which do not occur in frontal patients. Moreover, the percentage of other deviations (e.g., confabulation) is much lower in the nonaggressive schizophrenics, which differentiates them from groups with the frontal deficit.

There are also clear-cut qualitative differences between the four groups discussed so far (A, B, C, and D), and the group with posterior lesions (E) in spite of some quantitative similarities. Thus, although a tendency to digress from the main theme of a story occurs in patients with posterior brain damage, these patients do not generally exhibit confabulation. Likewise, describing pictures provokes these patients to incorrectly name objects. Thus, they may also be unable to correctly specify what is shown to them in a given picture or a picture story. Their misinterpretations, however, differ qualitatively from the misinterpretations made by frontal lobe patients. The following descriptions of the picture At the Dressmaker's (see Appendix B) illustrate these qualitative differences.

Accordingly, the patient with a parieto-occipital lesion says, "... There are ... some children ... They are making cutout ... And here are some ... scissors here ... There are two girls standing. They are cutting out something ... And here are some girls" (pointing to the picture hanging on the wall). Since visual perception disorders make it impossible for the patient to see what the picture shows, the patient tries to make sense out of snatches of the information he is able to perceive. All his failures result from his visual limitations. However, the patient with a posterior lesion is helped by the examiner to attain a correct interpretation of a given picture.

On the contrary, subjects with frontal lobe damage either produce stories that have no connection with the picture or respond to a visual fragment of the picture. Hence, they frequently state that the picture depicts a school or kindergarten. Here is a story elicited from the patient   S. D., a 62-year-old farmer with the meningioma in the right frontal lobe: "That is something like a school . . . There is a globe here . . . There is . . . a big . . . mirror here . . . a table . . . on the table a writing . . . a typewriter (pointing to a sewing machine) . . . Damn it, I can't recognize it . . . And four or five people . . . And here a cap (pointing to an iron) . . . a hat or a beret . . . ."

In describing The Birthday Party, the patient also stated that the picture depicts a school. At the same time, he saw nothing extraordinary about the fact that there were wine glasses on the table, and says: "Well, you may have a drink", and then: "Yes, it is ready to drink," etc. Moreover, he reacted with aggression to the hints of the examiner, who tried to make him see the obvious absurdity of his above statements.

As mentioned earlier, the same phenomenon may be observed in the narrative of schizophrenics with a history of a serious crime-behavior. A good example is the narration of the patient S. K., a 60-year-old farmer interned for homicide, on The Birthday Party. "Well, here job, people at work . . . at an alimentary wor- work. At the alimentary work . . . Some dumplings are here. At the alimentary work . . . It means they are, it means near near nearby, nearby there are . . . resting, resting nearby, aren't they? . . . That one here is a professor, here, a director or something . . . Well, he rebukes them. Those are young children. He is teaching them . . . Those are school children. He is teaching them. Well, those children are busy, they are listening to the professor . . . They are busy . . . This sonny, well, he is checking these wine glasses. He is checking the glasses . . . That daughter a basket, that daughter the basket wants to check, holds it . . . ."

It is characteristic of the patients with frontal deficits that they see nothing extraordinary in the fact that a schoolboy is "checking glasses," and they are reluctant to accept the clues given by the examiner. Such a type of information processing deficit impairs the ability to estimate the behavior, both of one's own and of others, leading to the inability to appreciate the wrongfulness of acts performed.

SYNTACTIC STRUCTURE

An information processing disability, which is sometimes referred to as "the poverty of thought" is frequently reflected in the structure of utterances produced by subjects with frontal lobe damage. Hence, their utterances tend to be grossly simplified. The most characteristic example of this phenomena is an increase in the frequency of simple sentences and a corresponding decrease of more complicated sentence structures. Our research has shown that the forensic evaluator can simply count the simple structures he or she finds in the narratives elicited from an individual with a suspected frontal lobe dysfunction. For example, we have found that if their frequency exceeds 30 percent of all sentence types, it may serve as an indicator of a frontal lobe deficit. Our studies have also demonstrated that the ratio of simple to complex structures is usually greater than 2 to 1. Another indicator is the percentage of repeated and part words. We have found that these patients frequently exceed 10 percent.

In order to permit the evaluator a precise and adequate estimation of the constructions found in the gathered language samples, a list of basic, simple sentence patterns is given below.

Following Kaznowski (1980, pp. 88–95) two basic criteria, generally accepted by grammarians regardless of the school to which they belong, have been identified: (1) the basic pattern includes one and only one finite verb predicator, and (2) all the other functional elements that occur are obligatory. The aforementioned criteria permit us to distinguish seven basic sentence patterns, which are listed below:

Basic Sentence Patterns

A. (S) + (P) consists of subject and predicator; the predicator being an intransitive verb.
   Examples: "It is raining."
               "The car stopped."
B. (S) + (P) + (Cs) consists of subject, predicator, and subject complement.
   Examples: "Mary is nice."
   "John is an engineer."
Beside the verb *be*, verbs of sensation can function as the predicator (e.g., look, feel, smell, taste).
   Example: "She looks pale."
Other verbs taking subject complement are: *seem, appear, remain, turn, come, fall, get, grow, keep, lie, look, become,* etc.
   Examples: "He seemed (to be) a fool."
               "All went wrong."
               "She remained our teacher."
C. (S) + (P) + (Ca) includes subject, predicator, and adverbial complement.
   Examples: "They are away."
               "He is sleeping in bed."
               "She goes to school."
D. (S) + (P) + (O) consists of subject, predicator, and object with the predicator being a nontransitive verb that requires one object only.
   Examples: "She buys a dress."
               "They are looking at her."
E. (S) +(P) +(Od) +(Oi) includes subject, predicator, direct object, and indirect object. The predicator here is a ditransitive verb requiring two objects.
   Examples: "I bought a hat for myself."
   "Mary has given him a present."
F. (S) + (P) + (O) + (Co) includes subject, predicator, object, and object complement.
   Examples: "They think him clever."
               "He accepted her as his partner."
Many verbs that take "as" after them admit of *to be* as an alternative structure.
Example:"He accepted her to be his partner."
G. (S) + (P) + (O) + (Ca) includes subject, predicator, object, and adverbial complement. The predicator is always a transitive verb of motion and the complement is obligatory.
   Examples: "She put the book on the shelf."
               "He showed Jane to the gate."
               "He will take them to London."

The examples given above should help the evaluator estimate the syntactic structure of the narratives elicited from the defendant.

It should be noted that language analysis has been accepted by a number of authors as a convenient diagnostic tool. For example, Andreasen, Hoffman, and Grove (1985) stated, "It is objective and lends itself readily to empirical study" (p. 202). Most importantly, however, is that linguistic capabilities of a given individual do not fluctuate with changing environmental settings. On the contrary, they are stable enough to justify the claim that the disturbances observed during the evaluation most likely occurred at the time of instant behavior. Thus, the way we speak not only reflects our personality, but also is automatic and subconscious to such a degree that the deliberate distortion of the structure of utterances produced by a person is practically impossible, especially if he is given the task of narration by focusing his attention upon its content.

At the same time, it must be recalled that language analysis is not sufficient in and of itself to diagnose the frontal lobe dysfunction. As pointed out in the previous sections of the book, it is necessary to obtain corroboration from a variety of interdisciplinary sources in order to establish the presence of a suspected frontal lobe syndrome.

CONCLUSIONS

The assumption of a frontal lobe defect in individuals with a history of violent crime has been supported by this chapter. The author's research findings demonstrate that frontal lobe deficits are more severe in individuals who exhibit aggressiveness. This leads the author to the conclusion that frontal lobe deficits produce a disturbance of executive functions. This is in agreement with the observations of Ingvar (1983), who reported evidence of activation of both the left and right prefrontal areas of the brain during goal-directed, temporally structured and serial abstract thinking, tasks that involved problem solving, categorization, discrimination, memorization, and recall as determined by regional blood flow and metabolic rate techniques. The same holds for both the expressive and receptive language. Moreover, Ingvar observed a decrease in regional blood flow and in the cerebral metabolism of old deteriorated schizophrenic patients, which was found to be correlated with the severity of psychotic symptoms.

The severity of brain impairments in the two aggressive groups was corroborated by the fact that symptoms of generalized encephalopathy could be observed in addition to salient features of frontal lobe deficits.

Another distinctive feature of the delinquent groups was their blunt affect, which reflects a lack of concern for the events of the surrounding world. This, in combination with their cognitive deficits, makes them unable to control their behavior when they encounter novel circumstances that exceed their limited coping abilities. This is best expressed by one of the patients who related the homicide he had committed in the following way: "I feel very unhappy in the psychiatric hospital. It has ruined my life. I've got a bit drunk at home, and they called an ambulance. And I've got a fright, and I killed my wife." It should be noted that he stated this in a flat, dull voice without showing any sign of emotion.

The need to feel that one is an agent acting upon an environment has been stressed by Brown (1985, 1987). At the same time, he also expressed the view that the feelings and affect that a given action generates are intertwined with the temporal unfolding of the action as well as with the volition, self-awareness, and monitoring of the action flow. As Brown (1985) puts it, "The loss of this active or colitional reaction to the world is, ultimately, the most profound effect of damage to the frontal lobes" (p. 63). He also emphasizes differences between the results of lesions of various parts of the frontal system that influence a hierarchy of "stages in the action sequence." It seems conceivable that more extensive defects, as those observed in our aggressive patients, should disrupt the control of the whole action.

A notion of Grafman (1989) is worth noting in this context. He introduced the idea of Managerial Knowledge Units (MKUs), which govern our behavior. The MKU is not only a schema or a script that makes possible performing complex actions in a routine way, but it is also concerned with the knowledge of when and how such a schema is to be utilized. Grafman believes that the MKU is closely integrated with the function of the frontal lobes, thus providing for the control of mood and behavior, as well as being able to act in accordance with social rules.

ACKNOWLEDGMENTS

Many thanks are due to Dr. Urszula Parol and Mariusz Hawryluk for their assistance in data gathering. A special note of thanks is extended to Dr. Henryk Knapik for statistical analyses.

REFERENCES

Ackerly, S. S. (1964). A case of paranatal bilateral frontal lobe defect observed for thirty years. In J. M. Warren & K. Akert (Eds.), *The frontal granular cortex and behavior* (pp. 192–218). New York: McGraw-Hill.

Andreasen, N. C., Hoffman, R. E., & Grove, W. A. (1985). Mapping abnormalities in language and cognition. In M. Alpert (Ed.), *Controversies in schizophrenia: Changes and consistencies* (pp. 199–227). New York - London: Guilford Press.

Baker, L., & Cantwell, D. P. (1982). Developmental, social, and behavioral characteristics of speech and language disordered children. *Child Psychiatry and Human Development, 12*, 195–207.

Baker, L., & Cantwell, D. P. (1987). A prospective psychiatric follow-up of children with speech/language disorders. *Journal of American Academy of Child and Adolescent Psychiatry, 26*(4), 546–553.

Bloor, D. (1977). The regulatory function of language. In J. Morton, & J. C. Marshall (Eds.), *Psycholinguistics: Developmental and pathological* (pp. 73–97). Ithaca, NY: Cornell University Press.

Brown, J. W. (1985). Frontal lobes and the microgenesis of action. *Journal of Neurolinguistics, 1*(1), 31–77.

Brown, J. W. (1987). The microstructure of action. In E. Perecman (Ed.), *The frontal lobes revisited* (pp. 251–272). New York: The IRBN Press.

Giannopoulou, S. (1990). *Attitudes of parents of children with language deficiency of aphasia type and the logopedic prognosis.* Lublin, Poland: University of Maria Curie Sklodowska (unpublished doctor's thesis, in Polish).

Goldberg, E., & Bilder, R. M. (1987). The frontal lobes and hierarchical organization of cognitive control. In E. Perecman (Ed.), *The frontal lobes revisited* (pp. 159–187). New York: The IRBN Press.

Goldstein, K. (1948). *Language and language disturbances.* New York: Grune & Stratton.

Grafman, J. (1989). Plans, actions, and mental sets: Managerial knowledge units in the frontal lobes. In E. Perecman (Ed.), *Integrating theory and practice in clinical neuropsychology* (pp. 93–138). Hillsdale, NJ: Lawrence Erlbaum Associates.

Ingvar, D. H. (1983). Serial aspects of language and speech related to prefrontal cortical activity. A selective review. *Human Neurobiology, 2*, 177–189.

Jackson, J. H. (1958). *Selected writings.* In J. Taylor (Ed.). London: Staples Press, v. 2.

Kaczmarek, B. L. J. (1984). Neurolinguistic analysis of verbal utterances in patients with focal lesions of frontal lobes. *Brain and Language, 21*, 52–58.

Kaczmarek, B. L. J. (1986). *Frontal lobes, language, and behavior.* Wroclaw, Poland: Ossolineum (in Polish).

Kaczmarek, B. L. J. (1987). Regulatory function of the frontal lobes. A neurolinguistic perspective. In E. Perecman (Ed.), *The frontal lobes revisited* (pp. 225–240). New York: The IRBN Press.

Kaznowski, A. (1980). *Essentials of English transformational syntax.* Warsaw: PWN.

Luria, A. R. (1961). *The role of speech in regulation of normal and abnormal behavior.* Oxford: Pergamon.

Luria, A. R. (1966). *Higher cortical functions in man.* New York: Basic Books.

Luria, A. R. (1973). *The working brain.* New York: Basic Books.

Luria, A. R. (1982). *Language and cognition.* New York: Wiley-Interscience.

Mazurkiewicz, J. (1980). *An outline of psychophysiological psychiatry.* Warsaw: PZWL (in Polish).

Milner, B. (1964). Some effects of frontal lobectomy in man. In J. M. Warren & K. Akert (Eds.), *The frontal granular cortex and behavior* (pp. 313–334). New York: McGraw-Hill.

Morice, R. (1986). Beyond language—Speculations on the prefrontal cortex and schizophrenia. *Australian and New Zealand Journal of Psychiatry, 20,* 7–10.

Morice, R., & Ingram, J. C. (1982). Language analysis in schizophrenia: Diagnostic implications. *Australian and New Zealand Journal of Psychiatry, 16,* 11–21.

Morice, R., & McNicol, D. (1986). Language changes in schizophrenia: A limited replication. *Schizophrenia Bulletin, 12,* 239–251.

Novoa, O. P., & Ardila, A. (1987). Linguistic abilities in patients with prefrontal damage. *Brain and Language, 30,* 206–225.

Pontius, A. A. (1974). Basis for neurological test of frontal lobe system functioning up to adolescence—A form analysis of action expressed in narratives. *Adolescence, 9,* 221–232.

Pontius, A. A., & Ruttinger, K. F. (1976). Frontal lobe system maturational lag in juvenile delinquents shown in narratives test. *Adolescence, 11,* 509–518.

Pontius, A. A., & Yudowitz, B. S. (1980). Frontal lobe system dysfunction in some criminal actions as shown in the narratives test. *The Journal of Nervous and Mental Disease, 168,* 111–117.

Sbordone, R. J. (1991). *Neuropsychology for the attorney.* Orlando: Paul M. Deutsch Press, Inc.

Stuss, D. T., & Benson, D. F. (1987). The frontal lobes and control of cognition and memory. In E. Perecman (Ed.), *The frontal lobes revisited* (pp. 141–158). New York: The IRBN Press.

Stuss, D. T., & Benson, D. F. (1990). The frontal lobes and language. In E. Goldberg (Ed.), *Contemporary neuropsychology and the legacy of Luria* (pp. 29–50). Hillsdale, NJ: Lawrence Erlbaum Associates.

Teuber, H. L. (1972). Unity and diversity of frontal lobe functions. *ACTA Neurobiologiae Experimentalis, 32,* 615–656.

APPENDIX A

Stories

A. Presented to the subjects
B. Propositions

The Fox and the Goat

A

Once upon a time a fox was running after a hen. But he did not notice the barrel which was dug in the ground and fell into it. The walls of the barrel were very high and he could not get out of it. After having looked around, he noticed a goat standing at the top. Then the fox pretended to drink the water and said it was very good. The goat also wanted some water and jumped into the barrel. That was what the fox waited for; he climbed onto the goat and ran away. And the goat was taken out by a farmer at night.

B

1. A fox was running after the hen.
2. The fox fell into the barrel.
3. The fox could not get out of it.
4. The fox saw a goat.
5. The fox pretended to drink the water.

6. The goat jumped into the barrel.
7. The fox climbed onto the goat.
8. The fox ran away.
9. The goat was taken out by a farmer.

The Gardener and the Bear

A

Once a gardener met a bear in the forest. He had been very frightened at first, but the bear wanted some company and he invited the gardener to have some berries. The gardener also was fed up with his loneliness, so he invited the bear to his home. They got on quite well together. The gardener was working in the garden, and the bear was cooking. The bear, however, liked to catch flies. One day when the gardener was sleeping in the garden, a fly sat on his nose. The bear wanted to kill the fly, but it managed to get away each time. The bear got very angry; he got a big stone and hit the fly with it. Killing the fly, he killed the gardener as well.

B

1. A gardener met a bear in the forest.
2. The bear invited the gardener to have some berries.
3. The gardener invited the bear to his home.
4. They were living together.
5. The bear liked to catch flies.

6. A fly sat on the gardener's nose.
7. The bear wanted to kill it.
8. He hit the fly with a stone.
9. Killing the fly, he killed the gardener, too.

Two Donkeys

A

Two donkeys were carrying heavy bags. One was carrying salt, and the other, sponges. When they came to a river, they decided to cross it. The first to cross was the donkey who carried the salt. After he came out of the water, it turned out that his bags became lighter since the salt had dissolved. The other donkey also wanted to make his load lighter, so he came into the deeper water. But when he came out onto the other bank, his bags turned out to be heavier.

B

1. Two donkeys were carrying the heavy bags.
2. One of them was carrying salt.
3. The other was carrying sponges.
4.   They decided to cross a river.

5. The first was the donkey carrying the salt.
6. His bags became lighter
7. Next was the donkey carrying sponges.
8. He went into the deeper water.
9. His bags became heavier.

APPENDIX B

Pictures

A. Pictures to be described
B. Propositions

A

Figure 1. The birthday party.

B

1. Two women are sitting on a sofa.
2. The women are talking.
3. A boy is standing near the sofa.
4. There is a table in the room.
5. There are cakes, fruits, drinks, and flowers on the table.

6. The guests are sitting around the table.
7. The girls are playing near the table.
8. This is a birthday party.

A

Figure 2. At the dressmaker's.

B

1. There is a sewing machine on the table.
2. There are scissors and some material on the table.
3. The dressmaker is adjusting the girl's coat.
4. The mother is watching them.
5. There is an iron on the ironing board.

6. There is some material there, too.
7. The model is standing near the desk.
8. The girl is looking at herself in the mirror.
9. There is a light over the table.
10. It is the dressmaker's shop.

A

Figure 3. Winter sports.

B

1. Children are playing in the snow.
2. They are sledding.
3. They are skiing.
4. They are skating.
5. One skater has fallen down.
6. One skier has fallen down.
7. The child is making a snowman.

APPENDIX C

Picture Stories

A. Stories to be described
B. Propositions

A

Figure 4. The bad helper.

B

1. The mother tells her son to water the vegetables.
2. The son is watering the vegetables.
3. Some children are playing ball behind the
   fence.
4. The boy has run to his friends.
5. He has left the gate open.
6. Some animals have come into the garden.
7. They are eating the vegetables.

A

Figure 5. Two cats and the sparrow.

B

1. Two cats are playing in the meadow.
2. The bird is sitting on a stump.
3. The cats have noticed it.
4. They have jumped to catch it.

5. They bump each other's head.
6. The sparrow has flown away.
7. The cats were frightened and ran away.
8. The sparrow is back on the stump.

A

Figure 6. The woodcutter and the bears.

B

1. A woodcutter is going to the forest with a saw.
2. He is sawing a tree.
3. He has left the saw stuck in the tree.
4. He has gone to look for help.

5. Two bears have gotten interested in the saw.
6. The bears are sawing the tree.
7. The tree is falling down.
8. The bears are running away.

Chapter 4

Neurobehavioral and Neuroimaging Data in the Medical-Legal Context

Ruben C. Gur
Raquel E. Gur

A question that may confront the legal handling of brain-injured individuals is to what extent behavioral deficits following the injury are related to disturbed brain functioning. To answer such a question it is necessary to understand how behavior is related to the anatomic integrity of brain regions as well as their level of activity. This has been very difficult since there were few techniques, until this past decade, for studying the living human brain.

We are presently undergoing a virtual revolution in neuroimaging technology. This has enabled unprecedented advances in the field of neuropsychology, particularly the study of regional brain function in relation to major behavioral dimensions. This chapter (1) briefly reviews the main neuroimaging techniques pertinent to evaluation of regional brain anatomy and physiologic activity, (2) summarizes major findings pertinent to brain–behavior relations, (3) describes a method we developed for comparing behavioral data with anatomic and physiologic findings, (4) enumerates some current limitations and pitfalls of this growing body of knowledge, and suggests short-term steps required to make them more powerful clinically applicable tools, and (5) raises possible issues that may face psychologists and other professionals when they introduce imaging measures in court.

NEUROIMAGING TECHNIQUES

It is beyond the scope of this chapter to give even a cursory description of the neuroimaging techniques and their clinical applications. Several comprehensive volumes contain such summaries (Phelps, Mazziotta, & Schelbert, 1986; Reivich & Alavi, 1985). Here we can mention the main purpose of each technique and illustrate the kind of information they yield.

Imaging Neuroanatomy

The two major techniques currently available for imaging brain anatomy are computed tomography (CT) and magnetic resonance imaging (MRI). MRI can clearly display with exquisite detail brain structures and many lesions (Fig. 1). If behavioral deficits occur after a brain injury, and a lesion is detectable on CT or MRI, then we can state with considerable confidence that at least some of the behavioral deficits have been caused by destruction of brain tissue.

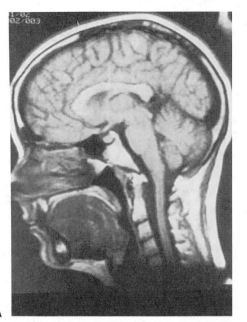 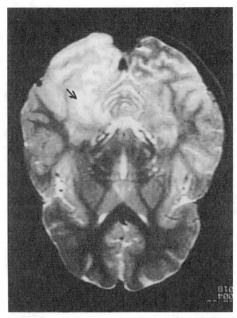

A   B

Figure 1. MRI: *A,* A saggital view of a normal brain. *B,* An axial view of a cerebral infarct.

In many respects MRI is superior to CT, particularly in brain areas near the skull or other bony tissue, where beam hardening effects of bone distort the CT scans. Some lesions can be missed by CT and detected by MRI. In comparison, abnormal signal intensity may occur in MRI scans of normal individuals, since the field still lacks standard scanning procedures and normative data. Very small lesions, or diffuse neuronal loss, such as occurs in Alzheimer's disease, can have deleterious effects on behavior and yet be undetectable by routine clinical reading of either CT or MRI. Computerized techniques for quantitating brain atrophy are currently being pursued, and should prove more sensitive for detection of such tissue loss.

Imaging Neurophysiology

Behavioral deficits can be more extensive than what is attributable to the death of neurons in regions showing anatomic destruction. They can be caused by brain cells that are not dead, but are either insufficiently active or too active. Some grave forms of brain dysfunction are caused by abnormalities in regional brain physiologic activity. For example, epilepsy has severe behavioral manifestations and there is evidence for interictal deficits in cognitive and emotional functioning (Dodrill & Wilkus, 1976). However, CT or MRI scans are frequently uninformative or even normal (Gastaut, 1970).

In the case of epilepsy, abnormalities in regional brain electric activity measurable by electroencephalography (EEG) have been reliably linked to seizure type and location. However, other brain disorders show abnormalities in electric activity that are too diffuse or varied to be of diagnostic value. Following stroke, for example, EEG slowing can be seen but the extent of slowing and its precise frequency and topographic distribution is difficult to assess from routine EEG evaluations. There are now methods of computerized EEG topography that can potentially be more helpful in localizing areas of abnormal brain electric activity. Imaging and quantitative assessment of regional brain physiologic activity is now also feasible with isotopic techniques for measuring regional cerebral blood flow and metabolism.

There are several techniques for generating topographic display of regional EEG measures. Duffy's brain electric activity mapping (BEAM) has received much attention (Duffy, 1986), but others such as Bio-Logic's Brain Atlas (Harner, Jackel, Mawhinney-Hee, & Sussman, 1987) and the technique of John (1977) follow similar principles. They quantify EEG parameters and produce topographic displays of EEG data such as is shown in Figure 2.

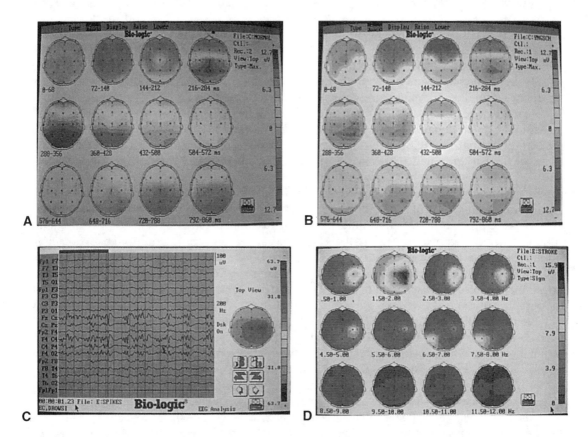

Figure 2. Presented are examples of topographic displays of electrophysiologic data: *A*, Integrated voltages of evoked responses for 12 latency windows following stimulus onset are mapped. In this case averaged evoked response amplitudes to a rare stimulus (oddball P300 paradigm) from a normal subject are shown. Note the posterior maxima in the 288–356 ms latency window. *B*, Similar data to *A*, but obtained from a schizophrenic patient. When compared with the normal subject, note the overall decreased amplitude as well as the right-sided skew the positive potential has, especially at the 288–356 ms latency window. *C*, In another example of a voltage map, the map displays the maxima of a spike obtained from an epileptic, which is indicated by a red cursor on the continuous EEG display. *D*, This display is of EEG that has been subjected to frequency analysis and the 12 integrated spectral bands are plotted topographically. In a patient with a right CVA, maximal amplitudes in the delta range (first three maps) are obvious over the right hemisphere.

Isotopic techniques for imaging neurophysiology make use of the fact that active neurons have metabolic needs for oxygen and glucose, and that cerebral blood flow rates change in response to these needs. Such measures can help identify regions of abnormal physiologic activation associated with behavioral deficits. Furthermore, such measures obtained during the performance of cognitive tasks could help delineate brain regions necessary for regulating cognitive processes.

These isotopic techniques for measuring cerebral metabolism and blood flow can be traced to the pioneering method of Kety and Schmidt (1948) for measuring whole-brain metabolism and blood flow. Their technique used intracarotid injection of nitrous oxide, and measurement of arterial-venous differences in concentration. It yielded accurate and reproducible data on brain metabolism and blood flow. However, this technique is not only limited to providing whole-brain values, but also by its invasiveness.

Safe regional measurements were first made possible by the introduction of the 133-Xenon clearance techniques for measuring regional cerebral blood flow (rCBF). The highly diffusible 133-Xenon can be administered as gas mixed in air or in saline. Its clearance from the brain is measurable by stationary scintillation detectors. The rate of clearance enables considerably accurate quantitation of rCBF in the fast clearing gray matter compartment, as well as calculation of mean flow of gray and white matter. Initial applications used carotid injections (Olesen, Paulson, & Lassen, 1971), which were invasive and only enabled measurements in one hemisphere at a time. Obrist and colleagues reported the 133-Xenon inhalation technique (Obrist, Thompson, Wang,, & Wilkinson, 1975), and presented models for quantifying rCBF with this non-invasive procedure. This technique permits simultaneous measurements from both hemispheres. The number of brain regions that can be measured depends on the number of detectors. Initial studies were performed with up to 16 detectors, eight over each hemisphere, but there are now commercially available systems with 32 detectors and recently a system has been introduced that enables the placement of up to 254 detectors. The quantitative data can be displayed topographically as is shown in Figure 3.

Note that rCBF is typically higher in the front of the brain. This "hyperfrontal" pattern has been observed routinely in normal subjects (Ingvar, 1979). The main limitation of the technique is that it is optimal for measuring rCBF only on the brain surface near the skull, and hence it can be used to study cortical brain regions only.

Positron emission tomography (PET) has made it possible to measure in vivo biochemical and physiologic processes in the human brain, with three-dimensional resolution. Initial work with animals used selectively labeled chemical compounds, called *radioisotopes*, to measure the rate of the biochemical process. This has been extended to humans by principles of CT (Reivich et al., 1979), and now the technique has been adapted to use several radionuclides that decay through the emission of positrons. Subjects are administered radionuclides that are unstable because their nuclei have an excess positive charge. The radionuclides are usually given intra-venously, and are taken up by tissue. Through the emission of a positron they get rid of their energy and undergo the process of annihilation where the positrons interact with a negatively charged electron. The two photons emitted from each annihilation travel in opposite directions while the energy generated is detected and measured by detector arrays. By CT principles, the coincidental counts are used to generate images reflecting the regional rate of radionuclide uptake. This information enables the calculation, depending on the specific radionuclide, of such density-varied physiologic parameters as oxygen and glucose metabolism, blood flow, or receptor density of neurotransmitters. In order to relate this physiologic information to anatomic regions of interest

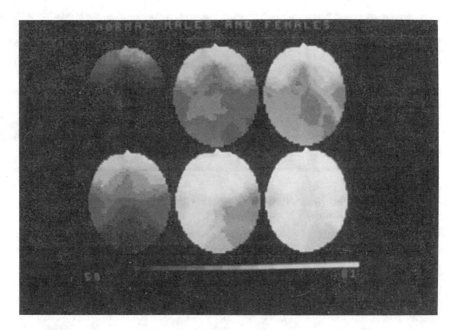

Figure 3. A topographic display of rCBF in a group of normal males (upper row) and females (lower row) during rest (1st column) a verbal analogies task (middle column), and a spatial line orientation task (last column). Note the hyperfrontal pattern at rest, the higher CBF in females, and the increased CBF in the left for the verbal and the right for the spatial task.

(ROI), an atlas of brain anatomy is required. These can be based on computerized images of sliced brains, or on CT or MRI scans. Multiple brain "slices" can be obtained with PET (Fig. 4).

Another technique recently introduced for three-dimensional imaging of rCBF is single photon emission computed tomography (SPECT). The technique enables three-dimensional imaging of CBF using radionuclides that, unlike positron emitters, do not require the availability of a dedicated cyclotron for their production. However, at present, reliable quantitation of rCBF with available radionuclides that can be safely administered is still very problematic, and much more work is required to make it applicable in systematic neurobehavioral research.

REGIONAL BRAIN FUNCTION AND BEHAVIOR

The application of these techniques to the understanding of human behavior is still in its infancy. We are still at the stage of identifying the sensitivity and limitation of some of these methods, and only crude dimensions of behavior have been examined in relation to what they measure. Here we will describe some of the findings and try to outline where this work could lead us.

Several studies have examined the relationship between cognitive dimensions and neuroanatomic data. For example, left hemispheric superiority in language processing has been related

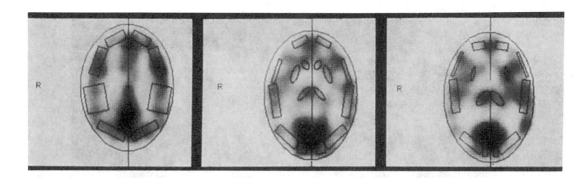

Figure 4. Placement of regions of interest. Reprinted from Gur, R. E., Resnick, S.M., Alavi, A., Gur, R. C., Caroff, S., Dann, R., Silver, F. L., Saykin, A. J., Chawluk, J. B., Kushner, M., & Reivich, M. (1987). Regional brain function in schizophrenia. I. A positron emission tomography study. *Archives of General Psychiatry, 44,* 119–125. With permission. Copyright © 1987, American Medical Association.

to CT evidence for asymmetry in size of language-related structures (see Naeser, 1985 for a review), while performance on cognitive tasks has been correlated with CT measures of atrophy. There seems to be a relationship between the extent and location of anatomic lesions and the severity and pattern of behavioral deficits (Raz, Raz, Yeo, Bigler, & Cullum, 1987). However, there is need for better normative data on control subjects and more precise quantitation of the CT and MRI results. The most widely used technique for obtaining neuroanatomic measures is to trace brain regions on the image and calculate the area using a technique called *planimetry*. A more rigorous method would be to apply segmentation algorithms to the actual data. While such procedures are currently being developed, their reliability and validity has yet to be established.

The physiologic neuroimaging techniques are more suitable for dynamic studies of brain-behavior relations. When applied to normal subjects, reliable patterns of physiologic activity have been observed. For example, as seen in Figure 3, the 133-Xenon technique consistently showed increased rCBF in anterior compared to posterior brain regions, "the hyperfrontal pattern" (Ingvar, 1979). PET shows higher glucose uptake in frontal regions, as well as in the posterior visual (calcarine) cortex (Fig. 4). Repeated measures in the same normal individuals demonstrate excellent reliability for the 133-Xenon technique (Warach, Gur, Gur, Skolnick, Obrist, & Reivich, 1987) and acceptable levels of reliability for PET indices (Gur, Resnick, Gur, Alavi, Caroff, Kushner, & Reivich, 1987). The techniques are sensitive to changes in brain activity produced by sensory stimulation and show specific effects for the visual, auditory, and somatosensory modalities (see Reivich, Gur, & Alavi [1983] and Gur & Reivich [1980] for a review).

The potential of the physiologic neuroimaging techniques for understanding brain-behavior relationships is particularly great because, unlike anatomy, the activity of brain regions is dynamic and changes in neurophysiologic activity have direct effects on behavior. To exploit this potential we need to establish links between regional brain activity and behavioral dimensions. For example, we evaluated whether metabolic activity, as measured by the techniques, shows changes during cognitive functioning. While several studies have answered this question affirmatively (Leli et al., 1982; Risberg & Ingvar, 1973), we decided to test the hypothesis that greater physiologic activation would occur in regions that serve specific cognitive functions. As a consequence we studied a sample of normal right- and left-handed males and females (Gur et al., 1982). Measurements of rCBF were performed with the 133-Xenon inhalation technique at rest, and during the performance of a verbal analogies and a spatial line-orientation task. We chose the verbal task because of evidence that performance of this task is impaired with left hemispheric damage. By contrast, performance on the line-orientation task is impaired with right hemispheric damage (Benton, Hannay, & Varney, 1975). Both tasks in our study reliably increased CBF in both hemispheres, but the increase was hemispherically asymmetric. The verbal task produced greater increase in left hemispheric rCBF whereas the spatial task produced greater increase on the right. The reason we examined left and right-handed males and females is that these dimensions of individual differences (handedness and gender) have been shown to influence the direction and degree of hemispheric cognitive specialization (Levy & Reid, 1976). In our rCBF study (Fig. 5), females had higher rCBF and left-handers differed from right-handers in their pattern of hemispheric activation. This indicated that rCBF measurement is sensitive not only to the effects of cognitive effort on regional brain activity, but also to individual differences known to influence the direction and degree of hemispheric specialization for cognitive function.

Subsequent studies with rCBF and PET have confirmed and extended these findings. In most cases some of the results related to hypotheses that had been generated from earlier observations, but as would be expected from this new technology, some of the results were unforeseen. Yet

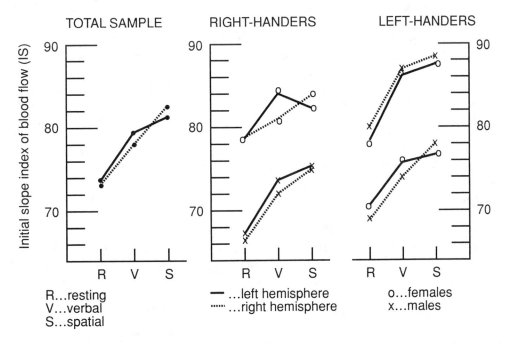

Figure 5. Initial slope (IS) index of blood flow to the left (——) and right (- - -) hemispheres for the total sample and for right- and left-handed females (o) and right- and left-handed males (x) during performance of resting (R), verbal (V), and spatial tasks (S). Reprinted from Gur, R. C., Gur, R. E., Obrist, W. D. et al. (1982). Sex and handedness differences in cerebral blood flow during rest and cognitive activity. *Science, 217*, 659–661. With permission. Copyright © 1982 by the AAAS.

other effects could not have been predicted from earlier theories, but the data helped explain our behavioral observations. For example, a PET study with the same verbal analogies and spatial-line orientation tasks described above showed asymmetric effects in the expected temporo-parietal regions that were implicated by the studies on behavioral sequelae of brain damage. However, a less established hypothesis proposed in 1972 by the British neuropsychologist Colwyn Trevarthen was also supported by the data. Trevarthen suggested that neural activation of lateralized cognitive processes could "spill over" to motor brain regions and produce orientation to the contralateral hemispace (Trevarthen, 1972). Thus, when people have verbal thoughts they would orient themselves to the right and when they have spatial cognitions they would orient themselves to the left. This hypothesis received some confirmation in studies examining the effects of verbal and spatial tasks on the direction of conjugate lateral eye movements while individuals were reflecting on the answers to test items. The PET study showed that the effects of the tasks were asymmetric not only in the temporoparietal regions, but also in regions controlling the orientation response (Gur et al., 1983).

Another behavioral dimension that received additional neurophysiologic corroboration from the new techniques is anxiety. For example, a behavioral "law" traced to the results of an animal study by the American neuropsychologists Yerkes and Dodson in 1908 posits a curvilinear, "inverted-U" relationship between anxiety and performance (Yerkes & Dodson, 1908). Performance is not very good when anxiety is extremely low, since the attentional and arousal components required for optimal performance are missing. At extremely high anxiety, however, performance deteriorates. The brain mechanisms responsible for the operation of this law could not be studied without the availability of the neuroimaging techniques. Initial findings with PET and the 133-Xenon technique have shown that the inverted-U relationship between anxiety and performance is paralleled by changes in cortical metabolism and blood flow. This suggests a neural mechanism that reduces cortical activity during high levels of anxiety, perhaps reflecting a shift toward activation of subcortical regions that play a prominent roll in fight-or-flight situations.

Other PET and 133-Xenon studies have examined regional brain involvement in attention. These studies helped establish, for example, the existence of a network of brain regions that animal neuroanatomic studies (Mesulam, 1981) have implicated in attentional processing. It was found that in humans these regions show greater right hemispheric activation. Further elaboration of attentional processes in relation to regional brain activity was elegantly carried out in a series of studies using PET measures of CBF (Posner, Petersen, Fox, & Raichle, 1988).

These early and preliminary studies seem to point to the possibility that neuroimaging techniques are sufficiently sensitive to detect the association between regional brain activity and behavior. These studies are encouraging and suggest that more systematic research using neuroimaging techniques to test hypotheses and generate new observations on brain-behavior relationships needs to be performed. This can be done by manipulating behavioral dimensions in normal subjects, and examining the effects of such manipulations on regional brain activity.

But how can the neuroimaging techniques be harnessed to understand the neural substrates of abnormal behavior? Initial studies have consisted of obtaining neuroanatomic data with the CT or MRI (Weinberger, Delisi, Perman, Targum, & Wyatt, 1982), while studies have obtained resting measures of rCBF and glucose metabolism (Buchsbaum et al., 1984; Gur et al., 1987a; Gur et al., 1987b).

The neuroanatomic studies suggested increased ventricular volume in schizophrenics, indicating neuronal loss in mesial brain structures (Andreasen et al., 1986; Weinberger, Torrey, Neophytides, & Wyatt, 1979). However, most of these studies used the CT scan, which is not optimal for measuring anatomic loss on the brain surface close to the skull (because of beam hardening effects of bone described above). Another limitation of most of these studies is the use of planimetric measures of surfaces as seen on the scans. As noted above, segmentation of tissue can be done more precisely by algorithms applied to the actual pixel by pixel data. This method was applied by Pfefferbaum et al. (1988), who used a semi-automated computerized approach for volumetric measurements. Diffuse cerebral atrophy distinguished schizophrenics from controls. Sulcal, more than ventricular enlargement, was implicated.

Physiologic studies examining regional brain abnormalities in psychiatric populations have typically used resting conditions. Initial reports suggested diffusely reduced CBF and metabolism in schizophrenia (Mathew, Meyer, Francis, Schoolar, Weinman, & Mortel, 1981; 1982), and evidence for "hypofrontality" (Buchsbaum, Ingvar, Kessler, et al., 1982; Farkas, Wolf, Jaeger, Brodie, Christman, & Fowler, 1984). Few studies have examined both resting and activated conditions. Gur et al. (1983) reported that resting rCBF was normal in medicated schizophrenics, but abnormalities were pronounced in the asymmetry of activation for the verbal analogies and the spatial line-orientation tasks. Schizophrenics failed to show the normal left hemispheric activation for the verbal task and showed a "paradoxical" left hemispheric activation for the spatial task. This supported Gur's (1979) hypothesis, based on behavioral studies, that schizophrenia is associated with left hemispheric dysfunction and overactivation of the left, dysfunctional hemisphere. Further support for the hypothesis was obtained in a sample of unmedicated schizophrenics (Gur et al., 1985a). In this group, resting CBF showed greater left hemispheric values, while abnormal activation of the left hemisphere was associated with increased symptom severity.

There have been other studies in schizophrenia as well as other psychiatric disorders such as depression, obsessive-compulsive disorders, and anxiety disorders. Such studies could improve diagnostic accuracy and may help identify patterns of abnormal activation in specific forms of psychopathology. A potentially productive strategy for such studies will be to a identify the regional abnormalities in brain anatomy and physiologic activity associated with focal and nonfocal brain disease, and relate the abnormal pattern to behavioral impairment. It is noteworthy that at this time it is not possible to examine a set of MRI, CT, PET, and rCBF data and arrive at a diagnosis of any psychiatric disease. Some neurologic diseases can be diagnosed with the help of CT and MRI (e.g., multiple sclerosis, brain tumors, stroke), but PET and 133-Xenon techniques have not yet been established as clinical diagnostic procedures.

A METHOD FOR INTEGRATING BEHAVIORAL AND NEUROIMAGING DATA

A key issue for future work centers is the integration of multifaceted data on regional brain function. In addition to the anatomic information on the integrity of brain regions, such as is now available from CT and from MRI scans, the PET and 133-Xenon techniques provide information on regional brain physiologic activity, while topographic EEG techniques complement our armamentarium of data on regional brain function with information on the electric activity of the brain. Imaging technology provides means for integrating such multifaceted data in a comprehensible manner, but a theoretical framework is needed to guide our understanding of how the activity of the brain is related to behavior. Thus the challenge is to integrate behavioral theories on regional brain function with anatomic and physiologic neuroimaging data.

Theories on brain regulation of human behavior have been tested in clinical populations by correlating behavioral deficits with clinical signs and postmortem findings. Neuropsychological testing in patients with brain disease provides measures of specific behavioral functions (e.g. memory, learning, praxis). In the process of formulating theories on brain regulation of behavior, the pattern of scores is used to test hypotheses on regional brain involvement for specific behavioral dimensions. The pattern of deficits is used in clinical practice to implicate brain regions putatively affected by a disease (Gur et al., 1985b; Gur, Saykin, Blonder, & Gur, 1988a; Gur, Trivedi, Saykin, & Gur, 1988b).

The process of testing neurobehavioral theories can be helped by quantification of theoretical statements concerning regional brain involvement in the regulation of behavioral dimensions. We have proposed an algorithm that applies such a quantification to standard neuropsychological test scores (Trivedi & Gur, 1986; 1989). The algorithm yields a value for each brain region, which reflects expectations that it is neurally compromised given the pattern of neuropsychological scores. These regional values can be examined statistically to test the behavioral hypotheses against clinical data and other neuroimaging data. They can also be presented topographically using standard procedures for translating numbers into a gray scale or a color scale. This can facilitate comprehension of the spatial distribution of implicated regions. Initial testing of the algorithm in clinical cases and populations was encouraging (Gur et al., 1988a; 1988b). There was consistency between the "behavioral images" and the location of lesion in patients with unilateral cerebral infarcts (Fig. 6).

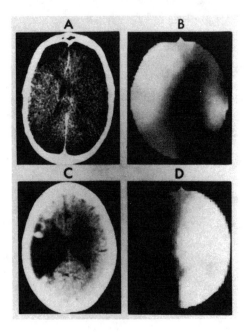

Figure 6. CT scans and corresponding behavioral images of two patients with cerebral infarcts, one in the right hemisphere (A and B for CT and behavioral image, respectively) and one in the left (C and D). The CT scans were reversed so that the left hemisphere is to the viewer's left. Reprinted from Gur, R. C., Trivedi, S. S., Saykin, A. J., & Gur, R. E. (1988). "Behavioral imaging"—A procedure for analysis and display of neuropsychological test scores: I. Construction of algorithm and initial clinical evaluation. *Neuropsychiatry, Neuropsychology, and Behavioral Neurology, 1,* 53–60. With permission.

The topographic displays showed correspondence with clinical and CT data, and were congruent with the clinical interpretation of the neuropsychological data. Note that in both cases the behavioral image suggested that regions considerably larger than the CT lesion were behaviorally "hypofunctional," including a contralaterally homotopic region. This was not detected by the clinical evaluation, and may reflect inadequacy in the "spatial resolution" of the behavioral images. However, it could also be a true behavioral manifestation of remote physiologic effects of focal lesions. As noted above, areas larger than the anatomic lesions have shown metabolic suppression in PET studies of local cerebral glucose metabolism using the 18-F-FDG technique (Kuhl et al., 1980; Kushner et al., 1984) and in studies of regional cerebral blood flow using the 133-Xenon clearance technique (Gur et al., 1987c). By comparing behavioral images with PET and CT scans it would be possible to evaluate which behavioral effects are accompanied by remote physiologic suppressions.

PRESENT LIMITATIONS AND FUTURE STEPS

The impact of neuroimaging technology is still only beginning to emerge. The techniques are still in the process of evolution toward optimal resolution and scanning procedures. Normative data are lacking, and only rudimentary steps were taken to identify neural networks regulating human behavior. Although already several brain diseases can be reliably detected by neuroimaging, the diagnostic utility of the techniques for the vast majority of neurologic and for all psychiatric diseases has not yet been established. It is already clear that no one technique will provide all the answers. Each has its relative advantages and limitations and yields data that are complementary but overlapping only in part. What are some immediate steps to advance our ability to harness this technology in the service of improved diagnosis and treatment?

Populations with behavioral deficits should be studied. Applying these techniques to patients with destructive brain lesions, such as are produced by stroke, head trauma, or brain tumors, could help in determining the extent and topographic distribution of anatomic brain damage and abnormal (suppressed or abnormally increased) metabolic activity. There is considerable evidence that metabolism is suppressed even in regions that appear anatomically intact when evaluated by techniques for assessing regional brain anatomy, such as CT scans and MRI. This could explain why so frequently patients show behavioral deficits that are more pervasive than what can be explained by regions of anatomic involvement. For example, when we applied the 133-Xenon technique to patients with unilateral stroke, we found that the extent of physiologic suppression was largest when right hemispheric stroke patients were performing a spatial task and, conversely, when left hemispheric stroke patients were engaged in a verbal task.

Other clinical populations of particular interest include Parkinson's disease and Alzheimer's disease. There is strong evidence that dopamine deficiency is responsible for the symptoms of the former, and some suggestions for the involvement of another neurotransmitter (cholinergic) system in the latter. The PET scan will enable imaging of the distribution of neurotransmitters, while studying the topographic distribution of metabolic abnormalities in these disorders could help understand how these neurotransmitter systems regulate behavior.

A complementary approach would begin with disorders of behavior where the brain pathology is unclear, where metabolic studies could help identify regional brain involvement. For example, reading disability and other learning disabilities could be studied, to test hypotheses on regional brain dysfunction that underlie these disorders. Understanding of psychiatric disorders could similarly be enhanced by techniques for measuring regional brain activity. In both psychiatric and neurologic populations it would be particularly informative to measure the physiologic activity not only at rest, but also while patients are engaged in pertinent cognitive behavior.

But looking at pathology and deficits is only one side of the coin. Normal individuals vary considerably in behavior and abilities, and studying the relation between this variability and regional brain physiology may shed light on the neural underpinnings of this variability. For example, exceptionally talented individuals in the sciences, art, and humanities could be evaluated. Again, this should be done at rest and during behavioral "challenged" procedures. How does regional brain activity of a mathematician differ from that of an architect? Which brain regions does a mathematician activate when attempting to develop a calculus for a particular problem? Which brain regions does a lawyer activate when preparing or presenting a case? Could we train individuals to activate appropriate brain regions and thereby enhance their abilities? The technology permits us to begin answering such questions.

Thus far the cognitive dimension has received the greatest attention, particularly in the examination of verbal and spatial tasks in relation to hemispheric activation. But emotional, conative, or motivational factors could also be studied with these techniques. Such studies could be informative in understanding regional brain involvement in the regulation of behavior and of considerable relevance to the diagnosis and treatment of dysfunction.

IMPLICATIONS FOR LEGAL PRACTICES

Given the focus of this book, it would be appropriate to speculate on how these techniques can be used to help within a medical-legal context. For example, if the issue is whether impaired behavior is the result of brain injury, evidence can be obtained from experts reviewing neurologic, psychiatric, and neuropsychologic data. In addition, CT and MRI scans may show the area of anatomic destruction. However, there are a variety of severe behavioral aberrations that are not produced by anatomic lesions, but may instead reflect metabolic abnormalities. In epilepsy, for example, seizures may occur in the absence of a lesion detectable by a CT scan. The abnormality, however, may be seen clearly in EEG and PET studies. Similarly, in the case of closed head injury, the CT lesion as seen on the CT scan may be much smaller than the area of metabolic suppression. Studies with PET or the (much more affordable) 133-Xenon inhalation technique for measuring rCBF typically will show the area of metabolic suppression. Regional reduction in brain activity may also be seen in computed EEG topography. The relation between the behavioral deficits and regional brain function can be established with neuropsychological testing. This can be particularly helpful when used in conjunction with the "behavioral imaging" techniques described above.

In the case of a patient who had suffered a closed head injury, these techniques were helpful in detecting regional deficit when test scores alone were unremarkable. This patient was a bright young man, college undergraduate, who complained of loss of concentration and memory. His test scores were all in the normal range, but for many of the tests the norms were inadequate for this highly educated individual. The "behavioral image" revealed a circumscribed area of brain deficit that corresponded to the area implicated by other evidence (Fig. 7).

Neuroimaging methods may also help evaluate the effectiveness and progress of a rehabilitation program. If a patient's memory deficit can be linked, for example, to suppression of neural

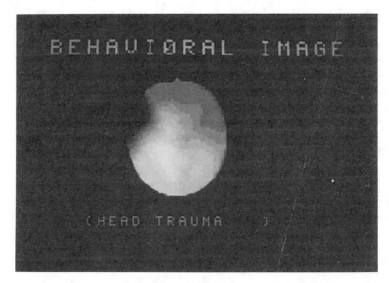

Figure 7. A behavioral image obtained from a patient with a
closed head injury.

activity in the temporal lobe, physiologic activation studies can show whether improved
memory is associated with improved tissue responsiveness to task demands.

Neuroimaging methods can also help settle questions of the accuracy of a particular psychiatric diagnosis arising, for example, in pleas of insanity. Although no specific pattern of physiologic disturbance has been established for schizophrenia, some specific patterns are emerging
(Gur, 1987). When such diagnostic markers are established, the determination of insanity will be
made on the basis of more objective data than is possible today.

Concerning the neurobehavioral evaluations, since many times individuals undergoing
neuropsychologic testing or a neuropsychiatric evaluation as part of court proceedings are
motivated to "fake bad," methods such as "behavioral imaging" could help determine whether
there is some regional coherence to the pattern of deficits. Another advantage of "behavioral
imaging" is the reduced need to rely entirely on experts who were hired by one of the parties.
Even without willful dishonesty, an expert's opinion can be influenced by the side that called for
the testimony. The theoretical weights used in the "behavioral imaging" algorithm can be supplied in advance of examining any particular case, since they can be obtained from remote and
well-established experts, while the computer does the rest since its impartiality could not be
questioned.

In dealing with expert testimony based on neuroimaging data, we believe a lawyer would do
best to rely on experts who do active research in the field. The technology is advancing fast. It is
"flashy" and hence appeals to charlatans, and level-headed appraisals are more likely to come
from someone close to the cutting edge of research, which exposes (on a daily basis) not only the
advantages but also the limitations of this technology. As indicated above, at present there is no
established pattern of abnormalities detectable by neuroimaging that is specific for any psychiatric disorder. While an expert witness may argue that a particular set of scans indicates that an
individual is schizophrenic, the reliability and validity of the evidence should be carefully
scrutinized.

SUMMARY

Despite their current shortcomings and limitations, neuroimaging techniques are already helpful in many clinical situations and their increased use in court is inevitable. We hope that this chapter, despite its brevity and lack of relative technical detail has nevertheless helped explain current neuroimaging techniques and what they measure. The preliminary applications for understanding brain-behavior relationships are presently being extended in an increasing number of research centers. As this technology becomes more available, advances will become more rapid. There are several specific steps that are needed for establishing the utility of neuroimaging in diagnosis and treatment of brain pathology, and these were outlined. The behavioral side of the equation has been particularly resistant to valiant attempts at objective quantitation, while the "behavioral imaging" algorithm was presented as a step toward addressing this problem. Finally, we addressed some issues on the applications of neuroimaging in court.

REFERENCES

Andreasen, N. C., Nasrallah, H. A., Dunn, V., Olson, S. C., Grove, W. M., Ehrhard, J. C., Coffman, J. A., & Crossett, J. H. (1986). Structural abnormalities in the frontal system in schizophrenia: A magnetic resonance imaging study. *Archives of General Psychiatry, 43,* 136–144.

Benton, A. L., Hannay, H. J., & Varney, N. R. (1975). Visual perception of line direction in patients with unilateral brain disease. *Neurology, 25,* 907–910.

Buchsbaum, M. S., Delisi, L. E., Holcomb, H. H., Cappelletti, J., King, A. C., Johnson, J., Hazlett, E., Dowling-Zimmerman, S., Post, R. M., Morihisa, J., Carpenter, W, Cohen, R, Pickar, D., Weinberger, D. R., Margolin, J., & Kessler, R. M. (1984). Anteroposterior gradients in cerebral glucose use in schizophrenia and affective disorder. *Archives of General Psychiatry, 41,* 1159–1166.

Buchsbaum, M. S., Ingvar, D. H., Kessler, R., Waters, R. N., Cappelletti, J., van Kammen, D. P., King, A. C., Johnson, J. L., Manning, R. G., Flynn, R. W., Mann, L. S., Bunney, W. E., Jr., & Sokoloff, L. (1982). Cerebral glucography with positron tomography. *Archives of General Psychiatry, 39,* 251–259.

Dodrill, C. B., & Wilkus, R. J. (1976). Relationships between intelligence and electroencephalographic epileptiform activity in adult epileptics. *Neurology, 26,* 525–531.

Duffy, E. H. (Ed.). (1986). Topographic mapping of brain electrical activity. Boston: Buttersworth.

Farkas, T., Wolf, A. P., Jaeger, J., Brodie, J.D., Christman, D. R., & Fowler, J. S. (1984). Regional brain glucose metabolism in chronic schizophrenia. *Archives of General Psychiatry, 41,* 293–300.

Gastaut, H. (1970). Clinical and electroencephalographic classification of epileptic seizure. *Epilepsia,11,* 102–113.

Gur, R. E. (1979). Cognitive concomitants of hemispheric dysfunction in schizophrenia. *Archives of General Psychiatry, 36,* 269–274.

Gur, R. E. (1987). Psychiatric disorders as brain dysfunction. *National Forum, 67,* 29–32.

Gur, R. C., Gur, R. E., Obrist, W. D., Hungerbuhler, J. P., Younkin, D., Rosen, A. D., Skolnick, B. E., & Reivich, M. (1982). Sex and handedness differences in cerebral blood flow during rest and cognitive activity. *Science, 217,* 659–661.

Gur, R. C., Gur, R. E., Rosen, A. D., Warach, S., Alavi, A., Greenberg, J., & Reivich, M. (1983). A cognitive-motor network demonstrated by positron emission tomography. *Neuropsychologia, 21,* 601–606.

Gur, R. C., Gur, R. E., Silver, F. L., Obrist, W. D., Skolnick, B. E., Kushner, M., Hurtig, H. I., & Reivich, M. (1987). Regional cerebral blood flow in stroke: Hemispheric effects of cognitive activity. *Stroke, 18,* 776–780.

Gur, R. E., Gur, R. C., Skolnick, B. E., Caroff, S., Obrist, W. D., Resnick, S., & Reivich, M. (1985a). Brain function in psychiatric disorders: III. Regional cerebral blood flow in unmedicated schizophrenics. *Archives of General Psychiatry, 42,* 329–334.

Gur, R. C., & Reivich, M. (1980). Cognitive task effects on hemispheric blood flow in humans. *Brain and Language, 9,* 78–93.

Gur, R. E., Resnick, S. M., Alavi, A., Gur, R. C., Caroff, S., Dann, R., Silver, F. L., Saykin, A. J., Chawluk, J. B., Kushner, M., & Reivich, M. (1987a). Regional brain function in schizophrenia. I. A positron emission tomography study. *Archives of General Psychiatry, 44,* 119–125.

Gur, R. E., Resnick, S. M., Gur, R. C., Alavi, A., Caroff, S., Kushner, M., & Reivich, M. (1987b). Regional brain function in schizophrenia. II. Repeated evaluation with positron emission tomography. *Archives of General Psychiatry, 44,* 126–129.

Gur, R. C., Saykin, A. J., Blonder, L. X., & Gur, R. E. (1988a). "Behavioral imaging": II. Application of the quantitative algorithm to hypothesis testing in a population of hemiparkinsonian patients. *Neuropsychiatry, Neuropsychology, and Behavioral Neurology, 1,* 87–96.

Gur, R. E., Skolnick, B. E., Gur, R. C., Caroff, S., Rieger, W., Obrist, W. D., Younkin, D., & Reivich, M. (1983). Brain function in psychiatric disorders: I. Regional cerebral blood flow in medicated schizophrenics. *Archives of General Psychiatry, 40,* 1250–1254.

Gur, R. C., Trivedi, S. S., Saykin, A. J., & Gur, R. E. (1988b). "Behavioral imaging"—a procedure for analysis and display of neuropsychological test scores: I. Construction of algorithm and initial clinical evaluation. *Neuropsychiatry, Neuropsychology, and Behavioral Neurology, 1,* 53–60.

Gur, R. C., Trivedi, S. S., Saykin, A. J., Resnick, S. M., Malamut, B. L., & Gur, R. E. (1985b). Behavioral imaging. *Journal of Clinical and Experimental Neuropsychology, 7,* 633.

Harner, R. N., Jackel, R. A., Mawhinney-Hee, M. R., & Sussman, N. M. (1987). Computed EEG topography in epilepsy. *Revue Neurologique (Paris), 143,* 457–461.

Ingvar, D. H. (1979). "Hyperfrontal" distribution of the cerebral matter flow in resting wakefulness: On the functional anatomy of the conscious state. *Acta Neurologia Scandinavica, 60,* 12–25.

John, E. R. (1977). *Neurometrics: Clinical applications of quantitative electrophysiology.* Hillsdale, NJ: Erlbaum Associates.

Kety, S. S., & Schmidt, C. F. (1948). The nitrous oxide method for the quantitative determination of cerebral blood flow in man: Theory, procedure and normal values. *Journal of Clinical Investigation, 27,* 476–483.

Kuhl, D. E., Phelps, M. E., Kowell, A. P., Metter, E. J., Selin, C., & Winter, J. (1980). Effects of stroke on local cerebral metabolism and perfusion: Mapping by emission computed tomography of 18 FDG and 13 NH3. *Annals of Neurology, 8,* 47–60.

Kushner, M., Alavi, A., Reivich, M., Dann, R., Burke, A., & Robinson, G. (1984). Contralateral cerebellar hypometabolism following cerebral insult: A positron emission tomographic study. *Annals of Neurology, 15,* 425–434.

Leli, D. A., Hannay, H. G., Falgout, J. C., Wilson, E. M., Wills, E. L., Katholi, C. R., & Halsey, J. H., Jr. (1982). Focal changes in cerebral blood flow produced by a test of right-left discrimination. *Brain and Cognition, 1,* 206–223.

Levy, J., & Reid, M. (1976). Variations in writing posture and cerebral organization. *Science, 194,* 337.

Mathew, R. J., Duncan, G. C., Weinman, M. L., & Barr, D. L. (1982). Regional cerebral blood flow in schizophrenia. *Archives of General Psychiatry, 39,* 1121–1124.

Mathew, R. J., Meyer, J. S., Francis, D. J., Schoolar, J. C., Weinman, M., & Mortel, K. F. (1981). Regional cerebral blood flow in schizophrenia: A preliminary report. *American Journal of Psychiatry, 138,* 112–113.

Mesulam, M. M. (1981). A cortical network for directed attention and unilateral neglect. *Annals of Neurology, 10,* 209–325.

Naeser, M. (1985). Quantitative approaches to computerized tomography in behavioral neurology. In M.M. Mesulam (Ed.). *Principles of behavioral neurology* (pp. 363–383). Philadelphia: F.A. Davis.

Obrist, W. D., Thompson, H. K., Wang, H. S., & Wilkinson, W. E. (1975). Regional cerebral blood flow estimated by 133-Xenon inhalation. *Stroke, 6,* 245–256.

Olesen, J., Paulson, O. B., & Lassen, N. A. (1971). Regional cerebral blood flow in man determined by the initial slope of the clearance of intra-arterially injected 133Xe. *Stroke, 2,* 519–540.

Pfefferbaum, A., Zipursky, R. B., Lim, K. O., Zatz, L. M., Stahl, S. M., & Jernigan, T. L. (1988). Computed tomographic evidence for generalized sulcal and ventricular enlargement in schizophrenia. *Archives of General Psychiatry, 45,* 633–640.

Phelps, M., Mazziotta, J. C., & Schelbert, H. R. (Eds.). (1986). *Positron emission tomography and autoradiography: Principles and applications for the brain and heart.* New York: Raven Press.

Posner, M. I., Petersen, S. E., Fox, P. T., & Raichle, M. E. (1988). Localization of cognitive operations in the human brain. *Science, 240,* 1627–1631.

Raz, N., Raz, S., Yeo, R. A., Bigler, E. D., & Cullum, C. M. (1987). Relationship between cognitive and morphological asymmetries in Alzheimer's dementia: A CT study. *International Journal of Neuroscience, 35,* 235–243.

Reivich, M., & Alavi, A. (Eds.). (1985). *Positron emission tomography.* New York: A.R. Liss.

Reivich, M., Gur, R. C., & Alavi, A. (1983). Positron emission tomography studies of sensory stimuli, cognitive processes, and anxiety. *Human Neurobiology, 2,* 25–33.

Reivich, M., Kuhl, D., Wolf, A. P., Greenberg, J., Phelps, M., Ido, T., CAsella, V., Fowler, J., Hoffman, E., Alavi, A., Som, P., & Sokoloff, L. (1979). The 18-F-fluorodeoxyglucose method for the measurement of local cerebral glucose utilization in man. *Circulation Research, 44,* 127–137.

Risberg, J., & Ingvar, D. H. (1973). Patterns of activation in the grey matter of the dominant hemisphere during memorizing and reasoning. *Brain, 96,* 737–756.

Trevarthen, C. (1972). Brain bisymmetry and the role of the corpus callosum in behavior and conscious experience. In J. Cernacvek & F. Podivinsky (Eds.), *Cerebral interhemispheric relations.* Bratislava: Publishing House Solvak Academy Sciences.

Trivedi, S. S., & Gur, R. C. (1986). Computer graphics for neuropsychological data. *National Computer Graphics Association:Technical Sessions Proceedings, 3,* 185–192.

Trivedi, S. S., & Gur, R. C. (1989). Topographic mapping of cerebral blood flow and behavior. *Computer Biology and Medicine 19,* 219–229.

Warach, A., Gur, R. C., Gur, R. E., Skolnick, B. E., Obrist, W. D., & Reivich, M. (1987). The reproducibility of the Xe-133 inhalation technique in resting studies: Task order and sex related effects in healthy young adults. *Journal of Cerebral Blood Flow Metabolism, 7,* 702–708.

Weinberger, D. R., Delisi, L. E., Perman, G. P., Targum, S., & Wyatt, R. J. (1982). Computed tomography in schizophreniform disorder and other acute psychiatric disorders. *Archives of General Psychiatry, 39,* 778–783.

Weinberger, D. R., Torrey, E. F., Neophytides, A. N., & Wyatt, R. J. (1979). Structural abnormalities in the cerebral cortex of chronic schizophrenic patients. *Archives of General Psychiatry, 36,* 935–939.

Yerkes, R. M., & Dodson, J. D. (1908). The relation of strength of stimulus to rapidity of habit-formation. *Journal of Comparative Neurology and Psychology, 18,* 458–482.

Chapter 5

Epileptic-Related Executive Dysfunction and Violent Crime

Robert J. Sbordone

Epilepsy has often been used as a possible medicolegal defense against violent crimes since it is not uncommon for the accused person to plead that he or she has no recollection of the criminal act of violence, and that the offense with which the accused is charged was committed in a state of automatism (a condition of impaired awareness in which an individual may perform an act, or series of complex acts often followed by complete amnesia for such acts, or partially imprecise recollection). Since the phenomenon of automatism occurs in epilepsy, there has been much interest in epilepsy as a possible medical defense against violent crimes (Gunn & Fenton, 1971).

Historically, this interest dates back to Lombroso (1911), who argued that there were three major types of criminals: the insane criminal, the born criminal, and the epileptic criminal, and that all three types of criminals stemmed from an "epileptoid base." Maudsley (1873), a prominent psychiatrist of his time, emphasized that epilepsy played an important role in aggressive crimes, such as homicide, suicide, and arson, since they were committed in such a "blind fury" that an epileptic process should be considered. He remarked, for example, "if it [the deed] has been done with great violence, without indication of premeditation, without apparent motive, and without secrecy, and if the accused person is discovered to be the victim of epilepsy, it is possible that it has been done in a paroxysm following an epileptic fit." East (1927), another prominent forensic psychiatrist, devoted an entire chapter in his textbook that emphasized the importance of examining for a previous history of epilepsy in cases involving violent crimes, and pointed out that the violent act should be a caricature of normal behavior and that amnesia for the violent act should usually be present. The relationship between epilepsy and violent behavior received further support when Hill and Pond (1952) reported that many murderers had abnormal electroencephalograms (EEG) and that a total of 18 out of 105 murderers were found to have epilepsy.

Further support for this relationship appeared in 1966 when Grinker and Sahs, in a major textbook in neurology, stated that during an epileptic attack, the patient is "likely to walk about, unbutton his clothes, expose himself, urinate, or commit acts of violence." Kolb (1968), in a major textbook of psychiatry, further strengthened this relationship by stating that "acts of violence may be committed in these automatisms and may be of a strikingly brutal nature, the patient pursuing his crime to a most revolting extreme." Mark and Ervin (1970) wrote a textbook on this issue, *Violence in the Brain*, which postulated a relationship between an abnormal brain activity, particularly in patients with psychomotor epilepsy, and violence. They also reported cases in which surgical destruction of certain areas of the limbic system would often result in a cessation or reduction of violence. Their book served as the impetus for Crichton's (1972) science fiction novel, *The Terminal Man,* which described a man with psychomotor epilepsy who frequently became violent at a moment's notice. This trend has continued in that a more recent psychiatric text by Kolb and Brodie (1982) stressed that psychomotor epilepsy was associated with aggressive acts of violence.

This chapter critically examines the relationship between epilepsy and violent behavior. It reviews both published clinical reports and controlled research studies, as well as examines some of the medicolegal issues confronting forensic experts and attorneys.

EPILEPSY

Epilepsy can simply be defined as a group of central nervous system disorders that result in recurrent seizures arising from disturbed electrical activity within the brain. Seizures can take a variety of different forms including episodes of disturbed movement, sensation, perception, and behavior, and frequently are accompanied by an alteration of consciousness (Trimble & Thompson, 1986). It has been estimated that at least 2 percent of the population of the United States suffers from some form of epilepsy. The onset of epilepsy, regardless of its etiology, tends to occur relatively early in life. For example, 77 percent of patients who are diagnosed as having epilepsy will have their first attack prior to the end of adolescence (Epilepsy Foundation of America, 1975).

Epilepsy can be divided into idiopathic and symptomatic categories. In the former, some form of inherited mechanism is believed to result in a propensity for low seizure thresholds. In the latter category, the etiology of the seizures are usually clearly defined and typically include such phenomena as tumors, intracranial infection, vascular lesions, head trauma, and anoxia. Seizures can generally be characterized into either partial or generalized (Gastaut, 1970). Partial seizures can be further broken down into seizures into which there is no impairment of consciousness (partial seizures with elementary symptomatology) and seizures generally accompanied by alterations of consciousness (partial seizures with complex symptomatology). In general, focal sensory and/or focal motor seizures fall under the former, while psychomotor attacks or temporal lobe seizures fall under the latter category (Dodrill, 1981). Patients with partial complex seizures typically present with a variety of experiences including hallucinations, affective disturbance, thought disturbances, and are typically complex in their manifestations. More importantly, however, such episodes are typically accompanied by the patient's inability to respond to situations in a purposeful and meaningful fashion. In this sense, executive-related deficits are always present when experiencing seizures.

Generalized seizures involve the entire brain and are accompanied by loss of consciousness or transient lapses of consciousness, which may be so slight as to be barely noticed by onlookers. Included within the category of generalized seizures are myoclonic seizures, infantile spasms, clonic seizures, tonic attacks, and tonic clonic seizures (often referred to as *grand mal epilepsy*), atonic seizures, and akinetic attacks. All epileptic seizures regardless of their type have in common their relatively sudden onset and origin in the brain. The complex and multifaceted aspects of seizure disorders have resulted in an appreciation of the heterogeneous rather than homogeneous aspects of epilepsy, and have caused many investigators to view epilepsy as a family of disorders, rather than as a single entity (Dodrill, 1981).

Typically, the diagnosis of seizure disorder is clinically determined, based on either observing a seizure or identifying as a seizure an episode reported by the patient or other observers. Since impairment of consciousness or a paroxysmal disturbance of the central nervous system can be produced by a variety of causes, such as vasovagal syncopal episodes, cardiac arrhythmias, transient ischemic episodes, migraine headaches, hypoglycemia, and behavioral disorders, it is important that the patient undergoes a careful neurologic examination and EEG. This is particularly important for patients who present with a history of only one episode of paroxysmal behavior disturbance, since it not uncommon for an isolated seizure to occur in response to stressors, such as sleep deprivation, fasting, or drug or alcohol withdrawal. If there is no evidence of neurologic disease, and these latter factors are present, and no epileptiform activity is seen on the EEG, then a diagnosis of epilepsy would not be appropriate (Ehle & Homan, 1980). However, when abnormal electrical patterns, which have been termed *epileptiform discharges*, are seen on the EEG in patients who have a positive clinical history, the diagnosis of epilepsy is typically made.

The difficulty with this diagnostic process is that the EEG is a relatively crude neurophysiologic tool (Kligman & Goldberg, 1975), and in a significant number of cases epileptogenic activity of subcortical structures may not be reflected in the EEG taken from scalp electrodes, since the EEG is handicapped by being unable to detect electrical potentials only a few millimeters from the most superficial layers of the cortex. To complicate matters further, the EEG recordings are made through the relatively thick insulating tissues of the head. An additional difficulty is that the EEG recordings usually last 30 minutes or less, and thus sample only a relatively small portion of the electrical activity of the brain (Dodrill, 1981). As a consequence, a number of individuals who are known to have seizure disorders on the basis of their history, often do not demonstrate a pattern of epileptiform discharges on their EEG.

PERSONALITY CHARACTERISTICS
OF EPILEPTICS

Bear, Levin, Blumer, Chetham, and Ryder (1982) compared the interictal behavior of hospitalized temporal lobe epileptics with patients suffering idiopathic psychiatric syndromes or other forms of epilepsy. They reported that when patients with temporal lobe epilepsy (TLE) were compared to patients with psychiatric disorders, patients with TLE exhibited a significantly greater frequency of excessive interpersonal clinging (viscosity), repetitive preoccupation with peripheral details (circumstantiality), religious and philosophical preoccupations, humorless sobriety, a tendency toward paranoid overinterpretation, and moralistic concerns. When TLE patients were contrasted with character disorders (e.g., sociopaths), the TLE patients were much more likely to accept responsibility for their violent outbursts and did not rely on the claim of amnesia or irresistible impulse. They also found that, while religious and moral concerns were prominent in TLE patients, they were only infrequently observed in patients with character disorders. In contrast to patients with affective disorders, TLE patients exhibited a significantly higher incidence of aberrant humor, circumstantiality, viscosity, paranoia, and religiosity. When TLE patients were contrasted with schizophrenics, viscosity was found to be the most single distinctive feature among the TLE group. In addition, they found that TLE patients exhibited a marked tendency to prolonged interpersonal contact with the interviewer, which contrasted markedly with the social awkwardness of schizophrenic patients. In addition, the TLE patients exhibited a propensity to write extensively (hypergraphia), which was rarely seen among schizophrenic patients. While alterations in sexual behavior occurred in both groups, TLE patients exhibited a decreased intensity of all sexual interests including self-stimulation and fantasy in comparison to the schizophrenic patients. In comparison to other epileptic groups, TLE patients exhibited a significantly higher level of religiosity and philosophical interest as well as deepened affect.

Dodrill and Batzel (1986) reviewed the research literature on this topic and concluded that the investigations of Bear and his associates (1982) were not objectively made and that some of the characteristics ascribed to TLE patients would be difficult to objectively demonstrate, which in turn made validation difficult even under the best possible circumstances. Dodrill and Batzel (1986) also reported that variables, such as the number of seizure types and history of psychiatric illness, tended to be ignored in many of these studies.

EPILEPSY AND VIOLENCE

It has been well recognized that patients with seizures often manifest irritable and aggressive behavior for a few hours or up to several days prior to having a seizure. This behavior often is alleviated after the patient has a seizure. Many family members and significant others, who bear the brunt of the patient's aggressive outbursts, will often report a relationship between seizures and aggressive behavior. For some patients the irritable, aggressive, and even explosive behavior may persist for long periods of time with or without a seizure, and produce a pattern of aggressive behavior that may require psychiatric intervention or incarceration.

A number of studies have reported an increased prevalence of violent and aggressive behavior in patients with epilepsy. For example, James (1960) examined adults with intractable TLE who had later undergone temporal lobectomies. He found that 20 of the 72 patients examined had a significant history of aggression. Serafetinides (1965) found that 36 out of 100 of these patients had a history of aggressive behavior. Thus, taken together, these investigators found that approximately one-third of these epileptic patients had a history of violence and aggressive behavior. However, they also found that the aggression was most likely to occur in males who had their first seizure prior to age 10 and in patients with low intelligence who required institutionalization. Rodin (1973) examined 700 unselected, noninstitutionalized epileptics and found that 4.8 percent were regarded as "destructive-assaultive." The majority, however, of this latter group appeared to be individuals with low average intelligence, poor employment records, and showed more evidence of organic brain disease on neurologic examination.

Ictal Violence

Because epilepsy has frequently been used as a justification for the diminished capacity and insanity defenses in crimes of violence, it is important to review the literature to determine whether violence or aggressive acts can occur during an epileptic seizure. Treiman and Delgado-Escueta (1983) reviewed 29 cases reported in the medical literature from 1972 through 1981 in which violent events were reported to be due to a seizure. They found that in only three of these cases was there evidence strongly suggestive of the relationship between the ictal event (epileptic seizure) and violent automatisms. In each of these three cases, the individuals developed what has been described as "resistive violence" in which they became violent when attempts were made to restrain them while they were in a postictal confusional state. Treiman (1986) has argued that the most probable explanation for resistive violence under these circumstances is a result of the differential recovery of the functional areas of the brain in that there is a relatively longer delay in the recovery of the higher level cognitive functions mediated by the frontal lobes as compared with the recovery of pure motor functions. Thus the patient may act with either lack of restraint or disinhibition similar to individuals whose social restraints have been compromised by alcohol or other centrally active drugs. Treiman has also argued that such an explanation may also provide an understanding of the "episodic dyscontrol syndrome" (intermittent explosive disorder) in which there is more permanent impairment of the frontal lobe function such that the patient lacks the normal capacity for social restraint of aggressive impulses. To the extent that it can be shown that a violent criminal act occurred at the time an individual was having a seizure or during the postictal confusional state, then the violent act, which occurred during the time that the individual had an alteration of consciousness, was most likely the result of the seizure. Under these conditions then, the individual should not be found guilty of the criminal act since a basic principal of the law is that in order for an act to occur, there must be intent. Clearly, when a patient is unconscious, there can be no voluntary intent.

Treiman (1986) reviewed a total of 75 kinds of violence in which epilepsy has been used as a defense, which has been reported in the appellate literature in the Federal and State courts of the United States. He found that in none of these cases, except in four cases of vehicular manslaughter, was there sufficient evidence to establish the ictal basis of the violent episode. In each of the cases of vehicular manslaughter, however, the act occurred as a result of a seizure. However, in one case there was evidence of alcohol consumption immediately preceding the accident and in two cases the defendant had previous seizures but chose to drive in spite of uncontrolled seizures. Thus, although the defendant lacked the intent, the defendant had consciously and intentionally operated his motor vehicle unsafely and was held criminally liable for vehicular manslaughter. Treiman has argued that one criterion that could be used in an epilepsy defense if violence or aggression occurs, is that the violent act is associated with an epileptic seizure and could not have been prevented by any action on the part of the defendant prior to or during the seizure.

Research Studies on Ictal Violence

Recently, techniques for the simultaneous recording of behavioral manifestations and electrical characteristics of ictal events have been utilized by researchers to shed light on the relationship between epileptic attacks and violent behavior. For example, studies by Delgado-Escueta and his colleagues (Delgado-Escueta, Bascal, & Treiman, 1982; Delgado-Escueta, Kunze, Waddell, Boxley, & Nadel, 1977; Delgado-Escueta & Walsh, 1985) have revealed three distinct types of complex partial seizures. The first and most common type began with an initial, motionless stare followed by stereotyped, oral-alimentary automatisms (consisting of lip smacking, swallowing, and mastication), followed by reactive quasi-purposeful automatisms during periods of impaired consciousness. The second seizure type began initially with complex quasi-purposeful bicycling motor automatisms, which were characterized by flailing movements of the extremities, bicycling movements of the legs, or karate-like movements which were often accompanied by ambulatory behavior. The third seizure type consisted of drop attacks during which the patient remained flaccid and totally unresponsive for 2 to 3 minutes followed by a period of reactive automatisms that usually lasted several minutes. These investigators have argued that because the patients were totally unresponsive during the stereotyped automatism phase of the seizure, it was unreasonable to expect that organized and directed aggression, particularly aggression involving complex acts, could constitute part of a complex partial seizure.

In another study by Delgado-Escueta and co-workers (1981), the clinical and EEG manifestations of approximately 5,400 patients with epilepsy were simultaneously observed. These investigators found a total of 19 patients who exhibited a total of 33 aggressive attacks during recorded seizures. The aggressive attacks were also rated as to their relative severity. On the basis of these ratings, four of the 19 patients exhibited evidence of spontaneous, nondirected, stereotyped aggressive movements and violence to property; were observed to shout or spit at persons; and exhibited what was judged to be mild to moderate violence toward another person during the height of their seizure. In two of these patients, however, these investigators noted that the observed aggressive behavior appeared to be a reaction to being held or being restrained (e.g., resistive violence). These investigators also reported that amnesia for aggressive acts was present in all cases, and that acts of aggression typically occurred during the beginning of a seizure and lasted an average of only 29 seconds, whereas complete complex and partial seizures lasted an average of 145 seconds. Furthermore, the aggressive acts were described as stereotyped, simple, unsustained, and were never supported by purposeful movements.

Interictal Violence

A number of well-respected clinicians and investigators have reported an increase in violent and aggressive behavior in epileptic patients between seizures. For example, Geschwind (1975) stressed that aggressive and violent acts were more frequently observed and were potentially more serious during the interictal period (between seizures). He also pointed out that the aggressive acts could frequently be provoked by relatively trivial events or minor frustrations. Bear et al. (1982) reported that the interictal aggressive acts were often planned out in clear conscience over a significant period of time and that the patient characteristically recalled and acknowledged his or her violent behavior and frequently expressed sincere remorse following such behavior.

Research Studies on Interictal Violence

Currie, Heathfield, Henson, and Scott (1971) examined the relationship between patients with TLE and the incidence of violent or aggressive behavior during the interictal period. While they found that 7 percent of the 666 patients studied exhibited an aggressive affect on mental status examination, none of these patients who had been diagnosed as having TLE exhibited aggressive behavior during their hospitalization. Rodin (1973) also found no evidence of increased aggressive behavior in TLE patients. Extensive reviews of the literature (Guerrant, Anderson, Fisher, Weinstein, Joros, & Deskins, 1962; Kligman & Goldberg, 1975; Tizard, 1962; Treiman, 1986) have concluded that issues of validity, reliability, and sampling bias prevent any firm conclusions from being drawn about the relationship between TLE and violent behavior.

There appears to be, however, a predilection for violent behavior in patients with organic brain pathology acquired as a result of traumatic brain injury (Lewis, Pincus, Feldman, Jackson, & Bard, 1986; Guerrant et al., 1962; Mignone, Donnelly, & Sadowsky, 1970; Small, Milstein, & Stevens, 1962; Small, Small, & Hayden, 1966). For example, Herman (1982) reported significantly more aggression and psychopathology in epileptic children with poor neurological functioning. In a more recent study, Lewis et al. (1986) evaluated the neurologic functioning of 15 death-row inmates who had been found guilty of acts of violence and were awaiting execution. A careful neurologic and neuropsychological evaluation of these prisoners revealed an overwhelming preponderance of neurologic dysfunction indicative of organic brain pathology. Detailed clinical histories also revealed that each subject had a history of multiple head trauma that resulted in significant brain pathology. EEG studies also revealed that six of the subjects satisfied the criteria for temporal lobe epilepsy. The results of this study, when combined with a review of this literature (Treiman, 1986), suggest a relationship between individuals with significant organic brain pathology, with or without epilepsy, and violent acts. For example, patients who sustain significant closed-head injuries, frequently resulting in damage to the orbital frontal and anterior temporal lobes, are well known for their aggressive outbursts. These individuals typically manifest poor frustration tolerance, irritability, impulsive behavior, emotional lability, poor judgment, and frequently exhibit evidence of significant impairment in recent memory on neuropsychological testing (Sbordone, 1984, 1988, 1990).

Sbordone (1987) has reported that a significant number of patients who sustain predominant right-frontal temporal lobe injuries are at high risk to develop what has been described as an "atypical bipolar depression" or organic affective disorder in which they exhibit rapid cycling manic-depressive symptoms frequently consisting of irritability and aggressive outbursts (during the manic phase) and suicidal ideation and attempts (during the depressive phase). Additionally, Shukla, Cook, Mukherjee, Godwin, and Miller (1987) reported a high incidence of secondary mania following closed head injuries in which the most predominant characteristic was irritability (which was found in 85 percent of these patients). These investigators also reported that post-traumatic seizure disorders were found in 50 percent of the patients studied and that there was a predominance of TLE among the seizure disorders.

NEUROBEHAVIORAL ASSESSMENT

Neurobehavioral assessment permits the neuropsychologist to detect subtle organic brain pathology. Neurobehavioral assessment places considerable emphasis on gathering a detailed history that includes developmental, clinical, and social factors, and reviewing educational, criminal, medical, and rehabilitation records (Sbordone, 1987). Included should be information from the patient's family and/or significant others, including the occupational, marital, and educational background of parents and siblings, as well as a history of substance abuse and marital, criminal, and psychiatric problems. A sexual history is important since it may shed light on strains (within a central love relationship). Information about the pattern of social relationships, including the history of the ability of the patient to both make and maintain friendships and the quality of those relationships, should also be obtained.

Behavioral observation of the patient across a variety of settings is an essential component of the neurobehavioral assessment process and should include, but not be limited to, open-ended and structured conversations, structured and unstructured settings, familiar and unfamiliar settings, rest breaks, and during formal testing procedures. The patient's behavior under each of these circumstances frequently conveys an enormous amount of information about the patient's communication skills, impulse control, motivation, cognitive abilities, and his or her ability to cope with the demands of the environment (Sbordone & Purisch, 1987).

Neuropsychological testing is also an essential component of the neurobehavioral assessment process. Testing should permit evaluation of basic areas of cognitive-communication functioning, such as attention-concentration, memory, motor and sensory-perceptual abilities, problem-solving skills, executive functions, mental flexibility, reasoning, planning, categorization, sequential thinking, language abilities, intellectual functioning, abstract reasoning, conceptual skills, visuospatial and constructional skills, speed of information processing, freedom from distraction, and academic skills, as well as emotional and social functioning. The choice of specific tests to be administered should reflect the patient's cultural, educational, and linguistic background; the particular complaints expressed by the patient and/or family; the severity of the patient's deficits; the length of time since the injury; specific referral questions; the patient's cooperation and motivation; previous testing; medications; and physical disabilities (Sbordone, 1988; 1991).

While neuropsychological tests have traditionally been utilized to evaluate the patient's cognitive functioning, the conditions of formal testing may compensate for or mask many of the patient's functional impairments (Baxter, Cohen, & Ylvisaker, 1985; Szekeres, Ylvisaker, & Holland, 1985; Sbordone, 1988, 1991). For example, the quiet and structured testing environment may help the patient compensate for problems of attention and concentration; frequent breaks and rest periods may compensate for the patient's problems of endurance, perseverance, and fatigue. The use of clear and repetitive instructions may mask the patient's difficulty in task orientation, flexible reorientation to new tasks, and problem-solving skills; and the interactive style of the examiner may mask the patient's motivational difficulties, problems with initiation, and response inhibition.

Neuropsychological tests also have a number of shortcomings. For example, the test items may have insufficient ecologic validity in the sense that they do not adequately test the patient in real-world situations; the tests may assess preinjury skills, abilities, or knowledge, rather than assessing cognitive functions sensitive to brain injury. As a consequence, many neuropsychological test reports tend to be "test bound" since they only report test data and omit information from significant others and behavioral observations of the patient during and outside of the testing situation. They tend to be acollateral in that they rarely contain interviews with significant others, and ahistorical, in that they fail to provide a chronological history of the patient's injury and contain an inadequate history of the patient prior to the injury (Sbordone, 1988; 1991).

The use of standardized neuropsychological tests to evaluate patients with epilepsy has been challenged by Dodrill (1981) and Trimble and Thompson (1986) since these tests were never designed to assess epileptics or validated for this population. As a consequence, these tests are often insensitive in discriminating patients with epilepsy from patients with organic brain pathology, or normal controls. Dodrill (1981; Dodrill, & Batzel, 1986) developed a specialized neuropsychological battery, which has been shown to be more effective in discriminating epileptics from normal controls and patients with organic brain pathology than standardized psychological (e.g., Wechsler Adult Intelligence Scale) or neuropsychological tests (e.g., Halstead-Reitan Neuropsychological Battery).

CONCLUSION

A review of the clinical and research literature reveals that ictal or even postictal aggression is rare, and that when aggression has been reported, it is typically resistive violence while the individual is being restrained at the end of the seizure rather than directed aggression. When aggressive acts have been observed as part of the documented seizure, they have been described as stereotyped, unsustained and unplanned, and never part of a consecutive series of complex acts. In addition, they did not occur in response to preictal provocation and were not premeditated.

Delgado-Escueta et al. (1981) have proposed the following criteria to be utilized to determine whether a violent crime was the result of an epileptic seizure:

1. The diagnosis of epilepsy should be established by at least one neurologist who has special competence in epilepsy assessment.
2. The presence of epileptic automatisms should be documented by the case history and by simultaneous behavioral and EEG recordings.
3. The presence of aggression during an epileptic automatism should be verified by a video-recorded seizure in which ictal epileptiform patterns are also recorded on the EEG.
4. The aggressive or violent act should be characteristic of the patient's habitual seizures, as elicited by the history.
5. A clinical judgment should be made by the neurologist attesting to the possibility that the act was part of a seizure.

Interictal violent behavior has been reported by a number of clinicians, but has not received much support from the research literature as a consequence of the failure of these studies to control the degree of organic brain pathology in their subjects. When epileptic patients were studied according to the severity of organic brain pathology, patients with more severe organic brain pathology appeared to have a significant predilection for violent behavior. Thus, persons arrested for acts of violence should be evaluated for organic brain pathology by competent forensic neuropsychologists and neurologists to determine the presence and severity of organic brain pathology as well as the manner and degree to which it may have contributed to the violent crime.

REFERENCES

Baxter, R., Cohen, S. B., & Ylvisaker, M. (1985). Comprehensive cognitive assessment. In M. Ylvisaker (Ed.), *Head injury rehabilitation: Children and adolescents.* (pp. 247-274).San Francisco: College-Hill Press.

Bear, D., Levin, K., Blumer, D., Chetham, D., & Ryder, R. (1982). Interictal behavior in hospitalized temporal lobe epileptics: Relationship to idiopathic psychiatric syndromes. *Journal of Neurology, Neurosurgery, and Psychiatry, 45,* 481–488.

Crichton, M. (1972). *The terminal man.* New York: Alfred A. Knopf.

Currie, S., Heathfield, K. W. G., Henson, R. A., & Scott, D. F. (1971). Clinical course and prognosis of temporal lobe epilepsy. *Brain, 94,* 173–190.

Delgado-Escueta, A. V., Bascal, F. E., & Treiman, D. M. (1982). Complex partial seizures on closed circuit television and EEG: A study of 691 attacks in 79 patients. *Annals of Neurology, 11,* 292–300.

Delgado-Escueta, A. V., Kunze, U., Waddell, G., Boxley, J., & Nadel, A. (1977). Lapse of consciousness and automatisms in temporal lobe epilepsy: A videotape analysis. *Neurology, 27,* 144–155.

Delgado-Escueta, A. V., Mattson, R. H., King, L., Goldensohn, E. S., Speigel, H., Madsen, J., Crandall, P., Dreifuss, F., & Porter, R. J. (1981). The nature of aggression during epileptic seizures (Special Report). *New England Journal of Medicine, 305,* 711–716.

Delgado-Escueta, A. V., & Walsh, G. O. (1985). Type I complex partial seizures of hippocampal origin: Excellent results of anterior temporal lobectomy. *Neurology, 35,* 143–154.

Dodrill, C. B. (1981). Neuropsychology of epilepsy. In S. B. Filskov & T. J. Boll (Eds.), *Handbook of clinical neuropsychology* (pp. 366–395). New York: Wiley.

Dodrill, C. B., & Batzel, L. W. (1986). Interictal behavioral features of patients with epilepsy. *Epilepsia, 27* (Suppl. 2), S64–S76.

East, W. N. (1927). *An introduction to forensic psychiatry in the criminal courts.* New York: Williams Wood.

Ehle, A., & Homan, R. (1980). The epilepsies. In R. Rosenberg (Ed.), *Neurology* (pp. 297–318). New York: Grune & Stratton.

Epilepsy Foundation of America. (1975). *Basic statistics on the epilepsies.* Philadelphia: F. A. Davis.

Gastaut, H. (1970). Clinical and electroencephalographical classification of epileptic seizures. *Epilepsia, 11,* 102–113.

Geschwind, N. (1975). The clinical setting of aggression in temporal lobe epilepsy. In W. S. Fields & W. H. Sweet (Eds.), *Neural bases of violence and aggression* (pp. 273–181). St. Louis: Warren H. Green.

Grinker, R. R., & Sahs, A. L. (1966). *Neurology* (6th ed.). Springfield, IL: Charles C. Thomas.

Guerrant, J., Anderson, W. W., Fisher, A., Weinstein, M. R., Joros, R. M., & Deskins, A. (1962). *Personality in epilepsy.* Springfield, IL: Charles C. Thomas.

Gunn, J., & Fenton, G. (1971, June 5). Epilepsy, automatism, and crime. *Lancet,* 1173–1177.

Herman, B. P. (1982). Neuropsychological functioning and psychopathology in children with epilepsy. *Epilepsia, 23,* 545–554.

Hill, D., & Pond, D. A. (1952). Reflections on one hundred capital cases submitted to electroencephalography. *Journal of Mental Science, 103,* 18–27.

James, I. P. (1960). Temporal lobectomy for psychomotor epilepsy. *Journal of Mental Science, 106,* 543–558.

Kligman, D., & Goldberg, D. A. (1975). Temporal lobe epilepsy and aggression. *The Journal of Nervous and Mental Disease, 100 (3),* 324–341.

Kolb, L. C. (1968). *Noyes modern clinical psychiatry.* Philadelphia: W. B. Saunders.

Kolb, L. C., & Brodie, H. K. H. (1982). *Modern clinical psychiatry* (10th ed.). Philadelphia: W. B. Saunders.

Lewis, D. O., Pincus, J. H., Feldman, M., Jackson, L., & Bard, B. (1986). Psychiatric, neurological, and psycho-educational characteristics of 15 death row inmates in the United States. *American Journal of Psychiatry, 143:7,* 838–845.

Lombroso, C. (1911). *Crime: Its causes and remedies.* (Translated by H. P. Horton, 1918). Boston: Little, Brown, and Co.

Mark, V. H., & Ervin, F. R. (1970). *Violence and the brain.* New York: Harper and Row.

Maudsley, H. (1873). *RBody and mind.* London : Macmillan.

Mignone, R. J., Donnelly, E. F., & Sadowsky, D. (1970). Psychological and neurological comparisons of psychomotor and non-psychomotor epileptic patients. *Epilepsia, 11,* 345–359.

Rodin, E. A. (1973). Aggression and epilepsy. *Archives of General Psychiatry, 28,* 210–213.

Sbordone, R. J. (1984). Rehabilitative neuropsychological approach for severe traumatic brain-injured patients. *Professional Psychology: Research and Practice, 15,* 165–175.

Sbordone, R. J. (1987). A conceptual model of neuropsychologically based cognitive rehabilitation. In J. M. Williams & C. J. Long (Eds.), *The rehabilitation of cognitive disabilities* (pp. 3–25). New York: Plenum.

Sbordone, R. J. (1988). Assessment and treatment of cognitive communicative impairments in the closed-head injury patient: A neurobehavioral-systems approach. *Journal of Head Trauma Rehabilitation, 3 (2),* 55–62.

Sbordone, R. J. (1990). Psychotherapeutic treatment of the client with traumatic brain injury: a conceptual model. In J. S. Kreutzer & P. Wehman (Eds.). *Community integration following traumatic brain injury* (pp. 139–156). Baltimore: Brookes.

Sbordone, R. J. (1991). *Neuropsychology for the attorney.* Orlando: Paul M. Deutsch Press, Inc.

Sbordone, R. J., & Purish, A. D. (1987). Clinical neuropsychology: Medico-legal application (Part 2). *Trauma, 6,* 61–94.

Serafetindes, E. A. (1965). Aggressiveness in temporal lobe epileptics and its relation to cerebral dysfunction and environmental factors. *Epilepsia, 6,* 33–42.

Shukla, S., Cook, B. L., Mukherjee, S., Godwin, C., & Miller, M. G. (1987). Mania following head trauma. *American Journal of Psychiatry, 144 (1),* 93–96.

Small, J. G., Milstein, V., & Stevens. (1962). Are psychomotor epileptics different? *Archives of Neurology, 7,* 187–194.

Small, J. G., Small, I. F., & Hayden, M. P. (1966). Further psychiatric investigations of patients with temporal and non-temporal lobe epilepsy. *American Journal of Psychiatry, 123,* 303–310.

Szekeres, S. F., Ylvisaker, M., & Holland, A. L. (1985). Cognitive rehabilitation therapy: A framework for intervention. In M. Ylvisaker (Ed.), *Head injury rehabilitation: Children and adolescents.* San Diego: College-Hill Press.

Tizard, B. (1962). The personality of epileptics: A discussion of the evidence. *Psychological Bulletin, 59,* 196–210.

Treiman, D. M. (1986). Epilepsy and violence: Medical and legal issues. *Epilepsia, 27* (Suppl. 2), S77–S104.

Treiman, D. M., & Delgado-Escueta, A. V. (1983). Violence and epilepsy. A critical review. In T. A. Pedley & B. S. Meldrum (Eds.), *Recent advances in epilepsy* (Vol. 1, pp. 179–209). London: Churchill Livingston.

Trimble, M. R., & Thompson, P. J. (1986). Neuropsychological aspects of epilepsy. In I. Grant & K. M. Adams (Eds.), *Neuropsychological assessment of neuropsychiatric disorders* (pp. 321–346). New York: Oxford Press.

Chapter 6

Demonstrating Relationships Between Natural History, Assessment Results, and Functional Loss in Civil Proceedings

Paul J. Bach

This chapter aids the clinician in organizing information about frontal lobe dysfunction with respect to the legal issue of damages as well as identifying for the court the extent to which the frontal lobe dysfunction may be related to the legal issue of liability.

Traumatic brain injury is the most likely cause of frontal lobe impairment of interest to the court. However, it is unclear the extent to which various environmental toxins may cause frontal lobe dysfunction, which could be an issue in personal injury proceedings (Hartman, 1988).

Chapter 1 of this text provided an overview of neuropsychological evaluation for the purposes of personal injury litigation. The reader may have prematurely arrived at the conclusion that a neuropsychological evaluation should be thorough because it will be exposed to painstakingly careful review by opposing counsel and his or her expert witnesses. However, this should not be the primary motivation for a thorough evaluation. It is necessary to assess subtle impairments of executive functions secondary to frontal lobe pathology for a number of purposes, particularly the prognosis for future. The patient, family, and rehabilitation service providers, no less than attorneys, judge, and jury, are particularly interested to know how well the patient may be expected to function in the future, the optimal conditions for functioning, and any foreseeable barriers to optimal functioning. Hence, personal injury litigation emphasizes the exhaustiveness, explicitness, and verifiability normally required of the clinical evaluation.

The task of the neuropsychologist testifying in personal injury litigation is quite different from criminal litigation. In criminal litigation the issue is how the patient's pathology played a causal role in specific behaviors at a specific time with the inference extended backward in time to circumscribed past behaviors. In personal injury litigation the question is how the patient's pathology interferes with adaptive behaviors, with the inference extended forward to future behaviors. With these differences of emphasis in mind, one should carefully recall the limitations of neuropsychological test data to future adaptive (vocational or interpersonal) behavior.

THE PROBLEMS OF ECOLOGICAL VALIDITY

The relationship between behaviors elicited on the neuropsychological evaluation and behaviors required of the traumatically brain-injured patient functioning in the everyday environment is an inferred relationship and not an experimentally demonstrated one. The phrase "ecological validity" refers to a conceptual relationship between observations made under controlled experimental conditions and predictions regarding events occurring under similar, but less well-controlled, conditions in the natural environment. The problem of ecological validity is a general, theoretical expression of the particular problem that occurs in neuropsychology when observations during neuropsychological assessment serve as the foundation for inferences made to predict the patient's future behavior in the natural environment. Hart and Hayden (1986) summarize their recent review of this theoretical problem by observing, "Our systems for classifying and describing (i.e., measuring) the behaviors related to brain injury do have predictive power for localizing an injury, but apparently less for understanding its effects on adaptive functioning."

The use of neuropsychological evaluations in personal injury suits amplifies the inferential difficulties when reasoning from test scores to future everyday functioning. The relationship between behavior on a specific measure (e.g., Wisconsin Card Sorting Test) and behavior on a specific job (e.g., choosing how the contents of a letter should be composed) is not easy to express in comprehensible, concrete language. The "real world" utility of behaviors required during neuropsychological evaluation is neither apparent nor easily expressed to the layman. The jury, judge, or cross-examining counsel may well appreciate that a person who cannot decide whether to use colors or shapes as a way of sorting cards suffers from some form of impaired reasoning. They may not, however, be so ready to conclude that this sort of impaired reasoning prohibits the individual from working. This practical difficulty in describing a relationship between assessment and real life simply illustrates the broader conceptual difficulties at this point in the evolution of empirical neuropsychological research. For instance, there is no clear relationship between specific behaviors observed during evaluation and specific behaviors that are adaptive in negotiating the demands of everyday life. The clinician who attempts to draw such a direct inference frequently does so with little or no experimental support and on the basis of experimentally unexamined assumptions regarding which elements of cognition or behavior are essential for specific adaptive tasks in the "real world."

The relationship between neuropsychological test scores and success in everyday life functioning may, of necessity , be only modestly correlated. The neuropsychologist who undertakes the search for empirically demonstrated relationships between neuropsychological test scores and specific vocationally related behaviors will find that such empirical evidence is "embarrassingly limited" (Brown, Baird, & Shatz, 1986). This specific relationship between test scores and occupationally significant behaviors is the ecological validity that is of interest to the clinical neuropsychologist. The relative dearth of demonstrated relationships between test scores and vocational behaviors exists for at least three different reasons, two of them statistical in nature.

First, it is clinically less interesting and perhaps theoretically trivial to note a specific correlation coefficient between a score on the Category Test and the ability to answer questions over the telephone in a competitively employable fashion. Even if such a relationship is found to exist, more significant questions remain: are scores on the Category Test related to competitive employability (the clinically significant issue)? What cortical function measured by the Category Test underlies the ability to answer telephone questions (e.g., abstract reasoning, cognitive flexibility, access to memory)? Hence, most of these studies that have been completed to date (reviewed extensively by Acker, 1986) have examined the relationship between neuropsychological test scores following traumatic brain injury and vocational or educational achievement. While the number of these studies is small and questions can be raised about their methodologic rigor, they generally indicate a modest correlation between some neuropsychological test scores and vocational outcome. However, one would only reasonably expect a modest significant correlation between neuropsychological test scores and vocational outcome, given the wide variety of behavioral demands included across a broad range of jobs. Statistically there is probably a rather low intratask correlation between vocationally relevant tasks for most persons in most job positions.

Within the experimental paradigm of relating specific test scores to employment success, Heaton, Chelune, and Lehman (1978) demonstrated that the best single predictors of "employability" as a general variable were scores on the Halstead Category Test, scales 2 and 4 of the Minnesota Multiphasic Personality Inventory, and, to a lesser extent, summary scores from the Halstead-Reitan Neuropsychological Test Battery, academic test scores, and scores on tests of memory functioning. By way of contrast, Klonoff, Costa, and Snow (1986) found that the neuropsychologically measured level of motor functioning was the single best correlate of "quality of life" as reported by traumatic brain injury patients, and "adjustment to injury," as reported by their relatives. Acker and Davis (1989) did *not* find frontal lobe measures uniquely related to late outcome of head injury, but instead found IQ and memory scores were generally predictive of functioning in the community. Nonetheless, Varney (1988) found very impaired vocational functioning in a group of 64 traumatic brain injury patients with frontal lobe contusions or orbitofrontal damage. Hence, reasoning capacity and emotional control seem essential to employability while memory, ambulation, and the ability to manipulate the external environment manually appear to be essential to living within the community. One reason for the modest correlations between neuropsychological test scores and daily functioning following traumatic brain injury is the broad variability of factors impinging upon successful functioning, for which no single factor or subset of variables can account in various jobs, living situations, and patients.

The second reason only modest correlations between frontal lobe measures and successful functioning has to do with the limited construct validity of predictor variables. For example, a cursory view of Lezak's (1983) encyclopedic work on neuropsychological assessment or Stuss and Benson's (1986) text on frontal lobe functions reminds one that neuropsychology does not have single, discrete measures of abstract reasoning, problem solving, or concept formation. What we do possess are more general measures that partially estimate combinations of these executive functions.

Third, and most important, in regard to the effects of traumatic brain injury upon frontal lobe functioning, is the functional anatomic nature of the frontal lobes themselves. For example, Damasio (1979) notes, "The frontal lobes are not anatomically homogenous structures, and therefore, there is no such thing as a single 'frontal lobe syndrome,' identical across patients and easily dissociable from other organic brain syndromes." Stuss (1989) offered the observation that the frontal lobes are likely to serve multiple, discrete, but highly interconnected functions.

The frontal lobes are made up entirely of sensory association cortex, which performs simultaneously a "sensory" and "effector" function. The frontal lobes are a major cortical monitor and modulator of limbic mechanisms, and therefore discrete functions performed by the frontal lobes or different anatomic regions of the frontal lobes are not be easily described or measured (Nauta, 1971). Finally, as Benson (1989) has pointed out, frontal lobe pathology is rarely discrete or focal, especially as a consequence of head trauma, since the variability of physical factors that create a traumatic brain injury are likely to result in widespread tissue destruction and thereby produce a variety of clinical syndromes. Therefore, research that demonstrates relationships between specific test scores thought to be related to frontal lobe functioning and vocationally relevant behaviors does not exist.

There is, however, a small but growing literature that suggests that neuropsychological frontal lobe measures are related to vocational outcome. Specifically, in two studies using a broad array of neuropsychological measures in a head-injured population (Heaton et al., 1978; Klonoff et al., 1986), two neuropsychological measures thought to be related to frontal lobe functioning (the Category Test and motor functioning tests within the Halstead-Reitan Neuropsychological Battery) have been shown to be related to employability and social adjustment following traumatic brain injury.

The traumatically brain-injured patients' ability to perform a task in a highly structured, one-on-one testing situation, may not be at all reflective of their ability to perform a similar task in a naturalistic environment where the external stressors are uncontrolled. Thus, scores on a standardized neuropsychological battery may actually overestimate a patient's ability to function in everyday life (Hart & Hayden, 1986). This is especially true since most neuropsychological tests measure well-rehearsed, overlearned functions that, for the most part, rely heavily on posterior cerebral structures. Neuropsychological evaluation, with its emphasis on optimum performance (e.g., only one examiner, one task, clear instructions, decreased environmental distractions) may compensate for some of the frontally impaired patients significant attentional and concentrational dysfunction, and thereby fail to demonstrate any significant impairment. To the extent the neuropsychological evaluation setting provides control, direction, and organization, this situation is capable of compensating for the brain-injured patient's frontal lobe pathology (Stuss, 1989).

Behavior during the neuropsychological evaluation is typically not the sole evidence utilized to infer behavioral or cognitive impairment that is likely to interfere with future adaptive functioning. It is determined by the absence of aberrant behavior prior to head injury, the appearance of such behaviors since the time of head injury, and the presence of aberrant behaviors during the evaluation, which provide the data base from which inferences regarding future behavior are made. Even though the ecological validity of behaviors observed and measured during neuropsychological evaluation has yet to be experimentally demonstrated, the inference from aberrant behavior based neuropsychological measures to everyday functioning can often be made possible by existing research and clinical data. For example, the literature is replete with clinical and experimental studies that describe the relationship between frontal lobe impairment and impaired performance on certain psychometric measures (Drewe 1974; Milner, 1963; Robinson, Heaton, Lehman, & Stilson, 1980; Stuss & Benson, 1984). Less extensive, but equally compelling, is the evidence that frontal lobe impairment significantly diminishes adaptive behavior in real world situations (Benton, 1968; Deutsch, Kling, & Steklis, 1979; Duncan, 1986; Varney, 1988). It is, then a matter of inference, although not a matter of demonstrated isomorphic causal relationship that performances on neuropsychological tests are related to behavior in the real world. For example, Newcombe (1987) has, with respect to forensic issues, stated that:

> The (legal neuropsychological) report reflects the most reasonable interpretation that can be made in the light of current knowledge. Unequivocal, long-term prognosis can rarely be undertaken

for moderate or severe cases. There is virtually no background information (*viz.* empirical research) that links long-term sequelae with behavioral outcome in any terms other than that of gainful employment. (p. 141)

DESCRIBING THE NATURAL HISTORY
OF FRONTAL LOBE SYNDROMES

Relating symptoms observed premorbidly and after traumatic brain injury with symptoms observed and measured during neuropsychological evaluation is a process of convergent description. The task of the forensic neuropsychologist in describing frontal lobe impairment of interest in a personal injury suit is to identify continuities of behavior across time so that a "natural history" of the symptoms emerges. In undertaking such a task, it is physiologically and neuropsychologically naive to expect that in all traumatic brain injury patients no "frontal lobe" symptoms are present until the day of the injury and, subsequently, all symptoms emerge, full-blown and easily identified, shortly after consciousness is regained, maintaining their severity until the time of neuropsychological evaluation and into the indefinite future.

Frontal lobe symptoms are extremely variable across patients (Damasio, 1979). The variability of presentations of frontal lobe syndromes is not surprising. For example, head injury patients frequently have quasipathologic conditions that can affect brain functioning (Dikman, Tomkinson, & Armsden 1989). The extraordinarily complex network of cortical and subcortical tracts projecting to and from the frontal lobe (Nauta, 1986), along with the possibility that different specific functions of the frontal lobes are affected by cortical areas relatively contiguous to each other (Stuss, 1989) means the presentation of frontal symptoms will vary a great deal depending upon the type of injury. The extreme variability in the mechanics of traumatic brain injury (velocity, direct trauma vs. acceleration—deacceleration pathologic effects, shearing vs. contusion vs. hematoma effects) is likely to produce considerable variability in frontal lobe pathology (Levin, Benton, & Grossman, 1982). Variable pathology superimposed upon highly complex neural structure predicts that a large variety of different symptoms of frontal lobe pathology will occur. For these reasons a relatively detailed investigation of cortically dependent cognitive domains is required to describe a particular case of frontal lobe dysfunction.

Obtaining the data (Table 1). A number of cognitive functions related to the integrity of the frontal lobe have been implied in this text (Chapters 1 and 2) and elsewhere (Stuss & Benson, 1986). The seven-part listing of cognitive functions utilized below is offered on the basis of its simplicity and general applicability to previous models.

Table 1. Schema for integrating information about frontal lobe functioning historically.

1. List frontal lobe symptoms in evidence before head injury.
2. List medical evidence for frontal lobe damage.
3. List evidence for frontal lobe symptoms following head injury.
4. List frontal lobe symptoms observed during evaluation.
5. List neuropsychological test failures on measures related to frontal lobe functioning.
6. List projected difficulties patient would have in future vocational/ interpersonal settings as a result of the above symptoms.

1. PREINJURY COGNITION AND BEHAVIOR. The time span over which symptoms are to be described are divided on the basis of from where the information originates. Description of preinjury behaviors as well as postinjury/preneuropsychological evaluation symptoms typically are best obtained from third party sources: relatives, friends, acquaintances, medical records, and in some cases (depending upon the time since injury, and the patient's level of dysfunction) the patient.

Tactile and motor functioning.   On a molar level, the neuropsychologist should inquire whether the degree of motor activity required in ambulation, manipulation (mechanical or writing), or strength required by the patient's premorbid vocational or educational status is commensurate with the current level of functioning. For example, did the patient have the sort of job in which impulsive behavior or bilateral dyscoordination would have resulted in poor job reports, lack of promotion, or termination? Was there a history of driving accidents or vocational accidents that might be consistent with impaired motor functioning? Premorbid tactile functions might be inferred from difficulties with fine motor control requiring tactile feedback such as electronic assembly, model-building, or needlework.

On a more atomistic level, can observers describe or do records suggest instances or periods of extreme exhaustion, motoric agitation, or extreme dyscoordination? Were there complex motor tasks (e.g., driving) that relatives or friends felt uncomfortable relinquishing to the patient? Was the patient technically inefficient or prone to simple errors (e.g., a "klutz")?

Language.   The patient's education can be evaluated in regard to its level, the quality of the institutions attended, grades obtained, and, if possible, the quality of work-based upon existing samples, and interviews with teachers, professors, or classmates.

More atomistically, did the patient exhibit notable instances of verbal impulsivity? Socially, was the patient known as foul-mouthed, verbally abusive, or socially offensive? Can specific instances be cited of the patient (in the absence of intoxication) "shooting off his mouth," "shooting from the hip," talking without thought to the impact upon the listener or upsetting others with coarse or abrupt honesty? Written letters may also be useful in obtaining evidence for spelling and language skills.

Visual-spatial/constructive functioning.   Some jobs (e.g., auto mechanics, engineering, architecture) and some avocations (e.g., hunting, bowling, needlepoint) require a degree of visual-spatial integrity; others do not. However, most every patient will have some history of operating an automobile and household mechanical device, the quality of which may have changed post-accident and thereby warrants inquiry. Sometimes, schemata drawn by the patient of spatial relationships that can be presumed as premorbidly intact (e.g., directions to a favorite fishing hole, route from home to work, layout of appliances and furniture in the kitchen or rooms in the home) can be used as evidence of current impairments in contrast with presumed premorbid integrity.

Attention and concentration.   Again, on a molar level, some vocations (e.g., accounting, drafting, nursing) and some avocations (e.g., woodworking, birdwatching) require careful attention to detail and sustained concentration so that inquiry is warranted. However, attention and concentration depends upon a variety of factors so that premorbid descriptions of these cognitive domains is often difficult.

Memory.   The effect of frontal lobes on memory seems to be primarily freedom from interference and temporal organization of elements in memory. However, memory can be significantly impaired as a consequence of emotional conditions (e.g., depression), endocrinologic disorders, medications, alcohol, and/or drugs. Thus, episodic memory can vary a great deal across normal individuals. Therefore, except in individuals obviously required to have exceptional episodic memory (e.g., physician, attorney, salesperson), this is a difficult area for inquiry of premorbid functioning.

Executive functions. What was the patient's level of complex responsibility for production at work, for the production of others as well as the verbal interaction (supervision and cooperation) with others? Is it plausible that a person demonstrating the patient's premorbid level of vocational or academic functioning could have suffered from regular impaired planning or concreteness? How reliable was the patient thought to be by virtue of responsibility in volunteer organizations? Did the patient act without thinking, seem unable to learn from experience, tend to strike out angrily, agree to disadvantageous agreements, act on the spur of the moment, or seem too often not to have a care for tomorrow in the way his or her money or time was spent? Was the individual described by others as "thick," unable to grasp a concept, able only to deal with the here and now, or to use words and ideas simply and directly? Did this person make the same mistake over and over again, seeming to get stuck in solving problems, being unable to change despite instructions from others? Was the patient able to use ideas, to learn from what he or she read or what others told him or her, or to apply that learning to new situations? Can others cite instances of the patient's ability to be creative and thoughtful in solving problems, or to exhibit novel ideas? Can notable instances be cited of the patient's inability to think ahead, tendency to get stuck in the middle of problems, or waste time and energy "spinning his or her wheels" in the middle of difficult problems?

Affective expression. How was the patient esteemed by co-workers and supervisors or others objectively unlikely to tolerate impulsive expressions of affect? From interview with the patient and spouse or significant others is there evidence of lasting interpersonal relationships that would be unlikely in the face of chronic lability, irritability, or asocial anergia? Was the patient socially active in or out of the home? To what extent was the patient relied upon by other members of the community that suggest the patient was liked, respected, and not labile? Is there evidence of a psychiatric history including not only inpatient hospitalization, psychoactive medication or psychotherapy, or frequent doctor visits for headaches, muscular pains, or gastrointestinal complaints?

Can co-workers cite instances of disruptive displays of affect at the work place? Was the patient, when working, judged to easily "run hot and cold," prone to notable periods of sadness or elation, prone to "fly off the handle" easily, or known to pick fights with or easily anger others? Socially, could the patient maintain long-term friendships in the church, community, on the golf course, or softball diamond? Was he or she sought out as a leader in church or volunteer organizations or left alone because "they were too emotional"?

2. MEDICAL EVIDENCE. At this point in the description of the "natural history " of the patient's symptoms, medical records for the time of hospitalization are germane. Neurosurgical records will describe the size and location of hematoma, dural tears, as well as any procedures performed. Neurosurgical or radiology records will include imaging—computerized tomography (CT) or magnetic resonance imaging (MRI), may give evidence of the localized contusion, encephalomalacia, edema, or fluid (CSF or blood) collection abnormalities. Skull series will identify skull fracture.

Undue weight ought not to be placed on imaging studies since the presence or absence of imaged abnormalities correlates poorly with neuropsychological findings (Bigler, 1988) since imaging demonstrates cerebral structure, while neuropsychological testing demonstrates cerebral functioning. Although the MRI is more likely to image frontal lobe pathology than the CT

(Levin & High, 1989) there is evidence to suggest that frontal asymmetry on CT is an unreliable finding, and not related to cerebral impairment (Palumbo, Naeser, & York, 1989)

Specific localization of an imaged abnormality in the frontal lobes should not be given undue interpretive weight, although some correlation can be made between various frontal lesions and their expected syndrome presentation (Rosvold, 1971; Sormon, Wassenstein, & Zappula, 1983). Benson (1989) differentiates between the "pseudopsychopathy" due to impairment of sequencing and planning seen in lateral frontal lesions with "pseudoretardation" characterized by apathy, akinesis, and adynamia typically seen in patients with medial frontal lesions. However, "pure" frontal lobe syndromes are rare following head injury. Conversely, rather "classic frontal lobe syndromes" can be seen following focal caudate and thalamus lesions (Eslinger & Gratten, 1989; Strub, 1989). Hence, specific differentiation of clinical syndromes with varying anterior lesions is unlikely to emerge from the traumatic brain injury literature.

Neurologic records will note behavior and mental status results of interest. For example, was anosmia noted? This can often be related to frontal impairment and may have prognostic value (Varney, 1988). Was there evidence of "frontal neglect," the grasp reflex, "utilization behavior," (Lhermitte, Pillon, & Serdau, 1986) or any other release of primitive reflexes from the normal inhibition of the frontal lobes that may be seen only shortly after injury and are documented only in these records? Psychiatric consultation notes may comment on verbal or motor disinhibition, digressiveness of speech, perseveration of content, flat affect, or the patient's inappropriate social behavior.

Patients with more severe head injuries will typically receive rehabilitation treatment. In that event, physiatric, speech, and occupational therapy notes may offer a wealth of information. For example, speech and language notes may mention a Broca's or transcortical motor aphasia (no longer in evidence at later neuropsychological evaluation), both of which implicate the frontal lobe pathology. More important than anything else, do not ignore nursing notes since they frequently contain a rich repository of verbal and behavioral data related to the acute recovery phase.

3. POSTINJURY SYMPTOMS. The same molar and atomistic level of description previously obtained regarding the patient's premorbid behavior, should also be obtained from the time of the traumatic brain injury to the neuropsychological evaluation in a chronologic fashion. However, this is a much shorter period of time than the premorbid time span, and is complicated by the recovery process from head injury. Therefore, the broad sweep of circumstances investigated by questioning regarding lifestyle is truncated and is typically individualized to the particular case. Anecdotal observations by relatives can be revealing but their generalizations are less compelling. The unit of interest for the neuropsychologist are the "changes" in the patient's behavior that have occurred post-accident. On the molar level, have there been significant social or familial changes? Has the family remained intact? Have relationships between patient and spouse or children remained unchanged? What comments from children, friends, acquaintances or spouse have been made regarding the patient's conduct? What changes have there been in the patient's level of educational or vocational functioning? Have relationships with teachers, professors, co-workers, or supervisors changed? What comments do these persons have about this person's behavior? Has the patient since the time of traumatic brain injury continued the same trajectory of success in educational or vocational endeavors? Has there been any progress, or decline? Can this be quantified in terms of grades, salary, or responsibilities assigned to the patient?

Data thus obtained from interview and record review is necessarily descriptive, anecdotal, at best demonstrative or provocative but never exhaustive or conclusive. However, it is useful and often essential. On a molar level it is often possible to demonstrate a notable disjunction between the patient's current clinical presentation and past performance in life. This sort of information is useful in avoiding "false positive" errors in clinical judgment. The greater the disjunction between past and current functioning, the greater the likelihood that the disjunction can be attributed to cerebral or frontal lobe pathology. On the more atomistic level of description it is often possible to obtain evidence of instances that occurred premorbidly that are so unlikely to occur with the patient's current, post-accident level of functioning so that evidence that avoids "false negative" errors can be identified. There are a number of specific behaviors during such an interview that are typical of frontal lobe patients. An attempt should be made to ascertain whether described instances of emotional lability, verbal disinhibition, or behavior impulsivity occurred on the basis of negligible or trivial interpersonal provocation, or are understandable given their social context. The more trivial the provocation, the more likely what is being described represents frontal lobe symptoms. Similarly, the more random the patient's behavior (the less predictable to the observer) is, the more likely frontal lobe impairment is being described. One specific instance of impulsivity often described by spouses is periods of hypersexuality uncharacteristic of the patient. Another example of concreteness or impaired abstract reasoning is the patient's denial, when questioned about reported behavior, that the "fault" is the patient's, that there is anything wrong with the patient, or that he or she is acting in an inappropriate or previously untypical fashion. This lack of understanding that there is something wrong in their conduct is typical of traumatic brain injury patients in general, not only frontal lobe patients.

Interviewees will sometimes be able to recount dramatic examples of behavioral or verbal perseveration that they observed on the part of the patient (e.g., the patient doing or saying the same thing over and over again in a way that is either bizarre or frightening to the observer). Interviewees should also be asked about their observations regarding the patient's capacity to formulate, plan, and carry out his or her goals. What do they observe about the patient's daily organization, use of time, and use of available supportive resources to remain organized?

Two problems complicate this form of data gathering from informants. For example, some individuals who are motivated by various personality or financial factors may be inclined to minimize or exaggerate symptoms. It has been suggested that relatives and patients rate their postmorbid behavior quite differently (Prigatano, 1986) thereby raising the issue of reliability of family report. The neuropsychologist should utilize a structured interview since it is likely to increase the reliability of family's reporting of symptoms (Kaye, 1990). Generally, the more consistency across informants and the more generalizaility across environments and over a time, the more confidence the clinician can have in reports of frontal lobe pathology.

Interviews of significant others and review of records undertaken as described above have not only gathered the very significant basal history, but have also identified medical evidence close to the time of traumatic brain injury for frontal lobe damage as well as evidence for frontal lobe symptoms following head injury up to the time of neuropsychological evaluation. The stronger the evidence is for the absence of frontal lobe symptoms prior to the time of traumatic brain injury, for positive medical indicators or description of "frontal lobe behavior" shortly after the time of injury (e.g., paramedic reports, emergency room records, and hospitalization), and for subsequent observation of frontal lobe symptoms by significant others, the more likely it is that the clinician is dealing with frontal lobe impairment. This chronologic organization of symptoms prior to, close to the time of, and following traumatic brain injury sets the stage for the description of behaviors and psychometric performances at the time of neuropsychological evaluation.

4. SYMPTOM OBSERVATIONS. At this point in the description of the patient's syndrome, the evaluator is not yet interested in neuropsychological test scores. Required first is the qualitative description of the frontal lobe syndrome as it is viewed in the neuropsychological laboratory. This is an important step in the inferential process. If the neuropsychological laboratory is an adequate environment for measuring the patient's cerebrally related behavior, instances should be observed of "frontal lobe behavior" as the evaluation proceeds, in addition to the neuropsychological test scores. For example, how did the patient make the appointment for neuropsychological evaluation, or who made the appointment for the patient? Was the patient on time? Did the patient find his or her way to the office in an expeditious fashion? Were the verbalizations upon presentation for evaluation cogent and responsive to the situation? Were the verbal interactions with secretarial staff, psychometricians, and clinicians indicative of verbal disinhibition or impulsivity?

It should be recalled, as various cognitive systems are reviewed below, that these impairments do not demonstrate frontal lobe tissue destruction as such, but instead they represent dysfunction of the control of the frontal lobes upon posterior systems (Stuss, 1987, 1989). In diffuse impairment, as is typically seen in traumatic brain injury, one likely outcome is the disruption of frontal connections with posterior cerebral regions (Goldberg & Bilder, 1987).

Tactile and motor functioning. Paralysis can be directly related to frontal lobe injury, while motor dysfunction can be attributed to various lesions to other parts of the brain (e.g., cerebellum) (Stuss & Benson, 1986). Peculiar to frontal lobe impairment is the dysfunction of alternating movements (Pribram, 1987), the organization and control of complex motor movement, as well as the rapid, smooth transition of motor control in complex motor movements (Stuss & Benson, 1987).

Behavioral impulsivity is the propensity of a patient to act without the ability to consider the predictable consequences of his or her actions, as those consequences impact upon his or her well-being or the well-being of others. This disorder may be related to what Nauta (1971) refers to as "the excessive vulnerability to interference of interfering events" observed in frontal lobe patients. The frontal lobe patient acts on the basis of information immediately impinging upon consciousness or recognition (e.g., stimulus-bound behavior), rather than on the basis of past learning or experience (Robinson et al., 1980; Derfaille & Heilman, 1987).

One interesting group of symptoms recently described by Lhermitte et al. (1986) has been termed *utilization and imitation behaviors.* These complex motor behaviors appear to be under the control of an inanimate object's expected functioning or the examiner's behavior, rather than the verbal instructions of the examiner or the adaptive intent of the patient. For instance, if handed a flashlight, the patient will begin to shine it on objects around the room. If handed a knife, the patient will find something to cut. Both occur in the absence of instructions to do so (utilization behavior). Similarly, if the examiner checks the time, cleans his or her glasses with a tissue, or absent-mindedly "fiddles" with a pen with the fingers of one hand, the patient is seen to imitate this behavior without instructions or indication that he or she should do so. What each of these behavioral symptoms appear to have in common is the inability to inhibit one's conduct based upon the (usually verbally encoded) norms and sanctions of interpersonal conduct that accrue over the years of an individual's experience. Instead, frontal lobe patients appear to act immediately, without forethought or reflection upon the past, without anticipation of another's reaction.

Although Luria (1966) describes a number of behavioral anomalies he observed in frontal lobe patients based on years of clinical experience, it is unclear how generalizable Luria's observations are to closed-head injury patients. For example, many of Luria's patients suffered from very destructive missile injuries and thereby may not be representative of closed-head injury patients (Hecaen & Albert, 1978). The sorts of behavioral anomalies described by Luria have received experimental verification in at least one investigation (Drewe, 1975). Finally, the tasks Luria used to elicit these behaviors, as they are most often utilized in the United States with the Luria-Nebraska Neuropsychological Battery, have been criticized for having a number of methodological problems (Lezak, 1983), but, more importantly, many of the examiners who utilize this battery lack an adequate background in behavioral neurology (Purisch & Sbordone, 1986).

Language functions. Specific aphasias are caused by frontal lobe lesions. Broca's aphasia with nonfluent verbal output, impaired repetition, and agrammatism, often accompanied by right hemiparesis, ideomotor apraxia, and aphemia (labored output with altered inflection or hypophonia) is the language disorder probably most often discussed in the literature as related to anterior lesions. However, transcortical motor aphasia, with truncated but intact grammar, reflectively spared repetition and comprehension, and impaired fluency characterized by poor narrative discourse and word listings, is likely associated with lesions anterior or superior to Broca's area (Benson & Geschwind, 1985).

Verbal disinhibition (or verbal dysdecorum) is a cardinal feature of the frontal lobe patient. The patient presents as if judgment regarding either the listener or social context (in which the speech occurs) plays no role in modulating the content of his or her speech. Scatologic or sexual innuendo or direct reference are frequent. Whether it be the facetiousness described by Hecaen and Albert (1978) as *Witzelsucht* or the caustic euphoria Damasio (1979) calls "moria" there is often in the frontal lobe patient a presumption of shared frivolousness that is totally out of keeping with the relationship between the patient and the examiner.

The verbal disinhibition extends not only to the content of the patient's utterances but also the ability to delay articulation of the patient's thoughts. Therefore, introjections, not always of a profane or scatologic content, punctuate or interrupt the conversation with the frontal lobe patient. In many ways, this symptom has the characteristic of the impetuous child who is so pleased with what he or she has to say that delay of utterance is impossible.

Such verbal disinhibition can be noted not only during conversation, but on the Vocabulary and Comprehension subtests of the Wechsler scales, the Absurdity subtest of the Stanford-Binet, or the "F" category of the Controlled Word Association Test.

Visual/spatial functions. Picture Arrangement on the WAIS-R may be the only visual-spatial task upon which frontal lobe dysfunction is regularly seen because of its emphasis on sequencing (Stuss, Benson, Kaplan, Della Malva & Weir, 1984). Motor perseveration, when it is seen in a drawing/copying task, is likely related to frontal impairment (Goldberg & Tucker, 1979).

Attention/concentration. Difficulties in these areas are more likely due to the diffuse impairment usually seen following closed head injury, but inattention to central features with perseverative attention to trivial details such as on the Cookie Jar test from the Boston Aphasia Examination or Hooper Visual Organization Test may well reflect frontal lobe dysfunction.

Memory. While there may be characteristic memory problems associated with frontal lobe impairment (Freedman & Cermak, 1986; Mayes, 1986), these problems are usually seen in combination with other frontal lobe symptoms and have recently come under experimental scrutiny and have been described clinically. As observed by Stuss and Benson (1987), "frontal lobe lesions do not cause a primary disturbance of memory but they do interfere with amnestic activity" (p. 150, Grafman, 1989). Problems with initiation of recall, or "forgetting to remember" as seen when free recall is impaired but cued structured recall approaches intact, may be related to frontal lobe dysfunction (Benson, 1989). Vulnerability to proactive inhibition has also been seen as a frontal symptom (Freedman & Cermak, 1986; Moscovitch, 1976).

Executive functions.   If the frontal lobe is conceptualized as primarily responsible for the application of rules and procedures to specific episodes or categories while the rules for generalization are obscure, then cognitive impairments, such as perseveration, concrete think-ing, and poor planning may be conceputalized as instances of impaired generalization.

Concreteness of thought or "abnormal inflexibility" (Nauta, 1971) refers to the phenomenon in which the patient's language and inferred cognition seems incapable of taking into account any but the most superficial elements of the object or circumstance immediately at hand.

The *perseveratory behavior* that is often seen accompanying frontal lobe impairment (Goldberg, 1986; Goldberg & Tucker, 1979; Sandson & Albert, 1984) essentially denotes the maintenance of a motor or verbal response (Golberg & Costa, 1986) long after the environment no longer directly elicits the response or has clearly changed, thus requiring a different response. Whether seen in its simpler forms of repetitive hand movements long after change in the movement has been requested or in more complex forms, as when the patient is unable to appear for an altered appointment time after becoming accustomed to a regular appointment time, the patient's ability to easily alter one's behavior on the basis of changed circumstances seems to be markedly impaired.

Impairment of *concept formation* or *abstract reasoning* is often discussed in the literature and observed clinically. Although various phenomena are doubtless referred to when these descrip-tive phrases are used, the frontal lobe patient essentially fails to consider various similar but not identical instances in arriving at a conclusion. Simply, inductive reasoning seems impaired and the ability to categorize in the service of conceptualization and reasoning seems very difficult. The patient seems unable to assess commonalities of various objects or instances that would facilitate the generalization of either what the patient knows about these objects or how he or she ought to act in these circumstances.

Also impaired in the frontal lobe patient is the capacity to successfully envision and proceed with a multistep process in an orderly fashion, retaining the integrity of each of the constituent elements of the process, as well as the sequence in which each of these constituent elements ought to be undertaken. This impairment is sometimes referred to as dysfunction in the areas of *underlying planning, carrying out*, and *effective performance*. In the frontal lobe patient's inability to plan, there is a loss of foresight, a decreased behavioral anticipation of behavioral options or contingent reactions to alternatives that may occur along the way. The frontal lobe patient seems unable to assess the value of a given activity in terms of reaching nonimmediate goals (Damasio, 1979). The frontal lobe patient presents as impaired in carrying out tasks. For example, tasks initiated go unfinished, while beginnings do not lead to completions, in the presence of intact memory and verbally stated intent that they ought to. As Nauta (1971) characterizes it, "Action programs fade out." Finally, as an end product, effective performance from beginning to end is severely impaired, as constituent elements of a performance are uncompleted, rearranged, or forgotten altogether, as "action programs become deflected along the way from their intended goal" (Nauta, 1971).

Concreteness of thought can be seen in answers to the Comprehension and Similarities subtests of the WAIS-R and Absurdities subtests of the Stanford-Binet. Perseveration can be observed, as well as directly measured, on the Wisconsin Card Sorting Test and Category test, along with indifference to environmental feedback and inability to learn from experience. Impairment of abstract reasoning can be seen in many of the tests related to frontal lobe functioning, but is perhaps most graphically seen on the Category and Wisconsin Card Sorting tests in those instances when the patient, during evaluation, articulates a wholly implausible solution strategy without any insight into its implausibility. The Porteus Maze illustrates not only the patient's impulsivity but inability to plan. Impairment in the patient's capacity to carry out plans can be seen not only on the Tinker Toy Test, but on the organization of the Rey-Osterreith Complex Figure as it is being copied.

Affective functions. Emotional lability is perhaps the best general descriptor of emotional sequelae related to frontal lobe impairment. Damasio (1979) describes apathy and indifference to environmental conditions as the baseline emotional reaction of the frontal lobe patient punctuated by marked emotional variability. For example, he describes the episodic facetiousness and boastfulness of the frontal lobe patient, interspersed by other episodes of sudden, short-lived, nonenvironmentally elicited, or inappropriately responsive anger. The frontal lobe patient, if he or she is demonstrating emotional sequelae to traumatic brain injury, will appear unpredictable to the objective observer, dramatically changed in comparison to his or her former self by those who have known him or her in the past, and will demonstrate an emotional responsiveness disproportionate or unrelated to events or persons in his or her environment (Blumer & Benson, 1975).

Blumer and Benson (1975) observe that the "pseudoretarded" presentation of some frontal lobe patients as apathetic, unconcerned, anergic, emotionally unresponsive with near normal intellect is associated with midline frontal gyri lesions. By contrast, the "pseudopsychopathic" presentation—impulsive, hedonistic, unempathic—is associated with lateral-orbital lesions.

Clinical observations of emotional lability are protean. Emotional lability may be observed as a function of frustration to the Category or Wisconsin Card Sorting Tests. If Lezak's Tinker Toy Test is used, an emotional reaction to "playing with toys" disproportionate to the clinical situation is occasionally seen. The correction of errors on Trails A or B may elicit a significant and untoward negative reaction. Resistance to the blindfold on the Tactual Performance Test may be frontally related negativism or impulsivity.

Behavioral description during the neuropsychological evaluation must inferentially precede interpretation of neuropsychological test scores. These observations of impaired motoric behavior, cognition, and emotion, both in "extra test" situations and as they are manifested directly in behavior during an evaluational task, provide the interpretive network for describing a frontal lobe syndrome. The preceding is not undertaken in order to simply observe symptoms. Nor is neuropsychological evaluation undertaken simply to document poor test performances. Instead, these observations allow the significant inferential link to be made about observed symptoms that interfere with test performances, resulting in poor test scores. In this way, the ecological validity of a particular test for a particular patient is demonstrated. It is in this fashion that impaired performances are not required to stand alone interpretively, but can be related directly to the frontal lobe impairment. Behavioral observations made during neuropsychological evaluation are demonstrated as the approximate cause of poor performances on neuropsychological test scores. For instance, the clinician is not limited to making comments regarding the number of errors made on the Wisconsin Card Sorting Test, but can comment directly upon the role of behavioral impulsivity in creating those errors. Further, the clinician can then describe the lack of behavioral impulsivity prior to the time of head injury and the emergence of behavioral impulsivity (similar in character to that observed in the laboratory) as a problematic behavior since the time of traumatic brain injury. It is this description of the "natural history" of behavioral symptoms that differentiates between "neuropsychological evaluation" and "psychological testing" with the intended inference that the former is preferred.

Neuropsychological test scores related to frontal lobe functioning are meaningfully interpreted only in the context of behavior observed during the evaluation and described prior to the evaluation.

5. NEUROPSYCHOLOGICAL TEST SCORES. These will only be briefly discussed since they have been previously discussed in the first two chapters of this book. Here it should be noted that they are of interest only in the context of the broader "natural history" of the patient's frontal lobe symptoms.

Motor/tactile functions. Only complex, bilaterally alternating motor tasks in the presence of verbal production indicating that the patient can describe the necessary movement is likely to be associated with a frontal lesion. The Graphic Pattern Generational Test (Regard, Strauss, & Knapp, 1982) is of interest, but as yet is without adequate norms (Vilkki & Holst, 1991).

Language. Impaired word fluency (Benton, 1968) as measured by the Controlled Word Association Test is most clearly related to frontal lobe dysfunction. However, even this consistent observation has been disputed (Vilkki & Holst, 1991). Evidence for Broca's or transcortical motor aphasia from the Benton Aphasia Examination or others is indicative of frontal dysfunction. Little organized output on Stuss's (1987, 1989) "The North" paragraph is said to be useful.

Visual/spatial factors. Poor performance on the Picture Arrangement (Stuss et al., 1984) is frequently suggestive of frontal lobe dysfunction. Failure to copy the Rey-Osterreith Complex Figure due to constructional disorganization of otherwise intact components is also suggestive of frontal lobe dysfunction.

Attention/concentration. Motor alteration on Trails B or verbal alteration on color naming from the Stroop Test (Peret, 1974) is difficult for frontally impaired patients. Correlation tasks (Glosser, Goodglass, Diamond, & Palumbo, 1989) as well as measures of sustained attention (Wikins, Shallice & McCarthy, 1987) appear to be particularly sensitive to frontal lobe dysfunction.

Memory. Recall after delay (Freedman & Oscar-Berman, 1986) or under the influence of proactive inhibition (Freedman & Cermak, 1986; Stuss, Kaplan, Benson, Weir, Chiulli, & Sarazin, 1982) is particularly vulnerable to frontal lobe impairment.

Executive functions. Shifting and sorting tasks, such as the Halstead-Reitan Category Test, Wisconsin Card Sorting Test, or Tower of Hanoi Test have all been demonstrated as sensitive to frontal lobe impairment, although the latter still lacks standardized administration procedures and composite norms. Poor performance on the Tinker Toy Test, as suggested by Lezak (1983), is also suggestive of frontal impairment.

Affective functions. Affective functions peculiar to frontal lobe dysfunctions are not uniquely measured by any current neuropsychological measurement, however, measures of empathy (Grattan & Eslinger, 1989) are lower in frontal lobe-impaired patients.

6. PROGNOSIS.

Prediction of future impaired adaptation to the interpersonal and academic or vocational demands of life draws upon data gathered from the entire neuropsychological evaluation and not from test scores alone. Too often, neuropsychological evaluation reports are read as if the author believes the patient will have difficulty functioning in the future because the patient's test scores were "bad," or "because brain damage is 'permanent,'" with little or no other inferential support to justify this claim. Such simplistic reasoning, of course, is flawed and does not adequately represent the reasoning of the clinician.

Neuropsychological evaluation of frontal lobe lesions for the purposes of personal injury litigation as outlined above allows the clinician in the individual case to speak with confidence despite the very thorny issues of ecological validity and lack of demonstrated statistical relationship between neuropsychological test scores and everyday functioning. By tracing the frontal lobe syndrome throughout its historic progression, the neuropsychological data become the quantifying measures of frontal lobe functioning, embedded in other historic, medical, and observational data, rather than the sole point from which all behavioral prognostication must be inferred.

To reiterate, on the basis of interview and medical data, the clinican is able to demonstrate the extent to which symptoms related to frontal lobe functioning were absent prior to the time of traumatic brain injury, the extent to which structural lesions were obvious at the time of injury, the extent to which medical observation shortly after the time of injury rendered the impression of frontal lobe impairment, and the progression of those frontal lobe symptoms up to the time of neuropsychological evaluation. In this way, the prognostication of future behavior is not based solely upon test scores, with the added old saw, "brain damage is permanent." Instead, it relies on one of the oldest and most reliable levels of inference available in clinical psychology. Whether in psychotherapy, in the prediction of future dangerousness, or the prediction of future behavior due to cerebral impairment, the best single predictor of future behavior is past behavior. The clinician is inferring that behavior described in the immediate past (the last year or two) will likely continue into the immediate future (the next several years) as it has been professionally observed and quantified at the point of neuropsychological evaluation.

Even then, one might object that such a prognostication ignores the plasticity of neural functioning and capacity for the individual's rehabilitation, a literature that is now burgeoning (Wilson, 1987; Meier, Benton, & Diller, 1987; Prigatano, 1986). When the clinician, however, ponders the rehabilitational capacity of frontal lobe patients, one is reminded that the literature to date has to do primarily with the rehabilitation of memory, attention, and concentration. We do not as of yet know the extent to which higher cortical functions are accessible to rehabilitation and in which patients since the literature on the effectiveness of the rehabilitation of patients with frontal lobe dysfunction is quite limited. Such rehabilitation will prove to be a formidable task in the patient who lacks the capacity to learn from past experience, and the capacity to generalize such learning, due to frontal lobe impairment.

In rendering a prognosis about future interpersonal and vocational functioning for the patient with frontal lobe impairment, the clinician has substantial data regarding the extent to which frontal lobe impairment has to date been disruptive of social interactions with significant others and on the job. The more severe the disruption in the immediate past, the more unlikely it is that the patient will be able to return to premorbid level of functioning in the immediate future.

On a more atomistic level of prognosis, it is essential to specify the requirements of the patient's job, social life, and family responsibilities. For example, a female patient who formerly worked as a receptionist, but who since the time of brain injury had been described as prone to cry at minimal frustration and to pepper her conversation with Anglo-Saxonisms, had lost her job as a receptionist because of these behaviors and exhibited these behaviors during evaluation, was unlikely to succeed at another job as a receptionist in the foreseeable future because patrons of the business for which she worked were likely to be offended, complain, and thereby demand her dismissal.

The question is then sometimes posed as to whether vocational functioning at a lower level is possible. While the behaviors described in the above example may be less disruptive if the patient is employed in a janitorial position, the possibility still exists that a foul-mouthed, episodically tearful person is less likely to obtain or hold such a position in a competitive workplace than another equally qualified person without these disruptive symptoms. The thesis that this example is intended to elucidate is that the frontal lobe patient's impairment is predictable not simply because it is a permanent impairment of brain functioning, but it is predictable because of a number of situational factors that are likely to elicit the impairment. A frontally impaired woman who is likely to be easily overwhelmed by a task and to respond with verbal disinhibition and emotional lability, will do so regardless of the type of frustration provided by various jobs. The question then is not, "Can she work as a janitress?" but instead, "Will employment as a janitress provide situations that will be cognitively overwhelming and frustrating, such that lability and disinhibition will prevent her competitive employment?" Hence, the question becomes, "How specifically can the clinician, from available data, specify the sorts of environmental conditions and cognitive tasks in response to which the patient has been known, both by history and upon evaluation, to exhibit frontal lobe symptoms?" The greater the specificity with which this relationship can be described the greater will be the specificity with which the clinican can address how the patient might react to future vocational or interpersonal demands.

There are, however, two additional complications to this sort of prognostication. First, as is well known, all cerbrally impaired persons, including those with traumatic brain injuries, function better in environments that are stable, routine, predictable, and nonchangeable. Their responses become less adaptive in environments that regularly present novel situations, new conditions, and changeable factors (Stuss, 1987). The extent to which the predicted future environment will be changeable rather than routine will allow the clinician one more mode of inference.

Additionally, as outlined above, a cardinal feature of patients with frontal lobe impairment is their unpredictability and propensity to overreact to even minimal provocation. Given their unpredictability, their increased likelihood of reacting negatively to what would in other instances seem to be only negligible environmental provocation, means the frontal lobe patient is more likely to react adversely.

7. A DEVELOPMENTAL POSTSCRIPT. The literature is conflicting regarding the effects of aging on test measures of frontal lobe functioning (Boone, Miller, Lesser, Hill, & D'Elia, 1990; Gavin, Isaac, & Adams, 1991). Until broad-based norms are available, some normal deterioration of scores of measures reflecting frontal lobe integrity after age 65 should be assumed by the clinician. Heaton, Grant, and Matthews (1991) is useful in this regard.

Developmental norms for the Wisconsin Card Sorting Test are available down to age 6 (Chelune & Baer, 1986), and other measures related to frontal dysfunction in children are being used experimentally (Passler, Issac, & Hynd, 1985; Becker, Isaac, & Hynd, 1987).

However, clincial measurement of frontal lobe functions in other than adults is still a largely unexamined area.

CLINICAL EXAMPLES

The following four clinical examples were chosen to elucidate the various ways with which premorbid history, psychological evaluation, and neuropsychological test results interact in arriving at a judgment regarding current level of impairment in frontally impaired patients.

Case One

Case One was a 23-year-old, right-handed male, who was seen 5 years after a physically destructive fist fight. The fight occurred as a result of the patient's mistaken identity by the perpetrator. There was no previous history of aggressive confrontation with other students. When he was admitted to the hospital, there was a diagnosis of significant laceration of the superior middle forehead and right frontal skull fracture with cerebral concussion. He was hospitalized for 2 weeks and upon discharge was diagnosed additionally as suffering from upper cervical strain, bilateral jaw sprain, and multiple chipped teeth. When seen on an outpatient basis for neurologic evaluation 5 months following the traumatic brain injury, he continued to complain of blurred vision, severe headaches, memory difficulties, and some motor and tactile anomalies. A neurologist noted modest social disinhibition in that he would blurt out socially inappropriate comments, at times alienating friends and acquaintances. EEG and CT scans at that time were read as normal.

When seen 5 years later for neuropsychological evaluation at the end of protracted personal injury litigation, he had just received his bachelor's degree in business administration with a 2.9 grade point average. The patient, prior to the accident, was a B student in high school, occasionally making the honor roll. He gave a long and detailed list of memory difficulties, both on the job as a retail salesperson and also at school. At work, he would often misplace objects essential for his job and would forget to or inaccurately relay telephone messages. At school, he took copious notes but would at times find they did not convey much meaning upon review. He had been married for 10 months at the time of this evaluation and was currently separated because of his wife's disinclination to deal with his emotional outbursts. He explained that he often became rageful in disproportionate reaction to something she had done, would curse impulsively and occasionally become quite verbally abusive, all behaviors untypical of him prior to his accident. His wife, on interview, verified these observations. His parents explained that he was, in fact, quite mild mannered and very pleasant in high school (prior to the accident) without any such history of angry verbal outbursts. An interview with the high school principal confirmed this impression. The patient was not known as a "fighter," had no legal record, and was thought in high school to perhaps be something of a "wimp." His parents offered the opinion that personality changes were notable only subsequent to the traumatic brain injury. Hence, we have a patient with a clear medical history of frontal lobe trauma, verbal and physical disinhibition and aggressiveness, memory complaints, none of which can be documented in the premorbid history. All informants (parents, wife, high school principal) indicate that this sort of irritability and disinhibition were uncharacteristic of him during his high school career.

Throughout the evaluation, this was a polite, responsive, at moments even charming fellow who was obviously impressed to be the subject of so much attention, when, in his opinion, he was doing "fine" except for not getting along with his new wife, which he attributed to his own immaturity and unwillingness to "understand her needs."

Verbal, Performance, and Full-Scale I.Q.s on the WAIS-R were respectively 98, 85, and 94. Subtest standard scaled scores ranged from 9 to 13. Memory testing, using the Denman Neuropsychology Memory Scale, obtained scaled scores from 6 to 10, with Verbal, Nonverbal, and Full-Scale Memory Quotients of 82, 85, and 80. The difference between memory and I.Q. scores is arguably indicative of some memory disturbance.

Controlled Word Association Test was excellent, with 41words produced. The Wisconsin Card Sorting Test was excellent, with all six categories completed with very few perseverative errors. The Category Test was completed with 32 errors, a normal performance. The Halstead Impairment Index from the Halstead-Reitan Neuropsychological Test Battery was 0.3, including an impaired performance on the Seashore Rhythm Test (10 errors) and Localization score on the Tactual Performance Test of four correct responses. Otherwise, test scores from the Halstead-Reitan Battery were normal. The most pronounced anomaly found in the battery was a much longer time during the second trial with the left hand on the Tactual Performance Test than during the first trial with the right hand consistent with right hemisphere disorder.

Although the left-right hand comparison on the Tactual Performance Test, as well as somewhat lowered memory scores, indicated some abnormalities, his overall level of impairment was found to be minimal. It was argued on the basis of this evaluation that he was still suffering from mild memory impairment and some cognitive dysfunction, as well as emotional lability secondary to the traumatic brain injury, which, taken together, were modestly disabling, primarily in regard to interpersonal relationships. Nonetheless, the normal performance on Category, Controlled Word Association, and Wisconsin Card Sorting Tests, as well as his lack of lability or impulsivity throughout the evaluation, were judged to not indicate frontal lobe impairment. Subsequently, a sizable out-of-court settlement was reached, more likely on the basis of the significant medical evidence and clear liability on the part of the defendant. The neuropsychological data were never entered into the court record, providing only weak evidence for continued dysfunction.

This, then, is an example of a very clearly unimpaired history premorbidly with significant evidence for frontal lobe damage at the time of hospitalization and moderate evidence for frontal lobe symptoms following the injury. Nonetheless, 5 years later, cognitive dysfunction attributable to the frontal lobe was not identified, and only the irritability and lability were presented as symptoms consistent with frontal lobe impairment. These latter symptoms were attributed to diffuse brain impairment rather than any specific localized frontal lobe dysfunction.

Case Two

Case Two was a regionally recognized medical specialist. She was the victim of a moving vehicle accident in which the automobile wherein she was a passenger collided with a cattle truck. She was subsequently unconscious for 2 1/2 weeks, with "massive" bilateral frontal hematomae surgically treated during that time. Post-traumatic amnesia was approximately 1 week retrograde and 1 month anterograde surrounding the time of the accident.

The patient was a graduate of a well-known Ivy League medical school, had graduated at the top of her class, and prior to her accident had a successful practice in a technically demanding medical specialty. Her husband and colleagues described her as methodical, excruciatingly careful, and extremely demanding of herself and of those with whom she worked prior to the time of the accident. When seen for neuropsychological evaluation 1 1/2 years following the accident, the patient's husband was considering divorce, and the Department of Family Services was investigating her for child neglect. Her husband expressed concern over a number of instances in which she had struck her 8-year-old daughter on the legs with her cane (she was still suffering from left-sided motor impairment, primarily in the leg, but also in the arm). Not only was she unable to care for the two school-aged children in any meaningful fashion, she was argumentative, abusive, and interfering with the children's care by the nanny who had been employed to take care of the children. Divorce was imminent. On one occasion while in the waiting room, she was seen by the receptionist to brandish her cane threateningly at a child accompanied by another parent in the waiting room, but no further incident ensued. The patient was perpetually late for appointments, argumentative and garrulous during them, with the result that the evaluation required five different appointments rather than the one or two typical at this clinic. Prior to each new portion of the evaluation, the patient would engage in a long series of tangential questions, apparently designed to demonstrate the patient's medical expertise and skepticism that anything meaningful was being accomplished during the evaluation. The receptionist at the clinic came to dread the appointment times and on one occasion another physician complained to the administrator about the patient's conduct in the waiting room.

Neuropsychological test results were uniformly impaired. Intelligence Quotients remained in the low 120s, while Memory Quotients were in the 80s. Picture Arrangement obtained a scaled score of 3, principally due to the patient's inclination to launch into long, disordered descriptions of what was going on in the pictures, thereby being overtime. Garrulousness on verbal subtests of the WAIS-R required 2.5 hours of administration time for intelligence testing alone. Halstead Impairment Index of 1.0 was obtained with poor to very poor performances across those seven tests. Eighty-two errors were made on the Category Test (from a woman with a full-scale I.Q. following serious traumatic brain injury of 123), while she failed to complete six complete categories and made 41 perseverative errors on The Wisconsin Card Sorting Test. She only produced 16 words on the Controlled Word Association. The Rey-Osterreith Complex Figure was extraordinarily disarrayed upon copy from design, suggesting extraordinary impulsivity, lack of planning, and inability to control motoric behavior. On Lezak's Tinker Toy Test, only eight of the 50 pieces were utilized to make a construction of undefinable shape or character, subsequently described by the patient upon injury as a "helimobile."

This still bright but obviously impaired physician was judged to suffer from serious neuropsychological impairment secondary to her head injury, including notable frontal lobe impairment. On the evaluation report and in subsequent testimony, the conclusion was offered that there was no indication in the patient's professional career of the behavioral impulsivity or emotional lability seen since the head injury, nor is it likely that impairments of abstract reasoning or planning, as seen on psychometric measures, existed during the patient's notable professional career. These behaviors emerged only after the head injury and continued in severity until the time of neuropsychological evaluation. In fact, between the time of the evaluation and actual testimony in court, the patient had accumulated a five-figure debt, using charge cards throughout the region in a remarkable binge of impulsive spending. She was further judged to be so impaired that return to an independent medical practice was impossible and she was wholly disabled in regard to her former career. The patient was encountered 7 years after the trial, without any intervening contact with this clinician. At that time, the patient had not resumed medical practice, but was involved with occasional consultation as a physician to facilities and institutions treating head-injured patients.

This case is similar to Case One in that the premorbid history was notably without behaviors or problems interpretable as frontal lobe dysfunction and provided notable evidence of frontal lobe impairment due to the trauma. It differs from Case One in that significant continued cognitive and behavioral impairment was found during the evaluation and on formal test scores. Substantial disability was judged to be present.

Case Three

Case Three was a 61-year-old, three-times-married, right-handed female referred by her attorney for neuropsychological evaluation. Her attorney was representing her in a malpractice suit against the state penitentiary for having failed to adequately treat encephalitis, resulting in neuropsychological dysfunction. Approximately 15 years prior to the encephalitis, the patient had suffered a compound skull fracture in the right orbital area, and right anterior hematoma secondary to a moving vehicle accident. The hematoma was surgically treated. Unconsciousness lasted approximately 10 days. Hospitalization was several months in duration, including acute care and rehabilitation medicine hospitalizations. Approximately 10 years prior to the cerebral infection, she was also hit in the right anterior region by a pistol. She was unconscious for 20 to 30 minutes and was observed in the emergency room, but there was otherwise no medical treatment. She was not hospitalized for that injury.

Skull x-rays and CT scans taken at the time of encephalitis revealed the above-noted old skull fracture and what appeared to the interpreting neurosurgeon to be an old lesion in the right frontal area. The patient's record included multiple arrests for felony theft and prostitution since the age of 19. There was a history of two psychiatric hospitalizations. There was admitted history of substantial substance abuse, primarily marijuana, but no alcohol abuse.

When seen for neuropsychological evaluation, intelligence scores were within normal limits, with subtest scores varying from 8 to 14. Memory scores, however, provided a Denman Verbal Memory Quotient in the low normal range, Nonverbal Memory in the normal range, with Verbal Memory subtest scores ranging from 7 to 10 and Nonverbal scores from 10 to 14. The differential between Verbal Memory and Verbal Intelligence was judged to be potentially consistent with cerebral impairment, including head injury. On the Halstead-Reitan Neuropsychological Test Battery, the patient was far slower and weaker than is normal with her left upper extremity than her right. A Halstead Impairment Index of 0.6 was obtained on the basis of impaired performance on TPT Localization, Speech Perception, Seashore Rhythm, and Finger Oscillation. Additionally, the Category Test and TPT total time were just short of the impaired range. Trailmaking Part B was performed, according to some norms, two standard deviations slower than normal, with two errors. The Wisconsin Card Sorting Test revealed numerous perseverative errors.

The testing was performed while the patient was incarcerated, but other than that inconvenience, the administration of tests was under normal conditions. Nonetheless, the patient's garrulousness, repeated inquiries about the psychologist's credentials, and long protracted description of history and past events extended the evaluation to 10 hours. At one point, when it appeared to the patient that the evaluation was not going to be supportive of her case, a few moments of marginally controlled verbal aggression ensued, and a guard was called. The appearance of a guard immediately calmed the patient down and the evaluation resumed. During a meal break, the patient was heard to be talking to herself in the testing room in a very loud voice in a way that could have either been poorly controlled verbalization or an odd attempt to impress the evaluator with her impairments.

This lady was found to be quite severely neuropsychologically impaired, although the evaluation was unable to identify the encephalitis as the primary contributing factor to her impairment. Certainly, the one very serious head injury was more or less consistent with the level of impairment. Equally notable is the patient's long legal history, poor marital history, and history of substance abuse, each of which bespoke a lifelong relative inability to control her impulsivity, or to conduct her actions in a planned, modulated fashion. As a result, no evidence was obtained in this evaluation that linked her neuropsychological impairments to a past history of encephalitis.

This case exemplifies an instance in which there were "frontal lobe signs" well before the instance in question (in this case, encephalitis) and, in fact, well before the head injuries. While there is no doubt that this woman was impaired, especially frontally impaired, it was impossible to link her impairments with the legal question at hand. As a consequence she continued to be incarcerated.

Case Four

Case Four is an instance in which, despite notable examples of disinhibited, dysfunctional behavior prior to the time of head injury, this woman was judged to suffer from a frontal lobe impairment directly resulting from a particular head injury and to be impaired secondary to that injury.

This patient was a 35-year-old, unmarried, right-handed female. Prior to the time of her head injury, she had obtained her GED and subsequently attended a vocational college, obtaining Ds. She had never been married, or engaged, and dated very little. She admitted to having been admitted to two different drug and alcohol programs prior to the time of the accident, although she denied substance abuse over the last 6 months. She admitted to DUI arrests in excess of a dozen times prior to her traumatic brain injury. In addition to occasionally attending classes at the technical school, she worked on and off as a painter, never holding a job for more than 18 months.

Three years prior to neuropsychological evaluation, she had fallen 30 feet off scaffolding, directly onto her head. She was seen in the emergency room with response to deep pain only and had been unconscious for approximately an hour prior to her first hospital admission. There were fractures noted to the right mastoid and superorbital bones in a skull series done at the time of admission. An EEG taken during the first day of hospitalization indicated moderately abnormal diffuse slowing across the right hemisphere. She was hospitalized for 2 weeks and was seen to be moderately cognitively impaired during a neurologic examination at the time of discharge. Since the time of discharge to the time of neuropsychological evaluation, she had not held a job and had been essentially "drifting," living with one group of friends or another.

The day just prior to the examination, she appeared, announcing that she would have to cancel the evaluation because she intended to move her residence. When it was pointed out to her that she had no new apartment rented, no public housing available to her, no means of transportation, either public or private, by which she could move her belongings, and that it was 28 degrees below zero on that day, she seemed unperturbed. It was obvious that she simply had the idea in her mind that moving was necessary, but the constituent elements of completing that task could not be planned or integrated by her. She was urged to contact her lawyer and not move on the next day.

Throughout the evaluation, the patient was talkative, presenting stories from her past in a disjointed, tangential fashion, in a style that was apparently amusing to her but to no one else. Circumlocutions were noted throughout her conversation. Sexual jokes were told on a number of occasions, not only to the male examiner, but to female clerical staff, in a very loud voice overheard by other patients. Her garrulousness was monumental. She spent approximately one-half hour conversing with the stenographer in the office, despite multiple attempts by the stenographer to ask her to sit down in the waiting room and allow her to continue with her work. On three occasions during the evaluation, she impulsively announced her need for a bathroom break, and on one occasion was unable to successfully return from the washroom to the examination laboratory, a distance of 10 yards. Disinhibited laughter was heard from the examining laboratory throughout the afternoon's evaluation.

Upon evaluation, she received a Verbal I.Q. of 120 and a performance I.Q. of 92. The 28-point difference between verbal and performance scores is suggestive of right hemisphere dysfunction. On the Denman Neuropsychological Memory Battery, she received a Verbal Memory Quotient of 96 and Performance Memory Quotient of 72. A difference was found between language and nonlanguage mediated scales with overall memory functioning being lower than overall intellectual functioning, consistent with cerebral dysfunction. On the Wisconsin Card Sorting Test, she was unable to finish the first category despite going through all 128 cards. Ninety-six errors were made on the Category Test.

This woman's educational, marital, and vocational history, along with a clear history of substance abuse, did not indicate stability or argue for cerebral intactness. Nonetheless, the combination of medical evidence immediately after her traumatic brain injury, decreased level of functioning vocationally and interpersonally, the amalgam of behavior symptoms seen during the evaluation, and the significant impairment on the Wisconsin Card Sorting and Category Tests, pointed to the conclusion that this woman suffered a frontal lobe trauma above and beyond what might be inferred from her premorbid level of functioning. She was subsequently judged permanently disabled and awarded disability benefits.

CONCLUSIONS

The foregoing case studies and discussion of the organization of data for neuropsychological evaluation are outlined to emphasize the necessity of integrating historical information, both before and after traumatic brain injury, with available medical information and neuropsychological and statistical data in order to arrive at a conclusion regarding the patient's current level of dysfunction and serve as a basis for prognostication for future functioning.

REFERENCES

Acker, M. B. (1986). Relationships between test scores and everyday life functioning In B. P. Uzell & Y. Gross (Eds.), *Clinical neuropsychology of intervention* (pp. 85–117). Boston: Martinus Nijof.

Acker, M. B., & Davis, J. R. (1989). Psychological test scores associated with late outcome in head injury. *Neuropsychology, 3,* 123–134.

Becker, M. G., Isaac, W., & Hynd, G. W. (1987). Neuropsychological development of nonverbal behaviors attributed to 'frontal lobe' functioning. *Developmental Neuropsychology, 3,* 275–298.

Benson, D. F. (1989). *Frontal influences on higher behavioral function.* Paper presented at the "Brain/Behavior relationships: An integrated approach" conference, Rancho Mirage, CA.

Benson, D. F., & Geshwind, N. (1985). Aphasia and related disorders. In M.M. Mesulan (Ed.), *Principals of behavioral neurology* (pp. 193–238). Philadelphia: F.A. Davis.

Benton, A. L. (1968). Differential behavioral effects in frontal lobe disease. *Neuropsychologia, 6,* 53–60.

Bigler, E. D. (1987). The clinical significance of cerebral atrophy in traumatic brain injury. *Archives of Clinical Neuropsychology, 2,* 293–304.

Bigler, E. D. (1988). Frontal lobe damage and neuropsychology assessment. *Archives of Clinical Neuropsychology, 3,* 279–297.

Blumer, D., & Benson, D. F. (1975). Personality changes with frontal and temporal lobe lesion. In D. F. Benson & D. Blumer (Eds.), *Psychiatric aspects of neurological disease: Vol. 1.* New York: Grune & Stratton.

Boone, K. B., Miller, B. L., Lesser, I. M., Hill, E., & D'Elia, L. (1990). *Performance on frontal lobe tests in healthy older individuals.* Paper presented at International Neuropsychological Society convention, Orlando, FL.

Brown, G. G., Baird, A. P., & Shatz, M. W. (1986). The effects of cerebrovascular disease and its treatment on higher cortical functioning. In I. Grand & K. M. Adams (Eds.), *Neurological assessment of neuropsychiatric disorders* (pp. 286–414). New York: Oxford.

Chelune, G. J., & Baer, R. A. (1986). Developmental norms for the Wisconsin Card Sorting Test. *Journal of Clinical Experimental Neuropsychology, 8,* 219–228.

Damasio, A. (1979). The frontal lobes. In K.M. Heilman & E. Valenstein (Eds.), *Clinical neuropsychology* (pp. 360–412). New York: Oxford.

Derfaellie, M., & Heilman, K. M. (1987). Response preparation and response inhibition after lesions of the medial frontal lobe. *Archives of Neurology, 44,* 1265–1271.

Deutsch, R. D., Kling, A., & Steklis, H. D. (1979). Influence of frontal lobe lesions on behavioral interactions in man. *Research Communications In Psychology, Psychiatry, and Behavior, 4,* 415–431.

Dikman, S. S., Tomkin, N., & Armsden, G. (1989). Neuropsychological recovery: Relatonship to psychosocial functioning and post-concussion complaints. In H.S. Levin, H. M. Eisenberg, & A. L. Bator (Eds.). *Mild head injury* (pp. 224–244). New York: Oxford.

Drewe, E. A. (1974). The effect of type and area of brain lesions on Wisconsin Card Sorting Test performance. *Cortex, 10,* 159–170.

Drewe, E. A. (1975). An experimental investigation of Luria's theory on the effects of frontal lobe lesions in man. *Neuropsychologia, 13,* 421–429.

Duncan, J. (1986). Disorganization of behavior after frontal lobe damage. *Cognitive Neuropsychology, 3,* 271–190.

Eslinger, P. J., & Gratten, L. (1989). A cortical and subcortical network of structures involved in cognitive flexibility. Paper presented at the International Neuropsychological Society Convention, Vancouver, B.C., Canada.

Freedman, M., & Cermak, L. S. (1986). Semantic encoding deficits in frontal lobe disease and amnesia. *Brain and Cognition, 5,* 108–114.

Freedman, M., & Oscar-Berman, M. (1986). Bilateral frontal lobe disease and selective delayed response deficits in humans. *Behavioral Neuroscience, 100,* 337–342.

Gavin, M. R., Isaac, W., & Adams, H. (1991). *The performance of healthy elderly adults on behavioral tasks associated with frontal lobe functioning.* Paper presented at International Neuropsychological Society Convention, San Antonio, TX.

Glosser, G., Goodglass, H., Diamond, H., & Palumbo, C. (1989). *Disorders of executive control among aphasic patients: Effects of frontal lobe lesions.* Paper presented at the International Neuropsychological Society Convention, Vancouver, B. C.

Goldberg, E. (1986). Varieties of perseveration: A comparison of two taxonomies. *Journal of Clinical and Experimental Neuropsychology, 6,* 710–726.

Goldberg, E., & Bilder, R. M. (1987). The frontal and hierarchical organization of cognitive control. In E. Perelman (Ed.), *The frontal lobe revisited* (pp. 159–188). New York: IRBN.

Goldberg, E., & Costa, L. D. (1986). Qualitative indices in neuropsychological assessment: An extension of Luria's approach to executive deficits following prefrontal lesions. In I. Grant & K. M. Adams (Eds.), *Neuropsycholical assessment of neuropsychiatric disorders* (pp. 48–64). New York: Oxford.

Goldberg, E., & Tucker, D. (1979). Motor perseveration and long-term memory for visual forms. *Journal of Clinical Neuropsychology, 1,* 273–288.

Grafman, J. (1989). Plans, actions and mental sets: Managerial knowledge units in the frontal lobes. In E. Pereman (Ed.), *Integrating theory and practice in clinical neuropsychology* (pp. 93–138). Hillsdale, NJ: Erlbaum.

Grattan, L. M., & Eslinger, P. J. (1989). Higher cognition and social behavior: Changes in cognitive flexibility and depth after cerebral lesions. *Neuropsychology, 3,* 175–185

Hart, T., & Hayden, M. D. (1986). The ecological validity of neuropsychological assessment and remediation. In B .P. Uzzell & Y. Gross (Eds.), *Clinical neuropsychology of intervention* (pp. 21–50). Boston: Martinus Nijhoff.

Hartman, E. E. (1988). *Neuropsychological toxicology: Identification and assessment of human neurotoxic syndromes.* New York: Pergamon Press.

Heaton, R. K., Chelune, G. J., & Lehman, R. A. W. (1978). Using neuropsychological and personality tests to assess the likelihood of patient employment. *The Journal of Nervous and Mental Disease, 166,* 408–416.

Heaton, R. K., Grant, I., & Matthews, C. G. (1991). *Comprehensive norms for an expanded Halstead-Reitan Battery.* Demographic corrections, research findings, and clinical applications. Odessa, FL: Psychological Assessment Resources.

Hecaen, H., & Albert, M. L. (1978). *Human neuropsychology.* New York: Wiley.

Kaye, T. (1990). *The NYU head injury family interview (Hi-Fi): Research and clinical applications.* Paper presented at New York University. "Head injury and family system" Conference at New York.

Klonoff, P. S., Costa, L. D., & Snow, W. G. (1986). Predictors and coordinators of quality of life in patients with closed-head injury. *Journal of Clinical and Experimental Psychology, 8,* 469–485.

Levin, H. S., & High, W. M. (1989). Contributions of neuroimaging to neuropsychological research on closed head injury. *Neuropsychology, 3,* 243–254.

Lezak, M. D. (1983). *Neuropsychological assessment* (2nd ed). New York: Oxford.

Lhermitte, F., Pillon, B., & Serdau, M. (1986). Human autonomy and frontal lobes. Part I: Imitation and utilization behavior: A neuropsychological study of 75 patients. *Annals of Neurology, 19,* 326–334.

Littleson, E. A. (1987). *Rehabilitation of memory.* New York: Guilford.

Luria, A. R. (1966). *Higher cortical functions in man.* New York: Basic Books.

Mayes, A. R. (1986). Learning and memory disorders and their assessment. *Neuropsychologia, 24,* 25–39.

Meier, M. J., Benton, A. L., & Diller, L. (1987). *Neuropsychological rehabilitation.* New York: Guilford Press.

Milner, B. (1963). Effects of different brain lesions on card sorting. *Archives of Neurology, 9,* 90–100.

Moscovitch, M. (1976). *Differential effects of unilateral temporal and frontal lobe damage on memory performance.* Paper presented at the International Neuropsychological Society convention, Toronto, Canada.

Nauta, W. J. H. (1971). The problem of the frontal lobe: A reinterpretation. *Journal of Psychiatric Research, 8,* 167–187.

Nauta, W. J. H. (1986). *Fundamental neuroanatomy.* New York: W.H. Freeman.

Newcombe, F. (1987). Psychometric and behavioral evidence: Scope, limitations, and ecological validity. In H.S. Levin, J. Grafman, & H. M. Eisenberg (Eds.), *Neurobehavioral recovery from head injury* (pp. 127–145). New York: Oxford.

Palumbo, C. L., Naeser, M. A., & York, A. P. (1989). Reliability of CT scan cerebral hemispheric asymmetry measurements across multiple CT scans and variability in CT scanning angulation. *Neuropsychology, 3,* 231–242.

Passler, M. A., Isaac, W., & Hynd, G. W. (1985). Neuropsychological development of behavior attributed to frontal lobe functioning in children. *Developmental Neuropsychology, 1,* 349–370.

Peret, E. (1974). The left frontal lobe of man and suppression of habitual responses in verbal categorical behavior. *Neuropsychologia, 12,* 323–330.

Pribram, K. H. (1987). The subdivision of the frontal cortex revisited. In E. Perecman (Ed.), *The frontal lobes revisited* (pp.11–40), New York: IRBN.

Prigatano, G. P. (1986). *Neuropsychological rehabilitation after brain injury.* Baltimore: Johns Hopkins University Press.

Purisch, A. D., & Sbordone, R. J. (1986). The Luria-Nebraska Neuropsychological Battery. In G. Goldstein & R. A. Tarter (Eds.), *Advances in clinical neuropsychology,* Vol 3. (pp. 291-316). New Jersey: Plenum Press.

Regard, M., Strauss, E., & Knapp, P. (1982). Children's Production on verbal and fluency tasks. *Perceptual and Motor Skills, 55,* 839-844.

Robinson, A. L., Heaton, R. K., Lehman, R. A. W., & Stilson, D. W. (1980). The utility of the Wisconsin Card Sorting Test in detecting and localizing frontal lobe lesions. *Journal of Consulting and Clinical Psychology, 48,* 406–614.

Rosvold, H. E. (1971). The frontal lobe system: Cortical-subcortical interrelationships. *Acta Neurobiological Experimentation, 32,* 439–460.

Sandson, J., & Albert, M. (1984). Varieties of perseveration. *Neuropsychologia, 22,* 715–732.

Sorman, P. B., Wasserstein, J., & Zappulla, R. (1983). *Cerebral correlates of cognitive regression and parallels with schizophrenic thought processes.* Paper presented at the meeting of the International Neuropsychological Society, Mexico City.

Strub, R. L. (1989). Frontal lobe syndrome in a patient with bilateral globus pallidus lesions. *Archives of Neurology, 46,* 1024–1027.

Stuss, D. T. (1989). Contribution of frontal lobe injury to cognitive impairment after closed head injury: Methods of assessment and recent findings. In H. S. Levin, J. Grafman, & H. M. Eisenberg (Eds.), *Neurobehavioral recovery from head injury* (pp. 166–177). New York: Oxford.

Stuss, D., & Benson, D. F. (1986). *The frontal lobes.* New York: Raven.

Stuss, D. T. (1989). *What's up front: Examination of executive functions.* Paper presented at the "Brain/Behavior relationships: An integrated approach" conference, Rancho Mirage, CA.

Stuss, D. T., & Benson, D. F. (1984). Neuropsychological studies of the frontal lobes. *Psychological Bulletin, 95,* 3–28.

Stuss, D.T., & Benson, D. F. (1987). The frontal lobes and control of cognition and memory. In E. Perecman (Ed.), *The frontal lobes revisited.* New York: IRBN Press.

Stuss, D. T., Benson, D. F., Kaplan, E. F., Della Malva, C., & Weir,W. S. (1984). The effects of prefrontal leucotomy on visual-perceptive and visual-constructive tests. *Bulletin of Clinical Neurosciences, 16,* 1085–1100.

Stuss, D. T., Kaplan, E. F., Benson, D. F., Weir,W. S., Chiulli, S., & Sarazin, F. F. (1982). Evidence for the involvement of orbitofrontal control in memory functions: An interference effect. *Journal of Comparative and Psychological Psychology,16,* 913, 925.

Varney, N. R. (1988). Prognostic significance of anosmia in patients with closed-head trauma. *Journal of Clinical and Experimental Neuropsychology, 10,* 250–254.

Vilkki, J. S., & Holst, J. P. (1991). *Word fluency and frontal lobe lesion.* Paper prsented at International Neuropsychological Socity convention, San Antonio, TX.

Walsh, K. (1987). *Neuropsychology: A clinical approach (2nd ed.)* New York: Churchill Livingstone.

Wilkins, A. J., Shallice, T., & Mc Carthy, R. (1987). Frontal lesions and sustained attention. *Neuropsychologia, 25,* 359–365.

Chapter 7

Linkage of Evaluation and Crime Behavior: Inventory of Defendant Competencies and Self-Control

Harold V. Hall

Based upon observation and theory/findings from the forensic neuropsychological literature, a decision model for the linkage of executive-related deficits and offense behavior is presented in this chapter. The information contained within this chapter represents an amplification of the self-control and linkage steps presented in Chapter 2. Linkage analysis is designed to synthesize previous material gathered for both the time of the evaluation and the instant offense. This synthesis is considered preparatory for the forensic neuropsychological conclusions that may follow, as set forth in a formal report and/or courtroom testimony.

LINKAGE MODEL

The linkage model presented in Figure 1 has been adapted from the executive model of Stuss & Benson (1986). This model proceeds from top to bottom. Initially, two sets of task responses are considered, corresponding to competencies representative of the various functional systems (e.g., attention, language, motor, memory) exhibited at the time of the offense and during the evaluation. Neuropsychological data from the evaluation are gathered first and presented in the standard format. Task responses during this time are assumed to reflect the best performance of the assessee.

Crime-related strengths and weaknesses are considered next. These refer to rudimentary skills and/or homeostatic activities of the defendant. They create the foundation for all self-control behaviors exhibited before, during, or subsequent to instant violence by the accused. In actual cases, the format for analysis may be as follows:

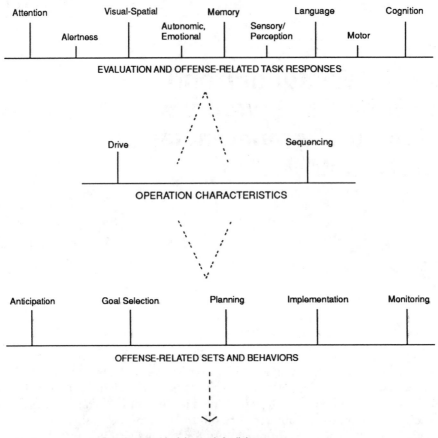

Figure 1. Executive functioning linkage.

	<u>Unknown</u>	<u>No</u>	<u>Yes</u>	<u>Specify</u>
Ability to sleep	_____	____	____	_____
Ability to eat/drink	_____	____	____	_____
Responds to autonomic pressure (e.g., incontinence)	_____	____	____	_____
Self-awareness (e.g., "I" statements)	_____	____	____	_____

(continued)   Unknown No   Yes Specify

	Unknown	No	Yes	Specify
Long-term memory skills (e.g., visual, auditory, tactile, olfactory)	_____	___	___	_____
Short-term memory skills	_____	___	___	_____
Reports cognitive activity	_____	___	___	_____
Awareness of surroundings (e.g., observations of environment)	_____	___	___	_____
Ability to estimate time	_____	___	___	_____
Ability to ambulate (e.g., voluntary movements)	_____	___	___	_____
Intact sensory skills (e.g., visual, olfactory, hearing)	_____	___	___	_____
Ability to express feelings (e.g., verbalizes anger, shows rage or fear)	_____	___	___	_____
Intact motor skills (e.g., grasping reflex, biting)	_____	___	___	_____
Withdrawal reflex from pain				
Voice recognition (e.g., of victim)	_____	___	___	_____
Self-grooming	_____	___	___	_____
Ability to maintain posture	_____	___	___	_____
Ability to show facial expression	_____	___	___	_____
Rudimentary chaining of behaviors (e.g., tracking and moving toward visual stimulus)	_____	___	___	_____
Other signs of basic self-regulation	_____	___	___	_____

The next level of the model concerns operation characteristics. Drive and sequencing, supra-model in nature, are the two principal operations. Both are almost always implicated in violence to others and subsequent evaluation-related behaviors. Difficulties usually represent either problems of excess or deficit. The key question at this level concerns whether neurobehaviors at the time of the evaluation and the crime are similar in function or operation. Only those conjoint neuropsychological behaviors for both times have relevance for linkage.

In terms of drive operations, for example, a "normal" activity level (relative to the defendant's own baseline) is expected. Look for hyperactivity-related responses, as with acting-out children, or hypoactivity, as in crimes of inaction (e.g., failure to assist), implicated in both the instant offense and evaluation behaviors.

The average person can perceive the emotional tone of sensory information as a further example of a drive-related competency. Did the defendant misinterpret cues from the examiner on his or her tests *and* from the victim or witnesses at the time of the instant offense? These cues need to be identified and ordered in terms of severity of deficits. Testing can be implemented to assess degree of deficits (e.g., TAT, Emotional Situations Test, Rorschach Test, Matching Facial Expressions Test). At the time of the alleged offense, data suggesting misinterpretation of the affective charge of sensory information can be scrutinized.

Sequencing operations for both the time of the evaluation and offense are next considered. In terms of deficits, intentionality in terms of a lack of congruence between intentions and actions can be assessed. Difficulty removing oneself from both the evaluation and crime context may reflect an abstraction problem. Long-range planning difficulties may yield impulsive, un-planned behavior. Defects in one's ability to control interference may manifest itself in distraction. An impaired ability to monitor the effects of one's output may result in perseveration or unawareness of consequences. In terms of long-range consequences, failure to learn from one's own offense-related responses predisposes one to repeat the behavioral pattern under similar contextual cues.

The key for both drive and sequencing operations is to consider as relevant those evaluation and crime-related behaviors that function or operate in a similar manner. Further and more importantly, since evaluation data are gathered under presumably optimal conditions, it is considered reflective of optimal responding. Therefore, only crime-related operations that represent a deterioration from evaluation behaviors (or history) have further relevance for linkage. How else could a presumably chronic cerebral lesion not show itself in violence at times other than the instant offense? In no case should a relevant crime behavior be less impaired than a comparable evaluation behavior, if indeed the accused asserts mental incapacity. Executive-related deficits at the time of the crime are thus always compared to a subsequent (i.e., evaluation) time in order to demonstrate loss of mental capacity.

The last level of the model, prior to conclusions, breaks up the crime sequence into discrete temporal categories before, during, and after the instant offense. All relevant data are synthe-sized into one of the five temporal periods (anticipation, goal selection, planning, implementa-tion, monitoring). Anticipation, for example, involves drive and sequencing operations that, in turn, are derived from the convergence and integration of the individual functional systems. This means that the competency of the accused in each of these areas must be considered. Victim and crime context factors must be incorporated into the temporal periods as they affect the defen-dant's behavior in discernable ways.

Characteristics of both the crime context and victim are considered by the evaluator prior to forming conclusions about each of the temporal periods. This is based upon the assumption that all violence to others is interpersonal by definition and represents a three-way interaction of perpetrator, victim, and context factors. A vulnerability analysis looks at features of the offense context in order to assess the impact on the defendant. Table 1 lists the principal factors to consider in the vulnerability analysis.

The victim in temporal interaction with the defendant can be scrutinized along any number of discrete dimensions. The Appendix lists perpetrator and victim characteristics at the time of the instant offense. Note, for example, the relative height and weight of the accused and the victim. Normally, aggressors choose victims who are shorter, slighter, or who possess charac-

Table 1. Vulnerability analysis of context.

Principal Factors	Assessment
Lighting pattern	_____
Visibility factors	_____
Security and weapons	_____
Presence of others	_____
Exits	_____
Locking system	_____
Background noise	_____
Temperature	_____
History of violence	_____
Architectural features	_____
Opportunities in concealment	_____

teristics that signal that the perpetrator would prevail if physical aggression occurred. The handedness of the victim and perpetrator should be compared, as a further example. Perpetrators usually use the dominant hand when aggressing with (one-handed) weapons; use of the nondominant hand is highly unusual and may suggest disorganized or incompetent responding. Victims typically show defensive wounds on both arms in an attempt to ward off the attack of the perpetrator.

Victim and perpetrator interaction on the day of the instant offense is particularly important to scrutinize. Victim provocation is common in assault cases, with many victims as the original aggressors who incurred more wounds than the arrested party. The procurement of weapons by the victim may have threatened, as an example, the defendant into inappropriate behavior. Table 2 presents a list of temporal interactive events to consider.

In general, after victim and crime context factors are taken into account, conclusions relevant to the defendant may be rendered individually for each temporal period. Deficits in anticipation of a crime, especially in physical assaults, may not substantially impair monitoring of one's previously violent behavior. Impaired monitoring, as in a poorly executed escape, may likewise not preclude a clear intention to engage in that criminal behavior. The next section amplifies each of the temporal periods.

Goal Formulation

Relevant to the time before the alleged violence, goal formulation taps the ability to systematically analyze and integrate the accused's awareness of self and environment. The capability of productively elaborating from a small number of cues from the crime context is also measured. Neuropsychological intactness and the ability to think of the violent act before it occurred, as evidenced by behaviors compatible with cognitive integration and volitional competence, is the central issue of this section.

Table 2. Day of alleged offense.

Event	Defendant		Victim	
	Time	Specify	Time	Specify
Significant events the night before	_____		_____	
Intoxicating substances ingested before instant violence occurred	_____		_____	
Procurement of weapons	_____		_____	
Presence of other people	_____		_____	
Arrival at instant violence scene	_____		_____	
First sighting of victim (accused)	_____		_____	
Verbal interaction with victim (accused)	_____		_____	
Time of instant violence	_____		_____	
Time left scene	_____		_____	
Destination	_____		_____	

	Unknown	No	Yes	Specify
Marked cognitive and/or behavioral focus	_____	___	___	_____
Ability to link thoughts with adaptive behavior (e.g., walking until food is found)	_____	___	___	_____
Verbal coherence and verbal fluency	_____	___	___	_____
Speaks to victim (e.g., requests money)	_____	___	___	_____
Appreciation of temporally distant need (e.g., need for more drugs to prevent withdrawal)	_____	___	___	_____
Knowledge of steps or elements in violent sequence	_____	___	___	_____

(continued)	<u>Unknown</u>	<u>No</u>	<u>Yes</u>	<u>Specify</u>
Cognitive mapping (e.g., navigating from home to crime scene)	_____	___	___	_____
Shows capacity for reflective thought about violence (e.g., verbalizations that involve comparisons)	_____	___	___	_____
Ability to think of alternatives to instant violence	_____	___	___	_____
Statements to others that he or she would harm the victim (e.g., for non-compliant behavior)	_____	___	___	_____
Other signs of goal formulation	_____	___	___	_____

Planning and Preparation

Relevant to the time before the alleged crime, this refers to the ability to show cognitive preparation for subsequent behaviors. Routine rehearsals for the alleged crime are the highest form of ability in this dimension.

	<u>Unknown</u>	<u>No</u>	<u>Yes</u>	<u>Specify</u>
Foreknowledge of alleged crime	_____	___	___	_____
Creation of time schedules	_____	___	___	_____
Temporal ordering of steps to complete task	_____	___	___	_____
Ability to revise plan given new information	_____	___	___	_____
Completes plan in reasonable time frame	_____	___	___	_____
Ability to interpersonally relate to others as planned	_____	___	___	_____
Motor or mental rehearsal of crime sequence	_____	___	___	_____
Other signs of planning/ preparation	_____	___	___	_____

Effective Performance

Occurring during the violence sequence, effective performance reflects the notion that the accused may simultaneously observe and change his or her behavior in response to a fluctuating environment, all in accordance with the goal or desired object of the action sequence. Hypothesis testing is the highest form of effective performance, as when the accused changes his or her own behavior (e.g., threatens victim, puts key in lock) in order to see the reaction (e.g., victim acquiescence, door becomes unlocked) and then changes his or own behavior accordingly (e.g., proceeds to rape victim, goes through door to bedroom). In essence, this skill taps the ability to show a concordance between intentions/plans and actions.

	Unknown	No	Yes	Specify
Able to view environment objectively (takes abstract attitude)				
Lured victim into defenseless position				
Demonstrates a variety of acts (flexible behavior as with several weapons)				
Displaying multiple sets of simultaneous motor behaviors				
Able to orchestrate multistep, multitask scheme (e.g., long connected chains of behaviors)				
Concerted effort in order to accomplish goal (e.g., despite victim resistance)				
Ability to show change in principle (e.g., from robbery to rape)				
Ability to show self-controlled somatic responses (e.g., sex with ejaculation, eating, drinking; all within violence sequence)				
Ability to delay responses				
Ability to monitor and self-correct ongoing behavior				

(continued)	Unknown	No	Yes	Specify
Nonstimulus boundedness (acts independent of environmental influences)	_____	____	____	_____
Ability to stop violence (e.g., response inhibition with no perseveration)	_____	____	____	_____
Ability to regulate tempo, intensity and duration of behaviors	_____	____	____	_____
Exhibited emotion is congruent with type of violence shown	_____	____	____	_____
Ability to avoid nonerratic behavior unless planned (e.g., deliberately becomes substance intoxicated)	_____	____	____	_____
Hypothesis testing	_____	____	____	_____
Awareness of wrongdoing during violence (e.g., from statements to victim)	_____	____	____	_____
Ability to hit/penetrate vital body target (e.g., deep knife penetration, shots to head)	_____	____	____	_____
Intact self-control (retrospectively reported by accused)	_____	____	____	_____
Evidence that offender disabled telephone, other utilities, or security devices	_____	____	____	_____
Victim was bound	_____	____	____	_____
Mouth was taped	_____	____	____	_____
Mouth gag was used	_____	____	____	_____
Blindfold placed over victim's eyes	_____	____	____	_____
Victim tied to another object	_____	____	____	_____
Perpetrator encourages bystanders to engage in violence to victim	_____	____	____	_____

(continued)	Unknown	No	Yes	Specify
Obliteration or destruction of evidence during instant violence	_____	___	___	_____
Other signs of effective performance	_____	___	___	_____

Recovery Period Behaviors

The accused may, after the instant offense, exhibit behaviors suggestive of memory/knowledge that a possible crime had been committed. These may include efforts ostensibly directed towards not getting caught for the alleged offense or of minimizing possible aversive consequences. Monitoring of the effects of violence may occur during this period.

	Unknown	No	Yes	Specify
Moves away when help arrives	_____	___	___	_____
Disposes of victim's body	_____	___	___	_____
Disposes of victim's clothing	_____	___	___	_____
Disposes of weapon used in offense	_____	___	___	_____
Disposes of other crime-related material	_____	___	___	_____
Cleans up own body	_____	___	___	_____
Washes own clothes used in alleged crime	_____	___	___	_____
Cleans/washes other material	_____	___	___	_____
Makes verbal statements of crime recall (e.g., spontaneous statements)	_____	___	___	_____
Relevant nonverbal gestures (e.g., points to victim's body)	_____	___	___	_____
Prevaricates incompatible behavior (e.g., makes up verifiably false story)	_____	___	___	_____
Writes confession	_____	___	___	_____
Other signs of recall for instant offenses	_____	___	___	_____

Post-Violence Depression Phase

For many violent perpetrators and suggestive of self-monitoring, a period of guilt and remorse is experienced after the exhibited aggression. This is especially true for episodic or rare violent offenders. The self-control to avoid self-punitive behavior is the focus of concern here (e.g., suicidal, self-mutilative gestures). Apology and remorseful behaviors are very common here and imply little about self-control at the time of the instant violence.

Routine Mental/Psychological Behaviors

Eventually, there is a return to baseline functioning for most individuals who perpetrate violence (see list of routine skills). A synthesis of all the above is presented in Table 3. Figure 2 portrays the same information in a simple three-way temporal period chart.

EVALUATION PROCESS AND CONCLUSIONS

The forensic neuropsychological evaluation in criminal settings is always focused on a temporal point different from that of the evaluation. Referral sources are interested in evaluation data only so far as they can be linked to (1) past events (e.g., insanity, diminished capacity); (2) near future activities (e.g., competency to proceed, pretrial hospitalization); or (3) distant future events (e.g., long-term dangerousness predictions, sentencing/treatment recommendations). The importance of conducting forensic neuropsychological examinations close to the temporal point of interest is the same as in nonforensic examinations. There is less chance of interference

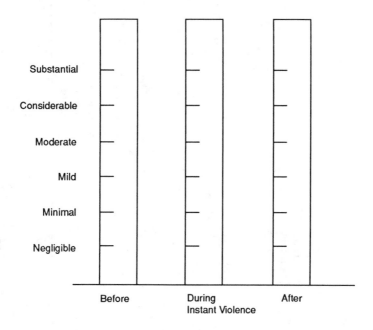

Combining all events within a time period, present the overall degree of self-control for BEFORE, DURING, and AFTER the instant violence on the above histogram.

NOTE: (See Table 3) BEFORE = A, B, C; DURING = D; AFTER = E, F, G.

Figure 2. Estimate of self-control by temporal period.

Table 3. Self-control of instant violence behaviors.

Synthesizing all self-control factors, judge whether the highest type of self-control called for at each of the levels has been attained. The suggested degree of maximum self-control this implies for the instant offense is presented on the left margin. Generic examples of each level of self-control are presented for each type.

Maximum level of self-control implied	Routine Mental/ Psychological Behaviors (Before)	Goal Formulation (Before)	Planning & Preparation (Before)	Effective Performance (During)	Recovery Period Behaviors (After)	Post-Violence Depression Phase (After)	Routine Mental/ Psychological Behaviors (After)
Substantial							
Considerable				Coordination of multiple behaviors to achieve objective goal; change in principle with shifting and monitoring			
Moderate			Ability to show cognitive and behavioral preparation for violence to follow; use of time in planning	Efforts to avoid detection & apprehension; ability to recall instant violence			
Mild	Awareness of inner & outer state and events; sensory & motor skills; short- and long-term memory; homeostatic & visceral activity		Ability to integrate internal & external information and to choose which action to follow; use of environmental cues			Ability to avoid suicidal or self-mutilative behavior; presence of remorse or apology	Awareness of inner & outer state and events; sensory & motor skills; short- and long-term memory; homeostatic & visceral activity
STAGE:	A	B	C	D	E	F	G

by a multiplicity of factors that render less reliable or less valid test results. If a disorder of executive functions is incurred after the previous violence, for example, by postcrime head trauma, it may invalidate the obtained results of the linkage assessment.

Judicial Considerations

The usual forensic neuropsychological evaluation involves the following sequence and considerations. Suggested degrees of certainty in evaluation conclusions are presented for the reader.

1. The accused engages in alleged violence.
2. Information is collected by police and other investigators.
3a. Court action is taken (e.g., grand jury, preliminary hearing); the key issue now is fitness to proceed.
3b. A referral question is framed regarding fitness responsibility, dangerousness, or treatment potential.
4. A forensic neuropsychologist (evaluator) is given authority to act:
   a. Collects information on #2;
   b. Adds to the data base information on perpetrator, victim, and crime context factors;
   c. Meets with accused over several points in time;
   d. Reaches conclusions; and
   e. Transmits information to the referral source.
5. A judicial disposition is reached. Dangerousness now emerges as the key issue. All forensic neuropsychological data submitted are now a permanent part of the record. Judicial feedback is automatic (e.g., appeal process, data retained for next conditional release hearing).

Recommended Procedures

A blowup of the evaluative role of the forensic neuropsychologist (evaluator) (#4), in terms of recommended procedures, is as follows:

BEFORE EVALUATION

1. The forensic neuropsychologist (evaluator) collects and reviews information in order to question the accused on alleged offense events.
2. Familiarizes self with literature relevant to the particular referral question and instant violence situation.
3. Makes expectations clear to retaining attorney (e.g., payment prior to submission of report unless governmental agency; all data are discoverable to both sides; dissemination of information through referral source).

DURING EVALUATION

1. The forensic neuropsychologist (evaluator) orients accused and attorney to (a) lack of guaranteed results, (b) the evaluation as an exception to privileged communication, and (c) test procedures.

2. Insists that attorneys/others are not present during testing as standardization does not involve the presence of significant/knowledgeable others, and results are thus contaminated.
3. Tapes procedures if possible for future review and/or replication of findings by others.

AFTER EVALUATION

1. The forensic neuropsychologist (evaluator) goes through the decision tree (see Chapter 2) to ensure all factors are taken into consideration. The report format should correspond to the retrospective decision path presented earlier.
2. Refers case to other sources if more data are needed (e.g., other forensic specialists, allied disciplines).
3. Comes to conclusions, writes reports, including attachments as needed, and provides copies for presiding judge, and defense and prosecuting attorneys.
4. Retains data until the death of the accused or for at least a decade, in order to provide a basis for reevaluation if necessary. In the civil cases that are based upon criminal actions, the statute of limitations need to be taken into account (e.g., wrongful death suits).
5. Does not send data to civil attorney or any source after court disposition since some verdicts are reversed, and the entire trial process may start anew.

CONCLUSIONS

Conclusions should be succinct, operationalized, and potentially replicable. The forensic neuropsychologist (evaluator) should:
1. State the decision path and key content factors that formed his or her conclusions.
2. Point out alternative explanations for the same data. Sociopathy or other psychogenic causes, for example, may account for a portion of the data.
3. Specify the degree of confidence in each conclusion rendered. Numerical probability figures, however, should be tied to base rate data. These ranges in part are suggested from the forensic literature (Stone, 1975).

Negligible—In essence, there is little or no evidence for a given conclusion. Degree of confidence is 0–10 percent.

Minimal—The evaluator here is asserting a very weak degree of confidence in his or others' assertions. Numerical probability is 11–25 percent.

Mild—The conclusion rendered may or may not be true as the evidence is somewhat weak. There is only a fair likelihood that this assertion is true, corresponding to a 26–50 percent probability range.

Moderate—More likely than not, the conclusion is true, corresponding to 51–75 percent probability of occurrence. A "preponderance of evidence" is the corresponding legal definition.

Considerable—In the evaluator's opinion, there is a strong likelihood that the conclusion is true, corresponding to a 76–90 percent probability of occurrence. This corresponds to the legal meaning of "clear and convincing."

Substantial—Here, the evaluator is almost certain of the conclusions, corresponding to a 91–100 percent degree of confidence. This corresponds to a legal definition of "beyond a reasonable doubt."

4. Specify the temporal limitations of the report. Ideally, these would be tied to the time period suggested by the base rate data utilized.
5. Provide feedback mechanisms for reassessment. Readministration of the same neuropsychological battery to see change over time may be suggested. Additional tests of executive functioning can be suggested.
6. Recommend intervention. Risk of dangerousness and possible intervention must be specified in many jurisdictions if an exculpating condition is found. Treatment may be recommended but should not be performed by the original evaluator as a double role develops.

THE EXPERT IN COURT

Under the Federal Rule of Evidence 702, which is followed by many state jurisdictions and is relevant to forensic evaluators, expert testimony is admissible when the expert is properly qualified and the subject matter of the expert testimony is such that the expertise of the witness will assist the trier-of-fact to understand the evidence or determine a fact in issue. This allows wide discretionary powers to any particular court that desires to receive testimony from a particular expert.

Frye v. U.S., 293 F. 1013 (D.C. Cir. 1923) establishes the prevailing standard for the admissibility of scientific testimony in federal jurisdictions. For example, the thing from which the deduction is made must be sufficiently established to have gained general acceptance in the particular field in which it belongs. The procedure or theory must have been around for a substantial period of time. *Frye* has been attacked on many grounds, not the least of which, if adopted in all jurisdictions, it would preclude input from experts with novel but promising methods. In psychology, in particular, there are hundreds of different diagnostic and intervention systems resting upon differing schools of thought and axiomatic bases.

In the case of neuropsychology, moreover, the bulk of the clinical and experimental lore rests upon the cerebrally impaired as opposed to normally functioning individuals and subgroups. Many of the reliability and validity coefficients of standard neuropsychological tests are quite modest. Entire batteries have been held in disrepute, basically because the claims of the investigators have not been replicated by independent evaluators (e.g., Luria-Nebraska Neuropsychological Battery; see Rogers, 1986). Yet, the clinical-forensic utility of neuropsychological assessment has been repeatedly demonstrated. In forensic settings and situations, even harsh critics of psychological and psychiatric expert evaluation have approved of its use (e.g., Ziskin, 1981).

The *Frye* test question remains. To date, psychologists are not accountable to meet *Frye* test requirements (e.g., see Blau, 1986), except in areas shared with other disciplines besides neuropsychology. The issue of hearsay, for example, involves the notion that information obtained from another person about the defendant (e.g., victim, relative, evaluator) is second-hand and should be excused unless demonstrated to be a reliable, valid, and usual and customary procedure or explanatory theory. Thus, many neuropsychologists in previous years, attacked on hearsay, testified on the cerebral functioning of defendants based upon test results obtained by psychometrists and technicians without having personally interviewed the defendant. This practice has changed drastically in recent years due to increasing antagonism by opposing attorneys. The court is keenly interested in whether the current neuropsychologist personally interviews the defendant.

The forensic psychologist's status is in question in terms of other testimonial admissibility issues. In *Coates v. Whittington*, 31 Tex. Sup. Ct. J. 659 (1988), a products liability case, the Texas Supreme Court held that a psychologist is not a physician and cannot, therefore, conduct a court-ordered mental examination. *Loomis v. Kaplaneris*, 519 So. 2d 1058 (Fla. 2d DCA 1988), held essentially the same thing. Psychologists are not considered "physicians" for purposes of the Florida Rules of Civil Procedure. In other jurisdictions (e.g., Oregon, Hawaii), psychologists are considered physicians.

Rule 35 of the Federal Rules of Civil Procedures was recently changed to include either a psychologist or a psychiatrist to examine and testify in a civil trial.

The federal jurisdictions allow psychologists on a par with psychiatrists in terms of assessment and testimony, yet both sets of experts cannot comment on ultimate issues in insanity cases. Instead, answers must be offered in terms of hypotheticals.

In the criminal court, some jurisdictions hold psychologists in low regard when compared to other experts. In *Commonwealth of Pennsylvania v. Webster*, 539 A 2d 804 (1988), an insanity case, the court allowed the psychologist to testify but stated that more qualified experts would follow. The trial judge's comments were targeted by the Supreme Court of Pennsylvania in that they were held to invade the province of the jury and, more importantly, deprive the defendant of a fair trial.

Cross-examination tactics by opposing attorneys represent a further hurdle for the expert psychologist witness. Several tables show a variety of approaches to question the expert from the point of view of a civil attorney (Table 4, McElhaney, 1989), a criminal psychologist attorney (Table 5, Ziskin, 1981), and from the prospective of the jury (Table 6, Tigar, 1982).

Synthesis

A double link is described by this book in joining neuropsychology and law in searching for commonalities between crime and evaluation behaviors. All else in this work is subordinate to the notion that offense-evaluation links can be uncovered, demonstrated, and presented in court or in a report with credibility. The value of behavioral science, in a general sense, must rest on the application of assessment principles to specific cases. In this, the editors hopes that this has been successful for a specific focus. Let us succinctly review the main points of the linkage phenomenon:

The defendant engages in both an instant offense and subsequent forensic evaluation. Victim and crime-context factors are taken into account. In both temporal situations, a discrete set of behaviors is exhibited, which are reflective of the various functional neural subsystems. If this is not the case, conclusions regarding linkage are not possible.

All behaviors are executed by definition. Therefore, they can be analyzed in terms of drive and sequencing operations for both the offense and evaluation. All offenses can be segmented in discrete temporal and neuropsychological periods. Drive and sequencing abilities, and lower to higher order executive skills, are operative within each of these crime time periods—anticipation, goal selection, planning, implementation, and monitoring. A substantial incapacity can exist within any time period during which the offense is put into action.

This model rests upon several assumptions. First, subsystem and executive-related responses for both the crime and evaluation must exist for comparison. The best (i.e., most competent)

Table 4. Expert witness cross-examination tactics.

Method	Principle/Example	Counteraction
1. "Make him your witness"	If you have a strong case on causation, create an ally instead of adversary (e.g., "You say he was epileptic?").	Anticipate and amplify on leading words/questions of cross-examiner.
2. "Attack his field"	Question his entire discipline (e.g., "Do I call you doctor, mister, or what?" "You have never physically examined a patient?").	Use as opportunity for educating the cross-eximiner and judge/jury.
3. "Attack his qualifications"	No matter how well trained or experienced he is, there are always levels he has not reached (often the vita is the basis for questioning).	See above; also eliminate unnecessary/meaningless information from vita.
4. "Expose his bias"	His integrity may be for sale if he spends much time in court or charges large fees.	Refer cross-examiner to your bookkeeper; know court experience/outcomes.
5. Attack his (second-order) facts"	Particularly suited for experts who do no factual investigation but rely on the reports of others.	Directly assess perpetrator, victim, and/or context.
6. "Vary the hypothetical"	Must have a factual basis. This method reveals the decision path of the expert.	Know the decision path leading to your ultimate conclusions.
7. "Impeach with a 'treatise'"	If an expert differs with others in his field, he may be wrong.	Do not accept a proffered treatise as authoritative.
8. "Attack him head-on"	The only direct method, this is dangerous and should be avoided in favor of above tactics.	Be thoroughly prepared; meet with your attorney prior to court.

Adapted from McElhaney, J. (1989). Nine ways to cross-examine an expert. *Journal of the American Bar Association, 9,* 99.

Table 5. Expert witness cross-examination tactics.

Method	Counteraction
1. Show that the forensic expert did not use the literature in reaching conclusions.	In all cases, use the general forensic literature with case-specific information.
2. Demonstrate that the psychologist did not have the medical training necessary to comment on the ultimate forensic issue.	In qualification, emphasize areas of training/ experience that are relevant to ultimate issue.
3. Demonstrate that the psychologist (psychiatrist) studied much that is not required for assessment/ training.	Partially admit; have illustrations showing how seemingly irrelevant areas amplify knowledge of forensic assessment.
4. Show that considerable controversy exists re status of assessment and therapy in psychology.	Use as opportunity to educate opposing attorney on recent developments.
5. (For board certified forensic experts) Have expert admit that his certifying board is new, did not require exams, and/or reflects only minimal competency.	Admit factual elements of certification; some data exists that rate of agreement with judge/jury outcomes may be higher (i.e., impact factor).
6. Suggest that the expert failed to take into account demand characteristics of assessment situation (e.g., that which is conducted in jail/prison).	Use multiple assessment devices at several different points in time.
7. Suggest that the examiner is biased due to language, cultural differences.	Demonstrate use of safeguards (e.g., use of interpreter, cross-cultural norm base for utilized tests).
8. Elicit data that show reliability and validity of utilized measures are poor or, at least, mediocre.	Ask which of the many types of reliability/ validity he is referring to; have list of correlational coefficients available.
9. Show that DSM III-R was not designed to illuminate forensic issues.	Admit, add that in every extant test of insanity, a mental condition must be proffered. An FDA is a separate issue.
10. Have him admit that clinical/forensic experience is not connected to accuracy of description/ prediction.	Know your own impact rating in court; have available your % of true positive and negative dangerousness predictions.

Adapted from Ziskin, J. (1981). *Coping with psychiatric and psychological testimony.* Venice, CA: Law & Psychology Press.

Table 6. Questions jury members want answered by the "expert."

1. How are you going to assist me in understanding the facts?
2. What makes you call yourself an expert?
   a. Are you an expert in life in general or is your expertise limited to a particular field? If so, which field?
   b. Are you an expert in something real, or just a theoretical academician?
3. Is your approach to your subject accepted?
   a. Is your approach controversial?
   b. Is it subject to responsible criticism from other experts in the field?
4. Do you concede that the other expert in the case is a respected, competent member of your profession?
   a. Then why should we believe you instead of him?
5. How did you arrive at your conclusions?
   a. Where did you get the tests upon which your conclusions are based?
   b. What tests did you do?
   c. Describe the tests that provided results inconsistent with your conclusions.
      1) Why shouldn't we believe these tests instead of the tests you rely on to form your conclusions?
6. Are you aware of the literature in your field that deals generally with the subject about which you are testifying?
   a. Are you aware of the treatise, _____, by Professor _____, which, at page _____, contradicts the validity of the conclusions you have drawn?
7. What about your previous testimony in the case of _____?
8. What about your treatise entitled, _____, which you published in _____? Doesn't your statement found at page ____, contradict what you have just told us?
9. Where did you get the facts to which you applied the tests?
   a. Were you there when the events you are talking about took place?
   b. Don't you think the source of your facts is biased?
   c. Why are the facts even relevant?
10. You weren't aware of these other facts: _____, _____, _____, that apply to this case?
    a. Now that you know them, wouldn't that change your conclusion?
11. What assumptions (or inferences) did you make to fill in the gaps between the facts?
    a. Why are your assumptions warranted?
    b. If these assumptions aren't true, wouldn't that change your conclusion?
    c. What if it really happened like this: _____. What is your conclusion now?
12. Why are you so boring? Don't you have any charts?
13. Are you objective?
    a. The State (County, Feds, etc.) pays your fees. Aren't you a pimp for the government?
    b. You don't want to disagree with your boss, Doctor _____, do you?
    c. This whole thing seems pretty fuzzy. Where are you coming from personally? How do you feel about law and order? Do you consider yourself a liberal or a conservative?
14. You appear rather pompous. Why do you appear so threatened by these questions?

Modified from Tigar, M. E. (1982). Handling the expert like an expert: Back to basics. *The Advocate*, *14*, 13.

responses from the evaluation represent the best responses capable by the defendant at the time of the offense, as optimal performance is provided for at the evaluation. Absent malingering or intervening cerebral/psychological deterioration, evaluation performance should represent the best performance of which the defendant is capable. Thus, it can be used as a dependent variable for post-hoc offense evaluation.

The defendant should have performed inferior to evaluation behavior if incapacity is asserted. In other words, there should be a deterioration from (optimal) evaluation performance. If not, the defendant may not have been impaired or disinhibited to the point of exhibiting violence and may have simply chosen that course of action for any number of reasons. Further, if crime responses match (or are superior to) evaluation behavior, then the defendant is performing at an optimal level. Hence, no disorganization occurs *compared to the defendant's own evaluation performance when criminal behavior is not engaged in*. Choice and deliberation are then implied.

A further assumption in the model is that a substantial impairment in any of the temporal periods before or during the crime renders mental incapacity for the entire crime. In all jurisdictions, state-of-mind applies to *all* elements of the offense—conduct, attendant circumstances, and results of conduct. An incapacity in any element exculpates the defendant for the crime charged. However, the law recognizes that a substantial impairment in monitoring (after the crime) does not necessarily render mental incapacity, as highly self-controlled and chosen goals/plans and crime methods may be followed by defendant disorganization, apology, or remorse.

Let us expand on the point of partial incapacity, implying substantial incapacity for the entire offense. In most jurisdictions, the four states-of-mind in terms of culpability and descending order (from most to least culpable) are (1) intentionally, (2) knowingly, (3) recklessly, and (4) negligently. Using the first state-of-mind, a person acts intentionally with respect to *conduct* when it is the conscious object to engage in such conduct. Goal selection clearly is implicated in this legal definition. Anticipation is necessary in order to select, plan, or practice behaviors necessary to successfully execute the offense.

A person acts intentionally with respect to *attendant circumstances* when there is awareness of the existence of such circumstances. Wrongly believing or even hoping for given attendant circumstances at the time of the offense qualifies for this criterion in many jurisdictions. Victim and crime-context factors thus must be considered, as well as the defendant's beliefs generated by his or her own behavior before or during the offense. Thus, analysis of behaviors within all the temporal periods may yield information on this criterion.

A person acts intentionally with respect to a *result* of conduct in most jurisdictions, when it is the specific intent or conscious object to cause a given result (e.g., a dead victim, a robbed bank). This is differentiated from the first criterion, which focuses upon the act itself rather than results from the same. Thus, information from the goal selection and implementation periods is important to consider here. Monitoring behavior may also shed light on the person's goal to obtain certain results.

In summary, law and neuropsychology of executive impairments will be increasingly intertwined as findings are applied to forensic settings and situations. Criterion-based quantitative models can be expected in the foreseeable future to assist in the evaluation of particular cases.

REFERENCES

Blau, T. (1986). *The psychologist as expert witness.* New York: John Wiley & Sons.

Coates v. Whittington, 31 Tex. Sup. Ct. J. 659 (1988).

Commonwealth of Pennsylvania v. Webster, 539 A 2d 804 (1988).

Frye v. U.S., 293 F. 1013 (D.C. Cir. 1923).

Loomis v. Kaplaneris, 519 So. 2d 1058 (Fla. 2d DCA 1988).

McElhaney, J. (1989). Nine ways to cross-examine an expert. *Journal of the American Bar Association,* 98–99.

Rogers, R. (1986). *Conducting insanity evaluations.* New York: Van Nostrand Reinhold.

Stone, A. (1975). *Mental health and the law: A system in transition* (DHEW Pub. No. ADM 76-176). Washington, DC: U.S. Government Printing Office.

Stuss, D., & Benson, D. (1986). *The frontal lobes.* New York: Raven Press.

Tigar, M. (1982). Handling the expert like an expert: Back to basics. *The Advocate, 14,* 13.

Ziskin, J. (1981). *Coping with psychiatric and psychological testimony.* Venice, CA: Law and Psychology Press.

APPENDIX

Perpetrator and victim characteristics at the time of the instant offense.

Please check as many as apply. Fill in the blanks when indicated.
P = Perpetrator; V = Victim

P	V		P	V	
		SEX			**ETHNICITY**
___	___	Male	___	___	Black
___	___	Female	___	___	White
___	___	Unknown	___	___	Hispanic
			___	___	Chinese
___	___	**KNOWN AGE**	___	___	Filipino
			___	___	Hawaiian
		ESTIMATED AGE	___	___	Japanese
___	___	Below 15 yrs	___	___	Polynesian
___	___	15–19 yrs	___	___	Portuguese
___	___	20–24 yrs	___	___	Samoan
___	___	25–29 yrs	___	___	Mixed/Combo
___	___	30–39 yrs	___	___	Other _____
___	___	40–49 yrs	___	___	Unknown
___	___	50–65 yrs			
___	___	Over 65 yrs			**BUILD**
			___	___	Skinny
		HEIGHT	___	___	Slim
___	___	Under 5'0"	___	___	Medium/Average
___	___	5'0" to 5'1"	___	___	Heavy
___	___	5'2" to 5'3"	___	___	Husky
___	___	5'4" to 5'5"	___	___	Muscular
___	___	5'6" to 5'7"	___	___	Fat
___	___	5'8" to 5'9"	___	___	Unknown
___	___	5'10" to 5'11"			
___	___	6'0" to 6'1"			**POSTURE**
___	___	6'2" to 6'3"	___	___	Stooped
___	___	6'4" to 6'6"	___	___	Bowed Legs
___	___	Over 6'6"	___	___	Bent to One Side
___	___	Unknown	___	___	Normal/Erect
			___	___	Stiff
		WEIGHT	___	___	Unknown
___	___	Under 100 lbs			
___	___	100 to 119 lbs			**GAIT**
___	___	120 to 139 lbs	___	___	Slow
___	___	140 to 159 lbs	___	___	Shuffle
___	___	160 to 179 lbs	___	___	Limp
___	___	180 to 199 lbs	___	___	Walks with Cane
___	___	200 to 219 lbs	___	___	Normal
___	___	220 to 239 lbs	___	___	Walks Fast
___	___	240 to 260 lbs	___	___	Runs
___	___	Over 260 lbs	___	___	Unknown
___	___	Unknown			

P	V		P	V	
___	___	**UNUSUAL MANNERISMS**	___	___	Lip, Upper
___	___	What? _____	___	___	Nose
___	___	Unknown	___	___	Ear(s), Pierced
			___	___	Other _____
		ACCENT			
___	___	What does it sound like? _____			
___	___	_____			**JEWELRY**
___	___	Unknown	___	___	What and where? _____
			___	___	_____
		INJURIES	___	___	_____
___	___	Where and what? _____			
___	___	_____			**OTHER** (e.g., hearing aid)
___	___	Unknown	___	___	What and where? _____
			___	___	_____
		TATTOOS	___	___	_____
___	___	Arm, Left			
___	___	Arm, Right			**HEAD HAIR—Color**
___	___	Back	___	___	Black
___	___	Chest	___	___	Brown
___	___	Fingers, Left	___	___	Blond
___	___	Fingers, Right	___	___	Dirty Blond
___	___	Hand, Left	___	___	Red
___	___	Hand, Right	___	___	Gray
___	___	Leg, Left	___	___	White
___	___	Leg, Right	___	___	Other _____
___	___	Other _____	___	___	Unknown
___	___	Unknown			
					HEAD HAIR—Style
		BODY SCARS	___	___	Straight
___	___	Abdomen, Left	___	___	Curly
___	___	Abdomen, Right	___	___	Wavy
___	___	Arm, Left	___	___	Afro
___	___	Arm, Right	___	___	Tied
___	___	Back	___	___	Braided
___	___	Chest	___	___	Neat
___	___	Hand, Left	___	___	Flat Top
___	___	Hand, Right	___	___	Wig
___	___	Leg, Left	___	___	Unknown
___	___	Leg, Right			
___	___	Wrist, Left			**HEAD HAIR—Length**
___	___	Wrist, Right	___	___	Bald
___	___	Other _____	___	___	Crew Cut
___	___	Unknown	___	___	Neck Length
			___	___	Shoulder Length
		FACIAL SCARS	___	___	Long
___	___	Cheek, Left	___	___	Unknown
___	___	Cheek, Right			
___	___	Chin			**FACIAL HAIR—Type**
___	___	Eyebrow, Left	___	___	Mustache
___	___	Eyebrow, Right	___	___	Goatee
___	___	Forehead	___	___	Beard
___	___	Harelip	___	___	Other _____
___	___	Lip, Lower	___	___	Unknown

P	V		P	V	
		FACIAL HAIR—Color	___	___	Brown
___	___	Black	___	___	Black
___	___	Brown	___	___	Clear
___	___	Blond	___	___	Moles
___	___	Red	___	___	Freckles
___	___	Gray	___	___	Blackheads
___	___	White	___	___	Acne/Pimples
___	___	Other _____	___	___	Pock-Marked
___	___	Unknown	___	___	Birthmark
			___	___	Other _____
		EYES—Color	___	___	Unknown
___	___	Black			
___	___	Brown			TEETH
___	___	Blue	___	___	Yellow
___	___	Gray	___	___	White
___	___	Green	___	___	Normal
___	___	Other _____	___	___	False
___	___	Unknown	___	___	Broken
			___	___	Braces
		EYES—Glasses	___	___	Missing
___	___	Bifocal	___	___	Stained
___	___	Other Prescription	___	___	Filled
___	___	Contact Lenses	___	___	Other _____
___	___	Sunglasses	___	___	Unknown
___	___	Reflective			
___	___	Other _____			MOUTH
___	___	Unknown	___	___	Alcohol Smell
			___	___	Saliva
		EYEGLASSES—Frames	___	___	Normal
___	___	Wire	___	___	Unusual Lips
___	___	Plastic	___	___	Mouth Concealed
___	___	Rimless	___	___	Other _____
___	___	Clear	___	___	Unknown
___	___	Color _____			
___	___	Unknown			HANDS
			___	___	Small
		EYES—Traits	___	___	Stubby
___	___	Crossed	___	___	Large
___	___	Squinting	___	___	Spotted
___	___	Bloodshot	___	___	Normal
___	___	Dilated/Constricted Pupil	___	___	Hairy
___	___	Lazy Eye	___	___	Injured
___	___	Wide	___	___	Other _____
___	___	Missing, Left	___	___	Unknown
___	___	Missing, Right			
___	___	Other _____			CLOTHING—Hat
___	___	Unknown	___	___	Baseball Cap
			___	___	Business
		COMPLEXION	___	___	Military
___	___	Pale	___	___	None
___	___	Fair	___	___	Other _____
___	___	Medium	___	___	Color _____
___	___	Ruddy	___	___	Designs _____
___	___	Tanned	___	___	Unknown

P	V		P	V	
		CLOTHING—Shirt/Blouse	___	___	Unknown
___	___	T-Shirt	___	___	Make _____
___	___	Pullover	___	___	Color _____ Year _____
___	___	Sport Shirt	___	___	Unusual Features _____
___	___	Dress Shirt	___	___	Decals _____
___	___	Blouse	___	___	License # _____
___	___	Other _____			
___	___	None			TYPE OF WEAPON
___	___	Unknown	___	___	Arson
___	___	Color _____	___	___	Ax
___	___	Sleeve Length _____	___	___	Blunt Instrument
___	___	Markings _____	___	___	Firearm
			___	___	Handgun _____ Cal.
		CLOTHING—Trousers	___	___	Shotgun _____ Ga.
___	___	Jeans	___	___	Rifle _____ Cal.
___	___	Dress Slacks	___	___	Machine Gun _____ Cal.
___	___	Shorts	___	___	Garrotte/Ligature
___	___	None	___	___	Hatchet
___	___	Casual	___	___	Knife, Large (6" or larger)
___	___	Corduroy	___	___	Knife, Small (less than 6")
___	___	Other _____	___	___	Odd/Unusual Weapon
___	___	Unknown	___	___	Physical Force
___	___	Color _____	___	___	Sharp Instrument (other than knife)
___	___	Length _____	___	___	Vehicle
___	___	Markings _____	___	___	Tire Tool
			___	___	Other _____
		CLOTHING—Shoes	___	___	Unknown
___	___	Barefoot	___	___	Color _____
___	___	Slippers	___	___	Composition _____
___	___	Dress Shoes	___	___	Container _____
___	___	Work Shoes			
___	___	Boots			FIRST SEEN BY OTHERS
___	___	Sandals	___	___	Car
___	___	Other _____	___	___	Club/Disco
___	___	Unknown	___	___	Date First Seen _____
___	___	Color _____	___	___	Estimated Time _____
___	___	Material _____	___	___	Health Club
					Hitchhiking
		CLOTHING—Dress	___	___	House/Apartment
___	___	Formal	___	___	Playground or Parks/Yards
___	___	Casual	___	___	Public Conveyance
___	___	Work	___	___	School
___	___	Unknown	___	___	Shopping
___	___	Color _____	___	___	Walking
___	___	Length _____	___	___	Work
___	___	Markings _____	___	___	City/State
			___	___	Other _____
		VEHICLE	___	___	Unknown
___	___	Automobile			
___	___	Bicycle			LAST SEEN BY OTHERS
___	___	Motorcycle	___	___	Car
___	___	Truck	___	___	Club/Disco
___	___	Other _____	___	___	Date Last Seen _____

P	V		P	V	
___	___	Estimated Time _____			**LIFESTYLE**
___	___	Health Club	___	___	Bisexual
___	___	Hitchhiking	___	___	Day Person—in early
___	___	House/Apartment	___	___	Heterosexual
___	___	Playground or Parks/Yards	___	___	Homosexual
___	___	Public Conveyance	___	___	Involved/Outgoing
___	___	School	___	___	Narcotics User
___	___	Shopping	___	___	Night Person—stays out late
___	___	Walking	___	___	Socializes Frequently
___	___	Work	___	___	Socializes Seldom
___	___	City/State	___	___	Withdrawn/Shy
___	___	Other _____	___	___	Other _____
___	___	Unknown	___	___	Unknown
		CRIMINAL OCCUPATION			**OCCUPATION**
___	___	Arson	___	___	Gas Station Attendant
___	___	Burglary	___	___	Business/Professional
___	___	Fraud	___	___	Homemaker
___	___	Gambling	___	___	Laborer/Services
___	___	Homicide	___	___	Street Person
___	___	Larceny	___	___	Student
___	___	Motorcycle Gang	___	___	None
___	___	Narcotics	___	___	Realtor
___	___	Organized Crime	___	___	Priest/Minister
___	___	Pornography	___	___	Store Clerk
___	___	Prostitution	___	___	Other _____
___	___	Robbery	___	___	Unknown
___	___	Other _____			
___	___	Unknown			

GLOSSARY

A

A Posteriori: "From the effect to the cause"; from what comes after. Denotes an argument based on experience or observation.

A Prior: "From the cause to the effect"; from what goes before. Denotes an argument which posits a general principle or admitted truth as a cause and deduces from it the effect which must necessarily follow.

Ab Initio: "From the first act"; from the beginning, referring to the validity of statutes and so forth. In contrast to ex post facto.

Abnormal: Maladaptive behavior detrimental to the individual and/or the group.

Abrogate: To cancel, annul, or destroy; to repeal a former law by a legislative act or by usage.

Absence Seizures: Petit mal seizures in children, shown by brief altered states of consciousness.

Absolute Refractory Phase: A period of complete unresponsiveness.

Acalculia: Impaired calculation abilities, more often associated with left parietal or occipital lesions.

Acapnia: A marked diminution in the amount of carbon dioxide in the blood.

Acceptance: An agreement to the act or proposal of another person.

Acetone Bodies: Acetoacetic acide, beta-hydroxybutyric acid, and acetone; found in blood and urine in increased amounts whenever too much fat in proportion to carbohydrate is being oxidized. Also called ketone bodies.

Acetylcholine (ACh): One of the best known synaptic transmitters. Acetylcholine acts as an excitatory transmitter at synapses between motor nerves and skeletal muscles but as an inhibitory transmitter between vagus nerve and heart muscle.

Acetylcholinesterase (AChE): An enzyme that inactivates the transmitter acetylcholine both at synaptic sites and elsewhere in the nervous system, thus halting its effects.

Achromatopsia: Impaired perception of colors due to cerebral dysfunction. Can be hemianopic or involve both entire visual fields.

Acidosis: Diminution in the reserve supply of fixed bases (especially sodium) in the blood.

Acquit: To set free or release from an obligation, burden or accusation; to legally certify the innocence of a person charged with a crime.

Action: A formal proceeding or complaint brought within the jurisdiction of a court of law in order to enforce any right.

Action Potential: Nerve impulse which flows along the membrane of the neuron. The membrane is receptive to potassium ions in the resting state and sodium ions when excited. The reversal in permeability causes the impulse.

Actuarial Approach: Application of probability statistics to human behavior, as in insurance.

Actus Reus: "Guilty act"; a wrongful act. As opposed to guilty, "mens rea."

Acute Alcohol Hallucinosis: State of alcoholic intoxication characterized by hallucinations.

Acute Paranoid Disorder: Psychoses characterized by transient and changeable paranoid delusions, usually related to an identifiable stressor and transient in nature.

Acute Posttraumatic Stress Disorder: Disorder in which symptoms develop within six months of an extremely traumatic experience instead of entering the recovery state.

Ad Hoc: "For this"; for a special purpose or particular action.

Adaptation: Adjustment to a stimulus; also used to denote changes in the retina on exposure to different intensities of light.
  A progressive loss of receptor sensitivity as stimulation is maintained.

Adenohypophysis: See anterior pituitary.

Adequate Stimulus: The type of stimulus for which a given sense organ is particularly adapted (e.g., light energy for photoreceptors).

Adhesion: Abnormal union of two surfaces as a result of inflammation.

Adipsia: A condition in which an individual refuses to drink.

Adjustment Disorder with Depressed Mood: Moderately severe affective disorder behaviorally identical to a dysthymic disorder or depressed phase of a cyclothymic disorder but having an identifiable, though not severe, psychosocial stressor occurring within three months prior to the onset of depression.

Admissible Evidence: Evidence that can be received by the court or judge.

Adventitia: The outermost covering of a structure that does not form an integral part of it.

Adversarial System: A legal system in which opposing parties content against each other by presenting arguments and information in the interest of their clients. The judge acts as a decision-maker. In contrast to the inquisitorial system.

Adversary Process: Having two opposing parties. In contrast to an ex parte proceeding.

Adverse Party: A person whose interests are opposed to the interests of another party to an action.

Adverse Witness: A witness who gives evidence which is prejudicial to the party examining him at the time. Commonly refers to a witness whose testimony is prejudicial to the party by whom he was called.

Afferent Fibers/Traits: Data going toward the brain through neuronal pathways from the peripheral area of the central nervous system.

Affidavit: A written or printed statement of fact, made voluntarily, signed and sworn before a person having the authority to administer such an oath (e.g., a notary public).

After Potentials: Positive and negative changes of membrane potential that may follow a nerve impulse.

Aggregation Theory: Proposed by Halstead, this theory held that discrete sensory areas within the cortex were joined by a multitude of cortical connections. The aggregation produces an integration of cortical function.

Aggression: Behavior aimed at hurting or destroying someone or something.

Agitation: Marked restlessness and psychomotor excitement.

Agnosia: Defect in object recognition not due to primary sensory system dysfunction.

Agrammatism: Speech deficits characterized by language abbreviation such as omission of articles, prepositions, and inflectional forms. Language is essentially reduced to substantives.

Agraphia: Disturbances in writing skills (not motor execution). Usually seen with aphasia.

Akathisia: A general motor restlessness together with elevated inner tension, subjectively reported by the patient.

Akinesia: Inability to move due to brain dysfunction.

Alarm and Mobilization Reaction: First stage of the general-adaptation-syndrome, characterized by the mobilization of defenses to cope with a stressful situation.

Albuminuria: Presence of albumin in the urine.

Alcoholic Intoxication: State reached when alcohol content of the blood reaches or exceeds a legally prescribed level (0.1 percent or above in many jurisdictions).

Alcoholism: Dependence on alcohol to the extent that it seriously interferes with life adjustment.

Aldosterone: A mineralocorticoid hormone that helps maintain homeostasis in the concentrations of ions in blood and extracellular fluid.

Alexia: Inability to read due to brain dysfunction. Refers to total loss of this ability due to a brain lesion, typically located in the posterior cerebral cortex.

Alexia Without Agraphia: Inability to read in the absence of other language deficit.

Alien Hand Syndrome: Also termed the "Dr. Strangelove effect," intermanual conflict between the two hands is seen, with patients learning to use their "obedient" hand to control the alien hand. Contralateral supplementary motor area (SMA) and corpus collosum lesions have been implicated.

Alkalosis: Increased bicarbonate content of the blood. It may be the result of ingesting large amounts of sodium bicarbonate, prolonged vomiting with loss of hydrochloric acid, or hyperventilation.

All-or-none: Refers to the fact that the amplitude of the nerve impulse is independent of stimulus magnitude. Stimuli above a certain threshold produce nerve impulses of identical magnitude (although they may vary in frequency); stimuli below this threshold do not produce nerve impulses.

Allesthesia: Sensation of being touched on the side ipsilateral to a lesion when contralateral stimulation was, in fact, presented.

Alpha Motoneurons: Motoneurons that control the main contractile fibers (extrafusal fibers) of a muscle.

Alpha Rhythm: A brain potential that occurs during relaxed wakefulness, especially at the back of the head; frequency 8-12 Hz.

Alzheimer's Disease (AD): A degenerative disease characterized by the presence of neurofibrillary tangles and senile plaques. The disease is progressive in that it starts with memory and affect problems, then goes on to speech and motor problems, and eventually to an immobile and confused bedridden status. The disease lasts from 1 to 15 years.

Amblyopia: Reduced visual acuity not caused by optical or retinal impairment.

Ameboid Movement: Movement of a cell by extending from its surface processes of protoplasm (pseudopodia) toward which the rest of the cell flows.

Amenorrhea: The absence of the menses.

Amicus Curiae: "Friend of the court." A person who petitions the court for permission to provide information to the court on a matter of law that is in doubt, or one who is not a party to a lawsuit but who is allowed to introduce evidence, argument, or authority to protect his interests.

Amnestic Syndrome: Inability to remember events more than a few minutes after they have occurred coupled with the ability to recall the recent and remote part.

Amorphosynthesis: Loss of ability to synthesize more than a few properties of a stimulus. Multiple sensory stimuli cannot be simultaneously processed. Ascribed to parietal lobe dysfunction.

　　　　Damage to part of one sensory system causing an inequality in the overall cerebral system. The hemisphere receiving the decreased stimulation due to damage now needs increased input to balance the level of awareness.

Amorphous: Without definite shape or visible differentiation in structure; not crystalline.

Ampulla: A saccular dilation of a canal.

　　　　An enlarged region of each semicircular canal that contains the receptor cells (hair cells) of the vestibular system.

Amusia: A temporal lobe deficit associated with inability or reduced skill in perception of tonal patterns, individual tones, singing or humming to a rhythmical pattern, or even enjoying music.

Amygdala: A structure of a limbic system associated with flight/fight and other primitive responses. Located at the base of the temporal lobe.

　　　　A group of nuclei in the medial anterior part of the temporal lobe.

Analgesia: Loss of sensitivity to pain.

Anaphylactic: Increasing the susceptibility to the action of any foreign protein introduced into the body; decreasing immunity.

Anarithmetria: Impaired primary calculation skills due to brain damage. Left hemisphere lesions are implicated.

Anastomose: To open one into the other; used in connection with blood vessels, lymphatics, and nerves.

Anergia: Decreased or absent motivation or drive.

Anesthesia: Loss of sensation.

Aneurysm: A dilation or bulging of a blood vessel which fills with blood. A sac formed by the dilation of the walls of an artery and filled with blood.

Angiogram: A technique for examining brain structure in intact humans by taking X-rays after special dyes are injected into cerebral blood vessels. Inferences about adjacent tissue can be made by examining the outline of the principal blood vessels.

Angiography: X-rays of the head subsequent to injection of a radiopaque contrast material into a major artery. Designed to enhance pictures of the cerebral vasculature.

Angiotensin II: A substance produced in the blood by the action of renin and which may be involved in control of thirst.

Angular Gyrus: A cortical convolution on the parietal lobe, associated with speech functions.

Anions: Negatively charged ions, such as protein and chloride ions.

Anomic Aphasia: A fluent aphasia characterized by difficulty in naming objects to confrontation. Comprehension and articulation may be unimpaired.

Anomia: Inability to name objects due to brain dysfunction.

Anorexic: Lacking in appetite for food.

Anosmia: Absence of the sense of smell.

Anosodiaphoria: Unconcern over, but admission of an actual neurological impairment. *See also* Anton's Syndrome.

Anosognosia: Denial of those affected with neglect syndrome that their paretic extremity belongs to them.

      Total ignorance with denial of obvious disability. Examples include Anton's Syndrome with denial of blindness, and denial of amputation, amnesia, and hemiplegia. Usually accompanied by confusion or clouding of awareness.

Anterior Aphasias: Primarily indicating a left frontal lesion, these include Broca's aphasia, aphemia, transcortical motor aphasia and supplementary motor area (SMA) disturbance.

Anterior Cerebral Artery (ACA): One of the two major vascular networks of the frontal lobes, the ACA and its branches feed the medial aspects of the anterior portion of the brain.

Anterior Pituitary: The front lobe of the pituitary gland which secretes tropic hormones; also called adenophpophysis.

Anterograde Amnesia: Inability to recall life events from the time of a previous trauma or condition. Inability to learn and poor short-term memory are associated features.

Anterograde Degeneration: Loss of the distal portion of the axon resulting from injury to the axon; also called Wallerian degeneration.

Antidiuretic Hormone (ADH): A hormone from the posterior pituitary that controls the removal of water from blood by the kidneys. Also called vasopressin.

Antigen: Any substance which, when introduced into the blood or the tissues, incites the formation of antibodies, or reacts with them.

Anton's Syndrome: See also anosognosia. Adamant denial of blindness, often associated with bilateral posterior CVA.

Antrum: A cavity, or chamber, especially one within a bone, such as a sinus; the pyloric end of the stomach.

Apathetico-akinetico-abulic Behavior: Produced by massive damage to the prefrontal areas, among others. This syndrome is characterized by low drive and reduced motor output. Ongoing behavior may be disorganized. The effector aspect of action seems to be impaired in what has been termed the "pathological inertia of existing stereotypes."

Aperture: An opening, or orifice.

Aphagia: Refusal to eat, often related to damage to the lateral hypothalamus.

Aphasia: Impairment in language understanding and/or production due to brain injury.

Aphemia: A poorly articulated, slow, hypophonic, breathy speech with no syntax deficits. Usually follows initial mutism and is associated with Broca's area lesions, or a subcortical undercutting of Area 44.

Apoplexy: A sudden loss of consciousness, followed by paralysis resulting from cerebral hemorrhage, or blocking of an artery of the brain by an embolus or a thrombus.

Appellant: The party who appeals a decision from one court or jurisdiction to another.

Appellate Court: A court having jurisdiction of appeal and review.

Appellee: The party against whom an appeal is taken in a cause; the party who has an interest opposed to the setting aside or reversing of a judgement.

Apperceptive Visual Agnosia: The inability to synthesize or integrate visual input. Awareness of discrete parts may be intact.

   Inability to perceive meaning in, or visually recognize objects, due to cerebral dysfunction, most likely in posterior areas. Patients act blind but can avoid obstacles, indicating preserved ability to see.

Apraxia: Refers to impaired goal-directed motor behavior in individuals with unimpaired comprehension and primary motor skills (e.g., coordination, strength).

Apraxia of Speech: Known also as verbal apraxia or Broca's aphasia. Speech movement/articulation problems may include: (1) articulation errors; (2) phoneme substitution; (3) greater latency of response; (4) greater trouble with initial than subsequent phonemes; (5) no major vocal musculature problems; (6) sparse output; (7) poor melody; and (8) articulation is with much effort.

Apraxic Agraphia: Deficit in forming graphemes when writing to dictation or spontaneously. Lesions are in the parietal lobe contralateral to the dominant (writing) hand.

Apraxic Agraphia without Apraxia: Preserved oral spelling with illegible graphemes in spontaneous and dictated writing. Normal praxis is apparent to include ability to hold/use a writing instrument. Associated with perietal lobe lesions.

Aprosodias: Deficits in the comprehension and expression of affect and emotion, traditionally associated with right hemisphere dysfunction.

Aqueduct: A canal for the conduction of a liquid; the cerebral aqueduct of Sylvius connects the third and the fourth ventricles of the brain.

Arachnoid Space: Allows for cerebrospinal fluid to move about the cerebrum. Filled with fibroid matter and is considered one of the three layers of the meninges.

Arbitration: A method of resolving a dispute by using an impartial third party by whose decision both parties agree in advance to abide.

Arteriovenous Malformation (AVM): Involving the frontal lobe preferentially and focally, AVMs are usually unrecognized until one or more episodes have occurred. Subsequent attacks by AVM hemorrhage widens the area of deficit.

Articulate: To join together so as to permit motion between parts; enunciation in words and sentences. Divided into joints.

Asphyxia: Unconsciousness owing to interference with the oxygenation of the blood.

Assertiveness Training: A behavior therapy technique for helping individuals become more self-assertive in interpersonal relationships.

Association Areas: Part of the cortex next to the motor or sensory cortex, involving an overlap of functions. Allows for integration of data; damage causes patterned rather than specific deficits.

Associative Visual Agnosia: Inability to visually recognize objects with intact ability to copy, draw, or match to sample.

Astereognosis: Inability to identify objects placed by touch in spite of intact appreciation of tactile sensation. Also called tactile agnosia.

Asthenia: Weakness.

Astrocyte: A star-shaped glial cell with numerous processes or extensions that run in all directions. Their extentions provide structural support for the brain and may isolate receptive surfaces.

Astrocytoma: Neoplastic disease arising from the astrocyte cells. Usually unencapsulated, intracerebral, and fatal.

Ataxia: Muscular coordination and balance problems due to brain dysfunction.

   A loss of the power of muscular coordination.

   Impairment in the direction, extent, and rate of muscular movement; often due to cerebellar pathology.

Athetosis: Slow, involuntary, twisting movements of the arms and legs. May occur either during movement or when at rest. Associated with lesions of the cortex and subcortex (especially globus pallidus and thalamus).

Atresia: Congenital absence, or pathologic closure, of a normal opening or passage.

Atrophy: A wasting, or diminution, in the size of a part of the body or brain.

Atropine: An alkaloid obtained from atropa belladonna; it inhibits the action of the parasympathetic division of the autonomic system.

Attention Deficit Disorder: Maladaptive behavior in children characterized by impulsivity, excessive motor activity, and an ability to focus attention for appropriate periods of time; also called hyperactive syndrome or hyperkinetic reaction.

Attest: To bear witness to; to affirm as true or genuine.

Attribution Theory: The theory of social psychology in which people explain causes of the behavior of others based on unseen or unrecognized qualities in themselves.

Auditory Affective Agnosia: Impaired ability to recognize or comprehend affectively intoned speech due to a cerebral disorder.

Auditory Agnosia: Impaired hearing due to cerebral dysfunction with intact receptive abilities, as measured by audiometry or other means.

Auditory Cortex: A region of the temporal lobe that receives input from the medial geniculate nucleus.

Auditory Sound Agnosia: Impaired ability to recognize nonspeech sounds due to cerebral dysfunction.

Auscultation: The act of listening for sounds within the body; employed as a diagnostic method.

Automated Assessment: Psychological test interpretation by electronic computer or some other mechanical means.

Automatism: Producing without effort or delay material learned by rote in childhood or for a given temporal period (e.g., alphabet, number series). Errors reflect attentional disturbances; non-acute condition-related errors may indicate significant memory dysfunction.

Autonomic Nervous System: Part of the peripheral nervous system that supplies neural connections to glands and to smooth muscles of internal organs. Composed of two divisions (sympathetic and parasympathetic) that act in opposite fashion.

Autosome: Any ordinary paired chromosome as distinguished from a sex chromosome.

Autotopagnosia: Disorientation of personal space. Associated with left frontal lesions and aphasic signs. The subject is typically assessed for ability to touch, name, or imitate the examiner in touching body parts. Associated with parietal lobe damage.

Axon Hillock: A cone-shaped area from which the axon originates out of the cell body. Depolarization must reach a critical threshold here for the neuron to transmit a nerve impulse.

Axoplasmic Streaming: The process that transports materials synthesized in the cell body to distant regions in the dendrites and axons.

Azygos: An unpaired anatomic structure; the azygos vein arises from the right ascending lumbar vein and empties into the superior vena cava.

B

Bailiff: An officer or attendant of the court who has charge of a court session in matters such as keeping order and having custody of the jury and of prisoners while in court.

Balint's Syndrome: A syndrome consisting of (1) oculomotor apraxia, or difficulty shifting focus from a near to a distant stimulus, (2) optic ataxia, shown by impaired visually guided movements, and (3) impaired visual attention in the absence of general attentional deficits, with initial random gaze until a stimulus is fixated upon.

Ballism: Uncontrolable violent tossing of the limbs due to basal ganglia dysfunction.

Ballistic: Classes of rapid muscular movements thought to be organized or programmed by the cerebellum. Contrast with ramp.

Bar: The entire body of attorneys, or the collective members of the legal profession.

Basal Ganglia: Forebrain nuclei including those in the amygdala, caudate nucleus, claustrum, globus pallidus, and putamen.
    A group of forebrain nuclei found deep within the cerebral hemispheres.

Bases: Components of a DNA or RNA molecule. DNA contains four bases (adenine, thyamine, cytosine, and guanine), a pair of which forms each rung of the molecule. The order of these bases determines the genetic information of a DNA molecule.

Basic Neuroglial Compartment: A level of brain organization which includes a single nerve cell with all its synaptic endings, associated glial cells surrounding extracellular space, and vascular elements.

Basilar Artery: An artery formed by the fusion of the vertebral arteries; it branches supply blood to the brainstem and to posterior portions of the cerebral hemispheres.

Basilar Membrane: A membrane in the cochlea containing the principal structures involved in auditory transduction.

Behavioral Teratology: Impairments in behavior produced by early exposure to toxic substances.

Bench: A seat of judgment for the administration of justice; the seat occupied by the judge in court; the aggregate of the judges of which the court is comprised.

Berry Aneurysm: A small sac formed by the dilation of the wall of a cerebral artery. The anterior portion of the circule of Willis is the site of about 90% of berry aneurysms.

Bifurcated Trial: A two-phase trial in which issues are tried separately, e.g., guilt is determined in the first phase and punishment in the second, or in sanity cases, guilty is determined in the first phase and sanity in the second.

Bill of Particulars: A written statement setting forth the demands for which a legal action is brought. Designed to inform the defendant of the specific information regarding the cause of action stated in the complaint.

Binocular Disparity: The slight difference between the views from the two eyes, important in depth perception.

Bipolar Neurons: Nerve cells with a single dendrite at one end of the nerve cell and a single axon at the other end. Found in some vertebrate sensory system.

Bitemporal Hemianopsia: Optic chiasm damage resulting in visual field loss in both temporal (as opposed to nasal) areas.

Blind Spot: A place through which blood vessels enter the retina. Because there are no receptors in this region, light striking it cannot be seen.

Blindsight: Denial of recognition in the face of previous correct recognition and stimulus responses.

Blood-brain Barrier: The mechanisms that make the movement of substances from capillaries into brain cells more difficult than exchanges in other body organs, thus affording the brain a greater protection from exposure to some substances found in the blood.

Body Schema: Body image.

Bolus: A rounded mass of soft consistency.

Bona: Good or virtuous.

Bradycardia: Abnormal slowness of the heart or pulse.

Bradykinesia: Motor slowing.

Brain Stem: Thalamus, hypothalamus, ganglia, midbrain, hindbrain, and associated structures.

Brain Stem Reticular Formation: Part of the brain stem involved in arousal.

Brandeis Brief: A form of appellate brief which includes social science principles along with legal arguments. Takes its name from Supreme Court Associate Justice Louis D. Brandeis, who used such briefs.

Brief: A written statement prepared by the attorney arguing a case in court, including a table of relevant cases, a summary of issues and facts, and an argument of law as it supports a litigant's position.

Broca's Aphasia: An expressive speech disorder with relatively intact auditory comprehension. A nonfluent speech is noticed that is slow, labored, dysarthric, incomplete, and concrete. Agrammatism consists of missing grammatical words and inflectional endings. Considered an anterior aphasia.

Broca's Area: An area in the frontal region of the left hemisphere involved in the production of speech.

Brown-Peterson Distractor Technique: Counting backwards by twos or threes upon presentation of a verbal or nonverbal stimulus. Rehearsal is prevented by the counting.

Bruit: A sound or murmur heard in auscultation, especially an abnormal one.

Buccolinguofacial Apraxia: An oral apraxia affecting voluntary movements of the larynxz, pharynx, tongue, lips, and related suborgans in which simple, automatic movements are intact. Commanded tasks may yield deficits (e.g., no swallowing, laughing) in the presence of noncommanded, contextual responses (e.g., swallowing food after eating, smiling).

   Deficit in performing voluntary buccofacial motor activities (e.g., chewing, swallowing, raising eyebrows) with intact ability to perform reflexive movements with the same muscle groups.

Buffer: Any substance that tends to lessen the change in hydrogen ion concentration which otherwise would be produced by adding acids or bases.

Burden of Proof: In the law of evidence, the duty of a party to affirmatively prove a fact in dispute. The obligation of a party to convince the trier of fact as to the truth of a claim by establishing by evidence a required degree of belief concerning a fact. In civil cases, proof must be by a preponderance of the evidence. In criminal cases, all crime elements must be proved by the government beyond a reasonable doubt. In some equity issues and more recent decisions of the Supreme Court, the standard of proof is clear and convincing evidence.

C

Calcitonin: A hormone released by the thyroid gland.

Calculus: A stone formed in any portion of the body.

Calorie: A unit of heat. A small calorie (cal.) is the standard unit and is the amount of heat required to raise 1 gm of water from 15 degrees to 16 degrees C. The large calorie

(Cal.) is used in metabolism and is the amount of heat required to raise 1 kg of water from 15 degrees to 16 degrees C.

Canaliculus: A small canal or channel; in bone, minute channels connect with each lacuna.

Capgras Syndrome: Involves the reduplication of relatives, friends, possessions and the like, and is often viewed as a psychiatric, as opposed to neurological, problem. The target person, almost always a close relative, is considered an imposter.

Carcinoma: A malignant tumor or cancer; a new growth made up of epithelial cells, tending to infiltrate and give rise to metastases.

Case Law: The sum of reported cases forming a body of law. The law of a certain subject as evidenced or formed by the adjudged case, as opposed to statutes or other sources of law.

Catabolism: Reactions in a plant or animal that result in the degradation, or exidation, of molecules.

Catalysis: Change in the speed of a reaction produced by the presence of a substance which does not form part of the final product.

Catalyst: Any substance which brings about catalysis.

Cataract: A loss of transparency of the crystalline lens of the eye or of its capsule.

Catastrophic Reaction: Intensely negative but temporary emotion reaction, associated with left hemisphere lesions. Often occurs when subjects are informed of their limitations or shortcomings, in response to task demands. A heightened sensitivity to one's limitations.

Caudal: An anatomical term meaning toward the tail end. Opposed to rostral.

Caudate Nucleus: One of the basal ganglia with long extension or tail.

Cell Differentiation: The prenatal stage in which neuroblasts acquire the distinctive appearance of cells characteristic of a region of the nervous system.

Cell Proliferation: The production of nerve cells.

Cellular Fluid: See intercellular fluid.

Central Deafness: Hearing impairments related to lesions in auditory pathways or centers, including sites in the brain stem, thalamus, or cortex.

Central Nervous System (CNS): The portion of the nervous system that includes the brain and the spinal cord.

Central Sulcus: Known also as the Fissure of Rolando, this sulcus divides the anterior from the posterior areas of the brain (frontal from parietal).

Cephalic: An anatomical term referring to the head end. Also called rostral.

Cerebellar Cortex: The outer surface of the cerebellum.

Cerebellar Fits: Not really seizures, these movements consist of periods of decerebrate rigidity. Associated with large midline cerebellar lesions.

Cerebellar Syndrome: Due to a lesion in the cerebellum, ambulation is unsteady with side-to-side swaying. Equilibrium is adversely affected.

Cerebellum: A structure located at the back of the brain, dorsal to the pons; it is involved in the central regulation of movement.

Cerebral Contusion: A brain bruise. Refers to superficial damage to gyri or other crests of the cortical convolutions.

Cerebral Cortex: The outer bark or cortex of the cerebral hemispheres which consists largely of nerve cell bodies and their branches.

Cerebral Hemispheres: The right and left halves of the forebrain.

Cerebrospinal Fluid: The fluid filling the cerebral ventricles.

Certiorari: "To be informed of." An action or writ issued by a superior court requiring an inferior court to produce a certified record of a particular case tried by the latter. The purpose of said action is to enable the higher court to inspect the proceedings to determine whether or not there were any irregularities. Most commonly used by the Supreme Court of the United States as a discretionary device to choose the cases it wishes to hear.

Cerveau Isole: An animal with the nervous system transected at the upper level of the midbrain (between the inferior and superior colliculus). Contrast with the encephale isole.

Cervical: Pertaining to the neck region.

Chalazion: A small tumor of the eyelid; formed by the distention of a meibomian gland with secretion.

Character Disorder: See Personality Disorder.

Cheiro-oral: Refers to the simultaneous twitching of the thumb and same-sided corner of the mouth. Occurs in epilepsy due to close proximity of motor execution zones for these body parts (i.e., the motor homonculus has its thumb in its mouth).

Chiasma: A crossing; specifically, the crossing of the optic nerve fibers from the medial halves of the retinae.

Child Abuse: The infliction of physical damage upon a child by parents or other adults.

Child Advocacy: A movement concerned with protecting the rights and ensuring the well-being of children.

Chlorpromazine: An antipsychotic drug, one of the class of phenothiazines.

Cholinergic: Refers to cells that use acetylcholine as their synaptic transmitter.

Chorda Tympani: A portion of the facial nerve that serves as taste receptors in the anterior two-thirds of the tongue.

Choreic Movements: Uncontrollable, brief, and forceful muscular movements related to basal ganglia dysfunction.

Chromidial Substance: Pertaining to granules of extranuclear chromatin seen in the cytoplasm of a cell.

Chromosome: A body of chromatin in the cell nucleus that splits longitudinally as the cell divides, one half going to the nucleus of each of the daughter cells; the chromosomes transmit the hereditary characters.

Ciliary: Relating to (1) any hairlike process, (2) the eyelashes, or (3) certain of the structures of the eyeball.

Cingulate Bodies: Limbic system tissue above or superior to the corpus callosum.

Cingulum: A region of medial cerebral cortex lying dorsal to the corpus callosum. Also called cingulate cortex.

Circadian Rhythms: Behavioral, biochemical, and physiological fluctuations during a 24-hour period.

Circle of Willis: A structure at the base of the brain formed by the joining of the carotid and basilar arteries.

Circulocution: Often seen in fluent aphasia, the substitution of an incorrect word for another word. The substitution may itself demand a specific but unobtainable word, thus producing a convoluted output.

Circumventricular Organs: Organs lying in the walls of the cerebral ventricles. These organs contain receptor sites that can be affected by substances in the cerebrospinal fluid.

Cistern: A closed space serving as a reservoir for fluid.

Civil: Of or pertaining to the state of its citizenry. Relates to an individual's private rights and remedies sought through civil action; in contrast to criminal proceedings.

Civil Commitment: Procedure whereby an individual certified as mentally disordered can be hospitalized, either voluntarily or against his will.

Civil Law: The body of law, concerned with civil or private rights and remedies, established by every particular municipality for itself; as opposed to the "law of nature."

Civil Rights: The body of law pertaining to personal, natural rights which are guaranteed and protected by the Constitution, such as freedom of speech and press, freedom from discrimination.

Clarendon Jury: In a procedure established by Henry II of England, at least twelve "good and lawful" men, reporting to the king's representative, were summoned as jurors to determine if a trial should be held and to decide actual innocence or guilt.

Clear and Convincing: A standard of proof greater than preponderance but less rigorous than reasonable doubt. Proof that should leave the trier of the facts with no reasonable doubt about the truth of the matters in issue.

Clear and Present Danger: A standard used to determine when one's First Amendment rights to freedom of speech and press may be curtailed. Pursuant to a doctrine in constitutional law, if necessary, government restrictions will be upheld in order to prevent grave and immediate danger to interests which government may lawfully protect.

Clinical Neuropsychology: That which deals with the psychometric or other objective psychological methods in the assessment of higher cortical functions in humans (Meier).

Coactivation: A central nervous system control program that activates or inhibits the skeletal motoneurons at the same time as it alters the sensitivity of the muscle spindles.

Cochlea: A snail-shaped structure in the inner ear which contains the primary receptors for hearing.

Cochlear Duct: One of the three principal canals running along the length of the cochlea.

Cochlear Microphonic Potential: An electrical potential produced by hair cells that accurately copies the acoustic waveform of the stimulus.

Cochlear Nuclei: Brainstem nuclei that receive input from auditory hair cells and send output to the superior olivary complex.

Coenzyme: A nonprotein substance that is required for activity of an enzyme.

Cognitive Dissonance: Condition existing when new information is contradictory to one's assumptions.

Collateral: Accompanying; running by the side of; not direct; secondary or accessory; a small side branch of an axon.

Colliculus: One of two pairs of structures on the dorsal midbrain. *See* inferior colliculus, superior colliculus.

Colloid: A state of subdivision of matter in which the individual particles are of submicroscopic size and consist either of large molecules, such as proteins, or aggregates of smaller molecules; the particles are not large enough to settle out under the influence of gravity.

Collusion: The making of an agreement between two or more persons with the purpose of defrauding another of his rights by the forms of law, or to obtain an object forbidden by law.

Coma: A state of profound unconsciousness from which one cannot be roused.

Coma Vigil: Immobility and unresponsiveness with eyes open and moving, associated with posteromedial-inferior frontal and/or hypothalamic damage.

Common Carotid Arteries: Arteries that ascend the left and right sides of the neck. The branch that enters the brain is called the internal carotid artery.

Common Law: The body of legal principles and rules of action which derives its authority from customs and general usage and rules of conduct existing among the people. In contrast to civil law. Originated in England.

Complaint: The original or initial charge by which a legal action is begun, naming a person by whom the offense was committed. In criminal law, a written statement containing the essential facts and legal theory upon which the charge is based.

Complex Cortical Cells: Cells in the visual cortex that respond best to a bar of a particular width and direction anywhere within a particular area of the visual field.

Complex Partial Seizures: Epileptic seizures in which consciousness is altered (complex) and are restricted or at least arise from a circumscribed area of the brain (partial).

Compos Mentis: Being sound of mind; mentally competent.

Compulsion: An irrational and repetitive impulse to perform some act.

Compulsive Gambling: See pathological gambling.

Compulsive Personality: A personality disorder characterized by excessive concern with rules, order, efficiency, and work.

Computer Assessment: Use of computers to obtain or interpret assessment data.

Computer Axial Tomogram: A technique for examining brain structure in intact humans through a computer analysis of X-ray absorption at several positions around the head. This technique affords a virtual direct view of the brain.

Computer Model: Use of computers to simulate psychological functioning.

Conciliation: The mode of adjusting and resolving a dispute through voluntary and unantagonistic settlement of the issues between opposing parties with a view towards avoiding litigation.

Concordance Rates: Rates at which a diagnosis or a trait of one person is predictive of the same diagnosis or trait in relatives.

Conduct Disorders: Childhood disorders marked by persistent acts of aggressive or antisocial behavior that may or may not be against the law.

Conduction Aphasia: A constellation of behaviors produced by a lesion in the white matter fibers connecting the posterior/anterior portions of the brain (near the arcuate fasciculus). A severe repetition deficit is apparent relative to good auditory comprehension and expression of speech.

A language disorder, involving intact comprehension but poor repetition of spoken language, related to damage of the pathways connecting Wernicke's area and Broca's area.

Cones: Receptor cells in the retina that are responsible for color vision. The three types of cones have somewhat different sensitivities to light of different wavelengths.

Confabulation: Production of bizarre, false, or unverifiable verbal/written responses, usually in association with amnesia. A close correlation exists between confabulatory tendencies and impairment in self-correction.

Congenital: Born with a person; existing at or before birth.

Consideration: The cause, price, or motivating factor which induces a party to enter into a contract.

Consolidation: A state of memory formation in which information in short-term or intermediate-term memory is transferred to long-term memory.

Conspiracy: A combination of two or more persons who propose to commit an unlawful or criminal act, or to commit a lawful act by criminal means.

Constructional Disorders: Deficits in constructional tasks (e.g., drawing, assembling) in which the spatial form of the target object may be lost. Associated with pathology of the nondominant (nonspeech) hemisphere.

Contempt of Court: An act or an omission which is calculated to obstruct or interfere with the orderly administration of justice or which is calculated to lessen the authority or dignity of the court.

Contingent Negative Variation (CNV): A slow event-related potential recorded from the scalp. It arises in the interval between a warning signal and a signal that directs action.

Contract: A binding agreement between two or more competent parties, based on mutual assent and made for a lawful purpose, which creates an obligation to do or not to do a specified thing.

Contralateral: Situated on, or pertaining to, the opposite side.

Contrast Sensitivity Function (CSF): A psychophysical function determined by finding the contrast necessary for perceiving different spacings of dark and light bars. Used to measure spatial acuity of the visual system.

Contrecoup: Refers to the contusion (bruise) in the area opposite the point of impact (coup).

Conversion Disorders: Neurotic condition is which symptoms of organic illness appear in the absence of any related organic pathology; previously called hysteria.

Coronal (plane): The plane dividing the body or brain into front and back parts. Also called frontal or transverse.

The band of axons that connects the two cerebral hemispheres.

Corpus Callosum: Intracerebral white matter connecting the right and left cerebral hemispheres.

Corpus Delecti: The body or material substance of a crime which provides objective proof that a crime has been committed.

Corpus Juris: A body of law. A term signifying a comprehensive book of several collections of law.

Cortical Deafness: Sell also cortical auditory disorder. Difficulty recognizing both verbal and nonverbal stimuli due to cerebral dysfunction. Most often associated with cardiovascular accident.

Corticotropin-releasing Hormone (CRH): A releasing hormone from the hypothalamus that controls the daily rhythm of ACTH release.

Cortisol: A glucocorticoid hormone of the adrenal cortex.

Court Martial: An ad hoc military court which is convened under the authority of government and the Uniform Code of Military Justice which has penal and disciplinary jurisdiction in trying and punishing offenses committed by members of the armed forces. The type (e.g., general, summary, special) and composition varies according to the seriousness of offenses.

Cranial Nerves: Originating from the brain, these are 12 pairs of nerves which transmit motor and/or sensory neuronic impulses to and from peripheral central nervous system sites.

One of the three main subdivisions of the peripheral nervous system, composed of a set of pathways mainly concerned with sensory and motor systems associated with the head.

Cretinism: Reduced stature and mental retardation caused by thyroid deficiency.

Creutzfeldt-Jakob Disease: A rare, transmittable (i.e., through virus which has a two-year incubation) dementia with a relatively short clinical course (nine-month average). Ten percent of cases may be inherited. Anxiety and memory loss first appear. Myoclonic jerking appears in conjunction with motor neurocerebellar, basal ganglion, or pyramidal tract lesions.

Dementia with progressive rigidity and mutism are end-stage symptoms.

Criminal Responsibility: Legal question of whether an individual should be permitted to use insanity as a defense after having committed some criminal act.

Cross Examination: The questioning of a witness during a trial, hearing, or deposition by the party opposing that which originally produced him to testify. Generally, the scope of cross examination is limited to matters addressed in direct examination.

Crossed Aphasia: Aphasic symptoms occurring, usually temporarily, in right-handed person with a right hemisphere lesion.

Cruel and Unusual Punishment: Punishment found to be unfair, shocking, or offensive to the ordinary person's reasonable sensitivity. The Eighth Amendment states that "excessive bail shall not be required nor excessive fines imposed nor cruel and unusual punishment inflicted."

Crystalloid: A body that, in solution, can pass through an animal membrane, as distinguished from a colloid, which does not have this property.

Culpable: Blamable; deserving of moral blame. Addresses fault rather than guilt.

Curare: A highly toxic extract that paralyzes muscle; it acts on the motor endplates.

Custody: The caring for, keeping, guarding, preserving of a thing or person. Implies responsibility for the protection and preservation of the thing or person in custody. When applied to a person, may mean lawfully authorized detention by means of restraint and physical control.

Cutaneous: Pertaining to the skin.

Cyanosis: A dark, purplish coloration of the skin and the mucous membrane caused by deficient oxygenation of the blood.

Cyclic Adenosine Monophosphate (cyclic AMP or cAMP): A second messenger involved in the synaptic activities of dopamine, norepinephrine, and serotonin.

Cyclothymic Disorder: Mild affective disorder characterized by extreme mood swings of nonpsychotic intensity.

Cytoarchitectonics: The study of anatomical divisions of the brain based on the kinds of spacing of cells and distribution of axons.

D

Dacrystic Epilepsy: Seizures where crying is the predominant ictal event.

Damages: A monetary compensation which may be recovered in court by any party who has suffered a loss or injury to person, property, or rights as the result of an unlawful act, negligence, or omission of another.

    Actual Damages: The amount awarded in compensation for a complainant's actual and real losses or injury which can readily be proven to have been sustained.

    Compensatory Damages: A monetary award to the injured party strictly for the loss of injury sustained.

    Double (or treble) Damages: An award for certain statutorily authorized kinds of injuries in an amount two to three times the damages normally awarded by a court or jury.

    Nominal Damages: A trivial sum awarded to a plaintiff in an action where there is no substantial loss or injury for which to be compensated. Or, in a case where there has been real injury, but the plaintiff's evidence fails to show its amount.

    Punitive (exemplary) Damages: Compensation in an amount greater than actual damages in cases where the wrong done to a plaintiff was aggravated by malice, violence, or fraud on the part of the defendant.

    Special (consequential) Damages: An award not arising directly or immediately from the act of a party, but only from the consequences or results of such an act.

De Bene Esse: Conditionally or provisionally; in anticipation of future need. Applies to proceedings taken provisionally and allowed to stand for the present but which may be subject to future challenges.

De Facto: In fact, actually, in reality. Characterizes an officer, government, past action, or state of affairs which is illegal or illegitimate, but for all practical purposes, must be accepted.

De Novo Hearing: A new hearing or a hearing for the second time in which the judgment of the trial court is usually suspended, with the reviewing court determining the case as though it originated in the latter court.

Decerebrate (rigidity): Extension and rigidity of the limbs caused by brain stem or cerebellar injury.

Deep Dyslexia: Deletion of grammatical morphemes with the presence of semantic paralexias, due to cerebral dysfunction. The loss of grapheme-to-phoneme processing is seen during reading.

Default Judgment: A decision of the court against a defendant because of his failure to respond to a plaintiff's action.

Defendant: The person from whom relief or recovery is sought in an action or suit. In a criminal case, the accused.

Defense: That which is offered and alleged by the party against whom an action or suit is taken, such as the lawful or factual reasons against the plaintiff recovering or establishing that which he seeks.

Delirium Tremens: Acute delirium associated with prolonged alcoholism; characterized by intense anxiety, tremors, and hallucinations.

Delirium: State of mental confusion characterized by clouding of consciousness, disorientation, restlessness, excitement, and often hallucinations.

Delusion: Firm belief opposed to reality but maintained in spite of strong evidence to the contrary.

Delusion of Persecution: False belief that one is being mistreated or interfered with by one's enemies. Often found in schizophrenia.

Delusion System: An internally coherent, systematized pattern of delusions.

Dementia Pugilistica: The "punch drunk" syndrome. Symptoms associated with repeated head trauma include dysarthria, tremor, seizures, and frontal signs. Memory
and concentration problems are marked.

Dendrites: Receptor structures of a neuron that project out in branch-like fashion.
Extensions of the cell body which are the receptive surfaces of the neuron.

Dendritic Branching: The pattern and quantity of branching of dendrites.

Dendritic Spines: Outgrowths along the dendrites of neurons.

Dendritic Tree: The full arrangement of a single cell's dendrites.

Deoxyribonucleic Acid (DNA): A nucleic acid present in the chromosomes of cells; it codes
hereditary information.

Dependent Personality: A personality disorder marked by lack of self-confidence and
feelings of acute panic or discomfort at having to be alone.

Dependent Variable: In an experiment, the behavior which is measured to determine
whether changes in the independent variable affect the behavior being studied.

Depersonalization Disorder: A dissociative neurotic disorder, usually occurring in
adolescence, in which individuals lose their sense of self and feel unreal or displaced
to a different location.

Depolarization: A reduction in membrane potential (the inner membrane surface becomes less negative in relation to the outer surface); this is caused by excitatory
neural messages.

Deponent: One who testifies to the truth of certain facts; one who gives a written statement,
deposition; a witness.

Deposition: A witness's testimony taken under oath outside of the courtroom in question-
and-answer form, reduced to writing and authenticated. Intended to be used at a
civil or criminal trial.

Depressive Disorder: Neurotic reaction characterized by persistent dejection and discour-
agement.

Depressive Neurosis: Depression of intermediate severity with little or no evidence of
personality breakdown or loss of contact with reality.

Depressive Stupor: Extreme degree of depression characterized by marked psychomotor
underactivity.

Derepression: The mechanism through which regions of the DNA molecule that are
repressed from transcription become unblocked. This process allows for the selection of genetic information that will be utilized by a particular cell.

Dermatome: A strip of skin innervated by a particular spinal root.

Desensitization: Therapeutic process by means of which reactions to traumatic experiences are reduced in intensity by repeatedly exposing the individual to them in mild
form, either in reality or in fantasy.

Deterrence: The premise that punishment for criminal offenses will deter that criminal and
others from future criminal acts.

Dexedrine: An amphetamine drug; a stimulant used to curb appetite or elevate mood.

Dextral: Refers to right-handedness. Opposed to sinstral, or left-handedness.

Dialysis Dementia: Chronic, degenerative intellectual problems (aphasia, memory difficulties), seizures, and motor signs (e.g., facial grimacing) seen occasionally as the result of long-term dialysis. The pathogenesis is unknown although the accumulation of aluminum in the brain has been implicated.

Dialysis Disequilibrium Syndrome: A consequence of the dialysis procedure itself, encephalopathy characterized by development of intermittent slowing speech, stuttering, and word finding problems. Progression of dyspraxia, memory loss, concentration problems, and (occasionally) psychosis. Shifts in sodium and potassium are associated with the disorder.

Diapedesis: The passage of blood cells through the unruptured walls of the blood vessels.

Diaschisis: Reduction of neuronal activity in brain sites outside the immediate perimeter of the lesion. Associated with acute, focal conditions.

Diastole: The rhythmic period of relaxation and dilatation of the heart, during which it fills with blood.

Diathesis: A predisposition or vulnerability toward developing a given disorder.

Diathesis-stress Model: View of abnormal behavior as the result of stress operating on an individual with a biological, psychosocial, or sociocultural predisposition toward developing a specific disorder.

Dichotic: Refers to studies where different stimuli are simultaneously presented to both ears, eyes, or tactilely to the subject.

Dictum (pl. dicta): A statement, remark, or observation of the law made by the court, not necessarily relevant or essential to the outcome of a case.

Diencephalon: The central core of the brain, which together with the telencephalon, forms the cerebrum. Consists of the thalamus, subthalamus, hypothalamus, and epithalamus.
    The posterior part of the forebrain; it includes the thalamus and hypothalamus.

Differential Reinforcement of Other Behavior (DOR): Behavior modification technique for extinguishing undesirable behavior by reinforcing incompatible behaviors.

Digitalis: The dried leaves of purple foxglove; it is used in the treatment of certain cardiac disorders.

Dilantin: An anti-convulsant medication often used in controlling epileptic seizures.

Diopter: The unit of refracting power of a lens; noting a lense whose principal focus is at a distance of 1 M.

Diploid: Having two sets of chromosomes, as normally found in the somatic cells of higher organisms.

Diplopia: Double vision, due to eye muscle imbalance, metabolic disturbances, or other causes.

Direct Examination: The initial questioning or examination of a witness by the party who originally called him to testify.

Directed Verdict: A verdict ordered by the judge when, as a matter of law, he rules that the party with the burden of proof has failed to present a prima facie case. The judge orders the jury to return a verdict for the opposing party.

Disconnection Syndromes: Disrupted neuronal transmission through the white matter that cut cortical pathways, thus disconnecting a cortical area from the rest of the brain. Corpus callosum disconnections are the most dramatic.

Discovery: A pretrial procedure by which one party can obtain vital facts and information material to the case in order to assist in preparation for the trial. The purpose of discovery being to make for a fair trial and to allow each party to know what documents and information the opponent has in his possession.

Disinhibition Syndrome: Inability to stop actions or impulses once initiated. Often attributed to frontal system deficits in exerting an inhibitory effect on on-going mental or behavioral processes.

Disintegration: Loss of organization or integration in any organized system.

Disorganized Schizophrenia: Subtype representing most severe disintegration of personality and poor prognosis for recovery; characterized by marked incoherence, silly, or inappropriate responses.

Dissociation: Separation or "isolation" of mental processes in such a way that they become split off from the main personality or lose their normal thought-affect relationships.

Dissociative Disorder: Psychoneurotic disorder characterized by amnesia, fugue, somnambulism, or multiple personality.

Distal: An anatomical term meaning toward the periphery or toward the end of a limb.

Diural: Daily.

Divergence: A system of neural connections that allows one cell to send signals to many other cells.

DNA: See deoxyribonucleic acid.

Docket sounding: A meeting between the judges and attorneys for the purpose of determining the schedule of cases for a specific period of time.

Dopamine (DA): A neurotransmitter produced mainly in the basal forebrain and diencephalon that is active in the basal ganglia, the olfactory system, and limited parts of the cerebral cortex. For location of dopaminergic fibers.

Dopaminergic: Refers to cells that use dopamine as their synaptic transmitter.

Dorsal: An anatomical term meaning toward the back of the body or the top of the brain; opposite of ventral.

Dorsal Root: Root at the back of the spinal cord.

Double-dissociation: Differential effects of lesions, allowing for comparison of both independent and dependent variables. Lesion X causes X but not Y whereas lesion Y causes Y but not X.

Double Tracking: The simultaneous operation of two mental operations. Digits backward on the Wechsler Adult Intelligence Scale (WAIS), for example, calls for memory and reversing operations at the same time.

Down's Syndrome: A form of mental retardation associated with an extra chromosome.

Due Process of Law: The regular course of law as administered through courts of justice. In each particular case, refers to the legal proceedings in accordance with the rules and principles established in our legal system to enforce and protect private rights.

Duplex Theory: A theory of pitch perception cominbing the place theory and volley theory. Volley theory operates for sounds from about 20 to 1000 Hz, and place theory operates for sounds above 1000 Hz.

Duplication of DNA: A process through which a cell duplicates (or replicates) its genetic information during mitosis.

Dura: First or outermost layer of the three layers of the meninges.

Durham Rule: The "irresistible impulse" test of criminal responsibility deriving from a 1954 decision of the United States Court of Appeals. States that a defendant is not criminally responsible if he suffered from a mental disease or defect at the time the unlawful act was committed if it is determined beyond a reasonable doubt that the act was a product of the mental disease or defect.

Duty: A legal or moral obligation or responsibility to perform an act or service.

Dyad: A two-person group.

Dynamic Formation: An integrated evaluation of a patient's traits, attitudes, conflicts, and symptoms that attempts to explain the individual's problem.

Dysarthia: Refers to speech disorders based on peripheral motor deficits. The quality of speech is affected, as in hypernasality, breathy phonation, and stridor (flaccid paretic dysarthria), slow, low pitch, harsh and difficult phonation (spastic paretic dysarthria), or explosive speech (ataxic or cerebellar dysarthria).

Dysfluency: Difficulty in generating words.

Dysmetropia: Defects in the visual appreciation of object size discrimination. Also called "past-pointing phenomenon" (i.e., in finger-to-nose exam). Associated with cerebellar lesions.

Dysnomia: Word-finding disability. Shown by failure to correctly name objects or by choosing words that are "off center." Associated with temporal lobe dysfunction.

Dysphagia: Difficulty in swallowing.

Dysthymic Disorder: Moderately severe affective disorder characterized by extended periods of nonpsychotic depression and brief periods of normal moods.

Dystonia: Prolonged abnormal posture as a consequence of involuntary muscle tension. Often a side-effect of neuroleptic medication.

E

Echopraxia: The mimicking of other's motor movements. Indicates that extant motor problems are not due to lack of inactivity.

Ectoderm: The outer cellular layer of the developing fetus; this layer gives rise to the skin and to the nervous system.

Ectopic: Out of the normal place.

Edema: An abnormal accumulation of clear, watery fluid in the lymph spaces of the tissues.

The swelling of tissue, especially in the brain, in response to brain injury.

Effusion: The escape of fluid from the blood vessels or the lymphatics into the tissues or a cavity.

Ego-Dystonic Homosexuality: Category of "mental disorder" in which the individual wishes to change his or her homosexual orientation.

Ejaculatory Incompetence: A male's inability to ejaculate.

Electric Synapse: Junctional region where the presynaptic and postsynaptic membranes approach so closely that the nerve impulse can jump to the postsynaptic membrane without being translated into a chemical message.

Electroencephalography (EEG): The recording and study of gross electrical activity of the brain recorded from large electrodes placed on the scalp.

Electrolyte: Any substance that, in solution, conducts an electric current.

Embolism: Obstruction, or occlusion, of a vessel by a transported clot, a mass of bacteria, or other foreign material.

Emotional Inoculation: Therapeutic procedures designed to prepare persons who face stressful situations, such as surgery, by providing the person with adaptive techniques.

Empiricism: The philosophical view based on the belief that knowledge is acquired through experience and observation.

Empyema: The presence of pus in any cavity.

Encephale Isole: An animal in which the brain stem is separated from the spinal cord by a cut below the medulla. Contrast with cerveau isole.

Encephalitis: A generalized viral infection of the brain's neurons or glial cell bodies.

Encephalomalcia: Cerebral tissue softening.

Encephalopathy: Brain degeneration.

Encoding: A process of memory formation in which the information entering sensory channels is passed into short-term memory.

Endocrine: Refers to glands that secrete products into the bloodstream to act on distant targets; opposite of exocrine.

Endorphins: Neurotransmitters that have been called the body's own narcotics.

Endothelial cells: The tightly fitting cells that make up the walls of the capillaries in the brain.

Enhancement: Independent of behavior, the increase in activity of some posterior parietal neurons by motivationally important visual stimuli. Responses to those stimuli are enhanced.

Enjoin: To command or require that a person perform or desist from a certain act.

Enuresis: Involuntary passage of urine after the age of three years.

Enzyme: A protein that catalyzes a biochemical reaction.

Epicritic: Sensory experiences that can be located on the body of the organism and are of brief duration (e.g., a sharp pain in the foot). Opposed to protocritic.

Epinephrine: A compound that acts both as a hormone (secreted by the adrenal medulla) and as a neurotransmitter; also called adrenalin.

Episodic Dyscontrol Syndrome: Totally unprovoked violence associated with an aura, consisting of rising anxiety, headaches, illusions, numbness, drowsiness, and hyperacusis. The attack lasts 15 minutes to two hours and is very violent, often directed towards property or persons. May be due to temporal-limbic structure dysfunction. Associated features include hypersensitivity to alcohol, multiple traffic accidents, and sexual impulsiveness, the last rising to the level of forensic concern.

Episodic Memory: Recall for events in one's life and experiences. It is therefore unique and anchored to distinct points in time and space.

Equilibrium Potential: The state in which the tendency of ions to flow from regions of high concentration is exactly balanced by the opposing potential differences across the membrane.

Equipotentiality: Notion that a lesion anywhere on the cortex will produce equivalent deficits. This holistic approach was espoused by Lashley.

Equity: A system of law and courts administered according to fairness and justness. Based on a system originated in England as an alternative to common law.

Estrogen: A hormone produced by female gonads.

Estrus: The period during which female animals are sexually receptive.

Eustress: Positive stress.

Evagination: A protrusion of some part of an organ.

Event-related Potentials: Gross electrical potential changes in the brain that are elicited by discrete sensory or motor events.

Excitatory Postsynaptic Potentials (EPSPs): Depolarizing potentials in the postsynaptic neuron caused by excitatory presynaptic impulses. These potentials may summate to trigger a nerve impulse in the postsynaptic cell.

Exclusionary Rule: The rule that defines whether evidence is admissible in a trial. In cases where evidence has been illegally obtained, it must be removed from consideration by the fact finders.

Exculpatory: Clearing or excusing a party from alleged fault or guilt.

Exemplary Damages: A monetary award in an amount over and above what is required to compensate a plaintiff for a loss in a case where the wrong was aggravated by violence, malice, or fraud on the part of the defendant.

Exhaustion and Disintegration: The third and final phase in the general adaptation syndrome, in which the organism is no longer able to resist continuing stress; at the biological level, may result in death.

Exner's Area: Formally seen as a "frontal writing center," located at the base of the second frontal convolution. Lesions in this area produce agraphia.

Exocrine: Refers to glands that secrete their products through ducts to the site of action; opposite of endocrine.

Exophthalmos: A protrusion, or prominence, of the eyeball.

Experimental Research: A research approach in which the experimenter manipulates the independent variable, controls outside conditions, and determines the effect on a dependent variable to test for causal linkages.

Expert Witness: A witness who has special knowledge in a field, obtained from education or personal experience.

External Validity: The degree to which experimental findings can reasonably be generalized to nonlaboratory situations.

Extinction: One of a stimulus pair simultaneously presented to different parts of the body, visual fields, etc., is not perceived.

Extinction to Double Simultaneous Stimulation: Failure to report the stimulus presented to the contralateral side of a lesion upon bilateral simultaneous stimulation.

Extracerebral: Extrinsic or outside of the brain hemispheres, as for example, between the skull and the brain on one of the three layers of meninges.

Extrapunitive: Characterized by a tendency to evaluate the source of frustrations as external and to direct hostility outward.

Extrapyramidal System: A motor system that includes the basal ganglia and some closely related brain stem structures.

Extravasation: The act of escaping from a vessel into the tissues; said of blood, lymph, or serum.

Extrinsic: Originating outside of the part where it is found or upon which it acts.

F

5HT: See serotonin

Fabrication: Relating imaginary events as if they were true without intent to deceive; confabulation.

Face-hand Test: Touching the face simultaneously with another body part, particularly same-sided. Suppression or displacement of the more peripheral stimulus indicates possible parietal lobe dysfunction.

Facial Nerve: A cranial nerve that innervates facial musculature and some sensory receptors.

Fasciculation: Localized contraction of muscle fibers, or an incoordinated contraction of skeletal muscle in which the fibers of one motor unit contract.

Feature Detector Model: A model of visual pattern analysis in terms of linear and angular components of the stimulus array. Contrast with spatial frequency filter model.

Felony: A crime of a more serious or harmful nature than a misdemeanor. Under federal law and many state statutes, any offense punishable by imprisonment for a term of more than one year or by death.

Fetal Alcohol Syndrome: Observed pattern in infants of alcoholic mothers in which there is a characteristic facial or limb irregularity, low body weight, and behavioral abnormality.

Fiduciary: A person having the duty to act in a relationship of high trust and confidence for another's benefit in the capacity of trustee, executor, or administrator.

Field Properties: Characteristics of the environment surrounding a living system.

Finger Agnosia: Inability to identify the fingers of one's own hand, or those of another person, due to brain damage.

Fistula: A pathologic, or abnormal, passage leading from an abscess cavity or a hollow organ to the surface, or from one organ to another.

Fixed Action Patterns: Complex preprogrammed species-specific behaviors triggered by particular stimuli and carried out without sensory feedback. *See also* modal action pattern.

Flaccid: Relaxed, flabby, soft.

Flashback: The recurrence of a drug experience, usually in a negative manner, without further ingestion of the drug.

Flatus: Gas or air in the stomach or the intestine; commonly used to denote passage of gas by rectum.

Flexion Reflex: Abrupt withdrawal of a limb in response to intense stimulation of the foot.

Flooding: Anxiety-eliciting technique involving placing the client in a real-life, anxiety-arousing situation.

Fluent Aphasia: Speech difficulty with incomprehension, jargon speech, and other signs such as lack of awareness. Often associated with posterior lesions. Nonfluent aphasia is associated with anterior lesions and almost always involves expressive speech deficits.

Folia: Folds or convolutions of the cerebellar cortex.

Folie à Deux: A psychotic interpersonal relationship involving two people; e.g., husband and wife both become psychotic with similar or complementary symptomatology.

Follicle-stimulating Hormone (FSH): A tropic hormone released by the anterior pituitary that controls the production of estrogen and progesterone.

Forcible Rape: An act of violence in which sexual relations are forced upon an unwilling partner who is over the age of 18.

Forebrain: The frontal division of the neural tube that contains the cerebral hemispheres, the thalamus, and the hypothalamus. Also called the prosencephalon.

Forensic Psychiatry: Branch of psychiatry dealing with legal problems relating to mental disorders.

Fornix: A fiber tract that runs from the hippocampus to the mammillary body.

Fovea: A cup-shaped depression or pit.

Fovea Centralis: Small central pit in the retina, packed with cones, where vision is sharpest and color accuracy most developed.

Frontal Amnesia: Difficulty in switching from one set of memory traces to another in the face of intact operating memory. "Forgetting to recall," as in disregarding instructions is an illustration.

Frontal Gait Disturbance: See magnetic apraxia and utilization behavior.

Frontal Inattention: A contralateral visual field defect caused by damage to particular frontal sites (arcuate sulcus in monkeys). Associated features may include conjugate deviation of the eyes, forced circling, the latter in the direction of the lesion.

Frontal Psychosurgery: Includes leukotomies aimed at severing frontal-thalamic connections, orbital undercutting, for example, by placement of radioactive yttrium pellets in the orbital tissues, cingulomotomy, stereotactic destruction of focal sites, and topectomy, ablation of selected frontal areas.

Frontal "Release" Signs: These are primitive reflexes which long have been considered frontal signs. The grasp reflex is associated with midline frontal pathology. Frontal system problems are indicated by rooting, sucking, and snout reflexes indicating a brain stem-diencephalic lesion.

Frye Test: A test emphasizing the subject of an expert witness's testimony must conform to a generally accepted explanatory theory. Named after the case in which the determination was made.

Fugue: A neurotic dissociative disorder which entails a loss of memory accompanied by actual physical flight from one's present life situation to a new environment or less threatening former one.

Functional Psychoses: Severe mental disorders attributed primarily to psychological stress.

Fundus: The bottom of a sac or hollow organ; the farthest removed from the opening.

Future Shock: A condition brought about when social change proceeds so rapidly that the individual cannot cope with it adequately.

G

Gambling: Wagering on games or events in which chance largely determines the outcome.

Gamma Efferents: Motors neurons by means of which the central nervous system controls muscle spindle sensitivity.

Ganglion: A collection of nerve cell bodies. Also called a nucleus.

Ganglion Cells: Cells in the retina whose axons form the optic nerve.

Gangrene: A form of necrosis combined with putrefaction; death of the tissue.

Gel: A colloidal system comprising a solid and a liquid phase that exists as a solid or semisolid mass; a jelly or solid or semisolid phase.

Gelastic Epilepsy: Seizures where laughter is the predominant ictal behavior.

Gene: An ultimate, ultramicroscopic, biologic unit of heredity; self-reproducing; located in a definite position on a particular chromosome.

General Adaptation Syndrome: Reaction of the individual to excessive stress; consists of the alarm reaction, the stage of resistance, and the stage of exhaustion.

General Paresis: A progressive mental deterioration due to syphilitic invasion of the central nervous system. Changes include deterioration of the entire range of mental functions due to brain atrophy. A loss of neurons with an increase in microglial cells and astrocytes is seen.

Generalized Seizures: Epileptic seizures that arise from pathology at brain sites that project to widespread regions of the brain. These seizures involve loss of consciousness and symmetrical involvement of body musculature.

Generator Potential: Local changes in the resting potential of receptor cells that mediate between the impact of stimuli and the initiation of nerve impulse.

Genome: The complete set of hereditary factors, as contained in the haploid assortment of chromosomes.

Gerstmann's Syndrome: The symptom cluster of ocalculia, agraphia, left-right spatial disorientation, and finger agnosia. Traditionally considered to involve the left parieto-occipital region of the brain.

Glabellar Tap Sign: The subject is tapped lightly just above and between the eyebrows in order to see whether blinking will normally and quickly habituate. Parkinson patients will continue to blink with each tap.

Glial Cells: Nonneural brain cells that provide structural, nutritional, and other supports to the brain. Also called glia or neuroglia.

Glioblastoma (Multiforma): A neoplasm arising from the glial cells, characterized by high degree of lethality and malignancy.

Gliomas: Brain tumors resulting from the aberrant production of glial cells.

Global Alexia: Inability to read letters or words.

Global Aphasia: Severe comprehension and articulation deficits associated with a large lesion of the entire perisylvian area of the frontal, temporal, and parietal lobes. Prognosis is grim.

Global Steropis: Depth perception in the presence of ambiguous stimulus forms. Presumed to be mediated by right hemisphere and is differentiated from a stereoacuity.

Glossopharyngeal Nerve: A cranial nerve that serves taste receptors in the tongue.

Glucocorticoids: Hormones released by the adrenal cortex that affects carbohydrate metabolism.

Golgi Tendon Organs: Receptors located in tendons that send impulses to the central nervous system when a muscle contracts.

Gonadotropin-releasing Hormone (GnRH): A hypothalamic hormone that controls the release of luteinizing hormone (or interstitial-cell-stimulating hormone). Also called luteinizing-hormone-releasing hormone.

Graded Potentials: Potentials that can vary continuously in size; also called local potentials; contrast with all-or-none potentials.

Gradient: An ascending or descending slope. In the body, gradients are determined by the difference in concentration or electric charges across a semipermeable membrane.

Grand Mal Seizures: A type of generalized epileptic seizure that involves nerve cells firing in high frequency bursts. These seizures cause loss of consciousness and sudden muscle contraction.

Grandfather Clause: Certain legal provisions permitting those engaged in a business or profession before the passage of an act regulating them to receive a license, power, or privilege without meeting the criteria established for those new to the field.

Grievance: A denial of legal right or an injury, injustice, or wrong which is grounds for a complaint due to being unjust, discriminatory, and oppressive.

Growth Hormone: A tropic hormone secreted by the anterior pituitary that influences the growth of cells and tissues. Also called somatotropic hormone (STH).

Guardian Ad Litem: A person appointed by the court to represent the interests of a minor or an incompetent in a litigation and to act on the person's behalf until the conclusion of the case.

Guilt: Feelings of culpability arising from behavior or desires contrary to one's ethical principles. Involves both self-devaluation and apprehension growing out of fears of punishment.

Gyri: The ridged or raised portions of a convoluted brain surface. Contrast with sulci.

H

Habeas Corpus: "You have the body." A writ or order commanding the authority who is detaining an individual to produce the body of the detainee before the court to determine whether the detainment is lawful.

Health Psychology: Subspecialty within the behavioral-medicine approach that deals with psychology's contributions to diagnosis, treatment, and prevention of behaviorally caused physical illnesses.

Hearsay: A statement made during a trial or hearing that is not based on the personal, firsthand knowledge of the witness.

Hearsay Rule: The regulation making a witness's statement inadmissible if it is not based on his personal knowledge.

Heat of Vaporization: The heat energy required to convert 1 Gm. of liquid into a vapor without a change in temperature of the substance being vaporized.

Hebephrenic Schizophrenia: Type of schizophrenia characterized by severe personality decompensation or disintegration.

Hematoma: An accumulation of blood within the meninges of the brain. Most often caused by head trauma.

Hematuria: The presence of blood in the urine.

Hemiparesis: Weakness on one side of the body.

Hemiplegia: Weakness or paralysis of one side of the body.

Hemispatial Neglect: Neglect of the hemisphere contralateral to a lesion. Also termed visuospatial agnosia or neglect, unilateral spatial neglect, or hemispatial agnosia.

Hemostasis: The arrest of bleeding; the checking of the flow of blood through any part of a vessel.

High-risk: Individuals showing great vulnerability to physical or mental disorders.

Hilus: A depression or pit, at that part of an organ where the vessels and nerves enter or leave.

Hippocampus: Actively concerned with memory consolidation functions, located at anterior temporal lobe.

Histrionic Personality: Personality pattern characterized by excitability, emotional instability and self-dramatization.

Holistic: A systematic approach to science involving the study of the whole or total configuration; the view of human beings as unified psychobiological organisms inextricably immersed in a physical and sociocultural environment.

Homeostasis: Tendency of organisms to maintain conditions making possible a constant level of physiological functioning.

Homologous: Corresponding; having similar relations.

Homonymous Field Cuts: Loss of vision in the same part of both visual fields.

Homonymous Hemianopsia: Loss of one-half of the visual field in each eye, right- or left-sided (e.g., right temporal/left nasal; right nasal/left temporal).

Huntington's Disease: A progressive, hereditary, dementing condition that affects the basal ganglia with atrophy of the frontal lobes and corpus callosum. Involuntary and spasmodic movements are associated features, along with declining cognitive and personality/social skills.

Hyaluronidase: An enzyme causing breakdown of hyaluronic acid in protective polysaccharide barriers, promoting invasion of cells and tissues by the invading agent; it is a spreading factor.

Hyperacusis: The perception of sounds as abnormally loud.

Hypergraphia: Overwriting, as when too many words are written in response to task demands.

Hyperplasia: The abnormal multiplication, or increase, in the number of normal cells in normal arrangement in a tissue.

Hypertrophy: The morbid enlargement, or overgrowth, of an organ or part, resulting from an increase in size of its constituent cells.

Hypnosis: Trancelike mental state induced in a cooperative subject by suggestion.

Hypnotherapy: Use of hypnosis in psychotherapy.

Hypnotic Regression: Process by which a subject is brought to relive, under hypnosis, early forgotten or repressed experiences.

Hypochondriacal Delusions: Delusions concerning various horrible disease conditions, such as the belief that one's brain is turning to dust.

Hypochondriasis: Condition dominated by preoccupation with bodily processes and fear of presumed diseases.

Hypophonia: Lowered voice volume. Contrasted to aphonia, or total lack of voice. The most common cause of both disorders is laryngitis.

Hypothalamus: Involved in homeostatic, motivational activities such as sexual activity, eating, drinking, and emotions, this structure is located in the limbic system, dorsal to the thalamus.

Hypothermia: Low temperature; especially a state of low body temperature induced for the purpose of decreasing metabolic activities and need for oxygen.

Hypotonia: The state of muscles tiring easily. Associated with cerebellar lesions.

Hypoxia: Refers to insufficient blood oxygen to the brain. Contrasted to anoxia which refers to a total lack of blood oxygen to brain structures.

Hysterical Amnesia: Loss of memory for emotional/psychological reasons without a know organic basis.

Hysterical Disorder: Disorder characterized by involuntary psychogenic dysfunction of motor, sensory, or visceral processes.

I

Iconic Memory: A very brief type of memory that stores the sensory impression of a scene.

Ideographic Methodology: A method of study emphasizing the individual case and the uniqueness of each personality.

Ideomotor Apraxia: Simple execution of motor responses (e.g., hitch hiking sign, salute, whistling) is impaired or absent in the presence of intact comprehension. Implies deficits in planning and initiation. Associated with left hemisphere lesions.

Idiopathic Epilepsy: A seizure disorder of unknown origin. Opposed to symptomatic epilepsy whose cause is known.

Illusion: Misinterpretation of sensory data; false perception.

Impeachment: A criminal proceeding against a public official before a quasi-political court. In regards to the testimony of a witness, to question the veracity of the evidence offered.

In Bank (en banc): "In the bench." Refers to a court session in which the entire membership of the court participates in making a decision instead of the regular quorum or one judge and jury.

In Camera: In chambers; in private. The hearing of a case before a judge in his private chambers, when all spectators are excluded from the courtroom, or when the judge performs a judicial act while the court is not in session.

In Loco Parentis: In place of a parent. A party charged to legally act in behalf of the parents.

In Re: In the matter of; concerning or regarding. The usual method of assigning a title to a case in which there are no adversary parties.

In Situ Research: Research in which real-life social situations are the emphasis of study.

In Vivo: Taking place in a real-life situation as opposed to the therapeutic or laboratory setting.

Inattention: Decreased/absent awareness of events occurring on the side of the body contralateral to the hemispheric lesion.

Incompetency: Lacking the physical, intellectual, or moral capacity or qualification to perform a required duty.

Independent Variable: The variable in an experiment that is controlled or manipulated by the experimenter.

Indifference Reaction: Denial, unawareness, or minimizing psychological/neuropsychological deficits, traditionally associated with right hemisphere lesions. Inappropriate elevated affect may be present.

Infarct: Impoverished or dead brain tissue associated with vascular occlusions.

Inferior Colliculus: The auditory center in the midbrain; it receives input from the brain stem auditory nuclei and sends output to the medial geniculate nucleus.

Inflammation: A series of reactions produced in the tissues by an irritant; it is marked by an afflux of blood with exudation of plasma and leukocytes.

Informed Consent: A person's agreement to the occurrence of a specified event based on a full disclosure of facts needed to make an intelligent decision.

Infra: Below, under, following; the opposite of supra.

Infundibulum: A funnel-shaped structure or passage. The stalk of the pituitary gland.

Inhibitory Postsynaptic Potentials (IPSPs): Hyperpolarizing potentials in the postsynaptic neuron caused by inhibitory connections. These potentials decrease the probability that the postsynaptic neuron will fire a nerve impulse.

Innervation Ratio: The ratio expressing the number of muscle fibers innervated by a single motor axon. The fewer muscle fibers an axon innervates (the lower the ratio) the finer the control of movement.

Inquisitorial System: A system in which the judge, as the primary figure in a trial, conducts his own investigation. The judge generally maintains more control over the proceedings than in the adversarial system.

Insanity: A social or legal term indicating a condition in which a person is unfit and lacks legal responsibility or capacity due to mental illness. As stated in the American Law Institute Penal Code, "A person is not responsible for criminal conduct if at the time of such conduct as a result of mental disease or defect he lacks substantial capacity either to appreciate the criminality or wrongfulness of his conduct or to conform his conduct to the requirements of the law."

Insanity Defense: "Innocent by reason of insanity" plea used as a legal defense in criminal trails.

Instrumental Use of Empirical Data: The application of concrete social science information of concepts to a case.

Integration: Organization of parts (psychological, biological functions) to make a functional whole.

Intent: A state of mind (inferred from the facts or from a person's actions) showing purpose, design, or resolve to act in a certain manner.

Intention Tremor: Also called kinetic tremor, this anomaly occurs at the end of a movement. Contrasted to "rest" tremor which occurs when no movement is present.
     A tremor that occurs only during a voluntary movement, e.g., when the person reaches out to grasp an object.

Interictal: Refers to behaviors/events between the time seizures occur. Adversive personality traits (e.g., irritability, obsessional traits) are associated features.

Intermediate Coup Lesions: Scattered areas of focal tissue damage in line with the point of trauma impact (coup) and possible terminal point of the damage (contrecoup).

Intermediate-term Memory: A form of memory lasting longer than short-term, and requiring no rehearsal, but not lasting as long as long-term memory.

Internal Carotid Artery: See common carotid artery.

Internal Validity:

Interstitial Policy Making: Laws that may be "made" by judges when the issues in a case fall "between the gaps"—interstices—of previous decisions.

Intracerebral: Intrinsic or inside of the brain hemispheres, usually referring to brain dysfunction caused by neoplasms or cardiovascular accidents.

Intracranial Steal: Complicating the finding of an arteriovenous malformation (AVM) location, here blood is shunted away from normal brain tissue to the AVM site. Thus, the unaffected area may show evidences of neuropsychological deficit.

Intravascular: Within a vessel or vessels.

Intropunitive: Responding to frustration by tending to blame oneself.

Invagination: The pushing of the wall of a cavity into the cavity.

Involution: The return of an enlarged organ to normal size; retrograde changes.

Ion: An electrically charged atom or group of atoms formed by the loss or gain of electrons.

Ipsilateral: Same side; homolateral; opposed to contralateral (opposite side), bilateral (both sides), unilateral (one side).

Ischemia: Cut-off of blood flow to an area of the brain or body organ.

Ischemic Infarction: A disruption of blood flow (infarction) creating dead or damaged tissue (infarct), resulting more from impaired or absent blood flow rather than from insufficient nutrients in the blood.

Isotope: An element that has the same atomic number as another but a different atomic weight. Radioactive isotopes, used clinically, usually refer to elements rendered radioactive by artificial means.

J

Jargon Aphasia: A form of paraphasias which have no meaning to those who hear the sounds.

Judicial Notice: The act by which a court, during a trial or while framing its decision, recognizes the existence and truth of certain facts which judges and jurors may take into consideration and act upon without proof because the facts are already known to them.

Jurisdiction: The authority and power by which courts and judicial officers hear and decide cases; the geographic area in which a court has jurisdiction.

Just-world Hypothesis: The hypothesis stating that the world is fair and that victims deserve what happened to them and, therefore, do not deserve help.

Juvenile Courts: A court system, established in the late nineteenth century, having special jurisdiction over delinquent, dependent, and neglected minors. Set up to treat youthful offenders separately from adults. The court acts in a parental, protective role.

Juvenile Delinquency: Legally prohibited behavior, such as disobedient, indecent, or immoral conduct, committed by minors.

K

Ketosis: The condition marked by excessive production of ketone bodies in the body.

Kinesthetic: Pertaining to muscle sense, or to the sense by which muscular movement, weight, position are perceived.

Kinesthetic Afferentiation: Gathering data concerning one's own current muscle tone, body position, oral status, etc. Considered a function of the posterior association areas.

Kinetic Afferentiation: Integration of input from parietal-occipital tertiary zones, basal ganglia, and premotor areas producing sequential and integrated actions. Depends initially on kinesthetic afferentiation.

Kinetic Apraxia: Disorgainzed transition of single movements (*see also* apraxia, echopraxia, apraxia of speech). Associated with lesions in basal gaglia-premotor areas. Subordination of movements to intentions is impaired.

Kluver-Bucy Syndrome: A condition manifested by hyperorality, hypersexuality, labile emotions, and inability to form new memories. Associated with temporal lobe or limbic system lesions.

Korsakoff's Psychosis: A progressive dementia considered subcortical in focus and associated with a nutritional deficiency of vitamin B_1 (thiamine). The condition is considered secondary to alcohol abuse. Memory impairments are paramount with associated confabulation, blandness, and passivity. Hippocampus lesions have been associated with this condition.

   A memory disorder, related to a thiamine deficiency, generally associated chronic alcoholism.

Kuru: A slow virus of the brain which produces trembling and, eventually, paralysis of the limbs.

L

Labeled Lines: A view of stimulus coding stating that particular nerve cells are intrinsically labeled for particular sensory experiences such as cold, touch, pain, and so forth.

Labile Memory: An early state of memory formation during which formation of a memory can be easily disrupted by conditions that influence brain activity.

Lacunar State: Multiple but small infarctions in the subcortical regions leaving lacunae. One of the end stages of hypertensive cerebrovascular conditions.

Laminar (form of organization): The horizontal layering of cells found in some brain regions.

Lateral: An anatomical term meaning toward the side; opposite of medial.

Lateral Geniculate Nucleus: Part of the thalamus which receives information from the optic tract and sends it to visual areas in the occipital cortex.

Lateral Hypothalamus (LH): A hypothalamic region involved in facilitating eating.

Lateral Inhibition: A phenomenon produced by interconnected neurons that inhibit their neighbors, producing contrast at the edges of the stimulus.

Law of Effect: Principle that responses that have rewarding consequences are strengthened and those that have aversive consequences are weakened or eliminated.

Leading Question: A question posed by a trial lawyer which is improper because it suggests to a witness the desired answer.

Lecithin: A monoaminomonophosphatide found in animal tissues, especially nerve tissue, semen, egg yolk, and in smaller amount in bile and blood.

Legal Fiction: An assumption of fact or a situation contrived by the law to decide a legal question.

Lethality Scale: Criteria used to assess the likelihood of an individual's committing suicide.

Leukemia: A disease of the blood marked by persistent leukodytosis, associated with changes in the spleen and the bone marrow, or in the lymphatic nodes.

Level of Aspiration: Standard by which the individual judges success or failure of his behavior.

Lexical Agraphia: Impaired ability to spell irregular or unknown works with an intact ability to spell regular words. Associated with lesions in the parieto-occipital lobule.

Limb-kinetic Apraxia: Complex/serial movement impairment in the presence of intact simple, repetitive movement. Brodman areas 4 and 6 are implicated in almost all cases.

Limbic System: Interconnected and primarily subcortial structures which are involved in emotional responses and memory.

Literal Paraphasia: Production of off-target sounds with effortless articulation. Associated with postrolandic lesions.

Litigant: One who is party to a lawsuit.

Local Circuit Neurons: Small neurons that make contact only with neurons that are within the same functional unit.

Localization of Function: The concept that specific brain regions are responsible for various types of experience, behavior, and psychological processes.

Locked-in Syndrome: Also known as de-efferentiation, this is due to bilateral pontine lesions and characterized by aphonia and quadraplegia. The patient is aware of his or her surroundings.

Logical Positivism: A philosophy which emphasizes the creation of knowledge and its verification through observation and experiment.

Long-term Memory: An enduring form of memory lasting for weeks, months, or years.

Lumbar: Referring to the lower part of the spinal cord or back.

Lumen: The space in the interior of a tubular structure such as an artery or the intestine.

Luteinizing Hormone (LH): A tropic hormone released by the anterior pituitary that influences the hormonal activities of the gonads. In males, this hormone is called interstitial-cell-stimulating hormone (ICSH).

Luteinizing Hormone-releasing Hormone: See gonadotropin-releasing hormone.

M

M'Naghten Rule: In most jurisdictions, the test applied for the defense of insanity. Under this test, an accused is not criminally responsible if he was suffering from a mental disease or defect at the time of committing the act and does not understand the nature and quality of his act or that what he was doing was wrong. In order to be considered "sane" and therefore legally responsible for the act committed, the defendant must know and understand the nature and quality of his act and be able to distinguish between right and wrong at the time the offense was committed.

Macula: A spot.

Magnetic Apraxia: Compulsive exploration of the immediate environment in the usual presence of intact comprehension skills. Forced hand grasping with difficultly "letting go" is an example. Prefrontal, mesial, and contralateral lesions are implicated.

Major Affective Disorders: Category of affective disorders in which a biological defect or other aberration renders a person liable to experience episodes of a more or less severe affective disorder.

Major Depression (unipolar disorder): A severe affective disorder in which only depressive episodes occur.

Malaise: A feeling of general discomfort or uneasiness; an out-of-sorts feeling, often the first indication of an infection.

Malfeasance: The commission of an unlawful, wrongful act; any wrongful conduct that affects, interrupts, or interferes with the performance of official duties.

Malleus Malleficarum: Infamous handbook prepared by two monks dealing with the "diagnosis" and "treatment" of witches and witchcraft.

Mammillary Bodies: Paired nuclei at the base of the brain slightly posterior to the pituitary stalk.

Mandamus: A writ or order issued from a superior court to a lower court or to a private or municipal corporation commanding that a specified act be performed. Used when other judicial remedies have failed.

Manic-depressive Psychoses: Older term denoting a group of psychotic disorders characterized by prolonged periods of excitement and overactivity (mania) or by periods of depression and underactivity (depression) or by alternation of the two.

Masked Fascies: An unblinking, bland, expressionless stare.

Masochism: Sexual variant in which an individual obtains sexual gratification through infliction of pain.

Mass Action: Proposed by Lashley, this notion stated that the degree of deficit showed by a lesion was a function of how much cortical tissue was destroyed.

Meatus: A passage, or channel, especially the external opening of a canal.

Medial: An anatomical term meaning toward the middle; opposite of lateral.

Medial Geniculate Nucleus: A nucleus in the thalamus that receives input from the inferior colliculus and sends output to the auditory cortex.

Mediation: A way of resolving disputes by using a third party to intervene between contending parties to bring them to a satisfactory settlement without resorting to litigation.

Medulla: The lowest part of the brain, also called myelencephalon.

Melokinetic Apraxia: Deficit in speech, skill, and coordination of movement, usually confined to a small muscle group. Unilateral and contralateral to lesion in premotor area.

Memory Traces: Persistent changes in the brain that reflect the storage of memory.

Meninges: Thin membranes on the brain—dura mater, pia mater, and arachnoid, which provide a venous drainage system.

Meningioma: Neoplastic growth arising from the meninges.

Menningitis: Inflammatory disease of the meninges with associated signs of fever, headache, and stiff neck.

Mens Rea: A guilty mind; having a guilty or wrongful purpose or criminal intent.

Mental Anguish: A compensable injury including all forms of mental, as opposed to physical, injury. In connection with a physical injury, includes the mental sensation of pain and accompanying feelings of distress, grief, anxiety, or fright.

Mesencephalon: The midbrain.

Mesmerism: Theories of "animal magnetism" (hypnosis) formulated by Anton Mesmer.

Messenger RNA (mRNA): A strand of RNA that carries the code of a section of a strand of DNA to the cytoplasm.

Metabolism: The sum of the chemical changes whereby the function of nutrition is affected; it consists of anabolism or the constructive and assimilative changes and catabolism or the destructive and retrograde changes.

Metamorphosias: Visual illusions where objects are distorted in size, shape, distance, or color. May occur with lesions anywhere in visual system, with substance intoxication, or in conjunction with psychiatric dysfunction.

Metencephalon: A subdivision of the hindbrain that includes the cerebellum and the pons.

Meter: A measure of length, 100 cm., the equivalent of 39.371 inches.

Methadone: An orally administered narcotic which replaces the craving for heroin and weans the individual from heroin addiction.

Microglia: Extremely small glial cells that remove cellular debris from injured or dead cells.

Microgram: One one-millionth of a gram, or 1/1000 of a milligram

Micron: One one-millionth of a meter or 1/1000 of a millimeter.

Microtubules: Hollow cylindrical structures in axons that are involved in exoplasmic streaming.

Midbrain: The middle division of the brain. Also called mesencephalon.

Middle Cerebral Artery (MCA): The MCA and its branches are one of the two major vascular networks of the frontal lobes. The lateral convexity is fed by anterior branches of the MCA.

Milieu: The immediate environment, physical or social or both; sometimes used to include the internal state of an organism.

Millimeter: One one-thousandth of a meter; about 1/25 inch.

Misdemeanor: An offense less serious than a felony, typically punishable by a fine or short-term incarceration.

Misfeasance: The improper performance to an act a person has a right or duty to perform.

Misoplegia: A type of unilateral inattention where the lesioned individual, usually hemiplegic, exhibits a strong dislike for the affected limbs or portions of the body. Intense hatred resulting in self-mutilation may be expressed.

Mistrial: A trial which is terminated before its normal conclusion and declared invalid prior to the returning of a verdict. A judge may declare a mistrial due to an extraordinary event (e.g., death of a juror), for a fundamental, prejudicial error that cannot be corrected by instructions to the jury, or because of the jury's inability to reach a verdict (hung jury). In a criminal case, may prevent a retial under the doctrine of double jeopardy.

Mitochondria: Organelles in the cytoplasm of cells; contain enzymes that make possible the reactions whereby energy is liberated from food and stored temporarily in the chemical bonds of ATP.

Mitosis: The process of division of somatic cells that involves duplication of DNA.

Model Psychoses: Psychotic-like states produced by various hallucinogenic drugs such as LSD.

Modulation of Formation of Memory: Facilitation or inhibition of memory formation by factors other than those directly involved in memory formation. Also called modulation of memory storage processes.

Modus Operandi: Manner or mode of behavior; a criminal's typical pattern of performing crimes.

Monopolar Neurons: Nerve cells with a single branch leaving the cell body which then extends in two directions—one end is the receptive pole, the other end the output zone.

Moot: A subject for debate; unsettled; undecided. A case is "moot" when a determination of a matter is sought which, when rendered, has no practical effect on the matter under dispute.

Moral Nihilism: Doctrine which denies any objective or real ground for moral beliefs, and holds that the individual is not bound by obligation to others or society.

Moral Therapy: Therapy based on provision of kindness, understanding, and favorable environment; prevalent during early part of the 19th century.

Motion: An application made to a court or judge, orally or in writing, requesting that a rule or order be given in favor of the applicant.

Motivational Selectivity: Influence of motives on perception and other cognitive processes.

Motive Pattern: Relatively consistent cluster of motives centered around particular strivings and goals.

Motoneurons: Nerve cells in the spinal cord that transmit motor messages from the spinal cord to muscles.

Motor Aprosody: Inability to sing or to change pitch or voice tempo with intact ability to recognize melodies.

Motor Cortex: A region of cerebral cortex that sends impulses to motoneurons.

Motor Extinction: Increased contralateral limb akinesia when simultaneously using ipsilateral extremities, due to cerebral dysfunction.

Motor Impersistence: Inability to maintain an initiated, voluntary (motor) behavior chain. Implies distraction due to interference factors. Common impersistences include lack of tongue protrusion, eyelid closure, mouth opening, breath holding, hand-grip pressure, and central gaze.

Motor Neuron: Spinal cord neurons involved in movement which extend to effector muscle sites.

Motor Unit: A single motor axon and all the muscle fibers it innervates.

Multi-infarct Dementia: A vascular disease that has a progressive, stepwise course caused by multiple strokes and arteriosclersosis. Cognitive symptoms usually precede personality problems. Motor anomalies are distinctive of this condition and reflect subcortical involvement.

Multiple Personality: Type of dissociative disorder characterized by the development of two or more relatively independent personality systems in the same individual.

Multiple Sclerosis (MS): A degenerative condition involving deterioration of the myelin sheath on nerve fibers. This disease therefore affects primarily the white matter. Multiple cognitive and emotional deficits are noted. The rate of progression of MS is extremely variable.

Multipolar Neurons: Nerve cells with many dendrites and a single axon.

Muscarinic: A cholingergic receptor (one responsive to acetylcholine) that mediates chiefly the inhibitory activities of acetylcholine.

Myasthenia Gravis: A neurological disease characterized by easy fatiguability and weakness of muscles.

Myelencephalon: A subdivision of the hindbrain; the medulla.

Myelin: The fatty insulation around an axon, formed by accessory cells; this improves the speed of conduction of nerve impulses.

Myelin Sheath: A thin cover on the axons of many neurons.

Myelinization: The process of formation of myelin.

N

Narcolepsy: A disorder involving frequent, intense episodes of sleep, which last from 5 to 30 minutes, and can occur anytime during the usual waking hours.

Narcosis: Stupor, or unconsciousness, produced by some narcotic drug.

Narcotherapy (narcoanalysis, narcosynthesis): Psychotherapy carried on while the patient is in a sleep-like state of relaxation induced by a drug such as sodium pentothal.

Narcotic Drug: Drugs such as morphine which lead to physiological dependence and increased tolerance.

Natural Law: A philosophy which refers to a system of rules and principles for the guidance of human behavior which arise from the rational intelligence of man. These rules are apart from enacted laws and stem from and conform to man's entire mental, moral, and physical constitution.

Necker Cube: An optical illusion using "rate of apparent change (RAC)" to differentiate normals from brain injured. Fewer and slower reversals are reported by brain injured, with damage associated with right hemisphere or frontal lobe lesions.

Necrosis: Local death of tissue.

Negative Feedback System: A regulatory system in which output is used to reduce the effect of input signals.

Negativism: Form of aggressive withdrawal which involves refusing to cooperate or obey commands, or doing the exact opposite of what has been requested.

Negligence: The failure to exercise the degree of care which a reasonable person, guided by ordinary considerations under similar circumstances would exercise.

Neocortex: The relatively recently evolved portions of the cerebral cortex.

Nerve Growth Factor: A substance that controls the growth of neurons of the spinal ganglia and the ganglia of the synmpathetic nervous system.

Nerve Impulses: The propagated electrical messages of a neuron which travel down from the axon to adjacent neurons. Also called action potentials.

Neural Tube: A prenatal structure with subdivisions which correspond to the future forebrain, midbrain, and hindbrain. The cavity of this tube will include the cerebral ventricles and the passages that connect them.

Neurasthenic Neurosis: Neurotic disorder characterized by complaints of chronic weakness, easy fatigueability, and lack of enthusiasm.

Neuroblasts: Early forms of cells during the stage of cell migration.

Neurofibrillary Tangles: Abnormal whorls of neurofilaments within nerve cells that are especially apparent in people suffering from dementia.

Neurofilaments: Small rod-like structures in axons that are involved in transport of materials.

Neuroglia: "Nerve glue" or glia, these cells make up about half the volume of the central nervous system and provide structural and metabolic support to neurons. *See* glial cells.

Neurohypophysis: See posterior pituitary.

Neurological Examination: Examination to determine presence and extent of organic damage to the nervous system.

Neuromodulators: Substances that influence the activity of synaptic transmitters.

Neuron: The basic unit of the nervous system, composed of a cell body, receptive extension(s), and a transmitting extension (axon).
     A cell of the brain or spinal cord (CNS) which is composed of a cell body (soma), axon, and dendrites.

Neuron Doctrine: A hypothesis which states that the brain is composed of separate cells that are distinct structurally, metabolically, and functionally.

Neuropathies: Perepheral nerve destruction.

Neurosecretory Cells: Neurons that manufacture and secrete hormones.

Neurospecificity: A theory of nervous system development which states that each axon grows to a particular site.

Neurotic Nucleus: Basic personality characteristics underlying neurotic disorders.

Neurotic Paradox: Failure of neurotic patterns to extinguish despite their self-defeating nature.

Neurotic Style: A general personality disposition toward inhibiting certain anxiety-causing behaviors; distinguishable from anxiety, somatoform, and dissociative disorders in that neurotic styles do not manifest themselves in specific, disabling neurotic symptoms.

Neurotransmitter: Biochemical substances which transmit information between neurons. *See* synaptic transmitter.

Nicotinic: A cholingergic receptor that mediates chiefly the excitatory activities of acetylcholine.

Night Hospital: Mental hospital in which an individual may receive treatment during all or part of the night while carrying on his usual occupation in the daytime.

Nigrostriatal Bundle (NSB): A dopaminergic tract that runs from the substantia nigra of the midbrain to the lateral hypothalamus, the globus pallidus, and the caudatepatamen.

Nihilistic Delusion: Fixed belief that everything is unreal.

Nociceptors: Receptors that respond to stimuli that produce tissue damage or pose the threat of damage.

Node of Ranvier: A gap between successive segments of the myelin sheath where the axon membrane is exposed.

Nomadism: Withdrawal reaction in which the individual continually attempts to escape frustration by moving from place to place or job to job.

Nomothetic Methodology: An approach in which the discovery of relationships between variables by studying large numbers of cases or events is emphasized.

Non Compos Mentis: Insane; not sound of mind. A very general term including all varieties of mental derangement.

Norepinephrine (NE): A neurotransmitter produced mainly in brainstem nuclei, also called noradrenalin.

Normal Pressure Hydrocephalus (NPH): A reversible condition involving obstruction of cerebral spinal fluid (CSF). Increased pressure leads to ventricle enlargement with the primary lesion in the midbrain reticular formation.

Nosology: The classification of diseases, including mental diseases.

NSB: See nigrostriatal bundle.

Nucleotide: A portion of a DNA molecule composed of a single base and the adjoining sugar-phosphate unit of the strand.

Nucleus: An anatomical collection of neurons, e.g., caudate nucleus.

Nystagmus: Abnormal to and fro movements of the eye during attempts to fixate. Rhythmic oscillation of the eyeballs, either horizontal, rotary, or vertical.

O

Occipital Cortex: The cortex of the occipital (posterior) lobe of the brain.

Ocular-dominance Histogram: A graph that shows the strength of a neuron's response to stimuli presented to either the left or right eye. Used to determine the effects of depriving one eye of visual experience.

Ondine Curse: A type of sleep apnea where automatic breathing during sleep is disrupted. Lesions of the reticulospinal tract have been implicated in this condition.

Oneirism: Prolonged dream state despite wakefulness.

Optic Aphasia: Inability to name visually presented objects with intact recognition. Spared recognition is shown by demonstration of use or matching (pointing) to the object when named.

Optic Ataxia: Inability to localize objects in space by visual guidance. Difficulty in shifting (stimulus boundedness) is an associated feature.

Optic Chiasm: The site where optic neurons from eye separate and cross over to the contralateral hemisphere. Located near the pituitary gland.

Optic Radiation: Axons of the lateral geniculate nucleus that terminate in the primary visual areas of the occipital cortex.

Optic Tract: The axons of the retinal ganglion cells after they have passed the optic chiasm; most terminate in the lateral geniculate nucleus.

Optokinetic System: A closed loop system controlling eye movement and keeping the gaze on target.

Organ of Corti: A structure in the inner ear that lies on the basilar membrane of the cochlea. It contains the hair cells and the terminations of the auditory nerve.

Orifice: Any aperture or opening.

Osmoreceptors: Cells in the hypothalamus that were thought to respond to changes in osmotic pressure.

Osmotic Thirst: The response to increased osmotic pressure in brain cells. Contrast with hypovolemic thirst.

Ostium: A small opening, especially one of entrance into a hollow organ or canal.

Overutilization Anoxia: Occuring during epileptic seizures, a lack of sufficient oxygen secondary to the abnormal electrical discharges. Seen as due to the high metabolic rates during seizures.

Oxidation: The combining of food and oxygen in the tissues; chemically, the increase in valence of an element.

Oximeter: An instrument for measuring the oxygen saturation of hemoglobin in the circulating blood.

Oxytocin: A hormone released by the posterior pituitary which triggers milk let-down in the nursing female.

P

Pacchionian Bodies: Small projections of the arachnoid tissue, chiefly into the venous sinuses of the dura mater.

Pain Asymbolia: Loss of appreciation for pain, associated with left parietal lesions.

Pain Cocktail: A concoction of all the medication a pain patient is taking in a single liquid that can be systematically controlled and reduced in strength.

Paleocortex: Evolutionary old cortex, e.g., the hippocampus.

Palilalia: Progressively more rapid and less loud speech productions, ending in an indistinguishable mutter. Associated with bilateral frontal lesions or with subcortical structures.

Palpitation: Forcible pulsation of the heart perceptible to the individual.

Papilledema: Edema of the optic disk, associated with increased intracranial pressure.

Paradigmatic Change: A new way of viewing the world.

Paradoxical Sleep: See rapid-eye-movement sleep (REM).

Parallel Processing: Using several different circuits at the same time to process the same stimuli.

Paralysis: A loss of power of voluntary movement in a muscle through injury or disease of its nerve supply.

Paranoia: Psychosis characterized by a systematized delusional system.

Paranoid Personality: Individual showing behavior characterized by projection (as a defense mechanism), suspiciousness, envy, extreme jealousy, and stubbornness.

Paranoid Schizophrenia: Subtype of schizophrenic disorder characterized by absurd, illogical, and changeable ideas of hallucinations of grandeur and persecution.

Paranoid State: Transient psychotic disorder in which the main element is a delusion, usually persecutory or grandiose in nature.

Paraphasias: Errors in word usage associated with aphasia. Substitutions for a correct word may occur (e.g., "I ate night") or substitution for syllables (e.g., "I ate rupper"). Neologisms may occur (e.g., "I ate ronks").

Parasympathetic Division: One of the two systems that compose the autonomic nervous system. The parasympathetic division arises from both the cranial and sacral parts of the spinal cord.

Paraventricular Nucleus: A nucleus of the hypothalamus.

Parenchyma: The essential elements of an organ; the functional elements of an organ, as distinguished from its framework, or stroma.

Parens Patriae: Literally, "parent of the country." Refers to the role of the state as sovereign or guardian of disabled persons, such as minors and insane and incompetent persons.

Parkinson's Disease: A degenerative neurological disorder involving dopaminergic neurons of the substantia nigra.

    A subcortical, progressive dementia that is primarily caused by neuronal degeneration of the basal ganglia, particularly the substantia nigra. There may also be cortical impairment. The three primary symptoms are tremor, rigidity, and bradykinesia. Egocentricity, irritability, and suspiciousness are common.

Partial Seizures: Epileptic seizures arising from pathological foci that to not have widespread distribution. These include focal repetitive motor spasms and do not involve loss of consciousness.

Parturition: Giving birth to young.

Path Analysis: Statistical technique which takes into account how variables are related to one another through time and how they predict one another.

Pathological Gambling: Addictive disorder in which gambling behavior disrupts the individual's life.

Pederasty: Sexual intercouse between males via the anus.

Perceptual Defense: A process in which threatening stimuli are filtered out and not perceived by the organism.

Perceptual Filtering: Processes involved in selective attention to aspects of the great mass of incoming stimuli which continually impinges on the organism.

Perimeter: An instrument delimiting the field of vision.

Peripheral Nerves: Neurons which lie outside the central nervous system.

Peripheral Nervous System: The portion of the nervous system that includes all the nerves outside the brain and spinal cord.

Permanent Planning: Placing children who are drifting through foster homes back into their original families.

Perseveration: Persistent continuation of a line of thought or activity once it is under way. Clinically inappropriate repetition.

Perseveration-consolidation Hypothesis: A hypothesis stating that information passes through two stages in memory formation. During the first stage the memory is held by perseveration of neural activity and is easily disrupted. During the second stage the memory becomes fixed, or consolidated, and is no longer easily disrupted.

Personality Disorder: A group of maladaptive behavioral syndromes originating in the developmental years and not characterized by neurotic or psychotic symptoms.

Perversion: Deviation from normal.

Petit Mal Seizures: A type of generalized epileptic seizure characterized by a spike-and-wave electrical pattern. During these seizures the person is unaware of the environment and later cannot recall what happened.

pH: The symbol commonly used in expressing hydrogen ion concentration. It signifies the logarithm of the reciprocal of the hydrogen ion concentration expressed as a power of 10.

Phantom Limb: The experience of sensory messages attributed to an amputated limb.

Phasic Receptors: Receptors that show a rapid fall in nerve impulse discharge as stimulation is maintained.

Phlebothrombosis: Thrombosis of a vein without inflammation of its walls.

Phonological Agraphia: Impaired ability to spell nonwords with intact ability for familiar words. Associated with lesions of the supermarginal gyrus or associated areas.

Phosphemes: Flashes of light caused by dysfunction of the auditory-visual association area. Visual hallucinations may also be produced, related or not to past experiences.

Photopic System: A system in the retina that operates at high levels of light, shows sensitivity to color, and involves the cones; contrast with scotopic system.

Phrenology: The belief that bumps on the skull reflect enlargements of brain regions responsible for certain behavioral faculties.

Pick's Disease: Similar to Alzheimer's disease, here neuronic damage is typically confined to the frontal and temporal lobes. Personality changes usually precede memory loss. Affects twice as many women as men.

Pilocarpine: An alkaloid that stimulates the parasympathetic division of the autonomic nervous system.

Pitch: A dimension of auditory experience in which sounds vary from low to high.

Pituitary Gland: A small complex endocrine gland located in a socket at the base of the skull. The anterior pituitary and posterior pituitary are separate in function.

Place Theory: A theory of frequency discrimination according to which pitch perceptions depends on the place of maximal displacement of the basilar membrane produced by a sound. Contrast with volley theory.

Plaintiff: A person who initiates an action or legal suit. In a civil suit, the party who complains or sues.

Planum Temporale: A region of superior temporal cortex adjacent to the primary auditory area.

Plea: In a legal action, the defendant's answer to the plaintiff's declaration.

Plea Bargaining: In a criminal case, the process in which the accused and the prosecutor negotiated a mutually satisfactory disposition of the case subject to the approval of the court. Usually involves the defendant pleading guilty to a reduced punishment or offense or to a lesser number of counts in a multi-count indictment.

Pleading: The formal allegations made by the opposing parties of their respective claims and defenses.

Pleasure Principle: In psychoanalysis, the demand that an instinctual need be immediately gratified regardless of reality.

Plexus: A network, or tangle, of interweaving nerves, veins, or lymphatic vessels.

Pneumoencephalogram: A technique for examining brain structure in intact humans by taking X-rays after a gas is injected into the ventricles.

Pons: A portion of the metencephalon.

Positive Law: A system of rules and laws enacted or adopted by the government of an organized political community for the purpose of controlling the conduct of its people.

Positron Emission Tomography (PET) Scan: A technique for examining brain structure and function in intact humans by combining tomography with injections of radioactive substances used by the brain. An analysis of metabolism of these substances reflect regional differences in brain activity.

Computer-assisted, X-ray procedure designed to analyze and track glucose utilization in the brain.

Postcentral Gyrus: Involved in sensory mediation, this cortical convolution is located just posterior to the Fissure of Rolando.

Posterior Pituitary: The rear division of the pituitary gland. Also called neurohypophysis.

Posthypnotic Amnesia: The subject's lack of memory for the period during which he was hypnotized.

Posthypnotic Suggestion: Suggestion given during hypnosis to be carried out by the subject after he is brought out of hypnosis.

Postpartum Disturbances: Emotional disturbances associated with childbirth.

Postsynaptic Potentials: See graded potentials.

Posttraumatic Amnesia (PTA): A form of anterograde amnesia seen as a post-concussional effect of head trauma. Correlates well with coma length and severity. Some retrograde amnesia may accompany PTA.

Posttraumatic Stress Disorders: Category of disorder in which the stressor is severe and residual symptoms occur following the traumatic experience.

Postural Tremor: A tremor that occurs when a person attempts to maintain a posture such as holding an arm or leg extended, resulting from pathology of the basal ganglia or cerebellum.

Precedent: A previous judgment or decision of a court considered as an authority for deciding later identical or similar cases. Under the doctrine of stare decisis, cases which establish that a rule of law are authoritative and must be adhered to.

Precentral Gyrus: Involved in the mediation of motor activity, this cortical convolution is located just anterior to the Fissure of Rolando.

Precipitating Cause: The particular stress which triggers a disorder.

Predisposing Cause: The factor which lowers the individual's stress tolerance and paves the way for the appearance of a disorder.

Predisposition: Likelihood that an individual will develop certain symptoms under given stress conditions.

Pressor: Excited vasoconstrictor activity, producing increased blood pressure; denoting afferent nerves that, when stimulated, excite the vasoconstrictor center.

Presumption: An inference resulting from a rule of law or the proven existence of a fact which requires such rule(s) or action(s) be established in the action. Presumptions can be irrebuttable, such as the presumption of incapacity in a person under seven years to act, or rebuttable, in which case it can be disproved by evidence.

Presumption of Innocence: A principle of criminal law in which the government carries the burden of proof beyond a reasonable doubt for every element of a crime, with the defendant having no burden of proof to prove his innocence.

Prima Facie Case: A case in which there is sufficient evidence for the matter to proceed beyond a motion for a directed verdict in a jury case or a motion to dismiss in a nonjury trial; it requires the defendant to proceed with his case.

Prima Facie Evidence: Evidence which, in the judgment of the law, is good and sufficient to establish a given fact or a chain of facts making up the party's claim or defense. If such evidence is unexplained or uncontradicted, it is sufficient to sustain a favorable judgement for the issue it supports; may be contradicted by other evidence.

Primary Reaction Tendencies: Constitutional tendencies apparent in infancy, such as sensitivity and activity level.

Privilege: A particular benefit or exemption enjoyed by a person, company, or class, beyond the common ones held by other citizens.

Privileged Communication: Statements that are made in a setting of legal or other professional confidentiality. Applies to certain persons within a protected relationship, such as husband-wife, attorney-client, which are legally protected from forced disclosure on the witness stand at the option of the witness.

Pro Bono Publico: For the welfare or good of the public, such as when an attorney or other professional handles a case without compensation to advance a social cause or represents a party who cannot afford to pay him.

Problem Drinker: Behavioral term referring to one who has serious problems associated with drinking alcohol. Term is currently preferable to alcoholic.

Process (Poor premorbid, Chronic) Schizophrenia: Schizophrenia pattern that develops gradually and tends to be long-lasting.

Prodrome: Behavioral/mood change preceding onset of a seizure. Prodromal signs may be apparent for several days before the seizure.

Progressive Supranuclear Palsy: An uncommon Parkinson-like condition that usually begins in the 50s with emotional lability, imbalance, and problems with downward gaze. A dementia develops with relative sparing of language and constructional abilities.

Projection Neuron: Large neurons that transmit messages to widely separated parts of the brain.

Prosecution: A criminal proceeding to determine the guilt or innocence of a person charged with a crime. Refers to the state or federal government as the party proceeding in a criminal action.

Prosencephalon: See forebrain.

Prosody: Rhythm, pitch, tempo, and like characteristics of speech. Important in communication of affective content. Typically seen as a right hemisphere activity.

Prosopagnosia: Inability to recognize faces of those with whom one was previously familiar. Loss of ability to recognize unfamiliar faces is a variant of this disorder. Usually associated with right association are lesions.

Protocritic: A diffuse type of sensory experience (e.g., temperature) that is common to all homeostatic internal mechanisms. Cognitive processing does not lead to identifying a discrete place or duration for the sensation. Opposed to epicritic.

Proximal: An anatomical directional term meaning near the trunk or center; opposite of distal.

Proximate Cause: An occurrence that, in a natural and unbroken chain of events, results in an injury and without which the injury would not have occurred. The event that is closest in the causal relationship to the effect.

Pseudo-community: Delusional social environment developed by a paranoiac.

Pseudobulbar State: Strong affective expressions to include laughing and crying, often simultaneously but also incongruous to the stated feeling of the person. Associated with lesions of connecting pathways between the frontal lobes and lower brain structures.

Pseudodementia: A pattern of deficit behavior resembling organically produced dementia. Depression is the primary factor causing the intellectual suppression.

Pseudodepression: The major pathology involves the dorsal-lateral frontal convexity, severe bilateral frontal pathology, or severing of frontal-thalamic pathways. This is a pathology of reduced/absent motor responses (e.g., mutism, inactivity, helpless unconcern). The subject may be aware of his deficit.

Pseudohemianopsia: Lack of attention to visual stimulation from the contralateral side despite intact visual fields.

Pseudopsychopathy: The major pathology involves the orbital frontal areas and reflects motor excess (e.g., peurile acts, restlessness, bursting into motion, impulsive antisocial acts). The subject knows but cannot control the motor behavior.

Psychic Cortex: Anterior portion of the temporal lobe which when stimulated produce recollection of previous experience (e.g., music, visual scenes). Temporal lobe tumors may produce hallucinations involving previous experiences.

Psychomotor Epilepsy: State of disturbed consciousness in which the individual may perform various actions, sometimes of a homicidal nature, for which he or she is later amnesic.

Psychosexual Dysfunction: Inability or impaired ability to experience or give sexual gratification.

Psychotogens: Substances that generate psychotic behavior.

Psychotropic Drugs: Drugs whose main effects are mental or behavioral in nature.

Pterygoid: Shaped like a wing.

Ptosis: Drooping eyelid caused by a lesion to the oculomotor cranial nerve.

Putative: Reputed or supposed.

Pure Agraphia: Writing deficits caused by brain damage in the absence of other significant language disturbance.

Pure Word Deafness: Inability to understand spoken words with an intact ability to read, write, and speak. Usually does not occur in isolation of other defects and is associated with cardiovascular accidents.

Purkinje Cell: A type of large nerve cell in the cerebellar cortex.

Pyramidal Cell: A type of large nerve cell in the cerebral cortex.

Pyramidal System: A motor system including neurons within the cerebral cortex and their axons with form the pyramidal tract.

Q

Quasi-experimental Design: A research study in which the experimenter has partial experimental control over the setting and variables.

R

Ramp Movements: Slow, sustained motions thought to be generated in the basal ganglia. Also called smooth movements. Contrast with ballistic.

Ramus: A branch; one of the primary divisions of a nerve or a blood vessel; a part of an irregularly shaped bone that forms an angle with the main body.

Random Assignment: An experimental method which ensures that every subject has an equal chance of being selected for the experimental or control group.

Range Fractionation: A hypothesis of stimulus intensity perception stating that a wide range of intensity values can be encoded by a group of cells each of which is a specialist for a particular range of an intensity scale.

Rape: An act of violence in which sexual relations are forced upon another person.

Raphe Nucleus: A group of neurons in the midline of the brain stem which contains serotonin, involved in sleep mechanisms.

Rapid-eye-movement (REM) Sleep: A state of sleep characterized by small-amplitude, fast EEG waves, no postural tension, and rapid eye movements. Also called paradoxical sleep.

Ratio Decidendi: The principal ground or reason for a court's written decision. The point in a case which is essential to determining the court's judgment.

Re-uptake: A mechanism by which a synaptic transmitter released at a synapse is taken back into the presynaptic terminal, thus stopping synaptic activity.

Reaction Formation: Ego-defense mechanism in which the individual's conscious attitudes and overt behavior are opposite to repressed unconscious wishes.

Readiness Potential: An electrical potential which occurs over widespread posterior regions of the scalp prior to the onset of a voluntary movement.

Reality Assumptions: Assumptions which relate to the gratification of needs in the light of environmental possibilities, limitations, and dangers.

Reality Principle: Awareness of the demands of the environment and adjustment of behavior to meet these demands.

Reasonable Doubt: The degree of doubt required to justify an acquittal of a criminal defendant, based on reason and arising from evidence or lack of evidence.

Reasonable Doubt Standard: A standard beyond which guilt must be shown.

Receptive Field: The stimulus region and features that cause the maximal responses of a cell in a sensory system.

Receptor: Nerve ending that receives a stimulus.

Receptor Proteins: Substances at synaptic receptor sites whose reaction to certain transmitters causes a change in the postsynaptic membrane potential.

Receptor Sites: Regions of specialized membrane containing receptor proteins located on the postsynaptic surface of a synapse; these sites receive and react with the chemical transmitter.

Receptors: The initial elements in sensory systems, responsible for stimulus transduction, e.g., hair cells in the cochlea or rods and cones in the retina.

Recess: A short interval during a trial or hearing when the court suspends business without adjournment.

Reduplicative Paramnesia: Associated with right parietal and/or frontal damage of a coarse nature. Involves relocating a place (e.g., hospital) to another place (e.g., one's home town).

Reflex: A simple, highly stereotyped, and unlearned response to a particular stimulus (i.e., an eyeblink in response to a puff of air).

Refractory: A period during and after a nerve impulse in which the axon membrane's responsiveness is reduced. A brief period of complete insensitivity to stimuli (absolute refractory phase) is followed by a longer period of reduced sensitivity (relative refractory phase) during which only strong stimulation produces a nerve impulse.

Regression: Ego-defense mechanism in which the individual retreats to the use of less mature responses in attempting to cope with stress and maintain ego integrity.

Remand: To send a case back to the court from which it came to have further action taken on it there.

Remedy: The means by which a right is enforced or the violation of a right is prevented or compensated.

Repression: Ego-defense mechanism by means of which dangerous desires and intolerable memories are kept out of consciousness.

Residual Schizophrenia: Category used for persons regarded as recovered from schizophrenia but will manifesting some symptoms.

Resistance: Tendency to maintain symptoms and resist treatment or uncovering of repressed material.

Resistance to Extinction: Tendency of a conditioned response to persist despite lack of reinforcement.

Resorption: The loss of substance through physiologic or pathologic means.

Respondent: The party answering a charge or the party contending against an appeal.

Resting Potential: Potential differences across the membrane of nerve cells during an inactive period. Also called membrane potential.

Retainer: A contract between an attorney and a client stating the nature of the services to be rendered and the cost of such services. By employing an attorney to act on his behalf, a client prevents him from acting for his adversary.

Rete Mirabile: A network of find blood vessels located at the base of the brain in which blood coming from the periphery reduces the temperature of arterial blood before it enters the brain.

Reticular: Netlike.

Reticular Activating System: Brain stem area which mediates level of arousal.

Reticular Formation: A region of the brain stem (extending from the medulla through the thalamus) which is involved in arousal.

Retinaculum: A special fascial thickening which holds back an organ or part; helps to retain an organ or tissue in its place.

Retrieval: A process in memory during which a stored memory is utilized by an organism.

Retroactive Amnesia: A type of memory loss in which events just before a head injury are not recalled.

Retrograde Amnesia: Inability to recall events previous to the onset of a trauma or condition. Recovery of remote events usually occurs first.

Retrograde Degeneration: Destruction of the nerve cell body following injury.

Reverse Tolerance: Situation in which a decreased amount of some psychoactive drug brings about the effects formerly achieved by a larger dose.

Rh Antigen or Factor: An agglutinogen, or antigen, first found in the erythrocytes of the rhesus monkey, hence the Rh. Rh positive and Rh negative terms, denoting the presence or absence, respectively, of this antigen.

Rhodopsin: The photopigment in rods that responds to light.

Rhombencephalon: See hindbrain.

Ribosomes: Organelles which appear as dots lining the endoplasmic reticulum; they are the protein factories of cells.

Right: A power or privilege, enforced legally, giving a person control over the actions of others.

Rigid Control: Coping patterns involving reliance upon inner restraints, such as inhibition, suppression, repression, and reaction formation.

Role Obsolescence: Condition occurring when the ascribed social role of a given individual is no longer of importance to the social group.

Roots: The two distinct brances of a spinal nerve, each of which serves a separate function. The dorsal root carries sensory information from the peripheral nervous system to the spinal cord. The ventral root carries motor messages from the spinal cord to the peripheral nervous system.

Rostral: An anatomical term meaning toward the head end; opposite of caudal.

S

Saccades: Rapid movements of the eyes which occur regularly during normal viewing.

Saccadic Suppression: The suppression of vision during saccades, which provides the viewer with perception free of these abrupt movements.

Sacral: Refers to the lower part of the back or spinal cord.

Sadism: Sexual variant in which sexual gratification is obtained by the infliction of pain upon others.

Sagittal Plane: The plane that bisects the body or brain into right and left halves.

Saltatory Conduction: The form of conduction seen in myelinated axons in which the nerve impulse jumps from one node of Ranvier to the next.

Schizo-affective Psychosis: Disorder characterized by schizophrenic symptoms in conjunction with pronounced depression or elation.

Schizoid Personality: Personality pattern characterized by shyness, over-sensitivity, seclusiveness, and eccentricity.

Schizophrenia: Psychosis characterized by the breakdown of integrated personality functioning, withdrawal from reality, emotional blunting and distortion, and disturbances in thought and behavior.

Schizophreniform Disorder: Category of schizophrenic psychosis, usually in an undifferentiated form, of less than six month's duration.

Schizophrenogenic: Qualities in parents that appear to be associated with the development of schizophrenia in offspring; often applied to rejecting, cold, domineering, overprotective mothers or passive, uninvolved fathers.

Schwann Cell: The kind of accessory cell that forms meylin in the peripheral nervous system.

Scotoma: A region of blindness caused by injury to the visual pathway.

Scotopic System: A system in the retina which responds to low levels of light intensity and involves the rods. Contrast with photopic system.

Second Messenger: A relatively slow acting substance in the postsynaptic cell which amplifies the effects of nerve impulses and can initiate processes that lead to changes in electrical potentials at the membrane.

Selective Vigilance: A tuning of attentional and perceptual processes towards stimuli relevant or central to goal-directed behavior, with decreased sensitivity to stimuli irrelevant or peripheral to this purpose.

Sella Turcica: A saddlelike depression on the upper surface of the sphenoid bone, in which the hypophysis lies.

Semantic Agraphia: Deficit or loss of ability to spell or write with meaning, produced by brain damage to various sites.

Semantic Memory: Memory for what is learned as knowledge. This recall therefore is considered "timeless and spaceless" (e.g., a number system, a foreign language).

Senile Dementia: A neurological disorder of the aged involving progressive behavioral deterioration including personality change and profound intellectual decline.

Senile Plaques: Neuroanatomical changes correlated with senile dementia. These plaques are small areas of the brain containing abnormal cellular and chemical patterns.

Sensorineural Deafness: A hearing impairment originating from cochlear or auditory nerve lesions.

Sepsis: A morbid condition resulting from the presence of pathogenic bacteria. From septic.

Septo-hypothalamo-mesencephalic (SHM)Continuum: One of three limbic mechanisms, the SHM continuum has distinct circuitry connecing the hypothalamus, the limbic midbrain area, and other sites. Only the prefrontal lobe has direct connections with the SHM continuum, out of the entire isocortex.

Serial Lesion Effect: The lessened severity of cerebral symptoms (e.g., due to diaschisis) when lesions are introduced in stages as opposed to all at once.

Serotonergic: Refers to neurons that use serotonin as their synaptic transmitter.

Serotonin (5HT): A neurotransmitter produced in the raphe nuclei and active in structures throughout the cerebral hemispheres.

A compound (5-hydroxytryptamine) found in the bloodstream; it has vasoconstrictive properties. It is possible that serotonin is concerned with some of the functions of the central nervous system.

Short-term Memory: Memory that usually lasts only for seconds or as long as rehearsal continues.

Significant Others: In interpersonal theory, parents or others on whom an infant is dependent for meeting all physical and psychological needs.

Simple Cortical Cells: Cells in the visual cortex that respond best to an edge or a bar of a particular width and with a particular direction and location in the visual field.

Simulation: An intentional imitation of the basic processes and outcomes of a real-life situation, carried out in order to better understand the basic mechanisms of the situation. In civil law, misrepresenting or concealing the truth, as when parties pretend to perform an act different from that in which they really are engaged.

Simultagnosia: The perception of one stimulus when two objects are presented. Often associated with inertia of gaze.

Sinus: A channel for the passage of blood; a hollow in a bone or other tissue; antrum; one of the cavities connecing with the nose; a suppurating cavity.

Sinusoid: A blood space in certain organs, as the brain.

Situational Stress Reaction (acute): Superficial maladjustment to newly experienced life situations which are especially difficult or trying.

Sleep Apnea: A sleep disorder that involves slowing or cessation of respiration during sleep, which wakens the patient. Excessive daytime somnolence results from frequent nocturnal awakening.

Slow-wave Sleep: Stages of sleep including stages 1 through 4, defined by presence of slow EEG activity.

Socialized-aggressive Disorder: Pattern of childhood maladaptive behaviors involving social maladaption, as stealing, truancy, gang membership.

Sodium Pentothal: Barbiturate drug sometimes used in psychotherapy to produce a state of relaxation and suggestibility.

Sodomy: Sexual intercourse via the anus.

Somatosensory Agnosia: Loss of tactile recognition due to cerebral dysfunction in the presence of intact somatosensory receptive functions.

Somatosensory Modalities: Refers to different types of body sensation (e.g., touch, pain, pressure). Distinguished from auditory and visual senses.

Somesthetic: Pertaining to somatesthesia, or the consciousness of having a body.

Somnolent Mutism: Immobility and unresponsiveness with eyes closed, associated with mesencephalic-diencephalic lesions. Intense stimulation yields minimal responses.

Spasm: An involuntary, convulsive, muscular contraction.

Spatial Acalculia: Spatial misarrangement of the numbers during arithmetic calculation with intact knowledge of correct principle. Associated with right hemisphere lesions.

Spatial Agraphia: Deficits in spatial-motor aspects of writing due to brain damage, located in the nondominant parietal lobe. Frequently associated with the neglect syndrome.

Spatial Summation: The summation of the axon hillock of postsynaptic potentials from across the cell body. If this summation reaches threshold, a nerve impulse will be triggered.

Special Vulnerability: Low tolerance for specific types of stress.

Specific Heat: The heat energy required to raise the temperature of one gram of a substance one degree centigrade.

Spectrally Opponent Cell: A visual receptor cell with opposite firing responses to different regions of the spectrum.

Spinal Nerves: The 31 pairs of nerves that emerge from the spinal cord.

Split-brain: Individuals who have had the corpus callosum severed, halting communication between the right and left hemispheres.

Squamous: Scalelike.

Stage 1 Sleep: The initial stage of slow-wave sleep involving small-amplitude EEG waves of irregular frequency, slow heart rate, and a reduction of muscle tension.

Stage 2 Sleep: A stage of slow-wave sleep defined by bursts of regular 14-18 Hz EEG waves that progressively increase and then decrease in amplitude (called spindles).

Stage 3 Sleep: A stage of slow-wave sleep defined by the spindles seen in stage 2 sleep mixed with larger amplitude slow waves.

Stage 4 Sleep: A stage of slow-wave sleep defined by the presence of high amplitude slow waves of 1-4 Hz.

Star Chamber: An ancient court of England which originally had jurisdiction in cases in which the ordinary course of justice was obstructed by one party to the extent that no inferior court would find its process obeyed. Abolished in modern jurisprudence.

Stare Decisis: The legal policy of courts stating that once a principle of law is laid down, it will be adhered to and applied to all future cases in which the facts are substantially the the same. Serves to ensure security and certainty of legal principles.

Static Phase of Weight Gain: A later period following destruction of the ventromedial hypothalamus during which the animal's weight stabilizes at an obese level and food intake is not much above normal.

Statistical Test of Significance: A standard of probability stating that an experimental finding is significant if, by chance alone, it could have occurred fewer than one or five times in one hundred occurrences. In the field of psychology, five times in one hundred is usually the standard of acceptability for statistical significance.

Statute: An act of legislation by which a law is created, as opposed to unwritten or common law.

Statutory Law: The body of law created by the legislature.

Statutory Rape: Sexual intercourse with a minor.

Stellate Cell: A kind of small nerve cell with many branches.

Stenosis: Narrowing or contraction of a body passage or opening.

Stereoacuity: The ability to discriminate small differences in visual depth by point-by-point matching in the retinas.

Stereopsis: The ability to perceive depth, utilizing the slight difference in visual information from the two eyes.

Stimulus Enhancement: The second stimulus in a pair adds rather than masks the neural effects of the first stimulus. Studies include those which present letters of one half of a word (first stimulus) and then letters of the remaining portion of the word (second stimulus).

Stimulus Masking: A second stimulus leads into or masks a first stimulus if the trace of the initial stimulus is long-lasting or otherwise suffiecient. The target stimulus (e.g., letters of the alphabet) is interfered with by the masking stimulus (e.g., patterned line segments).

Stimulus Persistence: Effects of external stimulation are lasting in the central nervous system, dependent on many factors. Stimulus persistence acting as an interference to new stimuli has been advanced to account for dificit perception in the older person.

Stipulation: An agreement made between opposing parties that certain facts or principles of law are true and applicable and will not be contested.

Stress-decompensation Model: View of abnormal behavior which emphasizes progressive disorganization of behavior under excessive stress.

Striate Cortex: A portion of the visual cortex with input from the lateral geniculate nucleus.

Strict Liability: Liability without a showing of fault, as when a person engages in a hazardous activity is totally liable for injuries caused by the activity even without negligence being shown.

Stricture: A circumscribed narrowing of a tubular structure.

Stroma: The tissue that forms the ground substance, framework, or matrix of an organ, as distinguished from that constituting its functional element, or parenchyma.

Sub Nom: Under the name. In the name of. Often used when the original name of a case must be changed due to a change in parties.

Subpoena: A command for a witness to appear at a certain time and place to testify in court on a certain matter.

Subpoena Duces Tecum: A command that a witness produce a specified document or record.

Substance-abuse Disorders: Pathological use of a substance for at least a month, resulting in self-injurious behavior.

Substance-dependence Disorders: Severe form of substance-use disorder involving physiological dependence on the substance.

Substance-induced Organic Disorder: Category of disorders based on organic impairment resulting from toxicity or physiologic changes in the brain.

Substance-use Disorder: Patterns of maladaptive behavior centered around regular use of substance involved.

Subventricular Zones: Regions around the brain ventricle which continue to manufacture the precursors of nerve cells after birth.

Sulci: The furrows of convoluted brain surface. Contrast with gyri.

Superior Colliculus: A structure in the midbrain that receives information from the optic tract.

Superior Olivary Complex: A brain stem structure that receives input from both right and left cochlear nuclei, providing the first binaural analysis of auditory information.

Supplementary Motor Area (SMA) Location: Areas 6 and partially 7, anterior to paracentral lobule. Function: Volitional (self-initiated) movements; perineal and leg movements are found in the medial extention of the motor homunculus. Considered also to be a secondary speech area.

Supra: Above, upon.

Supraoptic Nucleus: A nucleus of the hypothalamus.

Sympathetic Chains: One of two systems that compose the autonomic nervous system.

Synapse: An area composed of the presynaptic (axonal) terminal, the postsynaptic (usually dendritic) membrane, and the space (or cleft) between them. This is the site at which neural messages travel from one neuron to another. Also called the synaptic region.

Synaptic Assembly: A level of brain organization which includes the total collection of all synapses on a single cell.

Synaptic Bouton: The presynaptic swelling of the axon terminal from which neural messages travel across the synaptic cleft to other neurons.

Synaptic Cleft: The space between the presynaptic and postsynaptic membranes.

Synaptic Region: See synapse.

Synaptic Transmitter: The chemical in the presynaptic bouton that serves as the basis of neuro-neural communication. It travels across the synaptic cleft and reacts with the postsynaptic membrane when triggered by a nerve impulse. Also called neurotransmitter.

Synaptic Vesicles: The small, spherically shaped structures which contain molecules of synaptic transmitter.

T

Tactile: Pertaining to the sense of touch.

Tactual Hallucinations: Hallucinations involving the sense of touch, such as feeling cockroaches crawling over one's body.

Tardive Dyskinesia: Abnormal involuntary movements involving the extremeties or facial area (e.g., tongue, jaw, facial surface). Results as a late side effect of neuroleptic drug treatment and in many cases, is irreversible.

Involuntary movements—especially those involving the face, mouth, lips, and tongue—related to prolonged use of antipsychotic drugs, such as chlorpromazine.

Telecephalon: Consists of the cerebral cortex, corpus striatum, and medullary center.

The frontal subdivision of the forebrain which includes the cerebral hemispheres when fully developed.

Temporal Summation: The summation of postsynaptic potentials which reach the axon hillock at different times. The closer together they are, the more complete the summation.

Testosterone: A hormone produced by male gonads which controls a variety of bodily changes that become visible at puberty.

Tetany: Intermittent tonic muscular contractions of the extremities.

Thalamic Syndrome: Disturbance of the senses with initial hemianesthia, followed by a raised threshold to touch, pain, heat, and cold on the side opposite the lesion. The sensations may be extremely adversive when reached. Due primarily to a thalamic infarct.

Thalamus: The brain regions that surround the third ventricle.

Third-party beneficiary: A person who has enforceable rights created by a contract to which he is not party and for which he gives no consideration.

Thrombophlebitis: The condition in which inflammation of the vein wall has preceded the formation of a thrombus, or intravascular clot.

Thrombosis: The formation of a clot within a vessel during life.

Thrombotic Strokes: Results from blockage or occlusion by blood or tissue particles or overgrowth. Form most often where blood vessles branch.

Thrombus: A clot of blood formed within the heart of the blood vessels, usually caused by slowing of the circulation of the blood or by alteration of the blood itself or the vessel walls.

Thyroid-stimulating Hormone (TSH): A tropic hormone released by the anterior pituitary gland which increases the release of thyroxine and the uptake of iodide by the thyroid gland.

Thyrotropin-releasing Hormone (TRH): A hypothalamic hormone that regulates the release of thyroid-stimulating hormone.

Thyroxine: A hormone released by the thyroid gland.

Tinnitus: A ringing or singing sound in the ears.

Tolerance: Physiological condition in which increased dosage of an addictive drug is needed to obtain effects previously produced by smaller doses.

Tomogram: *See* computer axial tomogram.

Tonic Receptors: Receptors in which the frequency of nerve impulse discharge declines slowly or not at all as stimulation is maintained.

Tort: A private or civil wrong or injury, excluding a breach of contract, for which the court will provide a remedy in the form of an action for damages.

Toxicity: The poisonous nature of a substance.

Trabecula: A septum that extends from an envelope into the enclosed substance, forming an essential part of the stroma of the organ.

Transcortical Motor (TCM) Aphasia: Separation of general conceptual functions (posterior) from Broca motor output area (anterior). Lesions in the supplementary motor area (SMA) or in Broca's area. The patient can repeat words but has difficulty with comprehension and/or speech.

Transient Global Amnesia: A relatively brief (several hours to several days) amnestic condition with few neurological sequelae. Associated features include (1) a major symptom of anterograde amnesia, (2) some retrograde amnesia, (3) confusion and time/place disorientation, and (4) speech and orientation to person are unimpaired. There is usually a sudden onset and cessation with no prodromal symptoms or known cause.

Transient Ischemic Attacks (TIAs): Neurological dificits of sudden onset; less intense and temporary strokes that may precede thrombotic strokes. Last less than 24 hours by definition. About half of those who experience TIAs will have a major stroke.

Transient Situational Disorder: Temporary mental disorder developing under conditions of overwhelming stress, as in military combat or civilian catastrophes.

Transmethylation Hypothesis: A hypothesized explanation of schizophrenia suggesting that the addition of a methyl group to some naturally occuring brain compounds can convert some substances to hallucinogenic agents, or psychotogens.

Transverse: See coronal.

Tremor-at-rest: A tremor that occurs when the affected region, such as a limb, is fully supported.

Tremors: Rhythmic repetitive movements caused by brain pathology.

Trial: A judicial examination or determination, either civil or criminal, of issues between parties to an action.

Trigeminal Neuralgia: Intense and sudden pain in area of a trigeminal nerve lesion. The episodic pain may be set off by light stimulation such as touching the skin.

Tropic Hormones: Anterior pituitary hormones that affect the secretion of other endocrine glands.

U

Unconscious Motivation: Motivation for an individual's behavior of which he is unaware.

Undifferentiated Schizophrenia: Subtype in which the patient either has mixed symptoms or moves rapidly from one type to another.

Undue Influence: Any wrongful or improper persuasion whereby the person's will is overpowered, thereby causing him to act in a way he would normally not have acted.

Uniform Laws: A body of written laws, in various subject areas, approved by the Commissioners on Uniform State Laws, that are often adopted by individual states.

Unilateral Apraxia: Apraxia affecting one side of the body. Sympathetic and callosal types have been postulated. The sympathetic aspect occurs when other functions are likewise impaired (e.g., right hemiparesis, left-hand apraxia) and Broca aphasia produced by left motor association destruction of callosal fibers.

Unipolar Disorder: A severe affective disorder in which only depressive episodes occur, as opposed to bipolar disorders in which both manic and depressive processes are assumed to occur.

Unmyelinated: Refers to fine diameter axons that lack a myelin sheath.

Unsocialized Disturbance of Conduct: Childhood disorder in which the child is disobedient, hostile, and highly aggressive.

Urticaria: Nettle-rash; hives; elevated, itching, white patches.

Utilization Behavior: Considered a type of magnetic apraxia, here the afflicted individual pursues a stimulus to grasp within a set of actively exploring the environment. Considered a strong frontal sign. Gegenhalten occurs when contact is made. Walking is then impaired when attempted, with leg stiffening and no movement.

V

Vaginismus: An involuntary muscle spasm at the entrance to the vagina that prevents penetration and sexual intercourse.

Vagus Nerve: One of the cranial nerves.

Variant Sexual Behavior: Behavior in which satisfaction is dependent on something other than a mutually desired sexual engagement with a sexually mature member of the opposite sex.

Ventral: An anatomical term meaining toward the belly or front of the body or the bottom of the brain; opposite of dorsal.

Ventricles: Cavities in the brain which contain cerebrospinal fluid.

The four cavities in the brain which contain cerebrospinal fluid. The choroid plexus produces the cerebrospinal fluid

Spaces within the brain, filled with cerebrospinal fluid, which provide support and cushioning for the brain. Four in number.

Ventricular Layer: A layer of homogeneous cells in the neural tube of the developing organism which is the source of all neural and glial cells in the mature organism. Also called the ependymal layer.

Ventromedial Hypothalamus (VMH): A hypothalamic region involved in inhibiting eating, among other functions.

Venue: The particular geographic area in which a court with jurisdiction may hear and determine a case.

Verbal Adynamia: Diminished speech spontaneity. There is slow speech initiation and/or reluctance to continue verbal output. Usually accompanies general apathy.

Verdict: The formal decision or finding made by a judge or jury on the matters or questions submitted for their deliberation and determination.

Vertigo: Dizziness, giddiness.

Vesicle: A small bladder, or sac, containing liquid.

Vesicles (Synaptic): Small structures located at the end point (terminus) of the axon which are filled with neurotransmitter substances.

Vestibular: Pertaining to a vestibule; such as the inner ear, larynx, mouth, nose, vagina.

Vestibuloocular Reflex: A rapid response that adjusts the eye to a change in head position.

Viscosity: A condition of more or less adhesion of the molecules of a fluid to each other so that it flows with difficulty.

A behavioral pattern characterized by stickiness in interactional contexts. Associated with frontal system damage.

Visual Anosognosia: Denial of blindness caused by brain lesions. The subject attempts to behave as if the deficit was not present. *See* Anton's Syndrome.

Voir Dire: To speak the truth. The preliminary examination made by the court or by attorneys of one presented as a prospective juror to determine his competence to serve or as a witness to determine his competence to speak the truth.

W

Wada Technique: Designed to assess which hemisphere was language-dominant. Here, sodium amytal is injected into one carotid artery in order to deactivate an entire hemisphere. Changes in counting behaviors while the injection is in process indicate which hemisphere is dominant for speech and language.

Waive: To abondon, or give up a claim or right.

Waiver: An intentional and voluntary surrendering or giving up of a known right.

Warrent: A document directing a public official to perform a particular act.

Weight of the Evidence: The relative value of the credible evidence presented by one side balanced against the evidence presented by the other side. Indicates to the jury that the party having the burden of proof will be entitled to their verdict if they determine that the greater amount of evidence supports the issue before them.

Wernicke's Aphasia: A fluent disorder with severe auditory comprehension and process-ing deficits. Empty speech, press for speech, and a moderate to substantial naming deficit is apparent. Considered a posterior aphasia.

Wernicke's Area: A region of the left hemisphere involved in language comprehension.

White Matter: Consists of densely packed conduction fibers that transmit neural mes-sages between the cortex and lower centers (projection fibers), between the hemi-spheres (commissural fibers), or within a hemisphere (association fibers).

A shiny layer underneath the cortex consisting largely of axons with white, myelin sheaths.

Witness: One who testifies, under oath, to what he has seen, heard, or otherwise observed.

Word Deafness: Also called pure word deafness. Here, nonspeech sounds are recognized but not spoken words. Usually produced by subcortical lesion disconnecting auditory input from auditory processing.

Work Product: Work done by an attorney while representing a client, such as writings, statements, or testimony is regards to his legal impressions, tactics, strategies, and opinions, that are ordinarily not subject to discovery. Discovery may be obtained only when the party seeking it has a substantial need for the material to prepare his case and is unable to obtain the substantial equivalent of the material by other means without undue hardship.

Writ: An order issued by a court mandating the performance of a specified act, or giving authority to have it done.

XYZ

X cells: Retinal ganglion cells that continue to respond to maintained visual stimuli.

Xanthrochromia: Blood cells in the cerebrospinal fluid with discoloration due to an abnormal somatic condition.

Y cells: Retinal ganglion cells that respond strongly initially but rapidly decrease frequency of response as the visual stimuli is maintained.

A

Abarbanel, A. (1979). Shared parenting after separation and divorce: A study of joint custody. *American Journal of Orthopsychiatry, 50,* 320-329.

Abel, G. G., Barlow, D. H., Blanchard, E. B., & Guild, D. (1977). The components of rapists' sexual arousal. *Archives of General Psychiatry, 34,* 895-903.

Abel, G. G., Barlow, D. H., Blanchard, E. B., & Mavissakalian, M. (1975). Measurement of sexual arousal in male homosexuals: Effects of instructions and stimulus modality. *Archives of Sexual Behavior, 4,* 623-629.

Abel, G. G., Becker, J. V., & Skinner, L. J. (1980). Aggressive behavior and sex. *Psychiatric Clinics of North America, 3,* 133-151.

Abel, G. G., Blanchard, E., Becker, J., & Djenderedjian, A. (1978). Differentiating sexual aggressive-ness with penile measures. *Criminal Justice and Behavior, 5,* 315-332.

Abel, R. (1980). Redirecting social studies of law. *Law and Society Review, 14,* 805-829.

Abraham, H. J. (1980). *The judicial process* (4th ed.). New York: Oxford University Press.

Abrams, N. (1979). Definitions of mental illness and the insanity defense. *Journal of Psychiatry and Law, 7,* 441-456.

Abramson, M. F. (1971). Participant observation and attempted mental health consultation in a public defender agency. *American Journal of Psychiatry, 127,* 964-969.

Abt, L. E., & Stuart, I. R. (1979). *Social psychology and discretionary law.* New York: Van Nostrand Reinhold.

Adams, D. K., & Horn, J. L. (1965). Nonoverlapping keys for the MMPI Scales. *Journal of Consulting Psychology, 29,* 284.

Adams, K. M. (1980). In search of Luria's battery: A false start. *Journal of Consulting and Clinical Psychology, 48,* 511-516.

Adams, S. (1974). Measures of effectiveness and efficiency in corrections. In D. Glaser (Ed.), *Handbook of criminology.* Chicago, IL: Rand McNally College Publishing.

Adatto, C. P. (1949). Observations on criminal patients during narcoanalysis. *Archives of Neurology and Psychiatry, 69,* 82-92.

Adelman, R. M., & Howard, A. (1984). Expert testimony on malingering: The admissibility of clinical procedures for the detection of deception. *Behavioral Sciences and the Law, 2,* 5-20.

Adorno, T., Frenkel-Brunswick, E., Levinson, D., & Sanford, R. (1950). *The authoritarian personality.* New York: Harper.

Agnew, N. M., & Pyke, S. W. (1969). *The science game.* Englewood Cliffs, NJ: Prentice-Hall.

Ainsworth, M. (1973). The development of infant-mother attachment. In B. Caldwell & H. Riccioti (Eds.), *Review of child development research,* Vol. 3. Chicago, IL: University of Chicago Press.

Aker, J., Walsh, A., & Beam, J. (1977). *Mental capacity: Medical and legal aspects of the aging.* New York: McGraw-Hill.

Albers, A., & Pasewark, R. (1976). Involuntary hospitalization: The social construction of danger-ousness. *American Journal of Community Psychology, 4,* 129-131.

Albert, S., Fox, H. M., & Kahn, M. W. (1980). Faking psychosis on a Rorschach: Can expert judges detect malingering? *Journal of Personality Assessment, 44,* 115-119.

Alberts, W. E. (1963). Personality and attitudes toward juvenile delinquency: A study of Protestant ministers. *Journal of Social Psychology, 60,* 71-83.

Alexander, G. (1977). On being imposed upon by artful or designing persons: The California experience with the involuntary placement of the aged. *San Diego Law Review, 14,* 1083-1099.

Alexander, G. (1979). Premature probate: A different perspective on guardianship for the elderly. *Stanford Law Review, 31,* 1003-1033.

Alexander, J. (Ed.) (1973). *A brief narration of the case and trial of John Peter Zenger.* Boston, MA: Little, Brown.

Alexander, M. (1980). Protecting children from parents who provide insufficient care: Temporary and permanent statutory limits on parental custody. *Arizona State Law Journal,* 953-979.

Alker, H. A. (1978). Untitled review. In O. K. Buros (Ed.), *The eighth mental measurements yearbook,* Vol. 1. Highland Park, NJ: Gryphon.

Allen, R., Ferster, E., & Weihofen, H. (1968). *Mental impairment and legal incompetency.* Englewood Cliffs, NJ: Prentice-Hall.

Allen, R. M., & Young, S. J. (1978). Phencyclidine-induced psychosis. *American Journal of Psychiatry, 135,* 1081-1083.

Allen, R. P., Safer, D., & Covi, L. (1975). Effects of psychostimulants on aggression. *Journal of Nervous and Mental Diseases, 160,* 138-145.

Allyon, T., & Azrin, N. (1964). Reinforcement and instructions with mental patients. *Journal of Experimental Analysis of Behavior, 7,* 327-331.

Alpert, G. P., & Hicks, D. A. (1977). Prisoners' attitudes toward components of the legal and judicial system. *Criminology, 14,* 461-482.

Alpert, G. P., & Alpert, S. W. (1977). Personal communication.

Alpert, L., Atkins, B. M., & Ziller, R. C. (1979). Becoming a judge: The transition from advocate to arbiter. *Judicature, 62*(7), 325-336.

Allport, G. (1954). *The nature of prejudice.* Boston, MA: Addison-Wesley.

Alschuler, A. W. (1975). The defense attorney's role in plea bargaining. *Yale Law Journal, 84,* 1179-1191.

Alschuler, A. W. (1976). The trial judge's role in plea bargaining. *Columbia Law Review, 76,* 1059-1154.

Alschuler, A. W. (1979). Plea bargaining and its history. *Law and Society Review, 13,* 211-245.

American Bar Association, Standing Committee on Association Standards for Criminal Justice. (1983). *Criminal justice and mental health standards,* First draft. Chicago, IL: American Bar Association.

American Correctional Association. (1976). The use of prisoners and detainees as subjects of human experimentation: Position statement officially adopted. *American Journal of Corrections, 38*(3), 14.

American Law Institute. (1962). *Model penal code,* proposed official draft. Philadelphia, PA: ALI.

American Psychiatric Association. (1974). *Clinical aspects of the violent individual.* Washington, DC: American Psychiatric Association Task Force Report.

American Psychiatric Association. (1980). *Diagnostic and statistical manual of mental disorders* (3rd ed.). Washington, DC: APA.

American Psychiatric Association. (1983). American Psychiatric Association statement on the insanity defense. *American Journal of Psychiatry, 140,* 681-688.

American Psychological Association. (1973). *Ethical principles in the conduct of research with human participants.* Washington, DC: APA.

American Psychological Association. (1974). *Standards for educational and psychological tests.* Washington DC: APA.

American Psychological Association. (1977). *Standards for providers of psychological services.* Washington, DC: APA.

American Psychological Association. (1978). Report of the task force on the role of psychology in the criminal justice system. *American Psychologist, 33,* 1099-1113.

American Psychological Association. (1981). Ethical principles of psychologists. *American Psychologist, 36*(6), 633-638.

American Psychological Association. (1984). *Standards for educational and psychological testing.* Washington, DC: APA.

American Psychological Association. (1984). Text of position on insanity defense. *APA Monitor, 15,* 11.

American Psychological Association, Division of Industrial and Organizational Psychology. (1980). *Principles for the validation and use of personnel selection procedures.* Berkeley, CA: APA.

Anastasi, A. (1981). *Psychological testing* (4th ed.). New York: Macmillan.

Anderson, J. K., & Hayder, R. M. (1981). Questions of validity and drawing conclusions from simulation studies in procedural justice: A comment. *Law and Society Review, 15,* 293-304.

Anderson, K. (1982). American prisons. *Time, 11*(120), 38-82.

Anderson, N. H. (1974). Cognitive algebra: Integration theory applied to social attribution. In L. Berkowitz (Ed.), *Advances in experimental social psychology,* Vol. 7. New York: Academic Press.

Andreasen, N. C., Grove, W. A., Shapiro, R. W., Keller, M. B., Hirschfield, R. A., & McDonald-Scott, M. A. (1981). Reliability of lifetime diagnoses. *Archives of General Psychiatry, 38,* 400-405.

Andrew, J. M. (1974). Violent crime indices among community-retained delinquents. *Criminal Justice and Behavior, 2,* 123-130.

Andrews, D., Kiessling, J., Mickus, S., & Robinson, D. (1982). *The Level of Supervision Inventory: Interviewing and scoring guide.* Toronto: Ontario Ministry of Correctional Services.

Andrews, D. A., Young, J. G., Wormith, J. S., Searle, C. A. & Kouri, M. (1974). The attitudinal effects of group discussion between young criminal offenders and community volunteers. *Journal of Community Psychology, 1,* 417-422.

Andrews, R., & Withey, S. (1976). *Social indicators of well-being.* New York: Plenum Press.

Anthony, N. C. (1971). Comparison of client's standard, exaggerated, and matching MMPI profiles. *Journal of Consulting and Clinical Psychology, 36,* 100-103.

Antonio, J. D., & Innes, J. M. (1978). Attribution biases of psychiatrists and psychologists. *Psychological Reports, 43,* 1149-1150.

Applebaum, P., & Roth, L. (1982). Competency to consent to research: A psychiatric overview. *Archives of General Psychiatry, 39,* 951-958.

Applebaum, P. S. & Gutheil, T. G. (1980). The Boston State Hospital case: "Involuntary mind control," the constitution, and the "rights to rot." *American Journal of Psychiatry, 137*(6), 720-732.

Arboleda-Florez, J. (1978). Insanity defense in Canada. *Canadian Psychiatric Association Journal, 23,* 23-27.

Archer, R. L., Foushee, H. C., Davis, M. H., & Aderman, D. (1979). Emotional empathy in a courtroom simulation: A person-situation interaction. *Journal of Applied Social Psychology, 3,* 275-291.

Arenella, P. (1977). The diminished capacity and diminished responsibility defenses: Two children of a doomed marriage. *Columbia Law Review, 77,* 827-865.

Arens, R. (1967. The Durham rule in action: Judicial psychiatry and psychiatric justice. *Law and Society Review, 1,* 41-80.

Arens, R. (1974). *Insanity defense.* New York: Philosophical Library.

Arens, R., Granfield, D. D., & Susman, J. (1965). Jurors, jury charges and insanity. *Catholic University Law Review, 14,* 1-29.

Argyle, M. (1975). *Bodily communication.* New York: International Universities Press.

Armentrout, J. (1970). Relationships among preadolescents' reports of their parents' child-rearing behavior. *Psychological Reports, 27,* 695-700.

Armentrout, J. (1971). Parental child-rearing attitudes and preadolescents' problem behaviors. *Journal of Consulting and Clinical Psychology, 37,* 278-285.

Armentrout, J., & Burger, G. (1972). Factor analyses of college students' recall of parental child-rearing behaviors. *Journal of Genetic Psychology, 121,* 155-161.

Arnold, L. S., Quinsey, V. L., & Velner, I. (1977). Overcontrolled hostility among men found not guilty by reason of insanity. *Canadian Journal of Behavioral Science, 9,* 333-340.

Arnold, S. J., & Gold, A. D. (1979). The use of a public opinion poll on a change of venue application. *Criminal Law Quarterly, 21,* 445-464.

Arnold, W. R. (1965). A functional explanation of recidivism. *Journal of Criminal Law, Criminology, and Police Science, 56,* 210-220.

Arnold, W. R. (1965). Continuities in research: Scaling delinquent behavior. *Social Problems, 13,* 59-66.

Aronson, E., & Bridgeman, D. (1979). Jigsaw groups and the desegregated classroom: In pursuit of common goals. *Personality and Social Psychology Bulletin, 5*(4), 438-446.

Asch, S. E. (1960). Effects of group pressure on the modification and distortion of judgments. In D. Cartwright & A. Zander (Eds.), *Group dynamics* (2nd ed.). New York: Harper & Row.

Ash, P. (1966). The implications of the Civil Rights Act of 1964 for psychological assessment in industry. *American Psychologist, 21,* 797-803.

Ashford, J. W., Schultz, S. C., & Walsh, G. O. (1980). Violent automatism in a partial complex seizure: Report of a case. *Archives of Neurology, 37,* 102-122.

Atkinson, J. (1984). Criteria for deciding child custody in the trial and appellate courts. *Family Law Quarterly, 18,* 1-42.

Atkinson, J. W. (1965). Thematic apperceptive measurement of motive within a context of a theory of motivation. In B. I. Murstein (Ed.), *Handbook of projective techniques* (pp. 433-456). New York: Basic Books.

Atlas, R. (1982). Crime site selection for assaults in four Florida prisons. *Man-Environment Systems, 12,* 59-66.

Audubon, J. J., & Kirwin, B. R. (1982). Defensiveness in the criminally insane. *Journal of Personality Assessment, 46,* 304-311.

Ausness, C. (1978). The identification of incompetent defendants: Separating those unfit for adversary combat from those who are fit. *Kentucky Law Journal, 66,* 666-706.

Austin, W., & Williams, T. A. (1977). A survey of judges' responses to simulated legal cases: Research note on sentencing disparity. *Journal of Criminal Law and Criminology, 68,* 306-310.

Austin, W., Williams, T. A., Worchel, S., Wentzel, A. A., & Siegel, D. (1981). Effect of mode of adjudication, presence of a defense counsel, and favorability of verdict on observers' evaluations of a criminal trial. *Journal of Applied Social Psychology, 11,* 281-300.

Avanesov, G. (1982). *The principles of criminology.* Moscow, USSR: Progress Publishers.

Awad, G. A. (1978). Basic principles in custody assessments. *Canadian Psychiatric Association Journal, 23,* 441-447.

Azrin, N. (1967). Pain and aggression. *Psychology Today,* 27-33.

B

Bach-Y-Rita, G., Lion, J. R., Clement, C. E., & Ervin, F. R. (1971). Episodic dyscontrol: A study of 130 violent patients. *American Journal of Psychiatry, 127,* 1473-1478.

Bach-Y-Rita, G., Lion, J. R., & Ervin, F. R. (1970). Pathological intoxication: Clinical and electroencephalographic studies. *American Journal of Psychiatry, 127,* 689-703.

Bach-Y-Rita, G., & Veno, A. (1974). Habitual violence: A profile of 62 men. *American Journal of Psychiatry, 131,* 154-217.

Bacon, P. D., & Benedek, E. P. (1982). Epileptic psychosis in insanity: Case study and review. *Bulletin of the American Academy of Psychiatry and the Law, 10,* 203-210.

Balcanoff, E. F., & McGarry, A. L. (1969). Amicus curiae: The role of the psychiatrist in pretrial examinations. *American Journal of Psychiatry, 126,* 342-347.

Ballard, K. B., Fosen, R. H., Neiswonger, J., Fowler, R., Belasco, J., & Tyler, R. (1963). *Interpersonal Personality Inventory manual.* Vacaville, CA: Institute for the Study of Crime and Delinquency, California Medical Facility.

Bandewehr, L. J., & Novotny, R. (1976). Juror authoritarianism and trial judge impartiality: An experiment in jury decision making. *Journal of Experimental Study in Politics, 5,* 28-37.

Bandura, A. (1969). Principles of behavior modification. New York: Holt, Rinehart and Winston.

Bandura, A. (1971). Vicarious and self-reinforcement processes. In R. Glaser (Ed.), *The nature of reinforcement* (pp. 2228-2278). New York: Academic Press.

Bandura, A. (1973). *Aggression: A social learning analysis.* Englewood Cliffs, NJ: Prentice-Hall.

Bandura, A. (1978). The self system in reciprocal determinism. *American Psychologist, 33,* 344-358.

Bandura, A., & Walters, R. H. (1959). *Adolescent aggression.* New York: Ronald Press.

Banner, C. (1979). Child-rearing attitudes of mothers of under-, average-, and over-achieving children. *British Journal of Educational Psychology, 49,* 150-155.

Barbaree, H. E., Marshall, W. L., & Lanthier, R. D. (1979). Deviant sexual arousal in rapists. *Behavior Research and Therapy, 17,* 215-322.

Barbaree, H. E., Marshall, W. L., Yates, E., & Lightfoot, L. O. (1983). Alcohol intoxication and deviant sexual arousal in male social drinkers. *Behavior Research and Therapy, 21,* 365-373.

Barbour, G., & Blumenkrantz, N. (1978). Videotape aids informed consent decision. *Journal of the American Medical Association, 240,* 2741-2742.

Barkowitz, P., & Brigham, J. C. (1982). Recognition of faces: Own-race bias, incentive, and time delay. *Journal of Applied Social Psychology, 12,* 255-268.

Barland, G. G., & Raskin, DC (1975). An evaluation of field techniques in detection of deception. *Psychophysiology, 12,* 321-330.

Barnard, G. W., Holzer, C., & Vera, H. (1979). A comparison of alcoholics and non-alcoholics charged with rape. *Bulletin of the American Academy of Psychiatry and the Law, 7,* 432-440.

Barnett, N. J., & Feild, H. S. (1978). Character of the defendant and length of sentence in rape and burglary crimes. *Journal of Social Psychology, 104,* 271-277.

Barr & Suarez. (1965). The teaching of forensic psychiatry in law schools, medical schools, and psychiatric residences in the United States. *American Journal of Psychiatry, 122,* 612-616.

Barter, J. T., & Reite, M. (1969). Crime and LSD: The insanity plea. *American Journal of Psychiatry, 126,* 531-537.

Barthel, J. (1977). *A death in Canaan.* New York: Dell.

Bartol, C. R. (1983). *Psychology and American law.* Belmont, CA: Wadsworth.

Bash, I. Y. (1978). Malingering: A study designed to differentiate schizophrenic offenders and malingerers. *Dissertation Abstracts, 39,* 2973-B.

Bash, I. Y., & Alpert, M. (1980). The determination of malingering. *Annals of New York Academy of Sciences, 347,* 86-99.

Baskett, G. D., & Freedle, R. O. (1974). Aspects of language pragmatics and social perception of lying. *Journal of Psycholinguistic Research, 3,* 117-131.

Bauer, C. A., Schlottman, R. S., Kane, R. L., & Johnsen, D. E. (1984). An evaluation of the digit symbol component of the Russell, Neuringer, and Goldstein average impairment rating. *Journal of Consulting and Clinical Psychology, 52,* 317-318.

Bavolek, S. (1979). The emotionally disturbed delinquent adolescent: Manifestations of physical and sexual abuse. *Monograph of Behavioral Disorders,* 174-187.

Bavolek, S. (1980a). *Primary prevention of child abuse: Assessing the parenting and child-rearing attitudes of adolescents in inner city Baltimore.* Eau Claire, WI: University of Wisconsin, Department of Special Education.

Bavolek, S. (1980b). *Primary prevention of child abuse: Identification of high risk parents.* Eau Claire, WI: University of Wisconsin, Department of Special Education.

Bavolek, S. (1984). *Handbook for the adult-adolescent parenting inventory.* Schaumberg, IL: Family Development Associates.

Bavolek, S., & Comstock, C. (1982). *Nurturing program for parents and children.* Eau Claire, WI: University of Wisconsin, Department of Special Education.

Bavolek, S., Comstock, C., & McLaughlin, J. (1982). *The nurturing program: A validated approach for reducing dysfunctional family interaction.* Eau Claire, WI: University of Wisconsin, Department of Special Education.

Bavolek, S., Kline, D., McLaughlin, J., & Publicover, P. (1979). Primary prevention of child abuse: Identification of high risk adolescents. Child Abuse and Neglect. *The International Journal, 3,* 1071-1080.

Bazelon, D. L. (1974). Psychiatrists and the adversary process. *Scientific American, 230*(6), 18-23.

Bazelon, D. L. (1975). A jurist's view of psychiatry. *Journal of Psychiatry and Law, 3,* 175-190.

Bazelon, D. L. (1977). Can we afford not to live up to our moral pretenses? *New York State Bar Journal, 49,* 10-17.

Bazelon, D. L. (1982). Veils, values, and social responsibility. *American Psychologist, 37,* 115-121.

Beal, E. W. (1979). Children of divorce: A family systems perspective. *Journal of Social Issues, 35*(4), 140-154.

Becker, B. C. (1980, October). Jury nullification: Can a jury be trusted? *Trial,* 41-45.

Becker, W., & Krug, R. (1965). The Parent Attitude Research Instrument: A research review. *Child Development, 36,* 329-365.

Beis, E. B. (1984). *Mental health and the law.* Rockville, MD: Aspen Publications.

Bell, P. A., Fisher, J. D., & Loomis, R. (1978). *Environmental psychology.* Philadelphia, PA: W. B. Saunders.

Belli, M. (1982). The expert witness. *Trial, 17*(7), 35-37.

Bellows, G., & Johnson, E. (1971). Reflections on the University of Southern California clinical semester. *University of Southern California Law Review, 44,* 664-695.

Bellows, G., & Moulton, B. (1978). *The lawyering process: Materials for clinical instruction in advocacy.* Mineola, NY: Foundation Press.

Belsky, J. (1981). Early human experience: A family perspective. *Developmental Psychology, 17*(1), 3-23.

Belter, R., & Grisso, R. (1984). Children's recognition of rights violations in counseling. *Professional Psychology, 15,* 899-910.

Bem, D., & Allen, A. (1974). On predicting some of the people some of the time: The search for cross-situational consistencies in behavior. *Psychological Bulletin, 81,* 506-520.

Bendt, R. H., Balconoff, E. J., & Tragellis, G. S. (1973). Incompetency to stand trial: Is psychiatry necessary? *American Journal of Psychiatry, 130*(11), 1288-1289.

Benedek, E., & Benedek, R. (1972). New child custody laws: Making them do what they say. *American Journal of Orthopsychiatry, 42,* 825-834.

Bennett, D. (1968). Competency to stand trial: A call for reform. *Journal of Criminal Law, Criminology, and Police Science, 59,* 569-582.

Berg, K., & Vidmar, N. (1975). Authoritarianism and recall of evidence about criminal behavior. *Journal of Research in Personality, 9,* 147-157.

Bergler, J., Pennington, A., Metcalf, M., & Freis, E. (1980). Informed consent: How much does the patient understand? *Clinical Pharmacology Therapeutics, 27,* 435-440.

Berk, R. A. (1976). Social science and jury selection: A case study of a civil suit. In G. Bermant, C. Nemeth, & N. Vidmar (Eds.), *Psychology and the law* (pp. 283-297). New York: Lexington Books.

Berk, S. F., & Loseke, D. R. (1981). "Handling" family violence: Situational determinants of police arrest in domestic disturbances. *Law and Society Review, 15,* 317-346.

Berkowitz, L. (1983). Aversively stimulated aggression: Some parallels and differences in research with animals and humans. *American Psychologist, 38,* 1135-1144.

Berkowitz, L., & Le Page, A. (1967). Weapons as aggression-eliciting stimuli. *Journal of Personality and Social Psychology,* 202-207.

Berlyne, N. (1972). Confabulation. *British Journal of Psychiatry, 120,* 31-39.

Berman & Sales (1977). A critical evaluation of the systematic approach to jury selection. *Criminal Justice and Behavior, 4,* 219-240.

Bermant, G. (1977). *Conduct of the voir dire examination: Practices and opinions of federal district judges.* Washington, DC: Federal Judicial Center.

Bermant, G., Cecil, J. S., Chaset, A. J., Lind, E. A., & Lombard, P. A. (1981, August). *Protracted civil trials: Views from the bench and the bar.* Washington, DC: Federal Judicial Center.

Bermant, G., & Shephard, J. (1981). The voir dire examination, juror challenges, and adversary advocacy. In B. D. Sales (Ed.), *The trial process* (pp. 69-114). New York: Plenum Press.

Bernard, J. L. (1979). Interaction between the race of the defendant and that of jurors in determining verdicts. *Law and Psychology Review, 5,* 103-111.

Bersoff, D. (1981). Testing and the law. *American Psychologist, 36*(10), 1047-1059.

Bersoff, D. N. (1976). Therapists as protectors and policemen: New roles as a result of Tarasoff? *Professional Psychology, 7,* 267-273.

Bertelson, A. D., Marks, P. A., & May, G. D. (1982). MMPI and race: A controlled study. *Journal of Consulting and Clinical Psychology, 50,* 316-318.

Bevan, W. (1976). The sound of the wind that's blowing. *American Psychologist, 31,* 481-491.

Bickman, L. (1980). *Applied social psychology annual.* Beverly Hills, CA: Sage Publications.

Bienen, S. M. (1962). Verbal conditioning of inkblot responses as a function of instructions, social desirability, and awareness. (Doctoral dissertation, University of Maryland, 1961). *Dissertation Abstracts, 24,* 379.

Birk, L., Williams, J. H., Chasin, M., & Rose, L. I. (1973). Serum testosterone levels in homosexual men. *New England Journal of Medicine, 289,* 1236-1238.

Birren, J., Cunningham, W., & Yamamoto, K. (1983). Psychology of adult development and aging. In M. Rosenzweig & L. Porter (Eds.), *Annual review of psychology,* Vol. 34 (pp. 543-575). Palo Alto, CA: Annual Reviews.

Birren, J., & Schaie, K. (Eds.) (1977). *Handbook of the psychology of aging.* New York: Van Nostrand Reinhold.

Birren, J., & Sloane, R. (Eds.) (1980). *Handbook of mental health and aging.* Englewood Cliffs, NJ: Prentice-Hall.

Bittner, E. (1974). Florence Nightingale in pursuit of Willie Sutton: A theory of the police. In H. Jacob (Ed.), *The potential for reform of criminal justice.* Beverly Hills, CA: Sage Publications.

Black, C. (1960). The lawfulness of the segregation decisions. *Yale Law Journal, 69,* 421-430.

Black, C. (1976). Due process for death: Jurek v. Texas and companion cases. *Catholic University Law Review, 26,* 1-16.

Black, D. (1971). The social organization of arrest. *Stanford Law Review, 23,* 1087-1111.

Black, H. (1951). *Black's law dictionary* (4th ed.). St. Paul, MN: West Publishing.

Blair, D. (1977). The medical/legal aspects of automatism. *Medical Sciences and the Law, 17,* 167-182.

Blatt, S. J., & Berman, W. H. (1984). A methodology for the use of the Rorschach in clinical research. *Journal of Personality Assessment, 48,* 226-239.

Blau, T. H. (1959). *Private practice in clinical psychology.* New York: Appleton-Century-Crofts.

Blau, T. H. (1982). *The psychologist as expert witness: Compendium* (pp. 169-171). Tampa, FL: Psychological Seminars.

Blazer, D. (1978). The OARS Durham surveys: Description and application. In *Center for the Study of Aging and Human Development, Multidimensional functional assessment: The OARS methodology* (pp. 75-88). Durham, NC: Duke University.

Blinder, M. (1974). A response to Nietzel. *Judicature, 58,* 41-42.

Blinder, M. (1974). Understanding psychiatric testimony. *Judicature, 57,* 308-311.

Block, R. (1981). Victim-offender dynamics in violent crimes. In *Victims of crime, a review of research issues and methods.* Washington, DC: National Institute of Justice.

Bloom, J. D., Kinzie, D., & Shore, J. H. (1980). Residency curriculum in forensic psychiatry. *American Journal of Psychiatry, 137,* 730-732.

Bloom, J. D., Rogers, J. L., & Manson, S. M. (1982). After Oregon's insanity defense: A comparison of conditional release and hospitalization. *International Journal of Law and Psychiatry, 5,* 391-402.

Bloom, J. L., & Bloom, J. D. (1981). Disposition of insanity defenses in Oregon. *Bulletin of the American Academy of Psychiatry and the Law, 9,* 93-100.

Bluglass, R. (1979). The psychiatric court report. *Medical Science Law, 19*(2), 121-129.

Blumenthal, M. (1976). Violence in America: Still viewed by many as a necessary tool for social order, social change. *Institute for Social Research Newsletter, 4,* 2-23.

Blumer, D. (1976). Epilepsy and violence. Rage/hate/assault and other forms of violence, 207-221.

Blumer, D., & Migeon, C. (1975). Hormone and hormonal agents in the treatment of aggression. *Journal of Nervous and Mental Diseases, 160,* 127-137.

Bobbitt, J. M., & Hock, E. L. (1968). Order - and psychologist - in the court. *American Psychologist, 16,* 152.

Bockman, R. (1982, December 13). Expert: Leave insanity defense alone. *Tampa Tribune,* pp. B1-2.

Boffey, P. M. (1983, January 20). Psychiatric group urges stiffer rules for insanity pleas. *New York Times,* p. 8.

Bohman, M. (1978). Some genetic aspects of alcoholism and criminality. *Archives of General Psychiatry, 35*, 269-276.

Bohmer, C. E. R. (1977-1978). The court psychiatrist: Between two worlds. *Duquesne Law Review, 16*, 601-612.

Bohn, R. W. (1932). Sodium amytal narcosis as a therapeutic aid in psychiatry. *Psychiatric Quarterly, 6*, 301-309.

Bonnie, R., & Slobogin, C. (1980). The role of mental health professionals in the criminal process: The cause for informed speculation. *Virginia Law Review, 66*, 427-522.

Bonnie, R. J. (1977). Commentary: Criminal responsibility. In R. J. Bonnie (Ed.), *Diagnosis and debate*. New York: Insight Communictions.

Bonovitz, J., & Bonovitz, J. (1981). Diversion of the mentally ill into the criminal justice system: The police intervention perspective. *American Journal of Psychiatry, 138*, 973-976.

Borgida, E. (1979). Character proof and fireside induction. *Law and Human Behavior, 3*, 189-202.

Borgida, E. (1980). Evidentiary reform of rape laws: A psycholegal approach. In P. D. Lipsitt & B. D. Sales (Eds.), *New directions in psycholegal research*. New York: Van Nostrand Reinhold.

Borgida, E., & White, P. (1978). Social perception of rape victims: The impact of legal reform. *Law and Human Behavior, 2*, 339-351.

Bornstein, R. A. (1983). Verbal I. Q.-Performance I. Q. discrepancies in the Wechsler Adult Intelligence Scale-Revised in patients with a unilateral or bilateral cerebral dysfunction. *Journal of Consulting and Clinical Psychology, 51*, 779-780.

Boshier, R., & Izard, A. (1972). Do conservative parents use harsh child-rearing practices? *Psychological Reports, 31*, 734-736.

Botwinick, J. (1969). Disinclination to venture responses versus cautiousness in responding: Age differences. *Journal of Genetic Psychology, 115*, 55-62.

Botwinick, J. (1978). *Aging and behavior*. New York: Springer.

Boudouris, J. (1976). Criminality and addiction. *The International Journal of the Addictions, 11*(6), 951-966.

Boulding, K. (1967). Dare we take the social sciences seriously? *American Behavioral Scientist, 10*, 12-16.

Bouma, D. (1969). *Kids and cops: A study of mutual hostility*. Grand Rapids, MI: William B. Eerdmans Publishing.

Bouma, D., & Williams, D. G. (1972). Police school liaison: An evaluation of programs. *Intellect*, 119-122.

Boyanowky, E., & Griffith, C. (1982). Weapons and eye contact as instigators or inhibitors of aggressive arousal in police-citizen interaction. *Journal of Applied Social Contact, 12*, 398-407.

Bozzuto, J. C. (1975). Cinematic neurosis following "The Exorcist." *Journal of Nervous and Mental Disease, 161*, 43-48.

Bradburn, N. (1969). *The structure of psychological well-being*. Chicago: Aldine.

Bradford, J. M. W. (1983). The hormonal treatment of sex offenders. *Bulletin of the American Academy of Psychiatry and the Law, 11*, 159-169.

Bradford, J. M. W., & Smith, S. M. (1979). Amnesia and homicide: The Padola case and a study of thirty cases. *Bulletin of the American Academy of Psychiatry and the Law, 7*, 219-231.

Brakel, S. (1974). Presumption, bias, and incompetency in the criminal process. *Wisconsin Law Review*, 1105-1130.

Brakel, S., & Rock, R. (1971). *The mentally disabled and the law*. Chicago, IL: University of Chicago Press.

Brakel, S. J. (1978). Legal problems of people in mental and penal institutions: An exploratory study. *Research Journal, 4,* 565-645.

Branwhite, A. B. (1979). Malpractice liability and child psychology. *Bulletin of the British Psychological Society, 32,* 10-12.

Bray, R. M., Johnson, C. S., Osborne, M. D., McFarlane, J. B., & Scott, J. (1978). The effects of defendant status on the decisions of student and community juries. *Social Psychology, 41,* 256-260.

Bray, R. M., & Kerr, N. L. (1979). Use of the simultion method in the study of jury behavior: Some methodological considerations. *Law and Human Behavior, 3,* 107-119.

Bray, R. M., & Kerr, N. L. (1982). Methodological considerations in the study of the psychology of the courtroom. In N. L. Kerr & R. M. Bray (Eds.), *The pschology of the courtroom* (pp. 287-324). New York: Academic Press.

Bray, R. M., & Noble, A. M. (1978). Authoritarianism and decision of mock juries: Evidence of jury bias and group polarization. *Journal of Personality and Social Psychology, 36*(12), 1424-1430.

Brehm, J. W., & Cohen, A. R. (1962). *Explorations in cognitive dissonance.* New York: Wiley.

Brenner, M. (1977, October). Does employment cause crime? *Criminal Justice Newsletter, 24,* 5.

Brereton, D., & Casper, J. D. (1982). Does it pay to plead guilty? Differential sentencing and the functioning of criminal courts. *Law and Society Review, 16,* 45-70.

Bricklin, B. (1985). *Bricklin Perception Scales: Child perception of parent series.* Furlong, PA: Village Publishing.

Bricklin, B., Piotrowski, Z. A., & Wagner, E. E. (1978). *The hand test.* Springfield, IL: Charles C. Thomas.

Briddell, D. W., Rimm, D. C., Caddy, G. R., Krawitz, G., Sholis, D., & Wunderlin, R. J. (1978). Effects of alcohol and cognitive set on sexual arousal to deviant stimuli. *Journal of Abnormal Psychology, 87,* 418-430.

Bridgeman, D. L., & Marlowe, D. (1979). Jury decision-making: An empirical study based on actual felony trials. *Journal of Applied Psychology, 64*(2), 91-98.

Brigham, J. C. (1980). Perspectives on the impact of lineup composition, race, and witness confidence on identification accuracy. *Law and Human Behavior, 4,* 315-321.

Brigham, J. C. (1981). The accuracy of eyewitness evidence: How do attorneys see it? *Florida Bar Journal, 55,* 714-721.

Brigham, J. C., Maass, A., Snyder, L. D., & Spauling, D. (1982). Accuracy of eyewitness identification in a field setting. *Journal of Personality and Social Psychology, 42,* 673-681.

Briscoe, O. V. (1975). Assessment of intent: An approach to the preparation of court reports. *British Journal of Psychiatry, 127,* 461-465.

Brodie, K. H., Gartrell, N., Doering, C., & Rhue, T. (1974). Plasma testosterone levels in heterosexual and homosexual men. *American Journal of Psychiatry, 131,* 82-83.

Brodsky, S., & Smitherman, H. (1983). *Handbook of scales for research in crime and delinquency.* New York: Plenum Press.

Brodsky, S. L. (1977). The mental health professional on the witness stand: A survival guide. In B. D. Sales (Ed.), *Psychology in the legal process.* New York: Spectrum Publications.

Brodsky, S. L. (1980). Ethical issues for psychologist in corrections. In J. Monahan (Ed.), *Who is the client? The ethics of psychological interventions in the criminal justice system.* Washington, DC: American Psychological Association.

Brodsky, S. L., & Robey, A. (1972). On becoming an expert witness: Issues of orientation and effectiveness. *Professional Psychology, 3,* 173-176.

Brody, G. (1969). Maternal child-rearing attitudes and child behavior. *Developmental Psychology, 1*, 66.

Brody, J. E. (1983, March 29). Bonding at birth: A major theory being questioned. *New York Times, Science Times*, pp. 15, 16.

Broeder, D. W. (1965). Voir dire examination: An empirical study. *Southern California Law Review, 38*, 503-528.

Bromberg, W. (1969). Psychiatrists in court: The psychiatrist's view. *American Journal of Psychiatry, 125*, 1343-1347.

Bromberg, W. (1979). *The uses of psychiatry in the law: A clinical view of forensic psychiatry.* Westport, CT: Quorum Books.

Brooks, A. D. (1974). *Law, psychiatry, and the mental health system.* Boston: Little, Brown.

Brooks, A. D. (1980). *Law, psychiatry, and the mental health system: 1980 supplement.* Boston: Little, Brown.

Brown, F. (1965). The Bender Gestalt and acting out. In L. Abt & S. Weissman (Eds.), *Acting out: Theoretical and clinical aspects.* New York: Grune and Stratton.

Brown, J. S. (1963). *Techniques of persuasion.* London: Penguin.

Brown, L. M., & Dauer, E. A. (1978). *Planning by lawyers: Matrials on a nonadversarial legal process.* Mineola, NY: Foundation Press.

Brown, M. R. (1926). *Legal psychology.* Indianapolis: Bobbs-Merrill.

Brown, S., Burkhart, B. R., King, G. D., & Solomon, R. (1977). Roles and expectations for mental health professionals in law enforcement agencies. *American Journal of Community Psychology, 5*(2), 207-215.

Brownstone, H. (1980). The homosexual parent in custody disputes. *Queen's Law Journal, 5*, 119-240.

Bruning, O. M. (1975). The right of the defendant to refuse an insanity plea. *The Bulletin, 3*, 238-244.

Bryant, E. T., Scott, M. L., Golden, C. J., & Tori, C. E. (1984). Neuropsychological deficits, learning disability, and violent behavior. *Journal of Consulting and Clinical Psychology, 52*, 323-324.

Buckhart, B. R., Christian, W. L., & Gynther, M. D. (1978). Item subtlety and faking on the MMPI: A paradoxical relationship. *Journal of Personality Assessment, 42*, 76-80.

Buckout, R. (1974). Eye-witness testimony. *Scientific American, 23*(6), 23-31.

Buckout, R. (1975). Nearly 2,000 witnesses can be wrong. *Social Action and the Law, 2*, 7.

Buckout, R. (1977). Eyewitness identification and psychology in the courtroom. *Criminal Defense, 4*, 5-10.

Buckout, R. (1980). Eyewitness identification and psychology in the courtroom. In G. Cooke (Ed.), *The role of the forensic psychologist* (pp. 175-185). Springfield, IL: Charles C. Thomas.

Buechley, R., & Ball, H. (1952). A new test of "test validity" for the group MMPI. *Journal of Consulting Psychology, 16*, 299-301.

Bukatman, B. A., Foy, J., & DeGrazia, E. (1971). What is competency to stand trial? *American Journal of Psychiatry, 127*, 1225-1229.

Burak, C. S. (1978, Fall). The rhyme or reason for criminal responsibility. *Journal of Psychiatry and Law, 6*(3), 429-435.

Burger, G., & Armentrout, J. (1971). A factor analysis of fifth and sixth graders' reports of parental child-rearing behavior. *Developmental Psychology, 4*, 483.

Burger, G., Armentrout, J., & Rapfogel, R. (1973). Estimating factor scores for children's reports of parental child-rearing behaviors. *Journal of Genetic Psychology, 123*, 107-113.

Burger, W. E. (1980). *Year end review.* Washington, DC: United States Supreme Court.

Burke, M. (1963). The control of response choice on projective techniques. (Doctoral dissertation, University of Denver, 1962). *Dissertation Abstracts, 24*, 2119-2120.

Buros, O. (Ed.) (1933-1978). Mental measurement yearbooks (Vols. 1-8). *Tests in print: Educational, psychological and personality tests of 1933 and 1934*. Highland Park, NJ: Gryphon Press.

Bursten, B. (1982). What if antisocial personality is an illness? *Bulletin of the American Academy of Psychiatry and the Law, 10*, 97-102.

Burt, R. A., & Morris, N. (1972). A proposal for the abolition of the incompetency plea. *University of Chicago Law Review, 40*, 66-95.

Busch, K. B., & Schnoll, S. (1986). Cocaine abuse and the law. *Behavioral Sciences and the Law*.

Buss, A. H. (1961). *The psychology of aggression*. John Wiley and Sons.

Buss, A. H. (1963). Physical aggression in relation to different frustrations. *Journal of Abnormal and Social Psychology, 67*, 1-7.

Butcher, J. N. (Ed.) (1969). *MMPI: Research developments and clinical applications*. New York: McGraw-Hill.

Butcher, J. N., Braswell, L., & Rainey, D. (1983). A cross cultural comparison of American Indian, Black, and White inpatients on the MMPI and presenting symptoms. *Journal of Consulting and Clinical Psychology, 51*, 587-594.

Buxton, M., & Dubin, L. A. (1977). Teaching psychiatry to law students: Towards a replicable model. *New England Law Review, 13*, 233-245.

Bydder, G. M. (1983). Clinical nuclear magnetic resonance imaging. *British Journal of Hospital Medicine, 30*, 348-356.

Byers, E. S., Cohen, S., & Harshbarger, D. D. (1978). Impact of aftercare services of recidivism of mental hospital patients. *Community Mental Health Journal, 14*, 26-34.

Byrne, D. (1971). *The attraction paradigm*. New York: Academic Press.

Byrne, D. (1974). *An introduction to personality* (2nd ed.). Englewood Cliffs, NJ: Prentice-Hall.

C

Caesar, B. (1979, October). The insanity defense: The new loophole. *Crime and Delinquency, 25*(4), 436-449.

Cahn, E. (1955). Jurisprudence. *New York University Law Review, 30*, 150-169.

Calder, B. J., Insko, C. A., & Yandell, B. (1974). The relation of cognitive and memorial processes to persuasion in a simulated jury trial. *Journal of Applied Social Psychology, 4*, 62-93.

California State Psychological Association. (1980). Standards for professional services on court panels and other legal consultants. *California State Psychologist, 14*(2), 21-22.

California State Psychological Association. (1981). Two professioals urge ban on psychiatric testimony. *California State Psychologist, 15*(5), 1, 16.

Cameron, R. M. (1979). The mental health expert: A guide to direct and cross-examination. *Criminal Justice Journal, 2*, 299-311.

Campbell, A., Converse, P., & Rodgers, W. (1976). *The quality of American life: Perceptions, evaluations, and satisfactions*. New York: Russell Sage.

Campbell, D. T., & Ross, H. L. (1968). The Connecticut crackdown on speeding: Time-series data in quasi-experimental analysis. *Law and Society Review, 3*, 33-53.

Campbell, K. L. (1981). Psychological blow automatism: A narrow defense. *Criminal Law Quarterly, 23*, 342-368.

Caplan, N. (1977). A minimal set of conditions necessary for the utilization of social science knowledge in policy formulation at the national level. In C. Weiss (Ed.), *Using social research in public policy making.* Lexington, MA: DC Health.

Caplan, N. (1979). The two communities theory and knowledge utilization. *American Behavioral Scientist, 22,* 459-470.

Caplan, N., Morrison, A., & Stambaugh, R. (1975). *The use of social science knowledge in policy decisions at the national level.* Ann Arbor, MI: Institute for Social Research.

Caplan, N., & Nelson, S. D. (1973). On being useful: The nature and consequences of psychological research on social problems. *American Psychologist, 28,* 199-211.

Cardozo, B. (1921). *The nature of the judicial process.* New Haven, CT: Yale University Press.

Carlson, K. A. (1981). A modern personality test for offenders. *Criminal Justice and Behavior, 8,* 173-184.

Carp, A., & Shavzin, A. (1950). The susceptibility of falsification of the Rorschach psychodiagnostic technique. *Journal of Consulting Psychology, 14,* 230-233.

Carroll, J. S. (1978). Causal attributions in expert parole decisions. *Journal of Personality and Social Psychology, 36,* 1512-1520.

Carroll, J. S., & Coates, D. (1980). Parole decisions: Social psychological research in applied settings. In L. Bickman (Ed.), *Applied social psychology annual,* Vol. 1. Beverly Hills, CA: Sage Publications.

Carroll, J. S., & Payne, J. W. (1977). Judgments about crime and the criminal: A model and a method for investigating parole decisions. In B. D. Sales (Ed.), *Perspectives in law and psychology.* New York: Plenum Press.

Carroll, J. S., & Ruback, R. B. (1981). Sentencing by parole boards: The parole revocation decision. In B. D. Sales (Ed.), *The trial process* (pp. 459-480). New York: Plenum Press.

Carroll, J. S., & Weiner, R. L. (1982). Cognitive social psychology in court and beyond. In A. Hastorf & A. Isen (Eds.), *Cognitive social psychology.* New York: Elsevier-North Holland.

Casper, J. D. (1979). Reformers v. abolitionists: Some notes for further research on plea bargainig. *Law and Society Review, 13,* 567-572.

Cavanaugh, J. L., & Rogers, R. (1982). Convergence of mental illness and violence: Effects on public policy. *Psychiatric Annals, 12,* 537-541.

Cavanaugh, J. L., Rogers, R., & Wasyliw, O. E. (1981). Mental illness and antisocial behavior. In W. H. Reid (Ed.), *Treatment of antisocial syndromes* (pp. 3-19). New York: Van Nostrand Reinhold.

Center for Forensic Psychiatry. (1974, June). *Evaluation of guilty-but-mentally ill.* Seminar at Center for Forensic Psychiatry, Ann Arbor, MI.

Center for Study of Aging and Human Development. (1978). *Multidimensional functional assessment: The OARS methodology.* Durham, NC: Duke University.

Chalmers, P. K. (1969). Meanings, impressions, and attitudes: A model of the evaluation process. *Psychological Review, 76,* 450-460.

Chambers, M. (1983, January 21). Insanity defense backed by panel. *New York Times,* p. 15.

Chambers, W. N. (1974). Expert testimony regarding paranoia. *Florida Bar Journal, 48,* 633-636.

Champagne, A., & Nagel, S. (1982). The psychology of judging. In N. L. Kerr & R. M. Bray (Eds.), *The psychology of the courtroom* (pp. 257-286). New York: Academic Press.

Chapman, L. J., & Chapman, J. P. (1967). Genesis of popular but erroneous psychodiagnostic observations. *Journal of Abnormal Psychology, 72,* 193-204.

Chapman, L. J., & Chapman, J. P. (1969). Illusory correlation as an obstacle to the use of valid psychodiagnostic signs. *Journal of Abnormal Psychology, 74,* 271-280.

Chapman, L. J., & Chapman, J. P. (1971). Associatively-based illusory correlation as a source of psychodiagnostic folklore. In L. D. Goodstein & R. I. Landon (Eds.), *Readings in personality assessment*. New York: Wiley.

Charrow, B., & Charrow, F. (1979). Making legal language understandable: A psycholinguistic study of juror instructions. *Columbia Law Review, 79*, 1306-1374.

Chesterton, G. K. (1968). *"Tremendous trifles," Generally speaking*. Freeport, NY: Books for Libraries Press.

Chick, G. E., Loy, J. W., & White, W. E. (1984). Differentiating violent and nonviolent opiate-addicted reformatory inmates with the MMPI. *Journal of Clinical Psychology, 40*, 619-623.

Christie, R. (1976). Probability v. precedence: The social psychology of jury selection. In G. Bermant, C. Nemeth, & N. Vidmar (Eds.), *Psychology and the law*. New York: Lexington Books.

Christie, R., & Geis, F. (1970). *Studies in Machiavellianism*. New York: Academic Press.

Chorost, S. (1962). Parental child-rearing attitudes and their correlates in adolescent hostility. *Genetic Psychology Monograph, 66*, 49-90.

Christensen, A. -L. (1975). *Luria's neuropsychological investigation*. New York: Spectrum.

Church, T. W., Jr. (1979). In defense of "bargain justice." *Law and Society Review, 13*, 509-526.

Cialdini, R. B. (1980). Full-cycle social psychology. In L. Bickman (Ed.), *Applied social psychology annual*, Vol. 1. Beverly Hills, CA: Sage Publications.

Cipes, R. M. (1965). *Moore's federal practice: Rules of criminal procedure* (2nd ed.). New York: Matthew Bender.

Claeys, W., & DeBoeck, P. (1976). The influence of some parental characteristics on children's primary abilities and field independence: A study of adopted children. *Child Development, 47*, 842-845.

Clark, H. H. (1974). *Cases and problems in domestic relations*. St. Paul, MN: West Publications.

Clark, J. H. (1948). Application of the MMPI in differentiating AWOL recidivists from nonrecidivists. *Journal of Psychology, 26*, 229-234.

Clark, K. (1953). Desegregation: An appraisal of the evidence. *Journal of Social Issues, 9*, 1-77.

Clark, K. (1979). The role of social scientists 25 years after Brown. *Personality and Social Psychology Bulletin, 5*, 477-481.

Clark, R. A. (1965). Projective measurement of experimentally induced levels of sexual motivation. In B. I. Murstein (Ed.), *Handbook of projective techniques* (pp. 561-574). New York: Basic Books.

Clark, R. D., & Word, L. E. (1974). Where is the apathetic bystander? Situational characteristics of the emergency. *Journal of Personality and Social Psychology, 29*, 279-287.

Clausen, J. (1968). Perspectives in childhood socialization. In J. Clausen (Ed.), *Socialization and society* (pp. 130-181). Boston, MA: Little, Brown.

Cleary, E. (Ed.) (1972). *McCormick's handbook of the law of evidence*. St. Paul, MN: West Publishing.

Cleaver, P. T., Mylonas, A. D., & Reckless, W. C. (1968). Gradients in attitudes toward law, courts and police. *Sociological Focus, 2*, 29-48.

Clingempeel, W. G., & Reppucci, N. D. (1982). Joint custody after divorce: Major issues and goals for research. *Psychological Bulletin, 91*(1), 102-127.

Clopton, J. R. (1978). A note on the MMPI as a suicide predictor. *Journal of Consulting and Clinical Psychology, 46*, 335-336.

Coates, D., & Penrod, S. (1981). Social psychology and the emergency of disputes. *Law and Society Review, 15*, 655-680.

Cochran, W. C. (1973). *The law dictionary*. Cincinnati, OH: Anderson.

Cockroft, I. C. (1978, Winter). Governmental liability for mistakes in the parole and probation of dangerous convicts. *Criminal Justice Journal*, 2(1).

Cocozza, J., & Steadman, H. (1976). The failure of psychiatric prediction of dangerousness: Clear and convincing evidence. *Rutgers Law Review*, 29, 1084-1101.

Cocozza, J., & Steadman, H. J. (1978). Prediction in psychiatry: An example of misplaced confidence in experts. *Social Problems*, 25, 265-276.

Cofer, C. N., Chance, J. E., & Judson, A. J. (1949). A study of malingering on the MMPI. *Journal of Psychology*, 27, 491-499.

Cohen, F. (1966). The function of the attorney and the commitment of the mentally ill. *Texas Law Review*, 44, 424-469.

Cohen, F. (1968). Civil restraint, mental illness, and the right to treatment. *Yale Law Journal*, 77, 87-116.

Cohen, M. I., Groth, A. N., & Seigel, R. (1978, January). The clinical prediction of dangerousness. *Crime and Delinquency*, 24, 28-39.

Cohen, R. L., & Harnick, M. A. (1980). The susceptibility of child witnesses to suggestion. *Law and Human Behavior*, 4, 201-210.

Cohen, S. (1982, July 12). It's a mad, mad verdict. *The New Republic*, 13-16.

Cohn, A., & Udolf, R. (1979). *The criminal justice system and its psychology.* New York: Van Nostrand Reinhold.

Cole, W. G., & Loftus, E. S. (1979). Incorporating new information into memory. *American Journal of Psychology*, 92, 413-425.

Coleman, M., Ganong, L., & Brown, G. (1981). Effects of multimedia instruction on mothers' ability to teach cognitive abilities to preschool children. *Journal of Social Psychology*, 115, 89-94.

Colligan, R. C. (1976). Atypical response sets in the automated MMPI. *Journal of Clinical Psychology*, 32, 76-78.

Collins, G. (1982, December 20). Some broken families retain many bonds. *New York Times*, p. 17.

Collins, J. J. (1981). *Alcohol use and criminal behavior.* Washington, DC: National Institute of Justice.

Committee on Pattern Jury Instructions. (1979). *Pattern jury instructions* (Criminal cases). St. Paul, MN: West Publishing.

Committee to Develop Joint Technical Standards for Educational and Psychological Testing. (1982). *Standards for educational and psychological testing* (Draft). Washington, DC: American Psychological Association.

Comrey, A. L., Baker, E., & Glaser, M. (1973). *A sourcebook for mental health measures.* Los Angeles, CA: Human Interaction Research Institute.

Conley, J. M., O'Barr, W. M., & Lind, E. A. (1979). The power of language: Presentational style in the courtroom. *Duke Law Journal*, 1978, 1375-1399.

Constantini, E., & King, N. (1981). The partial juror: Correlates and causes of prejudgement. *Law and Society Review*, 15, 9-40.

Cook, P. (1975). The correctional carrot: Better jobs for parolees. *Policy Analysis*, 1, 11-54.

Cook, S. W. (1975). Social science and school desegregation: Did we mislead the Supreme Court? *Personality and Social Psychology Bulletin*, 5, 420-436.

Cook, T. D., & Campbell, D. T. (1979). *Quasi-experimentation: Design and analysis issues for field settings.* Chicago, IL: Rand-McNally.

Cook, W. W., & Medley, D. M. (1954). Proposed hostility and Pharisaic-virtue scales for the MMPI. *Journal of Applied Psychology*, 38, 414-418.

Cooke, G. (1969). The court study unit: Patient characteristics and differences between patients judged competent and incompetent. *Journal of Clinical Psychology, 25,* 140-143.

Cooke, G. (1980). *The role of the forensic psychologist.* Springfield, IL: Charles C. Thomas.

Cooke, G., & Jackson, N. (1971). Competence to stand trial: The role of the psychologist. *Professional Psychology, 2,* 373-376.

Cooke, G., Johnson, N., & Pogany, E. (1973). Factors affecting referral to determine competency to stand trial. *American Journal of Psychiatry, 130,* 870-875.

Cooke, G., & Pogany, E. (1975). The influence on judges' sentencing practices of a mental evaluation. *Bulletin of the American Academy of Psychiatry and the Law, 3*(4), 245-251.

Cooke, G., & Robey, A. (1971). The MMPI: A case study in dissimulation. *Journal of Consulting and Clinical Psychology, 36,* 355-359.

Cooke, G., & Sikorski, C. (1974). Factors affecting length of hospitalization in persons adjudicated not guilty by reason of insanity. *Bulletin of the American Academy of Psychiatry and the Law, 2,* 251-261.

Cooke, G. et al. (1974). A comparison of blacks and whites committed for evaluation of competency to stand trial on criminal charges. *Journal of Psychiatry and Law, 2,* 319-337.

Coons, J. (1977). Recent trends in science fiction. Sennano among the people of number. *Journal of Law and Education, 6,* 23-40.

Cooper, L. (1976). Voir dire in federal criminal trials: Protecting the defendant's right to an impartial jury. *Indiana Law Journal, 52,* 269-280.

Coopersmith, S. (1967). *The antecedents of self-esteem.* San Francisco, CA: Freeman.

Corotto, L. (1961). The relation of performance and verbal IQ in acting-out juveniles. *Journal of Psychological Studies, 12,* 162-166.

Coulton, C. (1979). Developing an instrument to measure person-environment fit. *Journal of Social Service Research, 3,* 159-173.

Cox, T. C., Jacobs, M. R., LeBlanc, A. E., & Marshman, J. A. (1983). *Drugs and drug abuse.* Toronto: Addiction Research Foundation.

Craft, M. (1978). The current status of xyy and xxy syndromes: A review of treatment implications. *International Journal of Law and Psychiatry, 1,* 319-324.

Cressen, R. (1975). Artistic quality of drawings and judges' evaluations of the DAP. *Journal of Personality Assessment, 39,* 132-137.

Criss, M. L., & Racine, D. R. (1980). Impact of change in legal standards for those adjudicated not guilty by reason of insanity, 1975-1979. *Bulletin of the American Academy of Psychiatry and the Law, 8,* 261-271.

Cromwell, R., Olson, D., & Fournier, D. (1976). Diagnosis and evaluation in marital and family counseling. In D. Olson (Ed.), *Treating relationships* (pp. 517-562). Lake Mills, IA: Graphic Publications.

Cronbach, L. (1970). *Essentials of psychological testing.* New York: Harper & Row.

Cronbach, L. (1971). Test validity. In R. Thorndike (Ed.), *Educational measurement* (pp. 443-507). Washington, DC: American Council on Education.

Cronbach, L., & Meehl, P. (1955). Construct validity in psychological tests. *Psychological Bulletin, 52,* 281-302.

Cross, J. (1969). College students' memories of their parents: A factor analysis of the CRPBI. *Journal of Consulting and Clinical Psychology, 33,* 275-278.

Crosson, B., & Warren, R. L. (1982). Use of the Luria-Nebraska neuropsychological battery in aphasia: A conceptual critique. *Journal of Consulting and Clinical Psychology, 50,* 22-31.

Crucitti, J. R. (1978). Cross-examination of psychiatric witnesses under the Vermont patient's privilege when the issue of insanity is raised. *Vermont Law Review, 3,* 191-216.

Crutchfield, R. (1955). Conformity and character. *American Psychologist, 10,* 191-198.

Curlee, J. (1973). Alcoholic blackouts: Some conflicting evidence. *Quarterly Journal of Studies on Alcohol, 34,* 409-413.

Curnutt, R., & Corozzo, L. (1960). The use of the Bender Gestalt cutoff scores in identifying juvenile delinquents. *Journal of Projective Techniques, 24,* 353-354.

Curran, W. J. (1972). Competency of the mentally retarded to stand trial: New rules from the Supreme Court. *New England Journal of Medicine, 287,* 1184-1185.

Curran, W. J. (1974). Legal psychiatry in the 19th century. *Psychiatric Annals, 4,* 8-14.

Curran, W. J. (1978). Comparative analysis of mental health legislation in forty-three countries: A discussion of historical trends. *International Journal of Law and Psychiatry, 1,* 79-92.

D

Dahlstrom, W. G., Welsh, G. S., & Dahlstrom, L. E. (1972). *An MMPI handbook: Clinical interpretation.* Minneapolis, MN: University of Minnesota Press.

Dahlstrom, W. G., Welsh, G. S., & Dahlstrom, L. E. (1975). *An MMPI handbook, Vol. 2: Research applications.* Minneapolis, MN: University of Minnesota Press.

Daley, M., & Piliavin, I. (1982). I. "Violence against children" revisited: Some necessary clarification of findings from a major national study. *Journal of Social Service Research, 5,* 61-81.

Dana, R. H. (1972). Thematic Apperception Test. In O. K. Buros (Ed.), *Mental measurements yearbook* (6th ed.) (pp. 492-495). Highland Park, NJ: Gryphon Press.

Dana, R. H. (1978). Rorschach. In O. K. Buros (Ed.), *Eighth mental measurements yearbook* (pp. 1040-1042). Highland Park, NJ: Gryphon Press.

Dane, F. C., & Wrightsman, L. S. (1982). The effects of defendants' and victims' characteristics on jurors' verdicts. In N. L. Kerr & R. M. Bray (Eds.), *The psychology of the courtroom* (pp. 83-118). New York: Academic Press.

Darley, J. M., & Latane, B. (1968). Bystander intervention in emergencies: Diffusion of responsibility. *Journal of Personality and Social Psychology, 8,* 377-383.

Dash, S. et al. (1969). Demonstrating rehabilitative planning as a defense strategy. *Cornell Law Review, 54,* 408-436.

Davidson, H. A. (1952). *Forensic psychiatry.* New York: Ronald Press.

Davidson, H. A. (1965). *Forensic psychiatry* (2nd ed.). New York: Ronald Press.

Davis, A. (1973). *The United States Supreme Court and the use of social science data.* New York: MSS Information.

Davis, F. B. (1966). *Standards for educational and psychological tests.* Washington, DC: American Psychological Association.

Davis, J. H. (1980). Group decision and procedural justice. In M. Fishbein (Ed.), *Progress in social psychology.* Hillsdale, NJ: Erlbaum.

Davis, J. H., Bray, R. M., & Holt, R. W. (1977). The empirical study of decision processes in juries: A critical review. In J. L. Tapp & F. J. Levine (Eds.), *Law, justice, and the individual in society: Psychological and legal issues.* New York: Holt, Rinehart & Winston.

Davis, J. H., Kerr, N. L., Atkin, R. S., Holt, R., & Meek, D. (1975). The decision processes of 6- and 12-person mock juries assigned unanimous and two-thirds majority rules. *Journal of Personality and Social Psychology, 32*, 1-14.

Davis, J. H., Stasser, G., Spitzer, C., & Holt, R. (1976). Changes in group members' decision preferences during discussion: An illustration with mock juries. *Journal of Personality and Social Psychology, 34*, 1177-1187.

Davis, K. R., & Sines, J. O. (1971). An antisocial behavior pattern associated with a specific MMPI profile. *Journal of Consulting and Clinical Psychology, 36*, 229-234.

Davis, W., & Phares, E. (1967). Internal-external control as a determinant of information-seeking in a social-influence situation. *Journal of Personality, 35*, 547-561.

Davis, W., & Phares, E. (1969). Parental antecedents of internal-external control of reinforcement. *Psychological Reports, 24*, 427-436.

Davison, G. C., & Stuart, R. B. (1975). Behavior therapy and civil liberties. *American Psychologist, 30*, 755-764.

Dawes, R. M. (1979). Robust beauty of improper linear model in decision making. *American Psychologist, 34*, 571-582.

Dawidoff, D. J. (1973). Some suggestions to psychiatrists for avoiding legal jeopardy. *Archives of General Psychiatry, 29*, 699-701.

DeCato, C. M. (1984). Rorschach reliability: Toward a training model for interscorer agreement. *Journal of Personality Assessment, 48*, 58-64.

Deese, J. (1972). *Psychology as science and art.* New York: Harcourt Brace Jovanovich.

Deffenbacher, K. A. (1980). Eyewitness accuracy and confidence. Can we infer anything about their relationship? *Law and Human Behavior, 4*, 243-260.

Deffenbacher, K. A., & Loftus, E. F. (1982). Do jurors share a common understanding concerning eyewitness behavior? *Law and Human Behavior, 6*, 15-30.

Deiker, T. E. (1974). A cross validation of MMPI scales of aggression on male criminal criterion groups. *Journal of Consulting and Clinical Psychology, 42*, 196-202.

Delgado-Escueta, A. V., Mattson, R. H., King, L., Goldensohn, E. S., Spiegel, H., Madsen, J., Crandall, P., Dreifuss, F., & Porter, R. J. (1981). The nature of aggression during epileptic seizures. *New England Journal of Medicine, 305*, 711-716.

Delis, D., & Kaplan, E. (1983). Hazards of standardized neuropsychological test with low content validity: Comments on the Luria-Nebraska neuropsychological battery. *Journal of Consulting and Clinical Psychology, 51*, 396-398.

Dellinger, R. W. (1978). High on PCP. *Human Behavior, 7*, 38-45.

Delman, R. P. O. (1980). Participation by psychologists in insanity defense proceedings: An advocacy. *Journal of Psychiatry and Law, 9*, 247-262.

Dent, H. R. (1982). The effects of interviewing strategies on the results of interviews with child witnesses. In A. Trankell (Ed.), *Reconstructing the past.* Deventer, Netherlands: Kluwer.

Department of Justice. (1978). *Criminal victimization in the United States.* Washington, DC: Superintendent of Documents, U. S. Government Printing Office.

DePaulo, B. M., & Rosenthal, R. (1979). Telling lies. *Journal of Personality and Social Psychology, 37*, 1713-1722.

Derdeyn, A. (1975). Child custody consultation. *American Journal of Orthopsychiatry, 45*, 791-801.

Derdeyn, A. (1976a). A consideration of legal issues in child custody contests. *Archives of General Psychiatry, 33*, 165-171.

Derdeyn, A. (1976b). Child custody contests in historical perspective. *American Journal of Psychiatry, 133,* 1369-1376.

Dershowitz, A. (1968). Psychiatry in the legal process: "A knife that cuts both ways." *Judicature, 51,* 370-385.

Dershowitz, A. (1978). The role of psychiatry in the sentencing process. *International Journal of Law and Psychiatry, 1,* 63-78.

DeVito, R. A. (1980). Some new alternatives to the insanity defense. *American Journal of Forensic Psychiatry, 1,* 38-51.

Diamond, B. L. (1957). With malice aforethought. *Archives of Criminal Psychodynamics, 2*(1), 1-44.

Diamond, B. L. (1959). The fallacy of the impartial expert. *Archives of Criminal Psychodynamics, 3,* 221-236.

Diamond, B. L. (1961). Criminal responsibility of the mentally ill. *Stanford Law Review, 59,* 82-83.

Diamond, M. J., & Lobitz, W. C. (1973). When familiarity breeds respect: The effects of an experimental depolarization program on police and student attitudes toward each other. *Journal of Social Issues, 29,* 95-109.

Diamond, S. S. (1974). A jury experiment reanalyzed. *University of Michigan Journal of Law Reform, 7,* 520-532.

Diamond, S. S. (1981). Exploring sources of sentence disparity. In B. D. Sales (Ed.), *The trial process* (pp. 387-412). New York: Plenum Press.

Diamond, S. S., & Zeisel, H. (1974). A courtroom experiment on juror selection and decision-making. *Personality and Social Psychology Bulletin, 1,* 276-277.

Dickey, W. (1980). Incompetency and the nondangerous mentally ill client. *Criminal Law Bulletin, 16,* 22-47.

Dickey, W. J., Remmington, S. J., & Schultz, D. (1980). Law, trial judges, and psychiatric witnesses: Reflection on how a change in legal doctrine has been implemented in Wisconsin. *International Journal of Law and Psychiatry, 3,* 331-341.

Dickinson, R. L. (1984). Indiana court condemns mentally ill man to die for murder. *Mental Health Reports, 8,* 1-2.

Diem, F. N. (1974). Evidence: The use of leaned treaties on cross-examination of a medical expert–treaties which an expert witness has used in his studies are acceptable for the sole purpose of impeaching his testimony. Seeley v. Eaton, 506 S. W. 2nd 719. *Texas Tech Law Review, 6,* 237-245.

Dietz, P. E. (1978). Forensic and non-forensic psychiatrists: An empirical comparison. *Bulletin of the American Academy of Psychiatry and the Law, 6,* 13-22.

Dillehay, R. D., & Nietzel, M. J. (1980). Constructing a science of jury behavior. In L. Wheeler (Ed.), *Review of personality and social psychology.* Beverly Hills, CA: Sage Publications.

Dillehay, R. D., & Nietzel, M. J. (1981). Conceptualizing mock jury-juror research: Critique and illustrations. In K. S. Larsen (Ed.), *Psychology and ideology.* Monmouth, OR: Institute for Theoretical History.

Directory of Law Teachers. (1983). St. Paul, MN: West Publishing and Foundation Press.

Dix, G. (1975). Determining the continued dangerousness of psychologically abnormal sex offenders. *Journal of Psychiatry and the Law, 3,* 327-344.

Dix, G. (1976). "Civil" commitment of the mentally ill and the need for data on the prediction of dangerousness. *American Behavioral Scientist, 19*(3), 318-334.

Dix, G. (1977). The death penalty, "dangerousness," psychiatric testimony and professional ethics. *American Journal of Criminal Law, 5,* 151-214.

Dix, G. E. (1971). Psychological abnormality as a factor in grading criminal liability: Diminished capacity, diminished responsibility, and the like. *Journal of Criminal Law, Criminology, and Police Science, 62*, 313-334.

Dix, G. E. (1977). Psychiatric testimony in death penalty litigation. *Bulletin of the American Academy of Psychiatry and the Law, 5*, 287-294.

Dix, G. E. (1981). Mental health professionals in the legal process: Some problems of psychiatric dominance. *Law and Psychology Review, 6*, 1-20.

Dix, G. E. (1984). Criminal responsibility and mental impairment in American criminal law: Response to the Hinckley acquittal in historical perspective. In D. N. Weisstub (Ed.), *Law and mental health: International perspectives* (pp. 1-44). New York: Pergamon.

Dixonn, T., & Blondis, R. (1976). Cross-examination of psychiatric witnesses in civil commitment proceedings. *Mental Disability Law Reported, 1*, 164-171.

Dolan, M. (1978). PCP: A plague whose time has come. *American Pharmacy, 18*, 22-29.

Domino, E. F. (1978). Neurobiology of phencyclidine: An update. In R. C. Petersen & R. C. Stillman (Eds.), *Phencyclidine (PCP) abuse: An appraisal* (pp. 18-43). Rockville, MD: National Institute on Drug Abuse.

Dreher, R. H. (1967). Origin, development, and present status of insanity as a defense to criminal responsibility in the common law. *Journal of the History of the Behavioral Sciences, 3*, 47-57.

Driver, E. (1968). Confessions and the social psychology of coercion. *Harvard Law Review, 82*, 42-61.

Druckman, D. (Ed.) (1977). *Negotiations: Social psychological perspectives*. Beverly Hills, CA: Sage Publications.

Drummond, F. (1966). A failure in the discrimination of aggressive behavior of undifferentiated schizophrenics with the Hand Test. *Journal of Projective Techniques and Personality Assessment, 30*, 275-279.

Dubin et al. (1977). Improving the relationship between mental health workers and lawyers. *Research Communications in Psychology, Psychiatry, and Behavior, 2*, 27-42.

Dubovsky, S. L., Feiger, A. D., & Eisman, V. (1984). *Psychiatric decision-making*. Philadelphia, PA: B. C. Decker.

DuCanto, J. (1967). Mental illness and child custody in matrimonial matters. *Journal of Family Law, 7*, 636-643.

Dudley, H. K., Jr. (1978). A review board for determining the dangerousness of mentally ill offenders. *Hospital and Community Psychiatry, 29*, 453-456.

Dullea, G. (1983, February 7). Wide changes in family life are altering the family law. *New York Times*, pp. 1, 12.

Duncan, E., Whitney, P., & Kunen, S. (1982). Integration of visual and verbal information on children's memories. *Child Development, 53*, 1215-1223.

Durand, R. M., Bearden, W. O., & Gustafson, A. W. (1978). Previous jury service as a moderating influence on jurors' beliefs and attitudes. *Psychological Reports, 42*, 567-572.

Dworkin, R. (1977). Social sciences and constitutional rights: The consequences of uncertainty. *Journal of Law and Education, 6*, 3-12.

Dysken, M. W., Kooser, J. A., Haraszi, J. S., & Davis, J. M. (1979). Clinical usefulness of sodium amobarbital interviewing. *Archives of General Psychiatry, 36*, 789-794.

D'Zurilla, T., & Goldfried, M. (1971). Problem solving and behavior modification. *Journal of Abnormal Psychology, 78*, 107-126.

E

Earls, C. M. (1983). Some issues in the assessment of sexual deviants. *International Journal of Law and Psychiatry, 6,* 431-441.

Ebbesen, E. B., & Konecni, V. J. (1975). Decision making and information integration in the courts: The setting of bail. *Journal of Personality and Social Psychology, 32,* 805-821.

Ebbesen, E. B., & Konecni, V. J. (1981). The process of sentencing adult felons: A causal analysis of judicial decisions. In B. D. Sales (Ed.), *The trial process* (pp. 413-458). New York: Plenum Press.

Ebel, R. (1972). Essentials of educational measurement. Englewood Cliffs, NJ: Prentice-Hall.

Edinger, J. D., & Bogan, J. B. (1976). The validity of the Rorschach prognostic rating scale with incarcerated offenders. *Journal of Clinical Psychology, 32,* 887-890.

Edwards, A. (1953). *Manual for Edwards Personal Preference Schedule.* New York: Psychological Corporation.

Edwards, A. (1957). *The social desirability variable in personality assessment and research.* New York: Dryden.

Edwards, D. W., Yarvis, R. M., & Mueller, D. P. (1979). Evidence for efficacy of partial hospitalization: Data from two studies. *Hospital and Community Psychiatry, 30*(2), 97-101.

Efron, M. G. (1974). The effect of physical appearance on the judgment of guilt, interpersonal attraction, and severity of recommended punishment in a simulated jury task. *Journal of Research in Personality, 8,* 45-54.

Egeth, H. E., & McCloskey, M. (1983). Expert testimony about eyewitness behavior: Is it safe and effective? In G. Wells & E. F. Loftus (Eds.), *Eyewitness testimony: Psychological perspectives.* London: Cambridge University Press.

Ehrenkranz, J., Bliss, E., & Sheard, M. H. (1974). Plasma testosterone: Correlation with aggressive behavior and social dominance in man. *Psychosomatic Medicine, 36,* 469-475.

Eichman, W. J. (1962). Factored scales for the MMPI: A clinical and statistical manual. *Journal of Clinical Psychology, 18,* 363-395.

Eisdorfer, C. (1983). Conceptual models of aging: The challenge of a new frontier. *American Psychologist, 38,* 197-202.

Eizenstadt, S. (1968). Mental competency to stand trial. *Harvard Civil Rights-Civil Liberties Law Review, 4,* 379-413.

Ekman, P., & Friesen, W. V. (1969). Non-verbal leakage and clues to deception. *Psychiatry, 63,* 88-106.

Ekman, P., & Friesen, W. V. (1972). Hand movements. *Journal of Communication, 22,* 353-374.

Ekman, P., & Friesen, W. V. (1974). Detecting deception from body or face. *Journal of Personality and Social Psychology, 29,* 288-298.

Ekman, P., & Friesen, W. V. (1975). Unmasking the face. Englewood Cliffs, NJ: Prentice-Hall.

Ekman, P., Friesen, W., & Scherer, K. (1976). Body movements and voice pitch in deceptive interaction. *Semiotica, 16,* 23-27.

Ellinwood, E. H. (1971). Assault and homicide associated with amphetamine abuse. *American Journal of Psychiatry, 127,* 1170-1176.

Ellis, R., & Milner, J. (1981). Child abuse and locus of control. *Psychological Reports, 48,* 507-510.

Ellison, K. W., & Buckhout, R. (1981). *Psychology and criminal justice.* New York: Harper & Row.

Ellsworth, P., & Levy, R. (1969). Legislative reform of child custody adjudication: An effort to rely on social science data in formulating legal policies. *Law and Society Review, 4,* 167-233.

El-Meligi, A. M., & Osmond, H. (1970). *Manual for the clinical use of the experiential world inventory.* New York: Mens Sana Publishing.

Elstein, A. S. (1976). Clinical judgment: Psychological research and medical practice. *Science, 194,* 696-700.

Elwork, A. (1984). Psychological assessments, diagnosis and testimony: A new beginning. *Law and Human Behavior, 8,* 197-203.

Elwork, A., Alfini, J. J., & Sales, B. D. (1982). Toward understandable jury instructions. *Judicature, 65,* 432-443.

Elwork, A., & Sales, B. D. (1980). Psychological research on the jury and trial processes. In C. Petty, W. Curran, & L. McGarry (Eds.), *Modern legal medicine and forensic science.* Philadelphia, PA: F. A. Davis.

Elwork, A., Sales, B. D., & Alfini, J. J. (1982). *Writing understandable jury instructions.* Charlottesville, VA: Michie/Bobbs Merrill.

Elwork, A., Sales, B. D., & Suggs, D. (1981). The trial: A research review. In B. D. Sales (Ed.), *The trial process* (pp. 1-68). New York: Plenum Press.

Emery, R., Hetherington, E., & Fisher, L. (1983). Divorce, children, and social policy. In H. Stevenson & A. Siegel (Eds.), *Children and public policy.* Chicago, IL: University of Chicago Press.

Emler, N. P., Heather, N., & Winton, M. (1978). Delinquency and the development of moral reasoning. British *Journal of Clinical Psychology, 17,* 325-331.

Endicott, J., & Spitzer, R. L. (1978). A diagnostic interview: The schedule of affective disorders and schizophrenia. *Archives of General Psychiatry, 35,* 837-844.

Endler, N., & Magnusson, D. (1976). *Interactional psychology and personality.* New York: Wiley.

Ennis, B. (1982). *Prisoners of psychiatry: Mental patients, psychiatrists, and the law.* New York: Harcourt Brace Jovanovich.

Ennis, B., & Emery, R. (1978). *The rights of mental patients.* New York: Avon.

Ennis, B. J., & Litwack, T. R. (1974). Psychiatry and the presumption of expertise: Flipping coins in the courtroom. *California Law Review, 62,* 693-752.

Epstein, L., & Lasagna, L. (1969). Obtaining informed consent—Form or substance? *Archives of Internal Medicine, 123,* 682-688.

Epstein, S. (1979). The stability of behavior: 1. On predicting most of the people much of the time. *Journal of Personality and Social Psychology, 37,* 1097-1126.

Erickson, B., Lind, E. A., Johnson, B. C., & O'Barr, W. M. (1978). Speech style and impression formation in a court setting: The effects of "powerful" and "powerless" speech. *Journal of Experimental Social Psychology, 14,* 266-279.

Eriksen, C. W., & Collins, J. F. (1968). Sensory traces versus the psychological moment in the temporal organization of form. *Journal of Experimental Psychology, 77,* 376-382.

Erlanger, H. S., & Klegon, D. A. (1978). Socialization effects of professional school: The law school experience and student orientations to public interest careers. *Law and Society Review, 13,* 11-35.

Eron, L., & Redmount, R. (1957). The effect of legal education on attitude. *Journal of Legal Education, 9,* 431-443.

Eron, L. D. (1965). A normative study of the Thematic Apperception Test. In B. I. Murstein (Ed.), *Handbook of projective techniques* (pp. 469-509). New York: Basic Books.

Eron, L. D. (1972). Thematic Apperception Test. In O. K. Buros (Ed.), *Mental measurements yearbook* (7th ed.) (pp. 460-462). Highland Park, NJ: Gryphon Press.

Etzioni, A. (1974). Creating an imbalance. *Trial, 10,* 28-30.

Eule, J. N. (1978). The presumption of sanity: Bursting the bubble. *UCLA Law Review, 25*(4), 637-699.

Evans, F. (1967). Suggestibility in the normal waking state. *Psychological Bulletin, 67*, 114-129.

Executive Committee, Family Law Section, NJSBA. (1983). Mediation committee report. *New Jersey Family Lawyer, 11*(5), 75-80.

Exner, J. E. (1969). *The Rorschach system.* New York: Grune & Stratton.

Exner, J. E. (1974). *The Rorschach: A comprehensive system.* New York: Wiley.

Exner, J. E. (1978). *The Rorschach: A comprehensive system, Vol. 2—Current research and advanced interpretation.* New York: Wiley.

Exner, J. E. (1980). Diagnosis versus description in competency issues. *Annals of the New York Academy of Sciences*, 20-26.

Exner, J. E., & Exner, D. E. (1972). How clinicians use the Rorschach. *Journal of Personality Assessment, 36*, 403-408.

Eysenck, H., & Eysenck, S. (1968). *Eysenck Personality Questionnaire.* San Diego, CA: Educational and Industrial Testing Service.

Eysenck, H., & Furneaux, W. (1945). Primary and secondary suggestibility: An experimental and statistical study. *Journal of Experimental Psychology, 35*, 485-503.

F

Fabianic, D. (1979). Relative prestige of criminal justice doctoral programs. *Journal of Criminal Justice, 7*, 135-145.

Faden, R., & Beauchamp, T. (1980). Decision making and informed consent: A study of the impact of disclosed information. *Social Indicators Research, 7*, 313-336.

Farberow, N. L., & MacKinnon, D. (1974). A suicide prediction schedule for neuropsychiatric hospital patients. *Journal of Nervous and Mental Disease, 158*, 408-419.

Farina, A., Fisher, J. D., & Getter, H. (1978). Some consequences of changing people's views regarding the nature of mental illness. *Journal of Abnormal Psychology, 87*, 272-279.

Farrell, R. A. (1971). Class linkages of legal treatment of homosexuals. *Criminology, 9*, 49-68.

Fauman, B. J., & Fauman, M. A. (1982). Phencyclidine abuse and crime: A psychiatric perspective. *Bulletin of the American Academy of Psychiatry and the Law, 10*, 171-176.

Fauman, M. A., & Fauman, B. J. (1979). Violence associated with phencyclidine abuse. *American Journal of Psychiatry, 136*, 1584-1586.

Federal Rules of Evidence for United States Courts and Magistrates. (1979). St. Paul, MN: West Publishing.

Feeley, M. M. (1979a). Perspectives on plea bargaining. *Law and Society Review, 13*, 149-210.

Feeley, M. M. (1979b). *The process is the punishment: Handling cases in a lower criminal court.* New York: Russell Sage.

Feher, E., Vandencreek, L., & Teglasi, H. (1983). The problem of art quality in the use of human figure drawing tests. *Journal of Clinical Psychology, 39*, 268-275.

Feighner, J. P., Robins, E., Guze, S. B., Woodruff, R. A., Winokur, G., & Munoz, R. (1972). Diagnostic criteria for use in psychiatric research. *Archives of General Psychiatry, 26*, 57-63.

Feild, H. S. (1978). Juror background characteristics and attitudes toward rape: Correlates of jurors' decisions in rape trials. *Law and Human Behavior, 2*, 73-93.

Feild, H. S. (1979). Rape trials and jurors' decisions: A psycholegal analysis of the effects of victim, defendant, and case characteristics. *Law and Human Behavior, 3*, 261-284.

Feild, H. S., & Burnett, N. J. (1978). Simulated jury trials: Students v. "real" people as jurors. *Journal of Social Psychology, 104,* 287-293.

Feld, S., & Smith, C. P. (1958). An evaluation of the objectivity of the method of content analysis. In J. W. Atkinson (Ed.), *Motives in fantasy, action and society.* Princeton, NJ: Van Nostrand.

Feldman, R. S. (1976). Nonverbal disclosure of teacher deception and interpersonal affect. *Journal of Educational Psychology, 68,* 807-816.

Feldman, W. S. (1981). Episodic cerebral dysfunction: A defense in legal limbo. *Journal of Psychiatry and Law, 9,* 193-210.

Felner, R., & Farber, S. (1980). Social policy for child custody: A multidisciplinary framework. *American Journal of Orthopsychiatry, 50,* 341-347.

Felstiner, W. L. F., & Williams, L. A. (1978). Mediation as an alternative to criminal prosecution: Ideology and limitations. *Law and Human Behavior, 2,* 223-243.

Fenster, C., Wiedemann, C. F., & Locke, B. (1977). Police personality: Social science folklore and psychological measurement. In B. D. Sales (Ed.), *Psychology in the legal process.* New York: Spectrum.

Ferguson, A., & Douglas, A. (1970). A study of juvenile waiver. *San Diego Law Review, 7,* 39-54.

Fersch, E. (1980). Ethical issues for psychologists. In F. Monahan (Ed.), *Who is the client? Ethics of psychological intervention in the criminal justice system.* Washington, DC: American Psychological Association.

Fillenbaum, G. (1978a). Conceptualization and development of the Multidimensional Functional Assessment Questionnaire. In Center for the Study of Aging and Human Development, *Multidimensional functional assessment: The OARS methodology* (pp. 16-24). Durham, NC: Duke University.

Fillenbaum, G. (1978b). Validity and reliability of the Multidimensional Functional Assessment Questionnaire. In Center for the Study of Aging and Human Development, *Multidimensional functional assessment: The OARS methodology* (pp. 25-35). Durham, NC: Duke University.

Fillenbaum, G., & Maddox, G. (1977). *Assessing the functional status of LRHS participants: Technique, findings, implications* (Technical report No. 2). Durham, NC: Duke University, Center for the Study of Aging and Human Development.

Fillenbaum, G., & Smyer, M. (1981). The development, validity, and reliability of the OARS Multidimensional Functional Assessment Questionnaire. *Journal of Gerontology, 36,* 428-434.

Fillenbaum, G., Dellinger, D., Maddox, G., & Pfeiffer, E. (1978). Assessment of individual functional status in a program evaluation and resource allocation model. In Center for the Study of Aging and Human Development, *Multidimensional function assessment: The OARS methodology* (pp. 3-12). Durham, NC: Duke University.

Filsinger, E. (1981). Parental attitudes toward child rearing and the psychological differentiation of adolescents. *Journal of Genetic Psychology, 139,* 277-284.

Filskov, S. B., & Goldstein, S. G. (1974). Diagnostic validity of Halstead-Reitan neuropsychological battery. *Journal of Consulting and Clinical Psychology, 42,* 382-388.

Fincham, F. D., & Jaspars, J. M. (1980). Attribution of responsibility: From man the scientist to man as lawyer. In L. Berkowitz (Ed.), *Advances in experimental social psychology,* Vol. 13 (pp. 82-139). New York: Academic Press.

Fingarette, H., & Hasse, A. F. (1979). *Mental disabilities and criminal responsibility.* Berkeley, CA: University of California Press.

Fink, L., & Hyatt, M. P. (1978). Drug use and criminal behavior. *Journal of Drug Education, 8,* 139-149.

Finkelstein, M. (1978). *Quantitative methods in law*. New York: Free Press.

Finney, J. C. (1965). Development of a new set of MMPI scales. *Psychological Reports, 17*, 707-713.

Finsterbusch, K., & Hamilton, M. R. (1978, March-June). The rationalization of social science research in policy studies. *International Journal of Comparative Sociology, 19*, 1-2, 90-106.

Fishbein, M., & Aizen, I. (1975). *Belief, attitude, intention and behavior: An introduction to theory and research*. Reading, MA: Addison-Wesley.

Fisher, C. M., & Adams, R. D. (1964). Transient global amnesia. *Acta Neurological Scandinavica, 40*, 46-72.

Fisher, E., & Fisher, R. (1976). Parental correlates of Rorschach human movement responses in children. *Perceptual and Motor Skills, 42*, 31-34.

Fisher, E., & Fisher, R. (1981). Parents of disturbed enuretic and nonenuretic children. *Perceptual and Motor Skills, 52*, 181-182.

Fisher, R. J. (1982). *Social psychology: An applied approach*. New York: St. Martin's Press.

Fishman, D. B., & Loftus, E. F. (1978). Expert psychological testimony on eyewitness identification. *Law and Psychology Review, 4*, 87-103.

Fitzgerald, J., Peszke, M., & Goodwin, R. (1978). Competency evaluations in Connecticut. *Hospital and Community Psychiatry, 29*, 450-453.

Fleishman, E. A. (1982). Systems for describing human tasks. *American Psychologist, 37*, 821-834.

Fontes, N. E., & Bundens, R. W. (1980). Persuasion during the trial process. In M. E. Roloff & G. R. Miller (Eds.), *Persuasion: New directions in theory and research*. Beverly Hills, CA: Sage Publications.

Ford, C., & Beach, F. (1951). *Patterns of sexual behavior*. New York: Harper and Row.

Forst, B., Rhodes, W., Dimm, J., Gelman, A., & Mullin, B. (1983). Targeting federal research on recidivists: An empirical view. *Federal Probation, 10*.

Fosdel, F. A. (1977). Contributions and limitations of psychiatric testimony. *Wisconsin Bar Bulletin, 50*, 31.

Foss, R. D. (1981). Structural effects in simulated jury decision making. *Journal of Personality and Social Psychology, 40*, 1055-1062.

Foster, H. (1978). Informed consent of mental patients. In W. Barton & C. Sanborn (Eds.), *Law and the mental health professions* (pp. 71-95). New York: International Universities Press.

Foster, H., & Freed, D. (1964). Child custody. *New York University Law Review, 39*, 423-443.

Foulds, G. A., Caine, T., & Creasy, M. A. (1960). Aspects of extra and intrapunitive expression in mental illness. *Journal of Mental Science, 106*, 599-610.

Foust, L. L. (1979). Research articles and comments. The legal significance of clinical formulation of firesetting behavior. *International Journal of Law and Psychiatry, 2*, 371-387.

Fox, J. L. (1984). PET scan controversy aired. *Science, 224*, 143-144.

Frank, J. (1930). *Law and the modern mind*. Magnolia, MA: Peter Smith Publisher.

Frank, J. (1950). *Courts on trial*. Princeton: Princeton University Press.

Frankel, M. (1972). Lawlessness in sentencing. *University of Cincinnati Law Review, 41*, 1-54.

Frankel, M. (1973). Comments of an independent variable sentencer. *University of Cincinnati Law Review, 42*, 667-671.

Franks, J. J., & Bransford, J. D. (1972). The acquisition of abstract ideas. *Journal of Verbal Learning and Verbal Behavior, 11*, 311-315.

Frederick, C. (1975). Determining dangerousness. In V. Bradley & G. Clark (Eds.), *Paper victories and hard realities: The implementation of the lethal and constitutional rights of the mentally disabled*.

Frederick, C. (1978a). *Dangerous behavior: A problem in law and mental health*. NIMH, DHEW Publication No. (ADM) 78-563 (pp. 153-191). Washington, DC: Superintendent of Documents, U. S. Government Printing Office.

Frederick, C. (1978b). An overview of dangerousness: Its complexities and consequences. In *Dangerous behavior: A problem in law and mental health*. NIMH, DHEW Publication No. (ADM) 78-563. Washington, DC: Superintendent of Documents, U. S. Government Printing Office.

Fredericks, M. (1976). Custody battles: Mental health professionals in the courtroom. In S. Koocher (Ed.), *Children's rights and the mental health professions* (pp. 41-52). New York: Wiley.

Frederiksen, N. (1972). Toward a taxonomy of situations. *American Psychologist, 27,* 114-123.

Freed, D. J., & Foster, H. H., Jr. (1981). Divorce in the fifty states: An overview. *Family Law Quarterly, 14,* 229-284.

Freed, D. J., & Foster, H. H. (1982). Family law in the fifty states: An overview as of September, 1982. *Family Law Reporter, 8,* 4065-4104.

Freedland, K., & Craine, J. (1981). Personal communication.

Freedman, D. X. (1984). Psychiatric epidemiology counts. *Archives of General Psychiatry, 41,* 931-933.

Freedman, L. Z. (1983). *By reason of insanity: Essays on psychiatry and the law*. Wilmington, DE: Scholarly Resources.

Freedman, L. Z., Guttmacher, M., & Overholser, W. (1961). Mental disease or defect excluding responsibility: A psychiatric view of the American Law Institute's model penal code proposal. *American Journal of Psychiatry, 118,* 32-34.

Freeman, H., & Weihofen, H. (1972). *Clinical law training*. St. Paul, MN: West Publishing.

Freeman, W., Pichard, A., & Smith, H. (1981). Effect of informed consent and educational background on patient knowledge, anxiety, and subjective responses to cardiac catheterization. *Catheterization and Cardiovascular Diagnosis, 7,* 119-134.

French, W. L., & Bell, C. H. (1978). *Organization development: Behavioral science interventions for organization improvement* (2nd ed.). Englewood Cliffs, NJ: Prentice-Hall.

Freud, S. (1959a). *Fragment of an analysis of a case of hysteria (1905)*. Collected papers, 3. New York: Basic Books.

Freud, S. (1959b). Psycho-analysis and the ascertaining of truth in courts of law (1906). In *Clinical papers and papers on technique, collected papers* Vol. 2 (pp. 13-24). New York: Basic Books.

Freund, K., Langevin, R., & Barlow, D. (1974). Comparison of two penile measures of erotic arousal. *Behaviour Research and Therapy, 12,* 355-359.

Fried, M., Kaplan, J. J., & Klein, K. W. (1975). Juror selection: An analysis of voir dire. In R. J. Simon (Ed.), *The jury system in America*. Beverly Hills, CA: Sage Publishing.

Friedman, H. (1972). Trial by jury: Criteria for convictions, jury size and type I and type II errors. *American Statistician, 26,* 21-23.

Friedman, L. (1967). Legal rules and the process of social change. *Stanford Law Review, 19,* 786-840.

Friedman, L. (1979). Plea bargaining in historical perspective. *Law and Society Review, 13,* 247-260.

Friedman, L. R. (1982). Unwrapping the riddle of the brain-injured patient by utilizing the beam EEG. *American Journal of Forensic Psychiatry, 3,* 47-52.

Friedman, S. (1969). Relation of parental attitudes toward child rearing and patterns of social behavior in middle childhood. *Psychological Reports, 24,* 575-579.

Fromm, E. (1973). *The anatomy of human destructiveness*. New York: Holt, Reinhart, and Winston.

Fukunaga, K., Pasewark, R., Hawkins, M., & Gudeman, H. (1981). Insanity plea: Interexaminer agreement and concordance of psychiatric opinion and court verdict. *Law and Human Behavior, 5,* 325-328.

Fuller, L. (1961). The adversary system. In H. Berman (Ed.), *Talks on American law*. New York: Vintage Books.

G

Gable, R. K. (1983). Malpractice liability of psychologists. In B. D. Sales (Ed.), *The professional psychologist's handbook* (pp. 457-491). New York: Plenum Press.

Gaines, I. D. (1956). The clinical psychologist as an expert witness in a personal injury case. *Marquette Law Review, 39*, 239-244.

Gaines, R., Sandgrund, A., Green, A., & Power, E. (1978). Etiological factors in child maltreatment: A multivariate study of abusing, neglecting, and normal mothers. *Journal of Abnormal Psychology, 87*, 531-540.

Galanter, M. (1974). Why the "haves" come out ahead: Speculations on the limits of social change. *Law and Society Review, 9*, 95-160.

Gallivan, G. M. (1978). Insanity, bifurcation and due process: Can values survive doctrine? *Land and Water Law Review, 13*, 515-555.

Garcetti, G., & Suarez, J. M. (1968). The liability of psychiatric hospitals for the acts of their patients. *American Journal of Psychiatry, 124*, 961-968.

Gardner, M. R. (1976). The myth of the impartial psychiatric expert: Some comments concerning criminal responsibility and the decline of the age of therapy. *Law and Psychology Review, 2*, 99-118.

Gardner, R. A. (1982). *Family evaluation in child custody litigation*. Creekskill, NJ: Creative Therapeutics.

Gass, R. (1978). The psychologist as expert witness: Science in the courtroom. *Maryland Law Review, 38*, 539-621.

Gauron, E. F., & Dickinson, J. K. (1966). Diagnostic decision-making in psychiatry: Information usage. *Archives of General Psychiatry, 14*, 225-232.

Gaylord, J. J. (1979). The aetiology of repeated serious physical assaults by husbands on wives (wife battering). *Medical Science Law, 19*(1), 19-24.

Geen, R., & Berkowitz, L. (1967). Some conditions facilitating the occurrence of aggression after the observation of violence. *Journal of Personality, 35*, 666-676.

Geis, G., & Meier, R. (1978). Looking backward and forward: Criminologists on criminology and career. *Criminology, 16*, 273-288.

Geizer, R., Burick, D., & Soldow, G. (1977). Deception and judgment accuracy: A study in person perception. *Personality and Social Psychology Bulletin, 3*, 446-449.

Geller, J., & Lister, E. (1978). The process of criminal commitment for pretrial psychiatric examination: An evaluation. *American Journal of Psychiatry, 135*, 53-60.

George, L., & Bearon, L. (1980). *Quality of life in older persons*. New York: Human Sciences Press.

Georgetown Law Journal Staff. (1980). Project: Tenth annual review of criminal procedure: United States Supreme Court and Courts of Appeal, 1979-80. *Georgetown Law Journal, 69*, 211-639.

Georgetown Law Journal Staff. (1981). Project: Eleventh annual review of criminal procedure: United States Supreme Court and Courts of Appeal, 1980-81. *Georgetown Law Journal, 70*, 465-860.

Gerbasi, K. D., Zuckerman, M., & Reis, H. T. (1977). Justice needs a new blindfold: A review of mock jury research. *Psychological Bulletin, 84*, 323-345.

Gergen, K. J. (1973). Social psychology as history. *Journal of Personality and Social Psychology, 26*, 309-320.

Giannoti, T., & Doyle, R. (1982, December). The effectiveness of parental training on learning disabled children and their parents. *Elementary School Guidance and Counseling*, pp. 131-136.

Gibbins, T. C. N., & Williams, J. E. H. (1977). Medical/legal aspects of amnesia. In C. W. M. Whitty and O. L. Vangwill (Eds.), *Amnesia: Clinical, psychological, and medical/legal aspects* (pp. 345-364). London: Butterworth.

Gibbs, E. L., & Gibbs, F. A. (1951). Electroencephalographic evidence of thalamic and hypothalamic epilepsy. *Neurology, 1*, 136-144.

Gifford, D. G. (1983). Meaningful reform of plea bargaining: The control of prosecutorial discretion. *University of Illinois Law Review*, pp. 37-98.

Gilberstadt, H., & Duker, J. (1965). *A handbook for clinical and actuarial MMPI interpretation*. Philadelphia, PA: Saunders.

Gilsinan, J. (1982). *Doing justice: How the system works as seen by the participants*. New York: Prentice-Hall.

Ginsberg, L. H. (1968). Civil rights of the mentally ill: A review of the issues. *Community Mental Health Journal, 4*, 244-250.

Glaser, G. (1979). Discretion in juvenile justice. In L. Abt & I. R. Stuart (Eds.), *Social psychology and discretionary law*. New York: Van Nostrand Reinhold.

Gleick, J. (1978, August 21). Getting away with murder. *New York Times*, pp. 21-27.

Glezor, D. (1981). Current contributions for psychiatry in rape cases. *Psychologie Medicale, 13*, 1583-1585.

Glick, I. O., Weiss, R. S., & Parkes, C. M. (1974). *The first year of bereavement*. New York: Wiley.

Glick, P. C. (1979). Children of divorced parents in demographic perspective. *Journal of Social Issues, 35*(4), 170-181.

Glueck, S. S. (1925). *Mental disorder and the criminal law*. Boston, MA: Little, Brown.

Glodofski, O. B. (1974). The psychology of testimony. *Vyestnik Prava, No. 16-18*, 185.

Goebel, R. A. (1983). Detection of faking on the Halstead-Reitan neuropsychological test battery. *Journal of Clinical Psychology, 39*, 731-742.

Gold, A. V. (1981). Drunkenness and criminal responsibility. In S. J. Hucker, C. D. Webster, & M. H. Ben-Arons (Eds.), *Mental disorder and criminal responsibility* (pp. 63-78). Toronto: Butterworth.

Gold, L. (1973). Discovery of mental illness and mental defect among offenders. *Journal of Forensic Sciences, 18*, 125-129.

Goldaber, I. (1979). A typology of hostage-takers. *Police Chief, 46*(6), 21-23.

Goldberg, L. R., & Rorer, L. G. (1963). Test-retest item statistics for original and reversed MMPI items. *Oregon Research Institute Monographs, 3*, (Serial No. 1).

Golden, C. J. (1979). Diagnosis of multiple sclerosis using double discrimination scales in the Luria-Nebraska neuropsychological battery. *International Journal of Neuroscience, 910*, 51-56.

Golden, C. J. (1980). In reply to Adam's "In search of Luria's battery: A false start." *Journal of Consulting and Clinical Psychology, 48*, 517-521.

Golden, C. J. (1984). The Luria-Nebraska neuropsychological battery in forensic assessment of head injury. *Psychiatric Annals, 14*, 532-538.

Golden, C. J., Ariel, R. N., McKay, S. E., Wilkening, G. N., Wolf, B. A., & MacInnes, W. D. (1982). The Luria-Nebraska neuropsychological battery: Theoretical orientation and comment. *Journal of Consulting and Clinical Psychology, 50*, 291-300.

Golden, C. J., Ariel, R. N., Moses, J. A., Wilkening, G. N., McKay, S. E., & MacInnes, W. D. (1982). Analytical techniques in the interpretation of the Luria-Nebraska neuropsychological battey. *Journal of Consulting and Clinical Psychology, 50*, 40-48.

Golden, C. J., Fross, K., & Graber, B. (1981). Split-half reliability and item consistency of the Luria-Nebraska neuropsychological battery. *Journal of Consulting and Clinical Psychology, 49*, 304-305.

Golden, C. J., Hammeke, T. A., & Purisch, A. D. (1978). Diagnostic validity of standardized neuropsychological battery derived from Luria's neuropsychological tests. *Journal of Consulting and Clinical Psychology, 46*, 1258-1265.

Golden, C. J., Hammeke, T. A., & Purisch, A. D. (1980). *The Luria-Nebraska battery manual*. Palo Alto, CA: Western Psychological Services.

Golden, C. J., Moses, J. A., Fishburne, F. J., Engum, E., Lewis, G. P., Wisniewski, A. M., Conley, F. K., Berg, R. A., & Graber, B. (1981). Cross validation of the Luria-Nebraska neuropsychological battery for the presence, lateralization, and localization of brain damage. *Journal of Consulting and Clinical Psychology, 49*, 491-507.

Golden, C. J., Moses, J. A., Zelazowksi, R., Graber, B., Zatz, L. M., Horvath, T. B., & Berger, P. A. (1980). Cerebral ventricular size and neuropsychological impairment in young chronic schizophrenics. *Archives of General Psychiatry, 37*, 619-623.

Golden, J., & Johnson, G. (1970). Problems of distortion in doctor-patient communications. *Psychiatry in Medicine, 1*, 127-149.

Goldfried, M., & D'Zurilla, T. (1969). A behavioral-analytic model for assessing competence. In C. D. Spielberger (Ed.), *Current topics in clinical and community psychology*, Vol. 1 (pp. 151-196). New York: Academic Press.

Golding, S., Roesch, R., & Schreiber, J. (1984). Assessment and conceptualization of competency to stand trial: Preliminary data on the Interdisciplinary Fitness Interview. *Law and Human Behavior, 9*, 321-334.

Goldman, B. A., & Saunders, J. L. (1974). *Directory of unpublished experimental mental measures*, Vol. 1. New York: Behavioral Publications.

Goldman, S., & Jahnige, T. (1976). *The Federal courts as a political system* (2nd ed.). New York: Harper & Row.

Goldstein, A. G. (1977). The fallibility of the eyewitness: Psychological evidence. In B. D. Sales (Ed.), *Psychology in the legal process*. New York: Spectrum Publications.

Goldstein, A. S. (1967). *The insanity defense*. New Haven, CT: Yale University Press.

Goldstein, G., & Shelly, C. (1984). Discriminative validity of various intelligence and neuropsychological tests. *Journal of Consulting and Clinical Psychology, 52*, 383-389.

Goldstein, J., Freud, A., & Solnit, A. (1973). *Beyond the best interest of the child*. New York: Free Press.

Goldstein, M. (1974). Brain research and violent behavior. *Archives of Neurology, 30*, 1-34.

Goldstein, R. L. (1973). The fitness factor, Part I: The psychiatrist's role in determining competency. *American Journal of Psychiatry, 130*(10), 1144-1147.

Goldstein, R. L., & Stone, M. (1977). When doctors disagree: Differing views on competency. *Bulletin of the American Academy of Psychiatry and the Law, 5*, 90-97.

Goldstein, S. G., Deysach, R. E., & Kleinknecht, R. A. (1973). Effects of experience and the amount of information on identification of cerebral impairment. *Journal of Consulting and Clinical Psychology, 41*, 30-34.

Goldzband, M. (1982). *Consulting in child custody*. Lexington, MA: Lexington Books.

Good, M. I. (1978). Primary affective disorder, aggression, and criminality. *Archives of General Psychiatry, 35*, 954-960.

Goodwin, D. W. (1969). Alcohol and recall: State-dependent effects in men. *Science, 163*, 1358-1360.

Goodwin, D. W., Alderson, P., & Rosenthal, R. (1971). Clinical significance of hallucinations in psychiatric disorders. A study of 116 hallucinatory patients. *Archives of General Psychiatry, 24,* 76-80.

Goodwin, D. W., Crane, J. B., & Guze, S. B. (1969). Phenomenological aspects of alcoholic "blackout." *British Journal of Psychiatry, 115,* 1033-1038.

Gordley, J. (1984). Legal reasoning: An introduction. *California Law Review, 72,* 138-177.

Gordon, L., & Mooney, R. (1950). *Mooney Problem Check List.* New York: Psychological Corporation.

Gordon, R. H. (1976). Diagnostic compliance in Rorschach interpretation as a function of group member status. *Journal of Consulting and Clinical Psychology, 44,* 826-831.

Gordon, R. I. (1976). The application of psychology to the law. *Law and Psychology Review, 2,* 1-8.

Gordon, R. W. (1978). Crystal-balling death? *Baylor Law Review, 30,* 35-65.

Gorenstein, G. W., & Ellsworth, P. C. (1980). Effect of choosing an incorrect photograph on a later identification by an eyewitness. *Journal of Applied Psychology, 65,* 616-622.

Gorman, W. E. (1984). Neurological malingering. *Behavioral Sciences and the Law, 2,* 67-74.

Gottfredson, D. M. (1971). Research: Who needs it? *Crime and Delinquency, 17,* 11-22.

Gottfredson, D. M., & Ballard, K. B., Jr. (1963, September). *Social agency effectiveness study* (Report Number One). Vacaville, CA: Institute for the Study of Crime and Delinquency, California Medical Facility.

Gottfredson, D. M., Hoffman, P. B., Sigler, M. H., & Wilkins, L. T. (1975). Making paroling policy explicit. *Crime and Delinquency, 21,* 34-44.

Gottfredson, G. D., & Dyer, S. E. (1978). Health service providers in psychology. *American Psychologist, 33,* 314-338.

Gough, H. G. (1947). Simulated patterns on the MMPI. *Journal of Abnormal and Social Psychology, 42,* 215-225.

Gough, H. G. (1950). The F-K dissimulation index for the Minnesota Multiphasic Personality Inventory. *Journal of Consulting Psychology, 14,* 408-413.

Gough, H. G. (1954). Some common misconceptions about neuroticism. *Journal of Consulting Psychology, 18,* 287-292.

Gough, H. G. (1955). *Reference handbook for the Gough Adjective Check List.* Berkeley, CA: Personality Assessment and Research Center.

Gough, H. G. (1957). *California Psychological Inventory manual.* Palo Alto, CA: Consulting Psychologists Press.

Gough, H. G. (1960). Theory and measurement of socialization. *Journal of Consulting Psychology, 24,* 23-30.

Gough, H. G., McClosky, H., & Meehl, P. E. (1951). A personality scale for dominance. *Journal of Abnormal and Social Psychology, 46,* 360-366.

Gough, H. G., McClosky, H., & Meehl, P. E. (1952). A personality scale for social responsibility. *Journal of Abnormal and Social Psychology, 47,* 78-80.

Gough, H. G., & Peterson, D. R. (1952). The identification and measurement of predispositional factors in crime and delinquency. *Journal of Consulting Psychology, 16,* 207-212.

Gough, H. G., Wenk, E. A., & Rozynko, V. V. (1965). Parole outcome as predicted from the CPI, the MMPI, and a base expectancy table. *Journal of Abnormal Psychology, 70,* 432-441.

Gourvitz, E. H. (1983). Divorce mediation: An alternative to the adversary approach. *New Jersey Family Lawyer, 11*(5), 81-85.

Gove, W., & Fain, T. (1977). A comparison of voluntary and committed psychiatric patients. *Archives of General Psychiatry, 34,* 669-676.

Gozansky, N. (1976). Court-ordered investigations in custody cases. *Willamette Law Journal, 12,* 511-526.

Graber, G. C., & Marsh, F. H. (1979, February). Ought a defendant be drugged to stand trial? *Hastings Center Report,* pp. 8-10.

Graham, J. R. (1977). *The MMPI: A practical guide.* New York: Oxford University Press.

Graham, M. H. (1977-1978). Impeaching the professional expert witness by a showing of financial interest. *Indiana Law Journal, 53*(35), 35-53.

Grand Jury Defense Office. (1982). The witness' appearance before the grand jury. In National Lawyer's Guild (Ed.), *Representation of witness before federal grand juries.* New York: Clark Boardman.

Grauer, H., & Birnbom, F. (1975). A geriatric functional rating scale to determine the need for institutional care. *Journal of the American Geriatric Society, 23,* 472-476.

Gray, R. A., Jr., & Hammond, S. R., Jr. (1978). Opinion and expert testimony. *Mississippi Law Journal, 49,* 1-30.

Graybill, D. (1978). Relationship of maternal child-rearing behaviors to children's self-esteem. *Journal of Psychology, 100,* 45-47.

Graybill, D., & Gabel, H. (1978). Factor analysis of the Children's Reports of Parental Behavior Inventory: A replication of preadolescents. *Psychological Reports, 42,* 953-954.

Grayson, B., & Stein, M. I. (1981). Attracting assault: Victim's nonverbal cues. *Journal of Communication, 31,* 68-75.

Grayson, H. (1951). *A psychological admissions testing program and manual.* Los Angeles, CA: Veterans Administration Center, Neuropsychiatric Hospital.

Green, R. K., & Schaefer, A. B. (1984). *Forensic psychology: A primer for legal and mental health professionals.* Springfield, IL: Charles C. Thomas.

Greenberg, D. F. (1974). Involuntary psychiatric commitments to prevent suicide. New York *University Law Review, 49*(2,3), 227-268.

Greenberg, J. (1976). *Judicial process and social change.* St. Paul, MN: West Publishing.

Greenberg, M. S., & Ruback, R. B. (1982). *Social psychology of the criminal justice system.* Monterey, CA: Brooks/Cole.

Greenberg, M. S., Ruback, R. B., & Westcott, D. R. (1982). Decision making by crime victims: A multi-method approach. *Law and Society Review, 17,* 85-104.

Greenberg, S. W. (1976). The relationship between crime and amphetamine abuse: An empirical review. *Contemporary Drug Problems, 5,* 101-130.

Greene, R. L. (1978). An empirically derived MMPI carelessness scale. *Journal of Clinical Psychology, 34,* 407-410.

Greene, R. L. (1979). Response consistency on the MMPI: The TR index. *Journal of Personality Assessment, 43,* 69-71.

Greene, R. L. (1980). *MMPI, an interpretive manual.* New York: Grune & Stratton.

Greenspan, E. L. (1978). Insanity and psychiatric evidence. *Crown's Newsletter, Crown's Attorneys of Ontario,* 1-40.

Gregory, C. O., Kalven, H., & Epstein, R. A. (1977). *Cases and materials on torts* (3rd ed.). Boston: Little, Brown.

Gregory, W. L., Mower, J. C., & Linder, D. E. (1978). Social psychology and plea bargaining: Applications, methodology, and theory. *Journal of Personality and Social Psychology, 36,* 1521-1530.

Greif, J. B. (1979). Fathers, children, and joint custody. *American Journal of Orthopsychiatry, 50,* 311-319.

Griffitt, W., & Jackson, T. (1973). Simulated jury decisions: The influence of jury-defendant attitude similarity-dissimilarity. *Social Behavior and Personality, 1*, 1-7.

Griffore, R. J., & Samuels, D. D. (1978). Moral judgment of residents of a maximum security correctional facility. *The Journal of Psychology, 100*, 3-7.

Grinspoon, L., & Bakalar, J. V. (1978). Drug abuse, crime, and the antisocial personality: Some conceptual issues. In W. H. Reid (Ed.), *The psychopath: A comprehensive study of antisocial disorders and behavior* (pp. 234-243). New York: Bruner-Mazel.

Grisso, T. (1980). Juveniles' capacity to waive Miranda rights: An empirical analysis. *California Law Review, 68*, 1134-1166.

Grisso, T. (1981). *Juveniles' waiver of rights: Legal and psychological competence*. New York: Plenum Press.

Grisso, T., & Pomicter, C. (1977). Interrogation of juveniles: An empirical study of procedures, safeguards, and rights waiver. *Law and Human Behavior, 1*, 321-342.

Grisso, T., & Vierling, L. (1978). Minors' consent to treatment: A developmental perspective. *Professional Psychology, 9*, 412-427.

Groethe, R. (1977). Overt dangerous behavior as a constitutional requirement for involuntary civil commitment of the mentally ill. *University of Chicago Law Review, 44*, 562-593.

Gronlund, N. (1968). *Readings in measurement and evaluation*. New York: Macmillan.

Gronlund, N. (1976). *Measurement and evaluation in teaching*. New York: Macmillan.

Grossman, J. (1980). The forensic psychologist and the rapist: Disposition and treatment. In G. Cooke (Ed.), *The role of the forensic psychologist*. Springfield, IL: Charles C. Thomas.

Grostic, J. M. (1978). The constitutionality of Michigan's guilty but mentally ill verdict. *University of Michigan Journal of Law Reform, 12*, 118-199.

Groth, A. N. (1979). *Men who rape: The psychology of the offender*. New York: Plenum.

Groth, A. N., & Birnbaum, H. J. (1978). Adult sexual orientation an attraction to underage persons. *Archives of Sexual Behavior, 7*, 175-181.

Groth, A. N., & Burgess, A. W. (1977). Rape: A sexual deviation. *American Journal of Orthopsychiatry, 47*, 400-406.

Groth, A. N., Burgess, A. W., Birnbaum, H. J., & Gary, T. S. (1978). A study of the child molester: Myths and realities. *LAE Journal of the American Criminal Justice Association, 41*, 17-22.

Group for the Advancement of Psychiatry. (1973). *The joys and sorrows of parenthood*. New York: Charles Scribner's Sons.

Group for the Advancement of Psychiatry. (1974). *Misuse of psychiatry in the criminal courts: Competency to stand trial*. New York: Committee on Psychiatry and the Law.

Group for the Advancement of Psychiatry. (1980). *Divorce, child custody and the family*. New York: Mental Health Materials Center.

Group for the Advancement of Psychiatry. (1983). Criminal responsibility and psychiatric expert testimony. In L. Z. Freeman (Ed.), *By reason of insanity: Essays on psychiatry and the law* (pp. 31-35). Wilmington, DE: Scholarly Resources.

Grove, W. M. (1985). Boot-strapping diagnoses using Bayes's Theorem: It's not worth the trouble. *Journal of Consulting and Clinical Psychology, 53*, 261-263.

Grover, S. C. (1981). *Toward a psychology of the scientist: Implications of psychological research for contemporary philosophy of science*. Calgary: University of Calgary Press.

Grow, R., McVaugh, W., & Eno, T. D. (1980). Faking and the MMPI. *Journal of Clinical Psychology, 36*, 910-917.

Grunder, T. (1978). Two formulas for determining the readability of subject consent forms. *American Psychologist, 33,* 773-775.

Gudeman, H. (1981). Legal sanctions and the clinician. *Clinical Psychologist, 34,* 15-17.

Gudjonsson, G. (1983). Suggestibility, intelligence, memory recall and personality: An experimental study. *British Journal of Psychiatry, 142,* 35-37.

Gudjonsson, G. (1984a). Interrogative suggestibility: Comparison between "false confessors and deniers" in criminal traits. *Medicine, Science and the Law, 24,* 56-60.

Gudjonsson, G. (1984b). A new scale of interrogative suggestibility. *Personality and Individual Differences, 5,* 303-314.

Gudjonsson, G., & Lister, S. (1984). Interrogative suggestibility in its relationship with self-esteem and control. *Journal of the Forensic Science Society, 24,* 99-110.

Gudjonsson, G., & Singh, K. (1984). Criminal convictions and its relationship with interrogative suggestibility. *Journal of Adolescence, 7,* 29-34.

Guion, R. (1974). Open a new window: Validities and values in psychological measurement. *American Psychologist, 29,* 287-296.

Guion, R. (1977). Content validity: Three years of talk–What's the action? *Public Personnel Management, 6,* 407-414.

Guion, R. (1978). Scoring of content domain samples: The problem of fairness. *Journal of Applied Psychology, 63,* 499-506.

Guion, R. (1983). Standards for psychological measurement. In B. D. Sales (Ed.), *The professional psychologist's handbook* (pp. 111-140). New York: Plenum Press.

Gulliver, P. (1979). *Disputes and negotiations: A cross-cultural perspective.* New York: Academic Press.

Gunn, A. (1977). Mental impairment in the elderly: Medical-legal assessment. *Journal of the American Geriatrics Society, 24,* 193-198.

Gunn, J., & Bonn, F. (1971). Criminality and violence in epileptic prisoners. *British Journal of Psychiatry, 118,* 337-343.

Gunn, J., & Fenton, G. (1969). Epilepsy in prisons: A diagnostic survey. *British Medical Journal, 4,* 226-328.

Gunn, L. M. (1979). California revises its insanity test: An analysis of criteria and practical effect. *Criminal Justice Journal, 2,* 253-269.

Gurel, L., Linn, M., & Linn, B. (1972). Physical and Mental Impairment-of-Function Evaluation in the aged: The PAMIE Scale. *Journal of Gerontology, 27,* 83-90.

Gurevitz, H. (1977). Tarasoff: Protective privilege versus public peril. *American Journal of Psychiatry, 134,* 289-282.

Gurland, B. (1973). A broad clinical assessment of psychopathology in the aged. In C. Eisdorfer & M. Lawton (Eds.), *The psychology of adult development and aging* (pp. 343-377). Washington, DC: American Psychological Association.

Gutheil, T. G. (1980). Restraint versus treatment: Seclusion as discussed in the Boston State Hospital case. *American Journal of Psychiatry, 137*(6), 718-719.

Gutheil, T. G., & Appelbaum, P. S. (1982). *Clinical handbook of psychiatry and the law.* New York: McGraw-Hill.

Guze, S. (1976). *Criminality and psychiatric disorders.* Oxford University Press.

Guze, S. B., Goodwin, D. W., & Crane, J. B. (1969). Criminality and psychiatric disorders. *Archives of General Psychiatry, 20,* 583-591.

Gynther, M. D., Altman, H., & Sletten, I. W. (1973). Replicated correlates of MMPI two point code types: The Missouri actuarial system. *Journal of Clinical Psychology, Monograph Supplement No. 39.*

Gynther, M. D., Altman, H., & Warbin, R. (1973). Interpretation of uninterpretable MMPI profiles. *Journal of Consulting and Clinical Psychology, 40*, 70-83.

Gynther, M. D., Altman, H., Warbin, R. W., & Sletten, I. W. (1972). A new actuarial system for MMPI interpretation: Rationale and methodology. *Journal of Clinical Psychology, 28*, 173-179.

Gynther, M. D., Burkhart, B. R., & Hovanitz, C. (1979). Do face-valid items have more predictive validity than subtle items? The case of the MMPI Pd scale. *Journal of Consulting and Clinical Psychology, 47*, 295-300.

Gynther, M. D., Fowler, R. D., & Erdberg, P. (1971). False positives galore: The application of standard MMPI criteria to a rural, isolated, Negro sample. *Journal of Clinical Psychology, 27*, 234-237.

H

Hackler, J. C. (1978). The dangers of political naivete and excessive complexity in evaluating delinquency prevention programs. *Evaluation and Program Planning, 1*, 273-283.

Hadar, I., & Snortum, J. R. (1975). The eye of the beholder: Differential perceptions of police by the police and the public. *Criminal Justice and Behavior, 2*(1), 37-54.

Haddock, M., & McQueen, W. (1983). Assessing employee potentials for abuse. *Journal of Clinical Psychology, 39*, 1021-1029.

Hafemeister, T., & Sales, B. (1984). The use of interdisciplinary teams of health related professionals in guardianship and conservatorship proceedings. *Law and Human Behavior, 8*, 335-354.

Hafner, H., & Boker, W. (1973). Mentally disordered violent offenders. *Social Psychiatry, 8*, 220-229.

Hain, J. D., Smith, B. M., & Stevenson, I. (1966). Effectiveness and processes of interviewing with drugs. *Journal of Psychiatric Research, 4*, 95-106.

Hall, H. V. (1982). Dangerousness predictions and the maligned forensic professional: Suggestions for detecting distortion of true basal violence. *Criminal Justice and Behavior, 9*, 3-12.

Hall, H. V. (1983). Guilty but mentally ill: Feedback from state attorney general offices. *Bulletin of the American Academy of Forensic Psychologists, 4*, 2-7.

Hall, H. V (1984). Predicting dangerousness for the courts. *American Journal of Forensic Psychology, 4*, 5-25.

Hall, H. V. (1985). Cognitive and volitional capacity assessment: A proposed decision tree. *American Journal of Forensic Psychology, 111*, 3-17.

Hall, H. V. (1986). The forensic distortion analysis: A proposed decision tree. *American Journal of Forensic Psychology, 4*, 31-59.

Hall, H. V. (1987). *Violence prediction: Guidelines for the forensic practitioner.* Springfield, IL: Charles C. Thomas.

Hall, H. V., Catlin, E., Boissevain, A., & Westgate, J. (1984). Dangerous myths about predicting dangerousness. *American Journal of Forensic Psychology, 2*, 173-193.

Hall, H. V., Price, A. B., Shinedling, M., Peizer, S. B., & Massey, R. H. (1973). Control of aggressive behavior in a group of retardates using positive and negative reinforcement procedures. *Training School Bulletin, 70*, 179-186.

Hall, H. V., Shinedling, M. A., & Thorne, D. E. (1973). Overcoming situation-specific problems associated with typical institutional attempts to suppress self-mutilative behavior. *Training School Bulletin, 70*, 111-114.

Halleck, S. L. (1967). *Psychiatry and the dilemmas of crime.* New York: Harper & Row.

Halleck, S. L. (1974). Legal and ethical aspects of behavior control. *American Journal of Psychiatry, 131,* 381-385.

Halleck, S. L. (1979). The reform of mental hospitals. *Psychology Today, 2*(10) 50-54.

Halleck, S. L. (1980). *Law in the pratice of psychiatry: A handbook for clinicians.* New York: Plenum Press.

Hallenstein, C. B. (1978, February). Ethical problems of psychological jargon. *Professional Psychology,* pp. 111-116.

Halpern, A. (1975). *Use and misuse of psychiatry in competency examination of criminal defendants.* New York: Insight Communications.

Halpern, A. (1980). The fiction of legal insanity and the misuse of psychiatry. *Journal of Legal Medicine, 2,* 18-74.

Halpern, A. L. (1982). Commentary: Reconsideration of the insanity defense and related issues in the aftermath of the Hinckley trial. *Psychiatric Quarterly, 54,* 260-264.

Hamilton, R. G., & Robertson, M. H. (1966). Examiner influence on the Holtzman Inkblot Technique. *Journal of Projective Techniques, 30*(6), 553-558.

Hamilton, V. L. (1976). Individual differences in ascriptions of responsibility, guilt, and appropriate punishment. In G. Bermant, C. Nemeth, & N. Vidmar (Eds.), *Psychology and the law* (pp. 239-263). New York: Lexington Books.

Hamilton, V. L. (1978a). Obedience and responsibility: A jury simulation. *Journal of Personality and Social Psychology, 36,* 126-146.

Hamilton, V. L. (1978b). Who is responsible? Toward a social psychology of responsibility attribution. *Social Psychology, 41*(4), 316-328.

Hamilton, V. L. (1980). Intuitive psychologist or intuitive lawyer: Alternative models of the attribution process. *Journal of Personality and Social Psychology, 39,* 767-772.

Haney, C. (1980). Psychology and legal change: On the limits of factual jurisprudence. *Law and Human Behavior, 4,* 147-200.

Haney, C. (1982). Employment tests and employment discrimination: A dissenting psychological opinion. *Industrial Relations Law Journal, 5,* 1-86.

Haney, C. (1984). Special issue. Death qualification. *Law and Human Behavior, 8*(1/2), 1-193.

Hans, V. P., & Slater, D. (1983). John Hickley Jr. and the insanity defense: The public's verdict. *Public Opinion Quarterly, 47,* 202-212.

Harbin, H. T. (1977). Episodic dyscontrol and family dynamics. *American Journal of Psychiatry, 134,* 1113-1116.

Hare, R. D., & Cox, D. N. (1978). Psychophysiological research on psychopathy. In W. H. Reid (Ed.), *The psychopath* (pp. 209-222). New York: Brunner-Mazel.

Harlow, C. (1985). *Reporting crimes to the police.* Rockville, MD: U. S. Department of Justice, Bureau of Justice, NCJ-99643.

Harrison, A. A., Hwalek, M., Raney, D. F., & Fritz, J. G. (1978). Cues to deception in an interview situation. *Social Psychology, 41,* 156-161.

Hart, H. L. A., & Honore, A. M. (1959). *Causation in the Law.* Oxford: Clarendon Press.

Hartman, K., & Allison, J. (1978). Predicting dangerousness. *Medical Trial Technique Quarterly,* pp. 131-136.

Hartogs, R. (1970). Who will act violently: The predictive criteria. In R. Hartogs & T. Artz (Eds.), *Violence: The causes and solution.* New York: Dell.

Harvard Law Review Staff. (1981). The Supreme Court, 1980 term. *Harvard Law Review, 95,* 91-345.

Harvey, M. A., & Sipprelle, C. N. (1976). Demand characteristic effects on the subtle and obvious subscales of the MMPI. *Journal of Personality Assessment, 40*, 539-544.

Harvey, O. J., & Lindgren, H. (1981). *An introduction to social psychology*. New York: John Wiley & Sons.

Hassett, J. M. (1980). A jury's pre-trial knowledge in historical perspective: The distinction between pre-trial information and "prejudicial" publicity. *Law and Contemporary Problems, 43*, 155-168.

Hathaway, S. R. (1946). The multiphasic personality inventory. *Modern Hospital, 66*, 65-67.

Hathaway, S. R., & McKinley, J. C. (1940). A multiphasic personality schedule: I. Construction of the schedule. *Journal of Psychology, 10*, 249-254.

Hathaway, S. R., & McKinley, J. C. (1948). *The Minnesota Multiphasic Personality Inventory*. New York: Psychological Corporation.

Hathaway, S. R., & Meehl, P. E. (1951). *An atlas for the clinical use of the MMPI*. Minneapolis, MN: University of Minnesota Press.

Hathaway, S. R., & Monachesi, E. D. (1957). The personalities of predelinquent boys. *Journal of Criminal Law, Criminology, and Police Science, 48*, 149-163.

Hattaway, C. A., & Poythress, N. (1977). A mental health critique of People v. Parney: Medical and non-medical expertise on competency to stand trial. *Michigan State Bar Journal, 56*, 784-792.

Hatvany, N., & Strack, F. (1980). The impact of a discredited witness. *Journal of Applied Social Psychology, 10*, 490-509.

Haward, L. (1976). Experimentation of forensic psychology. *Criminal Justice and Behavior, 3*, 301-314.

Haward, L. (1981). *Forensic psychology*. London: Batsford.

Haynes, S. (1978). *Principles of behavioral assessment*. New York: Gardner Press.

Hays, J., & Ehrlich, S. (1975). The ability of the mentally retarded to plead guilty. *Arizona State Law Journal, 4*, 661-676.

Hazard, G. (1967). Limitations on the uses of behavioral science in the law. *Case Western Reserve Law Review, 17*, 71-77.

Heaton, R. K., Baade, L. E., & Johnson, A. L. (1978). Neuropsychological test results associated with psychiatric disorders in adults. *Psychological Bulletin, 85*, 141-162.

Heaton, R. K., Grant, I., Anthony, W. Z., & Lehman, R. A. (1981). A comparison of clinical and automated interpretations of the Halstead-Reitan Battery. *Journal of Clinical and Neuropsychology, 3*, 121-141.

Heaton, R. K., & Pendleton, M. G. (1981). Use of neuropsychological tests to predict adult patients every day functioning. *Journal of Consulting and Clinical Psychology, 49*, 807-821.

Heaton, R. K., Smith, H. H., Lehman, R. A. W., & Vogt, A. T. (1978). Prospects of faking believable deficits in neuropsychological testing. *Journal of Consulting and Clinical Psychology, 46*, 892-900.

Hedegard, J. (1979). The impact of legal education: An in-depth examination of career-relevant interests, attitudes, and personality traits among first-year law students. *American Bar Foundation Research Journal, 4*, 791-868.

Heider, F. (1958). *The psychology of interpersonal relations*. New York: Wiley.

Heilbrun, A. B., Heilbrun, L. C., & Heilbrun, K. L. (1978). Impulsive and premeditated homicide: An analysis of subsequent parole risk of the murderer. *Journal of Criminal Law and Criminology, 69*, 108-114.

Hekimian, L. K., & Gershon, S. (1968). Characteristics of drug abusers admitted to a psychiatric hospital. *Journal of the American Medical Association, 205*, 125-130.

Heldt, N. (1978). The right of eccentricity. *Hastings Law Journal, 29*, 519-554.

Helfer, R., Hoffmeister, J., & Schneider, C. (1978). *A manual for use of the Michigan Screening Profile of Parenting*. Boulder, CO: Test Analysis and Development Corporation.

Heller, K., & Monohan, J. (1977). *Psychology and community change*. Homewood, IL: Dorsey Press.

Heller, M. S. et al. (1968). Developing clinical facilities in forensic psychiatry. *American Journal of Psychiatry, 124,* 1562-1568.

Hellman, D., & Blackman, N. (1966). Enuresis, firesetting, and cruelty to animals: A triad predictive of adult crime. *American Journal of Psychiatry.*

Helson, H. (1964). *Adaptation-level theory: An experimental approach to behavior*. New York: Harper & Row.

Helzer, J. E., Robins, L. N., Croughan, J. L., & Welner, A. (1981). Renard diagnostic interview. *Archives of General Psychiatry, 38,* 393-398.

Henderson, M. (1983). An empirical classification of non-violent offenders using the MMPI. *Journal of Personality and Individual Differences, 4,* 671-677.

Henderson, S., & Lance, G. N. (1979). Types of attempted suicide (para-suicide). *Acta Psychiatrica Scandinavia, 59,* 31-39.

Hendrick, C., & Shaffer, D. R. (1975). Effect of pleading the Fifth Amendment on perception of guilt and morality. *Bulletin of the Psychonomic Society, 6,* 449-452.

Hendrick, C., & Constantini, A. F. (1970). Effects of varying trait inconsistency and response requirements on the primary effect in impression formation. *Journal of Personality and Social Psychology, 15,* 158-167.

Henn, F. et al. (1977). Forensic psychiatry: Anatomy of a service. *Comprehensive Psychiatry, 18,* 337-345.

Hennigan, K. M., Flay, B. R., & Cook, T. D. (1980). "Give me the facts": Some suggestions for social science use in policy making. In R. F. Kidd & M. J. Saks (Eds.), *Advances in applied social psychology,* Vol. 1. Hillsdale, NJ: Erlbaum.

Hereford, C. (1963). *Changing parental attitudes through group discussion*. Austin, TX: University of Austin Press.

Herrmann, D. J. (1982). Know thy memory: The use of questionnaires to assess and study memory. *Psychological Bulletin, 92,* 424-452.

Hermann, D. J., & Neisser, U. (1978). An inventory of everyday memory experiences. In M. M. Grunberg, P. E. Morris, & R. N. Sykes (Eds.), *Practical aspects of memory*. New York: Academic Press.

Hersen, M. (1970). Sexual aspects of Rorschach administration. *Journal of Projective Techniques, 34,* 104-105.

Herz, M. I., Endicott, J., & Gibbon, M. (1979). Brief hospitalization. *Archives of General Psychiatry, 36,* 701-705.

Hess, H. (1977). Repressive crime and criminal typologies: Some neglected types. *Contemporary Crises, 1,* 91-108.

Hess, J., & Thomas, H. (1963). Incompetency to stand trial: Procedures, results and problems. *American Journal of Psychiatry, 119,* 713-720.

Hetherington, E. M., Cox, M., & Cox, R. (1979). Play and social interaction in children following divorce. *Journal of Social Issues, 35*(4), 26-49.

Hetherington, E. M., & Parke, R. (1975). *Child psychology: A contemporary viewpoint*. New York: McGraw-Hill.

Heumann, M. (1975). A note on plea bargaining and case pressure. *Law and Society Review, 9,* 515-520.

Heumann, M. (1978). *Plea bargaining: The experiences of prosecutors, judges, and defense attorneys.* Chicago, IL: University of Chicago Press.

Higgins, G. M. (1975). *The law enforcement perceptions questionnaire: Revised manual.* Munster, IN: Psychometric Affiliates.

Hilgard, E. R., & Loftus, E. F. (1979). Effective interrogation of the eyewitness. *International Journal of Clinical and Experimental Hypnosis, 27,* 342-357.

Hill, D., & Pond, D. A. (1952). Reflections on 100 capital cases submitted to electroencephalography. *Journal of Mental Science, 98,* 23-43.

Hill, E. F. (1972). *The Holtzman Inkblot Technique: A handbook for clinical application.* San Francisco, CA: Jossey-Bass.

Hill, R. W. (1981). Drunkeness and criminal responsibility: The psychiatrist's contribution. In S. J. Hucker, C. D. Webster, & M. H. Ben-Arons (Eds.), *Mental disorder and criminal responsibility* (pp 79-90). Toronto: Butterworth.

Hilliard, T., & Roth, R. (1969). Maternal attitudes and the non-achievement syndrome. *Personnel and Guidance Journal, 47,* 424-428.

Himelstein, P., & Grunau, G. (1981). Differentiation of aggressive and non-aggressive schizophrenics with the Hand Test: Another failure. *Psychological Reports, 49,* 556.

Hindelang, M. (1976). *An analysis of victimization survey results from eight cities.* Albany, NY: Criminal Justice Research Center.

Hindelang, M., & Gottfredson, M. (1976). The victim's decision not to invoke the criminal justice process. In W. F. McDonald (Ed.), *Criminal justice and the victim.* Beverly Hills, CA: Sage Publications.

Hirschi, T., & Hindelang, M. (1977). Intelligence and delinquency: A revisionist review. *American Sociological Review, 42,* 571-587.

Hirschi, T., & Selvin, C. (1967). *Delinquency research.* New York: The Free Press.

Hjelle, L., & Smith, G. (1975). Self-actualization and retrospective reports of parent-child relationships among college females. *Psychological Reports, 36,* 755-761.

Hoch, E. I., & Darley, J. G. (1962). A case at law. *American Psychologist, 17,* 623-654.

Hoffman, M. (1960). Power assertion by the parent and its impact on the child. *Child Development, 31,* 129-143.

Hoffman, P. J. (1960). The paramorphic representation of clinical judgment. *Psychological Bulletin, 57*(2), 116-131.

Hoffmeister, J. (1975). *Convergence analysis: A clinical approach to quantitative data.* Boulder, CO: Test Analysis and Development Corporation.

Hogan, R. (1973). Moral conduct and moral character. *Psychological Bulletin, 79,* 217-232.

Hogan, R. (1975). The structure of moral character and the explanation of moral action. *Journal of Youth and Adolescence, 4,* 1-15.

Hogan, R., DeSoto, C., & Solano, C. (1977). Traits, tests, and personality research. *American Psychologist, 32,* 255-264.

Hogarth, R. M. (1981). Beyond discrete biases: Functional and dysfunctional aspects of judgmental heuristics. *Psychological Bulletin, 90,* 197-217.

Hoiberg, B. C., & Stires, L. K. (1973). The effect of several types of pretrial publicity on the guilt attributions of simulated jurors. *Journal of Applied Social Psychology, 3,* 267-275.

Hoivath, F. (1977). The effect of selected variables on interpretation of polygraph records. *Journal of Applied Psychology, 62,* 127-136.

Holcomb, W. R., Adams, N. A., Ponder, H. M., & Anderson, W. P. (1984). Cognitive and behavioral predictors of MMPI scores in pre-trial psychological evaluations of murderers. *Journal of Clinical Psychology, 40*, 592-597.

Holderman, L. (1977). Joinder of criminal offenses in Nebraska: Judicial discretion v. fair and impartial trial. *Nebraska Law Review, 56*, 399-409.

Holland, J. (1973). *Making vocational choices: A theory of careers.* Englewood Cliffs, NJ: Prentice-Hall.

Holland, T. (1986, January). Personal communication. Chino, CA.

Holland, T., Holt, N., & Beckett, G. (1982). Prediction of violent versus nonviolent recidivism from prior violent and nonviolent criminality. *Journal of Abnormal Psychology, 3*, 178-182.

Holland, T. R. (1979). Ethnic group differences in MMPI profile pattern and factorial structure among adult offenders. *Journal of Personality Assessment, 43*, 72-77.

Holland, T. R., Holt, N., & Beckett, G. E. (1982). Prediction of violent versus nonviolent recidivism from prior violent and nonviolent criminality. *Journal of Abnormal Psychology, 91*(3), 178-182

Holmes, D. S. (1968). Dimensions of projection. *Psychological Bulletin, 69*, 248-268.

Holmes, D. S. (1974). The conscious control of thematic projection. *Journal of Consulting and Clinical Psychology, 42*, 323-329.

Holmes, T., & Rahe, R. (1967). The social readjustment rating scale. Journal of *Psychosomatic Research, 11*, 213-218.

Holmstrom, L. L., & Burgess, A. W. (1978). *The victim of rape: Institutional reactions.* New York: Wiley-Interscience.

Holmstrup, M., Fitch, W., & Keilitz, I. (1981). *Screening and evaluation in centralized forensic mental health facilities.* Williamsburg, VA: National Center for State Courts.

Holtzman, W. H., Thorpe, J. S., Swartz, J. D., & Herron, E. W. (1961). *Inkblot perception and personality.* Austin, TX: University of Texas Press.

Hook, E. B. (1973). Behavioral implications of the human xyy genotype. *Science, 179*, 139-179.

Hopwood, J. S., & Snell, H. K. (1933). Amnesia in relation to crime. *Journal of Mental Science, 79*, 27-30.

Horowitz, D. (1977). *The courts and social policy.* Washington, DC: Brookings Institution.

Horowitz, I. A. (1980). Juror selection: A comparison of two methods in several criminal cases. *Journal of Applied Psychology, 10*, 86-99.

Horowitz, I. A., Bordens, K. S., & Feldman, M. S. (1980). A comparison of verdicts obtained in severed and joined trials. *Journal of Applied Social Psychology, 10*, 444-456.

Horowitz, I. A., & Willging, T. (1984). *The psychology of law: Integrations and applications.* Boston, MA: Little, Brown.

Horstman, P. (1975). Protective services for the elderly: The limits of parens patriae. *Missouri Law Review, 40*, 215-278.

Hotchkiss, S. (1978). The realities of rape. *Human Behavior, 7*, 18-23.

Houlden, P. (1981). Impact of procedural modifications on evaluations of plea bargaining. *Law and Society Review, 15*, 267-292.

Houlden, P., LaTour, S., Walker, L., & Thibaut, J. (1978). Preference for modes of dispute resolution as a function of process and decision control. *Journal of Experimental Psychology, 14*, 13-22.

Houts, M. (1981). The accuracy/fallibility of eyewitness reporting. *Trauma, 23*, 1-6.

Howard, W. B. (1979). Some psychological strategies for dealing with the violent criminal. *Police Chief, 46*(5).

Howe, E. G. (1984). Psychiatric evaluation of offenders who commit crimes while experiencing dissociative disorders. *Law and Human Behavior, 8*, 253-282.

Howell, R. J. (1982). In defense of the insanity plea. *Bulletin of the American Academy of Forensic Psychologists, 3*(1), 1-2.

Huber, J., Jones, T., & Waters, C. (1981). Social science preferences of law students. *Journal of Psychology and the Law, 3,* 16-22.

Huckabee, H. M. (1973). Resolving the problem of dominance of psychiatrists in criminal responsibility decisions. *Southwestern Law Journal, 27,* 790-805.

Huckabee, H. M. (1980). *Lawyers, psychiatrists, and criminal law: Cooperation or chaos?* Springfield, IL: Charles C. Thomas.

Huesmann, L. R., Lefkowitz, M. M. & Eron, L. D. (1978). Sum of MMPI scales F, 4, and 9 as a measure of aggression. *Journal of Consulting and Clinical Psychology, 46,* 1071-1078.

Humphries, T., & Bauman, E. (1980). Maternal child rearing attitudes associated with learning disabilities. *Journal of Learning Disabilities, 13,* 459-462.

Hurst, J. W. (1950). *The growth of American Law: The law makers.* Boston, MA: Little, Brown.

Hyman, H. H., & Tarrant, C. M. (1975). Aspects of American trial jury history. In R. J. Simon (Ed.), *The jury system in America.* Beverly Hills, CA: Sage Publications.

Hyman, J. M. (1979). Philosophical implications of plea bargaining: Some comments. *Law and Society Review, 13,* 565-566.

I

Imperio, A., & Chabot, D. (1980). Male delinquents' perceptions of their parents: A factor analysis. *Perceptual Motor Skills, 51,* 829-830.

Inbau, F. E., & Reid, J. E. (1962). *Criminal interrogation and confessions.* Baltimore, MD: Williams & Wilkins.

Inhelder, B., & Piaget, J. (1958). *The growth of logical thinking.* New York: Basic Books.

Inman, D. J. (1977). Differentiation of intropunitive from extrapunitive female inmates. *Journal of Clinical Psychology, 33,* 95-98.

Insanity Defense Workgroup. (1983). American Psychiatric Association statement on the insanity defense. *American Journal of Psychiatry, 140,* 681-688.

Institute of Judicial Administration (American Bar Association). (1977). *Juvenile justice standards project.* Cambridge, MA: Ballinger.

Institute on Mental Disability and the Law. (1984). *The "guilty but mentally ill" verdict: Current state of knowledge.* Williamsburg, VA: National Center for State Courts.

Irvine, M., & Gendreu, P. (1974). Detection of the "good" and "bad" responses on the 16 personality factor inventory in prisoners and college students. *Journal of Consulting and Clinical Psychology, 42,* 465-466.

Isaacson, W. (1982, July 5). Insane on all counts. *Time,* pp. 22-26.

Izzert, R. R., & Sales, B. D. (1981). Person perception and the juror's reaction to defendants: An equity interpretation. In B. D. Sales (Ed.), *Perspectives in law and psychology: The trial process.* New York: Plenum.

J

Jacobs, P. A., Brunton, M., Melville, M. M., Brittain, R. P., & McClemont, W. F. (1965). Aggressive behavior, mental subnormality, and the xyy male. *Nature, 208,* 1351-1352.

Jaffe, S. (1903). Ein psychologische experiment in Kriminalistischen seminar der universitaet Berlin. *Beitraege zur Psychologie der Aussage, mit desonderer Bereuecksrchitigung der Rechspflege, Paedogogik, Psychiatrie und Geschichts forschung, 1,* 79.

James, R. M. (1959). Status and competence of jurors. *American Journal of Sociology, 64,* 563-570.

Janis, I. L. (1972). *Victims of groupthink.* Boston, MA: Houghton Mifflin.

Janus, S. S., Bess, B. E., Cadden, J. J., & Greenwald, H. (1980). Training police officers to distinguish mental illness. *American Journal of Psychiatry, 137*(2), 228-229.

Jarvik, L. et al. (1973). Human aggression and the extra Y chromosome. *American Psychologist, 28,* 674-682.

Jarvik, L., Eisdorfer, C., & Blum, J. (Eds.) (1973). *Intellectual functioning in adults.* New York: Springer.

Jeffrey, R. (1964). The psychologist as an expert witness on the issue of insanity. *American Psychologist, 19,* 838-843.

Jeffrey, R. W., & Pasewark, R. A. (1983). Altering opinions about the insanity plea. *Journal of Psychiatry and Law, 6,* 39-40.

Jencks, C. (1972). *Inequality, a reassessment of the effect of family and schooling in America.* New York: Basic Books.

Jensen, A. R. (1965). Rorschach. In O. K. Buros (Ed.), *Sixth mental measurements yearbook* (pp. 501-509). Highland Park, NJ: Gryphon Press.

Jesness, C. G. (1966). *The Jesness Inventory manual.* Palo Alto, CA: Consulting Psychologists Press.

Jillings, C., Adamson, C., & Russell, T. (1976). An application of Roth's Mother-Child Relationship Evaluation to some mothers of handicapped children. *Psychology Reports, 38,* 807-810.

Johnson, J. H. (1975). A cross-validation of seventeen experimental MMPI scales related to antisocial behavior. *Journal of Clinical Psychology, 31,* 564-565.

Johnson, N., & Cooke, G. (1973). Relationship of MMPI alcoholism, prison escape, hostility control, and recivism scales to clinical judgments. *Journal of Clinical Psychology, 29,* 32-34.

Johnson, O. G. (1976). *Tests and measurements in child development: Handbook II,* Vols. 1 and 2. San Francisco, CA: Jossey-Bass.

Joiner, C. (1962). *Civil justice and the jury.* Englewood Cliffs, NJ: Prentice-Hall.

Jones, A. (1977). Suicide by aircraft: A case report. *Aviation, Space, Environmental Medicine, 48,* 454-459.

Jones, E. E. (1979). The rocky road from acts to dispositions. *American Psychologist, 34,* 107-117.

Jones, E. E., Riggs, J. M., & Quattrone, G. (1979). Observer bias in attitude attribution paradigm: Effect of time and information order. *Journal of Personality and Social Psychology, 37,* 1230-1238.

Jones, R., Reid, J., & Patterson, G. (1975). Naturalistic observation in clinical assessment. In P. McReynolds (Ed.), *Advances in psychological assessment,* Vol. 3 (pp. 42-95). San Francisco, CA: Jossey-Bass.

Jones, T., Beidleman, W. B., & Fowler, R. D. (1981). Differentiating violent and non-violent prison inmates by use of selected MMPI scales. *Journal of Clinical Psychology, 37,* 673-677.

Jourard, S. M., & Landsman, M. J. (1960). Cognition, cathexis, and "dyadic effects" in men's self-disclosing behavior. *Merrill-Palmer Quarterly, 6,* 178-186.

Jurow, G. L. (1971). New data on the effect of a "death-qualified" jury on the guilt determination process. *Harvard Law Review, 84,* 567-611.

Justice, B., & Justice R. (1982). Clinical approaches to family violence: I. Etiology of physical abuse of children and dynamics of coercive treatment. *Family Therapy Collections, 3,* 1-20.

Justice, B., Justice, R., & Kraft, J. (1974). Early warning signs of violence: Is a triad enough? *American Journal of Psychiatry, 131,* 457-459.

K

Kadish, M. R., & Kadish, S. H. (1971). The institutionalization of conflict: Jury acquittals. *Journal of Social Issues, 27,* 199-218.

Kadish, M. R., & Kadish, S. H. (1973). *Discretion to disobey.* Stanford, CA: Stanford University Press.

Kahana, E. (1982). A congruence model of person-environment interaction. In M. Lawton, P. Windley, & T. Byerts (Eds.), *Aging and the environment* (pp. 97-121). New York: Springer.

Kahle, L., & Sales, D. (1980). Due process of law and the attitudes of professionals toward involuntary civil commitment. In P. Lipsett & B. Sales (Eds.), *New directions in psychological research.* New York: Van Nostrand Reinhold.

Kahn, M. W. (1967). Correlates of Rorschach reality adherents of murderers who plead insanity. *Journal of Projective Techniques, 31,* 44-47.

Kahn, M., & Taft, G. (1983). The application of the standard of care doctrine to psychological testing. *Behavioral Sciences and the Law, 1,* 71-84.

Kahneman, D., & Tversky, A. (1973). On the psychology of prediction. *Psychological Review, 80,* 237-251.

Kairys, D., Schulman, J., & Harring, S. (1975). *The jury system: New methods for reducing prejudice.* Philadelphia, PA: National Jury Project and National Lawyers Guild.

Kalven, H., Jr., & Zeisel, H. (1966). *The American jury.* Boston, MA: Little, Brown.

Kane, R., & Kane, R. (1981). *Assessing the elderly: A practical guide to measurement.* Lexington, MA: Lexington.

Kanfer, F. (1965). Vicarious human reinforcement: A glimpse into the black box. In L. Krasner & L. Ullman (Eds.), *Research and behavior modification* (pp. 244-267). New York: Holt, Rinehart and Winston.

Kanun, C., & Monachesi, E. D. (1960). Delinquency and the validating scales of the MMPI. *Journal of Criminal Law and Criminology, 50,* 525-534.

Kaplan, A. (1964). *The conduct of inquiry.* San Francisco, CA: Chandler.

Kaplan, L. V. (1977). The mad and the bad: An inquiry into the disposition of the criminally insane. *Journal of Medicine and Philosophy, 2,* 244-304.

Kaplan, M. F. (1982). Cognitive processes in the individual juror. In N. L. Kerr & R. M. Bray (Eds.), *The pyschology of the courtroom* (pp. 197-220). New York: Academic Press.

Kaplan, M. F., & Kemmerick, G. D. (1974). Juror judgments as information integration: Combining evidential and nonevidential information. *Journal of Personality and Social Psychology, 30,* 493-499.

Kaplan, M. F., & Miller, L. E. (1978). Reducing the effects of juror bias. *Journal of Personality and Social Psychology, 36,* 1443-1455.

Kaplan, M. F., & Schersching, C. (1980). Reducing juror bias: An experimental approach. In P. Lipsitt & B. D. Sales (Eds.), *New directions in psycholegal research.* New York: Van Nostrand Reinhold.

Kaplan, M. F., & Schersching, C. (1981). Juror deliberation: An informational integration analysis. In B. D. Sales (Ed.), *Perspectives in law and psychology: The trial process*. New York: Plenum.

Karrass, C. C. (1970). *The negotiating game*. New York: Thomas Y. Crowell.

Kassin, S. M., & Wrightsman, L. S. (1979). On the requirements of proof: The timing of judicial instruction and mock juror verdicts. *Journal of Personality and Social Psychology, 37*, 1877-1887.

Kassin, S. M., & Wrightsman, L. S. (1980). Prior confessions and mock juror verdicts. *Journal of Applied Social Psychology, 3*, 133-146.

Kassin, S. M., & Wrightsman, L. S. (1981). Coerced confessions, judicial instructions, and mock juror verdicts. *Journal of Applied Social Psychology, 11*, 489-506.

Kassirer, L. B. (1974). Behavior modification for patients and prisoners: Constitutional ramifications of enforced therapy. *Journal of Psychiatry and Law, 2*, 245-302.

Kastermeier, R., & Eglit, H. (1973). Parole release decision-making: Rehabilitation, expertise, and the demise of mythology. *American University Law Review, 22*, 477-1137.

Katz, A., & Debeaux, M. (1976). Trust, cynicism and Machiavellianism among entering first-year law students. *University of Detroit Journal of Urban Law, 53*, 397-412.

Katz, D. R. (1931). Attitude toward the law scale. In L. L. Thurstone (Ed.), *The measurement of social attitudes*. Chicago, IL: University of Chicago Press.

Katz, J., & Goldstein, J. (1964). Abolish the insanity defense—Why not? *Journal of Nervous and Mental Disease, 138*, 57-69.

Katz, L. (1975). Presentation of a confidence interval estimate as evidence in a legal proceeding. *American Statistician, 29*(4), 138-142.

Katz, L. S. (1968). The twelve man jury. *Trial, 5*, 39-42.

Katz, M., & Lyerly, S. (1963). Methods for measuring adjustment and social behavior in the community: 1. Rationale, description, and discriminative validity, and scale development. *Psychological Reports, 13*, 503-535.

Katz, S. (1971). *When parents fail: The law's response to family breakdown*. Boston, MA: Beacon Press.

Katz, S., Ford, A., Moskowitz, R., Jackson, B., & Jaffee, M. (1963). Studies of illness in the aged: The Index of ADL, a standardized measure of biological and psychosocial function. *Journal of the American Medical Association, 185*, 94-99.

Katz, S., Howe, R., & McGrath, M. (1975). Child neglect laws in America. *Family Law Quarterly, 9*, 1-372.

Kaufer, D., Steinberg, E., & Toney, S. (1983). Revising medical consent forms: An empirical model and test. *Law, Medicine and Health Care, 11*, 155-184.

Kaufman, R., & English, F. W. (1979). *Needs-assessment: Concept and application*. Englewood Cliffs, NJ: Educational Technology Publications.

Kaye, D. (1979). The laws of probability and the law of the land. *University of Chicago Law Review, 47*, 34-56.

Kaye, D. (1980). An then there were twelve: Statistical reasoning, the Supreme Court, and the size of the jury. *California Law Review, 68*, 1004-1043.

Kazen, B. A. (1977). *When father wants custody: A lawyer's view*. Austin: State Bar of Texas.

Keasey, B., & Sales, B. (1977a). An empirical investigation of young children's awareness and usage of intentionality in criminal situations. *Law and Human Behavior, 1*, 45-61.

Keasey, C. B., & Sales, B. D. (1977b). Children's conception of intentionality and the criminal law. In B. D. Sales (Ed.), *Psychology in the legal process* (pp. 127-146). New York: Plenum Press.

Keeton, R. E. (1973). *Trial tactics and methods* (2nd ed.). Boston, MA: Little, Brown.

Keilitz, I. (1981). *Mental health examinations in criminal justice settings: Organization, administration, and program evaluation.* Williamsburg, VA: National Center for State Courts.

Keilitz, I., & Fulton, J. P. (1983). *The insanity defense and its alternatives: A guide to policy makers.* Williamsburg, VA: National Center for State Courts.

Keller, M. B., Lavori, P. W., Andreasen, W. C., Grove, W. M., Shapiro, R. W., Scheftner, W. A., & McDonald-Scott, P. (1981). Reliability of assessing psychiatrically ill patients in a multi-center, test-retest design. *Journal of Psychiatric Research, 16,* 213-228.

Keller, M. B., Lavori, P. W., McDonald-Scott, P., Scheftner, W. A., Andreasen, W. C., Shapiro, R. W., & Croughan, J. (1981). Reliability of lifetime diagnosis and symptoms in patients with a current psychiatric disorder. *Journal of Psychiatric Research, 16,* 229-240.

Kelley, D. S. (1976-1977). Joinder of offenses: Louisiana's new approach in historical perspective. *Louisiana Law Review, 37,* 203-233.

Kelley, T. M. (1978). Clinical assessment and the detention, disposition, and treatment of emotionally disturbed delinquent youths. *Journal of Criminal Justice, 6,* 315-327.

Kelly, A. (1962a). An inside view of Brown v. Board. *Congressional Record, 108,* 19021-19026.

Kelly, A. (1962b). The school desegregation case. In J. Garraty (Ed.), *Quarrels that have shaped the Constitution.* New York: Harper-Torchbooks.

Kelly, C. (1976). *Crime in the United States: Uniform Crime Reports.* Washington, DC: Superintendent of Documents, U. S. Government Printing Office.

Kelly, J. E., & Llewelyn, S. P. (1978). Abuses of psychology for political purposes: Some critical remarks on the working party report. *Bulletin of British Psychological Society, 31,* 259-260.

Kelman, H. (1950). Effects of success and failure on "suggestibility" in the autokinetic situation. *Journal of Abnormal and Social Psychology, 45,* 267-285.

Keltikangas-Jarvinen, L. (1982). Alexithymia in violent offenders. *Journal of Personality Assessment, 46,* 462-467.

Kendall, P., & Norton-Ford, J. (1982). *Clinical psychology: Scientific and professional dimensions.* New York: Wiley.

Kerlinger, R. (1973). *Foundations of behavioral research.* New York: Holt, Rinehart & Winston.

Kerman, A. S. (1975). Value patterns among lawyers and their expert witnesses who are psychiatrists and psychologists. *Dissertation Abstracts International, 36,* 1409B-1410B.

Kerr, N. L. (1978a). Beautiful and blameless: Effects of victim attractiveness and responsibility on mock jurors' verdicts. *Personality and Social Psychology Bulletin, 4,* 479-482.

Kerr, N. L. (1978b). Severity of prescribed penalty and mock jurors' verdicts. *Journal of Personality and Social Psychology, 36,* 1422-1431.

Kerr, N. L. (1981a). Effects of prior juror experience on juror behavior. *Basic and Applied Social Psychology, 2,* 175-193.

Kerr, N. L. (1981b). Social transition schemes: Model, method, and applications. In H. Brandstatter & J. H. Davis (Eds.), *Group decision making processes.* New York: Academic Press.

Kerr, N. L. (1982). Trial participants' characteristics/behaviors and juries' verdicts: An exploratory field study. In V. Konecni & E. Ebbesen (Eds.), *Social psychological analysis of legal processes.* San Francisco, CA: W. H. Freeman.

Kerr, N. L., Atkin, R., Stasser, G., Meek, D., Holt, R., & Davis, J. H. (1976). Guilt beyond a reasonable doubt: Effects of concept definition and assigned rule on judgments of mock jurors. *Journal of Personality and Social Psychology, 34,* 282-294.

Kerr, N. L., & Bray, R. M. (Eds.) (1982). *The psychology of the courtroom.* New York: Academic Press.

Kidd, R., & Saks, M. J. (1980). What is applied psychology? An introduction. In R. F. Kidd & M. J. Saks (Eds.), *Advances in applied social psychology* (pp. 1-24). Hillsdale, NJ: Erlbaum.

Kiersch, T. (1962). Amnesia: A clinical study of 98 cases. *American Journal of Psychiatry, 119,* 57-60.

Kiesler, C. (1980). Psychology and public policy. In L. Bickman (Ed.), *Applied social psychology annual.* Beverly Hills, CA: Sage Publications.

Kiger, R. S. (1973). The psychiatrist as an expert witness in criminal court. *Hospital and Community Psychiatry, 24,* 613-615.

King, D. W., & Ajmone-Marsan, C. (1977). Clinical features and ictal patterns of epileptic patients with EEG temporal lobe foci. *Annals of Neurology, 2,* 138-147.

Kinnis, K. (1979). Plea bargaining: A critic's rejoinder. *Law and Society Review, 13,* 555-564.

Kinzel, A. (1970). Body-buffer zones in violent prisoners. *American Journal of Psychiatry, 127,* 59-64.

Kirby, C. (1976). Three years of adjustment: Where your ideals go. *Juris Doctor, 6,* 34-43.

Kirby, M. P. (1977). *The effectiveness of the point scale.* Washington, DC: Pretrial Services Resource Center.

Kirkham, J. F., Levy, S. G., & Crotty, W. J. (1970). *Assassination and political violence.* New York: Bantam.

Kirschner, S. (1982). Child custody determinations. In J. Henning (Ed.), *The rights of children: Legal and psychological perspectives* (pp. 117-140). Springfield, IL: Charles C. Thomas.

Klein, M. M., & Grossman, S. A. (1971). Voting competence and mental illness. *American Journal of Psychiatry, 127,* 1562-1565.

Kleinmuntz, B., & Szucko, J. J. (1982). On the fallibility of lie detection. *Law and Society Review, 17,* 85-104.

Klerman, G. L. (1977). Better but not well: Social and ethical issues in the deinstitutionalization of the mentally ill. *Schizophrenia Bulletin, 3*(4), 617-631.

Klieger, D. M. (1969). An investigation of the influence of response sets on the Holtzman projective technique (Doctoral dissertation, Iowa State University, 1968). *Dissertation Abstracts, 29,* 4848B.

Kline, M. V. (1979). Defending the mentally ill: The insanity defense and the role of forensic hypnosis. *International Journal of Clinical and Experimental Hypnosis, 27,* 375-401.

Klopfer, W. G., & Taubee, E. S. (1976). Objective tests. *Annual Review of Psychology, 27,* 543-567.

Kluger, R. (1975). *Simple justice.* New York: Knopf.

Knapp, M. (1978). *Nonverbal communication in human interaction* (2nd ed.). New York: Holt, Rinehart and Winston.

Knapp, M. L., Hart, R. P., & Dennis, H. S. (1974). An exploration of deception as a communication construct. *Human Communication Research, 1,* 15-29.

Knerr, C. R., & Carroll, J. D. (1978). Social scientists and the courts: The development of a testimonial privilege. *Social Science Journal, 15,* 103-113.

Knox, S. J. (1968). Epileptic automatism and violence. *Medical Sciences and the Law, 8,* 96-104.

Kohlberg, L., & Turiel, E. (1971). Moral development and moral education. In G. S. Lesser (Ed.), *Psychology and educational practice* (pp. 410-465). Glenview, IL: Scott, Foresman.

Kolodny, R. C., Masters, W. H., & Hendryx, J. (1971). Plasma testosterone and semen analysis in male homosexuals. *New England Journal of Medicine, 285,* 1170-1174.

Konecni, V., & Ebbesen, E. (1981). A critique of theory and method in social-psychological approaches to legal issues. In B. D. Sales (Ed.), *The trial process* (pp. 481-498). New York: Plenum Press.

Konecni, V., & Ebbesen, E. (1982). *The criminal justice system.* San Francisco, CA: W. H. Freeman.

Korer, J. R., Freeman, H. L., & Cheadle, A. J. (1978). The social situation of schizophrenic patients living in the community. *International Journal of Mental Health, 6*(4), 45-65.

Kosbab, F. P., & Kuhnley, E. J. (1978). Pathological intoxication. *Case Report, 15*, 35-39.

Koson, D., & Robey, A. (1973). Amnesia and competency to stand trial. *American Journal of Psychiatry, 130*, 588-592.

Kozol, H. (1975). The diagnosis of dangerousness. In S. Pasternack (Ed.), *Violence and victims* (pp. 3-13). New York: Spectrum.

Kozol, H. I., Boucher, R. J., & Garofalo, R. F. (1972). The diagnosis and treatment of dangerousness. *Crime and Delinquency, 18*, 371-392.

Kracke, K. (1981). A survey of procedures for assessing family conflicts dysfunction. *Family Therapy, 8*, 241-251.

Kraiger, K., Hakel, M. D., & Cornelius, E. T. (1984). Exploring fantasies of TAT reliability. *Journal of Personality Assessment, 48*, 365-370.

Kral, V. A. (1959). Amnesia and the amnestic syndrome. *Canadian Psychiatric Association Journal, 4*, 61-68.

Kral, V. A., & Durost, H. B. (1953). A comparative study of the amnestic syndrome in various organic conditions. *American Journal of Psychiatry, 110*, 41-47.

Kraus, J. (1972). Use of Bayes's theorum in clinical decision: Suicidal risk, differential diagnosis, response to treatment. *British Journal of Psychiatry, 120*, 561-567.

Kraut, R. (1978). Verbal and nonverbal cues in the perception of lying. *Journal of Personality and Social Psychology, 36*, 380-391.

Kray, F., & Berman, J. (1977). Plea bargaining in Nebraska: The prosecutor's perspective. *Creighton Law Review, 11*, 94-149.

Kreuz, L. E., & Rose, R. M. (1972). Assessment of aggressive behavior and plasma testosterone in young criminal population. *Psychosomatic Medicine, 34*, 321-332.

Krieger, M. J., & Levin, S. M. (1976). Schizophrenic behaviour as a function of role expectation. *Journal of Clinical Psychology, 32*, 463-467.

Kriger, S., & Kroes, W. (1972). Child-rearing attitudes of Chinese, Jewish and Protestant mothers. *Journal of Social Psychology, 86*, 205-210.

Kroger, W. S., & Douce, R. G. (1979). Hypnosis in criminal investigation. *International Journal of Clinical and Experimental Hypnosis, 27*, 358-374.

Krug, S. (1978). Further evidence on sixteen PF distortion scales. *Journal of Personality Assessment, 42*, 513-517.

Kubie, L. S. (1973). The Ruby case: Who or what was on trial? *Journal of Psychiatry and Law, 1*, 475-491.

Kuhn, T. S. (1970). *The structure of scientific revolutions*. Chicago, IL: University of Chicago Press.

Kunce, J. T., Ryan, J. J., & Eckelman, C. C. (1976). Violent behavior and differential WAIS characteristics. *Journal of Consulting and Clinical Psychology, 44*, 42-45.

Kuriansky, J., & Gurland, B. (1976). Performance test of activities of daily living. *International Journal of Aging and Human Development, 7*, 343-352.

Kurland, P. (1979). Government by judiciary. *University of Arkansas at Little Rock Law Journal, 2*, 307-322.

Kurland, P., & Casper, G. (1975). *Landmark briefs and arguments of the Supreme Court of the United States*. Arlington, VA: University Publications of America.

Kurlychek, R. T. (1978). Toward holding the criminally non-responsible defendant more responsible: Some therapeutic concerns. *Corrective and Social Psychiatry, 24*(4), 144-145.

Kurlychek, R. T., & Jordan, L. (1980). MMPI profiles and code types of responsible and nonresponsible criminal defendants. *Journal of Clinical Psychology, 36,* 590-593.

L

Laboratory of Community Psychiatry, Harvard Medical School. (1973). *Competency to stand trial and mental illness* (DHEW Publication No. ADM77-103). Rockville, MD: Department of Health, Education and Welfare.

Lachar, D. (1974). *The MMPI: Clinical assessment and automated interpretation.* Los Angeles, CA: Western Psychological Services.

Lachar, D., & Wrobel, T. A. (1979). Validating clinicians' hunches: Construction of a new MMPI critical item set. *Journal of Consulting and Clinical Psychology, 47,* 277-284.

Lacks, P. B., Colbert, J., Harrow, M., & Levine, J. (1970). Further evidence concerning the diagnostic accuracy of the Halstead organic test battery. *Journal of Clinical Psychology, 26,* 480-481.

Ladd, E. C., & Lipset, S. M. (1973). *Academics, politics, and the 1972 election.* Washington, DC: American Enterprise Institute for Public Policy Research.

Ladd, J. (1952). Expert testimony. *Vanderbilt Law Review, 5,* 414, 419.

LaFrance, M., & Mayo, C. A. (1978). *Moving bodies: Nonverbal communication in social relationships.* Monterey, CA: Brooks/Cole.

Lake, D. G., Miles, B., & Earle, R. B., Jr. (Eds.) (1973). *Measuring human behavior.* New York: Columbia University Teachers College Press.

Lamb, H. R., & Edelson, M. (1976). The carrot and the stick: Inducing local programs to serve long term patients. *Community Mental Health Journal, 12,* 137-144.

Lamb, H. R., & Goertzel, V. (1971). Discharged mental patients: Are they really in the community? *Archives of General Psychiatry, 24,* 29-34.

Lamb, H. R., & Goertzel, V. (1972). The demise of the state hospital: A pre-mature obituary? *Archives of General Psychiatry, 26,* 489-495.

Lamb, M. E. (1977). The development of mother-infant and father-infant attachments in the second year of life. *Developmental Psychology, 13*(6), 637-648.

Lambert, N. D. (1981). Psychological evidence in Larry P. v. Wilson Riles. *American Psychologist, 36,* 937-952.

Landwehr, L. (1982). Lawyers as social progressives or reactionaries: The law and order cognitive orientation of lawyers. *Law and Psychology Review, 7,* 39-51.

Landy, D., & Aronson, E. (1969). The influence of the character of the criminal and his victim on the decisions of simulated jurors. *Journal of Experimental Social Psychology, 5,* 141-152.

Langbein, J. H. (1978). Torture and plea bargaining. *University of Chicago Law Review, 46,* 12-13.

Langbein, J. H. (1979). Understanding the short history of plea bargaining. *Law and Society Review, 13,* 261-272.

Langevin, R., Ben-Aron, M. H., Coulthard, R., Heasman, G., Purins, J. E., Handy, L., Hucker, S. J., Russon, A. E., Day, D., Roper, V., & Webster, C. D. (1985). Sexual aggression: Constructing a predictive equation, a controlled pilot study. In R. Langevin (Ed.), *Erotic preference, gender identity and aggression in men: New research studies* (pp. 39-76). Hillsdale, NJ: Lawrence Erlbaum.

Langevin, R., Ben-Aron, M. H., Coulthard, R., Day, D., Hucker, S. J., Purins, J. E., Roper, V., Russon, A. E., & Webster, C. D. (1985). The effect of alcohol on penile erection. In R. Langevin (Ed.), *Erotic preference, gender identity and aggression in men: New research studies* (pp. 101-112). Hillsdale, NJ: Lawrence Erlbaum.

Langevin, R., Paitich, D., Orchard, B., Handy, L., & Russon, A. (1982). Diagnosis of killers seen for a psychiatric assessment: A controlled study. *Acta Psychiatrika Scandinavia, 66,* 216-228.

LaTour, S. (1978). Determinants of participant and observer satisfaction with adversary and inquisitorial modes of adjudication. *Journal of Personality and Social Psychology, 36,* 1531-1545.

LaTour, S., Houlden, P., Walker, L., & Thibaut, J. (1976). Procedure: Transnational perspectives and preferences. *Yale Law Journal, 86,* 258-290.

Laufer, W. S., Skoog, D. K., & Day, J. M. (1982). Personality and criminality: A review of the California Psychological Inventory. *Journal of Clinical Psychology, 38,* 562-573.

Laurie, W. (1978a). Population assessment for program evaluation. In G. Maddox (Ed.), *Assessment and evaluation strategies in aging* (pp. 100-110). Durham, NC: Duke University.

Laurie, W. (1978b). The Cleveland experience: Functional status and services use. In Center for the Study of Aging and Human Development, *Multidimensional functional assessment: The OARS methodology* (pp. 89-99). Durham, NC: Duke University.

Lawrence, S. B. (1978). *Manual for the Lawrence psychological-forensic examination for use within the criminal justice system.* San Bernardino, CA: Lawrence.

Lawson, J. S., & Inglis, J. (1983). The laterality index of cognitive impairment after hemispheric damage: A measure derived from a principal components analysis of the Wechsler Adult Intelligence Scale. *Journal of Consulting and Clinical Psychology, 51,* 832-840.

Lawson, R. G. (1968). Order of presentation as a factor in jury presentation. *Kentucky Law Journal, 56,* 523-555.

Lawton, M. P. (1972). Assessing the competence of older people. In D. Kent, R. Kastenbaum, & S. Sherwood (Eds.), *Research, planning and action for the elderly* (pp. 122-143). New York: Behavioral Publications.

Lawton, M. P. (1982). Competency, environmental press, and adaptation of older people. In M. P. Lawton, P. Windley, & I. Byerts (Eds.), *Aging and the environment: Theoretical approaches* (pp. 33-59). New York: Springer.

Lawton, M. P., & Brody, E. (1969). Assessment of older people: Self-maintaining and instrumental activities of daily living. *Gerontologist, 9,* 179-186.

Lawton, M. P., Moss, M., Fulcomer, M., & Kleban, M. (1982). A research and service oriented multilevel assessment instrument. *Journal of Gerontology, 37,* 91-99.

Lawton, M. P., Windley, P., & Byerts, I. (Eds.) (1982). *Aging and the environment.* New York: Springer.

Lee, J. F. (1970). *Manual for the law enforcement perception questionnaire.* Brookport, IL: Psychometric Affiliates.

Lefcourt, H. (1966). Internal versus external control of reinforcement: A review. *Psychological Bulletin, 65,* 206-220.

Lefcourt, H., & Wine. (1969). Internal versus external control of reinforcement and the deployment of attention in experimental situations. *Canadian Journal of Behavioral Science, 1,* 167-181.

Lefcowitz, M., Eron, L., Walder, L., & Heusmann, L. (1977). *Growing up to be violent.* New York: Pergamon.

Lehmann, V. (1963). *Guardianship and protective services for older people.* Albany, NY: National Council on Aging Press.

Leifer, R. (1964). The psychiatrist and tests of criminal responsibility. *American Psychologist, 19,* 825-830.

Leippe, M. R. (1980). Effects on integrative memorial and cognitive processes on the correspondence of eyewitness accuracy and confidence. *Law and Human Behavior, 4,* 261-274.

Leippe, M. R., Wells, G. L., & Ostrom, T. M. (1978). Crime seriousness as a determinant of accuracy in eyewitness identification. *Journal of Applied Psychology, 63,* 345-351.

Lempert, T. D. (1975). Uncovering "nondiscernible" differences: Empirical research and the jury-size cases. *Michigan Law Review, 73,* 643-708.

Lentle, B. C. (1983). Diagnostic imaging in transition. *Annals RCPSC, 16,* 555-559.

Leo, J. (1982, July 5). Insane on all counts. *Time,* pp. 22-27.

Leo, J. (1982, July 5). Is the system guilty? *Time,* pp. 26-27.

Lermack, P. (1979). No right number? Social science research and the jury-size cases. *New York University Law Review, 54,* 951-976.

Lerner, M. J. (1980). *The belief in a just world: A fundamental delusion.* New York: Plenum Press.

Lerner, M. J., & Simmons, C. H. (1966). Observer's reaction to the "innocent victim": Compassion or rejection? *Journal of Personality and Social Psychology, 4,* 203-210.

Lester, D., & Wright, T. (1978). Murderers and overcontrolled hostility. *Psychological Reports, 43,* 1202.

Levin, H., & Askin, F. (1977). Privacy in the courts: Law and social reality. *Journal of Social Issues, 33*(3), 138-153.

Levine, C. (1977). Hospital ethics committees: A guarded prognosis. *Hastings Center Report, 7,* 25-27.

Levine, M., Farrell, M. P., & Perrotta, J. (1981). The impact of rules of jury deliberation on group developmental processes. In B. D. Sales (Ed.), *The trial process* (pp. 263-304). New York: Plenum Press.

Levinson, R. M., & Ramsay, G. (1979). Dangerousness, stress, and mental health evaluations. *Journal of Health and Social Behavior, 20,* 178-187.

Levy, A. M. (1978). Child custody determination: A proposed psychiatric methodology and its resultant case typology. *Journal of Psychiatry and Law, 6*(2), 189-214.

Levy, M. R., & Kahn, M. W. (1970). Interpreter bias on the Rorschach test as a function of patient's socioeconomic status. *Journal of Projective Techniques, 34,* 106-112.

Levy-Shiff, R. (1982). The effects of father absence on young children in mother-headed families. *Child Development, 53,* 1400-1405.

Lewin, K. (1947). Group decisions and social change. In T. M. Newcomb & E. L. Hartley (Eds.), *Readings in social psychology.* New York: Holt, Rinehart & Winston.

Lewin, T. H. D. (1975). Psychiatric evidence in criminal cases for purposes other than the defense in insanity. *Syracuse Law Review, 26,* 1051-1115.

Lewis, D. O. (1976). Delinquency, psychomotor epileptic symptoms, and paranoid ideation: A triad. *American Journal of Psychiatry, 133,* 1395-1398.

Lewis, D. O., Pincus, J. H., Shanok, S. S., & Glaser, G. H. (1982). Psychomotor epilepsy and violence in a group of incarcerated adolescent boys. *American Journal of Psychiatry, 139,* 882-887.

Lewis, D. O., & Shanok, S. S. (1979). A comparison of medical histories of incarcerated delinquent children and a matched sample of nondelinquent children. *Child Psychiatry and Human Development, 9,* 210-214.

Lewis, G., Golden, C. J., Moses, J., Osmon, D., Purisch, A. D., & Hammeke, T. A. (1979). The localization of cerebral dysfunction with a standardized version of Luria's neuropsychological battery. *Journal of Consulting and Clinical Psychology, 47,* 1003-1019.

Lezak, M. D. (1983). *Neuropsychological assessment.* New York: Oxford University Press.

Lichter, D. H. (1981). Note: Diagnosing the dead. *American Criminal Law Review, 18,* 617-635.

Lidz, C. (1984). *A study of the clinical management of dangerousness* (Documents related to Research Grant MH-40030). Rockville, MD: Center for Antisocial and Violent Behavior, National Institute of Mental Health.

Lidz, C. W., Meisel, A., Zerubavel, E., Carter, M., Sestak, R. M., & Roth, L. H. (1984). *Informed consent: A study of decision-making in psychiatry.* New York: Guilford Press.

Lightcap, J., Kurland, J., & Burgess, R. (1982). Child abuse. *Ethnology and Sociobiology, 3,* 61-67.

Lind, E. A. (1982). The psychology of courtroom procedure. In N. L. Kerr & R. M. Bray (Eds.), *The psychology of the courtroom* (pp. 13-34). New York: Academic Press.

Lind, E. A., Erickson, B., Conley, J., & O'Barr, W. (1978). Social attributions and conversation style in trial testimony. *Journal of Personality and Social Psychology, 36,* 1558-1567.

Lind, E. A., & O'Barr, W. M. (1978). The social significance of speech in the courtroom. In H. Giles & R. St. Clair (Eds.), *Language and social psychology.* Oxford, England: Blackwell.

Lind, E. A., Thibaut, J., & Walker, L. (1973). Discovery and presentation of evidence in adversary and nonadversary proceedings. *Michigan Law Review, 71,* 1129-1144.

Lind, E. A., Thibaut, J., & Walker, L. (1976). A cross-cultural comparison of the effect of adversary and nonadversary proceedings. *Virginia Law Review,* 271-283.

Lind, E. A., & Walker, L. (1979). Theory testing, theory development, and laboratory research on legal issues. *Law and Human Behavior, 3,* 5-19.

Lindblom, M. J. (1977). Compelling experts to testify: A proposal. *University of Chicago Law Review, 44,* 851-872.

Lindemann, E. (1932). Psychological changes in normal and abnormal individuals under the influence of sodium amytal. *American Journal of Psychiatry, 88,* 1083-1091.

Lindley, D. A. (1977). Probability and the law. *The Statistician, 26,* 203-220.

Lindsay, R. C. L., & Wells, G. L. (1980). What price justice? Exploring the relationship of lineup fairness to identification accuracy. *Law and Human Behavior, 4,* 303-313.

Lindsay, R. C. L., Wells, G. L., & Rumpel, C. M. (1981). Can people detect eyewitness identification within and across situations? *Journal of Applied Psychology, 66,* 79-89.

Lindzay, G., & Tejessy, C. (1965). Thematic Apperception Test: Indices of aggression in relationship to measures of overt and covert behavior. In B. I. Murstein (Ed.), *Handbook of projective techniques* (pp. 575-586). New York: Basic Books.

Linn, M. et al. (1977). Hospital vs. community (foster) care for psychiatric patients. *Archives of General Psychiatry, 34,* 78-83.

Linn, M., Klett, J., & Caffey, E. M. (1980). Foster home characteristics and psychiatric patient outcome. *Archives of General Psychiatry, 37,* 129-132.

Lippold, S., & Claiborn, J. M. (1983). Comparison of the Wechsler Adult Intelligence Scale and the Wechsler Adult Intelligence Scale-Revised. *Journal of Consulting and Clinical Psychology, 51,* 315.

Lipsitt, P. D. (1970). *Competency screening test.* Boston: Competency to Stand Trial and Mental Illness Project.

Lipsitt, P. D., Lelos, D., & McGarry, A. L. (1971). Competency for trial: A screening instrument. *American Journal of Psychiatry, 128*(1), 137-141.

Lishman, W. A. (1971). Amnesic syndromes and their neuropathology. *Special Publication, British Journal of Psychiatry, 117,* 26-38(6).

Littlepage, G., & Pineault, T. (1978). Verbal, facial and paralinguistic cues to the detection of truth and lying. *Personality and Social Psychology Bulletin, 4,* 461-464.

Litwak, T. (1980). Competency to stand trial: Discussion. *Annals of the New York Academy of Science,* 38-43.

Litwak, T. R., Gerber, G. L., & Fenster, C. A. (1980). The proper role of psychology in child custody disputes. *Journal of Family Law, 18,* 269-300.

Livermore, J. M., Malmquist, C. P., & Meehl, P. E. (1968). On the justifications for civil commitment. *University of Pennsylvania Law Review, 117,* 75-96.

Llewelyn, K. (1960). *The common law tradition: Deciding appeals.* Boston, MA: Little, Brown.

Lobsien, M. (1904). Veber psychologie der aussage. *Zeitschrift feur Paedagogishe Psychologie, 6,* 161.

Lochner, P. (1973). Some limits on the application of social science research in the legal process. *Law and the Social Order,* 815-848.

Loevinger, J. (1957). Objective tests as instruments of psychological theory. *Psychological Reports, 3,* Monograph Supplement IX, 635-694.

Loew, C. A. (1967). Acquisition of a hostile attitude and its relationship to aggressive behavior. *Journal of Personality and Social Psychology, 5,* 335-341.

Loewen, J. W. (1982). *Social science in the courtroom.* Lexington, MA: Lexington Books.

Loftus, E. F. (1974). Reconstructing memory: The incredible witness. *Psychology Today, 8,* 116-119.

Loftus, E. F. (1975). Leading questions and the eye-witness report. *Cognitive Psychology, 7,* 560-572.

Loftus, E. F. (1979). *Eye-witness testimony.* Cambridge, MA: Harvard University Press.

Loftus, E. F. (1980a). The eyewitness on trial. *Trial, 16,* 29-35.

Loftus, E. F. (1980b). Impact on expert psychological testimony on the unreliability of eyewitness identification. *Journal of Applied Psychology, 65,* 9-15.

Loftus, E. F. (1981a). Eyewitness testimony: Psychological research and legal thought. In M. Tonry & N. Morris (Eds.), *Crime and justice: An annual review of research,* Vol. 3. Chicago, IL: University of Chicago Press.

Loftus, E. F. (1981b). Reconstructive memory processes in eyewitness testimony. In B. D. Sales (Ed.), *The trial process.* New York: Plenum Press.

Loftus, E. F. (1983a). Misfortunes of memory. *Philosophical Transactions of the Royal Society* (London), *B302,* 413-421.

Loftus, E. F. (1983b). Silence is not golden. *American Psychologist, 38,* 564-572.

Loftus, E. F., & Davis, G. (1984). Distortion in the memory of children. *Journal of Social Science, 40,* 51-67.

Loftus, E. F., & Greene, E. (1980). Warning: Even memory for faces can be contagious. *Law and Human Behavior, 4,* 323-334.

Loftus, E. F., & Loftus, T. R. (1980). On the impermanence of stored information in the human brain. *American Psychologist, 35,* 409-420.

Loftus, E. F., & Monahan, J. (1980). Trial by data: Psychological research as legal evidence. *American Psychologist, 35,* 270-283.

Loh, W. D. (1979). Psychology and law: A coming of age. *Contemporary Psychology, 24,* 164-166.

Lorei, T. (1970). Staff ratings of the consequences of release from or retention in a psychiatric hospital. *Journal of Consulting and Clinical Psychology, 34,* 46-55.

Lothstein, L. M., & Jones, P. (1978). Discriminating violent individuals by means of various psychological tests. *Journal of Personality Assessment, 42*(3), 237-243.

Louisell, D. W. (1955). The psychologist in today's legal world. *Minnesota Law Review, 39*(3), 235-272.

Lovaas, O. (1961). Effective exposure to symbolic aggression on aggressive behavior. *Child Development, 32,* 37-44.

Lovegrove, S. A. (1973). The significance of three scales identifying a delinquent orientation among young Australian males. *Australian and New Zealand Journal of Criminology, 6,* 93-106.

Lower, J. S. (1978). Psychologists as expert witnesses. *Law and Psychology Review, 4,* 127-139.

Lowery, C. R. (1981). Child custody decisions in divorce proceedings: A survey of judges. *Professional Psychology, 4*(12), 492, 498.

Lowery, C. R. (1984). The wisdom of Solomon: Criteria for child custody from the legal and clinical points of view. *Law and Human Behavior, 8,* 371-380.

Luepnitz, D. A. (1978). Children of divorce: A review of the psychological literature. *Law and Human Behavior, 2*(2), 167-169.

Luisada, P. V. (1978). The phencyclidine psychosis: Phenomenology and treatment. In R. C. Peterson & R. C. Stillman (Eds.), *Phencyclidine (PCP) abuse: An appraisal* (pp. 241-255). Rockville, MD: National Institute on Drug Abuse.

Lusky, L. (1975). *By what right?* Charlottesville, VA: Michie.

Lyerly, S. B. (1973). *Handbook of Psychiatric Rating Scales* (2nd ed.). Washington, DC: U. S. Government Printing Office.

Lykken, D. T. (1974). Psychology and the lie detector industry. *American Psychologist, 29,* 725-739.

Lykken, D. T. (1981). *A tremor in the blood: Uses and abuses of the lie detector.* New York: McGraw-Hill.

Lykken, D. T. (1984). Trial by polygraph. *Behavioral Sciences and the Law, 2,* 75-92.

Lyle, W. H., Jr. (1979). Temporary insanity: Some practical considerations in a legal defense. *Journal of Orthomolecular Psychiatry, 8*(3), 1-25.

Lynch, B. E. (1979). Detection of deception: Its application to forensic psychiatry. *Bulletin of the American Academy of Psychiatry and the Law, 7,* 239-244.

Lynch, B. E., & Bradford, J. W. (1980). Amnesia: Its detection by psychophysiological measures. *Bulletin of the American Academy of Psychiatry and the Law, 8,* 288-297.

M

Maass, A., & Brigham, J. C. (1982). Eyewitness identifications: The role of attention and encoding specificity. *Personality and Social Psychology Bulletin, 8,* 54-59.

MacCauley, S. (1979). Lawyers and consumer protection laws. *Law and Society Review, 14,* 115-171.

MacDonald, J. M. (1976). *Psychiatry and the criminal: A guide to psychiatric examinations for the criminal court.* Springfield, IL: Charles C. Thomas.

Machover, K. (1949). *Personality projection in the drawing of human figure.* Springfield, IL: Charles C. Thomas.

Magnusson, D., & Endler, N. (Eds.) (1977). *Personality at the crossroads: Current issues in interactional psychology.* Hillsdale, NJ: Erlbaum.

Mahoney, F., & Barthel, D. (1965). Functional evaluation: The Barthel Index. *Maryland State Medical Journal, 14,* 61-65.

Mahoney, M. J. (1976). *Scientist as subject: The psychological imperative.* Cambridge, MA: Ballinger.

Maier, N. R. S., & Thurber, J. A. (1968). Accuracy of judgment of deception when an interviewer is watched, heard, and read. *Personnel Psychology, 21,* 23-30.

Maletzky, V. M. (1973). The episodic dyscontrol syndrome. *Diseases of the Nervous System, 36,* 178-185.

Maletzky, V. M., & Klotter, J. (1974). Episodic dyscontrol: A controlled replication. *Diseases of the Nervous System, 37,* 175-179.

Malmquist, C. P. (1974). Empirical problems in the selection of the insanity defense. *Psychiatric Annals, 4,* 48-66.

Malmquist, C. P. (1979). Can the committed patient refuse chemotherapy? *Archives of General Psychiatry, 36,* 351-354.

Malpass, R. J., & Kravitz, J. (1969). Recognition for faces of own and other race. *Journal of Personality and Social Psychology, 13,* 330-334.

Mark, P. H., & Ervin, F. R. (1970). *Violence and the brain.* New York: Harper & Row.

Maning, M., & Mewett, A. (1976). Psychiatric evidence. *Criminal Law Quarterly, 18,* 325-354.

Mann, P. A. (1970, October). Police responses to a course in psychology. *Crime and Delinquency,* 403-408.

Margolies, P., & Weintraub, S. (1977). The revised 56-item CRPBI as a research instrument. *Journal of Clinical Psychology, 33,* 472-476.

Marin, B. V., Holmes, D. L., Guth, M., & Kovac, P. (1979). The potential of children as eyewitnesses. *Law and Human Behavior, 3,* 295-305.

Marks, J. (1953). The attitudes of the mothers of male schizophrenics toward child behavior. *Journal of Abnormal and Social Psychology, 48,* 185-189.

Marks, P., & Seeman, W. (1963). *The actuarial description of abnormal personality: An atlas for use with the MMPI.* Baltimore, MD: Williams & Wilkins.

Marks, P. A., Seeman, W., & Haller, D. L. (1974). *The actuarial use of the MMPI with adolescents and adults.* Baltimore, MD: Williams & Wilkins.

Markson, E. R., Greenland, C., & Turner, R. E. (1965). The life and death of Louis Riel: A study in forensic psychiatry. *Canadian Psychiatric Association Journal, 10,* 244-264.

Marsh, J., & Caplan, N. (1979, Autumn). Michigan's new rape law evaluated. *Institute for Social Research Newsletter,* 3-6.

Marshall, H. (1961). Relations between home experience and children's use of language in play interactions with peers. *Psychological Monograph, 75* (Serial No. 509).

Marshall, J. (1966). *Law and psychology in conflict.* Indianapolis, IN: Bobbs-Merrill.

Marshall, J. (1969). The evidence. *Psychology Today, 2*(9), 48-52.

Martin, G. A. (1981). Mental disorder and criminal responsibility in Canadian law. In S. J. Hucker, C. D. Webster, & M. H. Ben-Arons (Eds.), *Mental disorder and criminal responsibility* (pp. 15-32). Toronto: Butterworth.

Martin, J. A. (1977). The proposed "Science Court." *Michigan Law Review, 75,* 1058-1091.

Marvell, T. (1978). *Appellate courts and lawyers.* Westport, CN: Greenwood Press.

Marx, M. L. (1977). Prison conditions and diminished capacity: A proposed defense. *Santa Clara Law Review, 17,* 855-883.

Matarazzo, J. D. (1972). *Wechsler's measurement and appraisal of adult intelligence.* Baltimore, MD: Williams & Wilkins.

Matranga, J. T. (1976). The relationship between behavioral indices of aggression and hostile content on the TAT. *Journal of Personality Assessment, 40,* 130-134.

Mattes, J. A., Klein, D. F., Millan, D., & Rosen, B. (1979). Comparison of the clinical effectiveness of "short" versus "long" stay psychiatric hospitalization. *Journal of Nervous and Mental Disease, 167*(3), 175-181.

Matthews, A. (1970). *Mental disability and the criminal law: A field study.* Chicago, IL: American Bar Association.

Maudsley, H. (1898). *Responsibility in mental disease.* New York: D. Appleton & Co.

Mayfield, D. (1976). Alcoholism, alcohol intoxication, and assaultive behavior. *Diseases of the Nervous System, 37,* 288-291.

McArthur, C. C. (1972). Rorschach. In O. K. Buros (Ed.), *Seventh mental measurements yearbook* (pp. 340-343). Highland Park, NJ: Gryphon Press.

McBroom, P. (1980). *Behavioral genetics.* Rockville, MD: National Institute of Mental Health.

McCaldon, R. J. (1964). Automatism. *Canadian Medical Association Journal, 91,* 914-920.

McCary, J. L. (1956). The psychologist as an expert witness in court. *American Psychologist, 11,* 8-13.

McClain, P. (1982). Black female homicide offenders and victims: Are they from the same population? *Death Education, 6,* 265-278.

McClelland, D. (1973). Testing for competence rather than for "intelligence." *American Psychologist, 28,* 1-14.

McCloskey, M., & Egeth, H. (1983). Eyewitness identification: What can a psychologist tell a jury? *American Psychologist, 38,* 550-563.

McConaghy, N. (1974). Measurement of change in penile dimensions. *Archives of Sexual Behavior, 4,* 381-388.

McConahey, J., Mullin, C., & Frederick, J. (1977). The uses of social science in trials with political and racial overtones: The trial of Joan Little. *Law and Contemporary Problems, 41,* 205-229.

McCormick, C. T. (1945). Some observations on the opinion rule and expert testimony. *Texas Law Review, 23,* 109-136.

McCormick, S. (1976). Job task and job analysis. In M. Dunnette (Ed.), *Handbook of industrial and organizational psychology.* Chicago, IL: Rand McNally.

McCranie, E. W., & Mizell, T. A. (1978). Aftercare for psychiatric patients: Does it prevent rehospitalization? *Hospital and Community Psychiatry, 29,* 584-587.

McCreary, C. P. (1977). Training psychology and law students to work together. *Professional Psychology, 8,* 103-108.

McDonald, J. M. (1967). Homicide threats. *American Journal of Psychiatry, 124,* 61-68.

McElhaney, J. W. (1977). Expert witnesses and the federal rules of evidence. *Mercer Law Review, 28,* 463-495.

McFatter, R. M. (1978). Sentences, strategies and justice: Effects of punishment philosophy on sentencing decisions. *Journal of Personality and Social Psychology, 36,* 1490-1500.

McGarry, A. (1965). Competency for trial and due process via the state hospital. *American Journal of Psychiatry, 122,* 623-631.

McGarry, A. L. (1980). Psycho-legal examinations and reports. In W. J. Curran, A. L. McGarry, & C. S. Petty (Eds.), *Modern legal medicine, psychiatry, and forensic science* (pp. 739-760). Philadelphia, PA: F. A. Davis.

McGarry, A. L., Curran, W., & Kenefick, D. (1968). Problems of public consultation in medicolegal matters: A symposium. *American Journal of Psychiatry, 125,* 42-45.

McGillis, D. (1978). Attribution and the law: Convergence between legal and psychological concepts. *Law and Human Behavior, 2,* 251-273.

McGillis, D. (1981). Conflict resolution outside the courts. In L. Bickman (Ed.), *Applied social psychology annual,* Vol. 2 (pp. 243-262). Beverly Hills, CA: Sage Publications.

McGillis, D., & Mullen, J. (1977). *Neighborhood justice centers: An analysis of potential models.* Washington, DC: U. S. Government Printing Office.

McGlothlin, W. H., & Anglin, M. D. (1981). Shutting off methadone. *Archives of General Psychiatry, 38,* 85-89.

McGlynn, R. P., & Dreilinger, E. A. (1981). Mock juror judgement and the insanity plea: Effects of incrimination and sanity information. *Journal of Applied Social Psychology, 11,* 166-180.

McGraw, B. D., & Keilitz, I. (1984). Guilty but mentally ill: The legislative response to the insanity defense. *State Court Journal, 8,* 4-8.

McGuire, W. J. (1967). Some impending reorientations in social psychology: Some thoughts provoked by Kenneth Ring. *Journal of Experimental Social Psychology, 3,* 124-139.

McGurk, B. J. (1978). Personality types among "normal" homicides. *British Journal of Criminology, 18,* 148-161.

McGurk, B. J., & McGurk, R. E. (1979). Personality types among prisoners and prison officers. *British Journal of Criminology, 19*(1), 31-49.

McKay, S. E., & Golden, C. J. (1979). Empirical derivation of neuropsychological scales for the lateralization of brain damage using the Luria-Nebraska neuropsychological test battery. *Clinical Neuropsychology, 1,* 19-23.

McKay, S. E., Golden, C. J., Moses, J. A., Fishburne, F., & Wisniewski, A. (1981). Correlation of the Luria-Nebraska neuropsychological battery with the WAIS. *Journal of Consulting and Clinical Psychology, 49,* 940-946.

McKinley, J. D., & Hathaway, S. R. (1944). The MMPI: V, hysteria, hypomania and psychopathic deviate. *Journal of Applied Psychology, 28,* 153-174.

McLahon, J. F. C. (1976). A hostility scale for Form R of the MMPI. *Journal of Clinical Psychology, 32,* 369-371.

McNeil, B. J., Keeler, E., & Adelstein, S. J. (1975). Primer on certain elements of medical decision-making. *New England Journal of Medicine, 293,* 211-215.

McRuer, R. (1956). *Report of the Royal Commission on the law of insanity as a defense in criminal cases.* Ottawa: Queen's Printer.

Mednick, S. A., & Finello, K. M. (1983). Biological factors and crime: Implications for forensic psychiatry. *International Journal of Law and Psychiatry, 6,* 1-15.

Meehl, P. E. (1954). *Clinical versus statistical prediction: A theoretical analysis and review of the evidence.* Minneapolis, MN: University of Minnesota Press.

Meehl, P. E. (1965). Seer over sign: The first sound example. *Journal of Experimental Research in Personality, 27,* 32.

Meehl, P. E. (1970a). Psychology and the criminal law. *University of Richmond Law Review, 5*(1), 1-30.

Meehl, P. E. (1970b). Some methodological reflections on the difficulties of psychoanalytic research. In M. Radner & S. Winokur (Eds.), *Minnesota studies in the philosophy of science, Vol. 4. Analyses of theories and methods of physics and psychology* (pp. 403-416). Minneapolis, MN: University of Minnesota Press.

Meehl, P. E. (1971). Law and the fireside inductions: Some reflections of a clinical psychologist. *Journal of Social Issues, 27,* 65-100.

Meer, B., & Baker, J. (1966). The Stockton Geriatric Rating Scale. *Journal of Gerontology, 21,* 392-403.

Meerloo, J. A. M. (1964). Emotionalism in the jury and the court of justice: The hazards of psychiatric testimony. *Journal of Nervous and Mental Disease, 139,* 294-300.

Megargee, E. I. (1966). Undercontrolled personality types in extreme antisocial aggression. *Psychological Monographs, 80* (Whole No. 611).

Megargee, E. I. (1970). The prediction of violence with psychological tests. In C. Spielberger (Ed.), *Current topics in clinical and community psychology.* New York: Academic Press.

Megargee, E. I. (1976). The prediction of dangerousness. *Criminal Justice and Behavior, 3,* 1-21.

Megargee, E. I. (1977a). *The California Psychological Inventory Handbook*. San Francisco, CA: Jossey-Bass.

Megargee, E. I. (1977b). A new classification system for criminal offenders. *Criminal Justice and Behavior, 4*, 107-216 (Special issue).

Megargee, E. I., Cook, P. E., & Mendelsohn, G. A. (1967). Development and validation of an MMPI scale of assaultiveness in overcontrolled individuals. *Journal of Abnormal Psychology, 72*, 519-528.

Megargee, E. I., Lockwood, V., Cato, J. L., & Jones, J. K. (1966, August). The effects of differences in examiner, tone of administration, and sex of subject on scores of the Holtzman Inkblot Technique. *Proceedings of the 74th Annual Convention of the American Psychological Association*, 235-236.

Megargee, E. I., & Mendelsohn, G. A. (1962). A cross-validation of the twelve MMPI indices of hostility and control. *Journal of Abnormal and Social Psychology, 65*, 431-438.

Meisel, A. (1979). The exception to the informed consent doctrine: Striking a balance between competing values in medical decisionmaking. *Wisconsin Law Review*, 413-416.

Meisel, A., & Roth, L. (1981). What we do and do not know about informed consent. *Journal of the American Medical Association, 246*, 2473-2477.

Meisel, A., Roth, L., & Lidz, C. (1977). Toward a model of the legal doctrine of informed consent. *American Journal of Psychiatry, 134*, 285-289.

Melton, G. (1980). Children's concepts of their rights. *Journal of Clinical Child Psychology, 9*, 186-190.

Melton, G. (1981). Effects of a state law permitting minors to consent to psychotherapy. *Professional Psychology, 12*, 647-654.

Melton, G. (1983a). More on insanity reform. *Division of Psychology and Law Newsletter, 3*(2), 6-8.

Melton, G. (1983b). Training in psychology and law: A directory. *Newsletter, Division 41, American Psychology Association, 3*, 1-3.

Melton, G., Koocher, G., & Saks, M. (Eds.) (1983). *Children's competence to consent*. New York: Plenum Press.

Meltsner, M. (1973). *Cruel and unusual*. New York: Random House.

Mental Disability Law Reporter. (1978). Incompetency to stand trial on criminal charges. *Mental Disability Law Reporter, 2*, 615-663.

Menuck, M. (1983). Clinical aspects of dangerous behavior. *Journal of Psychiatry and Law, 11*, 277-304.

Menzies, R., Webster, C., & Sepejak. (1985). The dimensions of dangerousness: Evaluating the accuracy of psychometric predictions of violence among forensic patients. *Law and Human Behavior, 1*, 49-70.

Mesritz, G. D. (1976). Guilty but mentally ill: An historical and constitutional analysis. *Journal of Urban Law, 53*, 471-496.

Messick, S. (1975). The standard problem: Meaning and value in measurement and evaluation. *American Psychologist, 30*, 995-966.

Messick, S. (1980). Test validity and the ethics of assessment. *American Psychologist, 35*, 1012-1027.

Myers, T. J. (1965). The psychiatric determination of legal intent. *Journal of Forensic Sciences, 10*, 347-367.

Milgram, S. (1963). Behavioral study of obedience. *Journal of Abnormal and Social Psychology, 67*, 371-378.

Milgram, S. (1965). Some conditions of obedience and disobedience to authority. In T. D. Steiner & M. Fishbein (Eds.), *Current studies in social psychology*. New York: Holt, Rinehart & Winston.

Miller, C. (1970). *Handbook of research design and social measurement*. New York: David McKay Co., Inc.

Miller, G. R. (1980). On being persuaded: Some basic distractions. In M. E. Roloff & G. R. Miller (Eds.), *Persuasion: New directions in theory and research*. Beverly Hills, CA: Sage Publications.

Miller, G. R., & Boster, F. J. (1977). Three images of the trial: Their implications for psychological research. In B. D. Sales (Ed.), *Psychology in the legal process*. New York: Spectrum.

Miller, G. R., & Burgoon, M. (1973). *New techniques of persuasion*. New York: Harper & Row.

Miller, H. C., Lower, J. S., & Bleechmore, J. (1978). The clinical psychologist as an expert witness on questions of mental illness and competency. *Law and Psychology Review, 4*, 115-125.

Miller, R., & Willner, H. (1974). The two-part consent form. *New England Journal of Medicine, 290*, 964-966.

Miller, R. E., & Sarat, A. (1981). Grievances, claims, and disputes: Assessing the adversary culture. *Law and Society Review, 15*, 525-565.

Miller, T. (1977). Oregon's partial responsibility defense: Disposition of the defendant and burden of proof. *Williamette Law Journal, 13*, 347-364.

Miller, T. R., Bauchner, J. E., Hocking, J. E., Fontes, N. E., Kaminsky, A. P., & Brendt, D. R. (1981). How well can observers detect deceptive testimony? In B. D. Sales (Ed.), *Perspectives in law and psychology*, Vol. 2, The trial process. New York: Plenum.

Miller, W. (1958). A lower class culture as a generating milieu of gang delinquency. *Journal of Social Issues, 14*, 5-19.

Millon, T. (1981). *Disorders of personality: DSM III, axis 2*. Toronto: Wiley-Interscience.

Millon, T. (1982). *Millon clinical multiaxial inventory*. Minneapolis, MN: Interpretive Scoring Systems.

Mills, C. J., & Bohannon, W. E. (1980a). Juror characteristics: To what extent are they related to jury verdicts? *Judicature, 64*, 23-31.

Mills, C. J., & Bohannon, W. E. (1980b). Personality characteristics of effective state police officers. *Journal of Applied Psychology, 65*, 680-684.

Milner, J. (1980). *The Child Abuse Potential Inventory: Manual*. Webster, NC: Psytec Corp.

Milner, J. (1982). Development of a lie scale for the Child Abuse Potential Inventory. *Psychological Reports, 50*, 871-874.

Milner, J., & Ayoub, C. (1980). Evaluation of "at risk" parents using the Child Abuse Potential Inventory. *Journal of Clinical Psychology, 36*, 945-948.

Milner, J., Gold, R., Ayoub, C., & Jacewitz, M. (1984). Predictive validity of the Child Abuse Potential Inventory. *Journal of Consulting and Clinical Psychology, 52*, 879-884.

Milner, J., & Wimberley, R. (1979). An inventory for the identification of child abusers. *Journal of Clinical Psychology, 35*, 95-100.

Milner, J., & Wimberley, R. (1980). Prediction and explanation of child abuse. *Journal of Clinical Psychology, 36*, 875-884.

Mischel, W. (1968). *Personality and assessment*. New York: Wiley.

Mischel, W. (1973). Toward a cognitive social learning reconceptualization of personality. *Psychological Review, 80*, 252-283.

Mischel, W. (1977). On the future of personality measurement. *American Psychologist, 32*, 246-254.

Mischel, W. (1983). Alternatives to the pursuit of the predictability and consistency of persons: Stable data that yields unstable interpretations. *Journal of Personality, 51*, 578-604.

Mischel, W. (1984). Convergences and challenges in the search for consistency. *American Psychologist, 39*, 351-364.

Mitchell, H. E., & Byrne, D. (1973). The defendant's dilemma: Effects of jurors' attitudes and authoritarianism on judicial decisions. *Journal of Personality and Social Psychology, 25,* 123-129.

Mitford, J. (1973). *Kind and usual punishment.* New York: Random House.

Mnookin, R. (1975). Child custody adjudication: Judicial functions in the face of indeterminancy. *Law and Contemporary Problems, 39,* 226-293.

Molinari, J. B. (1974). The role of the expert witness. *Forum, 9,* 789-794.

Molinoff, D. (1977, May 22). Life with father. *New York Times Magazine.*

Monahan, J. (1973). Abolish the insanity defense? Not yet. *Rutgers Law Review, 26,* 719-740.

Monahan, F. (1975). The prevention of violence. In J. Monahan (Ed.), *Community mental health and the criminal justice system.* New York: Pergamon Press.

Monahan, J. (1976). Violence prediction. *Virginia Law Review, 27,* 179-183.

Monahan, J. (1977a). Empirical analyses of civil commitment: Critique and context. *Law and Society Review, 11,* 619-628.

Monahan, J. (1977b). Social accountability: Preface to an integrated theory of criminal and mental health sanctions. In B. D. Sales (Ed.), *Perspectives in law and psychology, Vol. 1, The criminal justice system.* New York: Plenum.

Monahan, J. (1978a). Prediction research and the emergency commitment of dangerous mentally ill persons: A reconsideration. *American Journal of Psychiatry, 135,* 198-201.

Monahan, J. (1978b). Report of the task force on the role of pscyhology in the criminal justice system. *American Psychologist, 33,* 1099-1113.

Monahan, J. (1978c). The prediction of violent criminal behavior: A methodological critique and prospectus. In A. Blumstein et al. (Eds.), *Deterrence and incapacitation: Estimating the effects of criminal sanctions on crime rates.* Washington, DC: National Academy of Sciences.

Monahan, J. (1980). *Who is the client? The ethics of psychological intervention in the criminal justice system.* Washington, DC: American Psychological Association.

Monahan, J. (1981a). *Predicting violent behavior: An assessment of clinical techniques.* Beverly Hills, CA: Sage Publications.

Monahan, J. (1981b). *The clinical prediction of violent behavior.* Rockville, MD: National Institute of Mental Health.

Monahan, J. (1986). Personal communication. Richmond, VA.

Monahan, J., & Hood, G. (1978). Ascriptions of dangerousness: The eye (and age, sex, education, location, and politics) of the beholder. In R. Simon (Ed.), *Research in law and sociology* (pp. 143-151). Greenwich, CN: Johnson.

Monahan, J., & Loftus, E. F. (1982). The psychology of law. *Annual Review of Psychology* (p. 1-47). Palo Alto, CA: Annual Reviews.

Monahan, J., & Monahan, L. C. (1977). Prediction research and the role of psychologists in correctional institutions. *San Diego Law Review, 14,* 1028-1038.

Monahan, J., & Steadman, H. (Eds.) (1983). *Mentally disordered offenders: Perspectives from law and social science.* New York: Plenum Press.

Money, J. (1970a). Behavioral genetics: Principles, methods, and examples from xo, xxy, and xyy syndromes. *Seminars in Psychiatry, 2,* 11-29.

Money, J. (1970b). Use of an androgen-depleting hormone in the treatment of male sex offenders. *Journal of Sex Research, 6,* 165-172.

Monroe, R. R. (1970). *Episodic behavior disorders.* Lexington, MA: Lexington Books.

Moore, M. S. (1979). Responsibility for unconsciously motivated action. *International Journal of Law and Psychiatry, 2,* 323-347.

Moos, R. (1973a). Conceptualization of human environments. *American Psychologist, 28*, 652-665.

Moos, R. (1973b). *Family Environment Scale Preliminary Manual.* Palo Alto, CA: Social Ecology Laboratory, Department of Psychiatry, Stanford University.

Moos, R. (1974). *The social climate scales: An overview.* Palo Alto, CA: Consulting Psychologists Press.

Moos, R. (1978). *Evaluating correctional and community settings.* New York: Wiley.

Moos, R., Grauvain, M., Max, S., & Mehren, B. (1979). Assessing the environments of sheltered care settings. *Gerontologist, 19*, 74-82.

Moran, G., & Comfort, J.C. (1982). Scientific juror selection: Sex as a moderator of demographic and personality predictors of impaneled felony juror behavior. *Journal of Personality and Social Psychology, 43*, 191-203.

Morris, G. (1975). *The insanity defense: A blueprint for legislative reform.* Lexington, MA: Lexington Books.

Morris, G. (1978). Conservatorship for the "gravely disabled": California's non-declaration of non-independence. *International Journal of Law and Psychiatry, 1*, 395-426.

Morris, H. (1979). Screening of police applicants: Issues of interviewing and psychological testing. *Police Chief, 46*(7).

Morris, N. (1974). *The future of imprisonment.* Chicago, IL: University of Chicago Press.

Morris, N. (1982). The criminal responsibility of the mentally ill. *Syracuse Law Review, 33*, 477-531.

Morrow, G., Gootnick, J., & Schmale, A. (1978). A simple technique for increasing cancer patients' knowledge of informed consent to treatment. *Cancer, 42*, 793-799.

Morrow, W., & Petersen, D. (1966). Follow-up on discharged offenders: "Not guilty by reason of insanity" and "criminal sexual psychopaths." *Journal of Criminal Law, Criminology, and Police Science, 57*, 31-34.

Morse, S. (1978a). Crazy behavior, morals and science: An analysis of mental health law. Southern *California Law Review, 51*, 527-654.

Morse, S. (1978b). Law and mental health professionals: The limits of expertise. *Professional Psychology, 9*, 389-399.

Morse, S. (1982a). Failed explanations and criminal responsibility: Experts and the unconscious. *Virginia Law Review, 68*, 971-1084.

Morse, S. (1982b). Mental health law: Governmental regulation of disordered persons and the role of the professional psychologist. In B. D. Sales (Ed.), *The professional psychologist's handbook* (pp. 339-422). New York: Plenum Press.

Morse, S. (1982c). Reforming expert testimony. *Law and Human Behavior, 6*, 39-43.

Morse, S. J. (1977). The twilight of welfare criminology. *New York State Bar Journal, 49*, 11, 18-23.

Morse, S. J. (1984). Undiminished confusion in diminished capacity. *Journal of Criminal Law and Criminology, 75*, 1-55.

Moses, J. A., Golden, C. J., Wilkening, G. N., McKay, S. E., & Ariel, R. (1983). *Interpretation of the Luria-Nebraska neuropsychological battery,* Vol. 2. New York: Grune & Stratton.

Mosher, D. L. (1965). Interaction of fear and guilt in inhibiting unacceptable behavior. *Journal of Consulting Psychology, 29*, 161-167.

Moskitis, R. L. (1976). The constitutional need for discovery of pre-voir dire juror studies. *Southern California Law Review, 49*, 597-633.

Mosteller, F., & Moynihan, D. (Eds.) (1972). *On equality of educational opportunity.* New York: Random House.

Moynihan, D. P. (1979). Social science and the courts. *Public Interest, 54*, 12-31.

Mullen, J. M. (1980). *The forensic psychiatric patient in Texas: Historical perspective and normative research on dangerousness.* Austin, TX: Texas Department of Mental Health and Mental Retardation.

Mullen, J. M., & Dudley, H. K., Jr. (1981). Development of an actuarial model for predicting dangerousness of patients in maximum-security mental hospitals. In J. R. Hays, T. K. Roberts, & K. S. Solway (Eds.), *Violence and the violent individual.* New York: SP Medical and Scientific Books.

Mullen, J. M., & Reinehr, R. C. (1982). Predicting dangerousness of maximum security forensic mental patients. *Journal of Psychiatry and Law, 10,* 223-231.

Mullen, J. M., Reinehr, R. C., & Swartz, J. D. (1982). Performance of forensic patients on the Holtzman Inkblot Technique: A normative study. *Perceptual and Motor Skills, 54,* 275-280.

Mulvey, E. P. (1982). Family courts: The issue of reasonable goals. *Law and Human Behavior, 6*(1), 49-64.

Mungas, V. (1984). Discriminant validation of an MMPI measure of aggression. *Journal of Consulting and Clinical Psychology, 52,* 313-314.

Munley, P. H., Devone, N., Einhorn, C. M., Gash, I. A., Hyer, L., & Kuhn, K. C. (1977). Demographic and clinical characteristics as predictors of length of hospitalization and readmission. *Journal of Clinical Psychology, 33*(4), 1093-1099.

Munsterberg, H. (1908). *On the witness stand.* New York: Doubleday, Page.

Murphy, G. E., Woodruff, M., & Herjanic, M. (1974). Validity of clinical course of a primary affective disorder. *Archives of General Psychiatry, 30,* 757-761.

Murphy, W. (1964). Elements of judicial strategy. Chicago, IL: University of Chicago Press.

Murray, D. M., & Wells, G. L. (1982). Does knowledge that a crime was staged affect eyewitness performance? *Journal of Applied Social Psychology, 12,* 42-53.

Murray, H. (1938). *Explorations in personality.* New York: Oxford University Press.

Murray, H. A. (1943). *Thematic Apperception Test manual.* Cambridge, MA: Harvard University Press.

Murstein, B. I. (Ed.) (1965). *Handbook of projective techniques.* New York: Basic Books.

Mutter, C. B. (1979). Regressive hypnosis and the polygraph: A case study. *American Journal of Clinical Hypnosis, 22,* 47-50.

Myers, D. G., & Kaplan, M. F. (1976). Group-induced polarization in simulated juries. *Personality and Social Psychology Bulletin, 2,* 63-66.

Myers, D. G., & Lamm, H. (1976). The group polarization phenomenon. *Psychological Bulletin, 83,* 602-627.

Myers, M. A. (1979). Rule departures and making law: Juries and their verdicts. *Law and Society Review, 13,* 787-797.

N

Nagao, D., & Davis, J. H. (1981). The effects of prior experience on complex social decisions: An illustration with mock jurors. Quarterly *Journal of Social Psychology, 43,* 190-199.

Naples, M., & Hackett, T. P. (1978). The amytal interview: History and current uses. *Psychosomatics, 19,* 98-105.

Nagel, S., Lamm, D., & Neef, M. (1981). Decision theory and juror decision making. In B. D. Sales (Ed.), *The trial process* (pp. 353-386). New York: Plenum Press.

Nagel, S., & Neef, M. (1975). Deductive modeling to determine an optimum jury size and fraction required to convict. *Washington University Law Quarterly*, 933-978.

Nagel, S., & Neef, M. (1976). Plea bargaining, decision theory, and equilibrium models. *Indiana Law Journal, 51*, 957-1024.

Nash, M. M. (1974). Parameters and distinctiveness of psychological testimony. *Professional Psychology, 5*, 239-243.

Nashel, H. M. (1974). Editorial. *Journal of Psychiatry and Law, 2*, 241-242.

National Advisory Commission on Criminal Justice Standards and Goals. (1973). *Program measurement and evaluation in criminal justice system*. Washington, DC: U. S. Government Printing Office.

National Conference of Commissioners on Uniform State Laws. (1971). Uniform marriage and divorce act. *Family Law Quarterly, 5*, 205-251.

Nehemkis, A., Macari, M. A., & Lettieri, D. V. (Eds.) (1976). *Drug abuse instrument handbook: Selected items for psychosocial drug research*. Washington, DC: U. S. Government Printing Office.

Neider, B. A. (1979). Criminal law: First degree murder–psychiatric testimony admissible on issue of intent. *Wisconsin Law Review*, 628-660.

Neisser, U. (1976). *Cognition and reality: Principles and implications of cognitive psychology*. San Francisco, CA: Freeman.

Nemeth, C. (1977). Interactions between jurors as a function of majority vs. unanimity decision rules. *Journal of Applied Social Psychology, 7*, 38-56.

Nemeth, C. (1981). Jury trials: Psychology and law. In L. Berkowitz (Ed.), *Advances in experimental social psychology*, Vol. 13. New York: Academic Press.

Nemeth, C., & Sosis, R. M. (1973). A simulated jury: Characteristics of the defendant and the jurors. *Journal of Social Psychology, 90*, 221-229.

Newson-Smith, J. G. B., & Hirsch, S. R. (1979). A comparison of social workers and psychiatrists in evaluating parasuicide. *British Journal of Psychiatry, 134*, 335-342.

Nierenberg, G. (1973). *Fundamentals of negotiating*. New York: Hawthorn Books.

Nietzel, M. T., & Dillehay, R. C. (1982). The effects of variations in voir dire procedures in capital murder trials. *Law and Human Behavior, 6*, 1-13.

Nordenberg, M. A., & Luneberg, W. V. (1982). Decision making in complex federal civil cases: Two alternatives to the traditional jury. *Judicature, 65*, 420-431.

Norton, J. E. (Ed.) (1981). *The anatomy of a personal injury suit* (2nd ed.). Washington, DC: Association of Trial Lawyers of America.

Nottingham, E. J., & Mattson, R. E. (1981). A validation study of the competency screening test. *Law and Human Behavior, 5*(4), 329-335.

Nutall, E., & Nutall, R. (1976). Parent-child relationships and effective academic motivation. *Journal of Psychology, 94*, 127-133.

Nydegger, C. (Ed.) (1977). *Measuring morale: A guide to effective assessment*. Washington, DC: Gerontological Society.

O

Oaks, D. (1970). Studying the exclusionary rule in search and seizure. *University of Chicago Law Review, 37*, 665-757.

O'Barr, W. M., & Lind, A. E. (1981). Ethnography and experimentation: Partners in legal research. In B. D. Sales (Ed.), *The trial process* (pp. 181-208). New York: Plenum Press.

O'Brien, D. (1980). The seduction of the judiciary: Social science and the courts. *Judicature, 64,* 8-21.

Office of the Secretary. (1978). HEW protection of human subjects: Proposed regulations in research involving prisoners. *Federal Register, 43*(3), 1050-1052.

O'Hagan, S. E. J. (1972). The validation of an MMPI scale of sociopathy. *FCI Research Reports, 4*(1), 1-26.

Okpaku, S. (1976). Psychology: Impediment or aid in child custody cases? *Rutgers Law Review, 29,* 1117-1153.

Ollendick, D., Laberteaux, P., & Horne, A. (1978). Relationships among maternal attitudes, perceived family environments, and preschooler's behavior. *Perceptual and Motor Skills, 46,* 1092-1094.

O'Neill, P., & Levings, D. E. (1979). Inducing biased scanning in a group setting to change attitudes toward bilingualism and capital punishment. *Journal of Personality and Social Psychology, 38*(8), 1432-1438.

Orne, M. T. (1961). The potential uses of hypnosis in interrogation. In A. D. Biderman & H. Zimmer (Eds.), *The manipulation of human behavior* (pp. 169-215). New York: Wiley & Sons.

Orne, M. T. (1971). The simulation of hypnosis: Why, how and what it means. *International Journal of Clinical and Experimental Hypnosis, 19,* 277-296.

Orne, M. T. (1972). On the simulating subject as a quasi-control group in hypnosis research: What, why and how. In E. Fromm & R. E. Shor (Eds.), *Hypnosis: Research developments and perspectives* (pp. 399-443). Chicago, IL: Aldine-Atherton.

Orne, M. T. (1979). The use and misuse of hypnosis in court. *International Journal of Clinical and Experimental Hypnosis, 27,* 311-341.

Orr, J. H. (1978). The imprisonment of mentally disordered offenders. *British Journal of Psychiatry, 133,* 194-195.

Orthner, D. K., & Lewis, K. (1979). Evidence of single father competence in child-rearing. *Family Law Quarterly, 13,* 27-47.

Osgood, C. E. (1962). *An alternative to war or surrender.* Urbana, IL: University of Illinois.

Ossipov, V. B. (1944). Malingering: The simulation of psychosis. *Bulletin of the Menninger Clinic, 8,* 39-42.

Oster, A. (1965). Custody proceedings: A study of vague and indefinite standards. *Journal of Family Law, 5,* 21-38.

Ostrom, T. M., Werner, C., & Saks, M. J. (1978). An integration theory analysis of jurors' presumptions of guilty or innocence. *Journal of Personality and Social Psychology, 36,* 436-450.

Overholser, J. (1962). Criminal responsibility: A psychiatrist's viewpoint. *American Bar Association Journal, 48,* 529-530.

Owen, D. R. (1972). The 47, xyy male: A review. *Psychological Bulletin, 78,* 209-233.

Owens, O. G., Johnstone, E. G., Bydder, G. M., & Kreel, L. (1980). Unsuspected organic disease in chronic schizophrenia demonstrated by computed tomography. *Journal of Neurology, Neurosurgery, and Psychiatry, 43,* 1065-1069.

P

Pace, R. (1969). *College and University Environment Scales: Technical manual.* Princeton, NJ: Educational Testing Service.

Pace, R., & Stern, G. (1958). An approach to the measurement of psychological characteristics of college environments. *Journal of Educational Psychology, 49,* 269-277.

Pacht, A., Kuehn, J., Bassett, T., & Nash, M. (1973). The current status of the psychologist as an expert witness. *Professional Psychology, 4*, 409-413.

Packer, I. K. (1981). Use of hypnotic techniques in the evaluation of criminal defendants. *Journal of Psychiatry and Law, 9*, 313-327.

Packer, K. (1983). A meta-analysis of the reliability and validity of the Rorschach. *Journal of Personality Assessment, 47*, 227-231.

Padawer-Singer, A. M., & Barton, A. H. (1975). The impact of pretrial publicity on jurors' verdicts. In R. J. Simons (Ed.), *The jury system in America.* Beverly Hills, CA: Sage Publications.

Padawer-Singer, A. M., Singer, A. N., & Singer, R. L. J. (1974). Voir dire by two lawyers: An essential safeguard. *Judicature, 57*, 386-391.

Padawer-Singer, A. M., Singer, A., & Singer, R. L. J. (1977). Legal and social-psychological research in the effects of pre-trial publicity on juries, numerical make-up of juries, non-unanimous verdict requirements. *Law and Psychology Review, 3*, 71-80.

Page, S. (1975). Power, professionals and arguments against civil commitment. *Professional Psychology, 6*, 381-392.

Page, S. (1982). Psychologist and physician diagnoses of hospitalized patients with similar MMPI symptomatology. *Canadian Journal of Psychiatry, 27*, 417-473.

Paitich, D. (1966). The clinical psychologist as an expert witness: A dialogue. *Canadian Psychologist, 7*, 407-412.

Palmer, J. (1983). *The psychological assessment of children.* New York: Wiley.

Panek, P. E., & Stoner, S. (1979). Test-retest reliability of the Hand Test with normal subjects. *Journal of Personality Assessment, 43*, 135-137.

Pankratz, L. (1981). A review of the Munchausen syndrome. *Clinical Psychology Review, 1*, 65-78.

Panton, J. H. (1962). Use of the MMPI as an index to successful parole. *Journal of Criminal Law, Criminology, and Police Science, 53*, 484-488.

Panton, J. H. (1970). *Manual for a Prison Classification Inventory (PCI) for the MMPI.* Raleigh, NC: Department of Rehabilitation and Control.

Panton, J. H. (1978). Personality differences appearing between rapists of children and non-violent molesters of female children. *Research Communications in Psychology, Psychiatry, and Behavior, 3*(4), 385-393.

Parker, G. (1977). *An introduction to criminal law.* Toronto: Methuen Publications.

Parker, K. (1983). Factor analysis of WAIS-R at nine age levels between 16 and 74 years. *Journal of Consulting and Clinical Psychology, 51*, 302-308.

Parwatikar, S. D., Holcomb, W. R., & Menninger, K. A. (1985). Detection of malingered amnesia in accused murderers. *Bulletin of the American Academy of Psychiatry and the Law, 13*, 97-103.

Pasework, R. (1981). Insanity plea: A review of the research literature. *Journal of Psychiatry and Law, 9*, 357-401.

Pasework, R., & Lanthorn, B. (1977). Disposition of persons utilizing the insanity plea in a rural state. *Journal of Humanics, 5*, 87-98.

Pasework, R., Pantle, M., & Steadman, H. (1979a). Characteristics and dispositions of persons found not guilty by reason of insanity in New York State, 1971-1976. *American Journal of Psychiatry, 136*, 655-660.

Pasework, R., Pantle, M., & Steadman, H. (1979b). The insanity plea in New York State, 1965-1976. *New York State Bar Journal, 52*, 186-189.

Patrick, J. (1984). Characteristics of DSM III borderline MMPI profiles. *Journal of Clinical Psychology, 40*, 655-658.

Patterson, G. (1977). Naturalistic observation in clinical assessment. *Journal of Abnormal Child Psychology, 5*, 307-322.

Patterson, G., Cobb, J., & Ray, R. (1972). A social engineering technology for retraining the families of aggressive boys. In H. Adams & I. Unikel (Eds.), *Issues in transient behavior therapy*. Springfield, IL: Charles C. Thomas.

Paulson, M., Schwemer, G., Afifi, A., & Bendel, R. (1977). Parent Attitude Research Instrument (PARI): Clinical vs. statistical inferences in understanding abusive mothers. *Journal of Clinical Psychology, 33*, 848-854.

Payne, J. W., Braunstein, M. L., & Carroll, J. S. (1978). Exploring predecisional behavior: An alternative approach to decision research. *Organizational Behavior and Human Performance, 22*, 17-44.

Peckins, D. M. (1976). Artificial insemination and the law. *Journal of Legal Medicine*, 17-22.

Penk, W. E., Charles H. L., & Van Hoose, T. A. (1978). Comparative effectiveness of day hospital and inpatient psychiatric treatment. *Journal of Consulting and Clinical Psychology, 46*, 94-101.

Penn, N. E. et al. (1969). Some considerations for future mental health legislation. *Mental Hygiene, 53*, 10-13.

Pennington, N., & Hastie, R. (1981). Juror decision-making models: The generalization gap. *Psychological Bulletin, 89*, 246-287.

Penrod, S., & Hastie, R. (1979). Models of jury decision making: A critical review. *Psychological Bulletin, 86*, 462-492.

Penrod, S., Loftus, E., & Winkler, J. (1982). The reliability of eyewitness testimony: A psychological perspective. In N. L. Kerr & R. M. Bray (Eds.), *The psychology of the courtroom* (pp. 119-168). New York: Academic Press.

Pepitone, A., & DiNubile, M. (1976). Contrast effects in judgments of crime severity and the punishment of criminal violators. *Journal of Personality and Social Psychology, 33*, 448-459.

Perlin, M. L. (1975). Psychiatric testimony in a criminal setting. *Bulletin of the American Academy of Psychiatry and the Law, 3*, 143-151.

Perlin, M. L. (1977). The legal status of the psychologist in the courtroom. *Journal of Psychiatry and Law, 5*, 41-54.

Perlin, M. L. (1980). The legal status of the psychologist in the courtroom. *Mental Disability Law Reporter, 4*, 194-200.

Perr, I. (1965). Liability of hospital and psychiatrist in suicide. *American Journal of Psychiatry, 122*, 631-637.

Perr, I. (1974). Independent examination of patients hospitalized against their will. *American Journal of Psychiatry, 131*, 765-768.

Perr, I. (1975a). Blood alcohol levels and "diminished capacity." *Journal of Legal Medicine, 3*(4), 28-396.

Perr, I. (1975b). Psychiatric testimony and the Rashomon phenomenon. *Bulletin of the American Academy of Psychiatry and the Law, 3*, 83-98.

Perr, I. (1976). Competency to "cop a plea." *Bulletin of the American Academy of Psychiatry and the Law, 4*, 45-50.

Perr, I. N. (1977). Cross-examination of the psychiatrist, using publications. *Bulletin of the American Academy of Psychiatry and the Law, 5*, 327-331.

Persons, R. W., & Marks, P. A. (1971). The violent 4-3 personality type. *Journal of Consulting and Clinical Psychology, 36*, 189-196.

Peterson, R. C., & Stillman, R. C. (Eds.) (1978). *Phencyclidine (PCP) abuse: An appraisal*. Rockville, MD: National Institute on Drug Abuse.

Petersilia, J., Greenwood, P., & Lavin, M. (1977). *Criminal careers of habitual felons*. Santa Monica, CA: Rand.

Petrella, R. D., & Poythress, N. G. (1983). The quality of forensic evaluations: An interdisciplinary study. *Journal of Consulting and Clinical Psychology, 51*, 76-85.

Petrich, J., & Homes, T. H. (1977). Life changes and onset of illness. *Medical Clinics of North America, 61*(4), 825-838.

Petrila, J. (1982). The insanity defense and other mental health dispositions in Missouri. *International Journal of Law and Psychiatry, 5*, 81-101.

Pettigrew, T. F. (1979, October). Race, ethics, and the social scientist. *Hastings Center Report*, 15-18.

Pfeiffer, E. (1975). A Short Portable Mental Status Questionnaire for the assessment of organic brain deficit in elderly patients. *Journal of the American Geriatric Society, 23*, 433-441.

Pfeiffer, E. (1978). Ways of combining functional assessment data. In Center for the Study of Aging and Human Development, *Multidimensional functional assessment: The OARS methodology* (pp. 65-71). Durham, NC: Duke University.

Pfeiffer, E., Eizenstein, R., & Dabbs, E. (1967). Mental competency evaluation for the federal courts: Methods and results. *Journal of Nervous and Mental Disease, 144*, 320-328.

Pfeiffer, E. et al. (1967). Mental competency evaluation for the federal courts: Appraisal and implications. *Journal of Nervous and Mental Disease, 145*, 18-24.

Philips, M. (1982). The question of voluntariness in the plea bargaining controversy: A philosophical clarification. *Law and Society Review, 16*, 207-224.

Phillips, B., & Pasewark, R. (1980). Insanity plea in Connecticut. *Bulletin of the American Academy of Psychiatry and the Law, 8*, 335-344.

Phillips, L. (1968). *Human adaptation and its failures*. New York: Academic Press.

Piciucco, L. (1976). *Personality effects of examiner on Rorschach scoring errors* (Doctoral thesis). San Diego, CA: United States International University.

Piersma, P., Ganousis, J., Volenik, A., Swanger, H., & Connell, P. (1977). *Law and tactics in juvenile cases*. Philadelphia, PA: American Law Institute-American Bar Association.

Piotrowski, Z. A. (1979). *Perceptanalysis*. Philadelphia, PA: Ex Libris.

Pipkin, R. (1976). Legal education: The consumers' perspective. *American Bar Foundation Research Journal*, 1161-1192.

Pizzi, W. (1977). Competency to stand trial in federal courts: Conceptual and constitutional problems. *University of Chicago Law Review, 45*, 20-71.

Platt, A. M., & Diamond, B. L. (1965). The origins and development of the "wild beast" concept of mental illness and its relation to theories of criminal responsibility. *Journal of the History of the Behavioral Sciences, 1*, 355-367.

Plotkin, L. (1972). Coal handling, steam-fitting, psychology and law. *American Psychologist, 27*, 202-204.

Podell, R., Peck, H., & First, C. (1972). Custody: To which parent? *Marquette Law Review, 56*, 51-68.

Pogrebin, M. R. (1979). The ambiguous role of the juvenile officer. *Juvenile and Family Court Journal, 30*(1), 17-20.

Pokorny, A. D. (1964). Suicide rates in various psychiatric disorders. *Journal of Nervous and Mental Disease, 139*, 499-506.

Pollack, M., Levenstein, D. S. W., & Klein, D. F. (1968). A three year post-hospital follow-up of adolescent and adult schizophrenics. *American Journal of Orthopsychiatry, 38*, 94-110.

Pollack, S. (1974). Forensic psychiatry: A specialty. *Bulletin of the American Academy of Psychiatry and the Law, 2,* 1-6.

Pollack, S. (1976). The insanity defense as defined by the proposed Federal Criminal Code. *Bulletin of the American Academy of Psychiatry and the Law, 4,* 11-23.

Pollack, S. (1977). Cross-examination of the psychiatrist using publications: Point counter-point. *Bulletin of the American Academy of Psychiatry and the Law, 5,* 332-335.

Pollack, S. (1982). The concept of dangerousness for legal purposes. In B. Gross & L. Weinberger (Eds.), *New directions for mental health services: The mental health professional and the legal system* (pp. 45-54). San Francisco, CA: Jossey-Bass.

Pollack, S., Gross, B. H., & Weinberger, L. E. (1982). Principles of forensic psychiatry for reaching psychiatric-legal opinions. In B. H. Gross & L. E. Weinberger (Eds.), *The mental health professional and the legal system* (pp. 25-44). San Francisco, CA: Jossey-Bass.

Pollak, L. (1959). Racial discrimination and judicial integrity: A reply to Professor Wechsler. *University of Pennsylvania Law Review, 108,* 1-34.

Poon, L. (Ed.) (1980). *Aging in the 1980s.* Washington, DC: American Psychological Association.

Pope, B., & Scott, W. (1967). *Psychological diagnosis in clinical practice.* New York: Oxford University Press.

Pope, T. (1975). Interpreter bias on the Rorschach test as a function of patients' social class and race. *Disseration Abstracts International, 36*(3-B), 1451-1452.

Post, R. M. (1975). Cocaine psychosis: A continuum model. *American Journal of Psychiatry, 132,* 225-231.

Potkay, C. R. (1972). Clinical judgment under varied informational conditions. *Journal of Consulting and Clinical Psychology, 39,* 513.

Pound, R. (1921). *The spirit of the common law.* Boston, MA: Little, Brown.

Powell, D. M. (1971). Reducing the size of juries. *University of Michigan Journal of Law Reform, 5,* 87-108.

Powitzky, R. J. (1979). The use and misuse of psychologists in a hostage situation. *Police Chief, 46*(6), 30-33.

Poythress, N. (1977). Mental health expert testimony: Current problems. *Journal of Psychiatry and Law, 5,* 201-227.

Poythress, N. G. (1978). Behavior modification, brainwashing, religion and the law. *Journal of Religion and Health, 17*(4), 238-243.

Poythress, N. G. (1980). Coping on the witness stand: Learned responses to "learned treatises." *Professional Psychology,* (1).

Poythress, N. G. (1982). Concerning reform in expert testimony. *Law and Human Behavior, 6,* 39-43.

Prandoni, J. R., & Swartz, C. P. (1978). Rorschach protocols for three diagnostic categories of adult offenders: Normative data. *Journal of Personality Assessment, 42,* 115.

Pratt, R. T. C. (1977). Psychogenic loss of memory, In C. W. M. Whitty & O. L. Vangwill (Eds.), *Amnesia: Clinical, psychological, and medical/legal aspects* (pp. 224-232). London: Butterworth.

Presidents' Commission for the Study of Ethical Problems in Medicine and Biomedical and Behavioral Research. (1982). *Making health care decisions.* Washington, DC: U. S. Government Printing Office.

Presidents' Commission on Law Enforcement and Administration of Justice. (1967). *Task force report: Juvenile delinquency and youth crime.* Washington, DC: U. S. Government Printing Office.

Presidents' Commission on Mental Retardation. (1976). *Mental retardation: Century of decision— Report to the President*. (DHEW Publication No. 76-21013). Washington, DC: U. S. Government Printing Office.

Press A. (1983, January 10). Divorce American style. *Newsweek*, pp. 42-48.

Prettyman, E. B. (1960). Jury instructions: First or last? *American Bar Association Journal, 46*, 1066.

Price, J. L. (1972). *Handbook of organizational measurement*. Lexington, MA: DC Heath & Co.

Price, W. H., Strong, J. A., Whatmore, P. B., & McClemont, W. (1966). Criminal patients with xyy sex chromosome complement. *Lancet, 1*, 565-566.

Prifitera, A., & Ryan, J. J. (1981). Validity of the Luria-Nebraska intellectual process scale as a measure of adult intelligence. *Journal of Consulting and Clinical Psychology, 49*, 755-766.

Pritchard, D. (1977). Stable predictors of recidivism. *Journal Supplement Abstract Service, 7*, 72.

PROMIS Research Project. (1977). *Highlights of interim findings and implications*. Washington, DC: Institute for Law and Social Research.

Pugh, R. (1973). The insanity defense in operation: A practicing psychiatrist views Durham and Brawnor. *Washington University Law Quarterly*, 87-108.

Purcell, K. (1956). The Thematic Apperception Test and antisocial behavior. *Journal of Consulting Psychology, 20*, 449-456.

Purisch, A. D., Golden, C. J., & Hammeke, T. A. (1978). Discrimination of schizophrenic and brain-injured patients by a standardized version of Luria's neuropsychological tests. *Journal of Consulting and Clinical Psychology, 46*, 1266-1273.

Putnam, W. H. (1979). Hypnosis and distortions in eye-witness memory. *International Journal of Clinical and Experimental Hypnosis, 27*, 437-448.

Pykett, I. L. (1982). NMR imaging in medicine. *Scientific American, 246*, 78-91.

Pyszczynski, T., Greenberg, J., Mack, D., & Wrightsman, L. S. (1981). Opening statements in a jury trial: The effect of promising more than the evidence can show. *Journal of Applied Social Psychology, 11*, 434-444.

Pyszczynski, T., & Wrightsman, L. S. (1981). The effects of opening statements on mock jurors' verdicts in a simulated criminal trial. *Journal of Applied Social Psychology, 11*, 301-313.

Q

Quen, J. M. (1974). Anglo-American criminal insanity: An historical perspective. *Bulletin of the American Academy of Psychiatry and the Law, 2*, 115-123.

Quen, J. M. (1978). Isaac Ray and Charles Doe: Responsibility and justice. In W. E. Barton & C. J. Sanborn (Eds.), *Law and the mental health professional* (pp. 235-250). New York: International Universities Press.

Quen, J. M. (1981). Anglo-American concepts of criminal responsibility. In S. J. Hucker, C. D. Webster, & M. H. Ben-Aron (Eds.), *Mental disorder and criminal responsibility* (pp. 1-10). Toronto: Butterworth.

Quinsey, V. L. (1975). Psychiatric staff conference of dangerous mentally disordered offenders. *Canadian Journal of Behavioral Science, 7*, 60-69.

Quinsey, V. L. (1979). Release from a maximum security psychiatric institution. *Criminal Justice and Behavior, 6*(4), 390-399.

Quinsey, V. L., Arnold, L. S., & Pruesse, M. G. (1980). MMPI profiles of men referred for a pre-trial psychiatric assessment as a function of offense type. *Journal of Clinical Psychology, 36*, 410-417.

Quinsey, V. L., Chaplin, T. C., & Varney, G. W. (1981). A comparison of rapists' and non-sex offenders' sexual preferences for mutually consenting sex, rape, and sadistic acts. *Behavioral Assessment, 3,* 127-135.

Quinsey, V. L., MacGuire, A., & Varney, G. W. (1983). Assertion and overcontrolled hostility among mentally disordered murderers. *Journal of Consulting and Clinical Psychology, 51,* 550-556.

R

Rabkin, J. G. (1979). Criminal behavior of discharged mental patients: A critical appraisal of the research. *Pscyhological Bulletin, 86*(1), 1-27.

Rachlin, S., Halpern, A. L., & Portnow, S. L. (1984). The volitional rule, personality disorders and the insanity defense. *Psychiatric Annals, 14,* 139-147.

Rada, C. M. (1977). MMPI profile types of exposers, rapists and assaulters in a court services population. *Journal of Consulting and Clinical Psychology, 45,* 61-69.

Rada, R. T. (1975). Alcoholism and forcible rape. *American Journal of Psychiatry, 132,* 444-446.

Rada, R. T. (1978). *Clinical aspects of the rapist.* New York: Grune & Stratton.

Rada, R. T. (1980). Plasma androgens and the sex offender. *Bulletin of the American Academy of Psychiatry and the Law, 8,* 456-464.

Rada, R. T., Kellner, R., & Winslow, W. W. (1976). Plasma testosterone and aggressive behavior. *Psychosomatics, 17,* 138-142.

Rada, R. T., Kellner, R., Laws, D. R., & Winslow, W. W. (1978). Drinking, alcoholism and the mentally disordered sex offender. *Bulletin of the American Academy of Psychiatry and the Law,* 296-300.

Rada, R. T., Laws, D. R., & Kellner, R. (1976). Plasma testosterone levels in the rapist. *Psychosomatic Medicine, 38,* 257-268.

Rada, R. T., Laws, D. R., Kellner, R., Stivastava, L., & Peake, G. (1983). Plasma androgens in violent and non-violent sex offenders. *Bulletin of the American Academy of Psychiatry and the Law, 11,* 149-158.

Radar, C. M. (1977). MMPI profile types of exposers, rapists, and assaulters in a court services population. *Journal of Clinical and Consulting Psychology, 45,* 61-69.

Rafkey, D., & Sealey, R. (1975). The adolescent and the law: A survey. *Crime and Delinquency, 21,* 131-138.

Rahaim, G. L., & Brodsky, S. L. (1982). Empirical evidence versus common sense: Juror and lawyer knowledge of eyewitness accuracy. *Law and Psychology Review, 7,* 1-16.

Rahe, R., & Holmes, T. (1966). Life crisis and major health change. *Psychosomatic Medicine, 28,* 774.

Rahe, R. H. (1972). Subjects' recent life changes and their near-future illness reports. *Annals of Clinical Research, 4,* 250-265.

Rakoff, V. M., Stancer, H. C., & Kedward, H. B. (1977). *Psychiatric diagnosis.* New York: Brunner-Mazel.

Ramsay, P. (1978). The Saikewicz precedent: What's good for an incompetent patient. *Hastings Center Report, 8*(6), 36-42.

Randolph, J., Hicks, T., & Mason, D. (1981). The Competency Screening Test: A replication and extension. *Criminal Justice and Behavior, 8,* 471-481.

Randolph, J., Hicks, T., Mason, D., & Cuneo, D. (1982). The Competency Screening Test: A validation in Cook County, Illinois. *Criminal Justice and Behavior, 9,* 495-500.

Rappeport, J. R. (1974). Personality disorders in the court. In J. R. Lion (Ed.), *Personality disorders: Diagnosis and treatment*. Baltimore, MD: Williams and Wilkins.

Rappeport, J. R. (1985). Reasonable medical certainty. *Bulletin of the American Academy of Psychiatry and the Law, 13*, 5-16.

Ratner, R. A., & Shapiro, D. (1978). The episodic dyscontrol syndrome and criminal responsibility. *Bulletin of the American Academy of Psychiatry and the Law, 7*, 422-431.

Rawlin, J. W. (1968). Street level abusage of amphetamines. In J. R. Russo (Ed.), *Amphetamine abuse* (pp. 51-65). Springfield, IL: Charles C. Thomas.

Read, J. D., Barnsley, R. H., Ankers, K., & Whishaw, I. Q. (1978). Variations in severity of verbs and eyewitnesses' testimony: An alternative interpretation. *Perceptual and Motor Skills, 46*, 795-800.

Rector, M. (1973). Who are the dangerous? *Bulletin of the American Academy of Psychiatry and the Law, 1*, 186-188.

Redlich, F., & Mollica, R. F. (1976). Overview: Ethical issues in contemporary psychiatry. *American Journal of Psychiatry, 133*, 125-136.

Redlich, F. C., Ravitz, L. J., & Dession, G. H. (1951). Narcoanalysis and truth. *American Journal of Psychiatry, 106*, 586-593.

Reed, A., & Kane, A. W. (1973). *Phencyclidine*. Rockville, MD: National Clearing House for Drug Abuse Information.

Regier, D. A., Myers, J. K., Kramer, M., Robins, L. N., Blazer, D. G., Hough, R. L., Eaton, W. W., & Locke, B. Z. (1984). The NIMH epidemiologic catchment area program. *Archives of General Psychiatry, 41*, 934-941.

Reich, T., Robins, L. N., Woodruff, R. A., Taibleson, M., Rich, C., & Cunningham, L. (1975). Computer-assisted derivation of screening interview for alcoholism. *Archives of General Psychiatry, 32*, 847-852.

Reiser, M., Ludwig, L., Saxe, S., & Wagner, C. (1979). An evaluation of the use of psychics in the investigation of major crimes. *Journal of Police Science and Administration, 7*(1), 18-25.

Reiser, M., & Nielson, M. (1980). Investigative hypnosis: A developing specialty. *American Journal of Clinical Hypnosis, 23*, 75-84.

Reitan, R. M. (1955). Certain differential effects of the left and right cerebral lesions in human adults. *Journal of Comparative and Physiological Psychology, 48*, 474-477.

Reitan, R. M., & Davidson, L. A. (1974). *Clinical neuropsychology: Current status and applications*. New York: Winston-Wiley.

Relinger, H., & Stern, T. (1983). Guidelines for forensic hypnosis. *Journal of Psychiatry and Law, 11*, 69-74.

Rembar, C. (1980). *The law of the land*. New York: Simon & Schuster.

Reppucci, N. (1984). The wisdom of Solomon: Issues in child custody determination. In N. Reppucci, L. Weithorn, E. Mulvey, & J. Monahan (Eds.), *Children, mental health, and the law* (pp. 59-78). Beverly Hills, CA: Sage Publications.

Resier, M. (1974). Hypnosis as an aid in homicide investigation. *American Journal of Clinical Hypnosis, 17*, 84-87.

Resnick, P. J. (1984). The detection of malingered mental illness. *Behavioral Sciences and the Law, 2*, 21-38.

Restak, R. M. (1977, September 4). Complex legal issues raised by Sam Case. *New York Times*, p. 12.

Revitch, E. (1977). Classification of offenders for prognostic and dispositional evaluation. *Bulletin of the American Academy of Psychiatry and the Law, 5*, 41-50.

Rey, A. (1941). L'examen psychologique dans les cas d'encephalophathie traumatique. *Archives de Psychologie, 28*(112), 286-340.

Rhodes, W. R. (1979). Future criminal justice information needs and systems. *Police Chief, 46,* 20-22.

Rice, G. P. (1961). The psychologist as expert witness. *American Psychologist, 16,* 691-692.

Richardson, S., Dohrenwend, B., & Klein, D. (1965). *Interviewing: Its forms and functions.* London: Basic Books.

Rieger, W., & Billings, C. K. (1978). Ganser's syndrome associated with litigation. *Comprehensive Psychiatry, 19,* 371-375.

Riesman, D. (1951). Some observations on law and psychology. *University of Chicago Law Review, 19,* 30-44.

Ring, K. (1967). Experimental social psychology: Some sober questions about frivolous values. *Journal of Experimental Social Psychology, 3,* 113-123.

Rioch, M. J., & Lubin, A. (1959). Prognosis of social adjustment for mental hospital patients under psychotherapy. *Journal of Consulting Psychology, 23,* 313-318.

Roback, H. B. (1968). Human figure drawings: Their utility in the clinical psychologist's armamentarium for personality assessment. *Psychological Bulletin, 70,* 1-19.

Robbins, I. P., & Sepler, H. J. (1978). A behavioral analysis of legal intent. *Law and Psychology Review, 4,* 19-41.

Roberts, A. C. (1982). The abuse of hypnosis in the legal system. *American Journal of Forensic Psychiatry, 3,* 67-78.

Roberts, B. (1978). A look at psychiatric decision-making. *American Journal of Psychiatry, 135,* 1384-1387.

Roberts, J. K. A., & Lishman, W. A. (1984). Use of the CAT handscanner in clinical psychiatry. *British Journal of Psychiatry, 145,* 152-158.

Robertson, K., & Milner, J. (1983). Construct validity of the Child Abuse Potential Inventory. *Journal of Clinical Psychology, 39,* 426-429.

Robey, A. (1965). Criteria for competency to stand trial: A checklist for psychiartists. *American Journal of Psychiatry, 122,* 616-623.

Robey, A. (1978). Guilty but mentally ill. *Bulletin of the American Academy of Psychiatry, 6,* 374-381.

Robins, L. N., Helzer, J. E., Croughan, J., & Ratcliff, K. S. (1981). National Institute of Mental Health Diagnostic Interview Schedule: Its history, characteristics, and validity. *Archives of General Psychiatry, 38,* 381-399.

Robinson, D. N. (1980). *Psychology and law.* New York: Oxford University Press.

Robinson, D. N. (1982, June 23). The Hinckley decision: Psychiatry in court. *Wall Street Journal,* p. 5.

Robinson, E. (1935). *Law and the lawyers.* New York: Macmillan.

Robinson, G., & Merav, A. (1976). Informed consent: Recall by patients tested postoperative. *Annals of Thoracic Surgery, 22,* 209-212.

Robinson, J. P., & Shaver, R. (1971). *Measures of social psychological attitudes.* Ann Arbor, MI: Institute for Social Research, University of Michigan.

Robinson, P. (1978). Parents of "beyond control" adolescents. *Adolescence, 49,* 109-119.

Robitscher, J. (198_). *The powers of psychiatry.* Boston, MA: Houghton Mifflin.

Robitscher, J. (1966). *Pursuit of agreement: Psychiatry and the law.* Philadelphia, PA: J. B. Lippincott.

Robitscher, J., Shah, S. A., & Zenoff, E. H. (1977). The limits of psychiatric authority. *Journal of Psychiatry and Law, 5*(4), 603-624.

Rockwell, D. A., & Oswald, P. (1968). Amphetamine use and abuse in psychiatric patients. *Archives of General Psychiatry, 18,* 612-616.

Rodin, E. A. (1973). Psychomotor epilepsy and aggressive behaviour. *Archives of General Psychiatry, 28,* 210-213.

Roesch, R. (1978). Competency to stand trial: An analysis of legal/mental health issues and procedures and a proposal for change. *Social Action and the Law, 4,* 39-42.

Roesch, R. (1979). Determining competency to stand trial: An examination of evaluation procedures in an institutional setting. *Journal of Consulting and Clinical Psychology, 47*(3), 542-550.

Roesch, R., & Golding, S. L. (1978). Legal and judicial interpretation of competency to stand trial statutes and procedures. *Criminology, 16,* 420-429.

Roesch, R., & Golding, S. L. (1980). *Competency to stand trial.* Urbana, IL: University of Illinois Press.

Rofman, E., Askinazi, C., & Fant, E. (1980). The prediction of dangerous behavior in emergency civil commitment. *American Journal of Psychiatry, 137,* 1061-1064.

Rogeness, G., Ritchey, S., Alex, P., Zuelzer, M., & Morris, R. (1981). Family patterns and parenting attitudes of teenage parents. *Journal of Community Psychology, 9,* 239-345.

Rogers, C., & Wrightsman, L. (1978). Attitudes toward children's rights: Nurturance or self-determination? *Journal of Social Issues, 34,* 59-68.

Rogers, J. L., & Bloom, J. D. (1982). Characteristics of persons committed to Oregon's Psychiatric Security Review Board. *Bulletin of the American Academy of Psychiatry and the Law, 3,* 155-164.

Rogers, R. (1983). Malingering or random? A research note on obvious vs. subtle subscales on the MMPI. *Journal of Clinical Psychology, 39,* 257-258.

Rogers, R. (1984a). *Rogers criminal responsibility assessment scales (RCRAS) and test manual.* Odessa, FL: Psychological Assessment Resources, Inc.

Rogers, R. (1984b). Towards an empirical model of malingering and deception. *Behavioral Sciences and the Law, 2,* 93-112.

Rogers, R. (1986). *Conducting insanity evaluations.* New York: Van Nostrand Reinhold.

Rogers, R., & Cavanaugh, J. L. (1980). Differences in select psychological variables between criminally responsible and insane subsamples. *American Journal of Forensic Psychiatry, 1,* 29-37.

Rogers, R., & Cavanaugh, J. L. (1981a). Application of the SADS diagnostic interview to forensic psychiatry. *Journal of Psychiatry and Law, 9,* 329-344.

Rogers, R., & Cavanaugh, J. L. (1981b). Rogers criminal responsibility assessment scales. *Illinois Medical Journal, 160,* 164-169.

Rogers, R., & Cavanaugh, J. L. (1981c). A treatment program for potentially violent offender patients. *International Journal of Offender Therapy and Comparative Criminology, 25,* 53-59.

Rogers, R., & Cavanaugh, J. L. (1983a). "Nothing but the truth"...A re-examination of malingering. *Journal of Psychiatry and Law, 11,* 443-460.

Rogers, R., & Cavanaugh, J. L. (1983b). Usefulness of the Rorschach: A survey of forensic psychiatrists. *Journal of Psychiatry and Law, 11,* 55-67.

Rogers, R., Cavanaugh, J. L., & Dolmetsch, R. (1981). Schedule of affective disorders and schizophrenia, a diagnostic interview in evaluations of insanity: An exploratory study. *Psychological Reports, 49,* 135-138.

Rogers, R., Cavanaugh, J. L., Seman, W., & Harris, M. (1984). Legal outcome and clinical findings: A study of insanity. *Bulletin of the American Academy of Psychiatry and the Law, 12,* 75-83.

Rogers, R., Dolmetsch, R., & Cavanaugh, J. L. (1981). An empirical approach to insanity evaluations. *Journal of Clinical Psychology, 37,* 683-687.

Rogers, R., Dolmetsch, R., & Cavanaugh, J. L. (1983). Identification of random responders on MMPI protocols. *Journal of Personality Assessment, 47*, 364-368.

Rogers, R., Harris, M., & Wasyliw, O. E. (1983). Observed and self-reported psychopathology in NGRI acquittees in court-mandated outpatient treatment. International Journal of Offender Therapy and Comparative Criminology, 27, 143-149.

Rogers, R., & Seman, W. (1983). Murder and criminal responsibility: An examination of MMPI profiles. *Behavioral Sciences and the Law, 1*, 89-95.

Rogers, R., Seman, W., & Stampley, J. (1984). Individuals evaluated for insanity: A comparative study of social and demographic variables. *International Journal of Offender Therapy and Comparative Criminology, 28*, 3-10.

Rogers, R., Seman, W., & Wasyliw, O. E. (1983). The RCRAS and legal insanity: A cross validation study. *Journal of Clinical Psychology, 39*, 554-559.

Rogers, R., Thatcher, A. A., & Cavanaugh, J. L. (1984). Use of the SADS diagnostic interview in evaluating legal insanity. *Journal of Clinical Psychology, 40*, 1538-1541.

Rogers, R., Thatcher, A. A., & Harris, M. (1983). Identification of random responders on the MMPI: An actuarial approach. *Psychological Reports, 53*, 1171-1174.

Rogers, R., Wasyliw, O. E., & Cavanaugh, J. L. (1984). Evaluating insanity: A study of construct validity. *Law and Human Behavior, 8*, 293-303.

Rogers, R., Wasyliw, O. E., & Dolmetsch, R. (1982). Accuracy of MMPI decision rules in DSM III diagnoses. *Psychological Reports, 51*, 1283-1286.

Rokeach, M., & Vidmar, N. (1973). Testimony concerning possible jury bias in a Black Panther murder trial. *Journal of Applied Social Psychology, 3*, 19-29.

Ron, M. A. (1983). The alcoholic brain: CT scan and psychological findings. *Psychological Medicine Monograph*, Supplement 3.

Roper, R. T. (1980). Jury size and verdict consistency: "A line has to be drawn somewhere." *Law and Society Review, 14*, 977-995.

Rose, B. (1981). Termination of parental rights: An analysis of Virginia's statute. *University of Richmond Law Review, 15*, 213-230.

Rosen, G. (1975). On the persistence of illusory correlations with the Rorschach. *Journal of Abnormal Psychology, 84*, 571-573.

Rosen, P. (1972). *The Supreme Court and social science.* Urbana, IL: University of Illinois Press.

Rosen, R. C., & Keefe, F. J. (1978). The measure of human penile tumescence. *Psychophysiology, 15*, 366-376.

Rosenberg, A. H., & McGarry, A. L. (1972). Competency for trial: The making of an expert. *American Journal of Psychiatry, 128*, 1092-1096.

Rosenberg, C. E. (1968). *The trial of assassin Guiteau: Psychiatry and law in guilded age.* Chicago, IL: University of Chicago Press.

Rosenhan, D. (1973). On being sane in insane places. *Science, 179*, 250-258.

Rosenhan, D. L. (1983). Psychological abnormality and law. In C. J. Scheirer & B. L. Hammonds (Eds.), *Psychology and the law* (pp. 89-118). Washington, DC: American Psychological Association.

Rosenthal, D. (1974). *Lawyer and client: Who's in charge?* New York: Russell Sage.

Rosett, A. L., & Cressey, D. R. (1976). *Justice by consent: Plea bargaining in the American courthouse.* Philadelphia, PA: Lippincott.

Roscow, I., & Breslau, N. (1966). A Guttman health scale for the aged. *Journal of Gerontology, 21*, 556-559.

Ross, H. C., & Campbell, D. T. (1968). The Connecticut speed crackdown: A study of the effects of legal change. In H. L. Ross (Ed.), *Perspectives on the social order: Readings in sociology*. New York: McGraw-Hill.

Ross, H. L. (1970). *Settled out of court*. Chicago, IL: Aldine.

Ross, L. (1977). The intuitive psychologist and his shortcomings: Distortions in the attribution process. In L. Berkowitz (Ed.), *Advances in experimental social psychology*, Vol. 10. New York: Academic Press.

Rossi, P. H. (Ed.) (1982). *Standards for evaluation practice* (Publication No. 15, New directions for program evaluation: Evaluation Reserch Society). San Francisco, CA: Jossey-Bass.

Roth, L., & Applebaum, P. (1982). What we do and do not know about treatment refusals in mental institutions. In A. Doudera & J. Swazey (Eds.), *Refusing treatment in mental health institutions: Values in conflict* (pp. 179-196). Ann Arbor, MI: AUPHA Press.

Roth, L., & Meisel, A. (1977). Dangerousness, confidentiality, and the duty to warn. *American Journal of Psychiatry, 134*, 508-511.

Roth, L., Meisel, A., & Lidz, C. (1977). Tests of competency to consent to treatment. *American Journal of Psychiatry, 134*, 279-284.

Roth, L., Lidz, C., Meisel, A., Soloff, P., Kaufman, F., Spiker, D., & Foster, R. (1982). Competency to decide about treatment or research: An overview of some empirical data. *International Journal of Law and Psychiatry, 5*, 29-50.

Roth, M. (1981). Modern neurology and psychiatry and the problem of criminal responsibility. In S. J. Hucker, C. D. Webster, & M. H. Ben-Aron (Eds.), *Mental disorder and criminal responsibility* (pp. 91-110). Toronto: Butterworth.

Roth, R. (1980). *The Mother-Child Relationship Evaluation: Manual*, 1980 edition. Los Angeles, CA: Western Psychological Services.

Rotter, J., & Rafferty, J. (1950). *Manual: The Rotter Incomplete Sentences Blank*. New York: Psychological Corporation.

Rozelle, R. M., & Baxter, J. C. (1978). The interpretation of nonverbal behavior in a role-defined interaction sequence: The police-citizen encounter. *Environmental Psychology and Nonverbal Behavior, 2*, 167-180.

Ruback, R. B. (1982). Issues in family law. In J. C. Hanson & L. Abade (Eds.), *Values, ethics, legalities and the family therapist*. London: Aspen Systems.

Rubin, A. B. (1982). Trial by jury in complex civil cases: Voice of liberty or verdict by confusion? *Annals of the American Academy, 462*, 86-103.

Rubin, B. (1972). Prediction of dangerousness in mentally ill criminals. *Archives of General Psychiatry, 27*, 397-407.

Rubin, J. G. (1974). Police identity and the police role. In J. G. Goldsmith & S. S. Goldsmith (Eds.), *The police community: Dimensions of an occupational subculture*. Pacific Palisades, CA: Palisades Publishers.

Rubin, J. Z., & Brown, B. R. (1975). *The social psychology of bargaining and negotiation*. New York: Academic Press.

Rubinstein, M. J., & White, T. J. (1979). Alaska's ban on plea bargaining. *Law and Society Review, 13*, 367-384.

Rudestam, K. E. (1977). Physical and psychological responses to suicide in the family. *Journal of Consulting Clinical Psychology, 45*(2), 162-170.

Rule, B., & Nesdale, A. (1976). Emotional arousal and aggressive behavior. *Psychological Bulletin, 83*, 851-863.

Rumsey, M. G., & Rumsey, J. M. (1977). A case of rape: Sentencing judgments of males and females. *Psychological Reports, 14,* 459-465.

Rundquist, H. C., & Sletto, R. F. (1936). *Personality in the depression.* Minneapolis, MN: University of Minnesota Press.

Russell, E. W., Nueringer, C., & Goldstein, G. (1970). *Assessment of brain damage: A neuropsychological key approach.* New York: Wiley-Interscience.

Russell, W. R., & Nathan, P. W. (1946). Traumatic amnesia. *Brain, 69,* 280-300.

Rutter, M. (1971). Parent-child separation: Psychological effects on the children. *Journal of Child Psychology and Psychiatry and Allied Disciplines, 12,* 233-260.

Rutter, M. (1972). Maternal deprivation reconsidered. *Journal of Psychosomatic Research, 16,* 241-250.

Rutter, M. (1974). *The quality of mothering: Maternal deprivation reassessed.* Harmondsworth, England: Penguin.

Ruzicka, W. J. (1979). *Psychodiagnostic assessment procedures in the criminal justice system.* Palo Alto, CA: Psychological Health Services.

Ryan, J. J., Prifitera, A., & Powers, L. (1983). Scoring reliability on the WAIS-R. *Journal of Consulting and Clinical Psychology, 51,* 149-150.

Ryan, J. P. (1981). Adjudication and sentencing in a misdemeanor court: The outcome is the punishment. *Law and Society Review, 15,* 79-108.

S

Saks, M. J. (1974). Ignorance of science is no excuse. *Trial, 10,* 18-20.

Saks, M. J. (1976, January). Social scientists can't rig juries. *Psychology Today,* 48-57.

Saks, M. J. (1977). *Jury verdicts.* Lexington, MA: Lexington Books.

Saks, M. J. (1981a). *Small-group decision making and complex information tasks.* Washington, DC: Federal Judicial Center.

Saks, M. J. (1981b). Innovation and change in the courtroom. In N. L. Kerr & R. M. Bray (Eds.), *The psychology of the courtroom* (pp. 325-352). New York: Academic Press.

Saks, M. J., & Baron, C. (1980). *The use/nonuse/misuse of applied social research in the courts.* Cambridge, MA: Abt Books.

Saks, M. J., & Hastie, R. (1978). *Social psychology in court.* New York: Van Nostrand Reinhold.

Saks, M. J., & Kidd, R. F. (1981). Human information processing and adjudication: Trial by heuristics. *Law and Society Review, 15,* 123-160.

Saks, M. J., & Miller, M. (1979). A systems approach to discretion in the legal process. In L. E. Abt & I. R. Stuart (Eds.), *Social psychology and discretionary law.* New York: Van Nostrand Reinhold.

Saks, M. J., & Ostrom, T. M. (1975). Jury size and consensus requirements: The laws of probability vs. the laws of the land. *Journal of Contemporary Law, 1,* 163-173.

Sales, B. D. (Ed.) (1977). *Psychology in the legal process.* New York: Spectrum.

Sales, B. D. (Ed.) (1981). *The trial process.* New York: Plenum Press.

Sales, B. D., Elwork, A., & Alfini, J. (1977). Improving comprehension for jury instructions. In B. D. Sales (Ed.), *Perspectives in law and psychology: The criminal justice system.* New York: Plenum.

Saltzburg, S. (1980). Foreword: The flow and ebb of constitutional criminal procedure in the Warren and Burger Courts. *Georgetown Law Journal, 69,* 151-209.

Sampson, E. (1981). *Introducing social psychology.* New York: Franklin Watts.

Sanborn, N., & Sanborn, J. (1976). The psychological autopsy as a therapeutic tool. *Diseases of the Nervous System, 37*(4), 7.

Sandy, J. P., & Devine, D. A. (1978). Four stress factors unique to rural patrol. *Police Chief, 9,* 42-44.

Santruck, J. W., & Warshak, R. A. (1979). Father custody and social development in boys and girls. *Journal of Social Issues, 35*(4), 112-115.

Sarason, I. G. (1966). *Personality: An objective approach.* New York: John Wiley.

Sarason, I. G., & Stoops, R. (1978). Test anxiety and the passage of time. *Journal of Consulting and Clinical Psychology, 46,* 102-108.

Sarat, A. (1976). Alternatives in dispute processing: Litigation in small claims court. *Law and Society Review, 10,* 339.

Sauer, R. H., & Mullens, P. M. (1976). The insanity defense: M'Naghten vs. ALI. *Bulletin of the American Academy of Psychiatry and the Law, 4,* 73-75.

Sawyer, J. (1966). Measurement and prediction, clinical and statistical. *Psychological Bulletin, 66,* 178-200.

Scanlon, J. C., & Weingarten, K. (1963). The role of statistical data in the functioning of courts. *Buffalo Law Review, 2*(12), 522-527.

Schaffer, K. (1981). *Sex roles and human behavior.* Cambridge, MA: Winthrop.

Scheflin, A. (1972). Jury nullification: The right to say no. *Southern California Law Review, 45,* 168.

Scheflin, A., & Van Dyke, J. (1980). Jury nullification: The contours of a controversy. *Law and Contemporary Problems, 43,* 52-115.

Scheib, K. (1978). The psychologists' advantage and its nullifcation. *American Psychologist,* 869-880.

Schein, E. H. (1969). *Process consultation: Its role in organization development.* Reading, MA: Addison-Wesley.

Schein, E. H. (1971). *Coercive persuasion.* New York: Norton.

Schein, E. H. (1980). *Organizational psychology* (3rd ed.). Englewood Cliffs, NJ: Prentice-Hall.

Schiffer, M. E. (1978). *Mental disorder and the criminal trial process.* Toronto: Butterworth.

Schneidman, E. (1967). Some current developments in suicide prevention. *Bulletin of Suicidology, 33,* 41.

Schneidman, E. (1976). *Suicidology: Contemporary developments* (pp. 351-352, 540-544). New York: Grune & Stratton.

Schneidman, E. S. (1978). *Voices of death.* New York: Bantam Books.

Schoenfeld, C. G. (1977). Recent developments in the law concerning the mentally ill: "A cornerstone of legal structure laid in mud." *University of Toledo Law Review, 9,* 1-29.

Schoenfeld, L. S., & Lehmann, L. S. (1981). Management of the aggressive patient. In C. E. Walker (Ed.), *Clinical practice of psychology.* New York: Pergamon Press.

Schubert, G. (Ed.) (1964). *Judicial behavior: A reader in theory and research.* Chicago, IL: Rand McNally.

Schuckit, M. A. (1979). *Drug and alcohol abuse: A clinical guide to diagnosis and treatment.* New York: Plenum.

Schuckit, M. A., & Morrissey, E. R. (1978). Propoxyphene and phencyclidine (PCP) use in adolescence. *Journal of Clinical Psychiatry,* 7-13.

Schulman, J., Shaver, P., Colman, R., Emricle, B., & Christie, R. (1973, May). Recipe for a jury. *Psychology Today,* 37-44, 79-84.

Schwade, E. D., & Geiger, S. G. (1956). *Diseases of the Nervous System, 17,* 307-317.

Schwade, E. D., & Geiger, S. G. (1960). Severe behavior disorders with abnormal eletroencephalograms. *Diseases of the Nervous System, 21,* 616-620.

Schwartz, F., & Lazar, Z. (1979). The scientific status of the Rorschach. *Journal of Personality Assessment, 43*, 3-11.

Schwitzegebel, R. K. (1974). The right to effective mental treatment. *California Law Review, 62*, 936-956.

Schwitzegebel, R. K. (1977). Professional accountability in the treatment and release of dangerous persons. In B. D. Sales (Ed.), *Perspectives in law and psychology*, Vol. 1, The criminal justice system (pp. 139-150). New York: Plenum Press.

Schwitzegebel, R. L., & Schwitzegebel, R. K. (1980). *Law and psychological practice*. New York: John Wiley.

Scott, R. L. (1982). Analysis of the need systems of 20 male rapists. *Psychological Reports, 51*, 1119-1125.

Scroggs, J. R. (1976). Penalties for rape as a function of victim provocativeness, damage, and resistance. *Journal of Applied Social Psychology, 6*, 360-368.

Sears, J. D., Hirt, M. L., & Hall, R. W. (1984). A cross validation of the Luria-Nebraska neuropsychological battery. *Journal of Consulting and Clinical Psychology, 52*, 309-310.

Sehulster, J. R. (1981a). Phenomenological correlates of the self-theory of memory. *American Journal of Psychology, 94*, 527-537.

Sehulster, J. R. (1981b). Structure and pragmatics of the self-theory of memory. *Memory and Cognition, 9*, 263-276.

Selby, J. W., Calhoun, L. G., & Brock, T. A. (1977). Sex differences in the social perception of rape victims. *Personality and Social Psychology Bulletin, 3*, 412-415.

Selye, H. (1976). *The stress of life* (2nd ed.). New York: McGraw-Hill.

Selye, H. (1978). The stress of police work. *Police Stress, 7*-8.

Severance, L. J., & Loftus, E. F. (1982). Improving the ability of jurors to comprehend and apply criminal jury instructions. *Law and Society Review, 17*, 153-198.

Shaffer, T. (1976). *Legal interviewing and counseling in a nutshell*. St. Paul, MN: West Publishing.

Shaffer, T., & Redmount, R. (1977). *Lawyers, law students and people*. Colorado Springs, CO: Shepard's.

Shah, S. (1963). Crime and mental illness: Some problems in defining and labeling deviant behavior. *Mental Hygiene, 53*, 21-33.

Shah, S. (1978a). Dangerousness: A paradigm for exploring some issues in law and psychology. *American Psychologist, 33*, 224-238.

Shah, S. (1978b). Dangerousness and mental illness: Some conceptual, prediction and policy dilemmas. In C. Frederick (Ed.), *Dangerous behavior: A problem in law and mental health*. NIMH, DHEW Publication Number (ADM) 78-563. Washington, DC: Superintendent of Documents, U. S. Government Printing Office.

Shanok, S. S., & Lewis, D. O. (1981). Medical history of abused delinquents. *Child Psychiatry and Human Development, 11*, 222-231.

Shapiro, A. (1977). The evaluation of clinical prediction: A method and initial application. *New England Journal of Medicine, 296*, 1509-1514.

Shapiro, D. L. (1984). *Psychological evaluation and expert testimony*. New York: Van Nostrand Reinhold.

Shapiro, M. (1964). Stability and change in judicial decision-making: Incrementalism or stare decisis? *Law in Transition Quarterly, 2*, 134.

Shapiro, M., & Tresolini, R. J. (1979). *American constitutional law* (5th ed.). New York: Macmillan.

Sharpe, G., & Richter, J. (1984). *Mental disorder project: Criminal law review* (Draft report). Toronto: Department of Justice.

Shaw, H. S. (1978). A paradigm for exploring some issues on law and psychology. *American Psychologist, 33,* 224-238.

Shaw, M. E., & Costanzo, P. R. (1970). *Theories of social psychology.* New York: McGraw-Hill.

Shepherd, J. W., & Ellis, H. D. (1973). The effect of attractiveness on recognition memory for faces. *American Journal of Psychology, 86,* 627-633.

Sheppard, B. H., & Vidmar, N. (1980). Adversary pre-trial procedures and testimonial evidence: Effects of lawyer's role and Machiavellianism. *Journal of Personality and Social Psychology, 39,* 320-332.

Sheppard, G., Gruzelier, J., Manchanda, R., Hirsch, S. R., Wise, R., Fracowiak, R., & Jones, T. (1983). O positron emission tomographic scanning in predominantly never-treated acute schizophrenic patients. *Lancet, 2,* 1448-1452.

Shimshak, G. (1979). Constitutional Law-Seventh Amendment-Right to jury trial in complex litigation. *Wisconsin Law Review,* 920-928.

Shinnar, S., & Shinnar, R. (1975). The effects of the criminal justice system on the control of crime: A quantitative approach. *Law and Society Review, 9,* 581-611.

Shoemaker, D. J., South, D. R., & Lowe, J. (1973). Facial stereotypes of deviants and judgments of guilt or innocence. *Social Forces, 51,* 427-433.

Shook, H. C. (1978). Pitfalls in policing. *Police Chief, 5,* 8-10.

Short, J. F. (Ed.) (1968). *Gang delinquency and delinquent subcultures.* New York: Harper & Row.

Shure, G. H., Meeker, R. J., & Hansford, E. A. (1965). The effectiveness of pacifist strategies in bargaining games. *Journal of Conflict Resolution, 9,* 106-117.

Shutt, D. (1982, August 25). Hinckley verdict reaction. Toledo, OH: *Toledo Blade.*

Siani, R., Garzotto, N., Zimmermann Tansella, C., & Tansella, M. (1979). Predictive sales for parasuicide repetition: Further results. *Acta Psychiatrica Scandivania, 59,* 17-23.

Sidley, N. T. (1976). On the distinction between medical and legal diagnosis. *Bulletin of the American Academy of Psychiatry and the Law, 4,* 244-250.

Siegel, R. K. (1978a). Phencyclidine, criminal behavior, and the defense of diminished capacity. In R. C. Petersen & R. C. Stillman (Eds.), *Phencyclidine (PCP) abuse: An appraisal* (pp. 272-288). Rockville, MD: National Institute on Drug Abuse.

Siegel, R. K. (1978b). Phencyclidine and ketamine intoxication: A study of four populations of recreational users. In R. C. Petersen & R. C. Stillman (Eds.), *Phencyclidine (PCP) abuse: An appraisal* (pp. 119-147). Rockville, MD: National Institute on Drug Abuse.

Siegel, S., & Fouraker, L. E. (1960). *Bargaining and group decision making.* New York: McGraw-Hill.

Sierles, F. S. (1984). Correlates of malingering. *Behavioral Sciences and the Law, 2,* 113-118.

Sigall, H., Braden, J., & Aylward, G. (1978). The effect of attractiveness of defendant, number of witnesses, and personal motivation of defendant on jury decision making behavior. *Psychology, 15*(3), 4-10.

Sigall, H., & Landy, D. (1972). Effects of the defendant's character and suffering on juridic judgment: A replication and clarification. *Journal of Social Psychology, 88,* 149-150.

Sigall, H., & Ostrove, N. (1975). Beautiful but dangerous: Effects of offender attractiveness and nature of crime on juridic judgment. *Journal of Personality and Social Psychology, 31,* 410-414.

Silber, D. E., & Courtless, T. F. (1968). Measures of fantasy aggression among mentally retarded offenders. *American Journal of Mental Deficiency, 72,* 17-27.

Silten, P., & Tullis, R. (1976). Mental competency in criminal proceedings. *Hastings Law Journal, 28,* 1053-1074.

Silver, S. G., & Spodak, M. K. (1983). Dissection of the prongs of ALI: A retrospective assessment of criminal responsibility by the psychiatric staff of the Clifton T. Perkins Hospital Center. *Bulletin of the American Academy of Psychiatry and the Law, 11,* 383-387.

Silverman, I. (1975). Nonreactive methods and the law. *American Psychologist, 30,* 764-769.

Silving, H. (1956). Testing of the unconscious in criminal cases. *Harvard Law Review, 69,* 683-705.

Simkins, L. D. (1960). Examiner reinforcement and situational variables in a projective testing situation. *Journal of Consulting Psychology, 24,* 541-547.

Simon, J. L. (1978). Guilt and innocence in the presentence psychiatric examination: Some ethical considerations. *Bulletin of the American Academy of Psychiatry and the Law, 6,* 41-44.

Simon, R. J. (1966). Murders, juries, and the press. Does sensational reporting lead to verdicts of guilty? *Transaction, 3,* 40-42.

Simon, R. J. (1967). *The jury and the defense of insanity.* Boston: Little, Brown.

Simon, R. J. (Ed.) (1975). *The jury system in America.* Beverly Hills, CA: Sage Publications.

Simon, R. J. (1977). Type A, AB, B murderers: Their relationship to the victims and to the criminal justice system. *Bulletin of the American Academy of Psychiatry and the Law, 5,* 344-362.

Simon, R. J. (1980). *The jury: Its role in American society.* Lexington, MA: Lexington Books.

Simon, R. J. (1983). The defense of insanity. *Journal of Psychiatry and the Law, 11,* 183-202.

Simon, R. J., & Cockerham, W. (1977). Civil commitment, burden of proof, and dangerous acts: A comparison of the perspectives of judges and psychiatrists. *Journal of Psychiatry and Law, 5*(4), 571-594.

Simpson, H. (1962). The unfit parent: Conditions under which a child may be adopted without the consent of his parent. *University of Detroit Law Journal, 39,* 347-392.

Sims, L., & Paolucci, B. (1975). An empirical reexamination of the Parent Attitude Research Instrument (PARI). *Journal of Marriage and the Family, 37,* 724-732.

Simson, G. (1976). Jury nullification in the American system: A sceptical view. *Texas Law Review,* 488-506.

Sines, L. K., Silver, R. J., & Lucero, R. J. (1961). The effect of therapeutic intervention by untrained therapists. *Journal of Clinical Psychology, 17,* 394-396.

Siomopoulos, V. (1978). Psychiatric diagnosis and criminality. *Psychological Report, 42,* 559-562.

Skolnick, J. (1973). A sketch of the policeman's working personality. In A. Niederhoffer & A. S. Blumberg (Eds.), *The ambivalent force.* San Francisco, CA: Rinehart Press.

Slater, P. E. (1958). Contrasting correlates of group size. *Sociometry, 21,* 129-139.

Slobogin, C., Melton, G. B., & Showalter, C. R. (1984). The feasibility of a brief evaluation of mental state at the time of the offense. *Law and Human Behavior, 8,* 305-320.

Slovenko, R. (1973). *Psychiatry and law.* Boston, MA: Little, Brown.

Slovenko, R. (1977). The developing law on competency to stand trial. *Journal of Psychiatry and Law, 5,* 165-200.

Slovenko, R. (1978). Reflections on the criticisms of psychiatric expert testimony. *Wayne Law Review, 25,* 37-66.

Slovenko, R. (1979). On the legal aspects of tardive dyskinesia. *Journal of Psychiatry and Law, 7,* 295-331.

Slovenko, R. (1983, February 14). Pleading insanity is here to stay; insanity plea or not. *New York Times,* p. 18.

Sluggs, D. L. (1979). The use of psychological research by the judiciary. *Law and Human Behavior*, 3(1/2), 135-148.

Smith, B. M., Hain, J. D., & Stephenson, I. (1970). Controlled interviews using drugs. *Archives of General Psychiatry*, 22, 2-10.

Smith, G., & Hall, J. (1983, March 30). Study: "Guilty but mentally ill" verdict have no effect on insanity cases. *Atlanta Journal*, p. 25-A.

Smith, G. A., & Hall, J. H. (1982). Evaluating Michigan's guilty but mentally ill verdict: An empirical study. *Michigan Journal of Law Reform*, 16, 80-85.

Smith, R. (1979). Mental disorder, criminal responsibility and the social history of theories of volition. *Psychological Medicine*, 9, 13-19.

Smith, R. S. (1983). A comparison study of the Wechsler Adult Intelligence Scale and the Wechsler Adult Intelligence Scale-Revised in a college population. *Journal of Consulting and Clinical Psychology*, 51, 414-419.

Smith, S. (1979). Psychological parents vs. biological parents: The courts' responses to new directions in child custody dispute resolutions. *Journal of Family Law*, 17, 545-585.

Snyder, S., Pitts, W. M., Goodpastor, W. A., Sajadi, C., & Gustin, Q. (1982). MMPI profile of DSM III borderline personality disorder. *American Journal of Psychiatry*, 139, 1046-1048.

Sobel, N. L. (1972). *Eyewitnesses: Legal and practical problems*. New York: Clark Boardman.

Sobeloff, S. G. (1958). From M'Naghten to Durham and beyond. In P. W. Nice (Ed.), *Crime and insanity*. New York: Philosophical Library.

Solomon, M. R., & Schopler, J. (1978). The relationship of physical attractiveness and punitiveness: Is the linearity assumption out of line? *Personality and Social Psychology Bulletin*, 4, 483-486.

Sommers, R. (1981). Packing them in: Part of the punishment. *APA Monitor*, 12, 2.

Somodevilla, S. A. (1978). The psychologist's role in the police department. *Police Chief*, 21-23.

Soskin, W. F. (1959). Influence of four types of data on diagnostic conceptualization in psychological testing. *Journal of Abnormal and Social Psychology*, 58, 69-78.

Span, M., & Cantor, D. W. (1983). Caution: Joint custody. *New Jersey Family Lawyer*, 2(5), 88-96.

Spector, R. G. (1977). Learned treaties in Illinois: Are we witnessing the birth of a new hearsay exception? *Loyola Law Journal* (Chicago), 9, 193-203.

Spector, R. S., & Foster, T. E. (1977). Admissibility of hypnotic statements: Is the law of evidence susceptible? *Ohio State Law Journal*, 38, 567-813.

Sperlich, P. (1978). Trial by jury: It may have a future. In P. Kurland & G. Casper (Eds.), *Supreme Court review*. Chicago, IL: University of Chicago Press.

Sperlich, P. (1980a). ...And then there were six: The decline of the American jury. *Judicature*, 63, 262-279.

Sperlich, P. (1980b). Social science evidence and the courts: Reaching beyond the adversary process. *Judicature*, 63, 280-289.

Sperlich, P. (1982a). The case for preserving trial by jury in complex civil litigation. *Judicature*, 65, 394-395.

Sperlich, P. (1982b). Was there a complexity exception to trial by jury in 1791? *Judicature*, 65, 396-414.

Sperlich, P. (1982c). Better judicial management: The best remedy for complex cases. *Judicature*, 65, 415-419.

Spiegel, D., & Spiegel, H. (1984). Uses of hypnosis in evaluating malingering and deception. *Behavioral Sciences and the Law*, 2, 51-65.

Spielberger, C. D. (Ed.) (1979). *Police selection and evaluation: Issues and techniques*. Washington, DC: Hemisphere Publishing.

Spielberger, C. D., Spaulding, H. C., & Ward, J. C. (1978). *Selecting effective law enforcement officers: The Florida police standards research project*. Tampa, FL: Human Resources Institute.

Spielberger, R. D. (1966). The effects of anxiety on complex learning and academic achievement. In C. D. Spielberger (Ed.), *Anxiety and behavior*. New York: Academic Press.

Spiers, P. A. (1981). Have they come to praise Luria or to bury him? The Luria-Nebraska battery controversy. *Journal of Consulting and Clinical Psychology, 49*, 331-341.

Spinetta, J. (1978). Parental personality factors in child abuse. *Journal of Consulting and Clinical Psychology, 46*, 1409-1414.

Spitzer, R. L., & Endicott, J. (1974). *Mental status evaluation record*. New York: Biometrics Research.

Spitzer, R. L., & Endicott, J. (1978). *Schedule of affective disorders and schizophrenia*. New York: Biometrics Research.

Spitzer, R. L., Endicott, J., & Rollins, E. (1975). Clinical criteria and DSM-III. *American Journal of Psychiatry, 132*, 1187-1192.

Spitzer, R. L., Endicott, J., & Rollins, E. (1978). Research diagnostic criteria for use in psychiatric research. *Archives of General Psychiatry, 35*, 773-782.

Spitzer, R. L., & Fleiss, J. L. (1974). A re-analysis of psychiatric diagnosis. *British Journal of Psychiatry, 125*, 341-347.

Spivack, G., & Shure, M. (1974). *Social adjustment of young children: A cognitive approach to solving real-life problems*. San Francisco, CA: Jossey-Bass.

Spivack, G., Platt, J., & Shure, M. (1976). *The problem solving approach to adjustment*. San Francisco, CA: Jossey-Bass.

Spohn, C., Gruhl, J., & Welch, S. (1982). The effect of face on sentencing: A reexamination of an unsettled question. *Law and Society Review, 16*, 71-88.

Spotts, J. V., & Spotts, C. A. (1980). *Use and abuse of amphetamine and its substitutes*. Rockville, MD: National Institute on Drug Abuse.

Squire, L. S. (1977). E. C. T. and memory loss. *American Journal of Psychiatry, 134*, 997-1001.

Stafford-Clark, D., & Taylor, F. H. (1949). Clinical and electroencephalographic studies of prisoners charged with murder. *Journal of Neurology, Neurosurgery, and Psychiatry, 12*, 325-330.

Standing Committee on Association Standards of Criminal Justice. (1983). *Criminal justice and mental health standards*. Chicago, IL: American Bar Association.

Stanley, B., & Howe, J. G. (1983). Identification of multiple sclerosis using double discrimination scales derived from the Luria-Nebraska neuropsychological battery: An attempt at cross validation. *Journal of Consulting and Clinical Psychology, 51*, 420-423.

Stanley, B., Stanley, M., Lautin, A., Kane, J., & Schwartz, N. (1981). Preliminary findings of psychiatric patients as research participants: A population at risk? *American Journal of Psychiatry, 138*, 669-671.

Stasser, G., & Davis, J. H. (1981). Group decision making and social influence: A social interaction model. *Psychological Review, 88*, 523-551.

Stasser, G., Kerr, N. L., & Bray, R. M. (1982). The social psychology of jury deliberations: Structure, process, and product. In N. L. Kerr & R. M. Bray (Eds.), *The psychology of the courtroom* (pp. 221-256). New York: Academic Press.

Staub, E. (1978). *Positive social behavior and morality: Social and personal influences*, Vol. 1. New York: Academic Press.

Steadman, H. (1973). Some evidence on the inadequacy of the concept and determination of dangerousness in law and psychiatry. *Journal of Psychiatry and Law, 1,* 409-426.

Steadman, H. (1975). Employing psychiatric predictions of dangerous behavior: Policy vs. fact. In C. J. Frederick (Ed.), *Dangerous behavior: A problem in law and mental health.* NIMH, DHEW Publication Number (ADM) 78-563, Washington, DC: Superintendent of Documents, U. S. Government Printing Office.

Steadman, H. (1976). Predicting dangerousness. In D. J. Madden & J. R. Lion (Eds.), *Rage-hate-assault and other forms of violence.* New York: Spectrum Publishers.

Steadman, H. (1977). A new look at recidivism among Patuxent inmates. *Bulletin of the American Academy of Psychiatry and the Law, 5,* 200-209.

Steadman, H. (1979a). *Beating a rap? Defendants found incompetent to stand trial.* Chicago, IL: University of Chicago Press.

Steadman, H. (1979b). The use of social science in forensic psychiatry. *International Journal of Law and Psychiatry, 2,* 519-531.

Steadman, H. (1980a). Insanity acquittals in New York State, 1965-1978. *American Journal of Psychiatry, 137,* 321-326.

Steadman, H. (1980b). The right not to be a false positive: Problems in the application of the dangerousness standard. *Psychiatry Quarterly, 52,* 84-99.

Steadman, H. (1981). A situational approach to violence. *International Journal of Law and Psychiatry, 5,* 171-186.

Steadman, H., & Braff, J. (1975). Crimes of violence and incompetency diversion. *Journal of Criminal Law and Criminology, 66,* 73-78.

Steadman, H. J., & Cocozza, J. J. (1974). *Careers of the criminally insane.* Lexington, MA: Lexington Books.

Steadman, H. J., & Cocozza, J. J. (1978). Psychiatry, dangerousness, and the repetitively violent offender. *Journal of Criminal Law and Criminology, 69,* 226-231.

Steadman, H. J., & Cocozza, J. J. (1979). The dangerousness standard and psychiatry: A cross national issue in the social control of the mentally ill. *Sociology and Social Research, 63.*

Steadman, H. J., & Cocozza, J. (1980). Prediction of violent behavior in the role of the forensic psychologist. In G. Cook (Ed.), *The role of the forensic psychologist.* Springfield, IL: Charles C. Thomas.

Steadman, H. J., Cocozza, J., & Melnick, M. (1978). Explaining the increased crime rate of mental patients: The changing clientele of State hospitals. *American Journal of Psychiatry, 135,* 816-820.

Steadman, H. J., Monahan, J., Hartstone, E., Davis, S., & Robbins, P. (1982). Mentally disordered offenders: A national survey of patients and facilities. *Law and Human Behavior, 6,* 31-38.

Steadman, H. J., & Morrissey, J. P. (1981). The statistical prediction of violent behavior. *Law and Human Behavior, 3*(4), 263-274.

Steadman, H. J., Vanderwyst, D., & Ribner, S. (1978). Comparing arrest rates of mental patients and criminal offenders. *American Journal of Psychiatry, 135*(10), 1218-1220.

Stearns, A. W. (1945). Isaac Ray, psychiatrist and pioneer in forensic psychiatry. *American Journal of Psychiatry, 101,* 573-583.

Steinman, S. (1981). The experience of children in a joint custody arrangement. *American Journal of Orthopsychiatry, 51*(3), 403-414.

Stelzner, L. G., & Pratt, R. (1983). The guilty but mentally ill verdict and plea in New Mexico. *New Mexico Law Review, 13,* 99-116.

Stephan, C., & Tully, J. C. (1977). The influence of physical attractiveness of a plaintiff on the decisions of simulated jurors. *Journal of Social Psychology, 101,* 149-150.

Stephan, W. G. (1978). School segregation: An evaluation of predictions made in Brown v. Board of Education. *Psychological Bulletin, 85,* 217-238.

Stephen, C. (1975). Selective characteristics of jurors and litigants: Their influences on juries' verdicts. In R. J. Simon (Ed.), *The jury system in America.* Beverly Hills, CA: Sage Publications.

Stephensmeier, D. J., & Faulknew, G. L. (1978). Defendants' parental status as affecting judges' behavior: An experimental test. *Psychological Reports, 42,* 939-945.

Stern, G. (1970). *People in context.* New York: Wiley.

Stevens, R. (1973). Law schools and law students. *Virginia Law Review, 59,* 551-707.

Stevenson, I., Buckman, J., Smith, B. M., & Hain, J. D. (1974). The use of drugs in psychiatric interviews: Some interpretations based on controlled experiments. *American Journal of Psychiatry, 131,* 707-710.

Stever, A. (1969). Legal vocabulary: Its uses and limitations. *Practical Lawyer, 15,* 39-55.

Stickney, S. (1974). Wyatt vs. Stickney: The right to treatment. *Psychiatric Annals, 4,* 32-45.

Stier, S. D., & Stoebe, K. J. (1979). Involuntary hospitalization of the mentally ill in Iowa: The failure of the 1975 legislation. *Iowa Law Review, 64,* 1284-1458.

Stolberg, A., & Ullman, A. (1983). *Single Parenting Questionnaire: Development validation and applications manual.* Richmond, VA: Department of Psychology, Virginia Commonwealth University.

Stone, A. (1971). Legal education on the couch. *Harvard Law Review, 85,* 392-441.

Stone, A. (1975). *Mental health and law: A system in transition.* Rockville, MD: National Institute of Mental Health.

Stone, A. (1976). The Tarasoff decisions: Suing psychotherapists to safeguard society. *Harvard Law Review,* 358-378.

Stone, A. (1977). Recent mental health litigation: A critical perspective. *American Journal of Psychiatry,* 273-279.

Stone, A. (1979). Informed consent: Special problems of psychiatry. *Hospital and Community Psychiatry, 30,* 321-327.

Stone, A. (1984). *Law, psychiatry, and morality: Essays and analysis.* Washington, DC: American Psychiatric Press.

Stone, L. A. (1965). Test-retest stability of MMPI scales. *Psychological Reports, 16,* 619-620.

Stone, W., & Belanger, J. (1978). Evaluating the competency of admissions to a state maximum-security service. *Hospital and Community Psychiatry, 29,* 425-426.

Storms, M. D. (1973). Videotape and the attribution process: Reversing actors' and observers' points of view. *Journal of Personality and Social Psychology, 27,* 165-175.

Stotland, E., & Berberich, J. (1979). The psychology of the police. In H. Toch (Ed.), *Psychology of crime and criminal justice.* New York: Holt, Rinehart & Winston.

Stouffer, S. A., Lunsdaine, A. A., Williams, R. M., Smith, M. B., Janis, I. L., Star, S. A., & Cottrell, L. J. (1949). *The American soldier: Combat and its aftermath.* Princeton: Princeton University Press.

Stratton, J. G. (1978). Police stress: An overview. *Police Chief, 5,* 58-62.

Strauss, S. A. (1972). Psychiatric testimony, with special reference to cases of post-traumatic neurosis. *Forensic Science, 1,* 77-90.

Strawn, D. U., & Buchanan, R. W. (1976). Jury confusion: A threat to justice. *Judicature, 5,* 478-483.

Strawn, D. U., Buchanan, R. W., Pryor, B., & Taylor, K. P. (1977). Reaching a verdict, step by step. *Judicature, 60,* 8.

Strawn, D. U., & Munstermann, G. T. (1982). Helping juries handle complex cases. *Judicature, 65,* 444-447.

Strawn, D. U., Taylor, J., & Buchanan, L. (1977). Finding verdict step by step. *Judicature, 60,* 383-392.

Strodtbeck, F. L., & Hook, L. H. (1961). The social dimensions of a twelve-man jury table. *Sociometry, 24,* 397-415.

Strodtbeck, F. L., James, R. M., & Hawkins, D. (1957). Social status in jury deliberations. *American Sociological Review, 22,* 713-719.

Strodtbeck, F. L., & Mann, R. (1956). Sex role differentiation in jury deliberation. *Sociometry, 29,* 3-11.

Strout, R. L. (1982, August 30). The American family: Winds of change. *Tampa Tribune,* p. 11-A.

Stukat, K. (1958). *Suggestibility: A factorial and experimental analysis.* Stockholm: Almqvist & Wiksell.

Suarez, J. M., & Pittluck, A. T. (1975). Global amnesia: Organic and functional considerations. *Bulletin of the American Academy of Psychiatry and the Law, 3,* 17-24.

Subcommittee on Criminal Law of the United States Senate Judicary Committee. (1982). *Hearings on limiting the insanity defense.* Washington, DC: U. S. Government Printing Office.

Sue, S., Smith, R. E., & Caldwell, C. (1973). Effects of inadmissible evidence on the decisions of simulated jurors: A moral dilemma. *Journal of Applied Social Psychology, 3,* 344-353.

Sue, S., Smith, R. E., & Pedroza, G. (1975). Authoritarianism, pretrial publicity, and awareness of bias in simulated jurors. *Psychological Reports, 57,* 1299-1302.

Sue, S., & Sue, D. W. (1974). MMPI comparisons between Asian American and non-Asian students utilizing a student health psychiatric clinic. *Journal of Counseling Psychology, 21,* 423-427.

Suggs, D., & Sales, B. D. (1978). The art and science of conducting the voir dire. *Professional Psychology, 9,* 367-388.

Suggs, D. L. (1979). The use of psychological research by the judiciary. *Law and Human Behavior, 3,* 135-148.

Summerlin, M., & Ward, R. (1978). The effect of parental participation in a parent group on a child's self-esteem. *Journal of Psychology, 100,* 227-232.

Sundberg, N., Snowden, L., & Reynolds, W. (1978). Toward assessment of personal competence and incompetence in life situations. In M. Rosenzweig & L. Porter (Eds.), *Annual review of psychology* (pp. 179-221). Palo Alto, CA: Annual Reviews.

Swartz, J. D. (1978). Thematic Apperception Test. In O. K. Buros (Ed.), *Mental measurements yearbook* (8th ed.) (pp. 1127-1130). Highland Park, NJ: Gryphon Press.

Swartz, J. D., Reinehr, R. C., & Holtzman, W. H. (1983). *Holtzman Inkblot Technique, 1956-1982: An annotated bibliography.* Austin, TX: University of Texas.

Swensen, C. H. (1957). Empirical evaluations of human figure drawings. *Psychological Bulletin, 54,* 431-466.

Swensen, C. H. (1968). Empirical evaluations of human figure drawings: 1957-1966. *Psychological Bulletin, 70,* 20-44.

Symonds, P. (1949). *Dynamics of parent-child relationships.* New York: Bureau of Publications, Teachers College, Columbia University.

Szasz, T. S. (1957). Psychiatric expert testimony: Its covert meaning and social function. *Psychiatry: Journal for the Study of Interpersonal Processes, 20,* 313-316.

Szasz, T. S. (1960). The myth of mental illness. *American Psychologist, 15,* 113-118.

Szasz, T. S. (1968). *Law, liberty and psychiatry.* New York: Collier Books.

Szasz, T. S. (1969). The crime of commitment. *Psychology Today, 2*(10), 55-57.

Szasz, T. S., & Alexander, G. J. (1972). Law, property and psychiatry. *American Journal of Orthopsychiatry, 42,* 610-626.

Szucko, J. J., & Kleinmuntz, B. (1985). Psychological methods of truth detection. In C. P. Ewing (Ed.), *Psychology, psychiatry, and the law: A clinical and forensic handbook* (pp. 441-466). Sarasota, FL: Professional Resource Exchange.

T

Talkington, L., & Reed, K. (1969). An evaluation of Rorschach indicators of psychosis among mentally retarded. *Journal of Projective Techniques, 33,* 474-475.

Talland, G. A. (1965). Deranged memory. New York: Academic Press.

Tanay, E. (1978). Psychodynamic differentiation of homicide. *Bulletin of the American Academy of Psychiatry and the Law, 6,* 364-369.

Tanford, S., & Penrod, S. (1982). Biases in trials involving defendants charged with multiple offenses. *Journal of Applied Social Psychology, 12,* 453-480.

Tanke, E. D., & Tanke, T. J. (1979). Getting off a slippery slope: Social science in the judicial process. *American Psychologist, 34,* 1130-1138.

Tapp, J. L. (1969). Psychology and the law: The dilemma. *Psychology Today, 2,* 16-22.

Tapp, J. L. (1976). Psychology and the law: An overture. In M. L. Rosenzweig & L. W. Porter (Eds.), *Annual review of psychology,* Vol. 27. Palo Alto, CA: Annual Reviews.

Tapp, J. L. (1977). Psychology and law: Look at interface. In B. D. Sales (Ed.), *Psychology in the legal process.* New York: Spectrum.

Tapp, J. L. (1980). Psychological and policy perspectives on the law: Reflection on a decade. *Journal of Social Issues, 36,* 165-191.

Tapp, J. L., & Kohlberg, L. (1977). Developing senses of law and legal justice. In J. Tapp & F. Levine (Eds.), *Law, justice, and the individual in society* (pp. 89-105). New York: Holt, Rinehart & Winston.

Tapp, J. L., & Levine, F. C. (Eds.) (1974). *Law, justice, and the individual in society.* New York: Holt, Rinehart & Winston.

Tavormina, J. (1975). Relative effectiveness of behavioral and reflecting group counseling with parents of mentally retarded children. *Journal of Consulting and Clinical Psychology, 43,* 22-31.

Taylor, D. A., Altman, I., Wheeler, L., & Kushner, E. N. (1969). Personality factors related to response to social isolation and confinement. *Journal of Consulting and Clinical Psychology, 33*(4), 411-419.

Taylor, J. (1975). Law school stress and the "deformation Professionalle." *Journal of Legal Education, 27,* 251-267.

Taylor, R. E. (1983, January 20). Insanity defense should be narrowed, psychiatrists say. *Wall Street Journal,* p. 18.

Taylor, S. P. (1967). Aggressive behavior and physiological arousal as a function of provocation and the tendency to inhibit aggression. *Journal of Personality, 35,* 297-310.

Taylor, S. P., & Leonard, K. E. (1983). Alcohol and human physical aggression. In R. G. Geen & E. I. Donnerstein (Eds.), *Aggression: Theoretical and empirical reviews,* Vol. 2 (pp. 77-101). New York: Academic Press.

Tedeschi, J. T., & Rosenfeld, P. (1980). Communication in bargaining and negotiation. In M. E. Roloff & G. R. Miller (Eds.), *Persuasion: New directions in theory and research.* Beverly Hills, CA: Sage Publications.

Teleki, J., Powell, J., & Dodder, R. (1982). Factor analysis of reports of parental behavior by children living in divorced and married families. *Journal of Psychology, 112*, 295-302.

Tenopyr, M. (1977). Content-construct confusion. *Personnel Psychology, 30*, 47-54.

Tepper, A., & Elwork, A. (1984). Competence to consent to treatment as a psycholegal construct. *Law and Human Behavior, 8*, 205-223.

Terman, L. M. (1931). Psychology and the law. *Los Angeles Bar Association Bulletin, 6*, 142-153.

Terman, L. M. (1935). Psychology and the law. *Commercial Law Journal, 40*, 639-646.

Theilgaard, A. (1983). Aggression and the xyy personality. *International Journal of Law and Psychiatry, 6*, 413-421.

Thibaut, J., & Walker, L. (1975). *Procedural justice: A psychological analysis*. Hillsdale, NJ: Erlbaum.

Thibaut, J., & Walker, L. (1978). A theory of procedure. *California Law Review, 66*, 541-566.

Thibaut, J., Walker, L., & Lind, E. A. (1972). Adversary presentation and bias in legal decision-making. *Harvard Law Review, 86*, 386-401.

Thomas, E., & Fink, C. (1963). Effects of group size. *Psychological Bulletin, 60*, 371-384.

Thomasson, E., Berkowitz, T., Minor, S., Cassle, G., McCord, D., & Milner, J. (1981). Evaluation of a family life education program for rural high-risk families: A research note. *Journal of Community Psychology, 9*, 246-249.

Thompson, G. N. (1965). Post-traumatic neurosis: A statistical survey. *American Journal of Psychiatry, 121*, 1043-1048.

Thornberry, T., & Jacoby, J. (1979). *The criminally insane: A community follow-up of mentally ill offenders*. Chicago, IL: University of Chicago Press.

Tierney, J. (1982). Doctor, is this man dangerous? *Science, 3*(5), 28-31.

Tigar, L. (1970). Foreword: Waiver of constitutional rights: Disquiet in the Citadel. *Harvard Law Review, 84*, 22-23.

Tinklenburg, J. R. (1973). Alcohol and violence. In T. Bourne & R. Fox (Eds.), *Alcoholism: Progress in research and treatment*. New York: Academic Press.

Toch, H. (1969). *Violent men*. Chicago, IL: Aldine.

Toch, H., & Schulte, R. (1961). Readiness to perceive violence as a result of police training. *British Journal of Psychology, 52*, 381-383.

Tomkins, S. S. S. (1947). *The Thematic Apperception Test: The theory and technique of intepretation*. New York: Grune & Stratton.

Toobert, S., Bartelme, K. F., & Jones, E. S. (1959). Some factors related to pedophilia. *International Journal of Social Psychiatry, 4*, 272-279.

Trachtman, J. P. (1970). Socio-economic class bias in Rorschach diagnoses: Contributing psychosocial attributes of the clinician. *Journal of Projective Techniques, 34*, 229-240.

Treffert, A., & Krajeck, R. W. (1976). In search of a sane commitment statute. *Psychiatric Annals, 6*, 283-294.

Tribe, L. H. (1971). Trial by mathematics: Precision and ritual in the legal process. *Harvard Law Review, 84*, 1329-1393.

Trunnell, T. (1976). Johnnie and Suzie, don't cry: Mommy and Daddy aren't that way. *Bulletin of the American Academy of Psychiatry and the Law, 4*, 120-126.

Tsai, L., & Tsung, M. T. (1981). How can we avoid unnecessary CT scanning for psychiatric patients? *Journal of Clinical Psychiatry, 42*, 452-454.

Tsubouchi, K., & Jenkins, R. L. (1969). Three types of delinquents: Their performance on MMPI and PCR. *Journal of Clinical Psychology, 25*, 353-358.

Tucker, G. W., Detre, T., Harrow, M., & Glaser, G. H. (1965). Behavior and symptoms of psychiatric patients and the electroencephalogram. *Archives of General Psychiatry, 12,* 278-286.

Turow, S. (1977). *One L.* New York: Putnam.

Tversky, A., & Kahneman, D. (1981). The framing of decisions and the psychology of choice. *Science, 211,* 453-458.

Twardy, S., & Siomopoulos, V. (1976a). Medical testimony—Mental Health Proceedings—Direct and cross-examination of a defendant's clinical psychologist—Part I. *Medical Trial Technique Quarterly, 23,* 66-104.

Twardy, S., & Siomopoulos, V. (1976b). Medical testimony—Mental Health Proceedings—Direct and cross-examination of a defendant's clinical psychiatrist—Part II. *Medical Trial Technique Quarterly, 23,* 187-232.

Tybor, J. R. (1982, May 2). Getting a verdict on jury predictability. *Wall Street Journal.*

U

Uhlman, T., & Walker, N. D. (1980). "He takes some of my time, I take some of his": An analysis of judicial sentencing patterns in jury cases. *Law and Society Review, 14,* 321-341.

Underwood, B. (1979). Law and the crystal ball: Predicting behavior with statistical inference and the individualized judgment. *Yale Law Review, 88,* 1409-1448.

Undeutsch, U. (1982). Statement reality analysis. In A. Trankell (Ed.), *Reconstructing the past.* Deventer, Netherlands: Kluwer Law and Taxation Publishers.

Unnever, J. D., Frazier, C. E., & Henretta, J. C. (1980). Race differences in criminal sentencing. *Sociological Quarterly, 21,* 197-213.

U. S. Department of Health, Education and Welfare. (1978). *Working document of patient care management.* Washington, DC: U. S. Government Printing Office.

V

Valenti, A. C., & Downing, L. L. (1975). Differential effects of jury size on verdicts following deliberation as a function of apparent guilt of a defendant. *Journal of Personality and Social Psychology, 32,* 655-663.

Van den Haag, E. (1960). Social science testimony in the desegregation cases: A reply to professor Kenneth Clark. *Villanova Law Review, 6,* 69-79.

Veach, R. (1977). Hospital ethics committees: Is there a role? *Hastings Center Report, 7,* 22-24.

Vega, A., & Parsons, O. A. (1967). Cross validation of the Halstead-Reitan test for brain damage. *Journal of Consulting Psychology, 31,* 619-625.

Verdun-Jones, S. N. (1979). The evolution of the defenses of insanity and automatism in Canada from 1843 to 1979: A saga of judicial reluctance to sever the umbilical cord to the mother country? *University of British Columbia Law Review, 14,* 1-76.

Victor, I., & Winkler, W. (1977). *Fathers and custody.* New York: Hawthorn.

Victoroff, V. M. (1977). Collaboration between Ohio psychiatrists and the legislature to update commitment laws. *American Journal of Psychiatry, 134,* 752-755.

Vidmar, N. (1979). The other issues in jury simulation research: A commentary with particular reference to defendant character studies. *Law and Human Behavior, 3,* 95-106.

Vincent, K. R. (1983). MMPI code types and DSM III diagnosis. *Journal of Clinical Psychology, 39*, 829-842.

Virkkunen, M. (1974). Incest offenses and alcoholism. *Medicine, Science and Law, 14*, 124-128.

Viukari, M., Rimon, R., & Soderholm, S. (1979). Attitudes toward criminal and other patients. *Acta Psychiatria Scandinavia, 59*, 24-30.

Von Rosensteil, L. (1973). Increase in hostility responses in the HIT after frustration. *Journal of Personality Assessment, 37*(1), 22-24.

Voss, H. L., & Hepburn, J. R. (1968). Patterns in criminal homicide in Chicago. *Journal of Criminal Law, Criminology, and Police Science, 59*, 499-508.

W

Wade, T. C., & Baker, T. E. (1977). Opinions in use of psychological tests: A survey of clinical psychologists. *American Psychologist, 32*, 874-882.

Wagner, E. E., & Medvedeff, E. (1963). Differentiation of aggressive behavior of institutionalized schizophrenics with the Hand Test. *Journal of Projective Techniques and Personality Assessment, 27*, 111-113.

Wald, M. (1976). State intervention on behalf of "neglected" children: A search for realistic standards. In M. K. Rosenheim (Ed.), *Pursuing justice for the child* (pp. 246-278). Chicago, IL: University of Chicago Press.

Waldo, G. P., & Dinitz, S. (1967). Personality attributes of the criminal: An analysis of research studies, 1950-1965. *Journal of Research in Crime and Delinquency, 4*, 185-202.

Waldo, G. P., & Hall, N. E. (1970). Delinquency potential and attitudes toward the criminal justice system. *Social Forces, 49*, 291-298.

Walker, E. (1961). Murder or epilepsy. *Journal of Nervous and Mental Diseases, 133*, 430-437.

Walker, L., Lind, E. A., & Thibaut, J. (1979). The relation between procedural and distributive justice. *Virginia Law Review, 65*, 1401-1420.

Walker, L., Thibaut, J., & Andreoli, V. (1972). Order of presentation at trial. *Yale Law Review, 82*, 216-226.

Walker, M. (1978). Measuring the seriousness of crimes. *British Journal of Criminology, 18*(4), 348-364.

Walker, R. (1972). The Brockton Social Adjustment Scale. *Diseases of the Nervous System, 33*, 542-545.

Wallerstein, J., & Kelly, J. (1974). The effects of parental divorce: The adolescent experience. In E. Anthony & C. Koupernik (Eds.), *The child in his family: Children at a psychiatric risk* (pp. 479-506). New York: Wiley.

Wallerstein, J., & Kelly, J. (1975). The effects of parental divorce: Experiences of the pre-school child. *Journal of the American Academy of Child Psychiatry, 14*, 600-616.

Wallerstein, J., & Kelly, J. (1976). The effects of parental divorce: Experiences of the child in early latency. *American Journal of Orthopsychiatry, 46*, 20-32.

Walshe-Brennan, K. S. (1978). Classification inconsistencies in defining the criminally mentally abnormal. *Medical Science Law, 18*(4), 283-286.

Walters, H. A. (1981). Dangerousness. In J. R. Moon (Ed.), *Encyclopedia of Clinical Assessment*, Vol. 2. San Francisco, CA: Jossey-Bass.

Ward, C. H., Beck, A. T., & Mendelson, M. (1962). The psychiatric nomenclature. *Archives of General Psychiatry, 7*, 198-205.

Wasyliw, O. E., Cavanaugh, J. L., & Rogers, R. (1985). Beyond the scientific limits of expert testimony. *Bulletin of the American Academy of Psychiatry and the Law, 13,* 147-158.

Watkins, C. M. (1981). Guilty but mentally ill: A reasonable compromise for Pennsylvania. *Dickson Law Review, 85,* 289-319.

Watson, A. (1968). The quest for professional competence: Psychological aspects of legal education. *University of Cincinnati Law Review, 37,* 91-166.

Watson, A. (1969). The children of Armageddon: Problems of custody following divorce. *Syracuse Law Review, 21,* 55-86.

Watson, J. B. (1913). Psychology as the behaviorist views it. *Psychological Review, 20,* 158-177.

Watt, W., & Maher, B. (1958). Prisoner's attitudes toward home and the judicial system. *Journal of Criminal Law, Criminology, and Police Science, 49,* 327-330.

Wax, D., & Haddix, V. (1974). Enuresis, fire setting, and animal cruelty in male adolescent delinquents: A triad predictive of violent behavior. *Journal of Psychiatry and Law, 2,* 45-71.

Webb, V. J. (1978). Criminal justice as an academic discipline: Costs and benefits. *Journal of Criminal Justice, 6,* 347-355.

Webster, C. D., Menzies, R. J., & Jackson, M. A. (1982). *Clinical assessment before trial: Legal issues and mental disorder.* Toronto: Butterworth.

Webster, J. S., & Dostrow, V. (1982). Efficacy of a decision-tree approach to the Luria-Nebraska neuropsychological battery. *Journal of Consulting and Clinical Psychology, 50,* 313-315.

Webster, W. (1982). *Uniform crime reports: Crime in the United States.* Washington, DC: Superintendent of Documents, U. S. Government Printing Office.

Webster-Stratton, C. (1982). The long-term effectiveness of a videotape modeling parent training program: Comparison of immediate and one-year follow-up results. *Behavior Therapy, 13,* 702-714.

Wechsler, D. (1955). *The Wechsler Adult Intelligence Scale.* New York: Psychological Corporation.

Wechsler, D. (1981). *The Wechsler Adult Intelligence Scale-Revised.* New York: Psychological Corporation.

Wechsler, H. (1959). Toward neutral principles of constitutional law. *Harvard Law Review, 73,* 1-35.

Wedding, D. (1983a). Clinical and statistical prediction in neuropsychology. *Clinical Neuropsychology, 5,* 49-54.

Wedding, D. (1983b). Comparison of statistical and actuarial models for predicting lateralization of brain damage. *Clinical Neuropsychology, 5,* 15-20.

Weinberg, H. I., & Baron, R. S. (1982). The discredible witness. *Personality and Social Psychology Bulletin, 8,* 60-67.

Weinberg, L. S., & Vatz, R. E. (1977-1978). Language and forensic psychiatry. *Duquesne Law Review, 16,* 583-600.

Weinberger, D. R. (1984). Brain disease and psychiatric illness: When should a psychiatrist order a CAT scan? *American Journal of Psychiatry, 141,* 1521-1527.

Weinberger, D. R., Wagner, R. L., & Wyatt, R. J. (1983). Neuropathological studies of schizophrenia: A slective review. *Schizophrenia Bulletin, 9,* 493-512.

Weiner, B. A. (1980). Not guilty by reason of insanity: A sane approach. *Chicago Kent Law Review, 56,* 1057-1085.

Weiner, J. M. (1966). An EEG study of delinquent and non-delinquent adolescents. *Archives of General Psychiatry, 15,* 144-148.

Weiner, R. D. (1983). Amnesia. In J. O. Cavenar & K. H. Brodie (Eds.), *Signs and symptoms in psychiatry* (pp. 575-596). Philadelphia, PA: J. B. Lippincott.

Weins, A., Matarazzo, J., & Gaver, K. (1959). Performance and verbal IQ in a group of sociopaths. *Journal of Clinical Psychology, 15,* 191-193.

Weisberg, R., & Wald, M. (1984). Confidentiality laws and state efforts to protect abused or neglected children: The need for statutory reform. *Family Law Quarterly, 18,* 143-212.

Weinstein, E. et al. (1970). The validity of the polygraph with hypnotically induced repression and guilt. *American Journal of Psychiatry, 129,* 1159-1162.

Weinstein, M. C., & Fineberg, H. B. (1980). *Clinical decision analysis.* Philadelphia, PA: W. B. Saunders Company.

Weiss, E., & Davison, M. (1981). Test theory and methods. In M. Rosenzweig & L. Porter (Eds.), *Annual review of psychology* (pp. 629-658). Palo Alto, CA: Annual Reviews.

Weiss, J., & Scott, K. F. (1974). Suicide attempters ten years later. *Comprehensive Psychiatry, 15,* 165-171.

Weissman, M. (1974). The epidemiology of suicide attempts: 1960-1971. *Archives of General Psychiatry, 30,* 737-746.

Weisstub, D. N. (1980). *Law and psychiatry in the Canadian context.* New York: Pergamon Press.

Weiten, W. (1980). The attraction-leniency effect in jury research: An examination of external validity. *Journal of Applied Social Psychology, 10,* 340-347.

Weiten, W., & Diamond, S. S. (1979). A critical review of the jury simulation paradigm: The case of defendant characteristics. *Law and Human Behavior, 3,* 71-94.

Weithorn, L., & Campbell, S. (1982). The competency of children and adolescents to make informed treatment decisions. *Child Development, 53,* 1589-1599.

Weitzman, L. J., & Dixon, R. B. (1979). Child custody awards. *Davis Law Review, 12,* 473-521.

Weld, H. B., & Danzig, E. R. (1940). A study of the way a verdict is reached by a jury. *American Journal of Psychology, 53,* 518-536.

Weld, H. B., & Roff, M. (1938). A study of the formation of opinion based on legal evidence. *American Journal of Psychology, 51,* 609-623.

Wells, G. L. (1978). Applied eyewitness research: System variables and estimator variables. *Journal of Personality and Social Psychology, 36,* 1546-1557.

Wells, G. L., Leippe, M. R., & Ostrom, T. (1979). Guidelines for empirically assessing the fairness of a lineup. *Law and Human Behavior, 3,* 285-294.

Wells, G. L., Lindsay, R. C. L., & Ferguson, T. J. (1979). Accuracy, confidence and juror perceptions in eyewitness testimony. *Journal of Applied Psychology, 64,* 440-448.

Wells, G. L., Lindsay, R. C. L., & Tousignant, J. P. (1980). Effects of expert psychological advice on human performance in judging the validity of eyewitness testimony. *Law and Human Behavior, 4,* 275-285.

Wells, G. L., & Loftus, E. F. (Eds.) (1983). *Eyewitness testimony: Psychological perspectives.* London: Cambridge University Press.

Wells, G. L., Ferguson, T. J., & Lindsay, R. C. L. (1981). The tractability of eyewitness confidence and its implications for triers of fact. *Journal of Applied Psychology, 66,* 688-696.

Wells, G. L., Leippe, M. R., & Ostrom, T. M. (1979). Guidelines for empirically assessing the fairness of a lineup. *Law and Human Behavior, 3,* 285-294.

Welsh, G. S. (1952). An anxiety index and an internalization ratio for the MMPI. *Journal of Consulting Psychology, 16,* 65-72.

Wenger, D. L., & Fletcher, C. R. (1969). The effect of legal counsel on admissions to a state mental hospital: A confrontation of professions. *Journal of Health and Social Behavior, 10,* 66-72.

Wenke, E. A., Robinson, J. O., & Smith, G. W. (1972). Can violence be predicted? *Crime and Delinquency, 18*, 393-402.

Werner, P., Rose, T., & Yesavage, J. (1984). Psychiatrists' judgments of dangerousness in patients on an acute care unit. *American Journal of Psychiatry, 141*, 263-266.

Wetter, J. (1972). Parent attitudes toward learning disability. *Exceptional Children, 38*, 490-491.

Wetzel, L., & Ross, N. (1983). Psychological and social ramifications of battering: Observations leading to a counseling methodology for victims of domestic violence. *Personnel and Guidance Journal, 61*, 423-428.

Wexler, D. (1975). Reflections on the legal regulation of behavior modifications in institutional settings. *Arizona Law Review, 17*, 132-143.

Wexler, D. (1981). *Mental health law*. New York: Plenum Press.

Wexler, D. et al. (1971). The administration of psychiatric justice: Theory and practice in Arizona. *Arizona Law Review, 13*, 1-260.

Whitaker, L. C. (1976). Psychological test evaluation. In J. M. MacDonald (Ed.), *Psychiatry and the criminal: A guide to psychiatric examinations for the criminal court* (pp. 151-178). Springfield, IL: Charles C. Thomas.

White, A. R. (1976). Intention, purpose, foresight and desire. *Law Quarterly Review, 92*, 569-590.

White, L. A. (1979). Erotica and aggression: The influence of sexual arousal, positive affect, and negative affect on aggressive behavior. *Journal of Personality and Social Psychology, 37*(4), 591-601.

Whitlock, F. A. (1963). *Criminal responsibility and mental illness*. London: Butterworth.

Wigmore, J. H. (1909). Professor Munsterberg and the psychology of evidence. *Illinois Law Review, 3*, 339-443.

Wigmore, J. H. (1940). *3 Wigmore on evidence* (3rd ed.). pp. 367-368.

Wildman, M. (1966). Selecting the jury: Defense view. *American Jurisprudence Trials, 5*, 249-285.

Willging, T., & Caplan, N. (1980). *Adversarial use of empirically tested data by lawyers in selected constitutional cases as a function of the training, practice, attitude and behavior of lawyers and their clients: Proposal to National Science Foundation*. Ann Arbor, MI: Institute for Social Research.

Willging, T., & Dunn, T. (1982). The moral development of the law student: Theory and data on legal education. *Journal of Legal Education, 31*, 306-358.

Willging, T., & Horowitz, I. A. (1981). *Legal negotiations: Skills and applications*. Washington, DC: Legal Services.

Williams, G. (1978). The mental element in crime: The law commission's report #89. *Criminal Law Review*, 588-599.

Williams, W., & Miller, K. (1977). The role of personal characteristics in perceptions of dangerousness. *Criminal Justice and Behavior, 4*, 241-251.

Williams, W., & Miller, K. (1981). The processing and disposition of incompetent mentally ill offenders. *Law and Human Behavior, 5*, 245-261.

Willick, D. H., Gehlkor, C., & Watts, A. M. (1975). Social class as a factor affecting judicial disposition. *Criminology, 13*, 57-77.

Wilson, J. (1977). The political feasibility of punishment. In J. Cederblom & W. Blizek (Eds.), *Justice and punishment* (pp. 107-123). Cambridge, MA: Ballinger.

Wing, J. D., Cooper, J. E., & Sartorius, M. (1974). *Measurement and classification of psychiatry symptoms*. New York: Cambridge University Press.

Winick, B. J. (1977). Psychotropic medication and competence to stand trial. *American Bar Foundation Journal, 3*, 769-816.

Winkel, G. H., & Sasanoff, R. (1967). An approach to objective analysis of behavior in architectural settings. In H. M. Proshansky, L. R. Rivlin, & O. H. Winkel (Eds.), *Environmental psychology: Man and his physical setting*. New York: Holt, Rinehart & Winston.

Winter, D. G., & Stewart, A. J. (1977). Power motive reliability as a function of retest instructions. *Journal of Consulting and Clinical Psychology, 45*, 436-440.

Witkin, H. A., Mendick, S. A., Schulisinger, F., Bakkestrom, E., Christiansen, K. O., Goodenough, D. R., Hirschhorn, K., Lundsteen, C., Owen, D. R., Philip, J., Rubin, D. B., & Stocking, M. (1976). Criminality in xyy and xxy men. *Science, 193*, 547-555.

Wolfgang, M. E. (1958). *Patterns in criminal homicide*. Philadelphia, PA: University of Pennsylvania Press.

Wolfgang, M. E. (1974). The social scientist in court. *Journal of Criminal Law and Criminology, 65*, 239-247.

Wolfgang, M. E., Figlio, R., & Sellin, T. (1972). *Delinquency in a birth cohort*. Chicago, IL: University of Chicago Press.

Wolfgang, M. E., Figlio, R., Tracy, P., & Singer, S. (1985). *National survey of crime severity*. Rockville, MD: U. S. Department of Justice, Bureau of Justice, NCJ-99643.

Wolinsky, J. (1982). Programs join "distrustful" disciplines. *APA Monitor, 13*(2), 15.

Woocher, F. D. (1977). Did your eyes deceive you? Expert psychological testimony on the unreliability of eyewitness identification. *Stanford Law Review, 29*, 960-1030.

Woods, S. M. (1961). Adolescent violence and homicide. *Archives of General Psychiatry, 5*, 528-534.

Woodward, R., & Armstrong, S. (1979). *The brethren*. New York: Simon and Schuster.

Woody, R. (1977). Psychologists in child custody. In B. D. Sales (Ed.), *Psychology in the legal process* (pp. 249-267). New York: Spectrum.

Woody, R. (1978). *Getting custody: Winning the last battle of the marital war*. New York: Macmillan.

Woolley, P. (1979). *The custody handbook*. New York: Summit.

Wrightsman, L. S. (1979). The American trial jury on trial: Empirical evidence and procedural modifications. *Journal of Social Issues, 34*, 4.

Wrightsman, L. S., & Deaux, K. (1981). *Social psychology in the 80s*. Monterey, CA: Brooks/Cole.

Wydra, A., Marshall, W. L., Earls, C. M., & Barbaree, H. E. (1983). Identification of cues and control of sexual arousal by rapists. *Behavior Research and Therapy, 21*, 469-476.

X-Y-Z

Yarmey, A. D. (1979). *The psychology of eyewitness testimony*. New York: Free Press.

Yesavage, J. A., & Freman, A. M. (1978). Acute phencyclidine (PCP) intoxication: Psychopathology and prognosis. *Journal of Clinical Psychiatry, 39*, 664-666.

Yochelson, S., & Samenow, S. (1976). *The criminal personality*, Vols. 1, 2, & 3. New York: Jason Aronson.

Zeegers, M. (1981). Diminished responsibility: A logical workable, and essential concept. *International Journal of Law and Psychiatry, 4*, 433-444.

Zeisel, H. (1971). ...And then there were none: The diminution of the federal jury. *University of Chicago Law Review, 38*, 710-724.

Zeisel, H. (1972). The waning of the American jury. *American Bar Association Journal, 58*, 367-370.

Zeisel, H., & Diamond, S. S. (1974). "Convincing empirical evidence" on the six-member jury. *University of Chicago Law Review, 41*, 281-295.

Zeisel, H., & Diamond, S. S. (1976). The jury selection in the Mitchell-Stans conspiracy trial. *American Bar Foundation Research Journal, 87,* 151-174.

Zeisel, H., & Diamond, S. S. (1978). The effect of peremptory challenges on the jury and verdict. *Stanford Law Review, 30,* 491-531.

Zelig, M., & Beidleman, W. B. (1981). The investigative use of hypnosis: A word of caution. *International Journal of Clinical and Experimental Hypnosis, 29,* 401-412.

Zigler, E., & Phillips, L. (1961). Social competence and outcome in psychiatric disorders. *Journal of Abnormal and Social Psychology, 63,* 264-271.

Zil, J. S., & Fineberg, D. E. (1978). A clinical laboratory for examination of psychiatric and legal labeling: CMHC inpatients with significant legal/social difficulties. *Corrective and Social Psychiatry Journal, 24*(4), 149-158.

Ziskin, J. (1981a). *Coping with psychiatric and psychological testimony.* Beverly Hills, CA: Law and Psychology Press.

Ziskin, J. (1981b). Use of the MMPI in forensic settings. *Clinical Notes on the MMPI, 9,* 1-13.

Ziskin, J. (1984). Malingering of psychological disorders. *Behavioral Sciences and the Law, 2,* 39-50.

Ziskin, J., & Coleman, L. (1981). Two professionals urge ban on psychiatric testimony. *California State Psychologist, 15*(5), 1-13.

Zonana, H. V. (1979). Hypnosis, sodium amytal, and confessions. *Bulletin of the American Academy of Psychiatry and the Law, 7,* 18-28.

Zubin, J., Eron, L. D., & Schumer, F. (1965). *An experimental approach to projective techniques.* New York: Wiley & Sons.

Zuckerman, M. (1971). Physiological measures of sexual arousal in the human. *Psychological Bulletin, 75,* 297-329.

Zuckerman, M., Larrance, D. T., Hall, J. A., DeFrank, R. S., & Rosenthal, R. (1979). Posed and spontaneous communication of emotion via facial and vocal cues. *Journal of Personality, 47,* 712-733.

Zuckerman, M., Lipets, M. S., Koivunaki, J. H., & Rosenthal, R. (1975). Encoding and decoding on verbal cues of emotion. *Journal of Personality and Social Psychology, 32,* 1068-1076.

Zuckerman, M., Ribbac, B., Monashkin, I., & Norton, J. (1958). Normative data and factor analysis on the Parental Attitude Research Instrument. *Journal of Consulting Psychology, 2,* 165-171.

Zunich, M. (1962). Relationship between maternal behavior and attitudes toward children. *Journal of Genetic Psychology, 100,* 155-165.

Zunich, M. (1971). Lower-class mothers' behavior and attitudes toward child rearing. *Psychological Reports, 29,* 1051-1058.

Zusman, J., & Simon, J. (1983). Differences in repeated psychiatric examinations of litigants to a lawsuit. *American Journal of Psychiatry, 140,* 1300-1304.

Zwick, R. (1983). Assessing the psychometric properties of psychodiagnostic systems: How do the research diagnostic criteria measure up? *Journal of Consulting and Clinical Psychology, 51,* 117-131.

Index

A

Abstraction, 44, 69
Abstraction factor, 44
Abstract reasoning, in frontal lobe dysfunction, 146
Acalculia, 19
Accident consequences and description, reluctance to describe, 14
Accuracy, of neuropsychologist, 26
Actus reus (deed of crime), 68
Acute confusional state, 63
Adaptability, 11
Adaptive dysfunctioning, significant, 6
Adaptive functioning, test sensitivity to, 23
Adversarial process, 1
Affective functions
    in frontal lobe syndrome, 95D96, 147-148
    linkage analysis and, 67
    neuropsychological test scores and, 148
    preinjury, 141
Aggression
    amnesia of, 128
    with frontal lesions, 89
Aggressive crimes, epileptoid base for, 123
Agnosia, 14, 19
Alcoholic dementia, 41
Alertness, linkage analysis and, 65
Alexythymia, 13
Alien hand phenomenon, 51
ALI guidelines (American Law Institute guidelines), 72-73
Alzheimer's disease, 41, 108, 117
American Board of Clinical Neuropsychology, 2
American Board of Professional Psychology, 2
American Law Institute guidelines (ALI guidelines), 72-73
American Psychological Association, Division of Clinical Neuropsychology, 2
Amnesia, 63, 68-69, 128
Anomia, 19
Anosognosia, 12, 14
Antisocial behavior, 44
Antisocial personality disorder, 20
Anxiety

performance and, 114
    symptoms of, 11-12
Anxiety reduction, 13
Aphasia, 8, 63, 145
Aphemia, 70
Arousal dysfunction, symptoms of, 9
Assessment, neuropsychological. See also Neuropsychological evaluation
    of executive functioning, 60D61
    for litigation, 3
    scientific bases for, 4
Attention. See also Concentration>
    deficits of
        symptoms of, 9
        test scores and, 63
    in frontal lobe syndrome, 41, 145
    in linkage analysis, 65
    neuropsychological test scores and, 148
    preinjury, 140
    regional brain involvement in, 114
Attorney
    attacks on expert witness, 31-32
    discovery process and, 21
    meeting in advance, for trial preparation, 29, 30
    neuropsychological education for, 4
Attribution, 2, 25
Atypical bipolar depression, 129
Authorization, 27D28
Automatism, 123
Autonomic systems, linkage analysis of, 67
Avoidance, 15
Awareness, lack of, 13-14

B

Background, in neuropsychological report, 25
Basal violence
    examination of, 71-72
    three-dimensional model of, 55-56
Baseline, preinjury
    comparison with, 22
    deficts comparisons with, 19
    establishment of, 18-19
    in neuropsychological report, 25